1,000,000 Books
are available to read at

Forgotten Books

www.ForgottenBooks.com

Read online
Download PDF
Purchase in print

ISBN 978-1-5280-3989-5
PIBN 10914871

This book is a reproduction of an important historical work. Forgotten Books uses state-of-the-art technology to digitally reconstruct the work, preserving the original format whilst repairing imperfections present in the aged copy. In rare cases, an imperfection in the original, such as a blemish or missing page, may be replicated in our edition. We do, however, repair the vast majority of imperfections successfully; any imperfections that remain are intentionally left to preserve the state of such historical works.

Forgotten Books is a registered trademark of FB &c Ltd.
Copyright © 2018 FB &c Ltd.
FB &c Ltd, Dalton House, 60 Windsor Avenue, London, SW19 2RR.
Company number 08720141. Registered in England and Wales.

For support please visit www.forgottenbooks.com

1 MONTH OF FREE READING

at

www.ForgottenBooks.com

By purchasing this book you are eligible for one month membership to ForgottenBooks.com, giving you unlimited access to our entire collection of over 1,000,000 titles via our web site and mobile apps.

To claim your free month visit:

www.forgottenbooks.com/free914871

* Offer is valid for 45 days from date of purchase. Terms and conditions apply.

English
Français
Deutsche
Italiano
Español
Português

www.forgottenbooks.com

Mythology Photography **Fiction** Fishing Christianity **Art** Cooking Essays Buddhism Freemasonry Medicine **Biology** Music **Ancient Egypt** Evolution Carpentry Physics Dance Geology **Mathematics** Fitness Shakespeare **Folklore** Yoga Marketing **Confidence** Immortality Biographies Poetry **Psychology** Witchcraft Electronics Chemistry History **Law** Accounting **Philosophy** Anthropology Alchemy Drama Quantum Mechanics Atheism Sexual Health **Ancient History Entrepreneurship** Languages Sport Paleontology Needlework Islam **Metaphysics** Investment Archaeology Parenting Statistics Criminology **Motivational**

To the Authorities
of the Toronto University
with the Author's best wishes
London.
May 23, 1890.

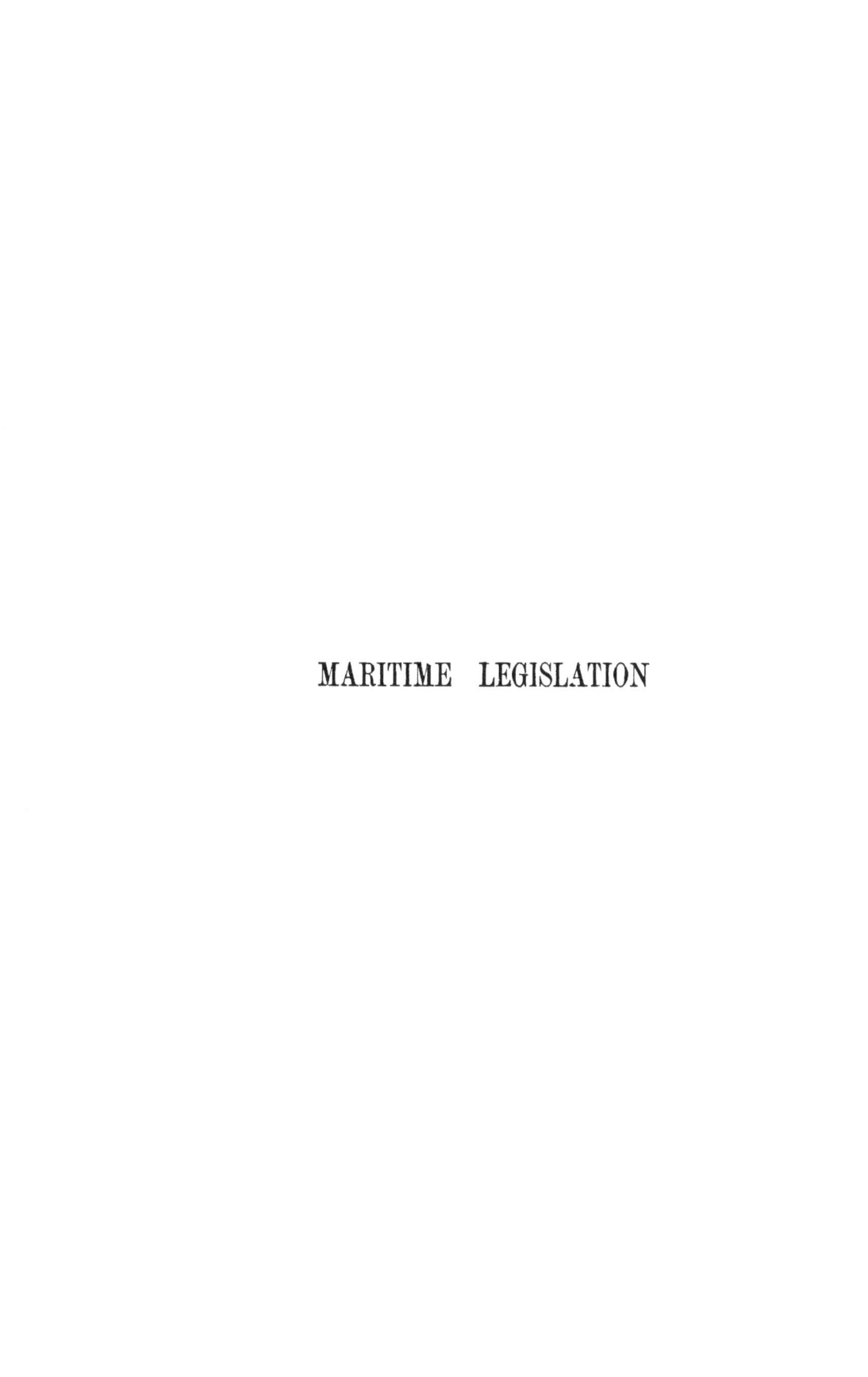

MARITIME LEGISLATION

PRINTED BY
SPOTTISWOODE AND CO., NEW-STREET SQUARE
LONDON

PAPERS

ON

MARITIME LEGISLATION

WITH A TRANSLATION OF

THE GERMAN MERCANTILE LAWS

RELATING TO MARITIME COMMERCE

BY

ERNEST EMIL WENDT, D.C.L.

THIRD EDITION

LONDON
LONGMANS, GREEN, AND CO.
AND NEW YORK: 15 EAST 16th STREET
1888

4339
14/11/80

PREFACE

TO

THE THIRD EDITION.

It is now seventeen years since the Second Edition of 'Papers on Maritime Legislation' was published, and in that time the subjects dealt with by me have been much discussed both in this country and in others. I have been asked to record these discussions—in many of which I have taken part—and their results in a permanent form, and I have endeavoured to carry this out in the present Third Edition of my papers.

In particular I have to the best of my power described the history of the General Average movement which preceded and has followed the issue of the York and Antwerp Rules, and of the struggle still pending with regard to the 'negligence' and other clauses of the Bill of Lading.

And, if I have ventured to express freely my own opinion in these pages, my excuse must be that they are at all events the result of many years' experience, as I have now been nearly thirty years the representative in this country of the more important maritime underwriters in all parts of the world, and have been personally conversant with the subjects treated for more than half a century.

With reference to the Appendix, I may remark that not only the translation of the German General Mercantile Law has been again very carefully revised, but that a translation of such laws as by the creation of the German Empire were in addition to the General Law required have been added.

It now remains only for me to express publicly to those who have so kindly assisted me in the preparation of one or the other of these three Editions my sincere gratitude, and these are :—Sir Travers Twiss, D.C.L., Q.C. (the last Advocate-General), Dr. Friedr. Sieveking (President of the Hanseatic Court of Appeal at Hamburg), Dr. Charles Stubbs, Mr. Fred. Stokes (the last Admiralty Proctor), and my present partner, Mr. Wm. Arnold.

4 & 6 Throgmorton Avenue:
July 1888.

PREFACE

TO

THE FIRST EDITION.

THE time for the reconsideration of the most important parts of our Maritime Enactments seems now so near at hand, that I have deemed it advisable to reproduce in the following pages some materials which will, I trust, be found useful by those who may be called upon to assist in the deliberations on the questions at issue.

15 FENCHURCH BUILDINGS, LONDON;
November 1867.

PREFACE

TO

THE SECOND EDITION.

THE necessity having arisen for the issue of a new edition of this volume, it appears to me to be my duty not only to express in this Preface my grateful acknowledgment of the favour with which the first edition has been received, but likewise to add, with respect to the subject-matter therein treated, a few remarks necessitated either by actual or attempted subsequent legislation.

But before I do so, I may be permitted for a moment to refer to certain critical observations which came to my notice soon after the publication of the first edition, and which characterised my work as an exposition of German views. I am, however, although a native of Germany, a British subject, and have been a resident in this country for more than twenty years, during which not only a close observance of everything relating to maritime commerce, but a careful study of our laws and customs, has been my constant duty.

So that, although the introduction of steam power and telegraphic communication has more than previously cemented *all the nations of the world into one and the some great Trading Community*, and therefore in the improvement of our laws not only British subjects, but the citizens of all other nations have a very material interest, my observations on them were never intended to be merely foreign views, which, if disagreeable to a very influential body of men, could readily be shelved, but the suggestions of a British subject, who has been for more than thirty years practically engaged in the consideration of matters of International and General Maritime Law, to an extent which falls to the lot of only few. This will readily be believed by those who are aware that I have been for years, and am now, honoured with the powers of attorney of more than Two hundred Marine Insurance Companies and Associations in different States of Europe and America, for the purpose of protecting their interests in cases of shipwreck within the United Kingdom of Great Britain and Ireland, and of conducting their lawsuits within this territory. This fact should, I think, give some weight to the remarks which I feel it my duty to submit; and here may I beg to remind my readers of a sentence which His Royal Highness the late Prince Consort uttered on a rather remarkable occasion to the following effect :—

> I conceive it to be the duty of every educated person closely to watch and study the time in which he lives, and, as far as in him lies, to add his humble mite of individual exertion to further the accomplishment of what he believes Providence to have ordained.
>
> Nobody, however, who has paid any attention to the peculiar features of our present era, will doubt for a moment that we are living at a period of most wonderful transition, which tends rapidly to accomplish that great end to which,

indeed, all history points—*the realisation of the unity of mankind.*

Not a unity which breaks down the limits and levels the peculiar characteristics of the different nations of the earth, but rather a unity, the *result and product* of those very national varieties and antagonistic qualities.

The alterations I have made in this edition are but few; the principal are the different order in which the contents appear, and, in consequence of a suggestion for which I feel very grateful, the reprint of the clauses of the Acts upon which my observations were intended to bear.

I trust that the class of readers for whom this second edition is more particularly intended will find this more systematical form an improvement, and that the same may be said for the addition made in reprinting the clauses of the different Acts.

Let me now review, as concisely as possible, the different subjects in their present order.

I.

I am sorry to be obliged to record that, in spite of the repeated attempts made by the Associated Chambers of Commerce to prevail upon the Board of Trade to make the International General Average Rules, as adopted at the Congress of Delegates at York, in September 1864, a subject of imperial legislation, nothing has been done.

Why not, may appear a mystery to those who remember that at the request of the Liverpool Chamber of Commerce the Foreign Office issued instructions to their principal consular officers abroad, for the purpose of urging upon the authorities where they were accredited the desirability of sending delegates to the York Congress, expressing at the same time the deep interest Her Majesty's Government felt in the result of the deliberations. Such result may have been unexpected, but it was to be hoped that the interest of the Government might survive the disclosure that some of our peculiarities were almost universally condemned.

II.

That under such circumstances the International Law of Affreightment, as adopted at a Congress held at Sheffield in 1865, which is of equal importance to the mercantile community generally, has not been brought by the Board of Trade before any branch of the Legislature, cannot surprise.

III.

It has often been remarked that if the late Lord Kingsdown had been sitting, such an infringement of International Law as the Judicial Committee of Her Majesty's Privy Council committed in the decision of the 'Marie de Brabant' could never have occurred; but it is more remarkable still that, notwithstanding the conclusions which I submitted in this correspondence, the Law Officers of the Crown should not have insisted on recommending the erasure of this blot from our Statute-book; or, is the influence of the large Steamboat Companies so great that they can with their power so easily defy the *clear and incontrovertible* right?

IV.

The Board of Trade not having considered it advisable to lay before Parliament my observations on the Acts here referred to, it will not occasion surprise that I have here reprinted them; especially when the different Bills laid before the House of Commons since have proved that the Board of Trade only approved my suggestion respecting the abolition of compulsory Pilotage, and left many other subjects with which I had dealt—not merely from the underwriters' point of view, but in an entirely *bonâ fide* spirit—altogether out of consideration.

That the Merchant Shipping Bill and the Merchant Shipping Code of 1870 and 1871, Mr. Farrer's two Memoranda on them, Sir William Mitchell's Review, Mr. H. C. Chapman's brief Review, the Report published by the Liverpool Chamber of Commerce, as well as Mr. Augustus Smith's notes, have had my serious attention, will readily be believed; and I may be permitted to say, that from all I have seen and heard, I am confirmed in the conviction that if Her Majesty's Government is really desirous of improving Maritime Legislation, so as to command not only the respect but the adhesion of *the great Trading Community of the whole World*, this can only be accomplished by appointing *a Royal Commission* to inquire into and report on the state of and the desired improvements in the whole of our Maritime Law, as well as to specify the subjects which ought to be more or less brought into harmony with the laws and customs of the other principal nations.

The task of such a Royal Commission will not be an

easy one, nor do I expect that its labours can be quickly accomplished; but if the members of the Commission really understand their duty—I mean if they are sufficiently versed in all the matters at issue—their Report or Reports are certain to enable the Legislature to amend the present law to the general satisfaction.

Mr. Farrer states that the suggestions and criticisms made by the members for the seaports, who assisted the Board of Trade at the conferences held at their office upon the Bill of 1870, have caused the Code now before the public to be improved. Now, there is an undoubted impression upon the public mind in general, that many more improvements would have been accomplished, if not only the Law Officers of the Crown had discussed the principles of the Code, but if the public in general had been officially heard in the only possible way, *i.e.* by a Royal Commission.

The delay thereby occasioned is sure not only not to be detrimental, but to lead to a great general benefit.

V.[1]

The subject of *Admiralty Jurisdiction* will naturally require a more than cursory remark; and the reason why I have not likewise reprinted the clauses of the Bill brought in during the session of 1867 is, because it was withdrawn altogether, and, as far as my observations can be still of interest, they are certain to be readily understood, even without the text of the Bill.

I will at once admit that there was no part of the

---

[1] This section was entitled: 'Observations on the Admiralty Jurisdiction Bill, dated April 16, 1867.'

Report of the Judicature Commission, dated March 25, 1869, for which I was less prepared, and the wisdom of which I must more doubt, than their recommendation to abolish the Admiralty jurisdiction, because the decisions of no Courts in the British Empire have commanded such universal respect as those of the High Court of Admiralty; and I heartily concur in the Protest with which the Judge of that Court, as a member of the Judicature Commission, recorded his dissent from that recommendation, and which is in the following terms, viz. :—

> (1) I think it is not expedient to destroy the special jurisdiction of the High Court of Admiralty. That Court has always administered, in peace and war, maritime international law. To no other Court has the Crown ever granted a Commission of prize; and even before the issue of such Commission, it has, in the opinion of Lord Stowell, an inherent jurisdiction in these matters. I may observe that the forms of pleading now in use in the High Court of Admiralty are as nearly as possible those which this report recommends to be generally adopted by all Courts.

In my introduction I stated why, according to my views, this jurisdiction should be increased, and I can therefore have no reason for entering on that subject again; suffice it to say, that from my own experience I would consider it a calamity if Sir Robert Phillimore's Protest remained unheeded, and the Legislature should decree the abolition of this most renowned jurisdiction.

Attention has recently been called by a memorial from the Associated Chambers of Commerce to the Judicature Commissioners to the present administration of this jurisdiction, which memorial was replied to by the Registrar of the High Court of Admiralty, and is likely to give rise to further discussion. Although, undoubtedly, some matters connected with the working of the Admiralty Court are open to improvement—and here I may refer to the very able letter which my friend, Mr. W. T. Pritchard, addressed to the Judge of the Court at the commencement of 1868, and which appeared in print—I am rather inclined to think that if the complaints of the memorialists are carefully sifted, it will be found that they might with equal or even greater justice be brought against any other Court in the United Kingdom.

The 'County Courts Admiralty Jurisdiction Act, 1868' (31 & 32 Vict. c. 71), the County Courts Admiralty Jurisdiction Amendment Act, 1869 (32 & 33 Vict. c. 51), and the Liverpool Admiralty District Registrars' Act, 1870 (33 & 34 Vict. c. 45), have, I am sorry to state, not been able to give that satisfaction—if any—which the general public anticipated, because there are few County Court Judges who can readily comprehend the subject-matters brought before them under these Acts, and if they can, their time is so fully occupied with the multifarious duties devolving upon them in the different towns of their district that one of the principal objects to be attained, viz. a quick despatch, is out of question altogether; and finally, the expenses are beyond everything anticipated.

The very fact that, since the first of these County Court Acts became law, every session has produced an Amendment or additional Act, has in itself been sufficient to prevent the Judges, Registrars, &c., of these Courts from becoming conversant with their duties, and it will hardly be believed that, in spite of all this piecemeal legislation, the cardinal necessity has been overlooked of making the Courts accessible to the owners of property salved as well as to the salvors, as was the case under the 460th section of the Merchant Shipping Act.

That under these circumstances attempts should have been made still further to extend the Admiralty Jurisdiction of the County Courts, and to establish Admiralty Registries with the same official duties as the Registry of the High Court, has taken me and many others by surprise.

What the general public really want are Admiralty Courts sitting, as in olden times, *de die in diem* (or *from tide to tide*, as expressed elsewhere), so that the hearing and determining of any cause can be proceeded with as soon as both parties have been able to collect their evidence, and to comply with such simple forms as are absolutely necessary in order to obtain complete justice; because it ought not to be overlooked that at present the preparatory proceedings for the hearing and determination of any cause require several weeks, unless both parties are equally anxious to push matters forward, and only too often delay is one of the weapons made use of for purposes of extortion. I imagine it would be considerably more conducive to the general interest, if, bearing in mind the suggestion as to the improvement in the despatch of the Admiralty business, in lieu of the County Courts with Admiralty jurisdiction, a certain number of Vice-Admiralty Courts, say at Liverpool, Cardiff, Falmouth, Deal, Great Yarmouth, Hull, and Newcastle-on-Tyne, were established for the purpose of exercising a jurisdiction identical with that of the High Court, for all cases which arise within a certain district attached to each of such Vice-Admiralty Courts; further, for all cases where plaintiff and defendant are resident within such district; and, finally, for all cases where plaintiff and defendant (non-residents) agree to such jurisdiction. The territorial limits to be fixed with regard to the peculiar Admiralty business which is principally expected at the particular Court, and which can easily be defined. The Appeal to go, as from the Colonial Vice-Admiralty Courts, direct to the Judicial Committee of Her Majesty's Privy Council.

I have no doubt that a carefully compiled return would prove that most of such Vice-Admiralty Courts, if not all, would be self-supporting.

VI.[1]

My observations under this head as well as under

VII.[2]

will, I trust, not be found out of place.

VIII.

My conviction, that in the interest of *bonâ fide* trade the addition there proposed to the International Criminal Law would be of immense advantage, remains unaltered.

IX.

I readily acknowledge that the subject here treated—depositions to be taken before the Receivers of Wreck—has had the favourable consideration of the Board of

---

[1] This section was entitled: 'Observations on the office of Judge in the Admiralty, Divorce, and Probate Courts Bill, dated June 19, 1867.'

[2] This section was entitled: 'Barristers' Petition against Extension of Admiralty Jurisdiction, and remarks thereon.'

Trade. Still, however, they have not been made, as I think they should be, compulsory.

X.[1]

The major part of the subjects herein enumerated remain yet open questions; a remark which likewise applies to

XI.[1]

and the Memorials alluded to under these heads.

In conclusion, I cannot but express the unfeigned gratification with which I have seen my translation of the German General Mercantile Law referred to and relied upon in the course of the important and interesting litigation which has not unnaturally resulted from the recent hostilities on the Continent. For the present edition this translation has been carefully revised, and some accidental—but happily unimportant—inaccuracies have been removed, and I sincerely trust that it may continue to be found worthy of attention in the course of further litigation as well as of future legislation.

[1] The letters here referred to in both Sections X. and XI. appear in this Third Edition, *sub* X.

15 FENCHURCH BUILDINGS, LONDON:
September 1871.

CONTENTS.

PAGE

INTRODUCTION xxiii

I.

INTERNATIONAL LAW OF GENERAL AVERAGE 1

II.

INTERNATIONAL LAW OF AFFREIGHTMENT IN CONNECTION WITH THE ATTEMPTS TO AGREE UPON UNIFORMITY IN THE WORDING OF BILLS OF LADING 295

III.

CORRESPONDENCE WITH THE BOARD OF TRADE RELATING TO THE INFRINGEMENT OF THE INTERNATIONAL LAW BY THE JUDICIAL COMMITTEE OF H.M. PRIVY COUNCIL IN THE DECISION OF THE 'MARIE DE BRABANT' 513

IV.

OBSERVATIONS, dated December 1886, on 17 and 18 Vict. cap. 104 (The Merchant Shipping Act, 1854); 17 and 18 Vict. cap. 120 (The Merchant Shipping Repeal Act, 1854); 18 & 19 Vict. cap. 91 (The Merchant Shipping Act Amendment Act, 1855); 25 & 26 Vict. cap. 63 (The Merchant Shipping Act Amendment Act, 1862) . . 527

V.

ADMIRALTY JURISDICTION OF COUNTY COURTS 621

VI.

SUGGESTIONS FOR THE IMPROVEMENT OF ADMIRALTY PRACTICE . . 624

VII.

FREIGHT, WHEN SHIP ABANDONED AT SEA 627

VIII.

Reasons why the making away with, or aiding and abetting in scuttling or otherwise destroying a vessel for the purpose of defrauding its underwriters, or those who have an interest therein, or in the cargo or freight, should, by agreement between the principal maritime nations, be declared an act of piracy 630

IX.

Merchant Ships' Logs, Protests and Depositions before Receivers 655

X.

Various papers showing how most of these subjects have been urged upon the Board of Trade 670

XI.

Appellate Jurisdiction in Maritime Causes 681

APPENDIX.

Translation of the German Mercantile Law relating to Maritime Commerce, and of— 687

   1. Regulation for seamen of December 27, 1872 790

   2. Law respecting the obligation of German merchant vessels to take home distressed seamen of December 27, 1872 . . 811

   3. Annex A to the above, viz.: Law respecting the nationality of merchant vessels, and their right to carry the flag of the Confederation, of October 25, 1867 813

   4. Law relating to registration and designation of merchant vessels of June 28, 1873 817

   5. Law respecting coast trading voyages of May 22, 1881 . . 817

Index 819

INTRODUCTION.

It ought never to be overlooked, that there is as much a law of the sea as there is a law of the land, and that, just as the Courts of Common Law and Equity have been established for the purpose of deciding differences arising within the territorial limits of the realm, the Court of Admiralty was, at a period beyond legal memory, established especially to take cognisance of all maritime contracts or torts, and all injuries or offences committed upon the high seas, in ports and havens, as far as the ebb and flow of the tide, in great rivers, beneath the first bridges thereof, and in all foreign parts, and based its decisions, as did the other European Admiralty Courts, on the Law Maritime and on the Roman Civil Law.

But attention should be paid to another difference between the Admiralty and the Municipal Courts, namely, that whereas in the latter, matters of fact are to be decided by a jury, the Judge of the former, assisted by nautical assessors, decides alike matters of fact and questions of law.

The consequence is, that the decisions in the Admiralty Court—in spite of the great expenses, and some other evils, which, however, may be easily rectified—have been much more approved by the mercantile communities here and abroad, than the decisions in the Common Law

Courts, where juries are frequently called upon to pronounce an opinion upon intricate commercial matters which they are incompetent to comprehend, and sometimes return verdicts utterly at variance with common sense.

Our North American cousins have, in their wisdom, left the Admiralty jurisdiction entirely intact as they received it from the British Crown, and anybody aiming at a Judgeship in their Courts clothed with Admiralty jurisdiction has to pass through a course of study of the Civil Law, which very few members of the English Bar have thought it necessary to master.

The great importance of this point ought not to be lost sight of, as in case, by certain positive enactments, the Judgeship in the Admiralty Court, and a seat in the Appeal Court, should not be reserved for learned civilians, it is difficult to see, not only how these Courts can be efficiently administered, but where the Foreign Office and the Lords of the Admiralty, as well as the general public, are in future to choose their advisers in matters of international and general Maritime Law, whom, for centuries, they have been accustomed to look for amongst the civilians.

I ought here to mention that, according to an official memorandum recently circulated, the present jurisdiction of the High Court of Admiralty of England embraces the following subjects :—

(Partly under old law, partly under recent statutes, 3 & 4 Vict. c. 65, and 24 Vict. 10.)

A. Collision, including all damage done by a ship.
B. Towage.

INTRODUCTION.

C. Pilotage.
D. Salvage, including Life Salvage.
E. Wages.
F. Bottomry and Respondentia Bonds.
G. Master's accounts.
H. Personal actions for damage between crew or passengers and owners.
I. Mortgages of ships.
J. Transfers of ships.
K. Right to possession of ships.
L. Questions between co-owners of ships.
M. Damage to, or detention of, imported cargo, where owner is not domiciled in England.
N. Necessaries when owner is not domiciled in England.
O. Building, equipping, or repairing a ship when under arrest.
P. Settlement of liability for personal and other injury in case of several claims against ship, and distribution of amount found due when ship is under arrest, Part IX., Merchant Shipping Act, s. 514, extended by 24 Vict. c. 10, s. 13.
Q. In addition, the Court has found it absolutely necessary to deal with other questions, such as freight and average, when those questions have arisen with respect to property in the hands of the Court (see 2 Moore's 'Privy Council Cases,' New Series, pp. 215, 235, 240; Place *v.* Potts, 5 'House of Lords,' 383),

and that it has been proposed to add the following subjects, viz. :—

A. Freight, and questions arising between Shipowner and Merchant on Charter-parties and Bills of Lading.
B. Demurrage.
C. Average.
D. Damage to, or detention of, cargo, when owner is domiciled in England, and under Charter-party.
E. Necessaries, when owner is domiciled in England.
F. Building, equipping, or repairing a ship when not under arrest.

G. Insurance.

II. In addition, there will be, no doubt, other matters arising out of, and incident to, the relations between Shipowner, Master, Merchant, and Underwriter.

With respect to the movement to obtain for County and other local Courts an Admiralty jurisdiction, it appears to me that the discussions which have taken place in and out of Parliament, so far as I have been able to follow them, have left entirely untouched the consideration of the following question:—

How a Court at Liverpool, for instance, or any other local Court, or any Admiralty Court but the High Court sitting at Westminster, can be expected to satisfy the requirements of any other than the local merchant or shipowner?

But before proceeding with my argument, I may state that there is, in my opinion, a very great difference of principle involved in the question, whether the anxiety which the merchants of some towns have evinced for a local Admiralty jurisdiction solely aims at Courts for the purpose of settling differences between merchants and others, where both plaintiff and defendant are residing in the same town, or, as generally has been assumed, at Courts where a non-resident plaintiff having a difference with a resident defendant, should be obliged to sue.

Now it is evident that to the former case alone the commonplace phrase of bringing justice to everybody's door can properly be applied; for neither a merchant of Newcastle, nor of London, nor of Hull, nor of Bristol, would consider it a sound application of this principle, if he were forced to pursue any claim he might have, not in the town where he resides, nor in the metropolis where all the other Courts of English judicature are efficiently conducted, and where, consequently, the whole forensic machinery of barristers, solicitors, and proctors is in perfect working order; but in Liverpool, for instance, where a non-resident plaintiff would have to encounter, as a stranger, difficulties at present entirely unknown to him.

The High Court of Admiralty, as a central tribunal, having so many cases of every description brought before it, has acquired great aptitude for the transaction of business, which must be impaired if that business be curtailed by the establishment in Liverpool and other towns of Admiralty Courts, with an identical jurisdiction to the High Court.

The late Lord Justice Knight-Bruce once said in an appeal before Privy Council, in which foreign merchants were interested, '*we ought not to forget that there are other people in the world besides ourselves,*' and these other people have quite as much interest that cheap and speedy justice should be done in our Admiralty Courts as we ourselves have. No Liverpool merchant who is to be sued by a London merchant, or *vice versâ*, can really maintain that there is a difference in the expenses of the suit, whether one of the parties with all his witnesses travels from London to Liverpool, or the other from Liverpool to London; and if the assertion, that Liverpool contributes in the number of cases coming before the Admiralty Court very little less than London, be correct, does that not show that very serious inconvenience and pecuniary loss would be inflicted upon a comparatively large number of merchants not resident in Liverpool, if they were to be forced to apply to a new and untried Court elsewhere?

As I pointed out above, if as a general rule all parties

to an Admiralty suit were resident in one and the same place, the desire for local Courts could not only be understood but would be highly appreciated; but as in the majority of cases which come before the High Court of Admiralty, the parties are either resident in or have more easy access to London, and their representatives reside for the most part in London, it is in my mind beyond a doubt that the result of the proposed innovation would be highly prejudicial to very important interests.

The proposed dispersion of the Admiralty business is also calculated to impair the efficiency of the practitioners. There are at present many more well-qualified practitioners who could be spared from the other branches of the law with safety to their clients than from the Admiralty Court, which has hardly recovered from the retirement of the great body of proctors. The few proctors and solicitors who habitually practice in it would have little encouragement to continue their staff of clerks, &c., if the present business of the High Court of Admiralty were to be dispersed amongst several local Courts.

I know that my excuse for venturing to touch upon these subjects can only be their vast importance to those enormous interests which could not but suffer if what appears to be the favoured scheme of some influential members of our Bar was really carried out.

Before concluding, I ought to observe that the reason for my adding a translation of the 'German Maritime Law,' as an Appendix to these Papers, is simply that the great care and research displayed in the framing of its different clauses entitle it to every consideration on the part of those who may be engaged in the preparation of a similar compilation for this country.

Nothing can be a better proof of the correctness of the assertion than the fact that, after the members of the late Germanic Confederation had decided in 1856 to convoke a meeting of delegates for the purpose of agreeing upon *one general mercantile law* for the whole of their territory, the Prussian Government appointed three committees of merchants, one in Stettin, one in Danzig, and one in Kœnigsberg, in order to investigate and collect the most desirable body of maritime law; and when the German commissioners met at Hamburg on April 26, 1858, their Prussian colleagues were enabled to lay before them a well-considered draft of a Common Maritime Law, together with carefully compiled reasons for the same.

The results of the deliberations of the commissioners, who were assisted by delegates from the most important mercantile communities of Germany, renowned for their practical knowledge of those matters, were referred to the different Governments for perusal, and after they had instructed their commissioners as to the different views they took of the draft, the commissioners met again and again for the revision and super-revision of it, and finally on March 1, 1862, the Government of Prussia set the example of adopting the revised draft as its public law in maritime matters.

That law has subsequently come into operation throughout the whole of Germany, and I cannot deny myself the satisfaction of here observing that the minutes or protocols of the deliberations of these commissioners, which have been fully published, afford the most interesting study on all questions of Maritime Law.

INTERNATIONAL LAW OF GENERAL AVERAGE.

ALTHOUGH the history of the movement which led to a very general adoption of the principles laid down for the uniform regulation of General Average by the so-called 'York and Antwerp Rules' has been written by Mr. Richard Lowndes in the third edition of his able work, 'The Law of General Average (English and Foreign),' 1878, and by several others, it has, as far as I am aware, not yet been attempted to reproduce in a collected form the discussions which paved the way and ultimately led to the adoption of those rules, and my object in reprinting some of them and printing others for the first time is, that future students of matters connected with this subject may have before them all the arguments advanced in relation thereto.

The initiation of this important movement was caused by the issue of the following circular to the principal Chambers of Commerce and bodies of Underwriters of Europe and America :—

National Association for the Promotion of Social Science.
3 Waterloo Place, London. May 3, 1860.

GENTLEMEN,—The system of General Average is one which, to prevent confusion and injustice, pre-eminently requires that the same principles should be acknowledged amongst the chief maritime nations. So far is this from being the case, however, that some of the most important rules vary not only in the same country, but in the same port. Uncertainty in law is always an evil; and, in regard to General Average, the evil is peculiarly felt. The ship may be owned in one country, insured in another, her cargo owned and insured in several, and the port of destination, where the General Average is made up, may be in a country which has different rules to any of the others. What is considered to be Particular Average on ship in one port is held to be General Average in another, so that the owner of an outward-bound ship may find himself unable to recover his loss either from his Underwriters at home, or as General Average abroad; or, on the other hand, he may be in a position to indemnify himself fraudulently twice over. A similar remark would apply to special charges on freight and on cargo. A very large proportion of the most important questions rests in England nominally upon the decision of that extremely vague authority, 'the custom of Lloyd's,' but really depends upon the idiosyncrasy of the particular adjuster who may be entrusted with the papers. Hence arise many cases where apparently injustice must be done to Assurer or Assured. Either the Assurer finds himself saddled with a loss against which he believed himself insured, or the Underwriter pays one which was not considered in the premium.

Much loss is occasioned to the mercantile community and to the country at large, and much valuable time is worse than wasted through business being impeded by misunderstandings and irritated feelings.

A still more crying evil resulting from the present uncertainty of law and custom, is the opening which it leaves for every sort of abuse. Attempts are daily being made to introduce charges of the most outrageous description, which do not even go into the pocket of the Shipowner, but which he feels himself helpless to resist from want of a law to appeal to; and he naturally considers himself hardly used should charges which he himself has paid be refused by his Underwriters, though these last are obliged to refuse in justice to themselves and to prevent the innovation becoming a precedent.

The evils of such a state of things are notorious and unquestioned, though it may be doubted whether many which are distinctly traceable to it, and are therefore removable, are clearly realised as proceeding from this source. Probably the chief reason which has hitherto prevented any general movement in favour of this reform, is an exaggerated estimate of the difficulties in the way of carrying it out. The difficulties are no doubt considerable, but they are far from being insuperable, and the importance of the end amply justifies an attempt to grapple with them.

Both the Assured and the Underwriter are interested in placing their mutual relations upon a footing which would effect a saving of time and temper, and would secure them against the annoying pecuniary loss to which they are at present exposed. It is not of so much importance how the disputed points of General Average are settled, as that they should be settled. Most of the questions are in the end merely matters of account between one set of Underwriters and another, and it would make little difference to any Underwriter upon which interest it might be determined the charge should fall. It is true that there are points, such as the allowance of wages and provisions in a port of refuge, which would raise questions between Shipowner and Underwriter, but for the sake of both it is to the last degree desirable that these should not be left as a bone of contention between Assurer and Assured, as they are at present, *e.g.*, when goods to America are insured in England.

The evils of the present system have already caused much dissatisfaction in America as well as in this country, and will become more and more intolerable as the commerce of the world increases, which it seems likely to do with a rapidity hitherto unexampled. The time then would seem to have come, when an attempt should be made to remove this most unnecessary element of irritation between Assured and Underwriter.

In the hope of coming to an understanding upon this question, the Council of the National Association for the Promotion of Social Science have determined that it shall be brought forward for discussion at their next meeting at Glasgow on Monday, September 24 next, and following days; and we earnestly trust that you will find it in your power to send representatives of your body to that meeting, as it is very desirable that delegates from the commercial bodies in different parts of the world which are chiefly interested should be present.

We are, Gentlemen,

Your obedient Servants,

BROUGHAM & VAUX, *President of the Council,* } NATIONAL ASSOCIATION FOR THE PROMOTION OF SOCIAL SCIENCE.
GEORGE W. HASTINGS, *General Secretary,*

DUNCAN DUNBAR, *Chairman of the General Shipowners' Society, London.*
THOMAS BARING, *Chairman of Lloyd's, London.*
WILLIAM WILSON SAUNDERS, *Chairman of the Association for the Protection of Commercial Interests, &c., London.*
W. J. TOMLINSON, *Chairman of the Chamber of Commerce, Liverpool.*
F. A. CLINT, *Deputy-Chairman of the Shipowners' Association, Liverpool.*
CHARLES LANGTON, *Chairman of the Underwriters' Association, Liverpool.*
WILLIAM M. MOSS, *Chairman of the Association for the Protection of Commercial Interests, &c., Liverpool.*
ALLAN GILMORE, *Chairman of the Shipowners' Association, Glasgow.*
WILLIAM P. PATON, *Chairman of the Chamber of Commerce and Manufactures, Glasgow.*
HENRY J. ATKINSON, *Chairman of the Shipping Committee of the Hull Chamber of Commerce and Shipping.*
WILLIAM BROWN ATKINSON & Co., *Managers of the Humber and Hull Mutual Insurance Association.*
JOHN SHUTE, *Chairman of the Chamber of Commerce, Bristol.*

Now, before entering upon what arose out of this circular, it may be expedient to remind my readers that the whole legislation on General Average is based upon a sentence in the Rhodian law (916 B.C.) which runs as follows: 'If goods are thrown overboard to lighten a ship, that which has been given for all shall be replaced by the contribution of all.'

This maxim found its way into the Roman civil law (Dig. lib. 14, Tib. 2, Fr. 1), and from thence, in nearly identical expressions, into the legislation of all the maritime nations of the world.

It can, therefore, be scarcely a matter of surprise that in process of time, measured by centuries, manifold conclusions were drawn from the enactments so promulgated by the parties who were entrusted with the administration of the law of General Average in the various cases which arose under different jurisdictions, so that when a comparative table of the laws and principles of General Average as actually administered was drawn up, a picture presented itself, for which even those most interested in the matter were scarcely prepared.

The divergent rules which arose have been so elaborately explained in Mr. Lowndes's work, above referred to, that they need not be recapitulated here, but I may at once refer to the proceedings of the Glasgow Congress and state that, a few days before its assembling, the following memorandum was issued:—

The adjustment of a General Average is governed by the laws and customs of the State in which it is adjusted. The laws and customs of different States vary materially, and that which is General Average in one country is not General Average in another. It is admitted that this is a great practical grievance, and the object of this meeting is to put an end to it.

The following are the principal points on which differences exist:—

1. Damage done to ship and cargo by voluntary stranding.
2. Damage done to ship and cargo in extinguishing a fire.
3. Chafage and breakage of cargo after jettison.
4. Damage done to cargo by discharging it at a port of refuge.
5. Cutting away the wreck of masts accidentally carried away.
6. Expenses of warehouse rent on cargo, re-shipping it, and outward port charges, at a port of refuge, when the original ship carries on the cargo from that port.
7. Carrying a press of sail.
8. Wages and provisions for the crew during the delay caused by putting into port.
9. Contributing values of ship, freight, and cargo.

The opinion of the meeting will be taken on each of these points:—

1st. As to the principle which should govern it—*i.e.* whether the loss is, or is not, in principle, allowable in General Average.

2nd. As to the expediency of adopting a practical rule to modify or prevent abuse of that principle.

All papers to be read at the meetings on this subject must be lodged with the secretary, at Glasgow, on or before Saturday, September 22. The reading of no paper must occupy more than fifteen minutes.

After all the papers have been read, a discussion will follow, in which every one may join. The opinion of the meeting will then be taken on each point, and measures will afterwards be adopted to carry out in practice the conclusions arrived at.

GEO. W. HASTINGS, *General Secretary.*

Thereupon Lord Brougham opened, on September 25, 1860, the first meeting by calling upon

MR. G. W. HASTINGS, the general secretary of the Association, who said he thought the best way to open the discussion would be for him to state in a few words how the movement had originated. The council of the Association was applied to in the early portion of the present year by several important commercial bodies, including Lloyd's in London and the Underwriters' Association of Liverpool, to take up the important question of international General Average, and, through the means of this Association at its meetings in Glasgow, to have a discussion on its principles, in order that some uniform system might be arrived at. The council accordingly issued circulars to the different commercial bodies of this country, and also to many parts of America and the continent of Europe. A considerable number of answers had been received to that circular and a large number of foreign delegates were present prepared to discuss the several questions. In order to confine the discussion to certain definite points they had prepared a short statement of nine points, which, as it seemed to him, were the principal points on which the discussion turned. And having said this much he would now suggest that Mr. Philip Rathbone, the honorary secretary of this meeting, and who had taken very great interest in the question, and to whom they were indebted for the discharge of many laborious duties in connection with the subject, should read to the meeting a statement of the question; and after that the different members, foreign and English, might give their opinions on the several questions, in the hope that some tangible results might be arrived at.

MR. P. H. RATHBONE then read the following statement: We are brought here to-day by the conviction that the differences of General Average are a serious detriment to the commerce of the country, entailing on those who are interested in it great pecuniary loss, and that which is worse in mercantile transactions, continual disputes. For instance, when a ship sails from New Orleans for Liverpool with a cargo of cotton, and on her passage meets with an accident which obliges her to put into a port of refuge to repair the injuries she has sustained, and at that port her cargo is discharged in order that she may be repaired, after she is repaired her cargo is reshipped, she proceeds on her voyage, and reaches her destination. Any mercantile man would expect that the General Average resulting from such simple and everyday facts would be the same wherever the average might be adjusted; but I am informed that that average adjusted in the United States might be *three* times as great as it would have been if it had been adjusted in the United Kingdom. Differences such as these—and their name is legion—give rise to constant disputes and feelings of injustice. A strong feeling has existed for a long time amongst commercial men that such a state of things ought not to be allowed to continue—that transactions between men of different nations (which General Averages are in most cases) should not be governed by the local laws or customs of the port of shipment, the port of destination, or the place of residence of the underwriter—that international or general maritime laws and customs should govern such subjects in the same way that collisions on the high seas are determined in our Admiralty Court, so that a General Average under any given circumstances should be the same in all countries. The difficulty has been how to bring about such a result. Some few have adopted practical remedies to meet the present grievance in our own particular cases, but this is only a partial and exceptional remedy. The generality are still daily sufferers, and the evil has become so great with the great increase of commerce, that application was made to this society to take up this subject and find a remedy. As the subject itself was of such great importance to a mercantile nation like ours, and the interests involved so vast, we did not hesitate to accede to the request, and the result is this meeting. On the end in view, viz. uniformity in the adjustment of General Average, we are not hampered with some of those difficulties which embarrass other questions, for it is admitted that there ought to be uniformity. We have, therefore, to consider only how we can practically accomplish it. When the present movement was first suggested a general revision of the principles which should govern the adjustment of General Average was contemplated, and it was argued, and with much reason, that if we could agree on the principles which ought to govern the adjustment of General Average we should have no difficulty in agreeing to act on these principles, and thus uniformity in practice would be obtained. The improbability of our all agreeing on these principles, in addition to other considerations, rendered it unadvisable to start upon that plan. It was then suggested that the attention of the meeting should be devoted solely to the formation of machinery for obtaining hereafter uniformity on any disputed point—*i.e.* to the formation of a court of appeal for all nations, to which all doubtful points should be submitted, and to whose decrees all nations should bow. This plan also has many arguments to recommend it, but it would involve indefinite delay before any practical results could be obtained, while it was felt that it was very desirable to obtain an immediate and practical remedy for the greatest of the existing evils. We were, therefore, induced, in the first instance, to make an attempt to procure an immediate decision on the points of the greatest and most pressing practical importance. This course will by no means preclude the consideration of the principles which ought to govern the subject, and naturally leads us to the discussion of the second, viz. the consideration of the expediency and practicability of forming a court of appeal for our government on all other questions which may be in doubt or disputed. It is not probable that we shall be unanimous on the abstract correctness of the principles which ought to govern any one of the points even now before us, still less on the practical rules which some may think it expedient to adopt to restrict or modify those principles. We are here from all parts of the world. Each country will naturally be favourable to its own customs and principles to which it is accustomed. Each of us will, therefore, be obliged to modify or abandon his own peculiar views in deference to those of the majority if we are to arrive at a practical result. Before we proceed to discuss the point before us, or even to read papers, we should consult and perhaps decide on the mode in which we are to arrive at the opinion of the meeting *as a body*, and after the points before us have been discussed, we must consider what available machinery can be framed for carrying out this opinion in practice and for rectifying hereafter other difficult, doubtful, or disputable points not included in our present programme. If we were all representatives with full power to bind our constituents, or even if all places were represented here to-day, we might perhaps devise such a plan, and carry it out in practice at once, but many of us are only present on our own account, although deeply interested in the subject no doubt, and from our position capable of influencing others. We must therefore submit our plans to the different mercantile communities before they either can or ought to be carried out in practice. This is a difficulty which calls for our attention. I have purposely abstained from commenting on any of the nine points to discuss which we have met here to-day, as it would be premature before the papers are read. I will, with these few observations, leave them in your hands, adding only on the part of this country that in which I am sure all Englishmen will agree—viz. that we feel deeply indebted to all those gentlemen who have crossed the seas, at so much personal inconvenience, for the purpose of attending here to-day, to promote unity amongst nations on this great mercantile question.

Mr. RATHBONE then said: I think perhaps it will be desirable to mention the course we propose to adopt. There are eight papers to be read—they are all very short—all to the point, which is not always the case, and, therefore, I think, perhaps, if my Lord Brougham agrees, that it will be better to read these papers first. I am sorry to say we have no paper from America, but I hope the delegates from America will say a few words after all the papers have been read. Perhaps it will be best at once to go to business upon the resolutions after reading the papers, and after we have heard the opinion from America. I think almost every other country has sent in its opinions in writing.

The Chairman. I think we have nothing from France.

Mr. Rathbone. I am sorry to say that, though the Association of Underwriters in Paris write most cordially, wishing us every success, the gentleman by whom they wished to be represented has unfortunately been prevented attending, by business.

The Chairman. When you talked of a court of appeal, did you intend it to be a court of appeal in General Average, or on all mercantile matters?

Mr. Rathbone. A general court of appeal, of which General Average would form a part.

The following papers were then read :—

Mr. William Richards (of London): Within the brief space of time permitted to us after receiving intimation of the course intended to be followed at the International Congress for the promotion of uniformity in the adjustment of General Average, to be held at Glasgow on September 25, 1860, it is impossible to enter upon the subject with the careful and mature consideration which it requires.

We can, therefore, only offer a few cursory reflections upon the general question.

Attention has frequently been drawn to the diversity of practice in the treatment of questions relating to General Average. From the remarks of Chief Justice Abbott,[1] and of Chief Justice Gibbs, in Taylor v. Curtis,[2] we learn that, although all the commercial states of Europe have adopted the rule as to General Average, contribution being made by all parties concerned in a sea adventure towards extraordinary expenses or losses, voluntarily incurred by one or more for the benefit of all—each of these states professing to follow the Rhodian law—yet they often differ from each other; that foreign jurists have often made very different comments

---

[1] 5th edition of *Abbott on Shipping*, p. 342.
[2] Hildyard's edition of *Parke on Insurance*, p. 282.

upon that law, and that no principle of maritime law has been followed by more variations in practice.

More than a century ago strenuous attempts were made to have the Marine Insurance law of this country reduced to a code as in many foreign states. The Legislature, however, have considered it better to avoid making positive enactments.

Marshall, in his preliminary discourse,[1] considers that it would be extremely difficult, if not wholly impracticable, to make positive laws to suit every case, and doubts whether, if such were made, they would be found to answer the purpose of preventing litigation; and the same writer maintains that, in consequence of the absence of any code, the practice of insurance in England had been in his time more conformable to principles and the usage of trade than that of foreign nations.

The present movement has for its intention to assimilate the General Average principles and practice of this and other countries, and thus to modify or put an end to the differences which exist between the laws and customs of different states in relation to General Average.

The mode adopted by the Association to obtain this desirable result is to a certain extent in accordance with the views of the late Mr. Stevens, the well-known writer on Average, who considered that the object of clearing up the uncertainty existing on many points would be most readily attained by men of experience communicating their knowledge to the world, and that repeated examination and discussion of the practice of insurance (and of average as arising out of it) would alone fix it on solid principles, and secure for them that universal assent which would probably never be yielded to the deliberations of any particular body of men.

In the case of Birkley v. Presgrove,[2] General Average was defined to be 'all loss which arises in consequence of extraordinary sacrifices, or expenses incurred for the preservation of ship and cargo.' The laws of foreign countries seem to recognise the same general principle as forming the basis of General Average. The question may therefore be asked, whence does such diversity arise

[1] *Treatise on Insurance.* London, 1808.   [2] 1 Eart. 220.

in the practice of different countries? No one will deny that a sacrifice made for the preservation of the lives and property at stake is General Average.

Mr. Benecke with justice says: 'The consequences deduced by legislators and commentators from this apparently simple rule differ materially from each other, and this is not surprising if we consider in what different senses the words *sacrifice* and *preservation* may be taken.'

The courts of law in England and America mutually regard the decisions in both countries on the subject of General Average with the highest respect, and the leading writers on General Average in each country give the greatest weight and consideration to the reasoning of those in the other. Yet, on some of the points proposed for discussion at the present meeting, the practice of the two countries is at variance, and the decisions and opinions of the greatest jurists have been conflicting.

If we refer to cases in our own courts we find that a leading principle is very frequently not considered as law until it has undergone discussion in more than one court, or has been submitted by appeal to the House of Lords. It is no wonder, then, that difficulties should arise in determining the construction to be put upon the principles referred to. And many cases of average arise in the course of practice which require close and careful investigation before a person well experienced in the study and practice of General Average can determine the principle which directly bears upon the point at issue. Although the adoption of the broad principles of General Average, as laid down in the case referred to above, is universal, the limit or extension of these principles varies in different countries to a very considerable extent, and it will be easily understood that to this cause is attributable the great diversity in practice. The practice as established in America allows in General Average the indirect consequences of a General Average act, while the practice of this country restricts such allowance to the direct and immediate consequences of such act. If we take the case of a mast cut away for the general preservation, we find the mast with yards, sails, rigging, &c., admitted as General Average in both countries, and if the ship has to bear up for a port of refuge to replace these losses, the wages and provisions of the crew from the time the vessel bore up till the repairs were effected would, in America, be chargeable in General Average, while in this country they would be placed to account of owners of the ship.

Again, if a ship, having been compelled by sea peril to put into a port of refuge, is obliged to unload her cargo to repair damage, the American practice allows in General Average the whole of the expense of unloading, warehouse rent, and reloading the cargo, as well as the wages and provisions of the crew; while the English practice charges in General Average the expense of unloading only; to the cargo warehouse rent; and to the freight the expenses of reloading and outward pilotage, &c.

These two instances may serve to illustrate, in the case of the American practice, the extension allowed and, in that of England, the limit put upon the general principle admitted in common by both countries.

In the time of Lord Mansfield, Mr. Millar, in the introduction to his able Treatise on Insurance,[1] says: 'The Trade of England has of late been so extensive and various as to increase, to a very great degree, the demand for insurance, and to bring under discussion a multiplicity of curious and interesting points.' This remark is still more applicable to the present day. Cases frequently arise which illustrate the accuracy or fallacy of admitted principles and usages, and although the learning and discrimination of the judges in the courts of law, and the researches of the writers of authority on this branch of the law, combined with the practical experience of those actually engaged in the business of insurance, have been progressively establishing fixed principles or usages, casualties nevertheless sometimes occur under circumstances which render them difficult of application to any recognised standard; and it is probable, therefore, that no attempt to completely assimilate the practice will succeed.

We may instance the case of voluntary stranding, the difference of opinion which exists on this subject being a fruitful source of complaint.

[1] Edinburgh, 1787.

Mr. Benecke, referring to voluntary stranding, writes as follows: 'When a vessel is purposely run on shore and afterwards got off with damage, the question whether the repairs of such damage belong to General or Particular Average, depends entirely upon the circumstances of the case. If the situation of the vessel were such as to admit of no alternative, so that without running her ashore she would have been unavoidably lost and that measure were resorted to for the purpose of saving the lives or liberty of the crew, no contribution can take place, because nothing in fact was sacrificed. But if the vessel and cargo were in a perilous, but not a desperate situation, and the measure of running her ashore was deliberately adopted as best calculated to save the ship and cargo, in that case the damage sustained, according to the fundamental rules, constitutes a claim for restitution.' 'Suppose,' continues Mr. Benecke, 'that a vessel having sprung a dangerous leak, the master, in order to save a valuable cargo, determines to run her ashore in a convenient place, although he might possibly have reached a harbour with a leaky vessel, at least if he had chosen to throw overboard part of the cargo; or suppose him to adopt the same measure if, pursued by an enemy, he considers this a more efficacious method of effecting her escape than lightening the vessel by jettison. Here we find all the necessary requisites for constituting a general contribution—imminent danger, a voluntary determination, and a sacrifice—and I can see no reason for distinguishing these cases from that of goods being thrown overboard, or of a mast being cut away in a storm.'

Mr. Benecke, in the above observations, appears to mark out a clear line of distinction in the treatment of claims for damage arising out of voluntary stranding. We may remark that, in the endeavour to assimilate the practice of General Average in relation to the allowance under this head of losses sustained, or expenses incurred, it is very important that full consideration should be given to the basis on which the values of the contributing interests should be established.

Magent says: 'The value of the ship and cargo to contribute to General Average is that value which they would have produced net for ready money, had they belonged to one person, and had no sacrifice been made.'

This is the basis adopted by the practice of this country, in cases where the average is adjusted after the arrival of the ship at her port of destination.

By the practice of Hamburg and other foreign states, any cargo is made to contribute upon the invoice value, without regard to the damage it may have sustained during the voyage.

This practice, considering the limited value usually put upon the ship, might not, when the cargo arrives in good order, be found to entail any very serious hardship on the owners of the vessel, but in the event of any particular shipment becoming greatly damaged during the voyage, such goods suffer an injustice by being forced to contribute upon a value which does not exist, and the owners of the same, in claiming under their policies, frequently become involved in difficulty and controversy.

In referring to the question of contributory values, we have only mentioned one point out of many which appears to require consideration.

The convenience now afforded of submitting a question of principle to the Judges, upon an admitted statement of facts, presents a means of gradually establishing a uniform system in this country, where established mercantile custom, ' once clearly ascertained in any of the supreme courts, acquires the force of law, without the sanction of legislative authority.'[1]

It is impossible, in the few minutes allowed for the reading of a paper, to touch upon the important matters which appear in the synopsis.

M. THÉODORE ENGELS (Chamber of Commerce, Antwerp): La Chambre de Commerce d'Anvers a reçu avec beaucoup de satisfaction l'invitation gracieuse de votre Comité de venir discuter en commun, les mesures à prendre dans un intérêt général à toutes les nations maritimes, des réglements qui régiront par la suite une matière aussi importante que celle des avaries communes.

Elle sait gré à l'Angleterre, le pays du progrès par excellence et des idées pratiques, d'avoir pris cette initiative et nous a chargés d'être auprès de vous l'interprète de ces sentiments. Vous trouverez, en notre pays, la plus grande sympathie et un appui

[1] Marshall, 21.

énergique, tant de la part du gouvernement que de celle du commerce, à faire prévaloir les mesures qu'une discussion générale et approfondie aura fait reconnaître comme les plus pratiques et les plus équitables.

En effet, Messieurs, en présence de tous les progrès qui se font jour, n'en est-il pas un des plus indispensables, dans l'intérêt général, que les répartitions d'avaries communes subies volontairement dans un moment de peril commun, se fassent sur un pied uniforme, que l'armateur, le négociant et l'assureur de toutes les nations sachent quelles sont les lois générales qui leur sont applicables et que, n'importe dans quel port du monde où son navire ou sa marchandise arrive, il soit traité d'après des bases fixes non sujettes à des interprétations arbitraires ou locales, qui donnent lieu à tout moment à des differences sérieuses et regrettables entre lui et ses assureurs.

La Belgique, Messieurs, ancien foyer d'industrie et de prospérité commerciale, ne reste jamais en arrière quand il s'agit d'inaugurer une innovation heureuse. Elle apprécie à leur juste valeur les nobles efforts que sont faits dans ce but, n'importe d'où ils arrivent, et on trouvera toujours en elle un concours loyal et actif.

Mr. Thomas R. Davison (Average Adjuster, London): If the section of the National Association, which has originated this movement, can succeed in its proposed object, the result, in a commercial point of view, will be, perhaps, more important than any subject brought under the notice of the Association.

The discordant practice of different countries, in reference to General Average, is a grievance to the mercantile community at large.

Some mode of apportioning General Average has existed since commerce originated. The early view taken of making a division of the losses or expenses incurred has been, that as an accident has happened, in which the entire interests of the ship, freight, and cargo were concerned, the charges should be distributed over the whole according to their respective values, without any attempt at discrimination.

This practice still prevails in some places, where probably closer investigation has not been entered upon, and in others it has been irregularly varied, without establishing any other principle: my object is to show that a more perfect examination of the subject would tend to bring about the agreement sought for.

In England the principles of General Average and its consequences have been a complete study and, among those who follow it as a profession, there is no difference of opinion except on some few inconsiderable points; upon great questions they are agreed.

General Average rules are to be considered without reference to Insurance: they are in reality a common-sense distribution of such losses and charges as belong to the united interest included in ship, freight and cargo. To arrive at a proper understanding of the apportionment of the losses and charges, it is necessary to look to the exact and immediate cause of them, and to avoid as much as possible including consequences. For this purpose I will consider No. 6, of the designated principal points on which differences exist: 'Expenses of warehouse rent on cargo, re-shipping it, and outward port charges at a port of refuge, when the original ship carries on the cargo from that port.'

In many countries it is the practice to put the cost of discharging cargo, warehouse rent and re-shipping into General Average, thus including therein the direct act of General Average and its consequences: no doubt this originated in the before-described idea that, as there was one general calamity, each interest should take its share according to its value. Our custom, the result of much study and experience, is to make such a separation of the charges as will make them apply as directly as possible to the respective interests for which they are incurred. A ship having sustained damage has sprung a leak, and it is requisite to discharge her cargo to repair; she could not otherwise proceed on her voyage, and therefore ship, freight, and cargo are interested in the discharge, and the expense of discharging the cargo is therefore General Average: the rent of the warehouse is a direct charge upon the cargo and should be so levied: it is a consequence of the accident, but so would the loss of the cargo be if it were burned in the warehouse, and I am not aware that it has ever been proposed to make damage in warehouse a subject of General Average;

the re-shipping and outward charges become a direct charge on the freight: the owner of the ship took in his cargo originally to earn a freight and must take it in again, after a casualty, to enable him to take it to its destination and so earn his freight.

In a case of accident and its consequences, every interest will incur some charges peculiar to itself, and it is not equitable to throw upon the general interest such share of the accident, enabling thereby the proprietor of one interest to escape at the expense of the others. The effect of putting the charges of rent and re-shipping into General Average is that the ship, having paid for its own particular average repairs of damage, is called upon to contribute to the charges belonging to cargo and freight, which pay nothing towards its repairs, and it might easily happen that a ship of high value having a bulky cargo, as of timber or coals, might have to pay, in addition to her own repairs, four-fifths of the rent and cost of re-shipping of the cargo to the ship's detriment and the advantage of the other two interests.

In reviewing the other points intended for consideration I will take No. 1. 'Damage done to ship and cargo by voluntary stranding.'

This cannot be taken to be General Average: it does not contain that first element of General Average which is the voluntary sacrifice of something which, being itself in a condition of safety, is intentionally destroyed or damaged for the general preservation. An anchor and chain by which a ship is riding in safety, is slipped to avoid a collision, or a danger of driving on shore; masts, when standing, cut away for the same cause; cargo taken out of the hold and thrown overboard to lighten the vessel— these are legitimate subjects of General Average; but a ship purposely run on shore is to prevent her sinking: before this were done she would be filling with water and be actually in a state of total loss: there could be no hope of saving the ship, and it could be done only in reality for a saving of life, the intention and expectation of saving the ship and cargo not being in fact contemplated. If it could be assumed to be General Average, it must fail as such for its own uncertainty; the value said to be sacrificed would be unascertainable: under such circumstances, a ship partially filled with water, and a cargo in such a state of damage could not be valued. In England, therefore, the damage to ship and cargo are treated as partial loss and not General Average.

No. 2. 'Damage done to ship and cargo by extinguishing a fire.' The damage to ship if by cutting the deck is voluntary and clearly visible, and its repair is General Average: the damage by water supposed to have got down by extinguishing the fire is incidental and not a voluntary act and is treated as partial loss.

No. 3. 'Chafing and breakage of cargo after jettison' is a consequence and not a voluntary act, and we make it partial loss.

No. 4. 'Damage done to cargo by discharging at a port of refuge.' I assume this to mean damage sustained in the act of discharging, which is General Average.

No. 5. 'Cutting away wreck of masts accidentally carried away.' Such wreck lying in the water is already lost, and is cut away as a nuisance, and is not General Average.

No. 7. As to 'carrying a press of sail,' I presume for the alleged purpose of keeping off a lee shore. The sails are doing no more than the duty required of them, and their being damaged is not General Average.

No. 8. 'Wages and provisions of the crew during the delay caused by putting into port' are not, by legal decision, recoverable in General Average in this country. The allowance of these charges in General Average is a very questionable advantage to the owner of the ship: it is an inducement to the master and crew to go into port upon slight or unnecessary occasions, and, even when necessary, to delay their departure; and the loss to the owner by the lengthening of his voyage is not compensated by his crew being paid their wages and board during detention. If it be no advantage to the owner of the ship it is most injurious to the owner of the cargo, whose market may be lost in addition to that of interest on his capital. If this portion of the system of General Average could be generally abandoned it would be a boon to the mercantile community.

No. 9. 'Contributing values of ship, freight, and cargo.' The rule in many places is to take half the value of the ship and half of the freight, taking also the net value of the cargo. There is an absence of any established principle in taking half the value of the ship and the full net value of the cargo: the value of the ship is her market value, less the repairs of her damage, and the freight is the freight due, less wages and charges, and that of cargo should be its net arrived value.

In most of the points considered above, if all interests—ship, freight, and cargo—were insured, the result might be of no importance to the proprietors of each interest, because they would recover their entire loss either under the head of General Average or partial charges or loss; but as it will frequently occur that some will be only partially, or not insured at all, it is as essential that an equitable mode of apportionment should be adopted as a unanimous one. If the warehouse rent of the cargo and charges thereon, which would follow, be included in the General Average, the owner of the ship uninsured would be materially prejudiced for the benefit of the cargo; so might the cargo be by having to pay its share of re-shipping charges.

For these reasons I am of opinion that in any apportionment of the charges arising out of a general casualty, whether those interested be insured or not, a separation according to the English custom will be found the most equitable.

In considering the whole proposed question of the promotion of uniformity in the adjustment of General Average I have to state that in my experience the opportunity has been afforded me of examining the General Average statements of perhaps every foreign country where such documents are usually made up. I have found statements made up in two ports of the same country differing entirely and materially. I have found in one city of most extensive commerce official statements made up on the most opposite principles. Throughout the whole which have come before me there appears an entire absence of any fixed principle and certainly there is no country in which there is a standard to which the general commercial community could conform with any advantage.

The English practice has been based on principles adopted after much study and experience, and I submit for the consideration of those whose minds have been directed to this question whether, as a whole, this may not be the best system to use as a guide to a general uniformity.

Dr. N. RAHUSEN (Representative of the Netherlands Trading Company). I must apologise for speaking a few words, in a language which is not my own, before the discussions on the various points of General Average are opened by the noble lord, our illustrious chairman.

We received in Holland, with great interest, the invitation of the National Society for the Promotion of Social Science, to meet at a congress in this thriving town of Scotland, for the purpose of discussing the system of General Average. I was appointed by the Netherlands Trading Society to be its representative. The committee of shipowners at Amsterdam also desired me to represent its interests. The object aimed at is to bring uniformity into the rules which regulate the statements of General Average. It cannot be denied that it is a vast project, for it will not be sufficient that there should be uniformity in the statements of the various seaports of one country, but the principles upon which they rely must be the same amongst all those nations which have a share in maritime transactions. If now we consider that in some countries the commercial codes have fixed the principles which regulate General Average, that those principles vary in the respective codes of commercial nations, and that there are other most important countries, as England and the United States, in which the system of General Average is only ruled by what is called custom and precedents, I believe I shall not have said too much, in giving my opinion, that the project is a vast one, and surrounded by difficulties. We may never forget that the law originates from the habits and the history of nations, and that, as long as there will be different nations, these nations will have their own history, their own law, their own application of science. We must fear that the legislative authorities in the various countries will not instantly accede to the rules which will be proposed by this meeting.

I frankly state my own opinion and do not conceal the difficulties connected with the subject. But, nevertheless, I may congratulate this Society for having adopted the idea, that the so discrepant principles of General Average should be brought into discussion, if I look around me and see in this congregation all those eminent men, and discussion will certainly be profitable to science. Various are the systems adopted in General Average, but truth is but one, and if we earnestly and without prejudice investigate this matter, we must come nearer to the truth, we must come nearer to the object which the Committee of International General Average has in view.

Gentlemen, one of the Roman emperors being asked by one of his præfecti for his decision in a case of stranding, gave this remarkable reply, which is preserved in the digests: 'I surely am the governor of the whole world, but the sea has its *own* law.' That was true in the time of the Roman empire, it is true yet in our days. For, although the practice and codification is different, yet in fact there is but one law of the sea. The more we study that law, that one law of the sea, the more unanimous we will be in its application, and if the result of our meeting is perhaps not so immediate, yet the seed is thrown into the earth and the fruit will ripen.

I shall be most happy to co-operate in your noble design.

Mr. J. A. W. Harper (Association for the Protection of Commercial Interests, London): Nearly all movements, such as the one in agitation on the subject of this section, have to encounter much opposition of a negative kind—not the less obstructive that it is negative—the opposition of apathy and indifference: a condition of mind which is formularised in the expression, 'Where's the good?'

I think that most of the gentlemen present here to-day must have become very familiar with that question lately. So far as I have had opportunities of forming an opinion, in the short space of time which has elapsed since I was first called upon to consider this subject, the great majority of persons immediately interested in it are deeply affected with this moral ague.

The underwriter I have found disposed to regard it in this manner. The difficulties occasioned by national differences in the adjustment of averages are only additional elements of risk: to reduce the number or diminish the urgency of such difficulties is, in effect, only to diminish the elements of risk; and if you proceed far in doing that, you will approach the extinction of all risk— and then, he asks, what has become of his craft? A register of premiums and a fair amount of capital will be the sum of an underwriter's requisites. At present he must have an extended and very various knowledge, and is compelled to exercise an intelligent vigilance: that knowledge and vigilance raise him from a dull mechanical tradesman into a thinking intellectual speculator, and he has no wish at all to descend again below that level; and so he looks upon your proceedings, to say the best, very coldly. He considers also his profits. His largest profits are extracted from the fluctuations of risks, which such difficulties as those you propose to remove give rise to.

The shipowner is disposed to regard the question in something like the same manner. Immediately he finds himself exposed to a new risk, such as that arising from the anomalies of average adjusting, he does his best to estimate it at a money value, and he covers it by an addition to his freight. Or, as is most commonly the case, the underwriter relieves him of the trouble of computing the risk—he estimates it for him, and charges it upon him in the shape of premium. The shipowner pays him and adds the amount to his freight. He cares nothing about these difficulties: and looks askance at your proceedings.

And so also the merchant. He covers all risks, computed in the same manner, by a charge against his profit, or by a premium paid to his underwriter; and in either case he raises his profit by the amount. And he, therefore, also makes little account of the discussions you are entering upon to-day.

Now what follows naturally, necessarily from these plain aspects of the question?

I have heard it said by some, whose view is not so clear as that of these experienced practical men—this is an underwriter's question only. Others look upon it as a shipowner's question; others again as a merchant's. I venture to maintain that it is neither one nor the other. It is simply a *consumer's* question. If the underwriter increases his premium to meet the additional risk; if the shipowner adds to his freight, for the same reason; or the merchant to his profit; in any case, he who ultimately bears the burden of the impost is the consumer. The increase is sure to find its way into the price of the commodity, and the buyer to be the ultimate sufferer.

This consideration should divest the question of its sectarian character, and elevate it to the importance of one affecting the whole community and all communities. But, regarded in its narrower aspect, if it be but regarded in a comprehensive *manner*, it will appear a question nearly affecting each man in his craft— each man who is labouring for profit in the consumer's service. Cheapness of productions stimulates their consumption, enlarges the area of the operations of all engaged in the production, relieves them of the excessive pressure of competition, and increases the amount of their gross periodical profits. In this way, although it may seem to the underwriter, the shipowner, and the merchant that, so long as the purchaser of commodities covers all their charges, it is of little consequence what those charges are, it is yet certain that in the end they will all find their account in any relief which accrues immediately to the consumer. And if they admit this, they will soon agree with us that differences in the law of General Average of various countries—inasmuch as they involve several risks, some certain, others indeterminate, and inasmuch as those risks enhance the price of commodities—are an evil which it is worth an effort to remove.

But the only one weighty objection to the proceedings of this section that I am aware of is this:—that there is no issue to your movement—that there can be no practical end to it and that you are beating the air. It is an objection which seems to have a sort of parasitical attachment to all considerable movements There has scarcely been any change of importance in the settled condition of things which, at the first conception of it, was not impossible. But yet the objection is one you must face, for it is a real and serious one. You may hope to effect the changes you look for through the medium of the Governments of the principal trading countries: in that case you must contemplate changes, more or less considerable, in the mercantile law of those countries. In order to appreciate the difficulties you would have to surmount to arrive at that, you have only to reflect for a moment upon what you must do to obtain any alteration in your own law; and of course you contemplate changes there. The law of General Average in England rests on the decisions of some of the ablest

Judges that ever adorned the Bench. And, whatever difficulty you might have to struggle with here, you will find yourselves confronted with similar ones in every other country.

But perhaps you hope for some general assent on the part of the trading communities in different countries, to a set of rules to be made operative by clauses of contract in documents of trade, such as bills of landing. The special obstacles to the progress of a scheme in this direction will, no doubt, be pointed out. One is prominent. The contracts will only bind the parties to them. Suppose an adjuster, employed upon the statement of a General Average, should find that half the bills of lading contain clauses binding the parties to them to the rules laid down in the new code, and the other half do not; and, suppose the law of the port of discharge differ from the code—half the interests would require an adjustment according to our principle, the other half according to another. What a provision for confusion we have here! If this prime difficulty can in any way be surmounted—if you can effect the necessary changes in the law, or frame a machinery for superseding the law, it is probable that you will accomplish all that you desire, and will confer important benefits on commerce.

Suffer me to refer, in conclusion, to one or two cases which may illustrate the mischiefs arising from want of uniformity in the laws of average.

A Spanish ship, with a cargo worth 200,000*l*., puts into a port of refuge a day or two after putting to sea, and is found to be rotten and wormed; the owner spends 8,000*l*. in repairing her, and then, having a fine new ship, takes on his cargo to a Spanish colony. There the General Average is adjusted, and the cargo contributes to the repairs. But the cargo is worth 200,000*l*.—the ship about 5,000*l*.; so that the cargo pays nearly all. When the English merchant is called upon to make this magnificent present there is some heart-burning, perhaps disputes or lawsuits.

An American ship is sinking; the captain runs her ashore; some of the cargo is saved, very badly damaged; the ship is recovered and repaired. By American law the stranding was voluntary, and the repairs are paid for by General Average contribution; and so the shipowner takes perhaps the whole of the saved cargo.

A Hamburg ship has a cargo of sugar worth 3,000*l*. She puts herself upon the strand; a great part of the sugar is washed out, the remainder sells for 300*l*. The ship is recovered and repaired for 2,500*l*. The cargo had to contribute to the General Average, not on the sold value, 300*l*., but on the invoice value, 3,000*l*. So that the merchant had to give up all his cargo that was saved and pay about 1,000*l*. for what was lost. The English underwriter had to pay it: it was Hamburg law.

A Dantzic vessel puts into Cowes in the beginning of winter; frost sets in in the Baltic; the vessel remains at Cowes all the winter and till the ports are open in the spring. During the repairs, which the rule I am going to mention has no tendency to expedite, the captain and crew enjoy themselves in the Isle of Wight at the general expense; for by the Prussian law their wages and keep are General Average. By English law it is not so; and when by-and-by, the English underwriter on the cargo is called upon to pay, the often-recurring disputes commence again.

The following is a curious case. A merchant shipped 8,000*l*. worth of goods for Sweden. Half (4,000*l*. worth) took sea-damage, the other 4,000*l*. worth arrived sound. There was a General Average contribution for damage and expenses. *Now first*—although the General Average act saved the goods, and therefore saved the freight, yet the freight (contrary to the practice of England) did not contribute: it had nothing to pay for being saved. *Secondly*, the sound half of the cargo was valued at its *invoice value*, which of course did not include the freight, &c. *But thirdly*, the damaged half was valued at its gross sold value—the gross amount it realised when sold, and that of course included the freight. So that the freight, in principle, in theory, was not to contribute at all. By the mode of settlement half did, in fact, contribute, half not. The statement was objected to, in this country, on all three grounds; but it was replied, from Stockholm, that such was the law of Sweden, and the adjustment stood its ground.

There is a vast number of cases of irregular adjustments, not made according to any known law. In Manilla an experienced shipmaster and respectable man of business are usually employed to invent the adjustments. In some places the notaries make them up. In some places the Chambers of Commerce provide the adjusters and dictate their law. In France, if an adjustment reaches, in any way, the Cour de Cassation, the Code Napoléon is applied to it.

But, practically, the Code scarcely reaches the ports of France. I am informed, by a very eminent adjuster, that the adjustments made up in Marseilles are very different from those made up in Le Havre. I have myself seen different adjustments made up in Antwerp, and signed by the number of adjusters, prescribed by the Belgian Code, upon quite different principles. And, finally, London is not always in accordance with Liverpool, nor London with itself.

Now, for all these latter cases the remedy, so far as they admit of remedy, is in the establishing of skilful professional adjusters; and this can only take place when the trade of a port becomes so considerable as to require it. For the differences in the laws of countries there may be a remedy: I hope that in your discussions you may light upon it.

MR. JAMES CADDOW (Average-stater, Liverpool). In presenting the following observations to the notice of the Association, I propose to draw attention to a few of the discrepancies and anomalies that mark the present system of General Average; their effect as regards owners of ship and cargo, and their underwriters; and the necessity for uniformity, and the mode of attaining it.

The discrepancies which exist in the usage of the different maritime countries in the world embrace—

1st. Those which arise in the disposal of the items which form the subject or claim for general contribution.

2nd. Those in the valuations on which the several interests are made to contribute their quota to the General Average.

Of the first of these two, the following constitute some of the principal points of difference.

The expenses of pilotage and towage inwards and outwards, and other charges incidental to a vessel's entering and departing from a port of refuge.

Discharging and reloading the cargo.

Warehouse rent.

Loss of, or damage to, cargo, through discharging and reloading.

Wages and provisions of crew during detention.

With regard to the above expenses the practice in England and America may be placed in juxtaposition, in order to illustrate those differences which it is our object to abolish. In America the whole of the above expenses are admitted as General Average, whilst in England the outward charges, the expenses of reloading, and the wages and provisions of the crew, are borne specifically by the owners of the ship, and the rent of the cargo, and the damage accruing to it from the forced discharge, fall upon its proprietors. In France a distinction is drawn between cases in which the putting in is the result of accidental damage, and those in which it is the result of a voluntary sacrifice of part of the ship. In the former case the charges are treated as special expenses, and in the latter they are all admitted as General Average.

Masts, spars, and rigging cut away.

Little, if any, diversity exists in the mode of settling this loss when the articles sacrificed are in perfect condition, and not what is technically termed 'in a state of wreck;' if, however, they have been previously carried away or damaged, a material difference exists in the practices prevailing in this and foreign countries. In Sweden, Denmark, and Prussia, the sacrifice of the above wreck is allowed as General Average. In England, however, it is—I think with propriety—disallowed, because it is incumbent upon the master in such circumstances to rid the ship of what is a mere incumbrance and impediment to her navigation.

A case came recently under my observation where a vessel, bound hence to Alicant, encountered tempestuous weather, in which the masts were sprung, and fell overboard with all attached. She put into Holyhead, and was towed to Liverpool, where the cargo was discharged in order to effect the repairs, on completion of which the cargo was re-shipped, and the vessel proceeded. In the foreign adjustment, the rent, discharge, and re-shipment of the cargo were included in the General Average, and not only was the cost of replacing the above spars and rigging admitted to the same column, but actually the cost of discharging and rent of cargo *at the port of destination*! This outdoes in liberality the practice which obtained in France some time since, and which included in General Average not only all the port charges and expenses involved in putting into a port of refuge, but also the extra cost of repairs at that port, beyond their estimated cost at the port of destination.

Damage done by carrying a press of sail, in order to avoid a lee shore, is allowed in America, and nearly everywhere but in England, where the rule laid down in the cases of Power *v.* Whitmore, and Covington *v.* Roberts, has long prevailed, and such loss is of course excluded from general contribution.

Damage by the voluntary stranding of a ship is also admitted in Prussia and Denmark, but rejected in this country.

Coppering, under certain circumstances, may form a subject of General Average, and the mode of adjustment is very different in the United States from the practice observed in England. In the former country the sheathing put on, less the proceeds of that stripped off, is carried to the one-third column. Here, however, the actual weight stripped off only, is allowed in full at the price of new, credit being given for the proceeds realised.

As regards credits for old materials sacrificed, the plan in vogue here again varies from that of the United States, where the shipowner, who is made to bear one-third of the cost of new, receives credit for one-third of the value of the old.

Commission collecting the General Average is an item invariably included in American adjustments, but not recognised in England.

Then, as to the contributory values, in America, England, and the Continental States widely different rules prevail.

For the ship.—In some cases she contributes for one-half her value. In some cases for four-fifths. In other cases for the actual value.

For the freight.—In some instances we find it contributing on one-half the gross amount. In some cases, on the gross amount, deducting wages and port charges. In others, deducting wages and provisions.

As regards the cargo, fewer or less prominent differences arise in this respect.

But it is clear that the whole system of contribution is of the most confused and contradictory kind, and requires revision, amendment, and assimilation.

With the above inconsistencies and irregularities before us, it cannot be matter of surprise than such an abnormal state of things should conduce to the most unsatisfactory results. Let us consider the effect as regards the parties concerned.

1. *On the shipowner.*—A British ship, outward bound, puts into an intermediate port, where the cargo is discharged, and during this operation considerable damage accrues to it. At the termination of the voyage he is called upon to pay his proportion of General Average, including, of course, this damage, but being insured in this country the underwriters ignore the foreign adjustment, simply paying him the amount of contribution computed in conformity with British usage, and he consequently suffers a loss he never contemplated.

2. *On the cargo-owner.*—It frequently happens that a vessel, bound hence to the United States, is compelled to seek a port of refuge, where, probably, a large amount of General Average charges is incurred; and on arrival in the States the adjuster includes in his statement, wages, provisions, and other items, which charges the owner of the cargo cannot recover from the underwriters here, who repudiate their liability on any other than an English adjustment.

3. *On the underwriters.*—From the above it will also be obvious that the insurers of ship or cargo *may* improperly be called upon to pay as Particular Average the damages which have already been recovered by the assured in the shape of General Average, and *vice versâ*.

It thus becomes the interest and duty of all parties to second the efforts now made to reform and remedy this anomalous state of things. Underwriters and average staters are painfully familiarised with the chagrin and disgust engendered in the minds of those who are the victims of a system which precludes the possibility of an assured obtaining that full indemnification which, after having paid his premium, he is naturally led to anticipate.

Whilst, however, our attention is directed to the diversity of practice and usage as between the various states of Europe and

America, the fact must not be overlooked that some rather serious differences exist in the mode of settlement adopted by the various average-staters in this country. For instance, it is by no means a settled point whether damage done to a vessel's bottom by the fall of spars cut away comes under the category of General or of Particular Average; and the same remark applies to the case of the remains of a parted chain being slipped, which some consider a General Average loss, whilst others charge it specially to the shipowner. In cases where a wreck of ship and cargo ensues, and the master and crew assist in saving property, some adjusters admit the wages from the date when the necessity for the condemnation becomes known; others again believe that the condemnation has a retrospective effect, and advocate their allowance from the date of actual wreck. Numerous other differences exist, chiefly in matters of detail, to which it is unnecessary to refer.

Another anomaly to which our attention may be directed, is the fact that the custom prevailing at Lloyd's is not unfrequently at variance with the legal decisions and opinions that have emanated from our Courts of Law. For instance, the judgments delivered in the cases of Gould v. Oliver, and Milward v. Hibbert, sanctioned the admission of jettison of deckload as General Average, when it is carried according to the usage of trade; and in the cases of 'The Copenhagen,' Da Costa v. Newnham, and Plummer v. Wildman, the tone of the Courts would lead us to infer that reloading and storage of cargo at an intermediate port are, in the eye of the law, subjects of General Average contribution. And latterly, in the case of Hall v. Jansen, the present Lord Chancellor, in delivering the judgment of the Court, incidentally referred to the expense of reloading as legitimately falling upon ship, freight, and cargo. And yet we know that in all such cases the judicial dicta are practically disregarded by the underwriting and mercantile community. Jettison also, although held by some of our learned writers on insurance to constitute a direct claim on the policy, is nevertheless invariably treated as a loss recoverable in General Average. Such an undefined state of the law, or rather such an antagonism between law and custom, should no longer be tolerated.

Without multiplying instances, I think that the defective state of the present General Average system has been abundantly evinced and sufficient has been said to force the conviction that a paramount necessity exists for having immediate recourse to measures calculated to remedy and eradicate the evils of which it is the fruitful parent.

For the attainment of uniformity, let the Chambers of Commerce and the Underwriting communities in each of the principal maritime states set to work vigorously, and if possible simultaneously, to form a committee or sub-congress, composed of individuals thoroughly conversant with the various questions in dispute; let them analyse the different regulations and customs which prevail in their respective countries, pointing out the peculiar advantages and disadvantages, and the equity and anomalies of the main features of their own system of General Average. Let a report on the subject emanate from every such committee. All the reports thus issued might then be laid before, and be considered by, a general International Congress, comprising delegates or representatives from the above sub-congresses, whose duty it would be to examine, discuss, and adjudicate on the subject, and whose decision on all the questions of general contribution would form the basis of a uniform legislation and codification of this branch of maritime law.

For my own part I can see no insuperable obstacle in the way of attaining an all but complete uniformity on this subject. In every maritime state the same interests are involved, the same sea perils are encountered, and the circumstances arising out of each marine adventure are similar in their nature; and the mutual interest each has in promoting the end in view, coupled with probably the same instincts and notions of justice, will doubtless facilitate and tend to the realisation of the important object of the Social Science Congress in regard to this question. There are, of course, matters of detail arising out of the peculiar nature of each particular case which must necessarily, and may safely, be left to the discretionary treatment of the adjuster; but in so comparatively limited a department of mercantile usage, it is surely not a utopian idea to believe that some assimilation, at least of general principles, will be effected, and that thus the present uncertainty of law and usage will be swept away, and an important advance be made in the direction of a general codification of our whole mercantile law.

To smooth the asperities and allay the irritations of commercial intercourse—to approximate more closely to sound principle and equal justice in settling the relations subsisting between the different parties to mercantile transactions—to arrive at a more definite and uniform system of legislation on matters inseparably connected with the existence of this country as a great maritime power, are assuredly objects worthy of energetic prosecution; and if by ventilating the various questions, of which the above is necessarily the merest outline, our efforts eventuate in entire or even partial success, this will certainly form not the least important feature of utility which has marked the career and operations of the 'National Association for the Promotion of Social Science.'

Mr. L. R. BAILY (Average-stater, Liverpool). In considering the points submitted to us in the notice issued by the Association, I will first state how I shall discuss them. I shall state,

    1st. The principles which I consider ought to govern each of the points.

    2nd. The reasons why I think it inexpedient to adhere to those principles on all of them.

As a means of obtaining a practical result from this meeting I shall then suggest,

    3rd. A plan for attaining the uniformity sought with as little deviation from principle as possible, and means for carrying out that plan in practice.

    1st. As to the principle which I consider ought to govern each of these points.

    (1) As to the damage done to a ship and her cargo by a voluntary stranding: this is, I think, allowable in General Average.

    (2) As to the damage done to a ship and her cargo by water let in or poured into the vessel to extinguish a fire:—this also, I think, is allowable in General Average.

    (3) As to the damage done to a cargo by chafing and breakage in consequence of a jettison:—this also, if unavoidable, is, I think, allowable in General Average.

(4) As to the damage done to a cargo by discharging it at a port of refuge :—this also, if unavoidable, is, I think, allowable in General Average.

(5) As to cutting away wreck of masts which have been accidentally broken :—this should not, I think, be allowed in General Average, for the wrecked state of the masts is the cause of the damage which renders their sacrifice necessary, and it is unreasonable, under such circumstances, to allow anything in General Average for such a sacrifice.

(6) As to the expense of warehouse rent on the cargo at a port of refuge, and the expense of re-shipping it, and the outward port charges at that port when the original ship carries on the cargo from that port :—they all should, I think, be allowed in General Average.

(7) As to the damage done to ship, freight, and cargo, by carrying a press of sail :—this, I think, should not be allowed in General Average.

(8) As to the wages and provisions of the crew whilst a vessel is delayed by putting into a port of refuge :—they are not, I think, allowable in General Average.

(9) The contributing values of ship, freight, and cargo should, I think, be the values at the time when they become liable for the General Average.

On these principles I have stated the conclusions only at which I have arrived, omitting the reasons for arriving at those conclusions; because, as you will see hereafter, I do not advise adherence to these principles, and because you may agree with me as to the correctness of the principles themselves, rendering an elaborate proof of that correctness unnecessary.

I will now consider :

2nd. The expediency of deviating from the above principles, and will apply it to the points under discussion.

1. *As to the expediency of deviating from principle on any point—*

It is not expedient to attempt to adhere to strict principle if the attempt must fail, if it will entail great evil and but small advantage, or if it will afford excuse for gross injustice and cause constant disputes.

It is expedient to deviate from principle by adopting practical rules for the government of all points on which it is practically impossible to agree on facts; otherwise there will be as many results, in any given case, as there are parties consulted about it.

To a merchant or shipowner it is, as a rule, of no consequence whether his loss be paid to him as General or as Particular Average, provided it *is* paid to him. To underwriters as a body, the same, provided they always pay the loss in the same way. The great object is *certainty*.

2. *As to the application of these remarks to some of the points under discussion—*

As to voluntary stranding. A vessel on the point of sinking is run on shore. The damage done to her, and the cargo, by this act is in principle allowable in General Average. So far the way is clear, but now comes the difficulty—what is the damage? It is reasonable to suppose that the vessel was much strained, and had much water in her, before the act was done, or she would not have been run on shore. Who can define the damage done before, and the damage done by the stranding, especially when it is borne in mind that evidence on this point is obtainable from parties interested on one side only, and thus great facilities for fraud are offered? Under such circumstances is it not better to obtain, by some practical rule, practical certainty combined in most cases with practical justice, rather than by aiming at theoretical equity, to attain only practical injustice in most cases and disputes in all?

I would suggest, therefore, in order to obtain uniformity with as little deviation from principle as possible, a practical rule which shall place voluntary stranding on the same footing as accidental stranding.

For similar reasons I would suggest practical rules which shall make Particular Average—the damage done to a cargo by chafing and breakage owing to a jettison, and the damage done to a cargo by discharging it at a port of refuge; because the allowance of these losses in General Average opens a wide door for fraud and error, it being assumed in practice, when these losses are allowable, that all the damage and loss which the cargo has sustained on the voyage was caused by the jettison or the discharge.

Not so as regards the damage done in extinguishing a fire. I do not see any practical difficulty, in the generality of cases, in determining what damage was done in that way and what damage was not done in that way. Nevertheless, in order to prevent disputes, I would suggest a practical rule for this point also, and for the following reasons: the damage done by the water to goods which are actually on fire is not, in principle, allowable in General Average. It is doubtful whether scorched goods should be governed by the same principle. To prevent disputes, therefore, I would suggest a practical rule, which should admit in General Average the damage by the water to the latter, but not to the former.

As regards cutting away the wreck of masts accidentally broken, I would suggest to those who differ from me in principle, a similar practical difficulty to that applying to voluntary stranding, viz.:—What is the value at which they are to be allowed? And, influenced by that consideration, I would have recommended a practical rule, excluding this loss from General Average, if I had held differently on the principle.

As regards wages and provisions for the crew, I cannot, in principle, draw any distinction between them and the wear and tear of the ship during the same period, which last is not recognised as General Average in any country, so far as I am aware. I do not, however, hope for general support in this opinion, and would therefore suggest a compromise by which the shipowners should, during the vessel's stay *at* the port of refuge, receive in General Average some compensation for this expenditure, which it may be expedient to calculate according to an established scale.

On the other points I would adhere to principle, excepting as regards the contributing value of freight.

I can see nothing to justify the customs that exist in some countries of contributing on half only of the values of ship and freight, of excluding freight altogether from contribution, or of not deducting freight from the value of the cargo in arriving at the contributing value of that cargo. I can see nothing to justify taking any values of ship, freight, and cargo, but their actual values at the time when they became liable for the General Average; but as regards freight I would suggest a practical rule. I cannot see anything to justify the custom common in this country of arriving at the contributing value of freight, by deducting from the gross freight, not only all the charges incurred *after* the General Average act, but also all those incurred *before* that act, such as the charges at the loading port; nor can I justify the practice in the English Admiralty Court in salvage suits, of making no deductions from the gross freight, in arriving at the freight's contributing value, but it is not unreasonable to deduct from freight the wages and port charges incurred *after* the General Average act, and therefore as a practical rule for arriving at the contributing value of *freight*, I would deduct from the gross freight the wages and port charges incurred *after* the General Average act.

3. *As to the plan I would suggest for carrying out these practical rules.*

I would call the conclusions we may arrive at 'The International Congress Rules for adjusting General Average,' I would then print them and bring them before the public—*i.e.* the shipowners, the merchants, the underwriters, and the average adjusters—and would, if practicable, obtain their approval of them on or before the 1st March next, a date which would give time for approval, and amendment if necessary. During this period a paid secretary will be necessary: his salary could easily be raised. On and after 1st July next, I would add a clause to policies of insurance and bills of lading, stipulating that 'General Average, if any, is to be adjusted according to the International Congress's printed rules.' There would be no practical difficulty in doing this; for a similar clause, 'General Average according to English custom,' is even now not uncommon in bills of lading. When the new clause is generally inserted in policies of insurance and bills of lading, it will govern the mode of adjusting General Average, and the uniformity sought will be attained.

To carry out the conclusions we may arrive at, or those which, on or before 1st March 1861, may be substituted for them, every one who approves of them must act energetically for himself, and if, as perhaps may happen, some of the merchants, shipowners, underwriters, or adjusters, before whom the conclusions are brought, do not express any opinion on them, those who do approve of them must act as if the conclusions had been generally approved of, for no reform was ever yet attained by waiting for the action of others.

As regards the future, I *could* suggest a permament ' International Court of Appeal ' for the redress of all other existing or future grievances, but *cui bono?* there is not even a reasonable probability that such a court could act. Throughout this paper I have looked to practical results only, and have avoided all *theoretical* remedies. The *practical* good must commence *now, whilst we are together*, or it will never come. The evils of the differences now before us are great: let us endeavour to find a speedy practical remedy for them. If we accomplish this, it will not be difficult to find a practical remedy for others.

P.S.—In suggesting this practical rule for voluntary stranding, I do not propose to exclude the damage done to a ship *above water in heaving her off*, when the expense of heaving her off is allowable in General Average. There are no great practical difficulties in ascertaining this damage.

The Chairman hoped that Judge Marvin, of the United States, would favour them with the views of America on the subject.

The Hon. Judge Marvin, (Delegate of the Chamber of Commerce of New York and of the Board of Underwriters of New York) said: I come here, gentlemen, from the city of New York more to listen and to hear what propositions may be brought forward by the various gentlemen concerned in the subject of General Average, than to bring forward any measures of our own. We, in the New World, although our commerce is very extensive, have not had the time since we were informed of this meeting to consider these questions as fully as you have on this side of the water. However, upon receipt of the circular to the Chamber of Commerce, that body thought it advisable to respond to the invitation, and asked me to attend in the capacity of its representative. There is a friend, also, here from Boston, representing the Board of Trade of that city; and there is a gentleman likewise from Mobile. None of us are prepared to read any paper on the subject under discussion. We are prepared, however, in the United States to co-operate in any movement that has a reasonable prospect of bringing about the object so much desired: the best means of bringing about that plan may be discussed here. I have listened to the paper of Mr. Baily as to the plan of producing the uniformity desired, after we have settled upon the principles. I don't know whether the plan which he suggests might be made effectual by clauses in the policy and bills of lading, binding the parties to submit the question of settlement to the rules prescribed by this Glasgow meeting. If that should be the idea acted upon and adopted by this convention, we ought to deliberate very calmly and consider the principles laid down very maturely, and not draw up rules with great haste and without the fullest consideration. I myself, however, see difficulties in the way. It is true that clauses inserted in the policy and bills of lading will bind the parties to the contract: but they will bind no one else. Some vessels in the United States are not insured at all; and as to them, they would not be bound by any policy of insurance they were not connected with. They might, perhaps, be bound by the bill of lading, but they might stipulate otherwise: their rights and remedies would be had upon the law of the land—they would appeal to their own judicial tribunals for justice. Mr. Harper, in his very interesting paper, which I listened to with great pleasure, alluded to the idea of legislation on the subject, and, to go a little into detail, my own view on that subject is this:—That this meeting ought not to come to any definite conclusion as to what the rules in General Average shall be, but that this congress shall provide the means of having these questions referred to some of the able jurists of this country, who should take into their counsel all the advice they can obtain; that those gentlemen, within the course of a year, should draw up the great doctrines of the law of General Average; that they shall define, in the form of a bill to be laid before Parliament, what is the meaning of the term 'General Average,' and what cases are to be included within the definition of General Average, and that when a case is determined to be a case of General

Average, then to specify, as near as well can be, what expenses shall be brought within it. Take a case: if a ship has to put into a port for repair, and supposing it to be a case of General Average, they shall determine whether the wages and provisions shall or shall not be one of the charges that make up the General Average. After those rules have been made up by the experience and knowledge of the gentlemen—after the language has been fully weighed by them—then I would suggest the idea of printing them, and the lines should be far apart to allow facilities for amendments. Then these should be sent to all parts of the world; and I will promise that in Boston, New York, and New Orleans any propositions coming from this side of the water will receive their consideration on that side. We will in America take up the rules that are furnished to us, and amend according to our view of the matter, by introducing alterations in the phraseology as we think necessary, or by the addition of entire sections, as might best conform with our views. They should be sent to France, Holland, and other commercial countries, and the people there will make them conform to their opinions. In this way you will collect the opinions of gentlemen who have had time for deliberation, and who are not prompted by the spur of the moment to give an opinion they do not, after deliberation, agree to. Then these papers should come back to London or Liverpool: the alterations and amendments are considered, and with the experience they have obtained and the information they have before them, the gentlemen will be able to draw up a Bill to be brought before Parliament, and to be made the law of Great Britain. A Bill thus matured by the experience of learned jurists and commercial men from the whole commercial world, I am inclined to think, notwithstanding the remarks of Mr. Harper to the contrary, would pass Parliament. Suppose it should become the law of a great nation like Great Britain, whose commerce is in every sea, and whose law has its influence all over the world, I do not think there would be any great difficulty in getting such a law enacted by the Congress of the United States. There would not, I think, be much difficulty in France and Holland. In this way, and by legal enactments, it seems to me, that in the course of three, or four, or five years, something like a great degree of uniformity may be produced on this subject. In this way you would arrive at a considerable degree of uniformity as to the definition of the general law, but utter and entire uniformity in the application of law to individual cases is hopeless, in my judgment. That, we cannot expect as long as the minds of men are unlike, and as long as different minds will take different views of the same question. Absolute uniformity and certainty do not belong to poor fallen humanity. Absolute uniformity in practice we cannot expect; but we may certainly expect a greater degree of uniformity in the definitions of the law. Now take the case that was put by Mr. Harper. A ship sails from New Orleans laden with cotton, she puts into a port in distress for repairs; those repairs are made, and she proceeds to Liverpool. In that case the wages and provisions of the master and crew during the time of detention will not be paid at Liverpool; the expenses will fall upon the shipowner. But let the same ship be bound for Amsterdam, with the same number of bales of cotton, and the provisions and wages would be allowed: it would be a case of General Average. So well is this understood, that masters of American vessels, when they have been disabled, congratulate themselves that they are bound to Amsterdam and not to Liverpool, because in the one case they would be allowed provisions and wages, and in the other they would not. In cases of temporary repairs to enable the vessel to carry on the cargo, there would be General Average in Havre and in America—not so in Great Britain. We are more inclined in the United States, in our general system of law on this subject, to be in accordance with the system prevailing upon the continent of Europe than with that which prevails at Lloyd's. The great mass of our common law came from the parent country, from England; but we have adopted many of the principles and ordinances of commercial law which are not particularly British. In the great international laws of the world we have been more inclined to approve of the equity and justice of the continental rules than we have been of those which have been established at Lloyd's, either by arbitrary adjustments or by usage. In the principles prevailing on the Continent, the general maritime law has its foundation in the great system of Roman civil law; and there never was a system so just in its details, so perfect in its provisions for the administration of justice between man and man, as the Roman civil law. Coming down from the Romans, and revived in the middle ages, it was repelled by the spirit of liberty in England, because it favoured despotic government; but, between man and man, the principles were sound and excellent; and the more the civil laws of Rome are studied, the more are our minds imbued with the principles of justice which characterised them. Being relieved from the trammels of the English system, our law on the subject of General Average is found to be, in some instances, in conflict with the usages that prevail at Lloyd's; and our practice will be found to conform more nearly with the practice and usage that prevails throughout the continent of Europe. Having now in this very rambling way addressed a few words to you, I submit to listen to what may be said by the gentlemen present.

Mr. J. Russell Bradford (Delegate of the Board of Trade Boston, Mass.) said: I have the honour of standing here to represent the Board of Trade of Boston. It is quite recently that I knew of my appointment, and until the last few days I was very uncertain whether my health would permit my being here. My friend from New York has in his closing remarks alluded to our laws as being based upon the old Roman law. Now we in America are inclined to think that, where there has been any deviation from the Roman law, that law was not at fault, but British practice is an innovation, and should be changed; and especially in Massachusetts we think we stand very nearly in accordance with the old Roman law. In the voluntary stranding of a ship no one with us supposes that any other damage is to be contributed for but the actual damage occasioned by the stranding. As to the damage caused to ship and cargo in extinguishing fire, the damage to ship by scuttling is allowable by English rule. We allow the *whole* damage done by water in extinguishing fire; but we distinguish very closely between the damage caused by fire and that caused by water: we allow the damage done by water *solely*. The wages and provisions we allow. Carrying a press of sail we do not allow: a decision in a case in the Supreme Court of the

United States was against it: the sails were used for their legitimate purpose, and, if lost by unusual press of wind, ought not to be allowed in General Average. In the contributing value of ship, freight, and cargo we follow the English rule, except with regard to the freight. I would say a few words in regard to the carrying out of any measures that we may arrive at here. I liked the remarks made by Mr. Baily, and it appears to me that the hints he gave, if followed, may attain the result desired much more speedily than my friend who last spoke suggests would be the case. I think well of that proposition, but I have some doubts of the passing of a law by our own Congress. It seems to me that the best way of meeting the matter is by a bill of lading, and to treat this subject as if there was no insurance in the world, taking as General Average that which is simply justice between man and man, for the matter of insurance will certainly adjust itself; and the great object we ought to have is to try and establish what is justice between man and man.

MR. DANIEL WHEELER (Representative of the Chamber of Commerce of Mobile) said he was glad of the opportunity of seeing the gentlemen present. Notwithstanding that the gentlemen from America had read no paper, there was evidence in the speeches which they had made that they had studied the subject. He was sure the United States of America, being the second commercial nation in the world, would willingly support the desire to have a uniform system of Average that would be just to all nations and to all people. The usage of the State of Alabama differed from that of New York and Boston; and in Mobile, which is in that state, and, though comparatively new, had a large commerce, they were exceedingly anxious to conform to the best usages of the great commercial nations. With regard to the plan of arriving at a uniform system, he differed from the gentlemen who had just spoken. He would look at it as a commercial matter, not as a national one. The laws were sufficient already, and he thought the movement should commence with the Chambers of Commerce of the various great commercial emporiums. He coincided with the gentleman from Boston that a much less time than four or five years would bring round a uniform system of Average, and he would be very much in favour of that plan if it should be proposed. Chambers of Commerce were composed of practical and commercial men, immediately interested and concerned in the settlement of the question; and he thought the movement should emanate from the Chambers of Commerce for the different commercial emporiums.

THE CHAIRMAN. The resolution which I see here is 'that the damage done to ship, cargo, and freight, by running a ship on shore'—that must mean a voluntary running the ship on shore. How would this be? I had the misfortune to be in a wreck on the coast of Yarmouth sixty years ago, I am sorry to say. Coming from Norway, after taking a pilot on board, we struck on a rock; and although it was in the middle of February, we had calms and very mild weather, and luckily for us that excessively moderate weather continued. Lord Stuart de Rothesay and I were together, and the first thing that happened to us was the crunch which we heard in our hammocks in the morning, before we got out. We went to the pumps, but all our efforts were vain. We found the rudder had been carried away, and there was a hole in the bottom sufficient to sink the vessel. She was water-logged in the course of three hours; but, luckily, the cargo was of timber, and she could not sink. Suppose this had happened: suppose she had not been laden with timber,—there she was in deep water, and with that hole in her bottom she was quite certain to sink if she had not been run on shore. Now, suppose she had not had a cargo of timber, and the Norwegian captain had run her ashore, would that have been a voluntary act—running her on shore to save her from being sunk? And another risk was this:—we remained off there for eight-and-forty hours, and could not get any boat; and then, though we were quite safe unless the wind had sprung up—and in the middle of February the probability was that a great wind would spring up either from the shore or from the sea, it did not signify which—but if a wind had sprung up she would have gone to pieces if she had been driven out to sea, or if she had been driven on shore. Would not the captain have been justified in that case in running the ship on shore to avoid these risks? He had two risks to avoid: the wind getting up and driving her out to sea or on shore; and supposing she had not been timber-laden she would have sunk. Would it have been voluntary stranding to run her on shore to avoid sinking? I cannot see that it would. The proposition is that the damage caused by running on shore should be General Average; that would only be a question of fact.

MR. LAURENCE R. BAILY then moved the first resolution: 'That the damage done to ship, cargo, and freight, by running a ship on shore (excepting the damage done to the ship above water in heaving her off, when the expense of heaving her off is allowable in General Average) shall not be allowed in General Average.' He did not know whether he ought to allude to the noble lord's remarks as to voluntary stranding, but perhaps it would be as well to do so. His lordship demurred to calling a ship run on shore, when she was on the point of sinking, a voluntary stranding. What is 'voluntary'? Anything which a man does himself from choice is 'voluntary.' If a man were standing on a line of railway, and a train were coming up, he must, as a reasonable man, jump off the line; but still, if he choose to abandon that character, he can remain on and be killed; and therefore his jumping off would be a voluntary act.

THE CHAIRMAN. Suppose a highwayman comes up to you and says, 'Give me your purse or your life,' and you give him your money to save your life, would you consider that a voluntary act?

MR. BAILY. Most certainly I would. Everything I do, which I can either do or leave undone, is a voluntary act. I call an act which a reasonable man performs, a voluntary act, although, if he continue to be a reasonable man, he must perform it. For instance, when I am on a line of railway, and jump off to save my life, jumping off is a voluntary act. If I am going to the bottom of the sea with my ship, and to save myself I cut away her masts, cutting away the masts is a voluntary act. When there is a choice of alternatives, it is clearly voluntary when you choose between them. Now as to the injury done: until a thing actually happens there is no certainty that it will happen. That sinking to which Lord Brougham alluded, might, for aught we know, have been prevented; and the railway train might have been stopped before it reached me. If, in such a case, you convert a doubt into a positive certainty, you have done the shipowner an injury. Whenever you convert a doubt—and a moral certainty, even, is but a doubt, *i.e.* an extreme degree of probability—into an actual certainty, and that certainty involves a loss, you do a man an injury. If you run a ship on shore, and that act occasions injury which is clearly traceable to the voluntary stranding only, that is an injury which it is possible might have been avoided. But, as I remarked in the paper which I read before the meeting, the practical difficulties are so great, that, however correct in theory it may be to allow such damages, I would in practice reject them from General Average; for when a ship is run ashore much water is already in her, and she and her cargo have both sustained much damage previously. By running her on shore these injuries may be increased; but who in the world is to say what that increase is? Is it not better to waive your principle and make a practical rule to prevent litigation? Principle even includes some only of the damage sustained by ship and cargo, for it excludes the damage which would have happened if the ship had not been run on shore. Referring to some remarks by some of the gentlemen present, that in practice the loss was not allowed, even in those countries in which the principle of allowing it was recognised, and therefore the abuse of principle was not to be feared, Mr. Baily added: As a matter of fact, I differ from some of the gentlemen who have spoken of the practical working of adhering to principle, for I have actually seen adjustments of voluntary stranding in which the whole ship and cargo have been allowed in General Average.

THE CHAIRMAN. You consider voluntary to be that which converts a moral certainty into an actual certainty; and, to revert to the case of the highwayman, when you run the risk of your life by refusing to give up your purse, and convert the moral certainty of his killing you into an actual certainty: that is suicide on your part.

MR. BAILY. Yes. I merely made these remarks to bring the question before you, in order that anybody who has anything to say on the resolution may do so; and I now beg formally to move the resolution.

MR. DAVISON asked whether they could come to any vote on the questions in a mixed company such as that present.

Mr. RATHBONE explained that voting papers would be sent round, on which gentlemen should write their names and the bodies they represented, if any; that the names would be printed, so that the voting would not be merely numerical, but would be considered in respect of the weight of the names voting for or against any proposition; and that he hoped no gentleman would vote except those who had given some time and attention to the subject.

Dr. RAHUSEN, of Amsterdam, said: Voluntary stranding was a measure justified only by extreme necessity. They must not forget that in the various commercial codes which admit voluntary stranding as General Average, as in the French, Dutch, and other codes, they had done so because, when the peril was extreme, there could be nothing more done to save the ship and cargo. But, in determining what ought to be allowed for this voluntary stranding, you must distinguish between the damage sustained before the voluntary stranding and the damage which is the direct consequence of the stranding. Before the ship was run ashore she might be in a very decayed or damaged state; only the damage that could be ascertained to be the direct consequence of the stranding could be allowed in General Average. We are told here that the English law is much better than the American, French, and Dutch laws; but they had heard that morning from the Lord Advocate that, theoretically, a law might be good, but practically bad. A theory might be correct and the practice inexpedient.

Mr. WERTHEIM said, when they considered the history of the Dutch laws, it was certain that they founded the first principles of their commercial law on the laws which they received from the Roman Empire; and a voluntary stranding would be contributed to by ship, cargo, and freight.

The CHAIRMAN. Then freight would pay as well as ship and cargo; that would be General Average.

Mr. WERTHEIM. That principle is laid down in 699 of the Dutch Commercial Code.

Mr. BRADFORD thought the resolution went too far. The vessel is not in a sinking condition in every case of voluntary stranding; in a great majority of cases where there was voluntary stranding, there was dragging or kedging towards the shore, where there might be rocks; and the master chose, instead of holding on with the anchor, to sacrifice the safety, whatever it was, and run the ship on shore. That was clearly the act of man—the judicious act of man. But the anchors might hold, for it was nothing unusual to bring up a ship after she had dragged; the master sacrificed that chance, and ran her on the strand. If he damaged his vessel and then ran her on shore, and said the cargo and freight should contribute for the value of the ship, he could not allow that; he never knew that to be allowed in General Average. The ship had no value, and where was the loss? There was a case in which a ship was tight, and was going towards the shore; still she might have held on; but the master, seeing a sandy beach, ran her so high and dry that she could not get off. The Court had decided, and the English adjusters had taken the same ground, that where there was a voluntary stranding they must pay for it. The master gave up a chance of safety, perhaps a good chance, and ran the ship on shore.

Mr. RATHBONE did not suppose that the captain of that ship intended to run her up so high that she could not float again; and that he only chose one kind of danger instead of a greater danger. The captain considered that, in running the ship on shore, he put her into greater safety than leaving her where she was. He thought there was no voluntary sacrifice in that case, and that the captain did the best he could for the ship, supposing there had been no cargo or freight whatever.

Mr. BRADFORD said they considered it was precisely the same as cutting away the masts. There might be a necessity for it, and they allowed it; and so also in jettison.

Mr. HARPER thought it should always be considered that the master made a sacrifice in electing to run his ship on shore; he did make a sacrifice, and therefore the value of the ship should be contributed for.

Mr. BAILY said the resolution was that the damage which they were discussing should *not* be allowed in General Average. He merely stated his own reasons for the vote he intended to give. Although he considered the damage done in this way was in theory allowable in General Average, yet from his practical experience he was of opinion that the disputes arising from treating it in that way in practice would be so numerous, that the little theoretical good that would be got from trying to follow principle would be more than counterbalanced by the annoyances and inconveniences the attempt would occasion, because they had to deal with facts, and facts were not easily ascertained in such cases. He would suppose a case in which the ship had been run ashore and the damage was to be allowed. Let there be twenty adjusters consulted as to the amount of the General Average, and no communication between them, and he would undertake to say that no two out of the twenty would agree in their adjustments of the case. The facts on which they had to decide were hypothetical, and no one could determine the exact amount of damage caused directly by the stranding. Another difficulty was this: the evidence was all on one side, that representing the ship. On the other side there could be nothing but argument. So, whatever they might think of the theory, it would be better to give up that theory on the ground of expediency.

MR. JAMES BROUN considered that if upon this resolution was intended to be founded an application for a legislative enactment they ought to oppose it; but if it were merely a recommendation to put a clause in the bill of lading, he had no objection to it. If, however, it was to be made law, it was, upon the very face of it, in the teeth of the principles upon which General Average was founded, because it was a voluntary act in law where the will of man interposed. But where the will of man interposed for the purpose of saving ship, cargo, and freight, that was General Average; and it was the policy of the law from the beginning, that if people did not make it a contributory loss, people would not make the sacrifice. In the case of goods thrown overboard, the theory was that as those goods were thrown overboard for the safety of all, a sacrifice was made for the common benefit, it was a common contribution. In cases of running the ship on shore, the captain would always consider whether other people would sustain the damage done to the vessel; but when he knew that there would be no contribution, he had no interest in doing so. Of course those who knew the practical difficulties of making up adjustments had all the facts before them, and ought to know whether they were insuperable.

Mr. Harper said when a ship was run ashore all parties were at an equal risk; there was no selection for the ship and cargo. They were all exposed to an equal danger in the hope of saving all. They were all—ship, cargo, and freight—put to an equal risk, a great risk, in the hope of saving them from a greater one.

Hon. Judge Marvin would suggest an amendment. In theory and principle the resolution was wrong; and he did not know why they should give up a good principle when they might avoid the inconvenience. Suppose they had an amendment something like this: 'Stranding of ships shall be deemed, *primâ facie*, to be involuntary, and not the subject of General Average; but if it shall appear that the case is one of intentional stranding with the view of the safety of all, then such a case does come within the principle of General Average, as an exceptional case.'

Mr. Baily observed that in practice every case that came before adjusters was the exception. When a ship is damaged, the only evidence that can be obtained is one-sided.

The Chairman. Suppose we take it in this way: that the damage done to ship, cargo, and freight, by running a ship on shore, shall not be allowed in General Average, although it was done for the benefit of ship, freight, and cargo.

Mr. Baily. Yes.

After some conversation, the first resolution, as originally proposed, was put to the vote, and negatived by a majority.

An amended resolution was afterwards carried upon this subject on the third day.

Hon. Judge Marvin then proposed the second resolution: 'That the damage done to ship, cargo, and freight, in extinguishing fire, shall be allowed in General Average.'

Dr. Rahusen suggested that the resolution should be altered to the 'damage done by water,' as that would make the meaning more clear.

Mr. Baily thought that if they confined it to the damage done by water, it would still leave the question unsettled, for there would still remain the damage done in getting at the fire, in order to extinguish it: such as cargo thrown overboard, breaking down a cabin, &c.

Mr. Richards objected to that being charged to General Average, on the same ground that he objected to the resolution on voluntary stranding. If the fire was in one part of the ship, and cargo that could be readily got at was in another part, they would take the goods out of another batch not affected by fire, and put them into lighters: but the damage done by water poured upon the fire was purely accidental, and the parties affected should treat it as Particular Average; and he saw no reason why they should change the system.

Mr. Baily, referring to some remarks that had been made that injury by water in such a case was not a sacrifice, as the ship and cargo on fire would have been lost but for the water, said they never had a General Average act, excepting when the ship was brought to a state in which it was supposed that she would be lost. On that principle, masts cut away should not be allowed; for, if the vessel were going to the bottom, cutting away her masts, and thus saving her, would be a positive benefit to her. With reference to Mr. Richards's remark about craft taking a portion of the cargo into safety, that must be an accidental circumstance, not to be dealt with as a matter of principle. When a fire was raging in a ship, they had to pour water into her as a means to put it out; and if they injured other portions of the ship's cargo by so doing, surely they had injured the owner of that property, and as they had done so for the general good, all the property that was saved ought to contribute in proportion to the benefit it had derived from the General Average act. If there were any little difficulties in the matter, it was better that they should have a general rule. It was undoubtedly the custom to exclude it in this country, but it was not so in foreign countries. In America and on the Continent he should say that, as a rule, they all allowed it, although there might be a few exceptions. He did not see any practical difficulties in getting at the damage done to ship and cargo by water and by fire.

Mr. Leathley said he thought it was due to the meeting to state the reasons why he did not wish to vote. Lloyd's, with which he was connected, wished well to this movement; but they, he believed, considered it premature to enter into the discussion of the details; and not having from them any commission to assent to or dissent from any resolution which should be proposed, he ought to abstain from voting. In anything he did, he wished it to be understood that he spoke simply in his individual capacity. He would adopt the suggestion which Judge Marvin had made: he would take into consultation the best advice he could possibly obtain— the most eminent men, persons whose education and habits entitled them to form opinions—taking a comprehensive and enlarged view in general, as well as particular cases. That being his position at the present time, he did not propose to give any expression of opinion, either as an individual or as representing the Committee of Lloyd's; though at the same time he wished the movement well, and hoped it would effect the result aimed at. No doubt it would take some time to produce any practical result, but so must every movement of this kind—no reforms were ever made in a day, and this was not a reform which was likely to occupy a very short time before it was effected.

Mr. RATHBONE observed that of course no one wished to interfere with Mr. Leathley's judgment; but many of the gentlemen present had given full consideration to such questions in different countries; and he doubted whether such an assembly as that present had met for the same purpose before. They were gentlemen whose opinions were of great importance, and he thought it was of the utmost value to have expressed the opinions of Antwerp, Amsterdam, Bremen, and America, even if they did nothing more.

The motion having been passed by a majority, and the time for rising having arrived, the section adjourned until the following day.

Wednesday, September 26.—Lord Neaves *presiding.*

The Chairman, in opening the proceedings, briefly explained the business which had been transacted at the previous meeting, and said it was of course understood that the only object of the resolutions was to ascertain, as a matter of fact, the predominant feeling and generally prevailing sentiment among those who were entitled to give an opinion on the matter; and where there were gentlemen assembled from all parts of the world, it was important that all their opinions should be ascertained, so that due effect might be given to them. If some gentleman would be so kind as to read the third resolution to be proposed, then he would be glad to hear anything that any gentleman had to say with regard to it.

MR. RATHBONE moved, *pro formâ*, the third resolution: 'That the damage done to cargo by chafing and breakage, resulting from a jettison of a portion of the remainder of the cargo, shall not be allowed in General Average.'

MR. W. J. LAMPORT, in the special interest of the shipowner, asked them to pause before they agreed to such a resolution. The question was whether the loss should fall upon the owner of the individual interest—*i.e.* be a Particular Average—or whether it should be a general contribution. There had been a disposition in some degree to adopt general principles by which practical expediency might be gained; and the question was, whether it was possible correctly to ascertain in an individual case whether the loss was particular or general; but with regard to the present resolution, he would remind the section that it would be absolutely necessary in every case to decide whether the chafing was the result of improper stowage or of a jettison; the question not being whether it be not a loss to fall on the individual interest or whether it be made good by general contribution, but whether, in order to prevent the trouble of ascertaining what the real facts of the case are, the burden of proof is not to be thrown on another class of people, the shipowners. The result of adopting that resolution would, in almost every case, be to throw the loss upon the shipowner unjustly. Could they ascertain the cause of chafing? The supporters of this resolution could not do so with anything like certainty: it might have arisen from improper stowage or from a jettison; and the only change effected by the resolution would be to throw the onus of proof from one set of shoulders to another.

THE CHAIRMAN inquired whether, supposing such and such damage did actually result from a jettison, was there any question as to the principle?

MR. BAILY. Some gentlemen near me dispute the principle.

THE CHAIRMAN said the question was whether they would give

up the principle on an ascertained statement of facts, or would the difficulty of drawing the line induce them to waive the principle altogether?

Mr. LEATHLEY thought there was one thing absent in the statement of facts which was an essential element in General Average, and that was the selection of some particular thing for destruction for the general benefit of the parties concerned. In the present case there was no intention to injure certain goods; it was simply an accident. The same principle ran through the whole spirit of English jurisprudence, and, he contended, correctly so. There was an absence of any intention to injure the property. There was another thing which, as a matter of principle, ought to be present, which was certainty. When a person had sustained injury it ought to be shown that the injury had been actually sustained; but when it was a question of chafing it was impossible to show when and how and where it had occurred; it might be chafed at one time or at another. The whole thing was involved in ambiguity, which, he contended, ought to withdraw it from General Average.

THE CHAIRMAN. The question involved is—Is it the result of a jettison for the general good or for a part?

Mr. LEATHLEY. I deny that it is a certainty. There may be, and sometimes is, a chafing after a jettison, but it is purely incidental.

Mr. HARPER. But the master contemplates the possibility.

Mr. BAILY said there was a particular way of stowing a cargo by which the whole was kept steady; and if the master took out the wedge that kept the goods fast, and thus permitted them to move about, the natural consequence was that, having loosened them, they would rub up against and chafe one another. This natural expectation of what would happen is followed in the case before us by the fact that it did happen. If a mast were cut away and in its fall knocked down another, those who support this resolution on principle would allow the second mast; and he therefore could not see, if they admitted that the chafe was the unavoidable consequence of throwing overboard a portion of the cargo, how they could resist on principle the allowance of the loss in General

Average. But there were several practical difficulties. The mere fact that the wedge was taken out, and that the chafing happened from it, was not sufficient to justify the allowance, if the loss could have been arrested, prevented, or checked. If you throw on an individual the responsibility of clearing himself, you get nearer to truth in practice than when you spread the loss over a large body. If the shipowner should clear himself in such a case, the practical rule will throw the loss on the underwriter of the goods chafed. The object of the rule was not somuch to throw the absolute responsibility or the difficulties of the case upon the master as to get at facts.

MR. W. J. TOMLINSON. Are we trying a question of principle or expediency?

MR. RATHBONE. The questions have all been put both upon principle and expediency.

THE CHAIRMAN. Where a resolution arises it may be supported or opposed on two grounds—on principle, or on the ground that, even supposing it to be consistent with principle, it is not expedient, from the difficulties of the investigation or from other inducements, to adopt it.

MR. TOMLINSON said one of the questions settled yesterday was on principle, and another on the ground of expediency. With reference to the resolution—if a cask were removed from the cargo and the next was uninjured by chafing, was it right that the shipowner should be made responsible for that? Was the shipowner to be made liable? No, certainly not. His own opinion was quite clear, both as to principle and to the expediency.

MR. RICHARDS said he quite agreed with the resolution in fact and in expediency. Unless there was a limit drawn as to what General Average was, they would get into interminable confusion. In the case of jettison of goods, that was of course a direct act, and of course General Average, but the consequence of that, the derangement of the cargo, ought not to follow as a General Average act. If it was meant to do so, there was no knowing to what extent it might go; and no line could be drawn unless you drew it between the immediate and direct, and the consequential and inferential result of the action. The jettison was a direct act, and was therefore General Average: the injury caused by the derangement of the ship's cargo was a secondary consequence, and therefore ought to be borne by the owners of the specific goods.

Mr. LEATHLEY, taking up the argument of Mr. Richards, asked where this liability as to consequential damage was to stop. Cargo would deteriorate to a certain extent by detention at a foreign port. He had known tea depreciate in value, to the amount of a farthing a pound, in consequence of detention. If the line was to be drawn anywhere, why not draw it between direct and secondary consequences? When articles were selected for the purpose of sacrifice, all well and good; but when you went beyond that point the loss might be traced to inferential consequences, and it was impossible to make any selection in that case.

Mr. LAMPORT thought that where the consequential damage was uncertain there should not be General Average; where it was certain, it should be General Average. If the chafing of goods was the certain and undoubted consequence of the jettison, then, he said, in principle it ought to be the subject of General Average. The question was as to the uncertainty. As a shipowner he was perfectly aware, from practical experience, that it was considered necessary, in order to relieve the shipowner from responsibility, that he should be in a position to prove that the damage did not occur from his default. As a matter of practice the onus of proof was undoubtedly thrown upon the shipowner. He would prove that the damage to the goods did not arise from improper stowage. Then what did it arise from? Of course from the jettison, and the chafing having certainly arisen from the jettison, the principle required that it should be made good by general contribution. There were peculiar kinds of cargoes which might be almost entirely lost by chafing, and if the loss was undoubtedly ascertained as the certain consequence of the jettison, what distinction was there between the cask thrown overboard and the cask broken in the hold and the contents leaked out? Each was the direct and consequent loss of the jettison, and ought to follow the same rule.

THE CHAIRMAN suggested whether the line might not be drawn at another place, for to draw it between direct and consequential was not easy—whether it would not do, occasioned by the jettison notwithstanding that the cargo was previously well stowed, and notwithstanding the jettison every care was taken to keep it all right, but that which was the result and undoubted consequence of the jettison.

Hon. Judge Marvin asked whether upon a policy of insurance upon cargo the underwriter would be liable for the breakage of cargo caused by the jettison.

Mr. Leathley replied that certainly he would be bound under the policy of insurance.

Hon. Judge Marvin thought, if the chafing and breakage were the immediate result of the jettison, it should be allowed; but if it were not the immediate consequence of the jettison, or if it were caused by the neglect of the ship-master, it should not be allowed. As the resolution stood, he would be compelled to vote against it; but he hoped the words 'not immediately resulting' would be introduced into the motion.

Mr. Baily, although he might differ with the principle, still thought very strongly that it was a question of expediency.

The resolution, on being put to the vote, was carried.

Mr. Rathbone next moved: 'That the damage done to cargo and the loss of it and the freight of it, resulting from discharging at a port of refuge in the way usual at the port with ships not in distress, shall not be allowed in General Average.'

Mr. Leathley thought this resolution involved exactly the same question as that included in the last. The spirit of the one was embodied in the spirit of the other; and those who supported the last would support this, and those who opposed the last would oppose the present resolution.

Mr. Baily thought otherwise, and observed that when a cargo is discharged there are some articles which it was not possible to avoid injuring, the mere effect of moving them was sufficient. With hides, for instance: the stowing of hides at the ports at which they were obtained was a peculiar trade, and in no other port except such ports could they be properly stowed. All the care in the world would not enable them to re-stow the hides at a port of refuge, not a hide port, without injury. Then again, they very often found, when a cargo was discharged, that it was necessarily injured from exposure to the weather, or it was lost between the ship and the warehouse. At the end of the voyage, again, they found that the cargo was short or injured, and the only way to account for it was that the losses had taken place at the port of refuge, and it could not have happened there if the vessel had not put into that port and been discharged there. Exposure to the atmosphere would cause injury to some kinds of cargo. All these questions must be considered. Again, when a cargo was taken out of the ship and put into a warehouse at a port of refuge, some of it might be stolen from the warehouse, or might be burnt, or, as had recently occurred in a case in which he was concerned, might be injured by a flood of water. All these cases had happened, and involved questions of great importance, and ought to be considered. Again, the mere handling of cargo sometimes caused injury. Many kinds of goods were put into bags which would bear twice handling—once in putting into the ship and another time in discharging—but they would not bear four times handling, and would therefore be injured by being twice discharged and loaded. It might be well, therefore, to split up the resolution into two parts—the damage done accidentally and that done naturally.

The Chairman. Is it quite apart from the question of loss of market?

Mr. Baily. Entirely.

Mr. Richards observed that in consequence of its detention and deterioration a cargo was sometimes unfit for the market for which it was intended, and that involved a loss of cargo.

Dr. Rahusen said he supposed the right point of this matter was adopted in the Dutch laws, which provided that the damage done to goods and loss of freight was General Average only when the vessel had not been brought into the port of refuge. For instance, it happened that a large vessel, drawing a great deal of water, could not get into the port, and had to be unloaded in lighters. The cargo while in the lighters was not yet saved, it was yet in danger, and was therefore General Average. It was at the port of distress, but it was not within the port of distress. In his opinion that was the right point. There might be a high sea, and the lighters might be thrown against the vessel, causing her damage.

THE CHAIRMAN. The resolution is quite clear: it is 'in' a port of refuge.

MR. BAILY said several gentlemen had asked whether this resolution drew any distinction between the damage done to cargo in the way he had mentioned and by the effects of climate— whether it might not be advisable to split the resolution into damage happening from accidental and from natural causes. Take, for instance, a cask of provisions. By an injury to a cask of pickled provisions the pickle might escape and the article would be damaged: that was an injury from without. A cask of dry provisions might be injured simply by keeping: and that was not the effect of injury from without.

MR. RICHARDS thought if the resolution said ' damage sustained by the cargo in consequence of discharging,' that would include every injury which the cargo might sustain while unloading.

MR. TOMLINSON explained that he was quite unable to vote on the question in its then indefinite shape: it was too vague.

The original resolution, with alteration of ' at a port of refuge ' to ' in a port of refuge ' was then put to the vote and affirmed.

MR. RATHBONE moved the fifth resolution: 'That the loss sustained by cutting away the wreck of masts accidentally broken shall not be allowed in General Average.'

DR. RAHUSEN said that, in his opinion, such was an act of General Average. It was a sacrifice for the common benefit in case of extreme necessity. There were a great many cases in which cutting away of wreck of masts or sails or booms was not General Average, but there were cases in which such certainly was General Average. When in a hurricane the three masts were blown down the hull was in danger, and then the captain cut away the wreck of those masts; that was a sacrifice in extreme danger, for the common benefit. The whole value of the masts and rigging must not, however, be allowed in General Average, but only that portion which was sacrificed.

MR. BAILY, as a matter of principle, did not think it was General Average. A man's property endangered his, and he removed that dangerous property. How could the man charge him for removing that property? It was unreasonable to ask him to pay. The danger must be removed; it was part and parcel of the original injury that the man had sustained. So far as principle went, it was an anomaly to ask them to pay for removing that which was the cause of the danger. Again, as a matter of expediency, how was it possible to estimate the value of an article that was in the sea in a gale of wind? They had to take into consideration the remote chance which there was of their being able to get it on board again, and the probability, after they had got it on board, of their being able to realise something for it at some distant period. On the ground of expediency, also, therefore, he would vote against allowing such a loss in General Average.

Dr. RAHUSEN considered that in principle it was General Average. How could the value of the broken mast be ascertained? That was only a matter of practice. Really the value of the broken mast, whatever it was, was sacrificed, and therefore it was General Average.

Mr. TOMLINSON observed that in principle it was General Average; but as a matter of expediency it was not advisable to consider it so.

Mr. BRADFORD quite agreed with Mr. Baily that it was not General Average in practice or in principle. It was utterly impossible to determine the value of the wreck cut away; and as far as American law was concerned, the custom was wholly against it throughout the United States. He had never allowed it and he never intended to do so.

The motion, on being put, was carried, with only two dissentients; and the Chairman expressed his regret for his Dutch and German friends (who voted against it), and hoped such a very decided expression of opinion on the subject would not be without its effects.

Mr. RATHBONE moved: 'That the expense of warehouse rent at a port of refuge on cargo necessarily discharged there, the expense of re-shipping it, and the outward port charges at that port shall, when the ship carries on the cargo from that port, be allowed in General Average.'

Mr. Lamport said he thought he recollected a decision in our English Courts that those charges were General Average.

Mr. Baily said there was no decision on the point, but there were dicta of the Judges to that effect.

Mr. Leathley said in principle he recognised the law, but there was not uniformity with reference to the law.

Mr. Richards was of opinion that these charges were not allowable in General Average. When the vessel and cargo were in safety at the port of refuge the General Average ceased.

Mr. Baily was of opinion that all these charges should be allowed in General Average. Physical safety was the end in some General Average acts only; in most cases the end was the arrival of the ship and cargo at their destination when that was possible. Towards this end, discharging a cargo, taking care of it whilst discharged, and re-shipping it were but steps; but for this end it was not necessary to discharge at all in many cases. The real object of putting into a port of refuge even is not to repair the ship, but to enable her to complete the voyage. If she could complete the voyage without being repaired it would not be justifiable to put into port. Terminating the General Average at the discharge of the cargo was cutting the General Average act in half.

This resolution having been carried, Mr. Rathbone moved the seventh: 'That the damage done to ship, cargo, and freight by carrying a press of sail shall not be allowed in General Average.'

The Chairman asked how such damage could arise.

Mr. Baily explained that if a vessel was on a lee shore she had to carry a press of sail; and the consequence was that her masts, spars, sails, and even the ship herself, were sometimes strained and damaged. A press of sail might likewise be carried to escape from a pirate or pursuit by an enemy.

After a discussion the motion was put to the vote and was carried.

It was then moved: 'That wages and provisions for the ship's crew shall be allowed to the shipowner in General Average, from the date on which his ship reaches a port of refuge under average until the date on which she leaves it—the allowance for provisions to be calculated at a fixed rate.'

Mr. W. H. Jones, of Liverpool, thought there was some ambiguity as to the expression 'under average.' If a ship put into a port to get new masts, after having had to cut them away in a hurricane, the expenses would be allowed; but if the ship sprung a leak, and was detained for some time to be repaired, that, he imagined, would not be allowed in General Average.

Mr. Baily said many ships came in from the Baltic, and ran into a port for shelter, to avoid threatening weather: if they admitted that into General Average, when there was nothing else wrong with the vessel, he apprehended that was not the real meaning of the resolution.

It was then agreed to amend the resolution by substituting for the words 'under average' the words 'in distress.'

Mr. Bradford said if he was not mistaken they would, according to the wording of the resolution, allow the wages and provisions of all hands, whether they were employed or not. That, he thought, would be unjust. The proper rule was to allow the wages and provisions of those men who were retained in the ship by the master; but it frequently occurred that, after going into a port of refuge, some of the men were discharged and some got other employments. The vessel was not at the expense of food for these men, and therefore no charge should be made for it. In the United States the law was to charge provisions and wages from the day on which the ship bore up for the port of refuge. Although he would vote for the resolution, he thought it should go further: the expenses should be allowed from the time the vessel makes an alteration in her course to bear up for the port of refuge.

Hon. Judge Marvin said, in the United States they adopted the principle of this resolution; and he believed they obtained it from England herself. But however it might be English law, it turned out not to be Lloyd's law. By Lloyd's law these wages and provisions were not allowed in the General Average act; they were not allowed by the underwriter upon the ship; they fell exclusively upon the shipowner; and when the shipowner was prepared to pay the full premium, why was he not fully indemnified? Why should he not be fully protected, either upon the General Average or upon the insurance?

MR. BAILY thought it was necessary that those who invariably shut out the expenses from General Average should say something on the matter. He himself thought it was not allowable in principle; he could draw no distinction between the wages and provisions of the crew and the wear and tear of the ship during the same period. It was one of those charges which attached to the shipowner—one of those charges which it must be held he had taken into consideration in entering into the contract. It was a casualty just like the wear and tear of the ship, which was of course greater the longer the voyage was protracted; but he did not think, if they were to aim at uniformity, that he could convert the whole world to his way of thinking; and therefore he accepted the resolution as a compromise to promote that uniformity. If they went as far as Mr. Bradford suggested they would get into endless disputes as to when the dividing-point in the course was reached — as to when the ship left the line of navigation proper for reaching her port of destination, *i.e.* when she entered upon her course for a port of refuge. If they would accept the resolution as a compromise between the two opinions he would be inclined to vote for it.

M. ENGELS did not think they should make any compromise in that which they did not agree to be right in principle. He was, however, in favour of the resolution, not as a compromise but as a matter of principle.

MR. BAILY observed that indirectly the English courts had decided that where a vessel put into a port of refuge the wages and provisions were not allowable.

The motion, on being put to the vote, was affirmed by a majority.

MR. RATHBONE moved the ninth resolution: 'That the contributing values of ship, freight, and cargo shall be their actual values to the owner of them at the time when they became liable for the General Average. That in fixing the value of freight, the wages and port charges up to the date of the General Average act shall not be deducted, and the wages and port charges after that date shall be deducted from the gross freight at the risk of the shipowner.'

At the suggestion of the Chairman, who observed that gentlemen might vote in favour of one part and against the other, Mr. RATHBONE first proposed the opening clause of the resolution.

Mr. BAILY thought there were some difficulties in the way of the resolution. Suppose some of the cargo of a ship had been thrown overboard, and afterwards the ship puts into a port of refuge and incurs expenses there, which are paid; after which she proceeds on her voyage, and subsequently goes to the bottom. She does not owe for the jettison till the end of the voyage: but what about the expenses actually incurred?

THE CHAIRMAN said a cargo might have a certain conjectural value if it reached a market at a given period; but when the voyage was actually completed it was found that that which had great invoice value was of no value, on account of a change in the market; should the person get off from contribution on the value of the article at the time the act was done, which was considered an act for the benefit of all?

MR. LEATHLEY said there was a question as to the value of the goods 'where,' as well as 'when,' for goods would have very different values in different places. The port of destination was the place for which the cargo was intended, and it might not be so valuable in any other port as at the place of destination.

MR. RICHARDS thought the port of destination was the proper place for the average to be made up. If taken to the port for which it was intended the cargo might be valuable; but at another place, where there was no market, it might be comparatively worthless. A valuation at an intermediate port could never, therefore, be a proper valuation.

MR. BAILY said there were always two questions to be considered in ascertaining a valuation—how much you could buy the article for, and how much you could sell it for. And he contended that the value of a ship was her value to the owner.

MR. HARPER said the value of goods to the owner was that at which they would sell if they had arrived at the time when they should have arrived—the proper time for the termination of the voyage if these interruptions had not taken place; not when the goods did in fact arrive, after a protracted voyage. He thought the value of the goods to the owner during the whole voyage was the value which he contemplated they would have brought when he made the venture. He made the venture for a certain market, and he calculated the vessel would have arrived within a certain time for that market.

DR. RAHUSEN said the ship had not always the same destination as the cargo, and the ship would not be at her port of destination when the cargo had arrived there; so that it would not be just to take the value of the goods at the port of destination. If there was a port of refuge into which the vessel put, they should take the value of the goods at that port. The freight was only earned at the port of destination, and if the vessel did not arrive there no freight was paid. The wages should also be deducted, for if the ship did not arrive at the port of destination no wages were paid, and no Particular Average on freight was paid.

MR. TOMLINSON thought they had no safe ground to go upon, except at the port of destination, and he should be quite prepared to leave that question in the hands of the average adjuster.

MR. RATHBONE. Perhaps instead of 'port of destination' 'termination of the adventure' would be better.

THE CHAIRMAN said the point seemed to be this: whether the values should be at the port of destination, with or without taking into view the depression from accident or changes of circumstances occurring after the time the General Average act was executed.

M. ENGELS said the voyage was not at an end until the ship and cargo came into the port of destination, and he considered that the values should be taken when the vessel arrived.

THE CHAIRMAN. Would 'the termination of the adventure' include the natural or assumed destination?

MR. BAILY. Whatever they agree upon with regard to the ultimate end of the adventure, the value in some cases may be less than the expenses.

THE CHAIRMAN asked if it ever happened that the liability was more than the *ad valorem* value of the goods?

MR. BAILY said the property was changed in value, and they ought not to apportion it according to the actual value. It would be very hard if, when expenses had been incurred at a port of refuge, and reasonably incurred, and the vessel was subsequently wrecked, that because he might be unfortunate enough to have some of his property saved, worth when saved say 600*l*., he should be compelled to pay 1,000*l*., whilst the man who was lucky enough to save nothing would have nothing to pay. If the amount ultimately saved came down below the expenses incurred, it would be very difficult to settle it.

Mr. RATHBONE inquired if there was anything objectionable in the principle adopted in England, to make the best of a bad job. The value of the property finally saved is set off against the amount, and the balance distributed over the estimated value of the property, as if the accident had not happened.

THE CHAIRMAN said there really were two questions before them, and that they could not adopt the resolution as it stood, as it was not clear what it meant, and as it would leave as many questions behind as it disposed of. But they all seemed to agree that the value must be taken to be the value of the article as at the termination of the adventure; but subject to this, which was open to a difference of opinion, namely, was the value of the ship to be affected or not by the depreciation occurring subsequent to the time when the act of General Average arose?

MR. RATHBONE then substituted for the motion, which he had previously submitted, the following: 'When the amount of the expenses is less than the value of the property finally saved, the contributing value of ship, freight, and cargo shall be their value to their owners at the termination of the adventure.'

DR. RAHUSEN. Do you mean by 'freight' only the freight of cargo, or also the freight of passengers?

MR. RATHBONE. That is a very different question. It is one of those questions which we cannot now raise, for if we once raise them we shall be settled for this day and to-morrow too. We must take it as freight as it is understood in each country.

THE CHAIRMAN. I don't know if there is any example of throwing a passenger overboard for the safety of the rest.

A MEMBER. There has been one instance, at least, in the case of Jonah.

MR. RATHBONE begged to move the resolution as he had already submitted it; and also 'That when the amount of expenses exceeds the value of property finally saved, the excess of expenses over proceeds shall be apportioned as if the whole property had reached its destination.' He also proposed a third resolution: 'That in fixing the value of freight, the wages and port charges, up to the date of the General Average act, shall not be deducted; and the wages and port charges after that date shall be deducted from the gross freight at the risk of the shipowner.'

MR. BAILY said the last resolution contemplated the ordinary case of freight being paid at the end of the voyage; but it was now frequently the case that a portion of the freight was paid at the port of shipment absolutely. The question was whether, if the shipowner had only a portion of the freight at risk, they should take off that portion all the port charges for the voyage or only part of them.

MR. RICHARDS said the owner had only a certain amount of money to put into his pocket when the ship arrived; but he had already been paid money on account of the freight, and it would be unjust that the entire amount of the wages incurred subsequently to the General Average act should be deducted from the small amount which he would receive at the end of the voyage.

After some conversation, the three motions were put to the vote, and all of them were carried by majorities.

HON. JUDGE MARVIN said it occurred to him that the resolutions which they had voted upon should now be referred to a committee, which should take them up, draft them into clear precise language, and introduce the various necessary qualifying terms. The language into which the resolutions should be put should be carefully considered, and afterwards they should be recommended by the committee for adoption. The resolutions ought to undergo careful revision at the hands of the committee, which ought to set to work as soon as may be, in order that the results of their deliberation might be circulated as soon as possible.

MR. RATHBONE. I think Judge Marvin means that we should not send forth as the resolutions of this meeting abominably bad English.

THE CHAIRMAN remarked that the functions of the committee would be to put the resolutions in more precise language where such was necessary.

Mr. Baily said they had not yet spoken to the practical way of carrying out the objects of the resolutions. Whilst they were at Glasgow they ought to discuss what were the best means of carrying out their resolutions, for if they considered that they had done their work when their votes were given it was a great mistake. When they came to add up the votes, they might find that a mere numerical majority was not of equal weight with the names of the gentlemen voting in the minority.

The Chairman said there was one thing which he hoped gentlemen would think of before they came to the discussion to-morrow, whether there was any objection, if it were thought advisable, that the names of the voters should be given. Gentlemen might not wish their names to be published; but there was no doubt it would be advisable to give the names of such as were agreeable.

Mr. Baily said each knew what he had done; and the public wished to know the value of the names which had voted. Lloyd's would of course pay more attention to some names than to others.

Mr. Rathbone thought it was understood from the first that that would be the case. There were some gentlemen who had taken part in the proceedings who represented large bodies, and in whose judgment everybody had great confidence, while there were others, perhaps, who had not the same experience.

Mr. Leathley explained that, although he was connected with Lloyd's, he simply voted in his individual capacity, and not as in any way representing them.

Mr. Baily also suggested that, before the names were published, gentlemen should have an opportunity of explaining whether they voted on the ground of principle or expediency, for he himself had voted for resolutions on different grounds.

The suggestions of Mr. Baily were acceded to; and a committee —consisting of Lord Neaves, Hon. Judge Marvin, Mr. Baily, Mr. Richards, Mr. Harper, and Mr. Rathbone—was appointed to consider the resolutions, the committee to report the results of their deliberations at the meeting to-morrow (Thursday).

The section then adjourned.

Thursday, September 27.—LORD NEAVES *presiding.*

A long discussion took place, in which almost all the gentlemen present took part. The purport of the discussion was the wording of a resolution which should practically exclude from General Average 'voluntary stranding,' without excluding it on the ground that it was wrong in principle to allow it. Even those who advocated the admission of the loss on principle felt the practical abuse it might lead to; and ultimately the following resolution, proposed by Lord Neaves, was agreed to, in the place of resolution No. 1, negatived on Tuesday: 'That, as a general rule in the case of the stranding of a vessel in the course of her voyage, the loss or damage to ship, cargo, or freight shall not be the subject of General Average, but without prejudice to such a claim in exceptional cases, upon clear proof of special facts.'

The meeting then proceeded to take into consideration as to how and in what form the business now concluded by this International Congress should be brought before the various Chambers of Commerce, and the mercantile public generally.

JUDGE MARVIN read a short statement of his views on the subject, which, after a discussion, in which the delegates from Holland and Denmark, Messrs. Leathley, Richards, and Baily took part, ended in the adoption of the following resolutions:—

1. 'That the meeting hereby requests the Council of the Association to assist by their counsels such person or persons as may be approved of by them, in drawing up a Bill, with a view to its being enacted into a law by the legislative authorities of the several nations of the world, which Bill shall define, as clearly as may be, the term "General Average," and describe more or less fully the cases intended to be included within the definition, and which shall also specify the nature of the loss, damage, or expense allowable in General Average, and the principle on which the amount of the loss, damage, or expense shall be ascertained; also, furnish a rule or rules for ascertaining the contributory values of the interests concerned, and which shall also contain such matters as the person or persons drawing up the Bill may think it advisable

to insert. That upon such Bill being drawn up and printed, copies thereof shall be transmitted to the several Chambers of Commerce, Boards of Underwriters, Shipowners' Associations, and other commercial societies in different parts of the world, accompanied by a copy of this resolution, and a request to them to examine and return the said copies, with such alterations or amendments as they may think proper to make therein, within six months from the time of the receipt thereof. That, upon the return of the said copies, or upon the expiration of the said six months, the said Bill shall be revised by the person or persons drawing up the same, enlightened by the information acquired as aforesaid. That, upon the Bill being perfected in the manner aforesaid, it be recommended to the legislative authorities of all commercial nations, to enact the same into a law.'

2. 'That, in the meantime, the meeting resolves to circulate as widely as possible, for general information, the rules embodied in the resolutions which have been passed by the meeting, as those which, under a uniform system, it might be desirable to consider.'

The business of the Congress being thus concluded, it was moved by JUDGE MARVIN, seconded by MR. LEATHLEY of Lloyd's, and carried unanimously : ' That this meeting offer their best thanks to Lords Brougham and Neaves for their kindness in acting as Chairmen, and for the able manner in which they have assisted its deliberations.' In seconding the resolution, MR. LEATHLEY said that Lloyd's took a warm interest in the question under discussion, and in the results that would follow this meeting at Glasgow.

A vote of thanks to Judge Marvin and to the other foreign delegates was also passed, and the meeting broke up.

It may not be out of place to reprint here the resolutions which were passed at a meeting of the Committee for managing the affairs of Lloyd's on the 10th of October, 1860, viz. :—

1. 'That the thanks of this committee be given to the several gentlemen who, at a great sacrifice of personal convenience, have come from abroad to attend the meeting at Glasgow on the subject

of General Average, and whom the committee had the honour of meeting by a deputation of their body.'

2. 'That this resolution be communicated to each of the gentlemen, and that they be assured at the same time that this committee take a strong interest in the subject discussed at Glasgow and that they will gladly co-operate in the endeavour to carry out the very desirable object sought to be attained.'

The draftsman to whom originally the task of framing a Bill—as a step towards the formation of a code to be adopted in the different countries—was entrusted, became, after his recovery from a serious illness, so overburdened with other engagements, that he was altogether disabled from undertaking the work, and the difficulty which in consequence arose in procuring a competent substitute caused such a delay in the preparation of the Bill that it was not drawn before the spring of 1862, when it appeared in the following terms, viz. :—

DRAFT OF A BILL

INTITULED

An Act to Consolidate and Amend the Laws relating to General Average Sacrifices and General Average Contributions.

Be it enacted by the Queen's most Excellent Majesty, by and with the Advice and Consent of the Lords Spiritual and Temporal, and Commons, in this present Parliament assembled, and by the Authority of the same, as follows:

Interpretation Clause.

1. For the Purposes of this Act (if not inconsistent with the Reason of the Thing or the Context), the following Terms and Phrases shall have the respective Meanings hereinafter assigned to them; (that is to say,)

'Master' shall include every Person having Command or Charge of any Ship:

'Seamen' and 'Crew' shall have the same Meaning, and shall each include every Person employed or engaged in any Capacity on board any Ship:

'Ship' shall include Man-of-War, Privateer, Merchantman, and every other Description of public or private Craft:

'The Ship' shall mean only the particular Ship in respect to which the General Average Loss in question shall have been made or incurred:

'Cargo' shall include every Description of Wealth on board the Ship except the Ship's Apparel and Outfit:

'Property' shall include the Ship, her Apparel and Outfit, the Freight and the Cargo, and every Article of Wealth at Hazard in the Adventure in which the Ship shall have been employed:

'Sacrifice' shall comprise the Destruction or Damage of or Injury to any Article of Wealth:

'General Average Act' shall comprise both General Average Losses and General Average Expenditures or Disbursements:

'General Average Act' and 'General Average Sacrifice' shall have the same Meaning:

'General Average Sacrifice' shall mean a prudent and extraordinary Sacrifice of Property made by the Master in order to avert an unusual and imminent Peril from the Ship, Freight, and Cargo, such Property so sacrificed as aforesaid not having been the Cause of such Peril as aforesaid, nor having been expressly stipulated for by the Parties to the Maritime Adventure in respect to which such Sacrifice as aforesaid shall have been made:

'General Average Loss' shall denote the Loss sustained by any Person in consequence of the Performance of a General Average Act or Sacrifice:

'General Average Expenditure' shall denote any Debt or Liability properly contracted in respect to a General Average Sacrifice by the Master of the Ship with a Person not having any Property at Risk in the Adventure:

'General Average Contribution' shall denote that Compensation which the Party who shall have suffered a General Average Loss shall be entitled to receive from the Owners of the Ship, Freight, and Cargo:

'Unusual Peril' shall comprise Enemies, Pirates, and formidable Robbers; and shall also comprise Storms, Swells, Shoals, Quicksands, Lee Shores, Rocks, Cliffs, and the Ship's straining or taking the Ground, provided that this latter Class of Perils shall not have been incident to the usual Course of the Voyage in prosecuting which the Ship shall have been employed at the Time when the Sacrifice in question shall have been made.

GENERAL PROVISIONS.

2. If the Majority of the Seamen on board the Ship shall concur in performing an Act, which, if done with the Master's Consent, would have been a General Average Act, such Act so performed by the Majority of the Seamen shall be deemed to be a General Average Act within the Meaning of this Act.

3. That all such Provisions of this Act as relate to a Ship shall (as far as is practicable) be deemed equally to apply to Boats of every Description, whether the same shall have been propelled by Oars or not.

4. That every Person who shall suffer a General Average Loss shall be entitled to receive from the Persons whose Property shall have been at Risk in the Adventure in respect to which such General Average Loss shall have been incurred a Sum of Money equivalent to the Loss (if any), properly and necessarily sustained by him in respect of such General Average Loss, and such Sum shall be contributed for by the Persons in respect of whose Property such General Average Act as aforesaid shall have been performed in proportion to the Values of their respective Interests in such Property as aforesaid, and such Values shall be estimated in the Manner hereinafter directed.

5. A General Average Expenditure shall give to the Person making the same a Right to a General Average Contribution, irrespectively of the final Success or Failure of the Adventure.

6. Subject to the Provisions of this Act, all Acts, Losses,

Expenses, Debts, or Liabilities which are either preliminary or necessarily incidental to a General Average Sacrifice or Loss, if such Acts, Losses, Expenses, Debts, or Liabilities could have been foreseen by the Master or other Person authorised by this Act to make a General Average Sacrifice as the natural and probable Consequence of such Sacrifice, shall be deemed to be General Average Acts within the Meaning of this Act.

JETTISON.

7. Subject to the Provisions of this Act, a Jettison shall, for the Purposes of this Act, be defined to be a prudent and extraordinary throwing overboard or Sacrifice of Property which shall have been on board, done or made by or by the Direction of the Master of the Ship, in order to avert an unusual and imminent Peril from the Property at Risk in the Adventure.

8. A Jettison shall be deemed to be a General Average Act within the Meaning of this Act.

9. The Loss or Damage necessarily done to Property in consequence of a Hole having been cut in the Ship in order to get Goods or Stores out for the Purpose of a Jettison, and the Loss or Damage of Goods occasioned by their being washed overboard or otherwise injured after having been brought on Deck either for the Purpose of being jettisoned themselves, or in order that less valuable Goods might be reached in order to be jettisoned, and the Loss or Damage of any Part of the Property on board on account of the Vessel's shipping Water in consequence of a General Average Act, shall be deemed to be Losses either preliminary, or (as the Case may be) necessarily incidental to a General Average Act.

10. Any Sacrifice, the Object of which could be properly and effectually accomplished by means of a Jettison, shall for the Purposes of this Act be considered as a Jettison.

11. A Jettison of Specie, Money, Jewels, or other like valuable Commodities shall not be made unless such Jettison shall be unavoidable.

SHIP, FREIGHT, AND CARGO.

12. Subject to the Provisions of this Act, a prudent and extraordinary Sacrifice of a Mast, Spar, Sail, Halyard, Yard, Rigging,

or other Apparel, Outfit, or Materials of the Ship, made by or by the Direction of the Master of the Ship, in order to prevent her from foundering, or to float her when stranded, to enable her to reach a Port of Refuge, to righten her when on her Beam Ends, to prevent her from being driven on Shore, to join Convoy, or to prevent her from being separated from the same, or in order to avert any unusual and imminent Peril from the Ship, Freight, and Cargo, shall be deemed to be a General Average Act or Loss within the Meaning of this Act.

13. The Loss sustained on account of any Part of the Bulwarks of the Ship having been cut away in order to relieve her of Water when flooding her Decks shall be deemed to be a General Average Loss within the Meaning of this Act.

14. When a Mainmast, after having been cut away for a General Average Purpose or Sacrifice, shall in its Descent have carried away the Mizenmast, or have injured the Boats or Bulwarks or any Part of the Ship or of the Cargo, then in such Case the Damage which such Mainmast shall have so done as aforesaid to the Mizenmast, Boats, Bulwarks, or other Part of the Ship, or to any Part of the Cargo, shall be likewise deemed to be a General Average Loss within the Meaning of this Act.

15. No Loss or Damage sustained by the Ship, Cargo, and Freight, in consequence of an intentional Stranding of the Ship, shall be deemed to be a General Average Loss within the Meaning of this Act; provided, that if the Property at Risk in the Adventure could have been equally efficaciously protected by means of a Jettison or other General Average Act, then in such Case such intentional Stranding shall be deemed to be a General Average Act as regards the Ship.

16. Subject to the Provisions hereinafter contained, all Loss or Damage properly and necessarily occasioned by or by the Direction of the Master to the Ship, her Apparel or Outfit, prior to the Discharge of the Cargo and for the Benefit of the Ship and Cargo, in heaving the Ship off after she shall have been either intentionally or accidentally stranded, shall be deemed to be a General Average Loss within the Meaning of this Act.

17. All Damage properly done to Property by the Master in

consequence of getting the Ship off the Ground after the Cargo shall have been discharged for that Purpose, shall be deemed to be a General Average Sacrifice, provided that the Cargo and Ship are subsequently reunited; or that, even if the Cargo and Ship are not subsequently reunited, the Value of the Ship shall not be improved by getting her off.

18. All Damage done to the Ship, Freight, and Cargo in consequence of a Measure properly taken by the Master to extinguish a Fire on board the Ship shall be deemed to be a General Average Loss within the Meaning of this Act.

19. All Expenses and Liabilities properly incurred by the Master of the Ship for the Purpose of extinguishing a Fire on board, shall be deemed to be General Average Losses within the Meaning of this Act.

20. The Loss or Damage caused to the Ship, Freight, and Cargo by carrying, crowding, or hoisting a Press of Sail shall not be deemed to be a General Average Loss within the Meaning of this Act.

21. When the Ship shall have been lost owing to the Want of an Anchor or Chain slipped from, such Loss of the Ship as aforesaid shall not be deemed to be a General Average Loss within the meaning of this Act.

22. No Sacrifice of the Wreck of a Mast, or of a Spar snapped or sprung by the Wind, or of the Rigging attached thereto, or of any other Portion of the Ship or her Apparel, that shall have been so damaged by Accident as to be unfit for its primary Function, shall be deemed to be a General Average Act within the Meaning of this Act.

23. The Sacrifice of any of the Ship's Guns, Ammunition, Outfit, Apparel, or Furniture, or of any other Property, made by or by the Direction of the Master of the Ship in lawful Defence against Capture, and the Expense of curing such Persons on board as shall have been wounded, maimed, or otherwise bodily injured in such Defence as aforesaid, shall be deemed to be General Average Sacrifices within the Meaning of this Act.

Note.—This Section is counter to the present Law on this Matter, but is recommended by its Policy in encouraging lawful and judicious Resistance.

24. No Loss of Interest or Profit on the Property at Risk in the Adventure, and no Loss occasioned by the Delay, Wear and Tear, Deterioration in Value, Loss of Market, or Change in Price of the Property at Risk as aforesaid, consequent upon a General Average Sacrifice, shall be deemed to be a General Average Loss within the Meaning of this Act.

25. No Sacrifice of Property that shall have been itself a Cause of Peril to any Portion of the Property at Risk in the Adventure, or which shall have been in a State of Wreck, or which shall have been carried on board the Ship in a Manner or at a Time not warranted by the usual Course of Trade in such Voyages as that in which the Ship shall at the Time of such Sacrifice have been employed, or which in any Manner shall have impeded the due Course of the Navigation of the Ship, shall be deemed to be a General Average Act within the Meaning of this Act.

26. No Loss occasioned by a contrary Wind or Calm, or by Frost or other Temperature of the Atmosphere, shall be deemed to be a General Average Loss within the Meaning of this Act, provided that, if the Master of the Ship shall, on account of the Performance of a General Average Act, have properly caused her to deviate from the Course of her Voyage for a Port or Place where she shall have been detained by a Severity of Climate usual at such Place, then, in such Case, the Cost of the Crew's Wages and Provisions occasioned by such Protraction of the Voyage shall, subject to the Provisions of this Act, be deemed to be General Average Losses within the Meaning of this Act.

27. Every General Average Act made on behalf of the Ship after Part of the Cargo shall have been placed in Lighters shall be deemed to be a General Average Sacrifice, likewise as regards that Part of the Cargo which shall have been placed in the Lighters (this will prevent undue Preferences on the Part of the Master).

28. When a General Average Sacrifice shall have been made of any Part of a Lighter, Long Boat, or small Craft into which Part of the Cargo shall have been placed or was about being placed in order to extricate the Ship from a Peril not incident to the usual Course of the Voyage, and when any General Average Expenditure shall have been incurred in respect to such Lighter, Long Boat, or

small Craft as aforesaid, all such said Sacrifices and Expenditures as aforesaid shall, subject to the Provisions of this Act, be deemed to be General Average Acts or Expenditures respectively as regards the Ship, Freight, and Cargo.

29. No Loss or Damage of Property by Worms, Insects, or Climate shall be deemed to be a General Average Loss within the Meaning of this Act.

Cargo.

30. Subject to the Provisions of this Act, the Jettison or other General Average Sacrifice of any Portion of the Goods placed in a Lighter, Boat, or other small Craft in their Passage from the Ship to the Shore shall be deemed to be a General Average Sacrifice as regards the Ship and the Lighter, Boat, or other like Craft and the Remainder of the Cargo.

31. The Shipper of Cargo by a Ship that shall have saved another at Sea shall be entitled to a Share of the Salvage proportionate to the Loss (if any), sustained by him by reason of such Salvage Services.

32. If Goods jettisoned or otherwise sacrificed by a General Average Act shall have been recovered, they shall be deemed to have continued to be the Property of the Person or Persons whose Property they were at the Time when they were jettisoned or otherwise sacrificed as aforesaid, but such Owner or Owners shall refund such General Average Contribution (if any) as shall have been received by him or them on account of such Jettison or other General Average Act, after having first deducted from the Amount of such Contribution a Sum that will be equivalent to the Value of the Damage sustained by the Goods so sacrificed as aforesaid together with the Costs of Salvage (if any).

33. The Loss or Damage of Cargo, and the Loss of Freight consequent upon a Discharge of any Part of the Cargo when the Ship shall have been stranded, shall be deemed to be a General Average Loss within the Meaning of this Act.

34. The Loss of, or on, Property by reason of its being properly sold by the Master of the Ship at a Port of Refuge in order to pay any Debts, Expenses, or Liabilities properly incurred by him in

respect to any Matter that is constituted by this Act a General Average Sacrifice, shall be deemed to be a General Average Loss within the Meaning of this Act.

35. No Damage occasioned to the Cargo on account of the Chafing or Breakage of any Part thereof in consequence of a Jettison or other General Average Act shall be deemed to be a General Average Loss within the Meaning of this Act.

36. No Loss of, or on, Cargo and Freight by discharging the Cargo at a Port of Refuge, except in Cases where such Discharge shall have been necessarily made in a Manner not usually adopted at such Port as aforesaid in respect of Ships not in Distress, shall be deemed to be a General Average Loss within the Meaning of this Act.

37. No Damage done to the Cargo by Water getting down the Hatches in consequence of a Jettison or other General Average Act being or having been made, shall be deemed to be a General Average Loss within the Meaning of this Act.

38. No Loss of, or on, Cargo by reason of its being properly shut out or left at a Port of Refuge shall be deemed to be a General Average Loss within the Meaning of this Act.

39. No Loss of, or on, Cargo caused by discharging it when the Ship shall have been condemned at a Port of Refuge, or in consequence of the accidental Wreck or Damage of the Ship, or accidental Damage of the Cargo, shall be deemed to be a General Average Loss within the Meaning of this Act.

40. If, or when, the Cargo shall have been necessarily discharged at a Port of Refuge, the loss of any part of the cargo at such Port as aforesaid by Fire, Theft, or any unusual and imminent Peril shall be deemed to be a General Average Loss within the Meaning of this Act.

41. No Sacrifice of Goods for which no Bill of Lading or other Note in Writing shall have been signed by the Master, or which shall have been taken on board by him barratiously or contrary to a Charter Party, or which the Owner of such Goods or his Agent shall without the Master's Consent have shifted to a Place in the Ship different from that allotted to them by the Master, shall be deemed to be a General Average Act within the Meaning of this Act.

Freight.

42. Subject to the Provisions of this Act, in all Cases in which the Sacrifice of any Part of the Cargo is constituted by this Act a General Average Loss, the Sacrifice of Freight sustained in consequence of such Sacrifice as aforesaid of any Part of the Cargo shall be deemed to be a General Average Loss of the Freight.

43. No loss of Freight on Cargo shut out at a Port of Refuge or on any Portion of the Cargo not sacrificed by a General Average Act, shall be deemed to be a General Average Loss within the Meaning of this Act.

Intermediate Expenses.

44. All extraordinary Expenses properly incurred by the Master of the Ship in order to join Convoy, or in consequence of his waiting for the same, shall be deemed to be General Average Sacrifices within the Meaning of this Act.

45. All Compensations and Ransoms properly paid to Pirates by the Master of the Ship on behalf of the Persons or Property on board shall be deemed to be General Average Acts within the Meaning of this Act.

46. The cost of Crew's Wages and Provisions and all other Expenses and Liabilities properly incurred by the Master in order to release the Property at Risk in the Adventure from Capture, Detention, or Embargo, suffered by Order of a Sovereign Power, shall be deemed to be General Average Losses within the Meaning of this Act.

47. If a Hostage shall, with his own consent and that of the Master of the Ship, have been properly given to secure a Compensation or Ransom, the Reimbursement to which such Hostage shall have been entitled for his Expenses and personal Inconvenience as such Hostage shall be deemed to be a General Average Loss within the Meaning of this Act.

48. All Sums of Money or Articles of Value properly and necessarily paid or given by the Master on account of the Services of another Ship in effecting a Re-capture of the Ship and Cargo

from an Enemy, shall be deemed to be General Average Losses within the meaning of this Act.

49. All Expenses and Liabilities properly incurred by the Master of the Ship for the Purpose of unloading her after she shall have been either intentionally or accidentally stranded, shall, except in Cases where the Cargo could have been discharged and forwarded to its Destination for an Outlay or Loss less in Amount than the Cost incurred in heaving the Ship off, be deemed to be General Average Losses within the Meaning of this Act.

50. All Expenses and Liabilities properly incurred by the Master in consequence of getting the Ship off the Ground, after the Cargo shall have been discharged for that Purpose, shall be deemed to be General Average Sacrifices, provided that the Cargo and Ship are subsequently re-united, or that even if the Cargo and Ship are not re-united as aforesaid, the Value of the Ship shall not have been improved by getting her off the Ground.

51. The Expense of re-shipping Cargo, after it shall have been put into Lighters to float or lighten the Ship when stranded, or when threatened with any unusual or imminent Peril, shall be deemed to be a General Average Loss within the Meaning of this Act.

52. The Crew's Wages and Provisions and all other Expenses consequent upon bearing up for a Port of Refuge shall (from the Date when the Ship deviates from the Course of her Voyage for the Purpose of such bearing up) be deemed to be General Average Losses within the Meaning of this Act.

53. The Inward Port Charges, such as Towage, Pilotage, Dockage, Health Fees, and the like, incurred at a Port of Refuge, whenever the bearing up for such Port shall have been rendered necessary either by a General Average Sacrifice, or by accidental Damage to the Ship or Cargo, Sickness of Crew, unexpected Want of Water or Provisions, shifting of the Cargo, Pumps choking, or other like Accident, shall be deemed to be General Average Losses within the meaning of this Act.

54. All Expenses consequent upon bearing up for a Port of Refuge, the Expense of discharging the Cargo there, and the Hire of Lighters in order to avoid discharging Part or the whole of the

Cargo there, if properly incurred by the Master, shall be deemed to be General Average Losses within the Meaning of this Act.

55. All Expense of Postages, Notarial Fees, Adjustment Fees, and Brokerage, properly incurred by the Master of the Ship at a Port of Refuge, shall be deemed to be General Average Losses within the Meaning of this Act.

56. The Cost of the Wages of Men properly employed by the Master to pump when the Cargo shall have been on board at a Port of Refuge, shall be deemed to be a General Average Loss within the Meaning of this Act.

57. The expense of Warehouse Rent at a Port of Refuge on Cargo necessarily discharged there, and the Expense of re-shipping it, except as to such Portion thereof as shall have been discharged in consequence of an Accident at such Port, and in all Cases the Outward Port Charges properly incurred by the Master at such Port, shall, in case the Ship shall carry on the Cargo from such Port, or when the original Contract of Affreightment shall not have been determined, be deemed to be General Average Losses within the Meaning of this Act.

58. If, or when, the Stowage of any Part of the Cargo shall have become, by means of Perils of the Sea, a Cause of Peril to the Property at Risk in the Adventure, all Expense properly and necessarily incurred for the Purpose of discharging the Cargo in order to restow it properly shall be deemed to be a General Average Loss within the Meaning of this Act.

59. All Expense properly incurred by the Master of the Ship in protecting the Property at Risk at a Port of Refuge shall be deemed to be a General Average Loss within the Meaning of this Act.

60. All Expense of Delay at Sea, properly incurred by the Master in order to refit, shall be deemed to be a General Average Loss within the Meaning of this Act.

61. The Expense of discharging the Cargo in order to cool it, or for any other Object, except it be to the Advantage of all the property at Risk in the Adventure, shall not be deemed to be a General Average Act or Loss within the Meaning of this Act.

62. The Expense of making permanent Repairs to the Ship at

a Port of Refuge, except in Cases where the Damage to repair which such Repairs shall be made shall have been a General Average Loss, shall not be deemed to be a General Average Loss within the Meaning of this Act.

63. The Expense properly incurred by the Master at a Port of Refuge in making Repairs which do not permanently improve the Value of the Ship shall be deemed to be a General Average Loss, provided that either such Repairs as aforesaid, or some other General Average Loss or Expense of an equal Amount should be necessarily incurred at such Port in order to the safe Prosecution of the Voyage, or in case that such Repairs as aforesaid shall have been made in order to avoid discharging the Cargo.

64. If, or when, the Ship shall have entered a Port of Refuge for the Purpose of having Repairs made which shall have been rendered necessary, partly on account of particular and partly on account of General Average Losses sustained by such Ship, the Expense of the Repairs, and of the Wages and Provisions for the Crew during the Time in which the Repairs are being made, shall be apportioned, so that so much only of such Expenses as aforesaid as shall have been rendered necessary in consequence of a General Average Sacrifice, shall be deemed to be a General Average Act or Loss.

65. Bottomry, Respondentia, and all other Interest and Commission, but not the Premiun of Insurance on Money expended, properly incurred by the Master at a Port of Refuge, with respect to a General Average Act, shall be deemed to be General Average Acts or Losses within the Meaning of this Act.

66. All Expenses incurred by the Master, which if incurred by another Person would have been Expenditures within the Meaning of this Act, shall be deemed to be Expenditures within the Meaning of this Act.

67. If, or when, the Ship, her Apparel or Outfit, or any Part thereof, shall have been properly and necessarily hypothecated by the Master, in order to discharge a General Average Liability, the Sum for which the Ship, her Apparel or Outfit, or any Part thereof, shall be so hypothecated as aforesaid, shall be contributed for as a General Average Loss, just as if the Shipowner had made a Jettison

of his Property of the Value of such Sum, provided that if the Cargo shall have been lost, and the Ship shall have remained safe, such Sum shall be contributed for as an Expenditure.

WRECKS.

68. In Case of Wreck, all prudent and extraordinary Sacrifices properly made, and all prudent and extraordinary Expenses and Liabilities properly incurred by the Master for the Benefit of the Property at Risk in the Adventure, shall be deemed to be General Average Losses within the Meaning of this Act.

69. In Case of Wrecks, the Cost of Crew's Wages, when the Crew shall have been employed for the Benefit of the Ship, Freight, and Cargo, after the Date at which the Shipowner could have legally dismissed them, and no Freight shall have been earned by him in the Adventure, shall be deemed to be a General Average Loss within the Meaning of this Act.

70. The Loss or Damage of any Part of the Ship's Stores caused by their being landed in case of Wreck in a disadvantageous Manner or at a disadvantageous Time, having been intended to facilitate the Discharge of the Cargo, shall be deemed to be a General Average Loss within the Meaning of this Act.

71. The Expense of landing the Cargo shall, when the Ship shall have been wrecked, or condemned at a Port of Refuge, be deemed to be a General Average Loss within the Meaning of this Act.

ESTIMATION OF GENERAL AVERAGE LOSSES.

72. The Amount of a General Average Loss of Ship's Stores shall, when the Ship shall have been wrecked before they shall have been replaced, be estimated at the Amount or Value which such Stores would have had if they had been on board when the Ship was wrecked.

73. The Amount of a General Average Loss of any of the Ship's Stores shall, when such Stores shall have been replaced before or at the Termination of the Adventure, be equivalent to the actual Expense of replacing such Stores; but, when such Stores shall have been replaced subsequently to the Termination of the

Adventure, the Amount of such General Average Contribution as aforesaid shall be equivalent to the Expense that would have been incurred if they had been replaced at the Termination of the Adventure.

74. The Amount of a General Average Loss of any Portion of the Cargo shall be estimated at the Price which it would have brought at the Ship's Port of Destination at the Time it would have been delivered there if it had not been sacrificed as aforesaid, deducting from such Amount as aforesaid all such Charges and Expenses as must have been paid if the Goods had been delivered at the said Port and shall have been avoided by the Goods having been sacrificed as aforesaid.

75. A General Average Sacrifice of Property at Risk in the Adventure shall not, if followed by a total Loss of the Ship and Cargo, be contributed for in any Manner.

76. For the Purposes of this Act, the Loss sustained by a General Average Sacrifice of Property at Risk in the Adventure shall, if followed by a Wreck of the Ship, be estimated at the Value which the Property so sacrificed would have had if it had also suffered the same Wreck.

77. The Loss sustained by a General Average Sacrifice of damaged or perishable Property shall be estimated at the Value which the Property so sacrificed would, if it had not been so sacrificed, have had at the Ship's Port of Destination, deducting from such Value all Charges and Expenses that should have been paid before such Goods as aforesaid could have been delivered there and shall have been avoided by their having been sacrificed as aforesaid.

78. The Value of Property to be contributed for in respect of a General Average Sacrifice made of the same, if such Value shall have been stated in the Bill of Lading lower than it really was, shall be its actual Value.

79. The Loss sustained in consequence of a General Average Sacrifice of Provisions intended to be consumed during the Voyage, or of the Effects of Sailors or Passengers, shall be estimated at the Amount for which the replacing of such Provisions or Effects shall, or would, have cost.

80. The Value of Goods to be contributed for after they shall have been sold to pay Expenses shall, when such Sale shall have been a General Average Loss within the Meaning of this Act, and shall have realised a less Sum than the Sale of the same Goods would have produced at the Ship's Port of Destination, be the probable Amount of the net Proceeds of such Goods at the Port of Destination; but, in case such Sale as aforesaid shall have produced a greater Sum than would have been obtained by a Sale of the same Goods at the Port of Destination, then in such Case the Value of such Goods so to be contributed for as aforesaid shall be equivalent to the net Proceeds of the Sale as aforesaid after deducting therefrom the Freight which the Shipowner would have earned if the Goods so sold as aforesaid had arrived at the Port of the Ship's Destination, provided that if such Deduction of Freight would lower the Proceeds of the Goods sold at such intermediate Port as aforesaid below the probable net Proceeds which would be obtained by a Sale of such Goods at the Port of Destination, then, in such Case, the probable net Proceeds of such Goods if sold at the Port of Destination, estimated according to the Provisions of this Act, shall be deemed to be the Value at which such Goods are to be contributed for.

81. In all cases where a Loss or contributory Interest is directed by this Act to be estimated at the Ship's Port of Destination, if it shall happen that the property so to be estimated shall not have a Price Current at such Port, and shall not be usually bought and sold there, then in such Case the Estimation of such Loss or contributory Interest (as the Case may be) shall be made according to the Value which the Property the Subject of such Loss or Contribution shall have at the nearest Port to the Ship's Port of Destination which, at the time of such Estimation as aforesaid, shall have Prices Current of such Property, or where such Property shall then be usually bought and sold.

82. Every Person who shall receive any General Average Contribution for any Portion of the Cargo shall pay Freight for the same, if such Portion of the Cargo as aforesaid would have been liable to Freight, in case the General Average Sacrifice on account of which he shall have received Contribution as aforesaid had not

been performed, but a like General Average Sacrifice had been performed by means of other Property, and the Amount for which he shall be liable in respect of such Portion of the Cargo for Freight shall be the Amount for which such Portion of the Cargo would have been liable in the Circumstances aforesaid, less an Amount equal to the Sum assessed on the Freight in the Adjustment of such General Average Contribution as aforesaid.

83. Subject to the Provisions of this Act, the Loss of Freight sustained in consequence of a General Average Sacrifice shall be estimated according to the Amount of Freight payable at the Ship's Port of Destination under the Bill of Lading.

84. If, or when, the Adjustment of a General Average Contribution shall be made at a Port where the Property in respect of which such Contribution shall have been made shall have been replaced by an Equivalent, the Property so sacrificed as aforesaid shall be contributed for at its Cost Price, together with the Shipping Charges, but without the Premium (if any) paid for its Insurance.

85. When Goods shall have been shipped at a Port of Refuge in the Place of Goods sacrificed by a General Average Act, an Amount equal to the net Freight payable in respect of the former Goods shall be deducted from the Freight Payable in respect of the latter Goods; but if the Goods shipped at a Port of Refuge shall not have been shipped in the Place of Goods sacrificed by a General Average Act, then, in such Case, only Half of the net Freight payable on the Goods shipped at such Port of Refuge as aforesaid shall be deducted from the Freight payable in respect of the Goods so sacrificed as aforesaid.

Contributory Interests and Values.

86. In the Case of a General Average Sacrifice made on behalf of a chartered Ship in Ballast, the Property liable to contribute in respect of such General Average Sacrifice shall be the Ship, and the Freight which she is earning under the Charter.

87. As regards a General Average Sacrifice made on behalf of a loaded Ship, the Property liable to contribute in respect of such

General Average Sacrifice shall be the Ship, the Freight, and the Cargo.

88. All Property at Risk in the Adventure shall be liable to contribute in respect of a General Average Sacrifice made in its Behalf irrespectively of the Question whether such Property as aforesaid could have been the Subject of a General Average Sacrifice or not.

89. If, or when, after Part of the Cargo shall have been discharged at a Port of Refuge, a General Average Sacrifice shall be performed in behalf of the Ship and the Remainder of the Cargo, the whole Cargo and the whole Freight shall contribute in respect of such General Average Sacrifice just as if no Part of the Cargo had been discharged previously to the Performance of such General Average Sacrifice as aforesaid.

90. In case a Ship laden with a Cargo which is liable to be confiscated for a Breach of International Law by the Shipper shall suffer a Loss which, if the Cargo had consisted of Articles that might have been lawfully shipped, would have been a General Average Loss, then, in such Case, such Loss shall be deemed to be a General Average Loss, but the Ship shall not, under such circumstances as aforesaid, be liable to contribute for any Loss sustained by the Cargo in order to evade Danger of such Confiscation as aforesaid.

91. If the Ship alone shall be liable to Confiscation, then, in such Case, no Portion of the Cargo shall be deemed liable to contribute in respect of any Loss sustained by the Ship in order to avoid the Danger of such Confiscation.

92. Arms, Ammunition, and other Munitions of War, such Provisions as are intended to be consumed during the Voyage, the Seamen's Wages and Luggage, Passengers' Luggage, Wearing Apparel, and such Money, Jewels, or other Articles as are being carried on the Bodies of Persons on board, Passage Money when not at Risk, and Money or Property lent or given on Bottomry or Respondentia, shall not be liable to Contribution in respect of any General Average Sacrifice.

93. In respect to General Average Sacrifices and General Average Losses, Jewels, Pearls, Diamonds, and other Ornaments

or Articles of Great Value not carried on the Person, and Gold and Silver, whether coined or uncoined, and not carried on the Person, shall be assessed for Contribution only at One Fourth the Amount at which they shall have been entered in the Bill of Lading: Provided that, if their Value shall not have been entered in the Bill of Lading, they shall be assessed for the Purpose aforesaid at One Fourth of their Value at the Ship's Port of Destination.

94. Every Person entitled to a General Average Contribution shall contribute towards such General Average Contribution, and towards all other General Average Contributions levied in respect to the same Adventure.

95. Subject to the Provisions of this Act, the contributory Value of Property in respect to a General Average Contribution shall be its Value at the Ship's Port of Destination.

96. For all Purposes of a General Average Contribution, the Value of all Duties, Landing Charges, Insurance Premiums, Commission Charges, Discounts, and Guarantees on Sales on Credit, and all other Charges, Claims, or Liens whatsoever to which the Ship and Cargo, or any Part of either, shall have been subject subsequently to the Performance of the General Average Sacrifice in respect to which the General Average Contribution shall be levied, shall be deducted from the Value of the said Property, when assessed as directed by this Act.

97. An Expenditure or Disbursement shall be contributed for by the Owners of the Property at Risk in the Adventure according to the Proportion of the Values of their respective Interests in such Property as aforesaid, estimated at the Time when such General Average Expenditure or Disbursement as aforesaid shall have been made.

98. If Property shall be liable to Contribution both in respect to a General Average Sacrifice and a General Average Expenditure or Disbursement, it shall be assessed on the different Principles ordained by this Act in respect to such Contributions respectively.

99. If any Property shall be properly and necessarily sold by the Master at another Place than that of the Ship's Destination, the Value of such Property in respect to its Liability to a General

Average Contribution shall be its Value at such Place of Sale as aforesaid.

100. Goods shipped into Barges for the Purpose of Safety, or of lightening and saving the Vessel and the Remainder of the Cargo (provided that such Shipment do not take place in the ordinary Course of Trade) shall, in respect to all other General Average Sacrifices not Expenditures made or incurred during the Adventure, be deemed to have continued on board throughout the entire Course of the Voyage.

101. The General Average Losses to which the Twenty-ninth Section of this Act relates shall be primarily contributed for by the Lighter, Longboat, or Craft referred to in the said Section, and the Cargo on board, and the Contribution of the Cargo of such Lighter, Longboat or Craft shall be apportioned among the principal Vessel and the Remainder of its Cargo.

102. If, or when, Part of the Property liable to a General Average Contribution shall have been sold on Credit, the Value of such Property in respect to its Liability to a General Average Contribution as aforesaid shall be its Price Current as defined by this Act, or its actual Credit Price, deducting therefrom the usual Discount and Guarantee.

103. If, after a Jettison or other General Average Sacrifice, the Ship shall, before completing her Voyage, return to the Port of Departure, or to any Port neighbouring thereto, where Articles of the Nature and Quality of the Goods jettisoned or otherwise sacrificed as aforesaid shall have been usually exposed for Sale, then in such Case, if the Owner of the Goods so jettisoned or sacrificed as aforesaid, or if any Agent of his at such Port as aforesaid, shall have had sufficient Time to purchase an equal Quantity of Goods of the same Description and Quality as the Goods so jettisoned or sacrificed as aforesaid, the General Average Contribution for such Jettison or other Sacrifice as aforesaid shall be made for a Sum equal to the Market Price of the Articles so jettisoned or sacrificed as aforesaid current at the Port of Departure or other neighbouring Port as aforesaid.

104. If any Portion of the Property which had been at Risk in the Adventure, on account of which a General Average Sacri-

fice shall have been incurred, shall, after a Wreck of the Ship, have been saved, such Property shall, in respect of such General Average Sacrifice, be liable to contribute for One Fourth Part of its actual Value after deducting therefrom the Costs of Salvage (if any).

105. Subject to the Provisions of this Act, the Value of the Freight in respect of its Liability to Contribution for a General Average Sacrifice shall be the Value of the Freight actually earned.

106. Subject to the Provisions of this Act, the Value of the Freight in respect to its Liability to a General Average Contribution shall be, in the Case of a loaded Ship, the Value of the Freight as specified by the Bill of Lading, but, in the Case of a Ship in Ballast, the contributory Value of the Freight shall be its Value under the Charter (if any) under which she shall have earned Freight in the Adventure in respect to which the General Average Act in question shall have been made.

107. In estimating the contributory Value of Freight with respect to General Average Contributions, the Value of the Wages, Port Charges, and other Expenses paid or incurred previously, but not any Wages, Port Charges, or Expenses incurred subsequently, to the Performance of the General Average Sacrifice in respect of which such General Average Contribution as aforesaid shall be levied, shall be deducted from the Value of the gross Freight.

108. Nothing in this Act contained shall affect the Rights of Parties having Interests in the Freight as between themselves.

109. If, or when, Goods shall have been transhipped by another Ship, the Value of the Freight as regards its Liability to Contribution in respect of a General Average Sacrifice performed in behalf of the Ship shall be the Value of the Freight as herein-before determined, deducting from such estimated Value the Amount of the transhipping Freight and increased Expenses attendant upon the Transhipment.

110. Subject to the Provisions of this Act, when the Ship shall have been chartered for an Outward and a Homeward Voyage by a single Charter, the Freight in respect to its Liability to Contribu-

tion for a General Average Act performed on the Outward Voyage, shall be apportioned, so that no Part of the Freight earned on the Homeward Voyage shall be liable to contribute in respect of such General Average Act as aforesaid.

111. When the Ship shall have been chartered for an Outward Voyage by one Charter and for a Homeward Voyage by another, the Homeward Freight under the Charter shall, in case such Charter shall have been effected before the Charter for the Outward Voyage, be liable to contribute in respect of a General Average Sacrifice incurred on the Outward Voyage.

112. The Freight paid by a Charterer of the Ship before the Contract shall have been performed shall be liable to Contribution in respect of a General Average Sacrifice made in its Behalf, and the Shipowner shall be *pro tanto* discharged from Liability to such Contribution as aforesaid.

113. When the Freight on Part of the Cargo is paid, 'lost or not lost,' on the Shipment of the Cargo, the Shipper of such Part of the Cargo as aforesaid, and not the Charterer, shall, in respect to such Portion of the Freight as aforesaid, be liable to Contribution in respect of a General Average Sacrifice performed in behalf of such Freight.

114. In respect to General Average Contributions, if the Freight for the Ship shall have been paid in advance, no Reduction shall be made of any Part of the Wages due or to accrue due in the Course of the Adventure, except for such Portion of the said Wages as may be dependent for Payment upon the successful Issue of the Adventure and shall have accrued due before the General Average Sacrifice in question shall have been performed.

115. When the Amount of an Expenditure or Expenditures as defined by this Act shall be less than the Value of the Property saved at the Termination of the Adventure, the contributory Values of the Ship, Freight, and Cargo shall be deemed to be their Values to the Owners of them respectively at the Termination of the Adventure.

116. When the Amount of an Expenditure or Expenditures as defined by this Act shall have been greater than the Value of the Property saved at the Termination of the Adventure, the Proceeds

of the Property so saved shall be applied towards the Liquidation of such Expenditure or Expenditures as aforesaid, and the Excess of the Amount of such Expenditure or Expenditures over the Proceeds of such Property as aforesaid shall be so apportioned amongst the Parties to the Adventure as that they shall be liable for such Expenditure or Expenditures in the Proportions in which they would have been liable if the whole Property which had been originally at Risk in the Adventure had safely reached the Ship's Port of Destination.

117. All Sacrifices, Expenses, or Losses which, as between the Shipowner, Charterer, Shipper, Passengers, and all Persons on board, are General Average Losses within the Meaning of this Act, shall also be deemed to be General Average Losses as between Underwriters and Assured.

118. Parties to a Contract may enter into any special Agreement in derogation of all or any of the Provisions of this Act, anything herein-before contained to the contrary notwithstanding.

PROCEDURE.

119. After a General Average Sacrifice shall have been made, the Master shall enter the Particulars thereof in his Log Book, and shall also draw up a Document stating the Circumstances which, in his Opinion, rendered such General Average Sacrifice necessary, and also containing a Description of the Property so sacrificed as aforesaid; and such Documents shall be signed by the Master, Seamen, and by such Owners of the Property at Risk in the Adventure as shall have been on board when the General Average Sacrifice was made; and the Master of every Ship, whether registered or unregistered, shall deliver a Copy of such Documents as aforesaid to the Shipping Master at the Port into which the Ship shall be first brought after the General Average Sacrifice shall have been made.

120. The Adjustment of General Average Contribution shall be made either at the Ship's Port of Destination, or at the Port into which she shall first properly and necessarily put after the

Performance of the General Average Sacrifice in respect of which such Contribution as aforesaid shall be levied.

121. No Foreign Adjustment of a General Average Loss shall be valid as between British Subjects unless such shall have been made in conformity with the Law of the Port of Destination of the Ship.

122. The Master of the Ship shall have a Lien upon and may retain all Property liable to a General Average Contribution until the same shall have been discharged by the Persons liable in respect thereof.

123. The Owner of Property or of Money which shall have been the Subject of a General Average Sacrifice may, after a Demand and Refusal of the General Average Contribution due to him in respect of such General Average Sacrifice as aforesaid, at his Election sue the Consignee or Shipper of the Property liable to such Contribution and the Master of the Ship either jointly or severally.

124. The Owner of Property sold by the Master of the Ship to discharge Liabilities properly incurred by him in respect of a General Average Act or Loss shall in all Cases, irrespectively of the Question whether the Master shall have given Security for such Liability or not, have a Right of Action against all Persons in respect of whose Property such General Average Act or Loss as aforesaid shall have been performed or sustained.

125. In case the Consignee of Property shall, after Demand, refuse to pay his share of a General Average Contribution due by him in respect of such Property, the Master of the Ship shall have a Right of Action against him and the Shipper of such Property, either jointly or severally, as he may think proper, but shall have no Claim against any other Person, in respect of such Contribution, in the event of the Refusal or Inability of the Consignee or Shipper to pay such Contribution.

126. In all Cases of Bankruptcy a Claim for a General Average Contribution shall, except as regards Debts of Record due to the Crown, take Priority of all other Debts or Liabilities of the Parties liable to such General Average Contribution.

After the labours of the Glasgow Conference had apparently so satisfactorily terminated, this was considered to be the most suitable form in which to obtain the consent of the legislatures to uniform enactments on the matter in question. For the reasons above set out, however, the Council of the Social Science Association had been unable to comply with that part of the Glasgow resolutions which desired that a period of six months previous to another conference should be given to the Chambers of Commerce and Underwriting Bodies there represented for the consideration of the Bill to be deliberated upon, and it was not until the month of April 1862 that the Bill was circulated among those concerned, together with a summons to meet for its discussion on June 6th following in the Guildhall of the City of London.

Now in order to shorten the public discussion on this Bill, such of the delegates and others interested as happened to be in town were invited to meet a few days previously, when the Antwerp delegates presented the following:—

Remarks on the General Average Consolidation Bill drawn up by the Care of the National Association for the Promotion of Social Science.

London: April 1862.

The Chamber of Commerce of Antwerp having communicated to the underwriters of this City the Bill on International General Average received from the Association for the Promotion of Social Science, some underwriters and persons competent in the matter assembled in order to examine the Bill.

These persons have fully appreciated all the merit and talent displayed in the framing of this important work, and on account of that merit itself it has been unanimously regretted that the short time allowed for consideration does not permit to frame the remarks with all the development required for a matter so important as that which concerns General Average, and which is in so close a connection with the contracts of affreightment, insurance, and bottomry.

The utility of uniformity in the matter being now universally recognised, this point needs not to be referred to; the remarks framed in these lines on account of the shortness of time allowed are only summary and chiefly based on expediency and practice, as they cannot be accompanied by commentaries or considerations on the origin of laws, doctrine or jurisprudence, neither on definitions, effects, consequences or incidents relating to a General Average Act.

1. Interpretation clause, perfect.

2. If the meaning of this article be well understood here, the crew may perform a General Average act without the consent or concurrence of the master. This principle appears to be dangerous, as it may bring in collision the master with the crew, who may contest his authority, so needful in a maritime expedition.

The Belgian and French laws appear to be more convenient, as the view of the master is always preponderating, though submitted to deliberation as much as circumstances permit to do so.

3 and 4. In conformity with the general principles.

5. Admits that a person who has made a General Average expenditure has a right to raise contribution, though the property at risk in the adventure be totally lost. In such a manner an agent at an intermediate port may apply to owners of property totally lost, to be repaid for the advances he had made in order to gain a commission or to procure a benefit to himself. Such agents ought to know that in case of failure of the adventure they have no right to claim. Besides, these advances may, in most circumstances, be covered by an insurance or bottomry.

The Belgian and French laws limit the contribution to the value of the property saved, and a shipowner is entitled to abandon ship and freight for expenses, debts, or liabilities incurred by the master, neither is the owner of a cargo lost bound to pay expenditures in case of total loss of his property; provided, nevertheless, that he has not directly interfered himself or contracted liabilities which, in that case, are obligations personal to the owner of ship or goods who have contracted them. An amendment in this sense is proposed.

6. Admitted.

7. It is proposed to add: 'The cases foreseen by Art. 25 always excepted.'

8. Admitted.

9. Is just, except the last section, relating to water spoiling goods in performing a General Average act, which ought to be suppressed in order to be in accordance with rule 37; or rule 37 to be amended and brought in concordance with rule 9.

10 and 13. Admitted.

14. It is asked if it would not be better to say: 'When a mast cut away . . . shall have carried away another mast and a . . .' instead of saying 'when the mainmast carries away the mizenmast?'

15. This article does not appear to be so clear as the resolution voted at Glasgow, which required 'Special facts clearly proved.' Further, the new article says: 'Shall be deemed General Average act as regards the ship.' Why should, then, the damage to cargo not be deemed General Average act?

16. Is in accordance with Art. 33, admitting equally the damage to the cargo.

17. The value of a stranded ship must necessarily improve by getting her off. How is this to be understood? The first paragraph of this article is very just and clear.

18 and 19. Agreed. It is understood the damage directly caused by the fire is necessarily Particular Average.

20. Agreed. Carrying a press of sail is a manœuvre the master is obliged to perform when circumstances require it.

22. Admitted. These objects having become by themselves a cause of peril, as is said in Art. 25.

23. Admitted. It would even be equitable to grant a remuneration to every person having become lame or incapable of working in consequence of having concurred in such a defence for the common interest.

24. It would perhaps be good to add the words 'leakage of liquids.'

25. This article is very good, but would it not be convenient to specify some articles excluded from General Average, as, for example, jettison of goods loaded on deck in any voyage whatever, and even from houses on deck, which impede the manœuvring, displace the centre of gravity, and cause the vessel to be thrown on her beam-ends when heavy seas are shipped? Jettison of water-casks, spars, and all other ship stores stowed on deck, cutting away the stern-boat, &c., ought neither to be considered as General Average losses.

26. The first paragraph of this article is just, but the second is very dangerous, as shipmasters may be induced to choose an intermediate port at their convenience to remain there during winter at the expense of the cargo. In order to prevent fraud and disputes, would it not be expedient to amend the rule in a manner that in such a case the cost of crew, wages, and provisions shall only be deemed General Average losses until the time when the vessel, being put again in a state of seaworthiness, should have been ready to leave such a port if she had not been impeded by the severity of climate?

27 and 28. Agreed.

29. Would it not be convenient to add 'leakage on liquids'?

30. Agreed.

31. This is very just, but does the word 'loss' comprehend only material loss, or does it even comprehend the incidental losses mentioned in rule 24?

In order to prevent abuses and disputes, it would perhaps be expedient to admit only material losses.

32. As the application of this rule will lead sometimes to difficulties, would it not be good to state, that in case of disagreement on the real value of the goods so recovered (undoubtedly in a damaged state), they shall be sold at public auction and the net proceeds divided between all the property in proportion of the amount they have contributed for?

33. This is logical, according to the dispositions of rule 16; nevertheless, would it not be more expedient not to admit such

losses, or at least only admit them in case the stranding has been deemed intentional, according to rule 15 ? At all events, the degree of damage resulting from such a discharge is very difficult to state.

34. It would perhaps be useful to explain that this loss is to be settled just in the same manner as a bottomry premium; that is to say, that loss apportioned *pro ratá* on the amount of General Average on the amount of special charges on cargo (if any), and on the amount of Particular Averages and charges on ship and owners (if any).

35 and 36. Agreed. According to the resolutions voted at Glasgow on points of expediency.

37. Is in contradiction with Art. 9, admitting as a General Average act the damage caused to the ship by cutting a hole in the deck, whilst rule 37 does not admit as a General Average act the water running down through that same hole and so damaging cargo.

Further: the last paragraph of rule 9 admits the damage by shipping water in consequence of a General Average act, and rule 37 does not admit it. As a matter of expediency, it would perhaps be desirable to suppress the last paragraph of rule 9 and to adopt rule 37 as it is framed in the Bill, though contrary to principle.

38. This appears really unjust, and seems to be contrary both to principles and to expediency. Abstraction made of the principle, let us examine only the expediency.

1st. That part of a cargo which cannot be put again on board the ship after repairs, and is necessarily left at a port of refuge, constitutes very often a total loss, as it is frequently too small a portion to be sent again to the port of destination by another vessel, which is not always at hand.

Why must the property of A remain there, and not that of B ?

Who is the supreme judge to decide whether A or B shall be put again on board or not ?

Rule 27 does not admit certain losses in order to prevent undue preferences on the part of the master. This reason alone would plead in favour of bringing a change in rule 38; the more so as rule 40 admits as General Average losses those occasioned by fire, theft, &c. We believe thus it is needless to bring forward other considerations, and think it utterly convenient to propose the framing of this rule as follows : ' The loss of, or on cargo, by reason of its being properly shut out or left at a port of refuge shall be deemed to be a General Average loss within the meaning of this Act.'

39. No objection.

40. Such losses appear to be very remote consequences of a General Average act, nevertheless they could be admitted as 'consequences' provided the loss on goods left at a port of refuge be likewise considered as 'consequences,' and accordingly to be deemed within the meaning of the bill as General Average losses.

41. On the ground of the same principle, and in order to prevent abuses and exaggerated claims, it would be desirable that the jettison or sacrifice of ship's provisions or stores be ruled in the same manner—*i.e.* (1st) that the master should be held to have on board duly verified accounts of such provisions or a list of such provisions certified by the competent authorities of the port of departure; (2nd) that the master should be held to have on board an authentic and certified list of all the objects of inventory or ship's stores, comprising also the spare stores; and (3rd) that the master shall be held to replace all such objects as are proved to have been lost as aforesaid, and not be paid by General Average contribution on the mere estimate of surveyors not accompanied by the proof of the objects having been replaced.

43. This rule ought to be brought in accordance with rule 38, if amended.

46. Could the time during which the wages and provisions are allowed not be more or less limited?

47. In what manner and by what authority will be valued the reimbursement to which the hostage shall be entitled?

49. As it would almost be impossible to appreciate beforehand if the costs of discharging and forwarding cargo to its destination should be less in amount than those to be incurred for heaving the ship off, it would perhaps be expedient to suppress the last paragraph of this rule.

50. Same observation as on rule 17, as it is not well understood how the value of the ship should not be improved by getting her off.

52. In order to bring in concordance this rule and rule 26, and to avoid abuses and difficulties in the application of this rule, would it not be expedient to admit only in General Average the crew's wages and provisions from the date of the arrival of the ship in the port of refuge until the day when the vessel, being again in state of seaworthiness, will be ready to put to sea, the allowance for provisions to be calculated at a fixed rate? See rule 26 on account of contrary wind, calm, frost, &c.; see also rule 74.

53. It appears that the costs resulting from a vessel putting in a port of refuge on account of sickness of the crew or want of provisions ought not to be deemed General Average losses; neither those resulting from shifting of the cargo, or pumps being choking, unless it be proved that these accidents do only arise from the perils of the sea and not from the fault of the master from not having scrupulously stowed the cargo, or the pumps being put in good order at the port of departure.

57. Is it understood that the expenses incurred in consequence ' of an accident at the port of refuge' refer to an accident on the ship?

58. We propose to add: ' Inasmuch as the master proves that the cargo has been properly stowed according to the regulations of the port of departure.'

60. It would perhaps be advisable, on account of expediency, to suppress this rule, as it might give rise to very exaggerated claims for wages and provisions.

What is the real meaning of the words ' delay at sea in order to refit'?

61. Heated goods being themselves a cause of peril, it is just that the expenses mentioned in this rule be not admitted as General Average expenses; but the words, ' except it be to the advantage of all the property at risk in the adventure,' can they not produce abuses, as the owner of such goods shall be led to pretend that the discharging of such goods is for the advantage of all the property which may become damaged or deteriorated if the dis-

charge does not take place? Would it not be better to suppress these words?

62. As concerns repairs to the ship, would it not be advisable to introduce a rule stipulating that, in order to compensate the supposed difference between the old objects sacrificed replaced by new ones, and according to the use now generally adopted,—'Shall be deducted from all repairs, replacements, workmanship, in consequence of General Average sacrifices, one-third from the justified cost of these works at the port where they have been made; nevertheless no deduction is to be made from the price of anchors and 15 per cent., or one-sixth only, from iron chain cable.'

64. The dispositions of this rule are very just and clear as concerns repairs, but on the point of crew's wages and provisions they are not in accordance with Arts. 52 and 53, which admit as General Average expenses those resulting from the vessel having put in a port of refuge either by a General Average sacrifice or by accidental damage to ship and cargo; as in practice the division of wages, and applying them partially on repairs for General Average, and partly on repairs for Particular Average could only be done in a very arbitrary manner, and lead to many abuses, for why, then, should not also the warehousing of cargo be divided in two parts—one during repairs for General, and one during repairs for Particular Average? We prefer to admit in General Average the wages during the whole time of detention, as is said in our observation on rules 52 and 53.

65. Why should not a person who has made an expenditure in a port of refuge be entitled to reimbursement of the premium of an insurance he had taken in order to cover himself for the loss of the sum expended, the more so, that by this insurance premium have been avoided the more considerable expense of a bottomry premium, which would have been considered a General Average loss?

72. Rule 75 states that in case of total loss of ship and cargo there shall be no contribution; how, then, is rule 72 to be understood as concerns loss of ship's stores when the ship shall have been wrecked before they shall have been replaced?

73. Is it to be understood that the value of sacrificed ship's

stores shall be reimbursed at the value of the port of destination, and that if they are not replaced the reimbursement will be effected on an estimation of surveyors who should value these provisions at their cost price at the moment of arrival of the vessel at its destination? On account of rule 41 we have already advised that it would be expedient, in order to prevent frauds and abuses, to oblige the master to replace all stores and objects proved to have been sacrificed, and not to admit estimations not accompanied by proof of the objects having been replaced.

Rule 79 states that the provisions shall be estimated at the amount for which the replacing of such provisions or effects shall or *would* have cost.

74. In accordance with rule 95; but according to rule 120 it is allowed to draw statements of General Average in ports of refuge.

How is it possible to be acquainted in such a port with the value the property would have at the port of destination? See Arts. 96 and 120.

75. Would it not be advisable to change rule 5 and make no distinction between a sacrifice and an expenditure in case of total loss of ship and cargo, as said in the observations on Art. 5?

76. The value of such property appears to be nought.

79. See observations on Art. 73.

82. The first paragraph of this article is very clear and just, but the last is totally unintelligible.

86. As concerns ships in ballast, it appears to us that the freight expected to be earned in virtue of a subsequent charter is too indirectly at risk in the adventure to be liable for contribution of a sacrifice made on board a vessel navigating in ballast though under charter.

This system presenting too many inconveniences, it has nearly universally been abandoned to draw statements on vessels in ballast.

And as it is now also nearly universally adopted to settle the General Averages on each voyage separately, it appears desirable to amend in that sense this rule as well as rules 110 and 111.

92. Money lent on bottomry ought to be liable to contribution,

for if a sacrifice saves the property at risk in the adventure this sacrifice saves also the loan which is lost for the lender in case of total loss of the property on which it has been lent.

93. The motives of this distinction are not understood. Why do articles of great value only contribute for one-fourth of the amount entered in the bill of lading, whilst the same articles of sacrifice are reimbursed for their whole value?

The admission of such a system does appear unjust, and it is deemed advisable that these articles should be liable to contribution on their real value at the port of destination, valued by competent surveyors. According to an English custom, landing specie in case of stranding, salvage or shipwreck is not to be considered as General Average; that specie pays its own expense, and does not contribute according to its real value in the general expenses of landing.

It would also be desirable that this should be abrogated by a rule as well, that of articles of great value and money only contributing for one-fourth of their value.

The preceding observations are not based on expediency, but on principle. From the most remote times to our days we do not find any laws establishing a difference between money or valuable articles in case of salvage or contribution.

Even the Roman law, which is generally admitted as the foundation of all our legislative system, does not make any difference in it, and this is very just. The following dilemma may be applied in the case:—

The sacrifice has, or has not, saved the property.

If the property be saved, it has to contribute according to its value saved.

If the property be not saved, it has not to contribute.

Thus, in case of contribution, no distinctions on account of valuable articles ought to be admitted.

95. If it is just and rational that the contributive values are those at the port of destination, would it not be desirable for elucidation to stipulate that it is understood these values are those of the property in the state in which it arrives at said port of destination?—as, for example,

The cargo being damaged shall have to contribute according to the value in its damaged state, subject to the deductions stipulated in Art. 96.

The ship equally in her damaged state, to which should be added the amount admitted in General Average for voluntary sacrifices.

If the vessel be repaired at an intermediate port of refuge, and arrive fully seaworthy at her port of destination, surveyors at that port should establish the value the vessel would have had if she had arrived at her destination in the same state of damage in which she was on the arrival at the port of refuge.

Vessels are frequently valued at the port of refuge, but this value being quite nominal in a port where they put in accidentally, this value may not be considered as the real value liable to contribution.

For the same motives it ought not to be permitted to draw up statements of General Average in ports of refuge unless the ship be legally sold there on account of unseaworthiness and the cargo sent home by another vessel, as we have observed at Art. 74. See also Arts. 120 and 121.

96. As the contributive value of cargo ought to be that really saved by a sacrifice, no other costs should be deducted from the market price at the port of destination than those which, in conformity with Art. 74, are to be deducted from the amount to be paid to the owner of jettisoned goods. These costs are: custom-house duties, landing, cartage, storage, and ordinary brokerage for sale.

97 and 99. As already said in Art. 5, it would be desirable not to admit a distinction between 'sacrifice' and 'expenditure.'

Further: how is it possible to appraise exactly the value of property at the time when the expenditure or disbursement has been made?

100. It is thereby understood that the loss of goods landed in barges in order to cross a bar in leaving the port of departure—as, for example, the bar of Sulina—be always excepted.

In that case we approve.

101. Would it not be convenient after the words, 'The principal vessel and the remainder of the cargo,' to add, ' and the freight '?

104. Why not the real values? This article ought to be put in accordance with Art. 32.

105 and 107. Does the contributory value of freight include primage? We think affirmatively.

As it is very difficult, if not impossible, in most circumstances to establish the precise moment of the sacrifice, it appears to be convenient to deduct from the freight all charges which would not have to be paid if the freight had not been earned.

For example, ought to be deducted the total amount wages due to the crew, less those advanced to the said crew before the beginning of the voyage, because these wages being earned at all events do no longer depend upon the successful issue of the adventure.

The port charges at the port of destination ought also to be deducted from the gross freight.

108. Appears superfluous, as not being directly in connection with General Average.

110 and 111. As we have remarked in Art. 86, it would be convenient that this Bill should stipulate that the General Averages be settled on each voyage separately, because the freight of goods not yet on board is only indirectly at risk in the adventure.

114. The wages dependent on the successful issue of the adventure are those not paid in advance, as observed on account of Arts. 105 and 107.

115 and 116. As said on account of Arts. 5 and 75, we consider it desirable that the present Act should stipulate that the liability of property is limited to its value saved as well as concerns sacrifices as expenditures or disbursements.

117. Underwriters ought also to be responsible only to the insured amount.

118. It would perhaps be preferable not to admit derogations.

120 and 121. As we have already observed on account of Arts. 74 and 95, we believe the settlement of a General Average in a port of refuge ought only to be allowed in the case we have quoted in our remarks on said articles.

123 and 125. We believe it ought not to be permitted to the master to sue at leisure the shipper or the consignee, the property

alone ought to the extent of the value saved, and not the shipper, who very often has sold the goods and has no longer interest in the property at risk in the adventure.

(Signed)   T. C. ENGELS,
President of the Committee of Underwriters of the First, Second, and Third Reunions.

(Signed)   ED. VAN PEBORGH,
Average Stater.

Antwerp: May 31, 1862.

In course of the preliminary discussions which took place on the different clauses of this draft Bill the following alterations were adopted, viz. :—

1. In the Interpretation clause—
    a. 'Ship' shall include; to strike out the word 'privateer.'
    b. To leave open for later discussion 'General Average sacrifice.'
    c. To leave open for later discussion 'General Average expenditure.'
    d. To add under 'Unusual Peril' after cliffs, the word: 'collisions.'
2. To be struck out altogether, as too dangerous to invite subordination.
5. To be left open for future discussion.
6. To strike out the words 'either preliminary or necessarily.'
9. To strike out the words 'either preliminary or (as the case may be) necessarily.'

10 and 11. To be struck out altogether.

14. To be amended as follows : ' When a mast, after having been cut away for a General Average purpose or sacrifice, shall in its descent have carried away another mast, or have injured the boats or bulwarks or any other part of the ship or of the cargo, then in such case the damage which such mast shall have so done as aforesaid to any part of the property at risk shall be likewise deemed to be a General Average loss within the meaning of this Act.'

15 and 17. To be left open for future discussion.

19. To be transposed before clause 44.

20. To strike out the words 'crowding or hoisting.'

21. To be struck out altogether.

28 and 29. To be left open for future discussion.

31. To be struck out altogether.

32. To be altered in conformity with the Antwerp proposal.

33, 35, and 36. To be left open for future discussion.

37. To be amended as follows : ' All damage done to the cargo by water getting down the hatches at the time of a jettison or other General Average act being or having been made, shall be deemed to be a General Loss within the meaning of this Act.'

38. To strike out the first word ' No,' and put instead the word ' All.'

39, 40, and 43. To be struck out altogether.

49. To strike out the words : ' Except in cases where the cargo could have been discharged and forwarded to its destination for an outlay or loss less in amount than the cost incurred in heaving the ship off.'

50. To be left open for future discussion.

52. To add the words, ' To the time of being ready for sea' before ' be deemed,' &c.

54. To be amended as follows : ' All expenses directly resulting from bearing up for a port of refuge, the expense of discharging the cargo there, and the hire of lighters in order to avoid discharging part or the whole of the cargo there, if properly and necessarily incurred by the master, shall be deemed to be General Average losses within the meaning of this Act.'

55. To be left open for future discussion.

57. To be amended as follows : ' The expense of warehouse rent at a port of refuge on cargo necessarily discharged there, and the expense of re-shipping it, and the outward port charges properly incurred by the master at such port, shall, when the original contract of affreightment shall not have been terminated, be deemed to be General Average losses within the meaning of this Act.'

60. To be struck out altogether.

62 and 64. To be altered in conformity with the Antwerp proposals.

65. To be amended as follows : ' Bottomry, respondentia, the

premium of insurance on money expended, and all other interest and commission properly incurred by the master at a port of refuge, with respect to a General Average act, shall be deemed to be General Average acts or losses within the meaning of this Act.'

68. To add the word 'all' before 'the property' &c.

69. To strike out the words 'and no freight shall have been earned by him in the adventure.'

70 and 71. To be struck out altogether.

73. The last part of the clause from the word 'but' to be struck out.

78. To be struck out altogether.

79. To strike out the words 'or would.'

80. To be left open for future discussion.

82 and 84. To be struck out altogether.

85. To be left open for future discussion.

86. To be left open for future discussion.

88 and 90. To be struck out altogether.

91. To be amended as follows: 'If the ship alone shall be liable to confiscation for a breach of international law, then in such case no loss sustained by the shipowner in order to avoid such confiscation shall be deemed a General Average loss within the meaning of this Act.'

92. The first words, 'arms, ammunition, and other munitions of war,' to be struck out.

93. To be struck out altogether.

94. To be left open for future discussion.

95. To be amended as follows: 'Subject to the provisions of this Act, the contributory value of property in respect to a General Average contribution shall be its value to its owner on the termination of the adventure as regards it.'

96. To be amended as follows: 'For all purposes of a General Average contribution, the freight, duties, landing charges, brokerage, discounts incurred subsequently to the performance of the General Average sacrifice, in respect to which the General Average contribution shall be levied, shall be deducted from the value of the cargo when assessed as directed by this Act.'

97 and 98. To be left open for future discussion.

99 and 100. To be struck out altogether.

101. To be left open for future discussion.

102, 103, 104, and 105. To be struck out altogether.

106. To be left open for future discussion.

107. To be amended as follows: 'In estimating the contributory value of freight with respect to General Average contributions, the value of those wages, port charges, and other expenses, the liability to which is contingent upon the earning of the freight, shall be deducted from the value of the gross freight only with two-fifths.'

108 and 109. To be struck out altogether.

110 and 111. To be left open for future discussion.

112 and 113. To be struck out altogether.

114. To be amended as follows: 'In respect to General Average contributions, no deduction shall be made under section 107 for any freight paid in advance.'

115. To be struck out altogether.

116. To be left open for future discussion.

117 and 119. To be struck out altogether.

120 and 121. To be left open for future discussion.

122. To be amended so as to give to the consignee a similar lien on the ship.

123, 124, 125, and 126. To be left open for future discussion. And that therefore only the following clauses passed without any alteration or amendment, viz.. 3, 4, 6, 7, 8, 12, 13, 16, 18, 22, 23, 24, 25, 26, 27, 30, 34, 41, 42, 44, 45, 46, 47, 48, 51, 53, 56, 58, 59, 61, 63, 66, 67, 72, 74, 76, 77, 79, 81, 83, 87, 89 and 118.

The following is the report of the preliminary committee communicating the result of their deliberations to Sir Travers Twiss, the President of what is known as the second International General Average Congress, viz. :—

NATIONAL ASSOCIATION FOR THE PROMOTION OF SOCIAL SCIENCE.

COMMITTEE ON GENERAL AVERAGE.

To the President of the VI. Department Trade and International Law, TRAVERS TWISS, Esq., Q.C., D.C.L.

3 Waterloo Place, Pall Mall: June 9, 1862.

Sir,—Having been elected to preside over this Committee, which was summoned by the Secretary to the Executive Committee of this Association for the preliminary discussion of the General Average Consolidation Bill, it is my duty to submit to you for the information of the sixth annual meeting of this Association the following report on the proceedings of this Committee.

I beg to hand you herewith a return of the gentlemen present at the proceedings of this Committee which has been assembled on the 4th, 5th, and 7th of this month, not only for the purpose of expressing their opinions on the Bill laid before them, but, if possible, to come to an understanding about the same.

Although the Committee has been in deliberation for nearly twenty hours during these three days it has been impossible to attain the latter so-much-desired result, and you will find on the copy of the draft of the Bill which I hereby enclose, that from the 126 sections which it contains the Committee has decided as follows:—

(1) That these 29 sections which are designated with a query could not be agreed upon, and were particularly left open for public discussion.

(2) That 22 sections were proposed to be altered as amended.

(3) That 30 sections were proposed to be struck out altogether.

(4) That the draftsman of the Bill was desired to alter five sections as instructed.

(5) And that only 40 sections passed as they were originally proposed.

The written remarks of the Antwerp delegates were handed to Mr. O'Hara as a guide for some of his amendments.

You will be kind enough to observe that the results of the

Committee's deliberations are marked in red on the draft of the Bill.—I have the honour to be, Sir,

Your obedient humble Servant,
(Signed)   Ernst Emil Wendt, *Chairman.*

Return of the Gentlemen present at the Proceedings of the Committee on General Average at their Meetings at 3 Waterloo Place, Pall Mall, on June 4, 5, and 7, 1862.

Remarks.—The I., II., and III. added to the names of every gentleman are to denote the meetings on which he has joined in the deliberations.

Amsterdam	{ E. N. Rahusen	I. II. III.
	J. Wertheim	I. II. III.
Antwerp	{ Théodore C. Engels	II. III.
	E. van Peborgh	I. II. III.
Boston, U.S.	J. Russell Bradford	I. II. III.
Copenhagen	{ Severin Gram	II. III.
	Svendson	II. III.
	Edward Thune	II. III.
Liverpool	{ L. R. Baily	III.
	Lowndes	III.
	P. H. Rathbone	III.
London	{ J. Brown	I. II. III.
	C. Leathley	III.
	O'Hara (*as Draftsman of the Bill*)	I. II. III.
	W. Richards	III.
	Ernst Emil Wendt	I. II. III.
Rotterdam	Driebeck	III.

(Signed)   Ernst Emil Wendt,
as Chairman.

London: June 9, 1862.

During the public discussions which followed in the Guildhall, it became evident that the Committee for managing the affairs of Lloyd's, which not only assisted in initiating this movement, but immediately after the Glasgow Congress passed the above set out highly complimentary resolution on the subject, was officially withdrawing from it. The letter which intimated this unexpected event ran as follows:—

Lloyd's (E.C.) : June 5, 1862.

Sir,—I have received and laid before the Committee for managing the affairs of Lloyd's your letter of May 30, stating that a discussion is to be held in the Trade and International Law Department of the National Association for the Promotion of Social Science, on the amendment of the law of 'General Average,' and inviting some representatives of the Committee to attend the meeting; also enclosing a copy of the Bill and documents relating to the subject.

I am directed to inform you in reply, that the Committee, having looked over the heads of the Bill, and given the subject full consideration, are so totally opposed to the several clauses contained in the Bill in question, that they are of opinion that no good could arise from any discussion on their part, and they therefore do not think it advisable to send a representative from their body to the meeting.

At the same time, they request me to assure you it is their earnest wish at all times to co-operate with parties interested in this question, when they see any opportunity of doing so with advantage to the very important interests at stake.—I am, Sir,

Your obedient Servant,
(Signed)   GEO. A. HALSTED, *Secretary.*

G. W. Hastings, Esq., Honorary Secretary,
  National Association for the Promotion
    of Social Science.

It can easily be understood that under such circumstances the first step which the assembled delegates took on June 6, when the congress had been opened, was to desire their President to address Lloyd's Committee with the view of inducing them to attend (as in Glasgow) by delegates. The meeting of the congress was thereupon adjourned to June 9, when, as no notice of this communication had been taken, the delegates authorised their President to write to the Chairman of Lloyd's the following letter :—

June 9, 1862.

Sir,—I have been authorised, as President of the Department of Trade and International Law, to transmit to you the first report of the Committee on General Average, as laid before me as President of the Department, with the result of their early deliberations. You will perceive that the provisions of the draft Bill have been submitted by them to a severe examination, and that they have only approved forty out of one hundred and twenty-six sections, whilst they have voted twenty-nine sections as questionable, and referred back twenty-two sections for amendment, having absolutely rejected thirty sections. I have laid before the Department the letters which I have received from the Secretary of your Committee; and in consequence of the impossibility, as expressed by the Secretary, of laying the communication, made by me on behalf of the Department, before the Committee until their meeting on Wednesday next, the Department has adjourned the further consideration of the question until Thursday next, in the confident hope that your Committee will delegate one or more of its members either to discuss the question before the Department, or to confer, if they prefer it, with the Committee on General Average, whose names you will find inscribed to their report. From the discussions which have already taken place, I am enabled to assure your Committee that it is the earnest wish of the Foreign members of this Association who are interested in the question of General Average, to act, if possible, in co-operation with Lloyd's, and that they desire very much to be favoured with their assistance upon many branches of the subject, in which their great experience is calculated to have great influence upon the decisions of the Committee.

I am, Sir, &c.,
(Signed) TRAVERS TWISS.

To this communication the President received the following answer:—

Lloyd's: June 11, 1862.

Sir,—Your letters of the respective dates of June 6, 7, and 9 have this day been read to the Committee of Lloyd's, and as they consider that you cannot be aware of the circumstances under which they felt precluded from sending any deputation of their body to the meeting of the Trade and International Law Department of the National Association for the Promotion of Social Science, they desire shortly to recount them.

In the month of April 1860, on the receipt of a letter from Mr. Rundell, Secretary to the 'Liverpool Committee on International General Average,' and also on the previous solicitation, personally, of Mr. Rathbone, of Liverpool, this Committee readily promised their assistance in aid of the Glasgow meeting, by obtaining through their agents abroad such information on the system of General Average as was desired.

In May 1860 this Committee proceeded further, and joined, through their Chairman, Mr. Thomas Baring, in the circular signed by about twelve of the Public Associations of this country, in asking the attendance of delegates from abroad at the meeting at Glasgow.

The Committee of Lloyd's, deeming it of importance that the Glasgow Conference should have as much information as possible, forwarded to the most important of their agents copies of the Liverpool Synopsis of Average for any remarks thereon, and in September 1860 again informed them of the necessity of their sending an early reply to Mr. Rundell. In September 1860, Mr. Leathley, a member of the Committee of Lloyd's, was requested to represent the Committee at the Glasgow meeting.

In October 1860, Mr. Leathley reported that he had so attended, and that resolutions, of which I enclose a copy, were passed, on which the cordial thanks of the Committee were given to Mr. Leathley for his trouble. The thanks of the Committee were also given to those gentlemen who had attended from abroad, and the assurance of the Committee was expressed that they would gladly co-operate in any endeavours to amend the laws referred to in the resolutions.

From that time until June 2 inst. the Committee of Lloyd's have received no further communication on the subject, but on Wednesday last the following letter, addressed to the Committee of Lloyd's, was read, dated Old Bond Street, May 30, 1862:—

'Gentlemen,—A discussion is to be held in the Trade and

International Law Department on the amendment of the law of General Average. We should be obliged if some representatives of your body would attend the meeting. I beg to enclose a copy of the Bill and documents relating to the subject.—I am, &c., (Signed) G. W. HASTINGS, *Honorary Secretary.*'

A course of proceeding so completely at variance with the decision of the Glasgow Congress, wherein six months' notice was provided, and the sudden call at a day's notice to consider and discuss a subject so difficult, and of such vast and varied importance, left the Committee of Lloyd's no option but respectfully to decline taking part therein.

I am further to convey to you the thanks of the Committee for your having informed the delegates from abroad that this Committee could not intend any discourtesy to them. The cordial support rendered by the Committee of Lloyd's in 1860 ought to prove it, and had the Committee been informed that those gentlemen had been invited to attend, they would with pleasure have joined in every mark of courtesy to delegates who at much personal inconvenience are now in London.

The Committee refrain from entering on the numerous objections which are apparent on the face of the proposed alterations by the Bill, but on receiving from the congress the result of their present discussions will be ready to give their best attention to it.

The Committee will feel obliged if you will read this communication at the meeting of your Department to-morrow.—I am, Sir,
Your obedient Servant,
(Signed)   GEO. A. HALSTED, *Secretary*.

To Doctor Travers Twiss, President of the
Department of Trade and International
Law, National Association for the
Promotion of Social Science.

This letter was presented at the meeting of the delegates on June 12, which thereupon jointly and separately made known their respective protests against the conduct of the Committee for managing the affairs of Lloyd's, and agreed unanimously that no public discussion on the subject of General Average should take place on this occasion in the Guildhall.

The delegates having then adjourned to my offices, a commencement was made with the deliberation of such clauses of the draft Bill which had in our preliminary meetings been reserved for future consideration, and the following alterations were adopted, viz. :—

1. Interpretation clause to be amended as follows :—

'General Average sacrifice' shall mean a prudent and extraordinary sacrifice of property made by the master in order to avert an unusual and imminent peril from the ship, freight, and cargo.

'General Average expenditure' shall denote any outlay properly made, or any liability on behalf of the property at risk properly incurred.

5. To be struck out altogether.

15. To be amended as follows :—

Loss or damage caused to the ship, cargo, and freight as the immediate and necessary consequence of a voluntary and prudent stranding of the ship shall be deemed to be a General Average loss within the meaning of this Act.

In order to complete the proceedings of this rather unfortunate second International General Average Congress, the draftsman's alterations to the Bill, which he based on the suggestions of the preliminary meetings of the delegates, are here subjoined :—

Interpretation Clause.

SECTION 1.—'General Average sacrifice' shall mean a prudent and extraordinary sacrifice of property at risk in the adventure made by the master in order to avert an unusual and imminent peril from the ship's freight and cargo.

Line 27.—'General Average expenditure' shall mean a prudent and extraordinary sacrifice of property or money not at risk in the adventure, in order to avert an unusual and imminent peril from the ship, freight, and cargo. (This section will prevent sales of goods at an intermediate port being contributed for, as they are at present contrary to principle, as expenditure.)

SHIP, FREIGHT, AND CARGO.

SECTION 15.—Loss or damage immediately and necessarily caused to the ship, cargo, and freight by a voluntary and prudent stranding of the ship shall be deemed to be a General Average loss within the meaning of this Act.

CARGO.

To SECTION 32, *subjoin*: Provided that, in case any disagreement shall arise respecting the real value of such goods so recovered as aforesaid, the same shall be sold by public auction, and the proceeds of such sale shall be apportioned amongst the parties to the adventure in proportion to the amounts of their respective contributions.

INTERMEDIATE EXPENSES.

SECTION 64.—Delete the words 'and of the wages and provisions for the crew during the time in which the repairs are being made.'

ESTIMATION OF GENERAL AVERAGE LOSSES.

SECTION 75.—A General Average sacrifice of property at risk in the adventure (such sacrifice not being an expenditure within the meaning of this Act) shall not, if followed by a total loss of the ship and cargo, be contributed for in any manner.

SECTION 80.—The owner of goods sold at an intermediate port to pay expenses incurred in respect of a General Average sacrifice shall in no case in which he shall be entitled to a General Average contribution suffer any detriment by reason of such sale having been made at an intermediate port instead of at the intended market of such goods if they had continued to be on board; but such owner as aforesaid may, on the other hand, retain any benefit resulting to him from such sale as aforesaid at an intermediate port by reason of such goods as aforesaid having fetched a higher price at such intermediate port than they would have fetched at their intended market.

CONTRIBUTORY INTERESTS AND VALUES.

SECTION 86.—A sacrifice made on behalf of a ship in ballast, whether chartered or not, shall not be deemed to be a General Average act within the meaning of this Act.

SECTION 91.—If the ship alone shall be liable to confiscation for a breach of international law, no loss sustained by the shipowner in order to avoid such confiscation shall be deemed to be a General Average loss within the meaning of this Act.

SECTION 95.—Subject to the provisions of this Act, the contributory value of property in respect to a General Average contribution shall be the value of such property to its owner at the termination of the adventure.

SECTION 107.—In estimating the contributory value of freight with respect to General Average contribution, two-fifths of the value of the wages, port charges, and other expenses shall be deducted from the value of the gross freight.

SECTION 114.—In respect to General Average contributions, no deduction shall be made under clause 107 for any freight paid in advance.

PROCEDURE.

SECTION 120.—The adjustment of a General Average contribution shall be made at the ship's port of destination, within fourteen days after her arrival at such port.

Some of the delegates having intimated the necessity of their returning home, it was not thought advisable to proceed any further with the task of remodelling the draft Bill, but in order to try if the so-much-desired result of one uniform system of General Average could not in any way be attained the following resolutions were unanimously agreed upon, viz. :—

1. That in consequence of the misconceptions which have taken place since the Glasgow meeting of the National Association for the Promotion of Social Science with regard to the General Average

question, another mode of proceeding on this very important question be adopted.

2. That, for the purpose of attaining this object, a committee be formed in order to decide upon and bring into shape a Bill, or series of resolutions, having for object the establishing one uniform system of General Average throughout the mercantile world.

3. That, in the opinion of this meeting, this object will be best attained if no steps be taken in this matter without the sanction of such committee.

4. That this committee consist of the following members [1]:—

E. E. Wendt, Esq., *Chairman of the Committee*	Wm. J. Lamport, Esq., *Liverpool*
Richard Lowndes, Esq., *Secretary*	Edouard van Peborgh, Esq., *Antwerp*
Laurence R. Baily, Esq., *Liverpool*	E. N. Rahusen, Esq., *Amsterdam*
J. Russell Bradford, Esq., *Boston*	P. H. Rathbone, Esq., *Liverpool*
L. C. Driebeck, Esq., *Rotterdam*	R. M. Smith, Esq., *Edinburgh*
Theodore C. Engels, Esq., *Antwerp*	J. J. Suenson, Esq., *Copenhagen*
S. Gram, Esq., *Copenhagen*	Edward Thune, Esq., *Copenhagen*
G. W. Hastings, Esq.	J. Wertheim, Esq., *Amsterdam*

This committee went vigorously to work. In order to secure a broad basis of action and so obtain the counsel and co-operation of those in all maritime countries who were most conversant with the subject of General Average, as well as to clear their own opinions by full discussion, it was determined by the committee to draw up a statement of the leading arguments on either side of what may be termed the disputed questions of General Average. This was published and communicated to the different members together with a *Projet de Code* (submitted by Messrs. Engels and van Peborgh of Antwerp), the compilation of the Danish Laws on General Average (emanating from Messrs. Gram, Suenson and Thune of Copenhagen), and the translation of the new German Law on Average and Salvage (issued by myself). The different members of the

[1] The names of the gentlemen who afterwards refused to act on the Committee have of course, been omitted.

committee were also invited to state their opinion upon the several questions raised in the statement and the reasons for and against them.

May 1, 1863, having been fixed as the date for the receipt of these statements, each member of the committee received a copy of the same, with the request that, before September 1, 1863, a final statement of opinion should be prepared, showing in what respects (if any) his previous opinion had been modified by the arguments of other members; and, if he retained his original opinion, stating any objection he might wish to urge against the arguments of those opposed to him.

Of the sixteen members of the committee, fourteen furnished their respective observations in ten pamphlets, and six members further supplied the committee, in five pamphlets, with their final statements of opinion on the questions at issue, and the following was the result:—

The report (this was the designation given to the statement of the leading arguments submitted to the committee), which was divided into six sections, viz.—first, preliminary observations; second, leading principles; third, definitions; fourth, sacrifices—*a*, of cargo—*b*, of ship's materials; fifth, extraordinary expenses; sixth, contributions—raised, in reality, twenty-three questions, on which an expression of opinion was considered serviceable; and as several members of the committee had not been present when the Glasgow resolutions were passed, it was quite natural that, in order to ascertain the opinions of all the members on *all* questions at issue in this controversy, the discussion on the Glasgow points should be reopened.

Now, the first nine questions raised by the report referred most immediately to the leading principles and definitions, in their different bearings, as to whether the *common safety* from danger of total loss, or the *common benefit*, that is, the completion of the adventure, should be considered the leading principle of the International General Average law.

It is well known that the common safety theory has been that which is commonly called the English practice; whereas upon the common benefit theory the other maritime nations of the world had mainly based their practice.

Of the fourteen members of the committee who expressed their opinion, only one was in favour of the common safety theory, while thirteen declared themselves in favour of the common benefit theory; so that the great principle which had been carried by the adoption of the Glasgow resolutions was confirmed by a very large majority.

The tenth question referred to cargo sacrificed on account of its *vice-propre*—a point not raised in Glasgow —and was unanimously decided as not allowable in General Average, for the article is by its own default itself the cause of the danger.

In the consideration of the eleventh question, referring to jettison of deck cargo—another point not raised in Glasgow—I imagine the enactment of the new German law, which only admits jettisoned deck cargo as General Average on coasting voyages, must have had considerable influence upon the opinions of the majority of the voting members; for although the business avocations of many must have made them aware that, for certain trades, particular vessels are built which will load one-fifth, or even one-fourth of their whole cargo on deck, the votes were expressed in a manner which showed that considerable doubt existed on the subject. I find five votes were given in favour of the proposal; five votes aimed at restricting the proposal to coasting voyages; and of the remaining two votes, one totally negatived the proposal, and the other in fact did the same by proposing that any such jettison should be divided between the shipowner and the owner of the deck cargo.

The twelfth question—damage to cargo in effecting jettison—corresponding to the third Glasgow resolution, produced five opinions in favour of reversing that resolution, while two of the five votes adhering thereto were accompanied by a declaration that such adhesion was only given because the resolution had been passed at Glasgow.

The thirteen votes given upon the thirteenth question —damage to cargo by forced discharge—entirely confirmed the fourth Glasgow resolution, to which it was similar.

The fourteenth question—damage to cargo in extinguishing a fire—treated of in the second Glasgow resolution, was confirmed by eight votes.

Upon the fifteenth question—loss of cargo by a sale to raise funds—the report proposed that such loss should be treated like a bottomry, that is, apportioned over the expenses for which it was sold, and that any profit should belong to the owner of the goods. Five of the eight votes given adopted the proposal purely; one added that the shipowner should be indemnified for loss of freight; and five were of opinion that, whereas the loss should be made good as proposed, any profit arising should not belong to the owner of the goods, but should be for the benefit of the common adventure.

The sixteenth question—the cutting away of wreck— was considered by the fifth Glasgow resolution not admissible in General Average. This was confirmed by ten votes against one vote.

The seventeenth question—damage by scuttling a ship to put out a fire—was included in the second Glasgow resolution, and here declared allowable in General Average by four votes against one.

The eighteenth question—damage by intentional stranding—proved to be most intricate. The first Glasgow resolution stated that such damage was, as a general rule, not admissible in General Average, but without prejudice to a claim in exceptional cases upon clear proof of special facts. The vagueness of the wording of this resolution must prove that the argumentations on both sides were so nice that it was impossible to come to an understanding upon any other basis. It is not unlikely that, this being the case, the first Glasgow resolution would have been confirmed by the majority of the committee, if the new German law had not made an enactment which, according to my humble opinion, ought to satisfy everybody, in consequence of its meeting, in the plainest terms, the principles involved. This enacts, in section 708, that such damages as are caused by the ship being purposely run ashore to prevent sinking or capture, and after being successfully got off is found capable of repair, is General Average. I find that four votes were decidedly in favour of the German enactment and one vote partially so; whereas one vote was given in favour of the Glasgow resolutions, and to the other eight votes various restrictions were attached.

Upon the nineteenth question—damage by carrying a press of sail—the seventh Glasgow resolution was confirmed by six votes.

The twentieth question—the port of refuge expenses —which had been declared by the sixth Glasgow resolution as admissible in General Average, was confirmed by thirteen votes against one vote.

The twenty-first question treated of two points—wages and provisions of the crew at a port of refuge, and loss of market. The first part of this question was, in conformity with the eighth Glasgow resolution, considered to be admissible in General Average by eleven votes, against three who held it inadmissible either on principle or for practical reasons. The seven votes which were given on the second part of the question were unanimous in not allowing the loss of market in General Average.

Upon the twenty-second question—contributing values —ten votes were given in conformity with the ninth Glasgow resolution, which considered the ultimate value liable, against one vote which was in favour of the value at the port of refuge.

The twenty-third and last question—deductions from freight—regulated by the eleventh Glasgow resolution, gave rise to a very interesting discussion in one of the preliminary meetings to the London Congress, where a proposal was made to modify the present practice by fixing upon a certain proportion of the freight to contribute to the General Average. The German law having adopted a similar principle, which, for practical reasons, would undoubtedly be very acceptable, it was to be regretted that only six members expressed their opinion on the subject at all, and these six were equally divided between adhering to the old practice and the adoption of a fixed proportion; so that, in reality, this remained an open question.

These different pamphlets, with the other papers referred to above, were bound together in a volume entitled 'Transactions of the International General Average Committee'; its circulation took place in January 1864.

Some months afterwards it was decided that the third International General Average Congress should meet on

September 26, 1864, in the city of York, and that the following draft of a Bill was to be taken as a basis for its deliberations:—

Whereas it is expedient that there should be uniformity in the law of General Average amongst all maritime communities, and that, in order to promote such uniformity, certain amendments should be made in the rules to be observed in the adjustment of claims for General Average made in any port or place within the United Kingdom of Great Britain and Ireland;

Be it therefore enacted, &c. &c. That on and after the day of the following rules shall be observed in the adjustment of all claims for General Average made in the United Kingdom of Great Britain and Ireland:—

SECTION I.—A jettison of timber or deals carried on the deck of a ship in pursuance of a general custom of the trade in which the ship is then engaged, shall be made good as General Average, in like manner as if such cargo had been jettisoned from below deck.

No jettison of deck cargo, other than timber or deals so carried as aforesaid, shall be made good as General Average; but if the shipment on deck have been made without the consent or sanction of the shipper or owner of such cargo, the loss resulting from such jettison shall be made good by the owner or owners of the ship; whereas, if such shipment have been made with the consent or sanction of such shipper or owner, the loss of cargo shall fall upon such shipper or owner.

Cargo, which is in a deck-house, poop, or topgallant forecastle, shall, for the purposes of this Act, be treated as cargo laden on deck.

SECTION II.—Damage done to goods or merchandise by water which unavoidably goes down a ship's hatches when opened for the purpose of making a jettison, shall be made good as General Average, in case the loss by jettison is so made good.

Damage done by breakage and chafing or otherwise from derangement of stowage consequent upon a jettison, shall not be made good as General Average, but shall fall upon the owners of the goods so damaged or their underwriters.

Section III.—Damage intentionally done to a ship or cargo for the purpose of extinguishing a fire on board ship, and damage done by water poured in or admitted through scuttle-holes or otherwise for the said purpose, shall be made good as General Average.

Section IV.—Damage done by cutting away the wreck, or remains of spars or other things which have previously been carried away, or permanently displaced by sea peril, shall not be made good as General Average.

Section V.—If a ship is intentionally run ashore in order to avoid capture or foundering, and is afterwards got off and repaired, all damage caused either to the ship or cargo on board by such running ashore shall be made good as General Average.

If a ship has been intentionally run ashore as aforesaid, but is not afterwards got off the shore, or being got off is found irreparably damaged, or so damaged as not to be worth repairing, no compensation in the way of General Average shall be made for the damage caused by such running ashore.

Section VI.—Damage occasioned to a ship or cargo by carrying a press of sail shall not be made good as General Average.

Section VII.—When a ship shall have entered a port of refuge under such circumstances that the expenses of entering the port are admissible as General Average, and when she shall have sailed thence with her original cargo, or a substantial part of it, the corresponding expenses of leaving such port shall likewise be so admitted as General Average; and whenever the cost of discharging cargo at such port is admissible as General Average, the cost of reloading and stowing such cargo on board the said ship, together with all storage charges on such cargo, shall likewise be so admitted.

Section VIII.—When a ship shall have entered a port of refuge under the circumstances defined in Section VII., the wages and cost of maintenance of the master and mariners, from the time of entering such port until the ship shall have been made ready to proceed upon her voyage, shall, subject to the provisoes undernamed, be made good as General Average.

Provided that, if reasonable dispatch be not used in repairing or otherwise getting the vessel to sea, no allowance for wages or maintenance shall be made in respect of the time so improperly expended.

Provided also, that no allowance shall be made for wages or maintenance as above in case the ship shall be condemned at such port as irreparable, or not worth repairing, or in case, for any other lawful cause, the cargo, or a substantial part of it, shall not be re-laden on board such ship for the purpose of further transport.

SECTION IX.—Damage done to cargo in the act of discharging it at a port of refuge shall not be admissible as General Average, in case such cargo shall have been discharged at the place and in the manner customary at that port with ships not in distress.

SECTION X.—The contribution to a General Average shall be made upon the actual values of the property at the termination of the adventure, to which shall be added the amount made good as General Average for property sacrificed; deduction being made from the shipowner's freight at risk of that portion of the crew's wages, and the port charges on the ship, the liability for which is contingent upon the earnings of such freights.

In case the amount to be made good shall exceed the aggregate of contributory values, computed as above stated, such aggregate shall, in the first instance, be taken towards satisfying the General Average, and the excess of the General Average shall then be apportioned as if the ship and entire cargo on board or at risk at the time of doing the act or measure which has given rise to the General Average had reached the port of destination free from damage.

The proceedings of this Congress were then opened on September 26, 1864, by the Right Honourable Sir James P. Wilde, Knight (now Lord Penzance), with the following words:—

We will, if you please, at once enter upon the business of the day; but before doing so I wish, on the part of the Social Science Association, of which I have the honour to be a member, to tender our best thanks to those gentlemen who have been good enough to come to attend this Congress, doubtless in some cases at great trouble or difficulty, from different parts of the world, to take part in this discussion. The Association feels that it is only by this sort of common effort on the part of those belonging to the mercantile community—gentlemen interested in the commercial affairs of the different countries to which they belong, such as those I now see before me—that any great practical measure can be successfully discussed and carried out. It is, therefore, right that our thanks should be tendered to all those who, by their presence on this occasion, show their willingness to aid us in the attainment of our present object. I will now call upon Mr. Wendt, the Chairman of the International General Average Committee, for his introductory observations.

MR. WENDT. It having been arranged that I, in my capacity as Chairman of the International General Average Committee, am to open the proceedings of the Third International General Average Congress with an introductory statement, I beg your attention to the following observations which I consider it my duty to address to you.

The first public step in favour of uniformity in legislation on General Average was made by the circular issued May 3, 1860, by the President and General Secretary of the National Association for the Promotion of Social Science, the Chairman of Lloyd's, the Chairman of the London General Shipowners' Society, the Chairman of Lloyd's Salvage Association, and the Chairmen of the Chambers of Commerce, the Underwriting Associations and others of Liverpool, Glasgow, Hull, and Bristol.

This circular contained, in the plainest possible language, the admission of these bodies that the system of General Average is one which, to prevent confusion and injustice, pre-eminently requires that the same principles should be acted upon by the chief maritime nations; that the uncertainty of the law on General Average is peculiarly felt; that much loss is occasioned to the mercantile community, and much valuable time is worse than wasted, through business being impeded by misunderstandings and irritated feelings; that the evils of such a state of things are notorious and unquestioned; that although the difficulties in the way of uniformity in General Average legislation are no doubt considerable, they are far from being insuperable; and that, in order to remove this most unnecessary element of irritation between assured and underwriter, the most important commercial bodies of the chief maritime nations should be invited to send delegates to that meeting, which is now better known as the First International General Average Congress at Glasgow.

After I had minutely referred to all the proceedings in Glasgow and London, and the preliminary steps taken by the International General Average Committee preparatory to this York Congress, all of which are fully set out in the foregoing pages, I concluded my address as follows:—

The committee is quite aware that this draft Bill does not contain everything which it might be desirable to embody in an Act on General Average; but it appeared to those members of the committee who had the principal charge of its action, that the differences of opinion still existing on the most important principles of General Average would inevitably necessitate at least a postponement of this public discussion, if they were not satisfied with those enactments which they have now been enabled to present; and I do not hesitate to say, that the amendments proposed by some very eminent and learned persons in the law of General Average, prove to me very decidedly that a very large and respectable majority is of the committee's opinion, that we do not absolutely require a complete codification on General Average. But for our purpose—I mean for the establishment of international uniformity—it will suffice that the important principles proposed in our draft Bill should be agreed upon and carried into effect.

I ought to observe, that Dr. Travers Twiss having revised and approved of the draft Bill now before you, it is sufficiently vouched as containing nothing objectionable in respect of legal phraseology.

I have now to say a few words as to some of the observations which are contained in the pamphlet of the learned delegate whom the governments of Hamburg and Lubeck did us the honour to send to this congress, and which I am sorry to say would, if the case as stated were in reality borne out by the facts, show considerable shortsightedness on the part of the members of the International General Average Committee. The learned delegate states that four classes of persons are principally interested in our movements, viz. :—1. The shipowners and merchants. 2. The underwriters. 3. The average-staters. 4. The lawyers.

Now, I think that, if he considers the various avocations of the sixteen members composing our committee, he will find that all these classes are fully represented in it; and there will then only remain his objection, that from the secluded life the committee has led, the different foreign Governments have not been sufficiently interested in the movement.

That her Majesty's Government views this movement with great interest, and is willing to assist, as far as lies in its power, in the attainment of uniformity in international General Average legislation, her Majesty's consular officers were authorised to declare to the Governments of their respective districts, at the request of the Liverpool Chamber of Commerce, which body was among the first originators of this movement.

With reference to the other Governments which are not represented among us, I can only say that a perusal of the correspondence and papers of the committee will satisfy everybody that we did what we possibly could to obtain the largest possible co-operation, both here and abroad. But if we consider that the principal obstacle to the attainment of uniformity in international General Average legislation does not arise abroad—for only slight differences on the minor points under discussion exist among the other maritime nations—but is attributable to the pertinacity with which, in this country, the principles hitherto acknowledged have been adhered to; then, I think, the most natural course of proceeding was to invite as much voluntary co-operation as possible from abroad, for the discussion and determination of what our international law ought really to be, without engaging to propose such law for the adoption of foreign Governments before it had been adopted and passed by the British Legislature.

The committee intend to follow with this law the same course as had been pursued with reference to some other enactments—as, for instance, the navigation clauses of the Merchant Shipping Amendment Act of 1862, which were first passed in this country, and adopted by the other maritime nations, who would certainly feel less objection when they saw that what the British Government submitted for their adoption was the result of the discussions of an international congress of gentlemen so well qualified to assist therein.

The committee has strengthened itself by inviting to its deliberations the delegates who have expressed their willingness to assist cordially in its labours, and it is to be hoped that, after this congress has arrived at a determination as to what clauses the draft Bill is to contain, the committee may be empowered to take immediate steps to lay the results of the labours of the congress before the Board of Trade, at the time most convenient to insure the attendance of the delegates who here honour us with their presence.

I sincerely hope that the third congress may really succeed in leading to a practical result.

THE CHAIRMAN. The statement that has just been read has placed us all in possession of a great deal of information very useful at this moment for the attainment of this most desirable end, and we shall presently proceed to consider the specific clauses of the Bill proposed to be brought before Parliament with that view. All present have, no doubt, acquainted themselves fully and entirely with the objects of this congress, and not only so, but also with the views of those who do not entirely agree with them; and as to those who have not done this, the printed book which I have before me[1] will place them in a position to judge of the matter. Before we proceed further, I think that we ought to ascertain to what extent different bodies of persons interested in this subject are represented here.

Captain Halsted, R.N., the secretary of Lloyd's, then handed the following letter to the Chairman, which he read:—

Lloyd's (E.C.): September 21, 1864.

Sir,—Within the year 1860, the subject of an 'International uniform system of adjusting General Average' was first brought under the notice of the Committee for managing the affairs of

[1] The above referred to: *Transactions of the International General Average Committee.*

Lloyd's, than whom probably no commercial body are better capable of appreciating the inconveniences resulting from the diversity of practice among different countries. They cheerfully co-operated with the promoters of the movement, and by the courtesy of their agents in foreign ports, much valuable information was afforded to the International Association.

The circumstances which prevented this Committee attending the meeting held in 1862, in London, have already been stated in a letter dated June 11, 1862, addressed to Dr. Travers Twiss, the then president of the meeting, and need not be further referred to.

As regards the forthcoming discussion in York, to which this Committee have had the honour to be invited, it would have been gratifying to them could they have felt themselves justified in taking part therein. But it is with surprise and regret, that on a perusal of the various preparatory papers and documents with which they have been favoured, this Committee find that the approaching meeting, instead of being constituted for the purpose of its original object (viz. the consideration of the laws of various countries, with a view to attempt their assimilation) has resolved itself into a committee for the purpose of effecting an alteration solely in the English law.

The draft Bill which is to be submitted seeks to establish uniformity in the adjustment of General Average by the sacrifice of some of the most valuable points in English custom, in favour of the most objectionable as administered abroad, and which the Committee consider would have a very prejudicial effect upon the liability of owners of cargo, whose interest throughout the proposed Bill would appear to be made subordinate to those of the shipowner. The proposed Bill would also largely add to the abuses and misunderstandings which arise under the existing system.

While this Committee are of opinion that, in the interests of the commercial world, whether merchants or shipowners, a uniform law is much to be desired, they do not see the means to attain this end in the proposals of the sub-committee, and therefore feel themselves compelled to refrain from the present agitation of the subject.

The secretary of Lloyd's, Captain Halsted, is requested to attend at the opening of the General Average congress, for the purpose of presenting this letter to the Chairman.—I am, Sir,

Your obedient Servant,
THOMAS BARING, *Chairman of Lloyd's.*

The Honourable Sir James Plaisted Wilde, President
of the Average Section of the Social Science
Association, York.

MR. J. A. W. HARPER, the Secretary of the Salvage Association, then handed the following letter to the Chairman, which he likewise read:—

ASSOCIATION FOR THE PROTECTION OF COMMERCIAL INTERESTS, AS RESPECTS WRECKED OR DAMAGED PROPERTY.

Lloyd's: Sept. 29, 1864.

To the Honourable SIR JAMES PLAISTED WILDE, *Chairman of the General Average Section of the Social Science Association, at York.*

Sir,—We, the Chairman and Vice-Chairman of the Association, beg, at the request of the Committee, to communicate to you, for information of the meeting of the above-mentioned section of the Social Science Association, the opinion of the Committee on the draft of the Bill which is intended to be laid before that meeting.

When the subject was first raised, the Committee regarded the meeting of the Social Science Association as a Congress of experts from various countries, assembled to discuss the principles of General Average, and especially the chief points of difference in laws and practice between various countries of Europe and America.

The Committee were informed that, as a result of the discussion at Glasgow, it was looked upon as not altogether impossible to obtain the adhesion of the leading maritime nations of the world to an International Code of General Average.

Although the Committee did not consider that the practical consequences of the conflict of laws, on the subject of General Average, are so serious as to require this great machinery to be put in force to avoid them, yet they were sincerely desirous to aid, as far as they could, any attempt that might be made with that object.

They observe, however, that, instead of an international code, it is intended to take the discussion on a proposed English Act of Parliament. The Committee presume, then, that all idea of an international code is abandoned. They are confirmed in this impression by the circumstance that some of the most important maritime nations have taken no part whatever in any of the proceedings up to this time.

Without saying what opinion they would entertain on any of the serious changes in English law contemplated in this Act, if they had been proposed as a part of a General International Law, the Committee regret that they find themselves compelled to decline taking any part in the consideration of them as simply reforms of the law of England.

At the same time that they do not consider they are called upon to say what course they would finally take under the above-mentioned conditions, they are anxious it should be understood that some of the provisions of the present proposed Bill seem to them so objectionable, that they can hardly imagine the circumstances under which they could be prepared to assent to them.

In thus abstaining from all active participation in proceedings which appear to be intended partly to effect large alterations of the law of this country, and, in part, apparently to commence a codification of the rest, but not with a view to establish an international code, the Committee are very desirous that it should not be supposed they would be backward to render any assistance in their power to all well-considered efforts towards facilitating the commercial intercourse of nations.—We have the honour to be, Sir,

Your obedient Servants,

WM. WILSON SAUNDERS, *Chairman*.
JOHN A. RUCKER, *Deputy Chairman*.

J. A. W. Harper, *Secretary*.

MR. LOWNDES. The following are the names of the representatives :—

EDWARD CRUSEMANN, Esq., *Chamber of Commerce, Bremen.*
CHARLES H. H. FRANCK, LL.D., *Chamber of Commerce, Hamburg;
  Chamber of Commerce, Lubeck.*
THEODORE T. ENGELS, Esq., *Belgian Government; Chamber of Commerce,
  Antwerp; Board of Underwriters, Antwerp.*
JULES DELEHAYE, Esq., *Comité des Assureurs Maritimes de Paris.*
G. KAMENSKY, Esq., *Russian Government.*
Captain E T. GOURLAY, *Sunderland Corporation.*
Dr. E. N. RAHUSEN, *Netherlands Trading Company.*
Dr. J. WERTHEIM, *Board of Underwriters, Amsterdam.*
D. W. MACKECHNIE, Esq., *Average Adjuster, Glasgow.*
HENRY J. ATKINSON, Esq., *President, Hull Chamber of Commerce.*
WILLIAM BONAR, Esq., *General Shipowners' Association, London.*
ED. VAN PEBORGH, Esq., *Belgian Government; Chamber of Commerce,
  Antwerp; Board of Underwriters, Antwerp.*
J. A. W. HARPER, Esq., *Salvage Association, Lloyd's.*
Captain HALSTED, R.N., *Lloyd's.*
L. R. BAILY, Esq., *Average Adjuster; Chamber of Commerce, Liverpool.*
P. H. RATHBONE, Esq., *Chamber of Commerce, Liverpool; Chairman
  of the Underwriters' Association, Liverpool.*
R. LOWNDES, Esq., *Average Adjuster; Chamber of Commerce, Liverpool.*
J. W. HALE, Esq., *Average Adjuster, London.*
R. M. HUDSON, Esq., *Shipowners' Society, Sunderland.*
JOHN J. KAYLL, Esq., *Sunderland Corporation.*
J. RUSSELL BRADFORD, Esq., *Average Adjuster; Board of Trade, Boston,
  U.S.; Board of Underwriters, Boston, U.S.*
Hon. JUDGE MARVIN, *Chamber of Commerce, New York; Board of
  Underwriters, New York.*
W. T. JACOB, *Shipowners' Association, Liverpool.*
WILLIAM RICHARDS, Esq., *Average Adjuster, London.*
MANLEY HOPKINS, Esq., *Average Adjuster, London.*
JOSEPH GREATED, Esq., *London.*

And then said : It is to a certain extent satisfactory to find that, with regard to Lloyd's, there has been some misconception, upon the removal of which we may fairly anticipate, from the tone of their letter generally, that, at all events, no opposition will be made to our intended Bill, and we may perhaps still hope for their continued assistance. I say they have acted under a misconception, for what is now proposed is not simply, as they imagine, to frame a Bill to be passed through the English Legislature, but to lay the basis of an International Code. This has been intended and understood all through. It is a movement not for England only, but for all parts of Europe and America.

THE CHAIRMAN. We had better now pass to voting upon the clauses or sections of the draft Bill, or to any discussion that may arise upon them.

MR. HASTINGS (General Secretary). With regard to the letters read, I think that, coming from bodies of such importance, I can hardly, as representative of the Council here, let them pass without saying that some authoritative reply should be given to those letters. If the statements are correct, which I hear they are not, then the committee would conceive that their object has not been carried out, because the resolution under which we appointed the committee—the resolution which induced the council to vote, more than once, money in aid of the expenses of these proceedings—was a resolution in favour of establishing an international code of General Average for the whole world. If the council had conceived that it was only for English purposes, they would not have thought it necessary to have had this meeting, but the question would have been treated and dealt with in our usual course of business. Therefore I trust that this section will be able to show to the council that their object is not merely to pass a Bill through the House of Commons and House of Lords for the altering of the English law, but for the establishing of a general international code of General Average. I have stated this now in order to avoid any future objection that might be taken.

MR. RATHBONE. We are, I believe, acting in strict accordance with the resolution passed at the Glasgow meeting of which I was secretary. On May 22 that resolution was sent to the committee. That resolution was submitted to Lloyd's immediately after the meeting on October 10, 1860, and I submit that we have not in any way altered the programme from what was then proposed. The directions given to the committee by the Glasgow Congress were as follows:—Mr. Rathbone read the resolution of the congress which directed the 'drawing up of a Bill, with a view to its being enacted into a law by the legislative authorities of the several nations of the world.'

THE CHAIRMAN. I think that the committee will consider that

what has been done has been merely to carry out what was done in Glasgow, and that the Bill has been drawn accordingly, and that it is contemplated in this resolution that it be recommended to the authorities of all commercial nations to adopt one uniform code. It seems to me, therefore, that the Committee of Lloyd's have unfortunately misunderstood the position we take; and under these circumstances it would be better to record the fact that the present meeting does not propose to restrict its action to British legislation, but to extend it to all foreign countries.

MR. RATHBONE. I am here for the Underwriters' Association of Liverpool, but I cannot commit that Association to anything that is done here, but I am merely to hear and watch and, if necessary, explain.

MR. MANLEY HOPKINS then read the following statement:—

The year 1860 saw the commencement in England of an endeavour which had, in a practical view, considerable importance. It was an attempt towards the unification of the laws, customs, and practice of all nations as they concern the subject of General Average, the final design being to procure an universal code for the regulation of all cases of General Average contribution.

The scheme was, perhaps, utopian, and its promoters may eventually find themselves obliged to succumb to special difficulties, which prove insurmountable. Nevertheless, there can be no doubt of the general benefit which attends the deliberation of a body of men met to consult upon the subject which most interests them, and upon which they are best informed. The danger which besets such a convention is a failure of practical result, and of the collision of many active minds ending in dialetic niceties, and a war of finely drawn distinctions, having no great difference at root.

The so-called International Congress, which assembled for the first time at Glasgow in 1860, consisted of 29 members. It took place under the presidency of the venerable Lord Brougham, Lord Neaves being also present. These 29 persons are, I observe in the proceedings, termed delegates by those foreign writers who have commented on the subject; but that name must be applied to them in a limited sense; and it is certain that the English members of the conference possessed no powers to bind or even to act for others. Of the entire number, 19 were from London and the principal ports of Great Britain, 2 from Antwerp, 2 from Amsterdam, 2 from Copenhagen, 1 from Hamburg, 1 from Bremen, and 2 from the United States of America.

I should here make the personal explanation, that I was not present at this meeting, nor at the subsequent meeting held in 1862. Under an anxiety to economise the time of the section, I condense my observations into the shortest compass, and, therefore, abruptly pass on to say that there is a consent among all maritime nations as to the intention of General Average, a term implying a sacrifice made by one individual in a marine adventure for the benefit of all concerned, entailing a contribution by all for the restitution of that individual's sacrifice. The unanimity extends only to the barest definition, and, even expressing the meaning of the term as generally as I have done, it is possible that each word may be objected to in detail. A divergence commences immediately, both as to principles and the practical adjustment of General Average. Each nation views this branch of distributive justice in its own manner; and even among the citizens of one country, individuals look at it variously, through their own particular spectacles. If the language of General Average is radically one, each trading community may be said to have its own dialect. This produces acknowledged inconveniences. Foreign commerce consists of an interchange of commodities between different nations, and these nations have different laws and customs. When claims arise between those mutually carrying on trade, they must be decided by the *lex loci* of the one terminus of the adventure or of the other. The result will be satisfactory on one side, but may interfere with the rights and laws on the other side. Commerce being essentially international, it required an international legislation to harmonise discrepancies, and to do away with these inconveniences. The congress of 1860 was meant to be the first step towards a consummation so devoutly to be wished for.

But is this possible? Has any advance been made in that direction? If not, what are the efficient causes of disappointment or delay? And if some are discovered, and appear to be insurmountable, what is the lower level of activity which might advantageously be pursued by those who anxiously desire greater unity in the regulation of General Average?

Taking the experience of the last four years as our guide in answering these questions, I think we must decide that an universal code of General Average is, at present, not to be looked for—first, because it is apparent that those who agree in desiring an international legislation are not agreed among themselves on first principles; and, secondly, because in homologating the existing systems, every step requires a change, or concession, from one community or the other; and in those countries where there is already a code or other legislation on the subject, even a mutation towards a proposed novelty will meet with opposition, because it will disarrange the existing law. I do not pretend to decide absolutely that it is so, and am far from wishing it to be the case; but I have stated my personal belief. The proceedings of to-day may show me to be wrong, but I never had faith in this cosmopolitan law-making, and so expressed myself shortly in print three years ago, and showed that a more useful field lay before the students and practitioners of this branch of science, in harmonising discordant views and methods, in our own country, by meetings at stated intervals for the consideration of difficult and doubtful points, and, by means of a majority of opinion, obtaining a reasonable and uniform practice.

I have carefully studied the various documents put forth by English and foreign members of the congress, and do not see, beyond a general desire for unity, any great promise of concession, even if the delegates were empowered to offer it. Since that meeting in 1860, Sweden has actually enacted a maritime code; and it would be against the known characteristics of the French nation to suppose that they would alter, on our account, their highly organised 'Code de Commerce,' which they so greatly admire and prize. Supposing, then, that the movement fails at present in its international character, the adoption of another effort is suggested for consideration at this congress, on that lower level I have already mentioned, and which the circular invites us to discuss, viz. home legislation on General Average. The project of a Bill, to be submitted to the Houses of Parliament, has been forwarded with a circular, by the International General Average Committee, the preamble of which recites, that whereas it is expedient that there should be uniformity in the law of General Average amongst all maritime communities, and that, in order to promote such uniformity, certain amendments should be made in the rules to be observed, in the adjustment of claims for General Average made in any port or place within the United Kingdom of Great Britain and Ireland, &c. The object of the proposed Act must, consequently, be so to legislate in our country, and with such concessions to the spirit of foreign laws and customs, as to bring our own system into harmony with the foreign system, whatever that may be.

But, again, even if the discussions of the section are narrowed to these limits, I see the same stumbling-block in the way of progress towards home legislation, as unfavourably effected in the international design, viz. the want of agreement amongst English members of the Association themselves, not only in practical details, but as to the very definition and the first principles of General Average.

Until this stumbling-block is taken away, by these differences disappearing or being reconciled, there can be no unity of action, even in England, or any satisfactory legislation.

Let us, then, see, in presence of the documents printed by the General Average Committee, embodying the views of English and foreign members of the Association, what these essential differences are.

First, it has been discussed, whether the term General Average relates to the act of sacrifice or to the subsequent contribution of all benefited parties to make good that sacrifice. I think we may easily dispose of this question by saying that, in the inexact language of commercial men, the term is sometimes used in the one sense or the other, or concretely for both. I do not think the question about name need distress us. But, secondly, the great principle is in contention, whether the aim and end of General Average be the restoration to physical safety of the imperilled interests—proceeding no further than their mere restoration to a state of safety—or, whether its vocation is the 'common benefit' of the associated interests, not merely in rescuing them from impending destruction, but conducing to their arrival at that intended terminus of the voyage where only they will have, in a true sense, a value. In other words, whether General Average means that—and all that—which, out of danger, tends to bringing the joint adventure to its proper termination; or, in the words of another writer, tends to the 'completion of the contract of affreightment when practicable, and to its termination when its completion is impracticable' (Baily). This is the cardinal question. There are many subsidiary points discussed in the published papers, but the scope of my present remarks goes no further than the great point of divergence of two schools of thought—one of which, the 'physical safety' school, may be called the dogmatic; the other, the 'final benefit' school, may be named the logical.

I have read, and with becoming attention, the views of the several writers whose separate papers and pamphlets have been collected into a volume. Had it been necessary, I should have been prepared to follow these writers in their conclusions with some detail; but this is not necessary, nor will our limited time for reading permit it. The copious and methodical observations of Dr. Franck, delegate from Hamburg, reached me as I was writing. Speaking generally, I may say that those who would limit General Average to a mere restoration to physical safety, are few in number. The view is only urged forcibly by one advocate, and he an Englishman, but his opinions are so careful and sincere as to be always entitled to respectful consideration. I speak of Mr. Lowndes, of Liverpool. I have named the holding of this view 'dogmatic,' because it involves the addition of a very arbitrary power—that of defining at what particular link of a chain of consequences the chain shall be broken as to joint responsibility. The act which gives birth to General Average generates also a train of consequences, and wave follows wave by a kind of natural necessity. But these *doctrinaires* place their finger on an imaginary point of demarcation, and pronounce it to be the dividing-line of solidarity. Then in a torrent of words, such as 'effects,' 'consequences,' 'incidents,' '*causa proxima*,' and '*causa remota*;' '*causa causans*,' and '*causa sine qua non*,' 'production of effects,' and 'induction of consequences;' 'common evil' distinguished from 'common danger'—we grow too giddy to reply, and, when the cloud of dust passes, lo! the magician is gone.

Nor must I here omit to notice another doctrine strongly held by one whose views have considerable influence—namely, that the condition precedent to an act of General Average is the 'moral certainty of destruction' as its alternative. This sentence jars strangely with the whole system, and for its decision requires a dangerously arbitrary treatment.

The 'logical' school—that which fearlessly follows legitimate consequences wherever they lead—is held pretty generally by the foreign members; in moderation by the English writers, '*à l'outrance*' by the Spanish and Swedish Codes, and, with some reservations, by the French 'Code de Commerce.' Many important points of detail will be examined and discussed to-day; but the distinction which I have dwelt on is the watershed of opinion—the groundwork of our contention. Whether the efforts of this meeting are directed towards the unification of our own and all foreign laws and customs, or whether they take the more special sphere of promoting home legislation, ideas will polarise themselves in reference to these cardinal points.

Our particular attention is, indeed, called on the present occasion to a project for a law for the regulation of General Average by our own Legislature. I shall not, therefore, detain the meeting longer with these preliminary remarks; but I would earnestly demand that, before any draft for an Act is placed in the hands of a Member of Parliament, the hearty concurrence of a large majority amongst its promoters should be secured for the proposed statute; that the danger should be remembered of reducing that liberty which is the life of trade, and fettering an ever-increasing commerce in its ever-multiplying changes and necessities.

We are told that, amongst the Locrians, any person proposing a new law stood forth in the assembly with a cord round his neck, and, if the law was rejected, the innovator was instantly strangled.

Perhaps it is too late in the day to revive that sharp and summary repression of law-making; and this meeting may, without such immediately fatal personal consequences, propose to our law-givers a scheme for regulating General Average. If the Houses of Parliament should think, in their wisdom, that the Association has not sufficiently made out a case, that enough unanimity does not exist for what is required, or that further legislation on the subject is not necessary at the time, the rope may still be used, although it is the projected law, and not its proposers, that will be strangled.

DR. FRANCK then read the following statement:—

Before commencing our discussion of the draft of Bill proposed by the honoured committee which hitherto managed the General Average movement, I beg leave to report a few facts to the congress now assembled, which might perhaps prove of some interest.

As the aim of our labours is to remove the difficulties and the inconvenience arising from the difference of the General Average laws and customs of the respective countries, it was and remains necessary to secure the active assistance of all countries with maritime interests, as well that of their commercial classes as that of their Governments, most of which have remained strangers to the question. Being penetrated by the truth of this observation, and very desirous to promote the important undertaking as best I could, I tried to interest influential persons, and particularly members of Governments, in this subject. I therefore wrote on this head to the Governments of France, Austria, Prussia, Sweden and Norway, Mecklenburg, Oldenburg and Hanover, and now beg leave to lay briefly before the honourable congress the poor results of my strenuous exertions for our common cause. As to Austria, the imperial Government did not think it proper to be represented here, because, by information it had from other Governments, it learned that the Congress of York was only a meeting of private persons. Prussia has been applied to, not only from mine, but from several parts. However, no Prussian member is present at our congress. France, I am very happy to observe, is, at last, this time represented by our most esteemed colleague, Mr. Director Delehaye, of Paris; this, however, being not my merit, but exclusively that of our very active member of the committee, Mr. Rathbone, of Liverpool. When I arrived at Paris, in order to secure us the presence of a French delegate, Mr. Delehaye had just been appointed the other day. As to Sweden, which hitherto took no part in the movement, I am glad to state that, although his Excellency the Swedish Minister of Justice, the Baron de Geer, informs us that the Swedish Government does not think it expedient to send a delegate to York, yet his Excellency authorises me to declare that, according to his personal opinion, the Swedish Government would, if invited by the English Government, most certainly send a plenipotentiary to a conference for settling finally the contents and shape of an universal General Average law. I am of the opinion that this declaration is the more to be valued if we consider that Sweden, after the most prolonged labours, at last just now has finished her new maritime law, which is to come into operation in the beginning of next year, and yet Sweden would be willing to adopt a new universal General Average law. His Excellency the Mecklenburg Minister of Justice, Dr. Von Schröter, had the kindness to write at great length on our undertaking, which he considers to be, as for Mecklenburg, of high importance. He authorises me to declare that the movement, so far as it concerns his country, may be sure of his active support. The Oldenburg Minister writes about to the same effect. All, however, decline to send official representatives to a private congress; but all will be ready to delegate plenipotentiaries, and to adopt, in the place of their own laws, an universal General Average law. I beg leave to state that the same is to be expected from the free cities of Hamburg and Lubeck, by whose Chambers of Commerce I have the honour of being delegated to this most honoured assembly. I beg to repeat that not the governments of these two cities are the delegating bodies, but their Chambers of Commerce. I, as well as most, perhaps all the other delegates, have no power of binding my constituents; they reserve to themselves the full right of considering the result of the congress, and then to decide on any further step which possibly ought to be taken afterwards. With respect to the voting, I beg leave to observe that my instructions from Hamburg compel me sometimes to vote in my capacity of delegate for Hamburg against my own convictions. Lubeck, however, having not fettered me by any instructions, my vote for Lubeck will be sometimes at variance with my vote for Hamburg.

Further, I beg leave to say, for safety's sake, a few words with respect to the circumstance that we now are making the draft of the Bill prepared by the honoured committee in the first place the basis of our discussion. I should have taken the liberty of opposing the mode of procedure but for the mutual understanding which I learn prevails, that as soon as the draft Bill has been discussed, amended, and passed, our congress will enter on the task of framing an universal code of General Average law as the second part of our labours. According to my opinion, it would perhaps have been better to enter immediately on the task of framing the code of General Average law, as the questions treated in the draft of the Bill have been discussed so very often, that most likely the members of our congress have already formed their ultimate opinion on them, and therefore another preliminary deliberation might perhaps be superfluous. But as the general opinion is in favour of considering in the first place the provisions of the draft of the Bill in question, and then in the second place the code, I submit, of course, to this mode of procedure.

Lastly, I take the liberty to observe that I should already at present put a resolution respecting the management of the whole General Average undertaking, as, from the reasons stated in my pamphlet, which is in the hands of the members of this congress, I am firmly convinced that our congress ought to be only a preliminary one, and that steps must be taken to induce her Britannic Majesty's Government to lend us in general their powerful assistance, and in particular to invite the other Governments to send competent delegates to a joint conference for agreeing finally on a complete, uniform, universal code of General Average law. But as I understand that it is the general wish to have this question settled after the draft of Bill has been considered, I shall delay the proposing of the resolutions until that time. However, as it is always of some use and interest to know as soon as possible, and beforehand, the proposals which will be made, I hereby beg to give the formal notice, that it is my intention to put the two following resolutions at issue as soon as the draft in question has been discussed.

I am in the painful situation of being compelled to make proposals, which I know, beforehand, though elsewhere entirely approved of, here will meet with but little sympathy and much opposition. But I am in duty bound to move for the said resolutions, as I am firmly convinced they would save our common cause from the peril of defeat in which it stands, and that they would lead us to success. More, perhaps, will be said when we come to discuss this subject; at present the foregoing is only a necessary declaration, an intimation of my intentions. I was compelled to give these explanations in order to remove any doubt as to the consequences of the circumstance that I do no longer oppose the draft of the Bill being now made the basis of the first part of our joint labour.

In accordance with the Chairman's suggestion, it was then resolved unanimously: 'That the object of this congress is simply to carry out the Glasgow resolution passed on September 27, 1860; and, that it is by no means intended that the Bill should be passed only by the English Legislature, but that, in the terms of that resolution, it should, when perfected, be recommended to the legislative authorities of all commercial nations, to enact the same into a law.'

THE CHAIRMAN. We will now proceed to consider the clauses of the Bill. We are to see to how much of it we can agree, and therefore to concentrate in it, as much as we can, our views on the subject. It would appear very desirable not to waste our time on comparatively unimportant points, but to apply ourselves to those points which seem capable of being passed without any great amount of opposition from one party or the other.

The first section of the Bill is this: 'A jettison of timber or deals carried on the deck of a ship, in pursuance of a general custom of the trade in which the ship is then engaged, shall be made good as General Average, in like manner as if such cargo had been jettisoned from below deck.

'No jettison of deck cargo, other than timber or deals so carried as aforesaid, shall be made good as General Average; but if the shipment on deck have been made without the consent or sanction of the shipper or owner of such cargo, the loss resulting from such jettison shall be made good by the owner or owners of the ship;

whereas if such shipment have been made with the consent or sanction of such shipper or owner, the loss of cargo shall fall upon such shipper or owner.

'Cargo which is in a deck-house, poop, or topgallant forecastle, shall, for the purposes of this Act, be treated as cargo laden on deck.'

It will be better to consider each paragraph of this section separately.

Dr. Rahusen proposed as an amendment that: 'No jettison of deck goods shall be made good as General Average.' Not only timber but cotton and many other kinds of goods were frequently carried on deck, and if the old-established principle of excluding deck loads from the benefit of contribution was broken in upon, it would be difficult to know where to stop. There seemed no clear distinction in principle between timber and other cargoes.

Mr. Rathbone seconded Dr. Rahusen's amendment. He believed many respectable shipowners engaged in the St. John's trade would prefer the clause to exclude deck loads from General Average, because they could then insure their freight on deck and invariably recover from their own underwriters in case of loss, without going into the difficult question as to whether the loss of the cargo was caused by a voluntary act, or directly by perils of the sea. Carrying cargoes of cotton from the Mediterranean on the decks of steamers had now become a general custom. Lastly, if deck loads were excluded from General Average, the assured would have to value them separately; which would enable underwriters to check, however imperfectly, the overloading of the cargo on deck; whereas at present the whole cargo was valued together, and it might appear the interests of shipowners to take on board freight which they would be perfectly prepared to jettison, knowing they could recover the loss in General Average.

Mr. H. J. Atkinson. I think there have been very few cases in which wood has been thrown overboard unnecessarily: a considerable portion of the loss generally falls upon the shipowner himself, and in most cases there is no clause in his policy on the ship to reimburse him for that portion. It has been asked, why draw a distinction between timber and cotton? Timber is not so damageable as cotton; merchants object to have cotton carried on deck. With timber, on the other hand, this is the customary mode of stowage. At a meeting of the Hull Shipowners' Association, they were unanimous in agreeing to this clause, and they considered that this was fair as between man and man. I think there is one omission; that is, after the word 'deals,' where it occurs in this paragraph, I should add 'or any other description of wood goods;' timber or deals would not carry everything in the timber trade.

MR. LOWNDES. It is a mere omission, and no doubt the committee will assent to that addition.

THE CHAIRMAN. It will be necessary to carry that amendment. The first amendment offered is in these terms: 'No jettison of deck cargo other than timber or deals, so carried as aforesaid, shall be made good as General Average; but if the shipment on deck have been made without the consent or sanction of the shipper or owner of such cargo, the loss resulting from such jettison shall be made good by the owner or owners of the ship: whereas if such shipment have been made with the consent or sanction of such shipper or owner, the loss of cargo shall fall upon such shipper or owner.' It would seem that the latter part of that clause would hardly be necessary to legislate upon.

MR. HUDSON. As a shipowner I think that, unless you pay double freight, you must allow the carrying of a deck load. As for overloading the ship, as Mr. Rathbone said, you can take the same precaution as for any other goods.

MR. GOURLEY. As a shipowner I can say there is no danger in carrying a moderate deck load of timber; as for overloading, captains will not knowingly do so, if only from a consideration of their own safety.

MR. CRUSEMANN. I quite concur in the amendment of Dr. Rahusen: the exclusion of deck loads does not, and ought not, however, to apply to the coasting trade.

MR. WENDT. Some vessels in the timber trade are particularly built for the purpose of carrying large deck loads; and I know it as a fact that in some ports of the Baltic vessels are constructed to carry as much as one-fifth to one-fourth of the whole loading capacity on deck. Timber goods, therefore, I think we are all justified in allowing to be carried on deck.

MR. BAILY. There is a flaw in this section, for with the latter part of the second clause we have nothing to do. The only question before us is, shall we, or shall we not, allow this loss in General Average? We shall therefore have to amend the words of this clause. Two points only are to be considered by us: first, what would be the effect on commerce generally of supporting the practice of carrying deck loads, by allowing in General Average jettisons of such deck loads? and secondly, what is a deck load?

THE CHAIRMAN. I would put these clauses separately—the one to be dealt with at present is the first: 'A jettison of timber or deals carried on the deck of a ship, in pursuance of a general custom of the trade in which the ship is then engaged, shall be made good as General Average in like manner as if such cargo had been jettisoned from below deck.'

MR. H. J. ATKINSON. I should like to hear Mr. Baily's views on that point.

MR. BAILY. Our House of Commons came to the conclusion, after an inquiry by its Committee, that it was so dangerous to carry a deck load between September 1 and May 1 that they would not allow it. If the danger was so great between those dates that the carriage of a deck load was during that time prohibited, it must be considerable in August and May, and, although less in July and June, must even then have existed. So long as danger results from carrying a deck load, the practice must be objectionable. It is true that this Act is now repealed, but it was repealed by a side wind, not on its merits.

MR. H. J. ATKINSON. What is now the common practice in cases of timber jettisons of deck loads between Liverpool and the Baltic, and other places?

MR. BAILY. Great difficulties and anomalies exist as regards the practice in this country of adjusting jettisons of deck loads. The owners of the cargo below deck have nothing to do with the jettison, but the value of their goods must form part of the contributing value. This raises the question who is to pay the portion falling on it—the owner of the ship, or the owner of the goods lost?

Mr. H. J. Atkinson. As a matter of principle the motion of Dr. Rahusen is a good one, although not likely to be fully adopted, but it would be well if the thing could be done. A general rejection of deck loads could not be admitted. It is the custom of our country to load certain cargoes on deck.

Judge Marvin. The present law and practice of the United States is, that the loss of any kind of deck cargo is not allowed as General Average. The rule is universal both as to foreign and coasting voyages. I see in this section that the law is laid down in the same manner, but there is an exception made in allowing the contribution of timber and deals. I had supposed it was brought forward by English gentlemen with a view to favour the trade carried on between Great Britain and her colonies, the Canadas and other places. I suppose this was brought forward to protect the English trade, and I am prepared, as one of the delegates of the United States, to concede to these gentlemen that it should be so. My vote will, therefore, depend upon the fact whether the English gentlemen desire an exception to be made in favour of timber and deals; but if they do not, I should vote that there be no contribution whatever.

The Chairman: That would be in conformity with the American law.

Judge Marvin: If it should be admitted, it would be on my part a concession to the English idea; for myself I would rather stand upon the universal law, but if the English think that the timber trade should be protected, then I should withdraw my objection and vote so.

Mr. Lowndes. The question is not whether timber should or should not be carried on deck; merchants themselves must decide that. It is a fact that a very large majority of timber cargoes are partially carried on deck. If this is a custom of shipowners which ought to be discouraged, surely it is for the Legislature of the country to take up the matter on the grounds of humanity or general policy, and declare whether cargoes shall be so carried or not. We have nothing to do with that. The real question with us is, which is most for the interest of commerce in general—accepting it as a fact that deck loads of timber are carried—whether, if they are jettisoned, the loss shall be a General Average or shall not be a General Average. It is not a matter of indifference to third parties whether such a sacrifice is made General Average or not: it affects the safety and the lives of the crew and passengers. It does so, by encouraging the timely throwing overboard of such cargoes when it is dangerous to delay; whereas if the captain knows that the loss will fall solely on the ship, he will be tempted to put off such a sacrifice to the last moment, when it may be too late. We cannot prevent the carrying of deck loads; the only question is, how is the matter to be managed so that the least mischief may be done? This appears to me the great argument in favour of the clause as it stands.

THE CHAIRMAN. I will put to the meeting for adoption first, Dr. Rahusen's amendment, taking, with his concurrence, the first proposition alone; suppressing the remainder, which might invite discussion. The amendment is, then, 'That no jettison of deck cargo shall be made good as General Average.'

DR. WERTHEIM. It would be against the principle of General Average for such jettisons to be allowed. Timber deck loads cause great peril to the rest of the cargo; for in a storm the timber goes over on one side, and hence it is that the captain throws over the deck load. I do not think that under such circumstances the loss should be made matter of General Average. Mr. Crusemann would exclude the coasting trade; I do not object to that.

The amendment was put.

For the amendment 8
Against it 12

MR. VAN PEBORGH: I beg to state that my vote against Dr. Rahusen's motion is not on the ground of principle, but only on that of convenience; as considering it impossible to have adopted in every country a universal rule abolishing the authorisation of loading timber on deck in voyages where it has been from all times customary to do so. Besides that, all other deck loads being prohibited, this will be really a sufficient improvement for commercial and insurance communities.

THE CHAIRMAN: We will now take the votes upon the first clause as it originally stood; still omitting those last words, which appear unnecessary.

For the clause 18
Against it 2

The clause was accordingly passed.

THE CHAIRMAN. I will now read to the meeting the next clause of this first section: 'No jettison of deck cargo other than timber or deals, or other wood goods, so carried as aforesaid, shall be made good as General Average.' There is an exception proposed by the representative of Bremen (Mr. Crusemann), as to goods carried in the coasting trade by permission of the law of the country to which the vessel belongs. The words following in the original draft Bill are, I think, by general consent to be omitted.

MR. GOURLEY. I would move as an amendment that there be inserted the words, 'tar, cotton, and tallow,' because those articles are carried as commonly now as timber.

MR. VAN PEBORGH. I strongly object to the amendments of Mr. Crusemann, and also to that of Mr. Gourley. They are contrary to all my experience of the rules of other countries. You would have to define what is a 'coasting voyage,' and this in a different way for different countries according as their laws or customs on this subject may differ. It would be impracticable.

MR. FISHER pointed out that the voyage from New York to California was only a coasting voyage. He wished to know how it was proposed to deal with cattle on deck.

JUDGE MARVIN. I would, as I said before, limit the allowance of deck-load jettisons as much as possible, the thing being, in my judgment, contrary to principle. We have conceded timber and deals; let us go no farther.

MR. RATHBONE. We are considered as going too far in this Bill as it is; do not let us go on to introduce other things into it, that every code on earth includes.

After some further conversation, Mr. Gourley's amendment was put and lost by a large show of hands.

THE CHAIRMAN. The next amendment is as to 'cattle' in addition.

Amendment put and lost by a large majority.

THE CHAIRMAN. The next amendment is that which has relation to the coasting trade, 'with the exception of goods so laden in the coasting trade by the permission of the laws of the country to which it belongs.'

Amendment put and lost by a large majority.

THE CHAIRMAN. I will now put the original clause.

    For the clause 15
    Against it 4

Clause carried accordingly.

THE CHAIRMAN. The next question is as to the last words of the section, viz. : 'Cargo which is in a deck-house, poop, or topgallant forecastle, shall for the purposes of this Act be treated as cargo laden on deck.'

MR. JACOB, as a delegate from the Shipowners' Association at Liverpool, was instructed by that body to move as an amendment the entire omission of this clause. The shipowners were very much dissatisfied with the proposed exclusion of cargoes in the poop from the benefit of a General Average. They thought the proposal must have been made without sufficient consideration of the magnitude of the interests involved. The quantity of cargo carried in the poops of ships was very great, and its value was even greater in proportion, since a great deal of silk and other light and valuable produce was carried in that manner. It would never do to exclude such cargoes. His instructions were to move for the entire omission of the clause. At the same time, speaking for himself, if the feeling of the meeting were (as he had been led to suppose it was) opposed to this view, he should be prepared to support the amendment which he understood Mr. Baily was about to propose, as he thought that would answer the purpose. He expressed regret at the course taken by Lloyd's committees and in London, because he was satisfied from practical experience, that some measure tending to a removal of the differences among different countries was very much wanted, and might really be carried out.

Mr. HUDSON seconded the amendment of Mr. Jacob. He thought it would be very unjust to treat poop cargo as cargo upon deck.

MR. BAILY. I beg leave to move this amendment: 'Every structure not built in with the frame of the vessel shall be considered to be a part of the deck of the vessel.' The poop is always built in with the frame of the vessel, and is recognised to be fit to receive such goods even as silk.

JUDGE MARVIN seconded Mr. Baily's amendment.

CAPTAIN GOURLEY thought that the expression 'built in the frame' was rather vague, and might give rise to dispute. Would it not be better to substitute, 'not included in the register tonnage'?

MR. JACOB. That would not do; for, under the Mercantile Marine Act, they measure in with the tonnage hurricane-houses, and many kinds of deck-houses which I should be very sorry to carry cargo in.

MR. GOURLEY thought Mr. Baily's amendment preferable to the entire omission of the clause. It really was desirable to define what was meant by the term 'deck,' since vessels are often built with three or four decks. Take the register tonnage, or some other rule; but at least have a rule. This was not an underwriter's question, but should be dealt with, as between shipowner and merchant, on general principles of justice.

DR. WERTHEIM wished to know what would be the effect of Mr. Baily's amendment. How would it bear on the case of houses built on to the beams?

MR. BAILY. I adopted the word 'frame' because I have been told by shipowners that it includes the ribs only, and not the beams. Houses of all kinds are objectionable for cargo. In a case which came before me, one of the regular American packets had a house for the crew, and it is reasonable to suppose that this house was at least a fair specimen, and yet it was swept away, and not one officer was left to the ship to bring her home, but the third mate, a boy. It may be supposed that whatever you put the crew into is a proper place for cargo, but it is not so.

MR. HUDSON. There is a description of houses called 'Liverpool houses' which are really part of the ship, built in the middle of the ship, and the deck is carried up to them. If any person can point out how they can be defined, I will say nothing more on the subject. The houses I refer to are as strong as the frame of the ship. A poop may be washed away, but that would only be by extraordinary weather, against which the shipowners have to insure. Let the words be 'permanent houses.' They must be sufficient to carry cargo, if sufficient to carry the crew.

DR. FRANCK. It would be better to leave this clause out

altogether. We rarely put into the deck-house anything but the crew. The crew will look to the safety of it themselves. Seamen have objected to berths, and would not ship in consequence of the accommodation not being what it ought to be. I therefore think it would be better that the clause be expunged.

Mr. JACOB withdrew his amendment, and the votes were then taken on Mr. Baily's amendment.

>   For the amendment 14
>   Against it 7

Amendment carried accordingly.

THE CHAIRMAN. The next section, the second, concerns the damage of goods at the time of the jettison: 'Damage done to goods or merchandise by water which unavoidably goes down a ship's hatches when opened for the purpose of making a jettison, shall be made good as General Average in case the loss by jettison is so made good.' We had better take this first clause only at present.

After some discussion as to the mode of wording the section, and a slight modification of it, Mr. Baily moved as an amendment that the word 'not' be inserted after 'shall.' He objected on practical grounds solely. It was a curious fact that claims of this nature were scarcely ever found to be made except in the case of such cargoes as were insured 'free of particular average.' The rule as proposed opened a door for frauds and disputes. There would constantly be put forward statements which it would be difficult to believe, but impossible to disprove.

MR. BRADFORD did not think the difficulty of proving the extent of the damage was a sufficient reason for excluding a loss which was confessedly admissible in principle. In many things besides this, it was difficult for the adjuster to make up his mind as to when, where, and how damage had occurred; but he had to find that out as well as he could. This was not a more difficult case than others. The claim had in each case to be supported by proof; if there were no proof, it must be rejected: that was no reason for rejecting it in cases where there was proof.

MR. BAILY. You must recollect that, when water goes down the hatches, the goods which it damages are very often thrown overboard, and when they are thrown overboard the rejection of such damage does not work any injustice. When they are not thrown overboard, the water finds its way to the bottom of the ship, and it then becomes impossible to distinguish between the damage done by the water admitted in this way and the damage done by water admitted in other ways.

Mr. Baily's amendment was then put.

For the amendment 1
Against it 20

The clause was then put and carried.

The Chairman. The next clause of this section is: 'Damage done by breakage and chafing or otherwise from derangement of stowage consequent upon a jettison shall not be made good as General Average, but shall fall upon the owners of the goods so damaged or their underwriters.'

Mr. Atkinson moved that the word 'not' be omitted. It seemed to him only reasonable to treat this loss, which was clearly a consequence of the jettison, in the same way as the jettison itself.

Dr. Wertheim seconded that amendment.

The amendment was put.

For the amendment 16
Against it 6

The amendment was therefore carried.

On the Right Honourable Chairman's vacating the chair, Mr. Wendt was called thereto.

The Chairman. The next section is No. 3: 'Damage intentionally done to a ship or cargo for the purpose of extinguishing a fire on board ship, and damage done by water poured in or admitted through scuttle-holes or otherwise for the said purpose, shall be made good as General Average.'

After some discussion as to the language of this section, it was agreed that it should stand as follows: 'Damage done to a ship and cargo by water or otherwise in extinguishing a fire on board the ship shall be made good as General Average.'

Dr. Rahusen proposed that the words 'and freight' should be added, but withdrew his amendment on the assurance that a clause should be added to the Bill, so as to attain his object in a more general way.

The section as amended was carried unanimously.

THE CHAIRMAN then put to the meeting section No. 4, viz.: 'Damage done by cutting away the wreck or remains of spars, or other things, which had previously been carried away or permanently displaced by sea peril, shall not be made good as General Average.'

A discussion arose as to the propriety of omitting the word 'permanently,' and it was eventually agreed to admit the words 'or permanently displaced.'

M. DELEHAYE did not approve of this clause. He thought, if wreck was cast away for common good, the value of that wreck, whatever it might be, ought to be replaced by general contribution. Such was at present the law of most maritime countries.

The clause as amended was carried by a large majority, three votes only being given against it.

Adjourned till to-morrow at 10 o'clock.

September 27, 1864.—SIR FITZROY KELLY *in the chair*.

Before the chair was taken, Mr. Wendt read a letter from the Portuguese consul, which stated that his Government had deputed him to attend the congress, and that, though prevented by illness from doing so, he wished to be supplied with some printed or other record of the proceedings, for transmission to his Government. Much satisfaction was expressed at the action of the Portuguese Government.

THE SECRETARY read the Minutes of proceedings of the 26th instant.

THE CHAIRMAN put to the meeting the fifth section, viz.: 'If a ship is intentionally run ashore, in order to avoid capture or foundering, and is afterwards got off and repaired, all damage caused either to the ship or cargo on board by such running ashore shall be made good as General Average. If a ship has been intentionally run ashore as aforesaid, but is not afterwards got off the shore, or being got off is found irreparably damaged, or so damaged as not to be worth repairing, no compensation in the way of General Average shall be made for the damage caused by such running ashore.'

MR. MANLEY HOPKINS considered the principle of allowing in General Average the damage done to a ship by intentional stranding to be perfectly sound. The practical difficulties of carrying out that principle, however, and the inconveniences it would occasion, were so considerable, that he would prefer to exclude it in all cases excepting that of running ashore to prevent capture. He had prepared an amendment to that effect, but would not at present bring it forward.

THE CHAIRMAN with great fulness and perspicuity explained the system on which the debate was to be carried on. Amendments were first to be taken; and, of these, those came first which dealt with the earliest portions of the clause; after all amendments had been dealt with, the clause in its amended form would have to be put to the meeting.

Some discussion ensued as to the amendments to be proposed, after which,

JUDGE MARVIN. I move the following amendment: In the third and fourth lines of the first paragraph I move to strike out the words 'and is afterwards got off and repaired.' I presume all here understand that there are two principles involved in this section. As it stands, it seems to be founded on the idea of the new German code, which limits the right to recover the damages sustained by voluntary stranding to those cases in which the vessel is afterwards gotten off and continues her voyage. I propose to allow such damage in General Average, independently of the circumstance whether the vessel be gotten off or not. The law of the United States upon this point is fully settled. Perhaps there is no question in the whole range of General Average law that has been so elaborately, and so learnedly, and so ably discussed in the Supreme Court of the United States, at Washington, as this very subject of voluntary stranding. I believe that all the points that could arise have been uncovered by the discussions of that court, which is the authoritative and the court of last resort. In a very able decision made about ten years ago, the Supreme Court adjudicated that where a vessel was driven ashore upon the rocks, and was to a very large extent beyond the control of the master—where she was irresistibly driving amongst the rocks, and must, under any circumstances, have gone ashore; but the master put up his helm, trimmed his sails, and managed with considerable skill, with the aid of his pilots and crew, to put her ashore on a sandy beach instead of on the rocks: by doing this he saved the cargo and lost the vessel, for the vessel was not got off: this was held to be a case of General Average. I propose by this amendment to place the law upon the same footing as that of the United States; at the same time I am prepared to assent to the proposition of Mr. BAILY which will be offered by-and-by. I propose, therefore, that such damage shall be allowed in General Average, whether the vessel is gotten off or not.

DR. RAHUSEN seconded the amendment.

DR. WERTHEIM: Mr. Marvin's amendment would tend to introduce the principle of the American law. The Dutch law has been so from the first time that we had any maritime law in Holland: that all damage done by intentional stranding should be paid for. Under section 99 of the Dutch code it is enacted 'that all damage done to a ship or cargo, in order to escape capture, or to avoid foundering, shall be paid for in General Average.' The only question to be asked is, whether it is done intentionally to avoid peril. When we look at the result of the discussions at the meeting held at Glasgow, we find that it was proposed that damage done to a ship in voluntary stranding should not be General Average. What was done there? It was decided by a large majority that as a general rule in the case of stranding it ought not to be the subject of General Average, *but subject to clear proof of special facts.* We think it ought to be asked for as General Average: we shall therefore vote for the principle of the amendment proposed by Judge Marvin, because it is that adopted by the maritime laws of Holland.

THE CHAIRMAN: The question that I am now to put is this, whether the words now proposed shall stand part of the clause. The real question is, whether the allowance in General Average of damage done by voluntary stranding, is or is not to be conditional on the ship's being got off and repaired.

    For the amendment 8
    Against it 9

THE CHAIRMAN. The amendment is rejected and these words stand part of the clause. Has any gentleman any amendment to propose after the fourth line?

MR. LOWNDES proposed that in place of the words 'or so damaged as not to be worth repairing,' be substituted, 'or so damaged that the expense of repairing would exceed the value of the ship when repaired, and if the ship shall not be in fact repaired.' He proposed this, merely to remove that which might be an ambiguity for foreigners, as in some countries a ship is treated as not worth repairing when the cost of repairing would exceed three-quarters of its value.

MR. RATHBONE seconded the amendment.

Amendment put.

    For the amendment 8
    Against it 9

MR. CRUSEMANN. I move also an amendment which will bring the section more within the German law on this subject. It is the obliteration of the words 'or so damaged as not to be worth repairing.'

On the vote there were—

    For the amendment 6
    Against it 8

THE CHAIRMAN. As the three partial amendments that have been proposed have now been disposed of, I will now put the general question. It is one of great importance. This clause which is proposed by the society to be introduced into the law of Great Britain, with the hope that it may be adopted by most, if not by all, the maritime nations of the world, is, that the intentional running ashore of a ship in order to avoid capture or foundering, shall, where the ship is got off and repaired, be made matter of General Average. Nations and courts of law have differed more or less upon this subject. It is a subject worthy the consideration of this meeting. I shall be very glad to hear any discussion upon it; and will only observe at the present moment, that the discussions of this meeting will no doubt have considerable weight with the House of Commons and the House of Lords in this country whenever such a Bill shall be introduced. I collect that it is the intention of those who are interested in this question to endeavour to bring forward a Bill carrying into effect these various provisions, and I shall be very glad to see that Bill brought into the House of Commons, of which I have the honour to be a member. I may, perhaps, be called upon to report as to my knowledge of it—to say what I may know of the general feeling and opinion of those who have an interest in, and have made themselves masters of, the subject. I shall therefore listen with great interest to the discussions on this Bill. The question is familiar to you all, and whatever may be the decision of this meeting, even if there happen to be differences of opinion, I shall take care to report, with all the weight that belongs to it, the practical opinion of this assembly whenever the case shall come under the consideration of the House of Commons. Any one may now move, upon the question being put, that this clause stand part of the Bill, or any one may move a negative, or move a clause of a totally opposite character.

Mr. BAILY. I move the following amendment; that instead of the first clause of section five, the following clause be substituted: 'When a ship is intentionally run on shore because she is sinking or driving on shore or rocks, no damage caused to the ship, the cargo, or the freight, or any or either of them, by such intentional running on shore, shall be made good in General Average.' We had a very long discussion at Glasgow on this subject. It seemed to be the general feeling that, on principle, you could not reject the damage done by voluntary stranding, but the allowance of it was open to so many abuses that the more it was limited the better it would be for underwriters, merchants, and shipowners generally. The resolution I propose is framed to meet these difficulties. The main objections to allowing voluntary stranding in General Average are these: When a vessel is on the point of foundering she has a quantity of water in her hold; if run ashore under these circumstances, it is often alleged that the whole damage, or nearly the whole damage, done to the cargo is owing to the straining of the ship by running her ashore. This allegation is not the fact, but it leads to a great deal of abuse and fraud; and, therefore, we were of opinion at Glasgow, that we had better exclude it in the case of foundering. When a ship is run ashore to avoid the fire of a battery, or capture, the same reasons do not apply, and there may be nothing to justify the exclusion of that damage from General Average. Those gentlemen even who are against the allowance of any damage done by running a ship ashore may sanction the amendment as a compromise, for there are not many practical objections to it; so that those who are opposed to all allowance may adopt this amendment, and those who are agreed that in principle such damage ought to be allowed, but that there are practical objections to it, may also pass it as a check on abuses.

JUDGE MARVIN. I second that amendment.

MR. ENGELS. As Mr. Baily now makes it, it is showing the way to the captain to avoid saying that the ship was foundering before he voluntarily stranded her, and so to get safe out of it. We have had instances of fraud—we all agree to that, and it is practically difficult to come at the value of the damage. I think we shall be showing to the captain how he is to act, and what he is to say, namely, that the ship was not sinking. On the principle we are all agreed that voluntary stranding should be admitted; but the amendment of Mr. Baily will, I think, produce a result different from that we all have in view, and I recommend, in preference, that we should adopt those resolutions on this subject which were agreed to in Glasgow.

MR. RATHBONE thought the Glasgow resolution decidedly more vague than that proposed by Mr. Baily. Most of the underwriters felt very strongly, and there had been very good reasons for their having a strong feeling against voluntary stranding—the reasons he wished not to be published. . . .

JUDGE MARVIN. I am favourable to the adoption of Mr. Baily's amendment; not that I like it in principle. I prefer the broad principle which I myself previously enunciated. We must, however, make a compromise of principle for the sake of policy: this is a departure from principle and founded on expediency; it is a concession to the views of the English underwriters and English average-staters. I believe they are against the principle of allowing as General Average any damage done by a voluntary stranding: this is a concession *pro tanto* to a certain point, but not of the whole thing. It still retains, after all, the great principle of the General Average doctrine that runs through the whole cases, because it simply excludes from General Average contribution some instances or cases of voluntary stranding, and leaves all the other cases that may arise to follow the general law of being made good in General Average. When a ship is intentionally run ashore to avoid sinking or driving on rocks, then it is not a General Average case. It fairly follows that all other cases are General Average. You thereby exclude that very class of cases stated by Mr. Rathbone. If the ship's state is such that she must go to the bottom, or if she is driving against the rocks and the master runs her on shore simply on the ground that she is already sinking, and in that inevitable condition or peril, and the master only selects another place to run her ashore (cases which would not very often arise), I should be willing that the thing should take its course and not let the loss fall on the General Average, leaving it to be determined as to what would be the result if the stranding had been done to avoid capture, or under other circumstances than those defined in the clause. I concede it; I like that better than the draft Bill, for I do not at all like the section as it stands in the draft.

MR. WENDT. There is, as experience has sufficiently shown, so much danger in allowing any case of stranding as General Average, that I would certainly propose to exclude them from General Average altogether.

MR. ATKINSON. I think that, under all the circumstances, the best plan will be to adopt the amendment contained in the proposition of Mr. Baily,

JUDGE MARVIN. I wish to repeat expressly that I regard this as a concession to the underwriters, because I believe that the Legislature of this country will affirm the doctrine of the United States, and that held in Holland and on the continent of Europe, and in everything that the text-writers have said on the subject, and will pass their law accordingly.

MR. DELEHAYE agreed with Judge Marvin in approving the

principle of universally treating a voluntary stranding as a case of General Average. If this were objected to, however, he preferred the resolution come to at Glasgow, which appeared to him as explicit as it was practicable to make one on this subject.

Mr. BRADFORD could not vote for the amendment, as he could not vote for anything which was against principle, on grounds of mere expediency. He admitted there were practical difficulties, but did not think these should be suffered to override a clear principle. He did not like the clause as it stood in the draft, for he could not see what difference it made whether the ship was afterwards got off, or not. He should be glad, like his friend Judge Marvin, to concede whatever he could to the English underwriters in a spirit of fairness, but not when it came to a question of principle. He believed the English courts of law, were the case to come before them, would arrive at the same conclusion as the American courts, and indeed those of the whole commercial world. He did not see that the carrying out of this principle was so very difficult. He had himself had within the last seven months to deal with three claims for damage by voluntary strandings, and had rejected them all; having satisfied himself in each case that the damage was not done by the stranding, but by previous sea peril.

DR. WERTHEIM. How does the principle stand in Mr. Baily's proposition?

THE CHAIRMAN. It leaves the law undetermined as to all cases except those defined in the proposition itself.

DR. WERTHEIM. There is an amendment to exclude only two cases; all other cases, then, are to be allowed?

THE CHAIRMAN. It leaves the law actually as it is, except as to the particular cases here named—that of an intentional running ashore because a vessel is sinking or driving ashore or on rocks.

DR. WERTHEIM. Then running ashore in all other cases is General Average, and is not prejudiced?

THE CHAIRMAN. Mr. Baily may probably explain that.

MR. ENGELS thought it best, as it was settled at Glasgow, to leave it to the average-staters, who were a most respectable body of men, to determine what cases should be treated as cases of voluntary stranding. By Mr. Baily's amendment, it was put into the mouths of captains what they should say in their protests, so as not to have their claims rejected. He thought there was great danger in pointing out one or two particular cases for exclusion. He could not but think that the Glasgow resolution had its merits.

MR. WENDT. If a vessel is put ashore in such a condition that it cannot keep afloat, it is, as a matter of course, a case of Particular Average, and not of General Average.

MR. HOPKINS. I have no hope that my amendment will be adopted by the meeting. My opinion has been before the world some years. I think we are making this an underwriters' question, whereas I understood that we were to take a national view of the thing. I think we ought not to appeal to the committee and say whether the underwriter is injured or not. We are expected to introduce general rules to be hereafter adopted by foreign countries. The average stater takes no view at all, he simply administers the law. These cases bring us a great deal of work in the way of business. Mr. Baily's amendment leaves open two results which will create quarrels and bring on as many difficulties as if the clauses were to stand; therefore, I think that if we are to legislate at all it should be for a very full measure. I only repeat that my idea is, that the only exception should be a case of threatened capture.

THE CHAIRMAN wished that all present should distinctly understand the actual position of the debate. The law of England, as it then stood, was, that where an injury had been *bonâ fide* done, whether to ship, freight, or cargo, by the voluntary act of the master, in order to prevent some greater calamity, then the consequences, whatever they might be, would belong to General Average. On this principle, the law, as regards voluntary strandings, would be the same in England as in the United States. If it were wished to leave this state of things untouched, there was no occasion to pass a clause at all. He understood that the amendment was proposed in the interests of the English underwriters. They were a body of persons who had suffered from the law as administered, not because the law, if duly administered, would be prejudicial to them, but because, unfortunately (and he did not solicit the silence of the press on this subject), there was a prejudice of juries against underwriters, as contrasted with other persons, which frequently led to a verdict of injustice. In no part of the Queen's dominions did that abuse prevail more than in the town of Liverpool. He himself had heard verdicts pronounced in Liverpool, he doubted not by able and well-intentioned juries, which went entirely to set aside the law and justice of the case, simply on account of their prejudice. Some of those present appeared to think, with Mr. Baily, that the underwriters should have some protection, yet without entirely overthrowing the principle of the law. Others, as was done at Glasgow, would exclude voluntary strandings altogether, except under some peculiar and exceptional circumstances, which they did not define. Another gentleman would exclude it in every case except that of a stranding to avoid capture. It was also open to them to abstain from making any clause. Between these views they had to choose. The learned gentleman proceeded to point out the proper course to be taken in discussing the various amendments.

After a short adjournment, MR. BAILY replied. In answer to Judge Marvin: This clause does not lay down as a principle that running a ship ashore is General Average in all other cases than those mentioned in the amendment, although that may be a fair inference from it. The amendment leaves it an open question in all other cases than those mentioned. In answer to Mr. Delehaye, who would prefer to say that special facts should make the damage General Average: We must look at the resolution as practical men; if we make exceptions, the case, whatever it may be, will always come within that exception. In every case which we can invent, some one will say that the case comes under the exception. A vague wording like that of the Glasgow clause creates or increases difficulties which we are trying to remove. In answer to Mr. Engels: When a man is in imminent danger of going to the bottom of the sea, he will not go to the bottom if he can avoid it; he will certainly not elect to go to the bottom because he cannot get the damage done to his ship allowed in General Average. Circumstances will force him to run the ship ashore, and he will not give

General Average a thought when he does it. With regard to pointing out to a captain that he must avoid saying that he ran the ship ashore to prevent her from sinking; if he does avoid it, the avoidance will not bring the damage into General Average; he must still assign a plausible and good reason for the act. When he has given his reasons, everybody can deal with the case as he thinks right. A man who runs his ship ashore without any reason will get nothing in General Average; he must assign some justifiable reason for doing it, and he will find it very difficult to bring all the actual circumstances to square with a reason which is not the true one, and in his efforts to do it he may find that he had something to pay to the owners of the cargo instead of something to receive for doing it. I know practically that there are great abuses, and I have endeavoured to frame a clause which will, I think, meet all your views, and not clash with the views of either those who hold that everything in such a case is General Average, of those who hold that some things are General Average and some are not, or of those who hold that nothing is General Average.

The amendment was then put.

> For the amendment 13
> Against it 6

The amendment carried accordingly.

THE CHAIRMAN. If any gentleman, before we proceed to the remaining clauses of the Bill, has to propose that some description of loss by voluntary stranding shall come within General Average, now is his time to do so. Mr. Baily does not intend to interfere with the principle of law as held in one country or another.

No further amendment having been proposed, the Chairman proceeded to put section six, viz.: 'Damage occasioned to a ship or cargo by carrying a press of sail shall not be made good as General Average.'

MR. ATKINSON proposed as an amendment that the clause should be altered by adding the words, 'except in cases where such sail is carried to keep off a lee shore.'

DR. FRANCK. I second that. I believe that every one here will be prepared to vote for it. I shall make no remarks.

Mr. RATHBONE. I hope it will not be carried, for I think it lays down most dangerous doctrine.

Amendment put.

 For the amendment 3

 Against it, the rest.

Amendment rejected accordingly.

Dr. FRANCK. I propose that the words 'unless it be proved that it was of an extraordinary kind and actually necessary to save the ship and cargo from a common peril.'

JUDGE MARVIN. I will second that, so as to give the opportunity of voting.

Amendment put.

 For the amendment 1

 Against it, the rest.

The clause in its original form was then put to the meeting, and carried, there being only two votes against it.

THE CHAIRMAN. Section seven must now be read: 'When a ship shall have entered a port of refuge under such circumstances that the expenses of entering the port are admissible as General Average, and when she shall have sailed thence with her original cargo or a substantial part of it, the corresponding expenses of leaving such port shall likewise be so admitted as General Average, and, whenever the cost of discharging cargo at such port is admissible as General Average, the cost of re-loading and stowing such cargo on board the said ship, together with all storage charges on such cargo, shall likewise be so admitted.' It would be more convenient to put this in the form of two questions.

MR. BAILY. I have to move some amendments, for one part is left rather vague. The cargo left behind at the port of refuge should not pay any part of the General Average provided for by this section. Then I object to the word 'substantial.'

THE CHAIRMAN. With reference to the word 'substantial,' I may simply observe that that word 'substantial' is only calculated to raise questions where no questions need be raised. The 'cargo' means a substantial part. The word 'substantial' may raise many legal questions.

Dr. Rahusen. I will second the motion that the word 'substantial' shall be struck out. [Agreed to.]

The Chairman. Will you give me the words in writing that you propose to have added?

Mr. Baily. 'As regards the ship, the cargo re-shipped, and the freight on it.'

Judge Marvin. I second the adoption of the amendment.

Dr. Rahusen. Jettisoned goods must then contribute to it.

Mr. Baily. Yes, I think so, but I do not think it is necessary to say so. Jettisoned goods are included in every adjustment.

The Chairman. It is very intelligible.

Dr. Rahusen. I do not see any difference between the cargo re-shipped and that to be sold in the port of refuge; the one part ought not to be left out of the General Average, but it ought all to be treated on the same footing; the one should not come into a better position than the other. Again, in exempting any part of the cargo, you make the other part of the cargo the sufferer, as it has to pay a higher percentage upon the General Average.

Mr. Baily. The voyage is at an end as to that part.

Dr. Rahusen. Cargo sold is, then, in a better position than that which is re-shipped.

The Chairman. This is a proper and judicious amendment. The effect of it is to limit the clause very much more than as it stood before. Mr. Baily proposes to limit the contributions towards the reloading and outward expenses, so as to bring in as contributories only the ship, the cargo re-shipped, and the freight on it; that is to say, he would exclude, from contribution towards such expenses, the cargo which may be sold at the port of refuge. This is at present the question for your consideration.

Dr. Wertheim considered that Mr. Baily's amendment raised a very important question of principle. In his opinion, Mr. Baily's view was opposed to the true principle of adjusting. When cargo is sold at a port of refuge, on account of its having been damaged, the shipowner is already a loser, through no fault of his; because he does not—at any rate, does not according to most laws—obtain his full freight. Mr. Baily, acting on the English law, would make him receive no freight at all; very many laws give him only a *pro ratâ* freight. As the shipowner is thus a loser, by the sale of the cargo for the sole benefit of the owner of the cargo, it did not seem reasonable to make him also a loser by excepting the cargo thus sold from paying its share of the outward expenses. The duty of the captain was merely to carry the goods from one place to another. He had nothing to do with whether they were damaged, or with what might be the best way of disposing of it. He ought not, then, to be in this way a loser by the sale of it.

MR. HOPKINS thought all Dr. Wertheim's objections might be answered, but that the amendment was wrong in other respects.

MR. BAILY. I brought this forward merely as a verbal alteration, believing that the principle was admitted. If goods are left at a port of refuge the voyage is at an end as regards them. The goods sold on the spot are no further interested at all.

DR. RAHUSEN. Mr. Baily's amendment, I must say, is very objectionable in principle. It leads directly to this unfairness, that the remaining part of the cargo is made to bear a much heavier portion of the outward charges from the mere fact of the sale of the sea-damaged part. This sale augments the General Average very much as to the rest, which must lead to injustice.

DR. WERTHEIM. If a part of any cargo is sold at a port of refuge, is that cargo to be on that account exempted from paying its share of the General Average occasioned by the putting into port? If there is any loss of masts, spars and stays, and so on, is the owner of the cargo left at the port of refuge to bear no part of that?

MR. BAILY. Of losses sustained before arrival at the port of refuge; but not after.

DR. WERTHEIM. You are not consistent there, I think.

THE CHAIRMAN. The question is whether, if the expenses of entering a port of refuge are already by law the subject of General Average, the expenses of leaving the port shall be the subject of General Average also, and whether, after the expenses of entering the port have been incurred, where a part of the cargo is left behind, and then there are after-expenses in leaving the port of refuge, that cargo is subject to General Average as to those expenses; that is very intelligible; but that does not apply to your case. If the masts, &c., are cut away in leaving the port, Mr. Baily says that any goods left behind at that port ought not to be subject to General Average, because the voyage is ended as to them.

Dr. Rahusen. In England and on the Continent the practice differs.

Mr. Baily. When a ship goes into port a second time, owing to damage sustained after she left the port of refuge, would you say that any part of that second General Average should be paid by the cargo left behind?

Dr. Rahusen. That would not be right. There is a great difference between a case where the whole cargo is to be sold and a case where only a part is to be sold. Where only part is sold the ship is bound to proceed to her port of destination. It is the uniform practice on the Continent to deal with it all under the same head, which is quite contrary to Mr. Baily's proposition: it is a new principle, and I should not like others to be taken by surprise.

The Chairman. I speak with submission to you. I do not understand that in any country, in Europe or in America, if a ship puts into a port of refuge and discharges and then leaves the port of refuge, and in so doing incurs certain expenses, that any part of the cargo left behind contributes to that part of the expenses.

Mr. Engels. The goods sold contribute but not those left behind.

Mr. Baily. If any part of the cargo is so damaged that it is necessarily sold, it does not in this country pay any subsequent General Average.

Dr. Rahusen. That seems to form a very intricate question.

Mr. Baily. I refer to goods left behind because they cannot be carried on owing to their state; as, for instance, because they are heated owing to sea-damage.

Mr. Crusemann. I would propose to make some alteration to that effect; because, in some cases when goods are sold, as, for example, when they are sold to raise funds, there is the question of the making good its market value at the port of destination, and other matters.

Mr. Baily. I will put it in any more definite form that will meet the case.

Mr. Lowndes. There is a very great principle involved in this discussion. The real question is this: do you allow the outward port charges because they are the consequences of going in, or for some other reason? If you allow them on the former ground, then, in whatever manner you charge the inward port charges, in the same manner you should charge the outward. On this view there would be no absolute inconsistency in making the goods sold at the port of refuge contribute towards the outward port charges. This is, in fact, the view commonly held on the Continent, as appeared in our discussion by pamphlets. But others, who dissent from this view, hold that the outward charges should be admitted into General Average on a perfectly distinct ground, viz. that they are incurred for the purpose of continuing the voyage, and are therefore in themselves—not looking back to any previous act of which they may be considered as the consequences—incurred for the common benefit. On this view, it is clear that they are only incurred for the benefit of that portion which leaves the port in company with the ship. The portion left behind does not share this benefit, and therefore should not contribute. The present discussion will oblige us to select between these two views. My own opinion is, for the reasons given in the pamphlets, that both views are erroneous. The draft Bill was framed simply in conformity with the opinion of the majority of the members. Perhaps Mr. Bradford will inform us what is the practice in America; whether cargo sold on account of sea-damage contributes to outward port charges or not.

The Chairman. If goods are sold merely because they are of a perishable nature, and it is expedient to determine the voyage, and the goods derive no subsequent benefit from the voyage, it seems clear that they should not contribute towards the expenses outwards.

Mr. Baily. Would it meet Mr. Crusemann's objections to say, 'As regards the ship, the property which leaves the port of refuge in her, and the property which is allowed in General Average subject to events happening subsequently to the vessel's leaving the port of refuge?'

Dr. RAHUSEN. You will agree that by selling one part of the cargo you augment the expenses of the other part.

Mr. BAILY. The cargo that is left at the port of refuge has nothing whatever to do with subsequent accidents. Test it by the case of a sale of the whole of the cargo.

Mr. BRADFORD. I was asked to speak with regard to the practice of America. Our law and practice is to charge the expenses, so far as they benefit all property, upon that property so benefited; but if it becomes necessary to sell a portion of the cargo, if for any justifiable reason a portion of the cargo is separated from the rest, whenever that occurs that cargo is not liable to the General Average charge, but becomes liable to a special charge for anything that is done for that special interest. I do not think that I can state it any more precisely than that, so long as the interests are bound together, so long the charges are General Average. When for any justifiable reason one portion of the cargo becomes separated from the other, that portion is freed from the General Average, and becomes liable to the special average charges. Therefore, if a portion of the cargo is left in port for any reason, it is not liable to the expenses incurred by that vessel in going out of port; it is simply liable for the expenses that had occurred before it was separated from the rest of the cargo. No portion of the outward port charges can be put upon that portion of the cargo remaining in port.

JUDGE MARVIN. The whole expression of this section in the draft Bill, to my mind, is very far from being desirable. If the whole were to be reconstructed, reconsidered, rebuilt, I think the time of the meeting would be saved.

Mr. RATHBONE. We cannot hope that any body of men can reconstruct these sections at once.

THE CHAIRMAN. I think that, as we have to deal with this Bill in the order in which we find the clauses, it will be better to go through them as we find them this afternoon, and if the gentlemen who have so much assisted us by their presence will, between this and the morning, draw up any amended clauses, and will prepare themselves for the purpose, we can have a fair and ample discussion on the subject to-morrow.

Postponement put and lost.

THE CHAIRMAN. I will now read Mr. Baily's amendment as altered: 'Except that any portion of the cargo left at such port of refuge on account of its being unfit to be carried forward, shall not be called on to contribute to such corresponding expenses.' But we must postpone that for the moment and put the remainder of the clause.

The remainder of the clause was then carried unanimously.

THE CHAIRMAN. I will now put Mr. Baily's amendment.

Amendment put.

    For the amendment 10
    Against it 5

Amendment carried.

MR. DELEHAYE. I propose the following amendment, that the words, 'and consignees' commission,' be added after 'all storage charges on such cargo.'

MR. BAILY. Agents' commissions are allowed as General Average in England, in most cases; but there may be cases where the commission ought not to be admitted in General Average.

DR. RAHUSEN. I propose an amendment that, to the words 'on board the said ship,' be added, 'or on board such ship as may have been chartered by the captain, for his own account, in case the original ship shall have been condemned.'

JUDGE MARVIN. I second it.

MR. BAILY. If you put this charge to General Average, you must put the forwarding freight to General Average also. In some countries they do so, but is it reasonable?

MR. VAN PEBORGH. What is to be done as to fire insurance on the cargo whilst in the warehouse?

THE CHAIRMAN. That is a charge on the cargo.

MR. VAN PEBORGH. It will be just to put it as a General Average charge.

THE CHAIRMAN. If it belong to the cargo and ship.

MR. BAILY. Excuse me; it does not follow that all losses resulting from accidents which follow a General Average act are to be allowed. A loss by fire in a warehouse is not allowable in General Average, although the goods may be in warehouse by a General Average act; therefore the fire assurance should not be allowed in General Average.

Amendments withdrawn.

THE CHAIRMAN. We now come to the eighth section: 'When a ship shall have entered a port of refuge under the circumstances defined in section seven, the wages and cost of maintenance of the master and mariners, from the time of entering such port until the ship shall have been made ready to proceed upon her voyage, shall, subject to the provisoes undernamed, be made good as General Average. Provided that, if reasonable dispatch be not used in repairing or otherwise getting the vessel to sea, no allowance for wages or maintenance shall be made in respect of the time so improperly expended. Provided, also, that no allowance shall be made for wages or maintenance as above, in case the ship shall be condemned at such port as irreparable or not worth repairing, or in case for any other lawful cause the cargo, or a substantial part of it, shall not be reladen on board such ship for the purpose of further transport.'

MR. RATHBONE. I think that wages should not be allowed. I move the insertion of the word 'not,' making it 'shall not be allowed as General Average.'

Amendment not seconded.

Amendment lost.

THE CHAIRMAN. Is there any objection that clause eight should stand?

MR. BAILY. The general feeling in this country as to wages, &c. is that they should not be allowed at all on any principle; but I shall vote for the resolution, because shipowners in this country feel the exclusion of them to be a great grievance, and the exclusion of them is contrary to most of the continental codes. I think, therefore, we ought to concede to that extent. Underwriters argue that, if you allow the wages and provisions, you hold out an inducement to the shipowner to remain in port unnecessarily. But is it likely that any shipowner will allow his captain to remain in port merely for the sake of getting back the wages which he spends by remaining in port, when by so doing he loses the use of his ship during such unnecessary delay? The principle which excludes them is, I think, this. Everything allowed in General Average should be caused by a General Average act. Now, the expenditure is not caused in any way by a General Average act, but by the contracts with the crew. It is an expense incident to the General Average act, but not caused by the General Average act, and on that ground I exclude them on principle; but I shall vote for the proposition on the ground of expediency.

Clause carried unanimously.

THE CHAIRMAN. I think there is no substantial difference of opinion on this clause. What Mr. Baily has now said suggests to me this consideration. Whenever this Bill shall come before the House of Commons, this clause will in all probability be met with a very serious opposition. I would recommend to Mr. Baily and the other gentlemen that, when the bill shall come before the House of Commons, they should append to it such suggestions to the member of that House who brings in the Bill as may be thought necessary. That member could hardly be expected to make himself master of all the most important considerations of this question or to understand it so well as Mr. Baily and others here who have dedicated their lives almost to the subject. You should, therefore, prepare what the lawyers call a brief, or series of arguments, for the member who is to introduce the Bill to the House. We now come to the provisoes. The first proviso is almost the common law at present; therefore we may let this proviso stand.

The first proviso was carried unanimously.

On the second proviso being brought forward,

MR. CRUSEMANN proposed, as an amendment, that in place of the second proviso in the draft Bill, the following proviso should be substituted: 'Provided also that in case the ship shall be condemned at such port as irreparable, or not worth repairing, no allowance shall be made for wages and maintenance beyond the date of condemnation; and no allowance shall be made in case, for any lawful cause, the cargo, or a substantial part of it, shall not be reladen on board such ship for the purpose of further transport.'

DR. FRANCK seconded that amendment.

Mr. LOWNDES was opposed to the amendment. It appeared to him that, whatever might be the case when a ship went into port to repair damage and then resume her voyage, it hardly admitted of doubt that, when she went into port and was there condemned, her only object for going in must have been to obtain physical safety, and that the General Average, and consequently the allowance for wages and provisions, ought not to extend beyond the attainment of safety. The clause as it stood was framed as a species of compromise, and he thought a stand should be made on that point.

Mr. BRADFORD. On the subject of the provisoes, I agree with Mr. Crusemann. I think that wages and provisions should be allowed until there is a separation of the interest in the voyage. I do not think it will be right to say, when you go into port and discharge cargo, that because you find the ship damaged so much that she cannot be repaired, therefore no wages or provisions shall be allowed. I suppose gentlemen all agree that if a vessel goes into port and the cargo is discharged, the discharge of that cargo is a General Average charge?

Mr. BAILY. No.

THE CHAIRMAN. It has not been so considered in England; it might have been elsewhere.

Mr. BRADFORD. The master has no reason to suppose that the voyage is to be ended. The cargo is discharged, and when it is taken out, it is found that the vessel is so much injured that she cannot be repaired, except at a cost that is unreasonable. As to the English law that the expense of going into port is not General Average, there is the expense of pilotage and tonnage; upon whom does the expense fall?

Mr. BAILY. In practice all the expenses of discharging the cargo are put to General Average; and if I am asked, Is that right? I say, Certainly not. When I became an adjuster, I found the custom was to put the expense of discharging in such a case to General Average; and I follow the custom, but I do not therefore think it right. It is a charge which should fall either on the owners of the cargo or on the shipowner.

Mr. BRADFORD. I think it ought to be General Average on principle. I say that, so long as the community of interests exists, so long are the ship, freight, and cargo bound together by the contract, and just so long any loss or any expense should be General Average. When it is decided that the voyage cannot be completed, then the General Average ceases—so the wages and provisions ought to be considered in General Average.

MR. CRUSEMANN'S amendment was then put :—

For the amendment 10
Against it 8

The amendment was therefore carried.

THE CHAIRMAN. Although very much called for in other departments, I will again to-morrow take the chair if you desire it. Although the motion of the learned judge Mr. Marvin has been rejected, it will not prevent him from proposing any amendments that he and his friends may wish. Considering that this Bill, when put into a more technical and legal form, with reference to our statutes, will probably be submitted next session to the Houses of Parliament, we ought to be ready to give the fullest consideration to any amendments any gentleman may be disposed to make.

Adjourned till to-morrow at half-past ten.

September 28, 1864.—MR. WENDT *was called to the chair*.

The minutes of the last day's proceedings were read and settled.

MR. LOWNDES. This is the proper time to move any amendment to clause eight as it now stands, modified by the amendment which was carried yesterday.

MR. BAILY. The clause as amended is, to allow wages up to the date of condemnation. The objection to this amendment is as follows: In the case of ships condemned at distant ports, captains are afraid to act; they hand the matter over to their owners, and often there ensues a long discussion between the owners and the underwriters, which involves great delay. Mr. Crusemann's resolution makes the cargo contribute to the wages and provisions of the crew during this delay—that is, during a delay occasioned by a dispute between the owner of the ship and his underwriters. Is this Mr. Crusemann's intention?

MR. CRUSEMANN. Yes.

Mr. Baily. I think the allowance of wages should stop as soon as any dispute arises, otherwise it may lead to great abuses. The owner of the cargo has a right to say to the captain, 'You are the man dealing with me, I have nothing to do with the people in a distant country. You have the estimates before you, showing what it will cost to repair the ship, and you ought to be able to, and must, tell me at once whether you are going to carry on my cargo or not. You are not only going to put me to all the inconvenience and loss of my cargo, but also to make me pay the expenses of your crew during that delay.' This resolution not only entails on the owners of cargo the annoyance and loss of having their goods kept at a port of refuge, but also calls upon them to pay the shipowner's expenses during the delay.

Judge Marvin. This may be carried out by a little change in the phraseology. Let it be provided that the wages and provisions of the crew shall not be allowed in General Average beyond the time when the ship is condemned or ought to be condemned upon the existing practice. That, I think, takes in both ideas.

Captain Gourley. I think Mr. Crusemann's clause had better remain as it is.

Mr. Lowndes. Suppose the ship is condemned and the cargo not reladen, if we apply the first half of Mr. Crusemann's clause we should allow wages and provisions down to the time of condemnation; if we apply the last half we shall not do so.

Mr. Wendt vacated the chair, which was taken by Sir Fitzroy Kelly.

Mr. Lowndes read the amendment which had been put by Mr. Crusemann and carried.

The Chairman. The object is to bring the Average down to the time the ship is condemned. May we now consider the eighth section with all its amendments as complete?

Mr. Baily. I have to move the omission of the words, 'and no allowance shall be made in case,' to the end of the paragraph, because Mr. Crusemann's clause is inconsistent. If you take the first part of the clause you give the compensation up to the time of condemnation; if you take the last part you do not give any.

The Chairman. The clause has been adopted with a qualification which it is now proposed to omit. Mr. Baily proposes to omit from 'and no allowance,' &c. to the word 'transport.'

MR. BAILY. I also propose to add to the middle of the clause, after the words 'date of condemnation,' 'or the time when the ship ought to have been condemned on the facts of the case.'

MR. LOWNDES seconded the amendment.

MR. GOURLEY. That nullifies Mr. Crusemann's proposition altogether, and I hope he will not consent to it.

MR. RATHBONE. I trust that that amendment may be carried. The wages and provisions of the crew might be going on for a whole year perhaps, during the dependence of a question arising with which the owners of the cargo would have nothing whatever to do. It cannot be right to charge the cargo therewith in General Average.

The amendment was put and carried.

MR. LOWNDES. I have now to move that after the words 'beyond the date of,' be inserted 'discharge of the cargo,' in place of the words 'condemnation of the ship or the time when the ship ought to have been condemned on the facts of the case.' I believe that this would be a more thorough way of obtaining that which by the votes, as given, it appears that we all have in view. I cannot see any ground for making the cargo contribute to General Average for the wages and provisions of the crew after the time when the cargo has been discharged: from that point the cargo ceases to be interested in any way in the detention, or in what may take place as to the disposal, or in the proceeds, of the ship: the connection between the ship and cargo is at that point terminated. What I fear is that, if we should frame a Bill which can be attacked on general principles on one important point, we may run the risk of losing the whole measure. It is easy to frame a Bill, but we must have one which will command the approval of jurists and persons acquainted with the subject in different countries.

MR. RATHBONE. I beg to second that amendment.

MR. WENDT. Is the whole or any part of the principle of the clause involved in this?

MR. RATHBONE. It is a mere detail.

THE CHAIRMAN. It relates only to the maintenance of the crew in the port of refuge. The question is whether that is or is not to be allowed beyond the time of the discharge of the cargo; that is to say, if it is to be made the subject of General Average, whether it shall cease from the time of the discharge of the cargo.

Mr. CRUSEMANN. I think that the wages and maintenance ought to be paid up to the same time as the storage and other expenses of the cargo; the storage and other expenses of the cargo will be charged in General Average up to the time of the condemnation of the ship, and it is therefore proper that the shipowner should be placed in as good a position as the owner of the cargo.

The CHAIRMAN. The whole question is between the discharge of the cargo on the one hand, and the condemnation of the ship on the other.

Dr. RAHUSEN. The proposal of Mr. Lowndes is very objectionable. By that amendment, from the moment the cargo was discharged, until the day of condemnation, the wages and maintenance of the crew would not fall upon General Average, but upon the shipowner, for he could not recover them from his underwriters as Particular Average. That would be contrary to all the principles of law that I ever heard of, and will be thought very unjust. After the date of the condemnation of the ship you may leave it for the shipowner alone to pay all expenses, because he then may pay off the crew, but not till then.

Mr. BAILY. If a vessel is condemned at a port of refuge, I hold that the cargo is not liable for any of this General Average.

The CHAIRMAN. Will any gentleman point out the difference between the period of condemnation of a ship and the period of the discharge of the cargo: that really is the point, it is a point of time only : whether these wages, &c. are to be allowed down to the time of condemnation or to the time of discharge of the cargo. Let us then consider what that time is, and why the rule should be applied to the one time rather than to the other.

Mr. BAILY. We are so thoroughly acquainted with the distinction that I will only say a few words upon it. One of the first steps is to discharge the cargo; after that, the ship is examined and sometimes is found to be in such a defective condition, that the captain, if he were the owner, would say, ' I will not repair the ship.' Not being the owner, he writes to the owner and asks him what he is to do; the owner goes to the underwriters, and discussions ensue that sometimes occupy months. A considerable time in consequence elapses before the captain receives his instructions, and during the whole of this time the cargo is kept at the port of refuge. Mr. Crusemann says the General Average should not cease until the ship is condemned, but I prefer Mr. Lowndes's amendment.

DR. WERTHEIM. Mr. Lowndes's amendment is quite contrary to the principle of law as to General Average, which is that, between the ship, the cargo, and the freight, the confraternity of interest ceases when the ship is condemned: up to that time General Average ought to rule; after that time nothing ought to be allowed. When a ship is condemned, all the expenses made by and on behalf of the common benefit and interest ought to be paid for in General Average by all the parties interested in them. Mr. Baily and Mr. Lowndes are of opinion, one one way and one another. The only principle upon which to act I say is this: so long as the confraternity exists, and no longer, all disbursements made on behalf of the parties should be allowed. How otherwise can we say when it shall cease so as to render justice to both, and who shall tell the moment of the ceasing of the confraternity? The only definite point of separation is the date of condemnation. Then there is the warehouse rent, &c. to be considered.

MR. BAILY. I should not put the rent to General Average. I repudiate that principle altogether.

DR. WERTHEIM. It is said in the seventh section that when, in order to repair the damage done to the vessel, the cargo is discharged, the warehouse rent should be admitted into General Average; yet now we are told by Mr. Baily that, if the ship happens to be not worth repairing, the cargo, and not the General Average, ought to bear this charge. This distinction cannot be founded on any principle; the question is treated as a mere matter of expediency on the part of the underwriters. This should not be. I am, in this as in all other cases, strongly opposed to the replacing of principle by expediency, and as a lawyer especially so. This expediency can be twisted any way.

MR. ENGELS. I quite agree with Mr. Baily. When does this confraternity between ship and cargo cease? That is the whole question. I agree with Mr. Baily that, from the moment that the cargo is discharged, the allowance in General Average ought to cease. You cannot certainly make the cargo pay the expenses of the wages and maintenance of the crew until a reply can be got from the owners, a proceeding which might extend over four or five months; the captain ought to know what he is to do.

MR. CRUSEMANN. That the confraternity ceases at the very moment the cargo is discharged is not the right view of the case. I think it is not so; it may cease for a time, but it does not cease ultimately and positively until the ship is condemned; and so long as it has not definitely ceased I should say all expenses must be borne by all interested. The date of condemnation can be the only time when the interests are separated.

DR. FRANCK. I should wish to move as follows: That from the words 'or in case' the clause be altered thus: 'but in case for any other lawful cause the cargo, or a substantial part of it, shall not be reladen on board such ship for purpose of further transport, no allowance shall be made for wages or maintenance of the crew.' I beg only to observe that, as soon as the cargo is left behind in the port of refuge, from any reason, the port of refuge becomes the port of destination of the different interests, *i.e.* the ship, the freight and the cargo, and as in the port of destination the charges in question are not General Average, so they are not in the port of refuge which has become the port of destination. It is impossible not to see at once that the port of refuge does in such a case become the port of destination.

MR. CRUSEMANN. Up to the time of the condemnation nobody has a right to dispose of the cargo. The shipper cannot take it away, the captain is not excused from keeping charge of it for the purpose of transit. The confraternity of interests therefore does not cease till after the condemnation.

MR. LOWNDES. With regard to the argument of Mr. Crusemann there is a case that constantly happens, to which it would not apply at all. As soon as the cargo has been discharged, it is at once seen that the ship is so damaged that she cannot be repaired on the spot, or at any place in the neighbourhood, so as to convey the cargo forward; the cargo is then at once sent forward in other vessels; then comes the question whether or not it will be possible by temporary repair to bring the ship to some place where she can be repaired more cheaply—to this country or some other port. I assume that any port at which the ship could be repaired would be so distant that the voyage would be completely at an end, and there would be no obligation to go back to fetch the cargo. In the case which I have supposed—a case which has more than once actually occurred within my knowledge—the question, whether the cargo should ever be carried on in the ship, or not, was determined at the very moment when the cargo was discharged. The subsequent fate of that ship was a matter of the most absolute indifference to the cargo. Surely in such a case as that it would seem unreasonable to make the cargo contribute to the expenses during the time that it had nothing to do with the ship. It is no doubt a theory which can be defended, that there is a community of interests continuing so long as there is a reasonable prospect of carrying the ship and cargo on together; but no one can say that the community should continue beyond that time. It is simply when they are engaged in one common enterprise that the community exists, and when that enterprise ceases the community ceases with it. Then comes the question, how are we to determine when that moment has arrived? In the case which I just put, there was no difficulty; the moment was determined as soon as the cargo was landed. In other cases, the state of the ship and the consequent impossibility of repairing may not be known until a later period. Still this impossibility existed from the first; and, when once it is ascertained, we should treat the matter as if it had been known from the first. All these matters are treated upon the basis of the ultimate result. Whenever it was known it was a fact that the ship was a total loss, or was unfit to complete the voyage, from the moment when she received the damage. This is the way in which we deal with all questions of insurance. Suppose the ship were insured by a time policy which terminated on January 1, and the ship received her damage in December, but was not surveyed and found irreparable until February, would you say that the underwriters were not liable for the total loss? To apply that to the present question, the community of interest between ship and cargo, which results from their being liable to a common risk, exists no longer than until both are in safety. That community of interests which results from the contract to carry the cargo to its destination, exists no longer than until it has become impossible to carry the cargo on; and this impossibility depends, not on the time when the extent of damage is known, but on the time when such damage takes place. I confess that I do regard with very great regret, and very great fears for the success of our undertaking, any alteration of this section, even in the provisoes. I feel that the prospect of carrying the Bill in this country is sensibly diminished. The section, with the provisoes, was, by those who framed it, intended as a species of compromise. By far the largest concessions have been made to the views of foreign countries; for, every English member believes the allowance of wages to be an erroneous course; and I regret to see the majority here moving step by step further in this direction. If gentlemen will press their objections to the full extent, the result will be, that the difficulties we shall have in this country will, I fear, be very much augmented. I regret what has already been done by carrying it on to this extent, and I shall indeed regret if we are induced to go still further.

MR. CRUSEMANN. We cannot vote against our convictions.

MR. ENGELS. We think we have made concessions in every possible way.

DR. WERTHEIM. Mr. Lowndes advocates the matter on the part of the underwriters; the concessions are to them. If the principle of allowing wages and provisions is correct, it should be carried out consistently. You should go all the way, not go half a mile, and then stop and hesitate. We must have a rule that we can act on. When are the wages, &c. to be paid, and when are they to cease? We must know as if we were consulting our watch, or else we shall not know how we stand.

MR. LOWNDES. I have said that I dissented entirely from the principle. The pamphlets and correspondence which show what our views are, the meeting are in possession of.

DR. RAHUSEN. Every nation has its own way of considering these questions. I would suggest that the first clause of this section remain, and then we should leave out altogether the provisoes and amendments which have sprung out of them; that we should pass the first part of the section only.

THE CHAIRMAN. This may be put as a separate motion afterwards. I must first take the votes on Mr. Lowndes's amendment.

Question put.
    For 5
    Against 8
Rejected.

THE CHAIRMAN. Dr. Rahusen may now make any remarks he thinks proper.

DR. RAHUSEN withdrew the motion to withdraw the provisoes.

MR. BAILY. I am sorry to hear that, for I must, in that case, move it myself.

THE CHAIRMAN. It will then stand thus: 'It is now moved by Mr. Baily that the provisoes be withdrawn, and that the clause shall remain.'

MR. ENGELS. I second it, because I think we ought to make concessions to English usages.

MR. WENDT. I am only afraid, if we pursue this course, we shall not be doing our work properly, or as we were sent to do it. We shall only have half-dealt with the question, for we shall leave it undetermined what is to be done in cases where the ship is not repaired.

MR. LOWNDES. In answer to Mr. Wendt, the real question is this: Will you have uniformity in all respects? or will you, by endangering the measure, run the risk of not obtaining uniformity at all? Let us not despise the work because 'it may be in some respects imperfect. If we can carry a measure which will produce uniformity on the leading points, the very fact of our doing so will tend indirectly to promote uniformity in the details which we are now compelled to leave open.

MR. CRUSEMANN. I only wish to say that those two provisoes made by the committee who drew up the Bill were certainly thought important enough to be brought into the Bill. I am sorry now to hear the contrary.

MR. LOWNDES. They were thought desirable as they stood originally, but not as they stand now, when they require us to do the direct contrary.

MR. BAILY. I would point out to the gentlemen present that

the essential part, namely, that affecting putting into port, which is an everyday occurrence, has been carried in favour of foreign views, and what we are considering now affects cases of condemnation only, cases which are of comparatively rare occurrence. We propose to leave it an open question, as you will damage the Bill by passing these provisoes.

Mr. WENDT. It is a rare case, and yet Mr. Baily lays great stress upon it.

Mr. BAILY. It is the last straw that breaks the camel's back.

Mr. BRADFORD. After the remarks of Mr. Baily I think we had better concede the point. I think the principle of allowing wages and provisions is very clear. The expenses of wages and provisions, like all other expenses, should continue just so long as the contract continues, or rather until it is broken up. It is not broken up, in my judgment, until the facts are ascertained. When the facts are ascertained, and the interests are not again to be united, then there is a cessation of the General Average charges. At the same time, if our English friends think that the success of this measure is in a great degree dependent on this article, I would concede it, as we have already settled the question of going into port. I would let the other go, because the object is to come to something universal; although it is contrary to every decision of which I am aware in the Courts of America.

Mr. CRUSEMANN. After the remarks I have heard I concede it also.

Motion put and carried without a division.

JUDGE MARVIN proposed the following amendment: 'To strike out the whole of the seventh and eighth sections,' and substitute the following: 'If, on account of the damage suffered by the ship in the course of the voyage, whether of a Particular or General Average nature, the sickness or mortality of the crew, the derangement of the stowage of the cargo, or other the like accidents of the sea, it becomes prudent and judicious in the master to deviate from the course of the voyage and go into a port of refuge, the expenses of entering such port, the port charges, the unloading of the cargo, the warehouse rent or storage thereon, the expenses of reloading the cargo on board, the wharfage or dockage of the ship while unlading and reloading, the wages and provisions of the crew, from the time that the ship shall bear up to enter such port of refuge until the time when the ship can again be got ready to resume her voyage, the expenses of leaving the port, and other incidental expenses necessarily incurred by the master for the common benefit, shall all be made good in General Average, in all cases in which the master shall resume and prosecute the voyage with the cargo on board. In case the voyage shall be abandoned in such port of refuge, the interests shall be deemed to be dissociated by such abandonment, and the General Average expenses shall cease thereon, and each interest shall thereafter bear its own expenses.' He objected against the seventh section as it stood, that it did not, in its first clause, at all specify what were the circumstances under which the expenses of entering a port of refuge should be admitted in General Average, and yet made all the subsequent clauses dependent for their operation upon this first clause; so that the section started with uncertainty and reasoned all through with uncertainty. He wished to do that which the clause as it stood had not done, viz.: to define the leading principle from which all was to follow. There were on this subject two principles between which they had to choose. By the law of Spain, and perhaps of some other countries, the mode of treating these expenses was dependent on whether the original cause which lead to the bearing up for a port was itself an accident or a sacrifice made for the common good. If the ship bore up because the masts had been cut away for the common safety, then all the expenses of going into and coming out of the port, and the crew's wages during her stay there, were treated as General Average. If, on the other hand, the master bore up for a port because the masts had been carried away by accident, that is, by Particular Average damage, then all these expenses incidental to the bearing up were treated as Particular Average. This was one intelligible principle; but it was not the principle adopted in England, France, Holland, the United States, and the great majority of maritime communities of the world. The principle most generally held was, that, whether the original cause of the damage were sacrifice or accident, so long as the putting into port was properly resorted to for the common good, under a necessity arising during the voyage, the consequent expenses were to be treated as General Average. That was evidently the principle intended to be embodied in the Bill, and he regretted that this intention had not been expressed more clearly. Brevity had been aimed at in the draft, at the expense of perspicuity. He had provided for all that in his amendment. It might be difficult to define all the possible cases; questions might be raised, for example, if the putting in were unnecessary, or if the ship were not seaworthy at starting; but so far as the thing could safely be defined, he thought he had done so. With regard to the latter portions of his amendment, it would be readily understood. He thought that the interests of ships, freight, and cargo might upon principle be considered as associated together—as being in a condition of 'confraternity' (which was a good phrase, though not often used in that sense by lawyers) up to the time when the master abandoned the voyage. The learned Judge then entered upon a comprehensive view of the principles of General Average, with especial reference to the question which had been much discussed in the pamphlets—whether the 'common safety' or the 'common benefit' were the true test of General Average. He held that both these conflicting theories might be reconciled by one more comprehensive. The 'common safety' theory seemed to be the better adapted to the case of sacrifices, such as jettisons or the cutting away of masts; but when it was a question of expenditures, as in the present case, it was necessary to resort to the more extensive theory of 'common benefit.'

The amendment was seconded by Dr. Wertheim, and put to the meeting.

    For the amendment 5
    Against it 10

The amendment was therefore negatived.

THE CHAIRMAN then read the ninth section, viz.: 'Damage done to cargo in the act of discharging it at a port of refuge shall not be admissible as General Average in case such cargo shall have been discharged at the place and in the manner customary at that port with ships not in distress.'

Mr. Baily moved the omission of the words 'in the act of,' and substitute the word 'by' before the word 'discharging.'

This was agreed to unanimously.

Mr. Delehaye thought that if the cargo was discharged for the common good, and was damaged in consequence, such damage should be treated as a sacrifice. He wished for some explanations on this head; and particularly, why insert the phrase 'in the manner customary at that port'?

Mr. Baily. I will explain to you why it is worded in this way. I am one of those who hold that damage done by a forced discharge of cargo at a port of refuge is General Average in principle; but the allowance of it opens the door to so much fraud and injustice that I, and many others who think that it ought to be admitted in principle, have, on the ground of expediency, agreed to exclude it. We do not, however, think that this practical objection applies to the discharge of vessels on shore and rocks or sandbanks; or to any discharge in a manner unusual at a port of refuge; and, therefore, we limit the exclusion to the case of an ordinary forced discharge at a port of refuge.

The clause was then put and carried, only one vote being given against it.

The Chairman. We now come to the tenth clause. I think it will be more convenient to read the first part of the first clause of the section first: 'The contribution to a General Average shall be made upon the actual values of the property at the termination of the adventure, to which shall be added the amount made good as General Average for property sacrificed,' without reference to the deduction. I put the question, that this portion of section ten to the word 'sacrificed' shall be adopted.

Carried unanimously.

The Chairman. Perhaps we had better now take the deduction here expressed: 'Deduction being made, from the shipowner's freight at risk, of that portion of the crew's wages and the port charges of the ship, the liability for which is contingent upon the earning of such freight.' The question is put that this part of the clause be adopted.

Mr. Baily. I have two amendments to propose—first, as to

the words, 'that portion of the crew's wages and the port charges on the ship, the liability for which is contingent upon the earning of such freight.' This clause has been worded rather with reference to the English law. The laws in different countries vary as regards the liability to the crew for wages, some making the wages payable up to the date of the loss of the ship; some holding that when there is no freight there are no wages. I propose, therefore, to avoid the difficulty by taking an arbitrary amount of the freight as the contributory value of that freight; and I suggest that we take three-fifths of the freight to contribute in all cases.

THE CHAIRMAN. Then the amendment is to this effect: 'Deduction being made from the freight of two-fifths of such freight, in lieu of crew's wages and port charges on the ship,' and you omit the rest of the original paragraph.

MR. RATHBONE. I beg to second that amendment.

MR. VAN PEBORGH was in favour of the amendment. The great argument in its favour was that it was the only practical method of producing uniformity. While the laws of different countries varied with respect to the payment of the crew, any rule of contribution based on that payment would necessarily be variable also. He wished, however, that the clause should be altered so as to lay down a rule touching the contribution of freight paid in advance. It ought to be clearly defined whether the shipowner or charterer should contribute in respect of such advances.

THE CHAIRMAN. We must confine ourselves at present to the question of two-fifths of the freight in lieu of crew's wages and port charges.

MR. LOWNDES preferred the clause in its original form, because they then would stand on a clear principle, as to which all might agree. To take an arbitrary proportion seemed to be a retrogression rather than an improvement. When a voyage was retarded, the freight might be entirely absorbed in wages and expenses. Why not have a rule which would meet this case? Enough would have been done towards uniformity if a uniform principle were adopted, though the application of it might vary in its details.

Mr. Baily's amendment was then put.

 For the amendment 7
 Against it 3

Amendment carried accordingly.

A discussion then took place as to several details of the deductions to be made from the contributory value of the freight. In order to avoid the disturbing effect of *pro ratâ* freight, as allowed in some countries, Mr. Baily proposed that no deduction for wages should be made from *pro ratâ* freight. This, however, was negatived. It was agreed that passage-money at risk should be put on the same footing as freight. And, on the suggestion of Mr. Crusemann, a clause was added to provide for the deduction from the contributory value of all charges incurred subsequently to the arising of the claim for General Average.

The clause, in its amended form, was then carried unanimously.

The Chairman. We now come to the last clause of the section. This is as follows: 'In case the amount to be made good shall exceed the aggregate of contributory values, computed as above stated, such aggregate shall, in the first instance, be taken towards satisfying the General Average; and the excess of the General Average shall then be apportioned as if the ship and the entire cargo on board or at a risk at the time of doing the act or measure which has given rise to the General Average had reached the port of destination free from damage.'

A discussion arose, and some alterations were agreed to in the wording of this clause, after which

Dr. Wertheim moved that the entire clause be rejected. He would simply cut it out, and substitute nothing in its place. It would be in vain to let stand part of the clause, when the whole clause is entirely against all the principles of law. When you go to the ancient law on the principle of General Average claims, you will find that no man is allowed to lose more than the entire value of his property which has been saved. Yet here, in 1864, we are called upon to depart from that good old principle. I am quite sure that America, Holland, Sweden and Belgium will keep to the true principle. When I have lost all my property, my purse, my money, and my dress—when I have no money, and even no pockets at all—then you are not satisfied to leave me in this forlorn condition, but you want me to pay something more. The only way left to me would be to raise the money from the underwriters, and the underwriters would not take the risk under such circumstances.

Mr. RATHBONE. I have often paid more than a hundred per cent., and a very uncomfortable state of things it is.

Dr. FRANCK seconded Dr. Wertheim's amendment.

Mr. LOWNDES. I will endeavour to answer the illustration of Dr. Wertheim, as to his pockets being emptied. If a shipowner has no other funds, and has lost all his property by the shipwreck, there is no way which has yet been made known of extracting anything more from him; but if he has property, not perhaps in that ship, but in another ship, or of any other description, it does not appear so clear that he ought not to pay the debts incurred in the unsuccessful endeavour to save his ship. If Dr. Wertheim were to happen to have his pocket picked, although he might lose all the money in that pocket or about his person, yet, if he chose to hire a detective to attempt to recover his property, although that attempt might prove unsuccessful, he would probably pay that detective for his services. In the same way a ship may be on the shore and in a position that makes it uncertain whether she will ever be got off. The owner deliberates as to employing a steamer to recover her; if he knows that he will be paid for the expense to be incurred whether the attempt is successful or not, the probability is that, if there is a reasonable prospect of getting the ship off, he will send down a steamer, and in this way much property may be saved that otherwise would not. A shipowner of any sense would be very careful indeed how he sent down a steamer, under such circumstances, for the benefit of underwriters, if he were to run the risk of having to pay for it out of his own pocket. The law of General Average supposes a reasonable expenditure and judicious conduct. It may be said, 'You have incurred expenses foolishly, beyond the probable value of the advantage to be derived, and acted unwisely in doing so'; but, if that could be established the parties would be excused from all liability. Supposing the measures to be taken in good faith and judiciously, so that any one would say it was for the benefit of all, why should the loss be thrown upon one person, more energetic than the rest, who takes the measures intended for the benefit of all?

JUDGE MARVIN. I will ask Dr. Wertheim a question on this. Did I understand him rightly to say that by the law of Holland the owner of the ship and the owner of the cargo cannot be called upon to lose any more than the whole ship and the whole cargo, that is, that the total loss is the boundary and extent of their liability? Then, what would they do in such a case as this? A vessel puts into a port of refuge, where various expenses are incurred for the purpose of enabling the master to complete the voyage. He has the cargo to unload, has warehouse rent to pay, and a variety of expenses are incurred. The vessel, after making the necessary repairs, proceeds on her voyage. There has been no bottomry bond given or taken; the master has obtained money by a bill on the owner of the vessel, or perhaps the owner of the vessel comes to the port of refuge himself and pays all the expenses, and every one is satisfied. Now then, the vessel starts on her voyage, sinks at sea, and goes to the bottom. I wish to submit to Dr. Wertheim this question: the shipowner having advanced this money, not only for his own benefit but also on account of the owner of the cargo, and all these expenses being General Average, the cargo having gone to the bottom, has not the shipowner, in some shape or other, a remedy against the owner of the cargo for the money he has advanced?

DR. WERTHEIM. When the shipowner or captain acts in that way, he is obliged, according to clause 334 of the Dutch code, to insure all that which he has disbursed on account of the common interest, because it is a new contract. If he is willing to take all risk for his own account, he is free to do that; but he is obliged, if he means to claim it again, to insure all the cost for repairs; in that way he has a remedy.

MR. BAILY. Suppose there are no insurance offices or underwriters, how does he manage then?

DR. WERTHEIM. In Holland he can do it; he can go to any insurance office or underwriter for that purpose.

DR. RAHUSEN. The shipowner will receive a bill of exchange drawn upon him: he can do as he pleases about accepting it; he need not to accept it unless he can insure it. If he insures it, he is safe. If he does not accept the bill, he is safe too; for if the ship be lost, he has only to abandon the ship and freight, and then he is clear. All that is quite simple.

Mr. BAILY. The flaw here is, that you render it almost impossible for a captain at a distant port to raise money by bill on his owners. He can never be secure of his bill being accepted, and no agent on the spot could prudently take a bill. In the generality of cases shipowners could not protect themselves by insurance under such circumstances. Besides, owing to telegrams, &c. it is not an unusual thing to hear of a loss at the same time as of a necessity for an insurance. Men will not run such risks when they advance money for other people.

JUDGE MARVIN. The proposition of Dr. Wertheim is sound as to sacrifices; if your goods are thrown overboard, there is an end of the matter, you ought not to pay any more. The same as to stranding; the same as to sacrifices, such as cutting away masts. The loss of the thing is the end of it; but when the master of the ship advances money for your benefit when in a port of distress, you ought to pay it. So that, as to expenditure made in a port of refuge, it appears to me there should be some provision made whereby he must be repaid where some of the property is lost, and the property saved is insufficient to pay the expenses.

Mr. ENGELS. In some instances it may not be easy, or even possible, to insure a vessel; in some places they will not insure all vessels. This is the risk which any shipowner has to consider; but there is a great deal of inconvenience and hardship in obliging me to pay all my property away because you choose to run me into debt. We have had in Belgium a shipowner of a certain vessel called the '———,' a small vessel, who was obliged to sell her off, even the beds, and was reduced to poverty. I am speaking of a shipowner who only has a ship or two. We say, 'You may have the liberty of abandoning the property,' and let the lender of the money look out for himself; he can protect himself by a loan on bottomry. That is the principle of the law laid down in Belgium, Holland, and elsewhere.

Mr. BAILY. The effect of the clause, as it stands, may be illustrated thus: If a steamer, the hire of which is 1,200*l.*, is sent down to save 2,000*l.* worth of property, which by casualties, after, or unknown at the time when the steamer is sent, is reduced in value to 1,000*l.*, that 1,000*l.* is credited to the 1,200*l.* expenses that have been incurred, and the balance, 200*l.*, is paid by all the property which it was intended to save, *i.e.* the 1,200*l.* I send down a steamer to save A and B's goods. A's goods are totally lost, and B's goods are saved. The proceeds of B's goods are put to the credit of the expenses, and the excess of expenses over the proceeds is paid by A and B. B cannot be made to pay the whole expenses, and you must repay the party who has incurred the expense.

MR. RATHBONE. Mr. Engels, you would not make B pay the expenses of A and B. The captain is simply the agent of the owner, and, therefore, making the captain responsible is making the owner responsible; is not that the case in Belgium as in England?

MR. ENGELS. He is only liable to the extent of the value of the vessel in that country.

THE CHAIRMAN. In England the expenses that are necessary are allowed.

MR. RATHBONE. These expenses have been incurred, and must be borne by somebody.

THE CHAIRMAN. Are you to go upon the owner of the property for the deficiency which the cargo saved will not meet?

MR. BAILY. Perhaps we had better withdraw the clause altogether.

THE CHAIRMAN. It is put to the committee that this latter part of the clause shall be struck out.

Carried unanimously.

MR. BAILY. There was one amendment postponed, at the end of section eight. I now propose to add, 'Except that any portion of the cargo left at such port of refuge on account of its unfitness to be carried by the ship, shall not contribute to such General Average.'

THE CHAIRMAN. Is it the pleasure of the meeting that these words shall be added?

MR. CRUSEMANN. I do not know that the word 'unfit' would be the proper expression there.

The Chairman. I do not think you will find a better word to express the meaning intended.

Mr. Crusemann. There may be goods remaining behind, because the ship cannot take them, the stowage not being in a state to take them. If you have a ship capable of stowing only 400 bales of cotton, it is impossible to bring 400 bales more in her, and therefore some part of the cargo must remain behind, and there these expenses would be apportioned on those goods remaining behind.

Mr. Baily. I do not wish to go into that.

The Chairman. It might be made to stand thus: 'either the unfitness of the goods to be conveyed or the unfitness of the ship to carry them.'

Mr. Lowndes. This proposition, as amended, is contrary to that proviso about which we had such a fight in the morning; it is undoing what was then done.

Mr. Baily. I will alter my amendment as proposed by our Chairman, and it will then stand thus : 'Except that any portion of the cargo left at such port of refuge on account of its unfitness to be carried by the ship, or the unfitness or inability of the ship to carry it forward, shall not contribute to such General Average.'

Mr. Lowndes was so unwilling by a side wind to defeat the arrangement come to in the morning, when the foreign members, after carrying their amendment, withdrew it out of deference to the wishes of the English members, and consented to leave the allowance of wages in the case of condemnation an open question, that he felt obliged to oppose Mr. Baily's proposition in its amended form. In cases of condemnation this clause would always come into operation through the words 'unfitness or inability of the ship to carry forward the cargo;' and thus in all these cases there would be no allowance of crew's wages in General Average. This was returning to the state of things first negatived, and then left an open question, in our discussion this morning.

The Chairman. Mr. Baily put forward last evening the matter now in hand, and it was understood that this was agreed to. Mr. Baily undertook to reframe the proviso. At first Mr. Crusemann seemed to have some objections. Mr. Baily has now corrected his amendment so as to meet his views. This addition applies solely to cases where the vessel goes into the port and out of the port with her cargo, and merely introduces an exception when some part of the cargo is left behind from having been sea-damaged. The words were added merely to define this, that the cargo which has finished its career does not contribute to the subsequent expenses, any more than to masts cut away in the future progress of the voyage. I think with perfect confidence it applies to the case in which the ship proceeds upon the voyage, not where the ship has been condemned; condemnation, therefore, is out of the question.

MR. BAILY. Mr. Lowndes is under a complete misapprehension as to the effect of my clause. It must be taken in connection with the rest of the sentence, which limits its operation to the case in which the ship 'shall have sailed from the port of refuge with her original cargo, or part of it.'

MR. LOWNDES. The principle contended for by Mr. Crusemann was this, that the communion between ship and cargo continued, even when the cargo was not reladen, beyond the discharge of the cargo. This view prevailed, but it was agreed to leave the matter open. Mr. Baily's clause certainly appears to contradict this view. Thus it is undoing our morning's work.

THE CHAIRMAN. I will now put the question whether this shall be adopted by the meeting or not.

For the resolution 11
Against it 2

The amendment carried.

MR. LOWNDES. In consequence of what took place at our sitting yesterday, I have drawn a clause in this form, to be made the eleventh section of the Bill: 'In every case in which a sacrifice of cargo is made good as General Average, the loss of freight, if any, which is caused by such loss of cargo, shall likewise be so made good.'

JUDGE MARVIN. I second that.

Carried unanimously.

JUDGE MARVIN. I wish to move that in the first section the words, 'or other wood cargo,' may be introduced.

The Chairman. I cannot interfere with the business of my predecessor in this chair. Section one and section two have been passed. If that which is now proposed has not been fully discussed, that would be a reason for my abstaining from introducing any alteration now, because it ought not to be introduced without further discussion.

The Chairman. I believe I may now announce to the meeting that their discussions upon the Bill, which it is proposed should be submitted to the Legislature, are closed. Before separating, I feel that, having so far performed my duty in presiding over your deliberations down to the settlement of the Bill, although I might conclude with merely thanking you for the willingness with which you have honoured my humble efforts to assist you, I should only have performed a part of my duty if I were to stop here. A great deal has yet to be considered and determined upon, and proceedings to be resolved on and adopted, before any practical results shall follow the deliberations in which we have now been engaged, and it is with a view to your assistance, to facilitate the efforts you have to make to give effect to this Bill, and to the exertions you have in common made to settle this question, that I have presided at this meeting. It will have been observed that I have myself cautiously abstained from expressing any opinion upon the different clauses which have come under consideration and been discussed. I have done so for two reasons; in the first place, upon a subject so complicated, a subject not merely involving questions of law, upon which, perhaps, I could have been prepared at any moment to express a definite opinion, but involving questions of expediency and public policy, not only throughout Great Britain but throughout the world, I have abstained from forming any opinion until I shall have referred to those who have made themselves masters of the subject, especially until I have referred to the treatises and works which have been published, and to which my very learned friend Judge Marvin has alluded. But there is another reason why I abstain. Sooner or later—I hope sincerely soon and not late—this Bill or some such Bill will come under the consideration of the Legislature. Having the honour to be a member of that Legislature, I would hold myself free and independent to take that course upon the Bill, or upon particular clauses of the Bill, which may appear expedient, not now only, but under the circumstances which may exist whenever that Bill may come before the Legislature. It is upon these grounds only that I have refrained from expressing any opinion myself; but so many gentlemen are here assembled who are perfectly adequate to form a sound judgment, that, had I been inclined to indulge in any opinion, I should have thought it unwise to express such an opinion. Let us consider, for a few moments, what are the steps about to be taken. If a Bill of this character be submitted to the House of Commons, or either branch of the Legislature, and it comes clothed and supported by the sanction and approval of the great majority of the mercantile community of the country: if the member who brings it forward can assert that it has received the approval of this and that Chamber of Commerce, and of a body of commercial persons who were in possession of the sentiments of the whole inhabitants, for example, of the towns of Liverpool, Manchester, Bristol, Glasgow, and Hull, and other great commercial communities, then, though there might be differences of opinion as to details, yet, if the House were satisfied that this Bill truly and adequately represents the opinions, the principles, and the wishes of the great majority of the mercantile community, the Bill is almost certain to receive the sanction of the Legislature. If, on the other hand, this Bill were to be the subject of great difference of opinion, such as would lead to much discussion in the House of Commons, the members for Liverpool insisting, perhaps, on one set of clauses, and those for Hull, for Glasgow, or Bristol for another set of clauses, so that the House of Commons might be ignorant as to whether they were or were not meeting the wishes of the great majority, then it would be impossible that the Bill could pass. Let me, therefore, recommend that the Bill should contain such provisions as the great majority of that community are willing and disposed to have passed and made into law. I think you may be pretty sure, after the discussion which has taken place, that what the great majority of those assembled here have deliberately approved of will receive the sanction of the commercial community. Let me advise every member to see that he has the sanction of the great commercial world in this matter. You must go to our Legislature, supported by the sanction and the approval of other countries also. It would be in vain for Great Britain to make an Act of Parliament in relation to the subject of General Average, already dealt with by the common law and acted upon in our courts, unless you were pretty sure of its becoming likewise the commercial law of the world, or that it was tolerably sure to receive the approval of the chief commercial countries of Europe and of America. I think you may well begin in this country, because, while I highly respect the Legislatures of many other nations, I think, considering the familiarity we in this country have acquired with every branch of commercial law, that, if the British Legislature were to pass an Act of this nature, it would become a precedent or an example which would be readily and immediately adopted, chiefly and first, I may hope, in the United States of America, that great maritime nation, and also in France, Germany, Spain, Belgium, Holland, and other great commercial communities of the world. I will suppose, therefore, that you have received the sanction of the other maritime and commercial nations of the world. Then will come the question—and here I have a few words to address to you which may be of some use to you—then will come the question how you are to bring forward this Bill in the Legislature. In the first place, you would have to engage some counsel at the bar, accustomed to the preparation of Acts of Parliament and drafts of Bills. If I may use such an expression, the substance, to the very letter, of this Bill as agreed, must be religiously adhered to, and not departed from in the least, but the phraseology must be altered in some immaterial instances; while the substance is almost religiously maintained, the form must be put into the usual form of an Act of Parliament. After this the Bill, thus put into shape, must be introduced into the House of Commons. To whom, there, are you to entrust this important office? One method is, to introduce the Bill by means of the Government of the country. It is in that case brought forward as a Bill which has received the sanction of the Government, which a member of the Government will introduce. Another method is, to have the Bill brought forward by an individual member of Parliament, who may or may not receive the support of the Government and of the House. If you can obtain the support of the Government, by all means do so, for then your Bill is almost sure to pass. If a member of the Government should bring forward a Bill, which has received the sanction of the commercial interests of Great Britain, and of the chief commercial nations of the world, it would pass through the House of Commons and the House of Lords with a great deal of support and no substantial opposition, and no material variation or modification might be made in it. If you can, therefore, do so, by all means obtain the sanction of the Government. The mode of doing that would be for a deputation to proceed to the President or Vice-President of the Board of Trade, and request him to confer with the Prime Minister of the crown, and to announce to him that the Bill had already received the sanctions to which I have alluded, and he might be induced to bring it forward in his place in Parliament, when it would be pretty certain to pass without opposition. It may be, however, that the Governmen, though perfectly willing to support such a measure, might not think it was within their province to bring it forward, especially if much pushed and pressed by other business, and then will come the task, and by no means an easy one, but a very delicate and difficult matter—to consider to what member or members you will entrust this Bill. Let me resort to the exhaustive process. You must not offer it to any individual member of the Government. If he represented a mercantile constituency, and could safely undertake it, he might be obliged, from some difference of opinion of his constituents, and likewise in the same way if one of his colleagues wished him to do so, to alter it, and thus endanger the measure. Neither should I recommend you to entrust the Bill to any one who, having been a member of a past Government, is likely to be a member of a succeeding one in case of a change in the Administration; and on this ground I must exclude and except myself. On the breaking up of the present Government, it might be that I should become a member of the following Government, and I might find myself embarrassed by the opposition of some of my colleagues. Avoid, therefore, a member of the Government, or a member of a past Government likely to be a member of a future Government; and then consider to what description of persons you may entrust the Bill. It should be entrusted to at least two members, one of whom should be a mercantile man, and representing a mercantile constituency. Then he must have the aid and the support of another member, who should be a member of the bar—a learned, and experienced, and accomplished lawyer. Without the advocacy of two gentlemen of that description—a mercantile man able to take his part in the debates that must ensue during the progress of the measure, and an able and experienced lawyer, able to take an active, prominent, and continual part in every stage of the passing of the Bill, there would be no hope that your Bill would succeed. Then you must take care to secure the support of as many members, mercantile and legal also, from both sides of the House as possible. There is always a danger arising in bringing in a Bill under the sanction of the members of one side of the House only. If the proposer and seconder and all the promoters of the Bill are on one side of the House, there is a danger of raising suspicion as to the party character of the Bill, which may be hazardous to its success. Whether myself a member of the Government, or out of the Government, if I shall be a member of either House of the Legislature when this Bill is brought forward, you may feel perfectly assured I shall not forget the business we have gone through to-day and yesterday, and you may rely upon every exertion I can make to give effect to your wishes.

Mr. Wendt. I think we all have to thank the Chairman for the kindness with which he has now addressed us, and the willingness and diligence with which he has aided our deliberations on this occasion.

Mr. Lowndes. I am quite sure we are all perfectly unanimous in expressing the extreme obligation which we all feel ourselves under to Sir Fitzroy Kelly. He has come to aid us, not considering it one of those things which were to be got through as a troublesome and irksome task, as many would have found it, but has taken a lively interest in the business of the committee, has given us advice of the greatest value, and has also throughout our discussions most materially benefited our cause. We are most warmly and deeply indebted to him; and though I can but inadequately express the feelings of the committee on this occasion, I trust he will accept our sincere thanks for the service he has rendered to us.

THE CHAIRMAN. I return my best thanks to yourselves; and, in taking my leave of you, can very sincerely assure you, not only that I have taken a most lively interest in all that has passed here, but also shall continue to feel a pleasure in the remembrance of these proceedings for a long time to come, and more particularly in having made the acquaintance of so many able and distinguished persons, whose acquaintance I hope I shall continue to enjoy for many years.

The Chairman withdrew.

Mr. Wendt was called to the Chair.

JUDGE MARVIN proposed the following resolution: 'Resolved that the thanks of this meeting be recorded to our Chairman, Sir Fitzroy Kelly, for his able and distinguished conduct while presiding over this committee.'

Seconded and carried unanimously.

The International General Average rules framed at the above congress are, therefore, as follows:—

Jettison of Deck Cargo.

I. A jettison of timber or deals, or any other description of wood cargo, carried on the deck of a ship in pursuance of a general custom of the trade in which the ship is then engaged, shall be made good as General Average, in like manner as if such cargo had been jettisoned from below deck.

No jettison of deck cargo, other than timber or deals, or other wood cargo, so carried as aforesaid, shall be made good as General Average.

Every structure not built in with the frame of the vessel shall be considered to be a part of the deck of the vessel.

Damage by Jettison.

II. Damage done to goods or merchandise by water which unavoidably goes down a ship's hatches opened, or other opening made, for the purpose of making a jettison, shall be made good as General Average, in case the loss by jettison is so made good.

Damage done by breakage or chafing, or otherwise from derangement of stowage consequent upon a jettison, shall be made good as General Average.

Extinguishing Fire on Shipboard.

III. Damage done to a ship and cargo, or either of them, by water or otherwise in extinguishing a fire on board the ship, shall be General Average.

Cutting away Wreck.

IV. Loss or damage caused by cutting away the wreck or remains of spars, or of other things which have previously been carried away by sea peril, shall not be made good as General Average.

Voluntary Stranding.

V. When a ship is intentionally run on shore because she is sinking or driving on shore or rocks, no damage caused to the ship, the cargo, and the freight, or any or either of them, by such intentional running on shore, shall be made good as General Average.

Carrying a Press of Sail.

VI. Damage occasioned to a ship or cargo by carrying a press of sail shall not be made good as General Average.

Port of Refuge Expenses.

VII. When a ship shall have entered a port of refuge under such circumstances that the expenses of entering the port are admissible as General Average, and when she shall have sailed thence with her original cargo, or a part of it, the corresponding expenses of leaving such port shall likewise be so admitted as General Average; and whenever the cost of discharging cargo at such port is admissible as General Average, the cost of reloading and stowing such cargo on board the said ship, together with all storage charges on such cargo, shall likewise be so admitted. Except that any portion of the cargo left at such port of refuge, on account of its being unfit to be carried forward, or on account of the unfitness or inability of the ship to carry it, shall not be called on to contribute to such General Average.

Wages and Maintenance of Crew in Port of Refuge.

VIII. When a ship shall have entered a port of refuge under the circumstances defined in Section VII., the wages and cost of maintenance of the master and mariners, from the time of entering such port until the ship shall have been made ready to proceed upon her voyage, shall be made good as General Average. Except that any portion of the cargo left at such port of refuge on account of its being unfit to be carried forward, or on account of the unfitness or inability of the ship to carry it, shall not be called on to contribute to such General Average.

Damage to Cargo in Discharging.

IX. Damage done to cargo by discharging it at a port of refuge shall not be admissible as General Average, in case such cargo shall have been discharged at the place and in the manner customary at that port with ships not in distress.

Contributory Values.

X. The contributions to a General Average shall be made upon the actual values of the property at the termination of the adventure, to which shall be added the amount made good as General Average for property sacrificed; deduction being made from the shipowners' freight and passage-money at risk, of two-fifths of such freight, in lieu of crew's wages, port charges, and all other deductions; deduction being also made from the value of the property of all charges incurred in respect thereof subsequently to the arising of the claim to General Average.

XI. In every case in which a sacrifice of cargo is made good as General Average, the loss of freight, if any, which is caused by such loss of cargo, shall likewise be so made good.

MR. LOWNDES, the secretary of the section, proposed the following resolutions, which were seconded and carried :—

1. That a short report of our proceedings be at once drawn up by the secretary, and presented to the council of the Social Science Association, with a request that it be entered on the minutes of the Association; and that a copy of the same be furnished to each member of the committee.

2. That a further report of the proceedings be afterwards drawn up by the secretary, printed, and circulated.

3. That the draft Bill as now amended in congress, ought, in the opinion of this congress, to be the basis of International General Average Law.

4. That in order to carry out this object, associations should be formed, or other measures taken in each of the countries represented in congress, and in other countries where practicable, for the purpose of causing this Bill to become the law and practice of such country.

5. That this end should be pursued through the Legislatures of each country where practicable, and also, pending legislation, by means of clauses to be introduced into bills of lading and charter parties.

6. That the clauses recommended for this purpose be the following: 'All claims for General Average to be settled in conformity with the International General Average rules, framed at York in 1864.'

7. That, for the execution of these resolutions in each of the places represented in this congress, the following representatives be appointed in the name of the York Congress:—

Holland.—E. Driebeek, LL.D.; E. N. Rahusen, LL.D.; J. Wertheim, LL.D.

Belgium.—Théodore J. Engels; Edward van Peborgh.

Maine (State of).—J. R. Bradford.

New York (do).—Hon. Judge Marvin.

Bremen.—Edward Crusemann, LL.D.

Hamburg and Lubeck.—Charles H. H. Franck, LL.D.

England.—H. J. Atkinson, Hull; L. R. Baily, Liverpool; E. Temperley Gourley, Sunderland; R. M. Hudson, Sunderland; W. T. Jacob, Liverpool; W. J. Lamport, Liverpool; Richard Lowndes, Liverpool; D. W. Mackechnie,

Glasgow; P. H. Rathbone, Liverpool; E. E. Wendt, London.

France.—Jules Delahaye.

Portugal.—

Russia.—G. Kamensky.

Denmark.—S. Gram; Jacques Suenson; Edward Thune.

8. That the representative or representatives of each country or place, as named above, shall charge himself or themselves with the task of organising an association or committee for such place, or taking such other measures as in his judgment shall be best conducive to the carrying out of the purposes laid down in the foregoing resolutions.

9. That each local association, organised as above, or the representative himself in the absence of an association, shall make an annual report to the council for the time being of the Social Science Association, setting forth what progress shall have been made in his or their district; and that such annual reports shall be continued until the task assigned to such local association or representative shall have been completely accomplished.

10. That in case any country or place, not here represented, shall hereafter wish to join in this movement, the council for the time being of the Social Science Association shall have power to appoint a representative or representatives for such country or place, who shall then have equal powers with the representatives here appointed.

11. That the cordial thanks of this congress are given to the National Association for the Promotion of Social Science, for the very valuable services which the Association has rendered to the congress.

12. That the objects of this congress having been attained, this congress and the 'International General Average Committee' be now dissolved.

A vote of thanks to Mr. Wendt was proposed and seconded, and carried unanimously, wherewith the labours of the congress terminated.

The general interest and approval with which the result of these labours were received in the mercantile and underwriting circles of the principal centres of trade could scarcely have been better proved than by the public discussions which followed the appearance of the very able reports which most of the delegates to the York Congress addressed soon after their return to their respective constituencies.

But, remarkable enough, neither such expressions of approval, nor the almost annual request which the Associated Chambers of Commerce, on the motion of the Hull Chamber, was for a number of years in the habit of addressing to the Board of Trade in order to obtain imperial legislation on the basis of the York rules, led to any practical result, and, if it is recollected that the Foreign Office not only formally sanctioned, but actually forwarded to H.M. Consular Officers abroad, official invitations for such commercial or underwriting bodies as might be established within their district, in order to induce them to send delegates to the York Congress, it is not easy to understand why no Government action was taken after the result of deliberations which were presided over by no less persons than the Judge of the Probate Court and Sir Fitzroy Kelly, who soon after became Lord Chief Baron of the Court of Exchequer, who were both no mean authorities on the subject under consideration.

In this unsatisfactory state the question rested for more than ten years, till, at the third annual Congress of the Association for the Reform and Codification of the Law of Nations at the Hague in 1875, one of its members drew attention to the desirability of considering the laws of General Average.

The fourth annual report of the same Association's conference, held at Bremen, states that on Tuesday, September 26, 1876, the subject upon the order of the day was General Average.

Mr. Theodore Hach, of Bremen, in a comprehensive paper, after giving an account of the Congresses of Glasgow (1860), presided over by Lord Brougham, London (1862), presided over by Sir Travers Twiss, and York (1864), presided over by the Lord Chief Baron of the Court of Exchequer of England, Sir Fitzroy Kelly, and alluding to the difficulties presented by inveterate practice and long-established custom, maintained that the Association ought not as yet to attempt to draft a complete code, but should agree to the following three propositions:—

1. That such a code is required.

2. That the principles asserted in it are right and generally recognised.

3. That the code is practicable.

He then entered into details as to the principles which he considered the true ones and moved the following resolutions:—

1. The fundamental principle of General Average is clearly and tersely expressed by the following words in the German General Mercantile Law: 'All damage done to ship, or cargo, or both, by the master, or by order of the master, with the object of saving both from a common danger, and all consequential damage resulting therefrom, and the expenses incurred thereby, are General Average; and General Average is borne by ship, cargo, and freight.'

2. The following are corollaries to this principle:—

(a) A temporary separation of ship and cargo during the voyage in consequence of circumstances inducing General Average does not terminate or suspend their common liability to General Average.

(b) Such damage only is to be deemed consequential as is caused by the original damage, not such as only follows accidentally.

3. This is the basis upon which an International Law of General Average ought to be founded; but, as there is no prospect of this object ever being attained without the initiative of the different Governments and Legislatures, the first efforts of the Association should be directed towards influencing those bodies.

4. A peculiarly suitable groundwork for the discussion of such

a law is to be found in that portion of the German General Mercantile Law which deals with General and Particular Average. Further valuable materials are contained in the reports of the three International General Average Congresses which have been held in England.

5. Provisionally, in order to obviate, as much as possible, the evil effects of the existing discrepancies in the laws of General Average, it is desirable that average statements made at the port of destination of a ship with the proper formalities and in accordance with the laws there obtaining should be everywhere recognised by insurers as binding.

6. That a committee be appointed by this meeting for the purpose of organising and keeping on foot the agitation necessary to give effect to Nos. 3 and 5 of these resolutions.

Mr. J. P. Schneider, of Bremen, followed with a paper upon General Average, in which he endeavoured to show that General Average rested entirely upon the principle of voluntary sacrifice. He went on to remark that it had long been the wish of the merchants and insurers of all maritime nations to see the laws of General Average assimilated, since the contributions to General Average were regulated by the laws of the country in which ship and cargo parted company, and very often had to be paid in different countries. The assimilation of the laws of Insurance was of less importance, since it was left to the choice of the insurer whether he would extend his insurance to foreign property and foreign countries; but that, too, was very desirable, since it constantly happened that insurer and insured belonged to different countries. The following, he said, were the principal points which called for reform:—

1. *Expenses of the ship during its detention by Governments and other higher powers.*—By the laws of some countries these expenses were apportioned as General Average. In the speaker's opinion it was wrong to assume that the expenses caused by the detention of ships carrying cargo always fell upon one party. Very frequently, when the cargo, by reason of the enforced detention, arrived too late for the market which was contemplated when it was shipped, the owner of the cargo suffered a greater loss than the shipowner, since a fall in prices could not be insured against, whereas the

shipowner could protect himself to any extent he pleased. Each party ought, therefore, to bear his own loss when a ship was forcibly detained.

2. *Expenses in ports of refuge.* — The above remarks were likewise applicable to port dues and wages and cost of maintenance of the crew when the ship was obliged to put into port on account of Particular Average or to procure necessaries for the voyage. If the expenses were apportioned as General Average, the insurer, who contracted to indemnify the shipowner against all losses, was released. When the cargo had to be landed for repairs, the expenses of landing and reloading the cargo ought to be borne by its owner, since the cargo ought not to stand in the way of the shipowner who was ready to do his duty.

3. *Damage done by collision.*—If, in a collision, the master of neither ship could be shown to be at fault, it seemed just that each should bear his own damage; if one only was at fault, he, of course, must alone be answerable; if both, neither ought to be able to claim compensation from the other. This was recognised by the German law, which was, however, silent as to the claims of the owners of cargo for damages in respect of collisions. In the speaker's opinion, the owners of cargo ought to look to the master only, to whom they had entrusted their goods, and the German Supreme Court for Mercantile Cases was wrong when, in a recent case, it decided in favour of the opposite view.

After further expressions of opinion from SIR TRAVERS TWISS, MR. O. SJÖSTRÖM, of Bremen, and others, MR. H. H. MEIER, at the conclusion of some remarks which he offered, moved, and it was resolved :—

'That à committee be appointed to consider the subject of General Average; and that Mr. Hach's resolutions and Mr. Schneider's paper be referred to that committee.'

The same report further mentions that on Thursday, September 26, 1876, the conference proceeded to the nomination of committees, and the following elections took place :—Committee upon International General Average Law : Sir Travers Twiss (*Chairman*), Dr. A. Hindenburg, of Copenhagen, and Messrs. E. E. Wendt, J. Wertheim, of Amsterdam, H. Th. Hach, and D. Murray. *Secretaries*: Mr. H. D. Jencken and Mr. R. S. Tredgold, of London.

This committee was during the following months considerably strengthened by the addition of most of the gentlemen who had in previous years evinced an interest on the subject, and, as soon as a decision was arrived at to meet in the autumn of 1877 in Antwerp for the purpose of trying seriously again to agree upon International General Average Rules, the committee used its best endeavours to secure a large attendance on that occasion, so that when, on Thursday, August 30, 1877, the meeting of those interested in the subject took place in the Town Hall of Antwerp, not less than sixty-eight gentlemen had assembled either as delegates of the most important mercantile and underwriting institutions in the world, or as on their personal account connected with the discussion.

SIR TRAVERS TWISS, being in the chair, called upon me to open the proceedings by delivering my address, which I did in the following words:—

The executive council of the Association having, since the Hague Congress in 1875, considered the subject of the laws of General Average worthy of its attention, the discussion which took place at last year's Bremen Congress on the matter led not only to the appointment of a standing committee on General Average at the headquarters of the Association, but to the formation of several local committees in different parts of the world.

As the result of the united exertions of the members of these committees the assembly here present may be taken, and, I am sure, we all sincerely hope not only that a practical international law of General Average may result out of our discussions, but that, after it has been agreed upon, the Governments whose flags are principally interested in the questions here to be considered may take the necessary steps in order to secure its enactment by the different Legislatures.

For although the executive council is well aware that if the principal shipowners, merchants, and their respective underwriters agree among themselves as to the principles upon which, in their joint maritime adventures, questions of General Average are to be treated, such agreements would be of legal force, but as they must be renewed for each maritime adventure separately, in a binding form, between the parties to it, the more convenient course would be to obtain their enactment at law by the authority of the different Governments, and some of them having evinced a not inconsiderable interest on the subject, we may hope that no insurmountable obstacles would be in the way to attain this desirable end in a reasonable time.

The transactions of the first International General Average Congress at Glasgow 1860, or the second at London 1862, and of the third at York 1864, being unfortunately out of print, reference as to the history of the previous endeavours to obtain uniformity in the international law of General Average must here be made to the well-known work of our friend Mr. Richard Lowndes, 'The Law of General Average,' second edition, and to the second edition of my ' Papers on Maritime Legislation.'

There it will likewise be found recorded that, in spite of repeated attempts made by the Associated Chambers of Commerce to prevail upon Her Britannic Majesty's Government to make the rules which were passed at the last congress in York (1864) a subject of imperial legislation, nothing has been done; and as the manner in which these so-called 'York Rules' were generally received, and have been reviewed by competent authority, has convinced the executive council that no better starting-point for discussion could be offered, it was decided to invite you to enter *seriatim* into the discussion of their different clauses.

But before you do so, let me allude to the reports which have been presented by the local committees of Bremen, Gothenburg, and Philadelphia.

The former document suggests the desirability of taking the well-known clauses of the German maritime law as a starting-point for our deliberations, but keeping in view that the York rules are a compromise between the parties who considered the 'common safety' principle as sufficient for a basis of the international General Average law, and those who insisted upon nothing less than that the *common benefit* of the maritime adventure should be the guiding principle of it—the Bremen committee discusses the York rules very fully, and submits in what form they should be amended in order to be brought into conformity with the German maritime law.

And, bearing in mind that the executive council, or rather those of its members upon whom the management of the affairs of all matters relating to General Average have devolved, owe an expression of opinion to their Bremen friends as an acknowledgment of the trouble they have kindly undertaken in the joint cause, I think it my duty on this occasion to make the following observations:—

As far as I recollect, there were certainly two reasons for the York Congress in not following the German law, and in omitting to place at the head of the York rules the definition of what is meant by a General Average act. The first was, that it was not easy to embrace in a few sentences all that it would have been considered necessary to express under this head; and the second was, that none of the definitions hitherto either enacted in foreign laws, or contained in the well-known authorities, did meet with general approval.

And the executive council will be glad to have your opinion whether you see any objection to our acceding to this part of the Bremen proposal and putting at the head of the international General Average Act law the combined Arts. 702 and 705 of the German law, which would then run as follows:—

'All damage done to ship or cargo, or both, by the master or by his orders, with intent to save both from a common danger, as also the consequential damages resulting therefrom, and the expenses incurred for the same purpose, are General Average.

'General Average is borne by ship, freight, and cargo in common.

'Average distribution takes place only when ship as well as

cargo, and both, either altogether or in part, have really been saved.'

The proposals then following, viz.: To make enactments: as to how the values are to be ascertained of any sacrifices made for the common benefit; how the contributory values are to be taken; whether the rights of claimants for General Average sacrifices are to be secured in any particular manner; and how the contributions to General Average are to be guaranteed—nay, if you think fit, be settled according to the usages of the port where the average statement is to be made up, as they hardly involve any question of principle.

But I think you will concur that with great propriety the port of destination, or the place where, in consequence of a General Average act, the maritime adventure is terminated, could be fixed upon as the place for the adjustment of the General Average, provided the parties interested do not agree upon any other course.

Such proviso has become the more necessary, as in some Eastern parts of the globe the custom of charging enormous commissions for making adjustments has lately induced the parties ultimately liable for General Average contributions to insist upon their being drawn up in some other place than the port of destination, and subject to this proviso, the Bremen proposal is recommended to the favourable consideration of the congress.

A reference to the report of the Bremen delegate to the York Congress, our late lamented friend Crusemann, would have convinced the Bremen committee that upon the consideration of no other part of the York rules more time was spent than upon the rules VII. (port of refuge expenses) and VIII. (wages and maintenance of crew in port of refuge), and it remains to be seen whether the discussions which must here take place on these most important subjects will lead to a more satisfactory working of these two rules.

But there is one observation in this part of the Bremen report which calls for a remark.

The most flagrant cases of leaving part of the cargo behind in ports of distress have occurred not—as here suggested—because the ship was overloaded from the beginning, but in consequence of cotton having been screwed into the ship's hold in conformity with the usages of the original port of loading, and from inability in the port of distress to restow it in the same manner.

The suggestion in the Bremen report that only the value of the repairs as *estimated* at the end of the voyage shall be deducted in order to arrive at the contributory value of the ship, may at first sight recommend itself to the favourable consideration of the meeting, but so many practical difficulties may be expected from the adoption of this suggestion that I am inclined to think this meeting will not recommend any alteration of the tenth rule.

Under the heading of 'Articles which might eventually be used as a compromise to English views'—under which term the York rules are apparently mentioned—the Bremen report consents to the wording of Rule V. (voluntary stranding), but suggests the propriety of enacting that damage done by defending a ship against enemies or pirates, and the expense of ransoming a ship after capture by enemies or pirates, should be made good in General Average —to which scarcely any objection can be raised. The same will be found with respect to their proposal to add to Rule I. (jettison of deck cargo): 'Provided that this rule applies only to such vessels as are expressly constructed and fitted up for such trade in such a way that the deck cargo does not cause any extraordinary risk to the navigation.'

The further suggestions under this head, namely, (*a*) that the contributory value of freight should not be reduced to less than one-half of the gross freight; (*b*) that any loss arising to cargo-owners out of the shipowner's inability to provide for his share to a bottomry bond should be rateably distributed among them; and (*c*) that in case of detention by *force majeure* the crew's wages and provisions should be dealt with as General Average, will undoubtedly give rise to some interesting discussions, so that I need not do any more in this place than call attention to them.

I come now to the recommendation in the Bremen report to reconsider the fourth rule (cutting away wreck), and I beg to express the hope that this recommendation will not be insisted upon, for this rule was passed in conformity with the well-known dictum of one of our most celebrated Judges, that the cutting away of that which, being in a state in which it cannot be saved, is already virtually lost, and moreover encumbering the navigation of the vessel, is therefore not such a sacrifice as to give a title to contribution.

The report of the Swedish committee draws very prominently our attention to the enactment in their law that no jettison of deckload is allowed in General Average, unless effected in order to lighten the vessel when aground; and if we take into consideration that this law is in existence in one of the countries which have most of the vessels trading under their flag which are especially built and fitted for carrying large deckloads, the principle here laid down is undoubtedly worthy of our most serious consideration.

The further suggestion that in case the voyage ends in a port of refuge no other expenses but those for entering the port, and for the maintenance of the crew till such resolution is arrived at, are allowable in General Average, appears self evident, and not requiring a special enactment.

The final suggestions in the Swedish report relating to the contributory values of ship, cargo, and freight will undoubtedly have the full consideration of the meeting, especially so far as it relates to the observation that the valuations of vessels are generally put lower than they ought to be, a calamity which, according to my own experience, can only be rectified by insisting in valuations made by appraisers who are not only competent, but sworn to be impartial.

The report of the Philadelphia committee, or rather the report of the committee on Adjustments of the Board of Marine Underwriters in that city, and addressed to the said Board, opposes the first rule (jettison of deck cargo) altogether, because deck cargo interferes—in their opinion—with the navigating and general management of the ship, endangering the safety of the cargo under deck, and because the act of jettison alone secures the earning of freight by the shipowner.

The report approves of Rules II. (damage by jettison), III. (extinguishing fire on shipboard), IV. (cutting away wreck), V. (voluntary stranding), VI. (carrying press of sail) entirely, but suggests to Rule VII. (port of refuge expenses) that as any portions of cargo which may have been left behind in a port of refuge have equally benefited with the rest by putting into port of refuge, they should not be exempted from contribution to General Average, and further suggests to Rule VIII. (wages and maintenance of crew in port of refuge) that such allowance should not only be made from the date of entering the port of refuge, but from the bearing away for that port, repeating at the same time the objection raised under the previous rule with respect to the exemption of cargo left at port of refuge from General Average.

Rule IX. (damage to cargo in discharging) is opposed because of the inability to see any difference in the method of discharging under the master's discretion.

The Rules X. and XI. (contributory values) are approved of, but an addition is suggested to the former—that even in the event of loss after departure from a port of refuge an apportionment in General Average of all expenses, with the exception of the wages and maintenance of the crew, should take place; a proposition which is not likely to obtain the assent of this meeting.

My reason for thus going more fully into the arguments upon which the resolutions of the Philadelphia report as stated are based is, that our friends there are not represented among us by a special delegate, whereas we have the satisfaction of seeing in this meeting delegates from Bremen and from Gothenburg, who, I am sure, will take care that their views shall be properly pressed upon the meeting. Before concluding, I ought to mention that the Executive Council has to thank Mr. Joh. Phil. Schneider, of Bremen, for the 'Rules for the adjustment of claims for General Average, and for averages from collision proposed for universal adoption;' but as the York rules had been previously suggested as a basis for our deliberations, the executive could not do more than circulate Mr. Schneider's rules and submit to the meeting, to consider how much of them could be used for the improvement of the York rules.

May our deliberations lead to a successful issue of an international General Average law!

THE CHAIRMAN then suggested that the York rules should be taken as a basis of discussion, but before the sense of the meeting thereupon could be ascertained, Mr. F. B. B. NATUSCH (one of the delegates from Lloyd's) rose and handed in the following letter:—

To the Chairman of the Meeting of the Association for the Reform and Codification of the Law of Nations.

AVERAGE LAW DEPARTMENT.

Lloyd's: August 1877.

Sir,—The Association for the Reform and Codification of the Law of Nations having invited the committee of Lloyd's to send representatives to the meeting at Antwerp, where the question of General Average is to be the subject of discussion, Messrs. F. B. B. Natusch and Joseph Hillman have been appointed by the committee as a deputation to represent them on that occasion, with Captain Henry Montague Hozier, the secretary of Lloyd's.

At the same time the committee think it right to place before the Association their views upon the subject, and the views which those who represent them will support.

There is a strong feeling in this committee that the differences which exist in various countries upon this subject would be best met by abolishing General Average altogether. Possibly this cannot now be done; and, if so, the committee consider that, so far as English practice is concerned, any difference should be met by curtailing, not by enlarging, the English rules.

The sacrifice of a part to avoid an impending peril was the foundation of General Average, and was the very essence of any claim. This ingredient should still form the basis of any claim, and without this basis the new element of common benefit should not be allowed to have any place.

From the fact that the York rules are to be adopted as a basis for discussion, it is clear that no return to first principles can be expected from the Antwerp meeting, for in the opinion of the committee those rules extend considerably, both in principle and amount, the area in which General Average may be recovered, and the attempt to establish uniformity is carried out solely by introducing into the law of England cases of General Average which are allowed abroad, but not in England, and which the committee consider most objectionable.

The committee think it right to bring these views to the attention of the Association, that it may be understood they are averse to any proposal for assimilating General Average which is based upon extending in any manner the English law, instead of reducing, both in principle and amount, the cases in which it can be claimed.—I have the honour to be, Sir,

Your obedient Servant,

(Signed)   GEORGE J. GOSCHEN,
Chairman of Lloyd's.

After the General Secretary had read the letter and the emotion caused by its contents had a little subsided,

MR. PH. H. RATHBONE (Chairman of the Liverpool Board of Underwriters) stated that he did not think that the position taken up by Lloyd's corporation was in any way justified; the doctrine and practice of General Average being of universal application, he could not admit the practicability of any other course than to discuss any amendments which might be suggested for the improvement of the York rules.

MR. JOHN GLOVER (Ex-Chairman of the General Shipowners' Society in London) thought that, in order to simplify the proceedings, the delegates of Lloyd's should be desired to explain the reasons which induced that body to send a letter of so serious a character.

MR. T. HILLMAN (one of these delegates) thereupon rose and explained that, in their view, General Average had become such an unbearable weight to commercial transactions that it would be for their benefit if it could be altogether abolished, and he considered himself the more justified to urge this view as everyone nowadays insured everything, so that the underwriter really becomes liable for whatever happened on the voyage, and it was immaterial to him whether it was paid in the shape of General or of Particular Average, or whether it was paid as expenses for the ship or for the cargo. He also criticised from a moral point of view the very prevalent tendency to speculate on the admission of certain items into General Average and the probability of causing jettisons by the overloading of vessels. He alluded further to the great delays and the heavy expenses which were caused by the adjustment of General Averages. He wound up his remarks by declaring his conviction that the evil of General Average was not a necessary one, and that the policies of insurance were quite sufficient to settle the different questions arising under this head.

MR. LAWRENCE R. BAILY (Representative of the Steam Shipowners' Association of Liverpool) observed that, although he might concede the correctness of the facts as stated by Mr. Hillman, he could not agree that the arguments brought forward by that gentleman, and which principally concerned England, could have any influence in considering the question whether it was advisable to frame 'International General Average Rules.' He did not believe it possible to abolish General Average altogether, and in defending his point of view he gave an example respecting the expenses in a port of refuge.

DR. E. N. RAHUSEN (Delegate of the Netherland Handels Maatschappij and the Shipowners' Association of Amsterdam) expressed his belief that the General Average customs would last longer than Lloyd's itself. He remarked that Mr. Hillman's allusion to jettisons caused by the overloading of vessels was inopportune, as in such cases no claim for General Average could be substantiated. He mentioned some other cases in which allowances in General Average would not take place. With respect to the long delays, he observed that they arose not in making the apportionment, but in examining the facts which had given rise to the case and in collecting the documents from the different parties interested. It was, moreover, not exact, certainly with regard to Holland, to say that all property was generally insured, and therefore the institution of General Average could not possibly be done away with.

MR. MANLEY HOPKINS stated that, although he and two of his colleagues (who had unfortunately been prevented from appearing) had been delegated to attend this meeting by the Average Adjusters' Association in London, he had to reserve to his clients the power to ratify or not to ratify the result of the deliberations at which this meeting would ultimately arrive. He was well aware that International Conventions could only arrive at results by mutual concessions of its delegates, who must have been instructed how far to go, and he was therefore highly interested as to the results he would be able to report to his colleagues.

MR. H. H. MEIER (President of the North German Lloyd of Bremen) was of opinion that the meeting should pass over the letter of Lloyd's to the order of the day as indicated by the President, viz. discuss the York rules and the concessions which could be made in order to arrive at distinct rules.

MR. JOHN GLOVER (Ex-Chairman of the General Shipowners' Society in London) did not concur in the extreme view the committee of Lloyd's intended to take upon this question, but suggested that the reasons given in the communication now under consideration should be used for the purpose of reducing not only the expenses, but also the items to be qualified as admissible in General Average as much as possible.

After a very lively discussion as to the future course of proceeding, in which the President, SIR TRAVERS TWISS, suggested that Mr. Goschen's letter should be entered on the minutes, MR. NATUSCH wished it to be understood that the committee of Lloyd's had only in view the prevention of the future development of the present system of General Average. MR. LOWNDES mentioned that, as Lloyd's, by sending three delegates to this meeting, had a perfect right to express their opinion, the passing to the order of the day was not intended to show any hostile feeling towards Lloyd's; whereupon it was unanimously resolved 'That the said letter should be entered on the minutes of the conference.'

The discussion on the letter from Lloyd's having thereby terminated, MR. H. H. MEIER formally proposed: 'That the York rules should be taken as a basis of discussion for this meeting.' This resolution was almost immediately adopted, after having been seconded by MR. R. LOWNDES, of the Liverpool Chamber of Commerce. This latter gentleman then proceeded to analyse and discuss the meaning of the first York rule, which runs as follows:—

RULE 1. *Jettison of Deck Cargo.*—A jettison of timber or deals, or any other description of wood cargo, carried on the deck of a ship in pursuance of a general custom of the trade in which the ship is then engaged, shall be made good as General Average in like manner as if such cargo had been jettisoned from below deck.

'No jettison of deck cargo other than timber or deals, or other wood cargo, so carried as aforesaid, shall be made good as General Average.

'Every structure not built in with the frame of the vessel shall be considered to be a part of the deck of the vessel.'

MR. LOWNDES advocated the adoption of this rule. DR. RAHUSEN, of Amsterdam, and MR. WINGE, of Christiania, together with some English speakers, having taken part in the debate on different sides, MR. MEIER, of Bremen, remarked that he reserved to himself the right to move an amendment in the event of Rule I., which he wished neither to oppose or support, being adopted. MR. CUPIER, of Newcastle, MR. HACH, of Bremen, MR. JACOBSEN, of Copenhagen, and SIR TRAVERS TWISS, President of the General Average Committee, examined from various points of view the principle at the bottom of the rule and the diverse eventualities which might present themselves. MR. J. LANGLOIS agreed with the opponents of the rule, because it is too difficult to prove what portion of the deck cargo has been voluntarily thrown overboard and what portion has been swept away by the sea.

MR. RATHBONE then moved that the first York and Antwerp Rule should run thus: 'No jettison of deck cargo shall be made good as General Average.'

DR. RAHUSEN seconded the motion. MR. AXEL WINGE, however, proposed as an amendment the addition of the words: 'Except in case of jettison to save the vessel.'

This amendment was seconded by MR. JACOBSEN, but lost by a large majority. Mr. Rathbone's resolution was thereupon submitted to the meeting and carried by 26 votes to 10.

The meeting of the committee broke up at six o'clock, adjourning till the next day at ten.

On August 31 the sitting was resumed. Sir Travers Twiss was in the chair, and was supported by Messrs. E. E. Wendt, Meier, Engels, Peborgh and Rand Baily, the Honorary Secretary of the Antwerp committee. After the formal business had been dismissed and Mr. Rand Baily had placed upon the table the further correspondence and papers, the discussion upon Rule I. was resumed by MR. RATHBONE, who was followed by MR. LOWNDES, MR. JACOBSEN, and MR. CAPPER. With reference to the word 'structure,' MR. NATUSCH defined what in his opinion ought to be considered the frame of an iron ship.

DR. RAHUSEN then submitted an amendment which ran as follows: 'That cargo laden in any structure not built in with the frame of the vessel shall be considered to be deck cargo.'

The amendment, which was seconded by MR. HILLMAN, having been advocated and opposed on various grounds by different members of the committee, was finally rejected without a division.

The rule as it then stood was now put by the Chairman, that: 'Every structure not built in with the frame of the vessel shall be considered to be a part of the deck of the vessel.'

MR. BROWN, of Hull, made some technical observations hereupon which were not approved by the auditory. DR. WERTHEIM read an extract from the report of the labours at York, in which Mr. Baily supported the paragraph which he was now desirous of suppressing. MR. BAILY retorted that he had taken this line of action precisely because of the difficulties that have presented themselves. MR. LOWNDES saw no difficulty in the interpretation of the word 'frame,' and proposed the maintenance of the word in question.

Dr. Rahusen's amendment: 'That cargo laden in any structure not built in with the frame of the vessel shall be considered to be deck cargo.' As it stood, the amendment, when put by the Chairman, was rejected, and the whole rule was then put to the meeting in the following form and adopted:—

'RULE I. *Jettison of Deck Cargo.*—No jettison of deck cargo shall be made good as General Average.

' Every structure not built in with the frame of the vessel shall be considered to be a part of the deck of the vessel.'

The meeting then proceeded to discuss

'RULE II. *Damage by Jettison.*—Damage done to goods or merchandise by water which unavoidably goes down a ship's hatches, opened or other opening made, for the purpose of making a jettison shall be made good as General Average in case the loss by jettison is so made good.

'Damage done by breakage and chafing, or otherwise from derangement of stowage consequent upon a jettison, shall be made good as General Average.'

DR. WERTHEIM proposed, and MR. HILLMAN seconded, that the first part of the second rule be adopted as printed. MR. HEIM pointed out that the French translation did not convey the meaning of the English text. MR. HILLMAN proposed that the word 'no' be introduced before the word 'damage,' the first word of the rule. MR. VAN PEBORGH declared that he only voted for it at York out of a spirit of concession, the great majority being then favourable to it. MR. MANLEY HOPKINS thought that it was difficult and perhaps inopportune to discuss this question, as it touched the general principle of what are the consequences of an average, a subject at present under consideration in London judicial circles. Mr. Hillman's amendment, opposed as it was to the first part of Rule II., was rejected by a large majority, and the original paragraph was adopted by a majority of 37 votes to 6.

As regards the second paragraph of Rule II., DR. RAHUSEN proposed to add the words : 'In case the loss by jettison is so made good.' MR. MEIER here remarked that it was desirable that every modification which only bore upon the change of words should be avoided by honourable members in order to expedite their labours, and, because, in any case, the resolutions of the congress, before passing into law in any country, would be the objects of a profound examination into the text.

Dr. Rahusen's amendment was then adopted, the second paragraph accordingly running: 'Damage done by breakage and chafing, or otherwise from derangement of stowage consequent upon a jettison, shall be made good as General Average, in case the loss by jettison is so made good.'

The meeting now proceeded to the consideration of Rule III., which was drawn up in the following terms:—

'RULE III. *Extinguishing Fire on Shipboard.*—Damage done to a ship and cargo, or either of them, by water or otherwise, in extinguishing a fire on board the ship, shall be General Average.'

Mr. POOLE, seconded by Mr. ENGELS, moved the adoption of the rule.

Mr. LOWNDES, however, proposed as an amendment the addition of the words· 'Except that no compensation be made for damage done by water to packages actually on fire.'

Dr. RAHUSEN seconded the amendment. On Mr. Meier's suggestion, the closing portion of the amendment was altered from ' packages actually on fire ' to ' packages which have been on fire.' Thus altered, the amendment was adopted by a majority of 36 votes to 4.

Rule IV. was next proceeded with.

'RULE IV. *Cutting away Wreck.*—Loss or damage caused by cutting away the wreck or remains of spars, or of other things which have previously been carried away by sea peril, shall not be made good as General Average.'

Mr. CAPPER, seconded by Mr. MURRAY, moved the adoption of the rule as it stood.

Mr. HACH, in the name of the German committee, asked for a reconsideration of the rule formulated at York, which he maintained to be perhaps too absolute for all contingencies, and stated that his friends only voted for it in a spirit of concession.

Mr. J. LANGLOIS was opposed to Rule IV., because the captain was thus likely to think of his own interest rather than of the general interest, and he asked for the reasons which had induced the proposition of Rule IV.

Dr. RAHUSEN thought that, when a thing which is overboard is cut away, the thing is already lost. It was not just to allow, as was done in Holland and in Belgium, the half of the value already lost. A mast which hangs alongside overboard, held to the ship only by a few ropes, was a lost mast. From another point of view, Dr. Rahusen went on, the captain, whose vessel was insured, would be tempted to modify his protest according to circumstances if the article was rejected.

Mr. HOPKINS admitted that Rule IV. was harsh, but it seemed difficult to do otherwise, and it is applied in England.

Mr. Middleberg, of Copenhagen, Mr. Winge, of Christiania, and Mr. Van Peborgh all supported the rule.

Mr. Rathbone remarked that, in order to accept it, one must be imbued with the general spirit of the rule, in virtue of which there is no sacrifice when the cause itself of the danger is to be sacrificed.

Mr. J. Langlois insisted on the objections which he had offered. If one does not give compensation for the mast which has been cut away, one should do so for the sails, yards, and so on, that are sacrificed at the same time.

Mr. Jacobsen pointed out that in these cases the sacrifice which the captain made was compulsory, and not voluntary, which is of the essence of General Average.

Rule IV. was then put to the vote, and adopted unanimously.

The committee now adjourned till two P.M. On its reassembling at that hour the chair was taken by Lord O'Hagan, who has since died, to the regret of his friends and admirers.

His lordship, who was supported by Sir Travers Twiss, Messrs. E. E. Wendt, Meier, Engels, Charles Clark, and Van Peborgh, read Rule V., of which the following is the text:—

'Rule V. *Voluntary Stranding.*—When a ship is intentionally run on shore because she is sinking or driving on shore or rocks, no damage caused to the ship, the cargo, and the freight, or any or either of them by such intentional running on shore, shall be made good as General Average.'

Mr. Natusch proposed, and Mr. Rathbone seconded, the rule, which was unanimously adopted.

Lord O'Hagan now read Rule VI. It is thus conceived :—

'Rule VI. *Carrying Press of Sail.*—Damage occasioned to a ship or cargo by carrying a press of sail shall not be made good as General Average.'

This rule, proposed by Mr. Murray, and seconded by Dr. Wertheim, was carried *nemine contradicente*.

Lord O'Hagan then read Rule VII., which was couched as follows:—

'Rule VII. *Port of Refuge Expenses.*—When a ship shall have entered a port of refuge under such circumstances that the expenses of entering the port are admissible as General Average, and when she shall have sailed thence with her original cargo, or a part of it, the corresponding expenses of leaving such port shall likewise be so admitted as General Average; and whenever the cost of discharging cargo at such port is admissible as General Average, the cost of reloading and stowing such cargo on board the said ship, together with all storage charges on such cargo, shall likewise be so admitted. Except that any portion of the cargo left at such port of refuge, on account of its being unfit to be carried forward, or on account of the unfitness or inability of the ship to carry it, shall not be called on to contribute to such General Average.'

Mr. Hach proposed the suppression of the last sentence in the rule beginning, 'Except that any portion of the cargo.' Mr. Meier seconded this amendment.

Mr. Hopkins remarked that this article was one of the most important. From the English point of view the responsibility of the freight entered into the reckoning as an element of appreciation.

Mr. Schneider, of Bremen, then read the following extracts from his work on the subject:—

'Section VII. Expenses and losses in a port of refuge shall be adjusted as General Average in the following cases only:

(a) When a vessel has entered for necessary repairs of damage voluntarily caused to it in the interest of all concerned;

(b) When a vessel has entered in order to escape from hostile men of war;

(c) When a vessel has entered for the purpose of waiting for instructions from the parties concerned, in case the port of destination is under hostile sway.

'Neutral goods shall, however, be free from contribution in the cases b and c.

'If a vessel, making for a port of refuge, is captured or perishes before having reached the port, each party bears its loss, although part of the cargo may have been saved in lighters.

'No General Average ensues from entry into another port in case the port of destination is blockaded by friendly forces or from detention by superior might.

'The expenses and losses in a port of refuge are, with reference to repartition in particular cases, to be distinguished as follows :—

'1. Expenses payable on the vessel's entry or departure.

'2. Lighterage and damage or loss sustained in the act of lightening the vessel.

'3. Expenses of discharging and reloading, and of carriage and warehouse rent, in case the vessel must be discharged for the purpose of repairs.

'4. Wages and maintenance of the ship's equipage during detention.

'5. Expenses of procuring money for defraying the charges incurred.

'If a vessel, after having reached a port of refuge, is not held worth repairing, the expenses and losses mentioned under 1 and 2 only shall be distributed as General Average.

'In case a vessel has entered a port of refuge for repairs of Particular Average the expenses under 1 and 4 shall be borne by the ship, the items under 2 and 3 ratably by the cargo, those under 5 by the parties for whose benefit the money has been expended.

'In case a vessel has entered a port of refuge for repairs of General and Particular Average the expenses incurred shall be divided in proportion to the importance of each description of average and be distributed as before stated.'

SIR TRAVERS TWISS proposed in the first place to discuss the amendment of Mr. Hach, which was then supported by MR. LOWNDES, and regarded from various points of view by MESSRS. BAILY, HILLMAN and NESBITT.

MR. COUDERT, of New York, brought to mind the reasons for which, by mutual concessions, the resolution of York had been taken; and did not believe that it was necessary to give them up any more than the exception which Mr. Hach desired by his amendment to suppress.

MR. JACOBSEN submitted some arguments in favour of the resolution of York, but neither did he admit the exception.

DR. BREDIUS, of Dordrecht, saw a contradiction between the exception at the end of the rule and the other part of it. 'The rejection of that exception,' he said, 'would be an injustice towards the ship, when a portion of the cargo is not suitable for reloading; and in case of the incapacity of the ship to take this cargo again on board, the former is already affected with the loss of its freight.'

Mr. Meier did not approve the point of view taken up by Mr. Coudert, but thought that the exception should be suppressed.

In reply to the observation of a member, Sir Travers Twiss observed that the final words, ' such General Average,' refer only to the case of 'reloading and stowing such cargo on board the same ship.'

After some observations had been made by Mr. Griffith, Lord O'Hagan put the amendment, which was carried by 31 votes to 13.

Mr. Schneider proposed to substitute section 7 of his report for Rules VII. and VIII., but found no support.

Lord O'Hagan then put it that Rule VII., omitting the last paragraph, be approved and adopted. This proposal was accepted by 39 votes.

Lord O'Hagan then read Rule VIII., which runs as follows :—

'Rule VIII. *Wages and Maintenance of Crew in Port of Refuge.*—When a ship shall have entered a port of refuge under the circumstances defined in Rule VII., the wages and cost of maintenance of the master and mariners, from the time of entering such port until the ship shall have been made ready to proceed upon her voyage, shall be made good as General Average. Except that any portion of the cargo left at such port of refuge on account of its being unfit to be carried forward, or on account of the unfitness or inability of the ship to carry it, shall not be called on to contribute to such General Average.'

Mr. Rathbone moved, and Dr. Rahusen seconded, the adoption of this rule. Mr. Hach proposed the omission of all words from the word 'except,' and Dr. Bredius seconded him. The amendment was carried by 32 votes to 2.

Mr. Nesbitt, however, opposed the whole rule, and proposed the insertion of the word ' not' between 'shall' and ' be made' in the final clause of the amended rule.

Mr. Meier remarked that this point was of great importance for the relations between shipowners and insurers. Policies could be easily effected at Lloyd's with the clause to pay according to foreign General Average statements. Now the expenses foreseen in Rule VII. are provided for thus, and Lloyd's have never raised any difficulties. It was astonishing that, although they continued to insure every day on such conditions, they came now into that room and declared here the whole subject of General Average to be a calamity.

MR. JOHN GLOVER said, as a delegate of the English shipowners, that his clients did not ask for the protection of English insurers. He added that there could not be any temptation for captains to prolong their stay in ports of refuge, because the loss of time to steamers was so considerable that reimbursement of the crews' expenses was as nothing in comparison to it; and opinion in England had long ago got the upper hand of the law on this point. In mutual assurance clubs wages were always allowed.

MR. CAPPER, representing the shipowners of the Bristol Channel, strongly supported the remarks of Mr. Glover.

MR. HILLMAN observed that, of course, Lloyd's could not exist if they refused to grant policies with such clauses as agreed with the foreign practice. In reply to other speakers, MR. HILLMAN declared that if the principle of this reimbursement was just, it should be further extended and allow also for the loss suffered through detention, interest, &c., and with regard to the usages of mutual assurance clubs, it could not be denied that they existed under very peculiar circumstances.

MR. RATHBONE thought that Rule VII. contained a concession, and confined itself within very wise limits. Lloyd's should congratulate themselves that these concessions were not carried to a wider extent.

MR. COUDERT was astonished to hear continual allusion made to the fear that the bad conduct of captains inspires. In his country these fears do not exist, and one would blush to be perpetually discussing on the hypothesis that maritime and commercial interests are constantly exposed to danger in the hands of captains. He was then for the full payment of wages.

Mr. Nesbitt's amendment, which was supported by the delegates from Lloyd's, was then rejected by 40 votes to 6.

Mr. Lowndes proposed to add the following words: 'Deducting, however, any saving in the expense actually made, or which ought to be made, by paying off the crew, or any portion of them, at the port of refuge.'

Mr. Rathbone seconded this amendment, and Mr. Hach opposed it.

One member of the committee remarked on the impossibility and danger of having the conduct of the captain on this point estimated by a third person. Besides, it was not in harmony with the general rule, according to which every captain who engaged a crew was bound to bring it home again unless authorised to pay it off, or unless the paying off took place by common consent. One could not then raise the objection that the captain would have been able at a certain moment to pay off his crew.

Mr. Lowndes's amendment was rejected, only four members voting for it. Rule VIII. was then put by Lord O'Hagan as originally proposed, and carried by 45 votes to 5.

Lord O'Hagan then submitted for consideration

'Rule IX. *Damage to Cargo in Discharging.*—Damage done to cargo by discharging it at a port of refuge shall not be admissible as General Average in case such cargo shall have been discharged at the place and in the manner customary at that port with ships not in distress,' which was moved by Mr. Coudert and seconded by Mr. Rathbone.

Mr. Manley Hopkins proposed that the rule should be altered to: 'Damage done to cargo by discharging it at a port of refuge shall be admissible as General Average.' This was seconded by Mr. Langlois.

Mr. Glover thought there was reason for not losing sight of the fact that the discharging might cause material losses which could not be confounded with such arrangement as one probably had in view.

Mr. Hopkins explained that discharging a cargo in a port of refuge was always the cause of an additional loss. Mr. Griffith strongly objected to the amendment.

Mr. Engels maintained that the large number of claims for losses on merchandise discharged in a harbour of refuge rendered desirable the maintenance of Rule IX. in the form in which it is proposed.

The amendment was then put and lost by a large majority, 37 being against and 8 for it. The original York rule as first read was then submitted to the committee by LORD O'HAGAN and adopted by 40 votes to 3.

Some members here proposed that the sitting should terminate, but the majority decided to proceed to the examination of the two last York rules.

LORD O'HAGAN then read

' RULE X. *Contributory Values.*—The contribution to a General Average shall be made upon the actual values of the property at the termination of the adventure, to which shall be added the amount made good as General Average for property sacrificed; deduction being made, from the shipowner's freight and passage-money at risk, of two-fifths of such freight, in lieu of crew's wages, port charges, and all other deductions; deduction being also made, from the value of the property, of all charges incurred in respect thereof subsequently to the arising of the claim to General Average.'

DR. RAHUSEN proposed, and MR. RATHBONE seconded, the adoption of this rule.

MR. HACH, seconded by MR. MEIER, proposed that the following clauses be substituted for Rule X.:—

'The cargo contributes with the actual net value of the goods at the end of the voyage, deducting the then still existing value of those repairs and supplies which have been made after the casualty.

' The freight contributes with two-thirds of its gross amount (eventually to concede three-fifths, or even one-half).

' To all these contributing values is to be added the amount made good in General Average objects sacrificed.'

And after having gone into the reasons for their proposal, which were further elucidated by MESSRS. JACOBSEN, LOWNDES, and BAILY, Mr. Hach's amendment was rejected by 28 votes to 8.

MR. COUDERT, seconded by MR. HILLMAN, proposed the following amendment: ' Freight contributed for must contribute at the rate contributed for,' which was opposed by Mr. Lowndes and Mr. Baily and rejected. Mr. Lowndes, supported by Mr. Driebeek, then proposed :

'That Rule X. be amended by the omission of the words " two-fifths of such freight in lieu of crew's wages, port charges, and all other deductions ; " and, in their place, that the following words be inserted : " such port charges and crew's wages as would not have been incurred had the ship and cargo been totally lost at the date of the General Average Act or sacrifice." '

After some remarks from Mr. Baily and Mr. Glover, the President read the rule and the proposed amendment, and there were 28 against and 11 for the amendment.

Lord O'Hagan then put to the meeting, 'That the rule as altered by Mr. Lowndes's amendment do pass,' and it was carried unanimously.

Lord O'Hagan then read

' Rule XI. *Loss of Freight.*—In every case in which a sacrifice of cargo is made good as General Average, the loss of freight (if any) which is caused by such loss of cargo shall likewise be so made good.'

Mr. Coudert proposed, and Mr. Glover seconded the rule, and it was thereupon unanimously adopted.

On Saturday, September 1, the chair of the General Average Committee was taken by Mr. Th. Engels, who was supported by Messrs. Wendt, Meier, and Van Peborgh.

The Honorary Secretary to the Committee, Mr. J. Rand Baily, read over the eleven rules approved and adopted on the previous day.

Mr. Coudert proposed, and Mr. Rathbone seconded, 'That the rules as now read are accurate, and should be adopted.'

Dr. Rahusen proposed that these rules, which will hereafter be known as the 'Rules of Antwerp,' should be officially translated into French.

Mr. Rathbone proposed that the new rules should be named 'The York Rules, amended at Antwerp.'

Mr. Meier was of opinion that the English text should remain the official one, and that local committees should charge themselves with the duty of making good translations of it, which would afterwards be communicated to the general council, and the general council, in case of doubt as to the sense, would make its observations on it.

Mr. Langlois asked that the English text should be always joined to the translated text. Errors, for example, had been committed in Belgium in the application of the rules as to collisions, because the French text was incorrect, and the errors had only been put right when the English text was produced in a court of justice.

Mr. Engels thought that this junction of the texts would be difficult in its official application.

Mr. Baily added that this was a question entirely for the interested countries.

The discussion having dropped, the Chairman called upon Mr. Hach to bring forward the additional rules suggested by the German Committee, upon which Mr. Hach suggested that the rules now agreed to should be preluded by a clear definition of General Average, and proposed the addition of a rule in the terms of Art. 702 of the German Commercial Code, page 3 of the Report of the German Committee, as follows:—

'All damage intentionally done to ship or cargo, or both, by the master, or by his orders, for the purpose of saving both from a common danger, together with any further damage occasioned by such measures, and likewise expenses incurred for the same purpose, are General Average. General Average is borne by ship, freight, and cargo conjointly.'

Dr. Rahusen considered it dangerous to formulate a general definition of General Average, and criticised the German formula.

Mr. Hopkins added that, if this path were entered on, the deliberations would last some days longer.

Mr. Capper also thought that it was not prudent to discuss what General Average should be; the congress had assembled to endeavour to make alike everywhere the laws on General Average, and in no way to discuss the definition and character of General Average.

Mr. MEIER considered that the York rules being far from comprising the greater part of the rules which present themselves in practice, it was, on the contrary, very wise to lay down a general principle, as had been done in the code of German commerce, for in defining only particular cases one exposed the Judges to the difficulty of having no sound rule of conduct in cases not foreseen.

Mr. GRIFFITH thought that, after having at York suppressed certain differences of detail between the usages of different countries, the Germans did well to seek to establish general principles, thus laying the foundations of the building before erecting it. It was, therefore, only a question to know if the proposed formula was good or incorrect, and whether it is within the province of the present labours of the congress to proceed to the examination of it.

Mr. LOWNDES said he considered that it would be impracticable and undesirable to attempt a definition. The rules, as being discussed, did not pretend to be a *code,* but only rules as to certain points on which countries differed.

Mr. COUDERT agreed with him.

Mr. VAN PEBORGH was of opinion that general definitions were necessary and proposed a formula.

Mr. LANGLOIS supported the formula of the German code.

Mr. NESBITT was disposed to adopt a good definition.

Mr. ENGELS submitted to the assembly the previous question: Should a definition be given or not?

After Mr. BAILY had made some objections, Mr. GAEMAERE remarked that the assembly could not settle absolutely and generally the question whether there was room for the introduction of a definition into the law or not; at the most it could declare whether it judged it opportune at the moment to express itself on that question. He asked the assembly therefore simply to decide that it does not judge it necessary to add at this moment to the York rules a definition of General Average.

Mr. Hach's motion was rejected by a large majority.

THE CHAIRMAN having asked if there were any further proposals to add to the rules, MR. HACH proposed to add a rule in the following words :—

'Average contribution takes place only when both ship and cargo, wholly or in part, have been actually saved.'

MR. BAILY requested Mr. Hach to explain what was meant by the word 'actually,' a word which he thought would cause difference of opinion.

MR. HACH agreed to substitute the word 'ultimately.' MR. MEIER seconded the amended motion. After some discussion, in which MESSRS. MANLEY HOPKINS, JACOBSEN, and RAHUSEN took part, MR. LOWNDES proposed the previous question. He considered the proposed addition involved the question of what was the ultimate ability of an owner, which would lead to great difficulty and danger.

MR. RATHBONE supported Mr. Lowndes's motion to propose the previous question.

MR. LANGLOIS agreed with the preceding speakers in finding the rule bad, or at least dangerous; but he would not support the previous question, because it was well to bring back the Germans from their error.

MR. COUDERT would also find utility in discussion, solely as the Germans do not themselves understand their law, and because at this very moment they had altered the most important term in it. He thought there was reason for opposing the previous question, as one found oneself, in effect, in the presence of two different traps.

MR. BAILY judged it opportune to prove to the Germans all that was defective in their law.

DR. SIEVEKING, of Hamburg, gave an explanation of the word 'actually.'

On an observation of MR. COUDERT the German delegates withdrew the word 'ultimately.'

After MR. LOWNDES had withdrawn his motion to propose the previous question, MR. WINGE quoted several cases to show how disadvantageously the German law had worked. MR. BAILY moved thereupon, as an amendment, that the following rule be added in the place of that proposed by Mr. Hach :—

'Whenever there is not any pecuniary benefit, or when the pecuniary benefit is less than the expense caused by a General Average act, the excess of that expense over that benefit shall be apportioned over the benefits which at the time when the General Average was performed it was intended that it should produce.'

Mr. NESBITT seconded this.

Mr. VAN PEBORGH opposed this amendment, as contrary to the general principle of most nations that value saved is the limit of the contribution.

Dr. RAHUSEN invoked the laws on responsibility, and the right of abandonment, which are different in different countries, in opposing the amendment of Mr. Baily.

Mr. CAPPER cited the case of a shipowner who had paid all the expenses of putting in at a port of refuge, and the ship and cargo afterwards perished before arriving at the port of destination; he asked if the shipowners ought to support all the loss.

MESSRS. ENGELS and MEIER: You shipowners ought to insure your advances.

MESSRS. BAILY and HACH declared themselves satisfied if they had succeeded in attracting for the future the attention of competent persons to this important question. MR. HACH withdrew his motion, and the CHAIRMAN put the previous question, which was carried unanimously.

MR. HACH then submitted for the acceptance of the committee the following proposition: 'The amount to be allowed for goods sacrificed is computed analogous to the contributory value by the actual net value of the goods in the same quality and condition at the end of the voyage.'

MR. MEIER seconded the adoption of this proposition; and, after some discussion between MESSRS. JACOBSEN and LOWNDES, MR. BAILY proposed, as an amendment, the adoption of the following rule: 'The value to be allowed for goods sacrificed shall be that value which the owner would have received if such goods had not been sacrificed.'

MR. MANLEY HOPKINS seconded, MR. MEIER opposed, the amendment. MR. RATHBONE was of opinion that, if MR. MEIER'S view were adopted, the owners of jettisoned goods would be placed in a better position than the owner of other goods.

THE CHAIRMAN put Mr. Baily's amendment, which was carried by a majority of 34 to 7. Thereupon MR. HACH withdrew his motion.

THE CHAIRMAN then put it to the vote: 'That the words of the amendment of Mr. Baily do form

'RULE XII. *Amount to be made good for Cargo.*—The value to be allowed for goods sacrificed shall be that value which the owner would have received if such goods had not been sacrificed.'

This was carried unanimously.

MR. HACH then submitted that 'the amount to be allowed for objects sacrificed of ship and ship's material is regulated by the usages of the port where the average statement is to be made up.' DR. RAHUSEN pointed out various objections to this amendment, which MR. HACH then withdrew.

MR. LANGLOIS, however, considered the point one which should be argued, and gave notice that he would bring it forward, with some modifications, at the afternoon sitting.

The committee then at one o'clock adjourned.

At the afternoon sitting of August 31, commencing at 2.30 P.M., M. T. Engels took the chair. He was supported by Messrs. Wendt, Meier, and Van Peborgh.

MR. LOWNDES, after pointing out the difference between the systems of England and other countries relative to articles replaced or repaired, submitted the following to be added as a new rule:—

' When new work replaces old the deduction shall be one-third, subject to the following exceptions, viz. :—

' 1. No deduction shall be made during the ship's first year.

' 2. Anchors are allowed in full.

' 3. Chain-cables are subject to one-sixth only.

' 4. In case of repairs at a port of refuge, the deduction shall not exceed one-third of the estimated cost of such repairs at the port of adjustment.

' 5. No deduction to be made for one-third of bottomry premiums, or commissions on advance.

' 6. No deduction is to be made from temporary repairs.'

Mr. Glover opposed the rule as suggested, inquiring if Mr. Lowndes proposed to make any distinction between wooden and iron ships.

Mr. Lowndes said he would be glad to modify his proposal by introducing such a distinction, but would like to know what was suggested.

Mr. Meier said it was perfectly ridiculous to want at the end of a year a reduction of one-third on iron ships. The speaker did not wish to make any proposition, because the building of iron ships was of too modern date for one to be able to form a sound estimate. Not to complicate the situation, he was of opinion that the subject should not be touched, otherwise he would propose that there should be no reduction during the five first years, and afterwards a sixth reduction during ten years.

Mr. Nesbitt said he considered the subject well worthy of discussion, but it could not be entered upon fairly or conveniently at this meeting; and after further remarks by Messrs. Hillman and Glover, the Chairman put the previous question, which was carried by 34 votes to 4.

Mr. Ahlers moved the insertion of the following rule : ' Either party whose property has been jettisoned or sacrificed for the common safety has a lien on the interests saved for contribution, which may be enforced by application to the proper tribunal or by retaining possession, where the party entitled to the lien is in possession.'

Mr. Hach seconded this, and after much discussion by Messrs. Rahusen, Glover, Rathbone, Natusch, Hillman, Murray, and Ahlers, the Chairman expressed a doubt whether the suggestion was practicable, as it would be impossible for a merchant to know whether goods of a similar kind saved were his or not.

The Chairman then put the previous question, which was carried by 24 to 9.

Mr. Lowndes suggested the addition of a rule as follows —:

' Damage done by defending the ship against enemies or pirates, ammunition expended in such defence, and compensation lawfully paid to wounded seamen, are General Average.'

Which was likewise negatived without discussion, the votes being—for the previous question, 15; against, 13.

MR. MEIER now said that the deliberations on the International General Average Congress having been concluded, it was time to think of the means most suitable to give practical effect to the rules voted by the congress. His proposition was therefore that the local committees should be moved to take such measures as they think suitable for obtaining the acceptance of the views of the congress by their respective Governments, and to render an account to the general council of the result of the steps so taken.

In this way, by the exercise of every influence they could bring about, they would eventually succeed in seeing the rules carried out which have actually been voted.

After DR. RAHUSEN had made some observations to the same effect, MR. JOHN GLOVER expressed a wish to see the delegates from Lloyd's working for the acceptance of the results of the congress.

MR. NATUSCH seized this opportunity, as a delegate from Lloyd's, to say that he believed he ought to declare that the results of the congress would not answer to the views of the insurers of Lloyd's. They knew this beforehand; but, invited to the congress, they considered that they would be performing an act of courtesy in sending delegates. He referred to the opinions of Lloyd's, and begged them to understand clearly that delegates from Lloyd's had taken no share in voting the 'Rules of York, amended at Antwerp.' He wound up by returning thanks for the kind reception the delegates had received.

MR. HILLMAN confirmed the remarks of his colleague. He would inform his constituents that they did well in sending delegates to the congress. He was convinced that the labours of the congress would produce good fruit in the future.

MR. RATHBONE, as President of the Underwriters of Liverpool and delegate from the Chamber of Commerce of that town, protested against the remarks of the delegates from Lloyd's, if they assumed to have spoken in the name of the majority of English underwriters, and declared that his constituents in the most loyal and complete fashion would endeavour to have passed in use and practice the rules here actually voted. (Applause.)

He regretted that Mr. Baily was not present at this moment, for he would undoubtedly ratify his declaration in the name of the Liverpool shipowners, and it was not, perhaps, needless to add that Mr. Baily represented about 800,000 tons of shipping. (Applause.)

Mr. Meier's motion was adopted.

This closed the proceedings of the committee.

At the suggestion of Mr. Jencken, it was agreed to frame a report, and, in pursuance of the practice of the Association, to submit the resolutions and report to the general meeting in conference. The members then adjourned into the principal hall, where his lordship was presiding.

The printed report of the General Average Committee was now submitted to the conference. It ran as follows:—

'Your committee adopted as the basis of its discussions the body of rules framed at York in 1864, and known by the name of "The York Rules." They first revised those rules in detail, and then proceeded to consider what additions, if any, should be made to them. The alterations which your committee have made in the York rules are as follows:—

' 1. The first York rule, which admitted into General Average one kind only of deck-load jettison, namely, that of wood goods, has been altered, and the rule now stands, that "No jettison of deck cargo shall be made good as General Average."

' 2. To the third York rule, which provided that damage done by the measures taken to extinguish a fire on shipboard should be treated as General Average, your committee has added the restriction that no compensation shall be made for damage done by water to packages which have been on fire.

' 3. The seventh and eighth York rules, after providing that, in certain cases, the cost of reloading cargo and leaving a port of refuge, and the wages and provisions of the crew, whilst in such port, should be treated as General Average, exempted from contribution to such General Average any goods that might have been sold at the port of refuge. Your committee has withdrawn that exemption.

'4. Whereas the tenth York rule had based the contribution of freight on three-fifths of its gross amount, your committee has considered that the gross freight should contribute, subject to the deduction of such port charges and crew's wages as would not have been incurred had the ship and cargo been totally lost at the date of the General Average act or sacrifice.

'With these modifications the York rules have been adopted, some of them unanimously and the remainder by very large majorities of your committee. After full consideration of a large number of proposed additional rules, your committee has determined to adopt no additional rule, excepting the following, which forms Rule XII. below, viz.:—

'"The amount to be allowed for goods sacrificed shall be that value which the owners would have received if their goods had not been sacrificed."

'The rules which your committee now lay before you as the basis of a uniform system of General Average for all maritime countries, and to which the title might be given of the "York and Antwerp Rules," are appended.

'In bringing their mission to a close, your committee, on the motion of Herr Meier, President of the North German Lloyd, unanimously agreed to submit to the conference the following resolution:—

'"That the local committees of this association be requested immediately to take such steps as they may deem expedient with a view to insuring a consideration of the rules as revised and the favourable attention and action of their respective Governments, reporting the result of such steps to the council of the Association."'

The York and Antwerp Rules.

Rule I. *Jettison of Deck Cargo.*—No jettison of deck cargo shall be made good as General Average.

Every structure not built in with the frame of the vessel shall be considered to be a part of the deck of the vessel.

Rule II. *Damage by Jettison.*—Damage done to goods or merchandise by water which unavoidably goes down a ship's hatches opened, or other opening made, for the purpose of making a jettison shall be made good as General Average, in case the loss by jettison is so made good.

Damage done by breakage and chafing, or otherwise from derangement of stowage, consequent upon a jettison, shall be made good as General Average, in case the loss by jettison is so made good.

Rule III. *Extinguishing Fire on Shipboard.*—Damage done to a ship and cargo, or either of them, by water or otherwise, in extinguishing a fire on board the ship, shall be General Average; except that no compensation be made for damage done by water to packages which have been on fire.

Rule IV. *Cutting away Wreck.*—Loss or damage caused by cutting away the wreck or remains of spars, or of other things which have previously been carried away by sea peril, shall not be made good as General Average.

Rule V. *Voluntary Stranding.*—When a ship is intentionally run on shore because she is sinking or driving on shore or rocks, no damage caused to the ship, the cargo and the freight, or any or either of them, by such intentional running on shore shall be made good as General Average.

Rule VI. *Carrying Press of Sail.*—Damage occasioned to a ship or cargo by carrying a press of sail shall not be made good as General Average.

Rule VII. *Port of Refuge Expenses.*—When a ship shall have entered a port of refuge under such circumstances that the expenses of entering the port are admissible as General Average, and when she shall have sailed thence with her original cargo or a part of it, the corresponding expenses of leaving such port shall likewise be admitted as General Average; and, whenever the cost of discharging cargo at such port is admissible as General Average, the cost of reloading and stowing such cargo on board the said ship, together with all storage charges on such cargo, shall likewise be so admitted.

Rule VIII. *Wages and Maintenance of Crew in Port of*

Refuge.—When a ship shall have entered a port of refuge under the circumstances defined in Rule VII., the wages and cost of maintenance of the master and mariners from the time of entering such port until the ship shall have been made ready to proceed upon her voyage shall be made good as General Average.

RULE IX. *Damage to Cargo in Discharging.*—Damage done to cargo by discharging it at a port of refuge shall not be admissible as General Average, in case such cargo shall have been discharged at the place and in the manner customary at that port with ships not in distress.

RULE X. *Contributory Values.*—The contribution to a General Average shall be made upon the actual values of the property at the termination of the adventure, to which shall be added the amount made good as General Average for property sacrificed; deduction being made from the shipowner's freight and passage-money at risk of such port charges and crew's wages as would not have been incurred had the ship and cargo been totally lost at the date of the General Average act or sacrifice; deduction being also made from the value of the property of all charges incurred in respect thereof subsequently to the arising of the claim to General Average.

RULE XI. *Loss of Freight.*—In every case in which a sacrifice of cargo is made good as General Average, the loss of freight, if any, which is caused by such loss of cargo shall likewise be so made good.

RULE XII. *Amount to be made good for Cargo.*—The value to be allowed for goods sacrificed shall be that value which the owner would have received if such goods had not been sacrificed.

The report having been read by MR. J. RAND BAILY, MR. E. E. WENDT, of London, moved:—

'That the York and Antwerp Rules be adopted and filed with the minutes of this congress.'

The motion was seconded by MR. RICHARD LOWNDES, of Liverpool, and carried unanimously.

LORD O'HAGAN, in the course of his valedictory address to the conference, remarked that 'he had been present at the deliberations of the legislative bodies of the greater number of the states of

Europe, but in no assembly had he ever heard questions debated with such earnestness, such cogency of logic, and such ease and precision of language as in the General Average committee-room. Nor was the reason far to seek; for in that room were gathered together those who knew most about the subject in hand, and whose interests would be most affected by the issue of the discussions.'

The fifth annual conference of the Association for the reform and codification of the Law of Nations broke up on Monday, September 3, 1877, and on that day the following letter was forwarded by the representatives of Lloyd's, before leaving Antwerp, to the secretary :—

'Antwerp: September 3, 1877.

'Sir,—We, the representatives deputed by the Committee of Lloyd's, on the invitation of the Committee of your Association, to attend the meetings, this day terminated, of the General Average section of the conference, request that it may appear in the protocol of the proceedings that we expressly declared that we had no intention, by our presence or otherwise, to accept, on behalf of our constituents, the decisions arrived at by the section, but that, on the contrary, we protested, on behalf of the Committee of Lloyd's, against certain of those decisions, and reserved the rights of our constituents in every respect.—We are, Sir,

'Your obedient Servants,

(Signed) { F. B. B. Natusch, Joseph Hillman.'

'H. D. Jencken, Esq.'

It can scarcely be a matter of surprise that, as soon as serious steps were taken to give practical effect to the York and Antwerp Rules by their embodiment in charter parties, bills of lading, and policies of insurance, an opposition was organised by those who either were antagonistic to all changes or had been induced by those members of the Committee of Lloyd's who thought that claims of General Averages might be got rid of altogether, to join in the general outcry against this innovation.

It cannot, however, be of any lasting good to republish the multifarious correspondence which the public press contained on this subject after the conference and until March 1879, because only arguments were advanced which had over and over again been stated and refuted, and it is, therefore, my intention to confine myself to print in the following pages only so much from the reports presented at different congresses of the Association for the Reform and Codification of the Law of Nations as will be necessary in order to bring the history of this movement down to the present day.

I may, therefore, begin with quoting from the Report of the General Average Committee presented to the Conference at Frankfort-on-Main on August 21, 1878, which commenced by recapitulating some historical facts to the above referred to concluding resolution at the Antwerp Congress, and then proceeded as follows:—

In pursuance of this direction, this Association has since that date employed all the means at its disposal to bring the matter before the Governments of the different European states and to stimulate the action of the various local committees which have been formed at the principal European ports for the purpose of insuring the adoption of the new rules. In England the conduct of this question was entrusted in the first instance to the General Shipowners' Association. Early in May the General Shipowners' Association convened a meeting of shipowners, underwriters and others and invited them to form a committee. On May 30 a general meeting was held at the Cannon Street Hotel, and, a committee having been formed, the following resolutions were passed:—

1. 'That in the opinion of this meeting it is desirable that the York and Antwerp Rules of General Average be carried into operation.'

2. 'That in the opinion of this meeting the most effectual

mode of procedure will be by a general agreement on the part of shipowners, merchants, and underwriters to insert in bills of lading and charter-parties the words, "General Average, if any, payable according to York and Antwerp Rules," and in policies of insurance to add to the foreign General Average clause the words, "or York and Antwerp Rules," so that the clause will run thus: "General Average payable as per foreign adjustment (or custom) or York and Antwerp Rules, if so made up."'

3. 'That a definite date should be fixed for the proposed change; and the date recommended by this committee is January 1, 1879.'

The committee has adopted the name of the 'English Central Committee.' It has issued a report, and its action has been most energetic. Steps have been taken to place in the hands of every shipowner, underwriter, and merchant in Great Britain a copy of the report.

It is satisfactory to be able to state that a large number of underwriters, shipowners, and merchants have already given in their adhesion, and it is confidently believed that by the close of this year the rules will be all but universally adopted.

Whilst the English Central Committee has thus with untiring perseverance pursued its course, supported by the Shipowners' Association, the Chamber of Shipping and the powerful commercial and shipping interests centred at Liverpool, the maritime states of the Continent and the great maritime ports of the United States have not been behindhand in evincing a lively interest in what was doing. A brief summary of what has been done will now be furnished.

Germany.—The Bremen Committee on General Average has been very industrious. On October 30, 1877, the President of the German Branch Association, Herr H. H. Meier, addressed a memorial to the Chancellor of the German Empire (Prince Bismarck), calling attention to the desirableness of having the York and Antwerp Rules introduced into the German Commercial Code. This memorial was followed by a petition, dated March 16, 1878, presented by the International Transport Insurance Association of Berlin to the German Reichstag, praying that the law of Germany might be altered by adopting (with, of course, necessary modifications) the York and Antwerp Rules; finally, the delegates of the North German ports and commercial cities have presented a memorial, dated May 22, 1878, to the German Government, approving and recommending the adoption of these rules. According to communications received from Herr Theodor Hach, it appears that the course intended to be pursued by the German Branch Committee is to follow the lead of England, but not to take the initiative.

The Netherlands.—This wealthy maritime state, with its vast shipping interests, has been likewise active. At the Antwerp Conference the Shipowners' and Underwriters' Associations and the great *Handelsmaatschappij* of Holland were represented by Dr. Rahusen, who took a prominent part in the proceedings. In the month of January 1878 a report[1] on the York and Antwerp Rules, drawn up by Dr. Rahusen, was presented to the Dutch Committee at Amsterdam and adopted, and at a meeting held in that month the following resolutions were voted:—

1. 'That it is highly desirable for shipowners and underwriters that the York and Antwerp Rules be adopted by all maritime nations.'

2. 'That this Committee address the Dutch Government and state to it the usefulness of the adoption of these rules to Holland and other maritime nations.'

Subsequently a memorial was addressed to the Government of the Netherlands by the members of the Dutch committee, calling attention to the York and Antwerp Rules and recommending that steps should be taken for embodying them in the commercial code of that country.

Belgium. In this country, since the date of the September Conference, great activity has been displayed in regard to the rules. The ' Société Commercielle et Industrielle ' of Antwerp, which at present has taken the place of the extinct Chamber of Commerce, has energetically taken up this matter. Early in the year a committee was appointed, consisting of Messrs. Th. C. Engels, E. van

---

[1] *Verslag van de Vergaderingen over de Internationale Avarij grosse Regeling, gehouden te Antwerpen, door E. N. Rahusen.*

Peborgh and G. Berdolt, to take steps to bring the subject to the attention of the Government of that country. The committee has placed itself in communication with M. Bara, Minister of Justice for Belgium, and has called his Excellency's attention to the York and Antwerp Rules, suggesting that the 'Code de Commerce' of Belgium might be altered so as to embody those rules. The Minister, we are informed, has given a favourable reply and promised to have this question investigated.

Sweden and Norway and Denmark.[1]—All these three countries were represented at the Antwerp Conference. At the seaports of Copenhagen,[2] Gothenburg, and Christiania committees have since been formed for the purpose of bringing this matter before their respective Governments. It is understood that their request is sure to meet with a favourable reception. For the present, the measures taken by these Governments in passing a common law on bills of exchange have, it is understood, absorbed their entire attention, and, until the report of the International Committee on Bills of Exchange has received the sanction of the Legislature of these kingdoms, the question of creating a common law for General Average losses will have to remain in abeyance.

Whilst these active measures have been taken in the states named, a lively interest in this question has been evinced in *Austria*, the matter having been submitted to the Government of that Empire by the Consul-General, the Chevalier Dr. Karl von Scherzer.

In *France* the attention of the Ministry has likewise been directed to this question, the Government of the Netherlands having been requested by the French Government to furnish them with a report on the York and Antwerp Rules. M. de Courcy, of Paris, has reported most favourably on these rules, pointing out that, as regards Italy and France, their adoption will not prove an insurmountable difficulty; that, in fact, these rules constitute a fair com-

---

[1] See Reports of Herr Axel Winge, December 1877.

[2] Mr. L. M. Hvidt, of Copenhagen, has by letter furnished a valuable summary of the law in Denmark; expressing his belief that, as the York and Antwerp Rules only slightly differ from the law of Denmark, their adoption may be regarded as all but certain.

promise between the English and Continental systems. Valuable contributions on this question have also been made by Mr. V. Labraque Bordenave.[1]

United States of America.—Having thus far given an account of what has been done in Europe, it becomes necessary to state the course that has been pursued in the United States of America. At the Antwerp Conference the Chamber of Commerce of New York and the Boards of Underwriters of that city and New Orleans were ably represented by Mr. F. R. Coudert; the Boston and Philadelphia Underwriters' Associations having communicated by letters their views in regard to the adoption of the York Rules. The favourable reception of the York and Antwerp Rules in that country was thus in part assured, and the hopes originally entertained as to their approval there have been fully realised. Mr. F. R. Coudert, in his report[2] on the York and Antwerp Rules, has not only pointed out the utility of the rules, but has shown that practically the law of the United States recognises the principle upon which they are based.

Several influential meetings have been held in New York, Boston, and Philadelphia, at which substantially these rules have been approved of. The Underwriters' Associations of New Orleans, and the Maritime Board of Underwriters of Boston, have intimated that they are prepared to follow the lead of England; the Underwriters of Philadelphia have adopted these rules with some slight modifications.

As regards the British Colonies, letters expressing the most lively interest have been received from Canada (Quebec), Australia (Sydney, Melbourne, Adelaide), India (Bombay, Calcutta), the Cape of Good Hope (Cape Town), and Mauritius (Port Louis), and also from Shanghai.

The only countries from which no expression of opinion has been elicited are Spain and Portugal; it is, however, apprehended that these countries would follow the lead of France, and in France,

---

[1] 'Règles d'York et d'Anvers sur les Avaries Communes' (*La France Judiciaire*, juillet 1878).

[2] Mr. F. Coudert's Report to the Chamber of Commerce and Board of Marine Underwriters, New York, November 1, 1877.

this Association has been informed, no doubt is felt that, should the English Government move in the matter, the French Government will seriously entertain the question.

Having thus far rendered a summary of what has been done in the past with regard to the adoption of the York and Antwerp Rules, it may not be out of place to point to the future.

No doubt can exist but that the shipowning interests, supported by the merchant in nearly all the European states,[1] favour the adoption of the York and Antwerp Rules. The necessity of establishing a common law, or rule, has become most urgent, and the only resistance to the introduction of a uniform system at present exists in the Underwriting Rooms at Lloyd's and some of the principal Marine Insurance Companies of London. The declaration of the Committee of Lloyd's Corporation, that it is desirable ultimately to abolish General Average altogether, explains the cause of this opposition. This suggestion has caused alarm amongst the shipowners, whose property would be imperilled if the losses occasioned by voluntary sacrifices incurred for the safety of all—for the vessel is the first and greatest sufferer in all cases of accident on the seas (anchors, masts, sails, &c., all first go to save the property and crew)—were burdened on the ship, and the cargo allowed to escape scot-free. Indeed, of such grave importance is this question, in the face of the active competition by other maritime states, that the shipowner, and behind him the merchant, it is true, reluctantly, have had to face their old friend the insurer and make him understand that the principal parties in all these questions are the owner of the ship and the owner of the cargo, and that an underwriter cannot, without imperilling his business, put at hazard those interests which the shipowner and the merchant regard as paramount.

HERR THEODOR HACH, of Bremen, thereupon moved: 'That this Association regards with great satisfaction the progress made in the matter of the adoption of the York and Antwerp Rules for the adjustment of General Average losses, and desires to express

---

[1] Reports on the Antwerp Conference on General Average have appeared in the following languages: English, French, Dutch, Danish, German, Italian, and Swedish.

its acknowledgment of the valuable services rendered both by the committees on the Continent and in the United States of America, and by the English Central Committee of underwriters and shipowners during the past year, and to express its sense of approval of the energetic measures taken by the English Central Committee to carry out those rules, and it adds an earnest request that the committees will continue their labours.'

The resolution, seconded by M. ENGELS, was carried unanimously.

In the following year (1879) the next conference of the Association was held in the Guildhall of the city of London, and the most interesting part of the Report of the General Average Committee presented there on August 13 reads thus :—

The course of action adopted by the Central Committee has been to issue a report laying the case distinctly before shipowners, merchants, and underwriters, and inviting the first-named to sign a declaration of their individual approval of the York-Antwerp Rules, and of their intention, on and after January 1, 1879, to insert the clause above referred to in their bills of lading and charter parties, unless under exceptional circumstances.

This invitation has been largely responded to. No less than 789 steam and sailing ship-owning companies or firms, representing 2,296,085 tons, or more than two-fifths of the entire registered tonnage of Great Britain, have signed this declaration. The new clause has likewise been adopted by a large proportion of the mutual insurance associations of Great Britain.

At this moment the York-Antwerp clause is actually in force for a large percentage of the commerce of this country; and its adoption is extending itself every day.

‘ No practical difficulty has been found on the part of underwriters; though in the first instance, owing to the unfavourable attitude taken up by the Committee of Lloyd's and by influential persons connected with one or two insurance companies in London, there appeared to be some danger that this might be the case.

From the first the Underwriters' Association of Liverpool cordially and loyally supported the new rules. There is now no difficulty in obtaining insurances at Lloyd's on the usual terms. We are informed that no extra premium has in any instance been required. The change, as a matter of voluntary contract, is now quietly and steadily extending itself, and opposition is rapidly dying away.

In this country it so happens that the proposed change is greatly facilitated by the present condition of the law, as distinguished from the practice, of General Average. Principles have been laid down by the courts which have not yet been completely carried out in practice, but which are gradually asserting their supremacy, and by degrees transforming our practice, as point after point is brought before the attention of the Judges. The principles thus enunciated are precisely those which the York-Antwerp Rules are founded on; the practices thus undergoing the gradual process of being broken down are precisely those which the rules strive to change. The rules, therefore, are in no respect adverse to English law; and it may perhaps be regarded as only a question of time, whether our vicious practices will be first reformed by the Courts or by the voluntary adoption of the York-Antwerp Rules.

The progress made towards the adoption of the York-Antwerp Rules on the continent of Europe and in trans-oceanic states may be briefly summarised as follows :—

In Norway and Sweden, more especially the former country, the York-Antwerp Rules have been agreed to by an overwhelming majority of the ship and steamship owners and also by the marine insurance clubs and companies of those kingdoms.

The Danish ship and steamship owners and marine insurance companies have adopted a resolution approving of the rules, whenever their use does not clash with pre-existing rights.

The German Committee has reported favourable progress. An imperial commission appointed to consider the question of their adoption terminated its sittings in February last and has approved of them. Since that date the ship and steamship owners of Bremen have unanimously voted their adoption, and the concurrence of the Hamburg, Altona, and Stettin shipowners and marine insurance companies has to a great extent been secured.

In the Netherlands the adoption of the rules has, subject to some minor modifications, been secured.

In Belgium the 'Société Commerciale et Industrielle,' which society now represents in that country the former Chambers of Commerce, has voted their adoption and a recommendation of their insertion in contracts of affreightment.

The marine insurance companies of Russia and Austria-Hungary and some of the French and great Swiss insurance companies have, conjointly with the countries already named, agreed (the former all but unanimously) to recognise the York-Antwerp Rules in settlements of General Average losses.

In France and Italy some shipowners have evinced a spirit of opposition, the clause contained in the codes of these countries limiting the contribution to one-half of the value of the ship being deemed too favourable to the shipowners to be relinquished at present. The important Chamber of Commerce of Lyons has, however, sent in its unqualified approval of the rules, thus proving that, at all events, a powerful section of the merchants of France favours the change.

As regards the British colonies, those of British North America have to a great extent approved and adopted the rules. The Melbourne Chamber of Commerce and the Shipowners' Society of that city have likewise approved of them. In our East Indian possessions foreign-going vessels are all but exclusively in the hands of British shipowners. The marine insurance companies of England transact the whole of the insurance business of India, and thus the action of those dependencies is regulated entirely by that of the capitalists in the home country.

The leading insurance companies of the United States of America have agreed to recognise the rules, and upwards of one hundred of the great ship and steamship owning firms have assented to inserting them in their bills of lading and charter-parties. The Chambers of Commerce of New York and San Francisco have, in opposition to this favourable movement, voted by small majorities against their adoption, whilst the Board of Trade of Baltimore has approved of them.

A favourable feature in the course of the progress made towards the universal adoption of the rules is the fact that, without public announcement or subscribing to any declaratory document of assent, the ship and steamship owners and merchants in different countries are inserting them in their contracts of affreightment. A movement so widespread, including many countries and affecting the interests of commercial and shipping men in all parts of the world, could hardly be expected to take place without interfering with interests more or less affected by the change. Hitherto the resistance offered in some quarters has been vastly overbalanced by the success obtained in other parts; and a reasonable hope may be entertained that at no very distant period the York-Antwerp Rules will have accomplished a complete change, in all the great commercial countries of the civilised world, in this branch of maritime law.

Having thus reported what has been done in the interval between the meeting at Antwerp and the present meeting, we may be allowed to say a few words on the question, what steps may with advantage, in our opinion, be taken now in furtherance of the object before us.

There can be no doubt that the York-Antwerp Rules constitute —though by far the most important and difficult step—yet a step only towards an international law. The rules deal only with a portion of the subject. There should, eventually, be an International Code, dealing with the whole matter. The framing of such a code is now, accepting the York-Antwerp Rules, a matter of no great difficulty. The fundamental principle of the law is identical in all countries; there is no dispute or difference as to the more important instances to which this principle is applied; what differences of detail at present exist are, substantially, now settled by the York-Antwerp Rules. Thus the work of codification would seem to be little more than the expressing in precise and clear language of conclusions already settled, a declaration, not a change, of the law.

Nevertheless, it appears by no means clear that it would be judicious, at the present stage, to proceed forthwith to draw up such a code. It would be better, in our opinion, first to consolidate and extend the adoption of the York-Antwerp Rules as they stand.

A few years' practical experience of the working of these rules, in as many countries as can be induced to adopt them, would, in the first place, be of itself so much clear gain and would, in the second place, render the framing of an International Code so much easier, that its success, and eventual adoption, generally, if not universally, might be regarded as certain.

For these reasons we venture to think that the most judicious course to be taken this year is to content ourselves with some general expression of opinion, such as may have the effect of stimulating and extending the movement in the direction in which it is going on, recommending, if possible, to other countries the line of action which is working so well in England, pointing, perhaps, to a code, as something to be aimed at in the future, but not, for the present, attempting to go beyond the York-Antwerp Rules.

The secretary also laid upon the table two papers upon the York-Antwerp Rules, written respectively by Dr. W. Lewis,[1] Professor in the University of Berlin, and Mr. Dexter H. Walker, of New York.

HERR H. H. MEIER, of Bremen, President of the North German Lloyd, observed that in Germany people were fairly agreed as to the merits of the York-Antwerp Rules, and the rules had made their way in practice too, although doubts were felt by some whether the provisions of the law would not override the contract of the parties. In his opinion the rules had everywhere so far asserted their right to general adoption that to desist from further action, though only for a time, would be an excess of caution. He thought that the moment had arrived when the English Secretary of State for Foreign Affairs might be asked to use his influence in bringing about a conference of the seafaring nations with a view to an international code of General Average being framed.

MR. JOHN GLOVER, Chairman of the English Central Committee upon General Average, considered that Herr Meier had acted wisely in not moving a resolution in accordance with his views.

[1] This treatise, which gives the history of the General Average question and its literature and also contains an enlightened *critique* of the York-Antwerp Rules, together with some valuable reflections upon the best mode of effecting the assimilation of the laws of different nations, is to be found printed in full in the *Zeitschrift für Handelsrecht*, vol. xxiv.—ED.

The opposition of Lloyd's in England had relaxed, but was not entirely overcome, and it was desirable to let that opposition die out altogether before trying to set the Governments in motion. The time of which Mr. Meier spoke was, no doubt, not far distant, but its arrival would be retarded by an undue eagerness to press orward.

DR. E. N. RAHUSEN, of Amsterdam, counsel to the Nederlandsche Handelsmaatschappij, spoke to the same effect, and said that the law should follow, rather than lead, custom. He had often encountered the York-Antwerp Rules in practice; this showed that the proper kind of propaganda was actively going on. He could not doubt that the justice and expediency of the rules would eventually make themselves felt even at Lloyd's. He was in a position to state on the best authority that there would be no difficulty in effecting the necessary changes in the law, so far as Holland was concerned.

M. THÉODORE ENGELS, of Antwerp, President of the Belgian Lloyd, stated that he was able to give the same assurance with regard to Belgium. The subject had been broached to M. Bara, the Belgian Minister of Justice, who had warmly approved of the rules and of the movement. He instanced, as showing the equity of the rules, that in England they were considered too favourable to the shipowner, in France the contrary. It seemed to him that the Association should jealously watch for the earliest opportunity of taking further action.

MR. H. J. ATKINSON, Chairman of the Hull Chamber of Shipping, gave an amusing account of the rapidity of the progress made by the rules at Hull. When they had once become fairly known, only one large merchant and one small one had refused to adopt them, and the former of the two had soon found it prudent to make his submission.

M. E. VAN EETEN, Delegate of the Société Commerciale et Industrielle (= Chamber of Commerce) of Antwerp, touched upon the present relation of Antwerp to the York-Antwerp Rules and expressed an opinion that without legislative enactment the rules would soon have the force of law in Antwerp. He said:—

'There can be no doubt that in the case of a ship arriving at

Antwerp with the York-Antwerp clause in her bills of lading the General Average, if any, would be settled according to the rules. But I think that in a very short time the York-Antwerp Rules will be applied, whether there be a clause to that effect in the contract of affreightment or not. My reasons for saying so are these. According to the present law of Belgium the contributory value of the ship is one half, and the wages and provisions of the crew during the vessel's stay at a port of refuge are not admitted as General Average, while the code says nothing whatever about the apportionment of any other port of refuge expenses. Those expenses have so far been regulated by the local custom; that is to say, when the cargo is entirely discharged for the ship to be repaired, the cargo alone bears all the expenses of landing, warehousing, and re-shipping. A new law on the subject of General Average has already been voted by the Chamber of Representatives and has been recently adopted by the Senate. According to the new law the contributory value of the ship will be her entire value at the port of destination, and the wages and provisions of the crew at a port of refuge will be allowed, but again nothing is said as to other ports of refuge expenses. Now, supposing a ship to enter the port of Antwerp without the York-Antwerp clause in her bills of lading, wages and provisions having to be admitted according to the new law, it would evidently be unfair to continue to saddle the cargo with the expenses of landing, storing, and re-shipping and with its share of the wages and provisions besides. It will, therefore, be necessary to change the local custom of Antwerp, and the York-Antwerp Rules will, no doubt, be resorted to and soon become the custom of Antwerp.'

Mr. J. HORNE PAYNE, of London, observed that the justice of the rules in one particular had lately been triumphantly vindicated by a decision of the Queen's Bench Division of the English High Court of Justice,[1] by which, in spite of the inveterate contrary practice of average adjusters, the English law relating to port of refuge expenses had been brought into harmony with No. 7 of the rules.

M. EDOUARD CLUNET, of Paris, pointed out that the only

[1] *Attwood* v. *Sellar* (L. R. 4 Q. B. D. 342).

radical innovation which the adoption of the rules would introduce into the laws of France was the provision contained in Rule X., to which the French shipowners were naturally opposed, seeing that by the existing code the contribution of the ship was limited to one half of its value.

CAPTAIN N. JACOBSEN, of Copenhagen, reminded the meeting of the action already taken by the German Government in referring the rules to an imperial commission and of the willingness of that Government to proceed further in the matter, and urged that, if the Association as such was to remain quiescent for the present, it might at least be enjoined upon the local committees to seize the earliest opportunity of endeavouring to induce their respective Governments to countenance and actively promote the movement.

MR. BRISTOWE (Chairman of the Australian and New Zealand Underwriters' Association) described the interest which the rules had awakened in the colonies, where many, he said, wished to see them obtain everywhere the force of law.

MR. MANLEY HOPKINS (of London), MR. E. H. CAPPER, Delegate of the Central Committee on General Average at Cardiff, and MR. LAWRENCE R. BAILY, Delegate of the Steamship Owners' Association of Liverpool, also took part in the discussion, which closed with some remarks from SIR TRAVERS TWISS.

It may be imagined with what satisfaction I read at the Conference of the Association on August 26, 1880, at Berne, the following report :—

At the request of the executive council of this Association I have undertaken to report to this conference what has taken place since our last meeting with respect to the international law of General Average, as embodied in the York and Antwerp Rules.

And I think it is a matter of sincere congratulation to the members of this Association that I am able to record that the first judgments (of the Queen's Bench and the Appeal Courts) in matters of General Average not only ratified, as far as the subject under consideration was concerned, the principle upon which that part of the York and Antwerp Rules was based, but actually pronounced that the custom or practice which for at least eighty years had prevailed among the English average adjusters, and according to which they adopted a contrary system of adjustment, was at variance with the common law of England.

The case in which this satisfactory result was attained was that of Atwood v. Sellar, which came, on a so-called special case, first before the Queen's Bench Division, consisting of Lord Chief Justice Cockburn and Justices Mellor and Manisty, and afterwards before the Court of Appeal, consisting of the Lords Justices Bramwell, Baggallay, and Thesiger.

The circumstances under which it arose were, that the ship 'Sullivan Sawin,' during a voyage from Savannah to Liverpool in February 1877, encountered severe weather, which compelled the master to cut away the foretopmast, the fall of which having occasioned further damage to the vessel, he was forced to put into Charleston for repairs. These could not be effected without the discharge of a portion of the cargo, and the expenses thus incurred for landing, warehousing, and re-shipping the same, as well as for pilotage and other charges paid in respect of the ship, were, on arrival at Liverpool, all brought into the General Average column by our friend Mr. Lowndes. This being against the view which the members of the Average Adjusters' Association had hitherto adopted, and according to which, where ships have put into port to refit, whether such putting into port had been occasioned by a General Average sacrifice or a Particular Average loss, the expense of discharging the cargo was treated as General Average, the expense of warehousing it as Particular Average on the cargo, and the expense of the re-shipment of the cargo, pilotage, port charges, and other expenses incurred to enable the ship to proceed on her voyage, as Particular Average upon the freight, the principal underwriters interested on the cargo agreed to contest this innovation upon a practice of more than eighty years' standing, but they were disappointed in the result.

After a very elaborate argument of counsel before the Queen's Bench Division, it was only Mr. Justice Manisty who stood out for the old practice, whereas the majority of the Court, Lord Chief Justice Cockburn and Mr. Justice Mellor, condemned it in somewhat remarkable terms; and although the limits of this report will prevent me from giving a full reprint of the Lord Chief Justice's argument, I think I may venture so much as to quote the most instructive passages verbatim.

After some introductory observations his lordship says: 'Two questions present themselves: First, what, independently of this practice of average adjusters, is the principle or rule of law applicable to the case? Secondly, whether, assuming the practice to be inconsistent with what otherwise should be the law having subsisted for so long a time it must be taken to give the rule properly applicable to such a case;' and after alluding to some conflicting decisions to which reference had been made in the course of the argument, he states:—

'That the expenses which, according to the practice of average adjusters, are thus treated as Particular Average, should, according to legal principles, be made the subject of General Average, appears to me to flow necessarily from the fundamental principle on which the whole doctrine of General Average rests, namely, that all loss which arises from extraordinary sacrifices made or expenses incurred for the preservation of the ship and cargo must be borne proportionably by all who are interested.

'The contract between the goods owner and the shipowner on a charter-party or a bill of lading being for the conveyance of the goods to a given port, there occurs in the course of the voyage a state of things which is not provided for by the contract.

'A storm arises, the vessel is in danger, but a port is within reach, into which, in the common interest of all concerned, it would be prudent to take refuge, or it becomes necessary to cut away a mast, and as a consequence of so doing to seek an intermediate port in order to replace it. Or the ship sustains damage from the violence of winds or waves, which renders it necessary for the common safety of ship and cargo, and for the further prosecution of the adventure, to seek a port at which repairs which have become necessary for the safe prosecution of the voyage may be effected.

'The result is that, in theory at least, a new arrangement not contemplated or provided for by the original contract, takes place between the partners, who in theory, as formerly in fact, must be supposed to be present each in the practice of modern times represented by the master, to whom the interests of both are committed. If we could suppose both parties to be actually present and under a sense of imminent danger to concur in the necessity of seeking a port of refuge, but discussing the question as to how the expenses incidental to such a course shall be borne, what arrangement could be more reasonable or just than that these expenses, being extraordinary expenses incurred for the common benefit, should be borne in common, on the same principle as that which has been established from the earliest times in the case of actual jettison?

'Applying this principle with reference in the first place to the expenses incurred by the ship, it is admitted on all hands that the expenses of entering the port of refuge should be carried to General Average. Logically it would seem to follow that as the coming out of port is—at least where the common adventure is intended to be, and is afterwards further prosecuted—the necessary consequence of going in, the expenses incidental to the later stage of the proceeding should stand on the same footing as the former. The further prosecution of the voyage was in the contemplation of the parties, or of the master representing them in going in; the coming out, therefore, must equally have been in view when the resolution to go in was formed. But it is said—and it is upon this ground that the difference between these two sets of expenses is alleged to be founded—first, that it is the shipowner's duty, under his contract, to keep the ship in a navigable state, and consequently, to repair any damage she may have sustained; secondly, that when the ship has been repaired, it is the owner's duty, under his contract, to re-ship the goods and to set forth again on the voyage, and to that end to incur the cost of quitting the port and of employing a pilot or a tug if necessary. The whole of this reasoning appears to me to be based on an assumption altogether fallacious. The shipowner is not bound to repair for the purpose of carrying on the cargo, nor, having repaired, does he become bound to re-ship the cargo and complete the voyage under the original contract, but if bound at all to do so, is bound only under that contract as modified by the altered circumstances of the case.

'The contract, it should be remembered, expressly exempts the shipowner from performance of his obligations under it, when performance is prevented by perils of the sea. The ship having become incapacitated from prosecuting the voyage, and performance of the contract having been prevented by the excepted cause, the shipowner is under no obligation, so far as the goods owner is concerned, to repair. He cannot, it is true, expose the goods of the freighter to further peril by persisting in carrying them on if, having the opportunity of putting into a port of refuge, he cannot or will not, repair the ship; but, if he chooses to forego his right to freight, he may repair or not, as may best suit his interest.'

A little further on the following passages occur:—

'In legal theory we must suppose the parties to be present. In contemplation of law the master, as representing both, makes for them both the agreement, which it is reasonable to suppose that, if present, they would have made for themselves. The common purpose is twofold. The first and immediate purpose is that of saving ship and cargo by bringing both into harbour. The second is that of repairing the ship with a view to the further prosecution of the voyage, if such repair should prove reasonably practicable, with certain reservations on the part both of the shipowner and the goods owner, which probably may lead to the abandonment of the further prosecution of the voyage. The second of these purposes involves several subordinate operations and expenses incidental thereto. The state of the ship and the degree of damage she has sustained have first to be ascertained. To effect this, as well as to do the necessary repairs, it may be necessary to unship the cargo; to preserve the goods from harm they will have to be warehoused. The repair to the ship having been completed, the cargo must be reshipped. Lastly, all things having been completed, the ship will have to leave the port and put to sea. In respect of each of these stages, expenses will have to be incurred for which, as being altogether outside the original contract, that contract wholly fails to provide. They are extraordinary expenses, incurred for the preservation of ship and cargo, and in furtherance of the common adventure under circumstances in which the ship and cargo would otherwise have perished or the common adventure would have been abruptly brought to a termination. Upon whom should the expenses of these different operations fall? The practice of the average adjusters makes the unloading of the cargo matter of General Average, and as it seems to me on principle rightly so. On what ground the distinction between the cost of unshipping the cargo and of warehousing it, which is thrown on it as Particular Average, and that of re-shipping, which is treated as Particular Average on the freight, is founded, I wholly fail to perceive. Looking to the common purpose for which all these operations are performed, it seems only reasonable and just that the expenses should be borne ratably by all parties concerned; in other words, be treated as General Average, so far, at all events, as the common purpose has been effected.

'It is true that it not unfrequently happens that the primary purpose of putting into port having been accomplished, the ulterior purpose, that of further prosecuting the voyage, fails. There may be no means in the port of refuge for repairing the vessel. The cost of repairing may be so great as not to make it worth the owner's while to repair in order to earn the freight. As regards the alternative of transhipment, there may be no opportunity to tranship, or only at an increased rate of freight, on which account the shipowner may decline to tranship, except on account of the goods owner. On the other hand, the cargo may be of a perishable nature, or it may be so damaged that it cannot be carried on further without becoming worthless; or the repairs to be done to the ship will take so long a time that in the interest of the goods owner the master would not be justified in detaining the goods, but, acting as the agent of the latter, becomes bound to forego the right of carrying on the goods, and so earning the freight, and must deal with them in the interest of their owner alone. In such cases it may well be that only the expense of putting into the port of distress could properly be made matter of General Average, and that expenses thus incurred, from which no benefit results to the common adventure, should be treated as Particular Average to ship or goods, as the case may be. But we are here dealing with a case in which every expense has been incurred with a view to, and has resulted in, the further prosecution of the common adventure. The ship and cargo have been saved from destruction by being brought into port; the ship has been repaired, the cargo, having in the meantime been preserved by being warehoused, has been re-shipped, the voyage has been resumed and brought to a safe conclusion, and the goods have been delivered; in a word, the common purpose, the fulfilment of the contract of affreightment, has been effected. But how has this result been brought about? By the series of operations which have taken place from the ship's going into port to her putting to sea again inclusively. But the whole of these operations were necessary to the resumption of the voyage; the expenses of carrying them out were each of them incurred in furtherance of the common purpose. Not being expenses within the scope of the original contract, but extraordinary expenses incurred for the common benefit of ship and cargo, the conclusion appears to me irresistible that, with the exception of the cost of repairs to the ship, all these expenses should be charged to General Average.'

Then, after referring to one of the reported cases, and to the American and other laws, the judgment proceeds:—

'We have next to consider whether the practice of average adjusters in this country, which is said to have existed for seventy or eighty years, if thus found to be at variance with legal principles, shall nevertheless prevail, and must be considered as having settled the law. I am not aware of any principle on which the affirmative of this proposition can be maintained, or of any authority by which it can be upheld. It is not a usage of trade by which the terms of a contract may be interpreted or modified. It is not a custom which can be presumed to have a legal origin. It is not the *inveterate praxis* of a Court or Courts having judicial authority, and which must therefore be taken to be the law, though inconsistent with general principles. The authority of average adjusters may be said to be of an anomalous character. By the consent of shipowners and merchants they act as a sort of arbitrators in the settlement of matters of average. But they are bound in the adjustment of such claims to follow the law. And in the practice they have adopted, they have not acted or intended to act on or give effect to any mercantile usages, but have intended to give effect to what they believed to be the law; but they have mistaken it.'

And after having made the following remark, 'If a custom prevailing in a Court which, though an inferior Court, is still a Court of law, if inconsistent with law cannot prevail, surely the same rule must apply to a practice of average adjusters. When a practice of this kind is brought to the test of a legal decision, and is found to be erroneous and inconsistent with law, it cannot be permitted to override the law and acquire the force of law,' the Lord Chief Justice concludes as follows :—

'The case of Stewart v. ThePacific Steamship Company (Law Reports, 8 Q. B. p. 88), so far from supporting the defendants' case, appears to me a strong authority the other way. There, by the terms of the bill of lading, average (if any) was to be adjusted according to British usage. A fire having broken out in the ship, water was poured in to extinguish it, and bark shipped on board by the plaintiffs was seriously damaged thereby. The plaintiff claimed as for General Average; but it appeared that it was the practice of average adjusters in this country to treat such damage as Particular Average. The Court expressly declared the practice to be at variance with the law applicable to such a case, and would assuredly have given judgment in favour of the plaintiffs, had not the latter, by the terms of the bill of lading, expressly agreed to make the custom a part of the contract. "If," says Mr. Justice Quain, in delivering the judgment of the Court, "the present case depended wholly on the common law applicable to General Average, we think the plaintiffs would be entitled to recover; but as the parties have agreed to make the custom a part of their contract, the case must be decided according to the custom, and the result is that our judgment must be for the defendants." To which the learned Judge added, "It is to be hoped, however, that in future there will be no difference between law and custom on this point, and that average adjusters will act on the law as now declared, and that bills of lading will also be framed in accordance with it." There being no such term in the present contract, I see no reason for treating the practice with more consideration than the practice then before the Court received at its hands in that case.

Walthew v. Mavrojani (Law Reports, 5 Ex. p. 116) was altogether different from the present; it was a case of stranding, and the question was whether expenses incurred for the purpose of getting the ship off, after the goods had been taken out of her, and removed to a place of safety, could be made the subject of General Average, and it was held that they could not. But of the six Judges in the Exchequer Chamber, Bovill (Chief Justice), Mellor, Montague Smith, Lush and Hannen (Justices) base their judgment on the ground that while it was essential to the owner of the ship to get his ship off so as to be able to resume the voyage and earn the freight, it was indifferent to the goods owner, the goods being in safety, whether they were carried on in the same ship or in another. " It is not shown," says the Chief Justice, "that any advantage resulted to the goods from their being carried on in that ship rather than in any other." It was indifferent to the owners of the cargo whether the ship floated or not, and there was, therefore, no sacrifice made, or extraordinary expense incurred to save both ship and cargo, or for the common benefit of both. " I draw the inference," says Mr. Justice Montague Smith, " that it was indifferent to the owner whether the goods went forward to England in the ' Southern Belle,' the ship in question, or any other." Mr. Justice Hannen says: "It is unjust that expenses incurred by the owner of the ship for the benefit of all should be borne by him alone, but the expenses in question were not such, for it is indifferent to the owner of goods whether his goods are taken on by the same ship, except where they would not otherwise be carried on at all, or only at a greater expense." Even Mr. Justice Brett, who appeared to have been disposed to lay down the rule more generally, treats these expenses as incurred solely for the benefit of the shipowner.

'In like manner, in the earlier case of Hallett v. Wigram (9 Common Bench, p. 580), in which a claim for contribution had been made where part of the cargo had been sold to raise money to repair the ship, which had put back by reason of damage sustained by ordinary perils of the sea, Wilde (Chief Justice) in giving judgment, says: " It is in respect only of the incapacity of the particular ship to carry the goods forward to their destination that the pleas show that the cargo was in danger of being wholly lost. It is difficult to see how the repair of the ship could be for the benefit and advantage of the plaintiff. The plaintiff's goods were of a description not to be deteriorated to any great extent."

'These two decisions are, no doubt, sufficient authority for saying that, according to English law, expenses incurred for the benefit of the ship alone, without any concomitant benefit to the cargo, such as the expense of getting off a stranded vessel after the goods have been discharged, or repairing a vessel in a port of refuge, in the absence of special circumstances such as were referred to in Walthew v. Mavrojani, will not give a claim to General Average; but they are inapplicable to a case like the present. There is nothing here to show that the goods carried have been sent on in another vessel; and what is of more importance, the expenses were all incurred in furtherance of the common purpose and for the benefit of the cargo as well as the ship. Of the ship, as an opportunity was thus afforded of repairing it, and enabling it to take on the cargo; of the cargo, as it was thus enabled to be carried on to its destination. I am therefore of opinion that our judgment must be for the plaintiff, and as my brother Mellor concurs in the view I take, both as regards the result and as regards the reasons for it, there will be judgment for the plaintiff.'

The defendants appealed against this judgment, and both parties having fortified themselves respectively with two leading counsel, eminent in matters of commercial law, long and learned arguments were addressed to the Court of Appeal, which confirmed the first judgment, and pronounced its unanimous reasons through the mouth of Lord Justice Thesiger —

'The question raised by this appeal is whether, in the case of a vessel going into port in consequence of an injury which is itself the subject of General Average, the expenses of warehousing and reloading goods necessarily unloaded for the purpose of repairing the injury, and expenses incurred for pilotage and other charges on the vessel's leaving the port, are the subject of General Average also.

'The matter came before the Court below in the form of a special case, and upon it the Court decided in favour of the plaintiffs, who assert that the expenses in question are the subject of General Average.

'The special case states a long-continued practice of British average adjusters, in adjusting losses in cases where ships have put into port to refit, whether such putting into port has been occasioned by a General Average sacrifice or a Particular Average loss, to treat the expense of discharging the cargo as General Average; the expense of warehousing it as Particular Average on the cargo, and the expense of the re-shipment of the cargo, pilotage, port charges and other expenses incurred to enable the ship to proceed on her voyage as Particular Average upon the freight. It was not, however, and could not reasonably be contended for the appellant, that the practice could be put so high as a custom impliedly incorporated in the contract between the parties; and during the course of the argument we intimated our opinion, founded upon the language of the special case with regard to this practice, and especially the language of the fifth paragraph, that the question between the parties must be decided in accordance with legal principle and authority, which the practice of the average adjusters professes to follow.

'The law governing the case is admittedly English law, for the expenses in dispute arose upon a voyage the proper and actual termination of which was an English port.

'As a matter of principle we are clearly of opinion that the judgment of the majority of the Court below in favour of the plaintiffs was right. The principle which underlies the whole doctrine of General Average contribution, is that the loss, immediate and consequential, caused by a sacrifice for the benefit of cargo, ship, and freight, should be borne by all.'

After some further observations, the judgment thus proceeds :—

'A vessel which has put into port to repair an injury occasioned by a General Average sacrifice, may be, and generally is, when in port, in perfect safety; and if by the expression " common danger " be meant danger of actual injury to vessel and cargo, there is no more danger to the goods when on board, the vessel being in port, than when stowed in a warehouse on shore, and indeed in many cases only a portion of the goods is removed from the vessel in order to do the repairs to her, while the remainder of the goods is left on board.

'If, on the other hand, by "common danger" be meant the danger of the vessel with her cargo being prevented from prosecuting her voyage, then there is no more reason why the expenses of warehousing and reloading, and the expenses incurred for pilotage and other charges paid in respect of the vessel leaving port and proceeding upon her voyage, should not constitute General Average than there is reason for saying that unloaded and warehoused goods should not contribute, as it is clear in a case of voluntary sacrifice that they must, to the expenses of the necessary repairs to the vessel. Both classes of expenses are extraordinary expenses, consequent upon the voluntary sacrifice, and necessary for the due prosecution of the voyage by the vessel with her cargo. Neither class can as a general proposition be said to be incurred exclusively for the benefit of either vessel or cargo. In some cases it might be for the interest of a shipowner to terminate the voyage at the port where his vessel puts in to repair a disaster, while it would be all-important for the goods owner to have his goods carried on by the same vessel; in other cases the position of the parties in this respect might be reversed. But however this may be, the going into port, the unloading, warehousing, and reloading of the cargo, and the coming out of port, are at all events parts of one act or operation contemplated, resolved upon and carried through for the common safety and benefit, and properly to be regarded as continuous. The shipowner is, at least, entitled to re-ship the goods and prosecute his voyage with them, and the expenses necessary for that purpose, being *ex hypothesi* consequent upon a damage voluntarily incurred for the general advantage, should legitimately be the subject of General Average contribution; or, to use the language of Lord Tenterden in his work on shipping: "If the damage to be repaired be in itself an object of contribution, it seems reasonable that all expenses necessary, although collateral to the reparation, should also be objects of contribution: the accessory should follow the nature of its principal."

'But it is said for the appellants that if this be so, and the principle be carried out to its logical consequences, expenses incurred for wages of crew and provisions, should equally form the subject of General Average; and that inasmuch as it is, as they suggest, undeniable that they do not, the principle itself must either be faulty or at least not recognised in English law. As a matter of fact, it is extremely doubtful whether the expenses for wages of crew, and provisions in a port of refuge, have ever been disallowed by our Courts as constituting a claim for General Average in a case where the ship has put into the port to repair damage itself belonging to General Average; but even if the assertion were correct, the conclusion drawn would by no means follow.

'That the principle in question is not faulty we have endeavoured to show in the observations already made, and the view we have taken upon the point is strongly confirmed by the fact that it is recognised and carried to its so-called logical consequences as regards the wages of crew and provisions in all other countries than our own.

'That the principle is not recognised in English law is not proved by showing that expenses incurred for wages of crew and provisions have been under certain circumstances disallowed as the subject of General Average, unless it be shown, which it has not been to us at the same time, that they have been disallowed upon grounds that negative the principle, and is disproved if it be found that, notwithstanding such disallowances, the expenses in question in this case have been allowed. All that in such a case can be said is, that either the Courts have made a mistake in limiting the application of the principle, or that its limitation is due to some real or supposed rule of public policy. This at least may fairly be asked: What is the principle if this is not? If then the question before us stood only upon principle, we should have no hesitation in deciding it according to the principle we have stated, and it at least may fairly be asked: What other principle, if it be not correct, is to be substituted in its place? But the authorities remain to be considered, and it is the more necessary that they should be examined with attention, seeing that the practice of the average adjusters professes to follow them.'

And after a careful review of the different authorities quoted on both sides as bearing upon the subject under consideration, the judgment continues:—

'We have, therefore, the law as laid down by the Courts for a considerable portion of the period over which the practice of average adjusters, stated in the special case, extends, running counter to that practice by recognising as regards port of refuge expenses a distinction between cases where a ship puts into a port of distress for repair of damage done by a voluntary sacrifice, and cases where it so puts in for repair of damage caused by perils of the seas, and admitting in the former cases as a matter of principle, if not of express decision, expenses such as those in question in this case, to be the subject of General Average contribution.

'This distinction in principle is to be found asserted by Benecke, who was a member of Lloyd's, in his valuable work on the principles of Indemnity in Marine Insurance, published in 1824. At page 191 he says: "If, setting aside all laws and received opinions, the case is examined merely according to the fundamental maxims which regulate General and Particular Average, it will in the first instance appear evident that not only all the port charges, such as pilotage, harbour dues, lighterage, &c., but also the charges of unloading and reloading, repairs, and crews' wages, will be General Average, if the ship put into port for the mere purpose of repairing a damage voluntarily incurred for the general advantage. For all these expenses, being the necessary consequences of a measure taken for the general benefit, belong to General Average;" and then turning to the case where the port is entered in consequence of a particular damage sustained, by which the vessel is rendered unfit to prosecute her voyage, as when masts, sails, or other requisite apparel are lost in a storm, or the vessel has sprung a dangerous leak, he adds: "All the expenses of entering the port are a subject of General Average, being the consequence of a measure voluntarily taken for the preservation of the whole. But as soon as the object of putting the vessel and her cargo in safety is accomplished, the cause for general contribution ceases; for whatever is subsequently done is not a sacrifice for the benefit of the whole, or for averting an imminent danger, but is the mere necessary consequence of a casual misfortune." Benecke then claims the allowance even of wages of crew and provisions, where the putting into port is the consequence of a damage belonging to General Average; on the other hand, he contends for the disallowance even of the expenses of unloading cargo, where it is the consequence of a damage belonging to Particular Average. In Stevens "On Average," and Bailey "On Average," the distinction referred to is not adopted except as regards the repairs of the ship; but both writers assert, as a matter of principle, that, where a ship necessarily puts into a port to repair damage, whether the original cause of damage be a voluntary sacrifice or any ordinary peril of the sea, the expenses of warehousing and reloading, as well as those of unloading the cargo, and the outward as well as inward port charges, should be the subject of General Average contribution. (See "Stevens," p. 22, and "Bailey," p. 119.) They look not to the more remote damage which undoubtedly was a Particular Average loss, but to the proximate act of putting into port for the safety of ship and cargo, which would belong to General Average, and in answer to the argument that their views, if logically carried out, would lead to the allowance as General Average of the cost of repair of the ship, Bailey, at p. 119, replies that the damage which necessitated that repair, being caused by a peril of the sea, the repair should be treated as Particular Average, but that the ship does not put into the port of refuge because she wants repairs, but because the voyage cannot be continued until she is repaired, or a total loss of ship and cargo will follow if she does not go into port. He adds: "The immediate cause for putting into the port of refuge is the impossibility of completing the voyage in her then state, or the expected total loss of ship and cargo; the damage which the ship has sustained is the remote cause only, for under other circumstances the crew are not justified into putting into port, although the vessel may have sustained damage which it will be necessary ultimately to repair."

'The views thus expressed are substantially those which are recognised in American law and practice, and they are carried out to the length of including the expense of wages of crew and provisions at the port of refuge in the amount to be contributed for in General Average in all cases where a vessel puts into port for the common safety, whether owing to injury from a peril of the sea or a voluntary sacrifice. (See Phillips "On Insurance," 3rd edition, sections 1,322, 1,326, and 1,328.) To return to the text-writers of this country, Mr. Arnould, in his work upon "Marine Insurance, 3rd edition, vol. ii. p. 789, after discussing the principles relating to General Average, says: "From these principles it follows that where a ship has either cut away her masts or rigging, or has been so damaged by a storm that it is necessary for the safety both of ship and cargo to put into a port of distress for repairs, all the expenses inseparably connected with the act of first putting into and afterwards clearing out of such a port of distress, give the shipowner a claim to a General Average contribution, and this upon the plain ground that these expenses are a necessary consequence of an extraordinary measure taken for the general preservation."'

And the judgment concludes in the following terms:—

'The result of this review of the authorities is to confirm the opinion which, apart from authority, we entertain, and have already expressed upon the questions submitted to us.

'The practice, then, of the average adjusters, as stated in the special case, appears to us to be neither founded upon true principles, nor to be in accordance with the views of the text-writers; and so far as there is case authority upon the matter, it appears to us to be opposed to legal decisions. It is a practice, too, which has not been, as the practice in Stewart v. The West India and Pacific Steam Ship Company (Law Reports, 8 Q. B. p. 88) was made, part of the contract between the parties, and therefore constitutes no impediment to our giving effect to the objections to its validity, and in deciding as we do that the judgment of the authority of the Court below was right and should be affirmed, it is satisfactory to us to know that the law as laid down in the judgment of the Court below and of this Court is placed upon a footing which more nearly assimilates it, in matters in which assimilation is desirable, to the law obtaining in other mercantile and maritime communities.'

I should be only too happy if I could add that the antagonists to the York and Antwerp Rules, taking into their consideration the arguments in the above-quoted judgments, would now cheerfully and cordially join us in adopting them altogether, for as Mr. Lowndes in his address at the last meeting of the Average Adjusters' Association very truly stated:—

'It is a somewhat remarkable circumstance that, of all the

changes proposed by the York rules—I call them for the moment by their old name, because I am now referring to the state of things when they were drawn up—all except two have been since adopted into the law and practice of this country. At the time when those rules were drawn up, it was an innovation on our practice to propose that damage to cargo by opening the hatches to make a jettison, or by derangement of stowage consequent on a jettison, or by pouring down water to extinguish a fire, should be treated as General Average; or that damage either to ship or cargo by a voluntary stranding should be treated as General Average under any circumstances; or that damage done to cargo by discharging at a port of refuge should be treated as General Average under any circumstances; or that the deductions from the contributory value of freight should be confined to those expenses which were incurred subsequently to the General Average act. All these innovations have now been adopted, some under the compulsion of legal decisions, others without that compulsion, into our practice; and in all these respects our practice at this day conforms to the very words of the York-Antwerp Rules. So much of our labours at York and at Antwerp has borne fruit. This is a fact which every adjuster knows or ought to know. The only portion of our work which at this moment remains unaccomplished is the carrying out of Rule 7, which is identical in substance with the resolution we are now considering, and Rule 8, which declares that the wages and maintenance of the crew during a vessel's detention in a port of refuge ought to be replaced as General Average.'

As to the wages and maintenance of the crew during a vessel's detention in a port of refuge, I can only repeat what I have on previous occasions given as the result of my practical experience, that if such expenditure is not *bonâ fide* allowed, means are found to recover them under the denomination of labourage, and if we believe some of our friends who have been professionally engaged at the Cape of Good Hope and at other ports frequently entered by vessels in distress, the charges for labourage are often very much in excess of what crews' wages and provisions during such stay could possibly amount to.

So far as I have been able to ascertain the case stands thus :

whereas the Liverpool and Glasgow adjustments are generally drawn up in conformity with the 'Attwood v. Sellar' case, i.e.—carrying the principle involved in that case to its apparently legitimate extension in conformity with the York-Antwerp Rules—the London adjusters continue still to adhere to the old practice in all cases except those which are absolutely on all-fours with Attwood and Sellar. That such a difference of practice cannot continue stands to reason, especially if it is considered that the York and Antwerp Rules are inserted in almost all policies on ships and cargoes, so that practically the work of their general adoption is steadily, although slowly, going onwards. Further litigation will undoubtedly be resorted to, and it is not improbable that at our next meeting we may hear that our jurisprudence has made a fresh advance towards that uniformity which has so long been our goal.

There is only one subject—and our much respected friend, Mr. Lawrence R. Baily, having mentioned it in his opening address as Chairman to the Average Adjusters' Association, my alluding to it need scarcely require an apology—to which I wish to call the attention of the conference.

It is well known, and not only laid down by the most eminent Judges and text-writers, but everywhere conceded, that the adjustment of any General Average occurring in the course of a maritime adventure is to be drawn up at the port of destination, and in conformity with the there prevailing laws, customs, or practices, whatever they are. On this point Mr. Baily stated:—

'In most cases this would create no inconvenience, but when as in Mediterranean steamers, which have on board goods for and from different countries, say England, Greece, Turkey, destined for other countries, say Greece, Turkey, Spain, &c., the laws and customs in each of which differ from those in every other—such a doctrine would produce chaos. There is no one port of destination as regards all the cargo in such a case. Would it not be reasonable and create less confusion if the law of the flag of the ship were adopted in such a case? General Average under such a system would be intelligible, and all could protect themselves by insurance against such a General Average.'

I think that the suggestion here made is worthy of the very

best consideration at the hands of all who have an interest in the question; but with how much more satisfaction would the alteration be received if the York and Antwerp Rules had in the meantime secured the adhesion of all the leading maritime nations!

Now the Transactions of the Association for the years 1881 (Cologne), 1882 (Liverpool), and 1883 (Milan) contain only one sentence on this subject, and that is in the report of the council to the Cologne Conference, which reads thus :—

Mention has been made in the last report of the increasing acceptance of the York and Antwerp Rules to regulate General Average contributions, and the council have the satisfaction to announce that these rules have become all but universally adopted.

This meant, of course, not by legal enactment or by decisions of courts of law, but by agreement between shipowners and merchants and their respective underwriters.

I come now to the last legal feature as far as our English jurisprudence is concerned on this subject, which is fully set out in the following report which I read at the Hamburg Conference of the Association in 1885, and runs thus :—

At the request of the executive council of this Association, I have undertaken to inform this meeting of such incidents as have occurred in England with regard to the international law of General Average—as embodied in the York and Antwerp Rules—since I had the honour of bringing the subject before the Berne Conference (1880) of this Association.

It was then my good fortune to report that, owing to a decision of the Judges of the Queen's Bench Division, confirmed by the unanimous judgment of the Lords Justices of the Court of Appeal, it was settled law in England, that if a vessel had to put into a port of distress in consequence of a General Average act, all expenses thereby incurred should be apportioned upon all the interests of the maritime adventure.

The language used in the judgments upon this occasion (Attwood v. Sellar) led some members of the Average Adjusters' Association to consider themselves authorised to apportion in an equal manner all port of distress expenses, even if the putting in had not been caused by a General Average act.

This gave rise to another lawsuit (Svendson v. Wallace), which was taken to the House of Lords, and has only lately been decided there.

The circumstances of the case were that the Norwegian vessel 'Olaf Trygvason,' with a cargo of rice from Rangoon to Liverpool, met with heavy weather and sprang a serious leak, in consequence of which the master was compelled, for the preservation of ship and cargo, to put into St. Louis, Mauritius, where the vessel had to be discharged and the cargo to be stored, and, after the completion of the vessel's repairs, to be re-shipped.

Now, according to the average adjustment, which our friend Mr. Richard Lowndes issued in conformity with his interpretation of the principles recognised in Attwood v. Sellar, the proportion due from the owners of the cargo ex 'Olaf Trygvason' amounted to 770l. 2s. 4d.; but, although the owners of the cargo—in conformity with an average statement drawn up by the well-known London adjusters, Messrs. Wm. Richards & Sons—admitted their liability to repay the cargo's proportion of the expenses of putting into port, as well as the landing charges and warehouse rent of the cargo at St. Louis, amounting to 681l. 13s. 1d., they denied their liability to contribute to the expenses of re-shipping the cargo, and in the port charges, pilotage, and other expenses subsequent to its reloading, amounting to 88l. 19s. 10d.

Under these circumstances several witnesses were called at the trial, whose evidence was to the effect that for sixty or seventy years the practice of average adjusters had been in conformity with the cargo-owners' contention, but the learned Judge held that this was not evidence of a custom of trade which could be left to the jury, a decision which was upheld by the Divisional Court in very elaborate judgments delivered by Mr. Justice Grove and Mr. Justice Mathew.

Thereupon a special case was agreed upon between the parties, and argued before Mr. Justice Lopes, who decided that he was bound by the principles laid down in the case of Attwood v. Sellar, and concluded his judgment as follows :—

'It seems to me that the point relied on by the defendant, that the expenses of going out of port are not chargeable to General Average because the cargo is in safety when the port is reached, is unsustainable. The cargo is in safety when the port is reached; still it must be admitted that the expenses of unloading are General Average expenses. Such an argument would be equally cogent whether the cause of putting into port was a General or a Particular Average damage. In Attwood v. Sellar, however, it was held that the expenses of going out of port were General Average expenses. I am of opinion that the plaintiffs are entitled to judgment for 88*l*. 19*s*. 10*d*. with interest in the usual way and costs. I have not thought it necessary to cite authorities. So far as the principle involved in Attwood v. Sellar is concerned, the authorities are most exhaustively dealt with by Thesiger, L.J., in his most able judgment in that case in the Appeal Court. With regard to the other question raised in this case not decided in Attwood v. Sellar, there is little authority to be found.'

The cargo-owners, not content with this decision, took the case to the Court of Appeal, where the Master of the Rolls and Lord Justice Bowen pronounced judgment in their favour, Lord Justice Baggallay, the other member of the Court, being of a contrary opinion. From a perusal of the judgment delivered by the Master of the Rolls (Sir Wm. Baliol Brett),[1] it will be seen that he condemns the principle upon which the York and Antwerp Rules were based, and which was approved of by five of the most learned of our Judges in the Attwood v. Sellar case—the principle that the common benefit or the completion of the maritime adventure should be the guiding motive of the General Average law. He insists upon the axiom that as soon as the common safety of the maritime adventure is insured from danger of total loss, no apportionment of any further expenses may take place.

The members of this Association will easily understand the line

---

[1] Now Lord Esher.

of argument of the Master of the Rolls from the following passage out of his judgment :—

'The governing principle or proposition, which has been adopted in its terms by a succession of English Courts as the true statement of the governing principle, is that which was stated by Mr. Justice Lawrence in Birkley *v.* Presgrave. It has been considered to be one of the many happy expositions of mercantile law made by that learned person, in terms so broad and yet so accurate as show that he was one of the greatest mercantile lawyers who has ever adorned our profession in this country. His proposition is thus expressed : "All loss which arises in consequence of extraordinary sacrifices made or expenses incurred for the preservation of the ship and cargo come within General Average, and must be borne proportionably by all who are interested." This proposition, read with regard to expenses, will read thus : All loss which arises in consequence of extraordinary expenses incurred for the preservation of the ship and cargo comes within General Average. But the loss which arises from an expense is the expense itself. Therefore, we must read thus : Every expense incurred for the preservation of the ship and cargo comes within General Average. Applying this rule in its ordinary sense to each item successively claimed as an item of expenditure in respect of which a General Average contribution in any given case is due, the question must be : was the item of expenditure at the moment it was incurred, incurred for the safety of both the ship and cargo ? The word "benefit" is not used by Mr. Justice Lawrence, but it is used by Lord Kenyon in the same case. He says: "for the benefit of the whole concern." But the word "benefit," thus used by him with regard to the same facts in the same case in a judgment agreeing with the judgment of Mr. Justice Lawrence sitting by his side, must have been intended to mean the same as the word "preservation" used by that learned Judge. The words have been usually used as equivalent.'

Lord Justice Bowen arrived at the same conclusion in a very elaborate judgment, in which he criticises the arguments used by the late Lord Chief Justice Cockburn and the late Lord Justice Thesiger in the Attwood *v.* Sellar case, and his observations cannot but remind one of the time when in Glasgow, London, York, and Antwerp, the same arguments were used in behalf of what was then called Lloyd's practice.

The terms in which Lord Justice Baggallay announced his dissent from the conclusions to which his two colleagues arrived were as follows:—

'I feel bound to express the opinion at which I have arrived, and to state concisely the reasons by which I have been influenced in forming that opinion. In doing so I propose, in the first place, to compare the circumstances under which the decision in Attwood *v.* Sellar was arrived at, with those with which we have to deal on the present appeal; for conciseness and convenience of comparison I will refer to the ships as A and B, and will deal with them as having encountered the same storm and as having sought the same port of refuge. The circumstances may be then stated as follows: two ships, A and B, each on a voyage from a foreign port to Liverpool, and having a valuable cargo on board, encountered a violent storm; the master of A, to avoid a more serious injury, cut away one of his masts; B sprang a dangerous leak; both, for the safety of ship and cargo, put into a port of refuge to repair the injuries they had sustained; to effect such repairs and to enable the ships to prosecute their respective voyages, it became necessary in the case of each ship to discharge the whole or a portion of her cargo; in addition to the port dues and other expenses incident to her entering the port, further expenses were incurred in respect of each ship in unloading, warehousing, and reloading her cargo whilst she remained in port, and for pilotage and other charges on leaving the port to prosecute her voyage.

'The only difference between the circumstances of A and those of B was in the nature or character of the injury, which occasioned her putting into port. The cutting away of one of the masts of A was the subject of General Average; in other words, her putting into the port of refuge was occasioned by a General Average sacrifice; whilst the putting into port of B was occasioned by her springing a dangerous leak, which was a Particular Average loss. But in each case the putting into port for the safety of ship and cargo was an act of sacrifice giving rise to claims for General Average contribution; in the case of A this act of sacrifice followed, or was a continuation of the original act of sacrifice, whilst in the case of B. it was itself the original act of sacrifice; in each case the proximate cause of the extraordinary expenses incurred was the putting into the port of refuge.

'If it had been left to average adjusters, previously to the decision in Attwood v. Sellar, to adjust the losses in respect of the expenses incurred by the two ships, they would, in accordance with a practice of many years' duration, have dealt with them as follows: in respect of each ship they would have treated the expenses incurred in entering the port and of discharging the cargo as General Average, those incurred in warehousing the cargo as Particular Average on the cargo, and the pilotage and other charges incidental to leaving the port as Particular Average on freight; the fact that in the case of A the putting into port was occasioned by a General Average sacrifice, whilst in the case of B it was occasioned by a Particular Average loss, would in no way have affected the adjustment of the losses incurred by reason of the putting into port; and properly so, if I am correct in the view which I have expressed, that in each case the putting into port was an act of sacrifice and the foundation of a claim for General Average contribution.

'That the practice of the average adjusters was based upon the principle that the putting into port to refit is in itself an act of sacrifice, is evidenced by their treating the expenses incidental to entering the port of refuge and of discharging the cargo as the subject of General Average contribution; upon no other principle could the practice be supported. But the decision in Attwood v. Sellar established that, whilst the practice of the average adjusters was in accordance with legal principles, so far as it treated the expenses of entering the port of refuge and of discharging the cargo as the subject of General Average contribution, it was erroneous, in the case of A, in limiting the expenses, which were the subject of General Average contribution, to those last mentioned, and that the expenses of warehousing and reloading the cargo and those incidental to leaving the port were equally the subject of General Average contribution. But if, in the case of A, the expenses of warehousing and reloading the cargo and of leaving the port were properly held to be the subject of General Average contribution, I am unable to suggest any reason, satisfactory to myself, why the like principle should not be applied in the case of B; in that case the expenses of unloading, warehousing, and reloading of the cargo and the coming out of port were as consequent upon the putting into port as they were in the case of A; if they ought not to be treated as the subject of General Average contribution in the case of B they ought not, according to the view which I take of the circumstances of the two cases, to have been so treated in the case of A.

'It has been pressed upon us in argument that in the judgment which was delivered in Attwood v. Sellar care was taken to avoid intimating any opinion as to how a case similar to that now under consideration should be dealt with. I cannot assent to this view of the scope of the judgment; it is doubtless true that it was not intended to express any decided opinion upon the question referred to, but attention is distinctly directed to the case of a ship which has been damaged by perils of the sea, and has subsequently put into a port of refuge, and a distinction as regards any claim to General Average contribution is drawn between a case in which the goods are unshipped and in safety, and the common danger consequently at an end, before the ship puts into port, and one in which the goods are not unshipped until after the ship has put into port, and in which there is consequently a common danger at the time when the ship put into port. And similar views are indicated in the comments upon the case of Job v. Langton. For the reasons which I have thus concisely stated, I am of opinion that Lopes, J., arrived at a correct conclusion, and that the appeal should be dismissed.'

Strangely enough, the expectations which were formed, by the mercantile community in general, of the view the learned members of the House of Lords would take of the case have not been fulfilled. After very long arguments, the apparently unanimous opinion of Lord Blackburn, Lord Watson, and Lord FitzGerald, before whom the hearing took place, was delivered by Lord Blackburn on May 12 last. The House dismissed the appeal, thereby ratifying the views of the Master of the Rolls and Lord Justice Bowen, and dissenting from those of Mr. Justice Lopes and Lord Justice Baggallay.

Lord Blackburn, at the commencement of his judgment, minutely stated the course usually adopted in matters of this description, as far as the settlements between the interests to a maritime adventure were concerned. Having then given a full history of the case, and explained what caused the 'Olaf Trygvason' to enter the port of distress, what happened there with respect to her, and how the different contentions ultimately arose, he proceeded as follows:—

'In Simonds v. White (2 Barnewall & Cresswell, 111) Chief Justice Abbott says: "The principle of General Average, namely, that all whose property has been saved by the sacrifice of the property of another shall contribute to make good his loss, is of very ancient date and of universal reception among commercial nations. The obligation to contribute, therefore, depends not so much upon the terms of any particular instrument, as upon a general rule of maritime law. The obligation may be limited, qualified, or even excluded, by the special terms of a contract as between the parties to the contract, but there is nothing of that kind in any contract between the parties to this cause. There are, however, many variations in the laws and usages of different nations as to the losses which are considered to fall within this principle."'

His lordship drew from this judgment the well-known and generally adopted conclusion that average statements have to be made in conformity with the laws of the port of destination. He then approved of Mr. Justice Manisty's dictum in Attwood v. Sellar to the effect 'that general practice, long continued amongst English adjusters, affords strong ground for thinking that the practice is one which is not in general inconvenient, and that it throws a considerable onus on those who impugn it to show that the particular circumstances are such as to render an adherence to the practice in that case against principle.'

His lordship continued:—

'Before proceeding further, I think it desirable to consider what is the question raised on the issue reserved for further consideration. The plaintiffs claimed the sum which Messrs. Lowndes and Ryley made payable, viz. 770*l.* The defendants had paid the sum which Messrs. W. Richards and Sons made payable by them. The issue was whether all that was really due had been paid. It is to be observed, first, that the points on which Messrs. W. Richards and Sons differ from Messrs. Lowndes and Ryley are not all in favour of the defendants. If the 190*l.*, which represents the warehousing rent, and fire insurance, is properly charged to cargo, the defendants have to pay the whole of it. If it is properly charged to General Average, they have only to pay their proportion of it, or somewhat less than one-half. That, if it stood alone, would make nearly 100*l.* more payable by the defendants. But if the 450*l.*, which is the cost of re-shipping, is properly charged to freight, the defendants are not liable to pay any portion of it. If it is properly charged to General Average they would have to pay about half of it. So that that item makes a difference of about 230*l.* If, in addition, the 20*l.* for the cost of going out of port is properly charged to freight, that makes a further difference of about 10*l.* It is not, therefore, necessary to decide anything more than whether these two items are, under the circumstances of the case, properly chargeable to General Average or not. If they are not so chargeable, the order appealed against is right, for the defendants have paid enough, and more than enough, whether the 190*l.* is properly chargeable to cargo or not, and it is unnecessary to consider that question, except in so far as it may throw light on the principles which are to guide the decision of the first and most important one.

'I do not think it necessary to inquire what would be the proper course, if the seeking the port of refuge had been solely for the purpose of doing repairs, the cargo not being in any danger. Such a case may perhaps sometimes, though rarely, occur. Nor do I think it necessary to inquire what would be the proper course if the ship and cargo were both safe in the harbour of refuge, and the unloading of the cargo was entirely for the purpose of facilitating the repairs. Such a case seems more likely to happen than that first supposed. I think, on examining the two adjustments, and exercising the power which I have assumed to be given, there can be no doubt that the cargo on board the ship, leaking to the extent which she did, was not safe even in harbour until the ship was so far lightened that she could be taken into dry dock. Should the expense of reloading her, after the repairs were made, be charged to freight, the goods having been taken out under such circumstances? I think it should.

'I am afraid I have not understood the reasoning on which Chief Justice Cockburn, in his judgment in Attwood v. Sellar (Law Reports, 4 Q. B. D. 354) comes to a contrary conclusion. If I have, I must express dissent from it.

'The ordinary contract between shipowner and merchant is that the goods shall be carried to their destination, and shall there be delivered, unless prevented by the excepted perils. And this generally should be done in the original ship. Whenever the ship is disabled it must, in order literally to fulfil this contract, be necessary to repair the ship so far as to make her fit to carry on the cargo, and if any part of the cargo has been taken out, to reship it.'

And in Rosetta v. Gurney (11 Common Bench, 188) the decision of the Court comes to this:—

' "If the voyage is completed in the original ship it is completed upon the original contract, and no additional freight is incurred. If the master tranships because the original ship is irreparably damaged without considering whether he is bound to tranship or merely at liberty to do so, it is clear that he tranships to earn his full freight, and so the delivery takes place upon the original contract." There never was in the present case any question as to the "Olaf Trygvason" being irreparably damaged; but she was so far damaged that it was certain that there would be some delay (it turned out to be about six weeks) before the "Olaf Trygvason" was in a fit state to carry the goods on to Liverpool. And if there had been a good ship at St. Louis willing to carry the goods to their destination for less than the agreed freight from Rangoon, it might have been for the benefit of all that the goods should be shipped on that vessel at once, carried on and delivered to the consignee without delay. Such was the course pursued in Shipton v. Thornton (9 Adolphus & Ellis, 314), where the original shipment was from Singapore to London in the "James Scott." She put into Batavia in distress, and there the goods were transhipped into the "Mountaineer" and the "Sesostris," carried to London, and there delivered to the owner of the "James Scott," at a cost less than the amount of freight which he would have earned had the goods been carried on in the "James Scott." He delivered them to the consignee, who produced the original bill of lading by the "James Scott." The consignee refused to pay freight at the rate in the bill of lading of the "James Scott" from Singapore to London, though he paid that from Batavia agreed in the bills of lading of the "Mountaineer" and the "Sesostris." The decision was, that whether or not the captain was bound to tranship he was at liberty to do so, and having done so, had earned his full freight. The expense which he had incurred to earn it being certainly not General Average, but I think a Particular Average, paid by the shipowner to earn his freight. My conclusion is that if, instead of transhipping, the captain waits till the original ship is repaired, and then re-ships on that original ship, the cost of so doing should not be General Average but Particular Average to earn the full freight. Chief Justice Cockburn seems to think that in all cases where the ship is disabled, whether she can be repaired or not, the original contract is dissolved and a new one formed by law. This seems to me in direct conflict with the two decisions I have just cited; and even if it were so, I think it is somewhat in the nature of a *petitio principii* to say that one of the terms of the new contract should be that the cost of transhipment or re-shipment, as the case may be, should be General Average.

'The judgment, however, of the Court of Appeal, delivered by Lord Justice Thesiger, does not proceed on this ground. I have some difficulty, after reading the statement as to the grounds on which the Court of Appeal proceeded, given by Lord Justice Baggallay in his judgment in the present case, in saying on what ground it does proceed.

'The special case in Attwood v. Sellar was express that the ship was injured by a voluntary sacrifice, and was thereby compelled to put into Charleston to repair the said damage. It is not expressly said either way whether the cargo was in any danger. Lord Justice Baggallay, who was a party to that judgment, says that it was decided on the ground that putting into the port of refuge was necessary for the safety of both ship and cargo, and that he, at least, thought that it was immaterial what was the cause of that necessity. Yet I think there is much reason for doubting if Lord Justice Thesiger quite agreed in this. He says: "The principle which underlies the whole law of General Average contribution is that the loss, immediate and consequential, caused by a sacrifice for the benefit of cargo, ship, and freight, should be borne by all. This principle is in the abstract conceded by counsel for the defendants, and its application to the present case is admitted to the extent of allowing the expenses of unloading the goods, for the purpose of doing the necessary repairs to enable it to proceed on the voyage, to be the subject of General Average contribution; but they attempt to distinguish such expenses from those of warehousing and reloading the cargo, and of outward port and pilotage charges, by the suggestion that the common danger to the whole adventure is at an end when the goods are unloaded, and that General Average ceases at the point of time when the common danger ceases." This is, I think, a fair statement of the argument of the respondents' counsel in the present case. Afterwards, he says: "The going into port, the unloading, warehousing, and reloading, are at all events parts of one act or operation contemplated, resolved upon, and carried through for the common safety and benefit, and properly to be regarded as continuous." This was much relied on by the counsel for the respondents. If I thought it was the state of the case before the House, I should consider whether, in such a case, it might not fairly be argued that the whole of these operations were to be considered as parts of the expense of repairing the damage, and therefore in a case where the cause of the damage was such that the expense of repairing it ought to be borne by all, as was the case in Attwood *v.* Sellar, to be borne by all; but that in a case where the cause of the damage was such that the expense of repairing it ought to be borne by the ship only, which is the present case, to be borne by the ship only. But having come to the conclusion that such is not the state of the case before the House, I do not enter into this inquiry.

'Having come to the conclusion that, under the circumstances of this case, the expenses of reloading, &c., should not be placed to General Average, and that being enough, if your lordships agree with me, to show that the respondents have paid more than enough, it is not necessary to consider whether the smaller sum of 20*l*. ought also to have been charged to ship or freight and not to General Average. I agree with Lord Justice Bowen in what he says at p. 90, that that is a more difficult question than the other. And as the amount is not sufficient to turn the scale, it is not necessary to decide it. I should think it seldom involved any sum so great as to be of practical importance, and I prefer leaving it undecided.

'I shall therefore move that the Order appealed against be affirmed, and the appeal dismissed; the appellants to pay the costs.'

It is sincerely to be regretted that this report must end with a communication so unsatisfactory to the members of this Association, who had every reason to expect, from the general applause with which the York and Antwerp Rules were accepted by the mercantile community in general, that the judicial luminaries of this country would, with an overwhelming majority, sanction the principles therein adopted, and thereby proclaim the uniformity of the law of General Average. Instead of this we now have the declaration of the highest tribunal of the land that the uniformity arrived at for more than a quarter of a century by the mercantile communities of the principal nations of the world cannot be sanctioned. And why? Because the view that the interests to a maritime adventure are bound together till its termination, the 'common benefit' theory of all other maritime nations, has not found such favour with some of our English adjusters as to induce them to give up their favourite 'common safety' theory.

Before I conclude, I would state that the Association of Average Adjusters in London, which has been in existence since 1873, for the purpose of securing the greatest possible uniformity in the preparation of average statements entrusted to the adjustment of their individual members, have agreed upon the following rules of practice in adjusting claims :—

Contributory Value of Freight.

That freight at the risk of the shipowner shall contribute to General Average upon its gross amount, deducting the whole of, and no more than, such port charges as the shipowner shall incur after the date of the General Average act, and such wages of the crew as the shipowner shall become liable for after that date.

Basis of Contribution to General Average.

When property saved by a General Average act is injured or destroyed by subsequent accident, the contributing value of that property to a General Average which is less than the total contributing value, shall, when it does not reach the port of destination, be its actual net proceeds; when it does it shall be its actual net value at the port of destination on its delivery there; and in all cases any values allowed in General Average shall be added to and form part of the contributing value as above.

The above rule shall not apply to adjustments made before the adventure has terminated.

Damage by Water used to Extinguish Fire.

That damage done by water poured down a ship's hold to extinguish a fire, be treated as General Average.

Damage caused by Water thrown upon Burning Goods.

That goods in a ship which is on fire, or the cargo of which is on fire, affected by water voluntarily used to extinguish such fire, shall not be the subject of General Average if the packages so affected be themselves on fire at the time the water was thrown upon them.

Towage from a Port of Refuge.

That if a ship be in a port of refuge at which it is practicable to repair her, and if, in order to save expense, she be towed thence to some other port, then the extra cost of such towage shall be divided in proportion to the saving of expense thereby occasioned to the several parties to the adventure.

Cargo Forwarded from a Port of Refuge.

That if a ship be in a port of refuge at which it is practicable to repair her, so as to enable her to carry on the whole cargo, but, in order to save expense, the cargo, or a portion of it, be transhipped by another vessel, or otherwise forwarded, then the cost of such transhipment (up to the amount of expense saved) shall be divided in proportion to the saving of expense thereby occasioned to the several parties to the adventure.

Agency Fees Chargeable by Shipowners.

That neither interest nor commission (excepting bank commission), nor any other charge by way of agency or remuneration for trouble, is allowed to the shipowner in General Average or Particular Average on ship, or as a special charge in respect of payments made, or services rendered, at the port at which the managing owner for the time being resides, excepting that a commission or agency fee is allowable in respect of payments made, or services rendered on behalf of cargo, when such payments or services are not involved in the contract of affreightment.

Damage caused to Cargo during Forced Discharge.

That whenever the cost of discharging cargo is General Average, all loss or damage necessarily arising to cargo therefrom shall be allowed in General Average.

From the foregoing pages, I think, the readers of this volume will gather, with great satisfaction, that, although the intention to prepare a code of General Average by general consent of those most interested in the commerce of the world, for the purpose of submitting it to their respective Governments to be enacted by them as laws, has not been realised, the intricate and very puzzling subject of General Average has been so thoroughly thrashed out, that those who are really anxious for uniformity will not have much difficulty in obtaining it if they choose to continue to expose the fallacy of the 'common safety' theory.

II.

THE INTERNATIONAL LAW OF AFFREIGHTMENT IN CONNECTION WITH THE ATTEMPTS TO AGREE UPON UNIFORMITY IN THE WORDING OF BILLS OF LADING.

The York Congress of 1864 having resulted in an agreement upon certain principles or rules of General Average, the attempt naturally followed to come to some similar arrangement upon the subject of Freight, as it was evident that a uniform system of General Average could not be put into practice unless there was an agreement as to the payment of freight where the ship is condemned and the cargo forwarded, where the cargo is sold at an intermediate port, and in other cases where the voyage is interrupted. With the object, therefore, of setting this matter in motion, the able delegates of the Belgian Government to the International General Average Congresses, Messrs. Theodore C. Engels and Edouard van Peborgh prepared the following 'projet de loi':—

Projet de Loi.

1. To establish as a general rule that freight shall not be due until the voyage be accomplished, *i.e.* until delivery of the cargo at the port of destination.

2. If in the course of the voyage the ship, in consequence of the perils of the sea, and not through any default on the part of the captain or owner, has become unseaworthy and not in a state to accomplish her voyage, the captain shall be bound to forward

the cargo to its destination by other vessel or vessels, and in this case he shall, upon delivery, have a claim for the whole of the freight due under the original charter-party (or bill of lading), although, in consequence of the cargo having been forwarded, the goods have been transported at a lower freight. But the captain of the original vessel is liable for the forwarding freight.

If, on the contrary, the forwarding freight is equal or greater than the original freight, the captain can claim no freight, but the owner of the cargo will be liable for the whole of the forwarding freight. If the captain does not forward the cargo he has not any claim for freight.

The system of *pro ratâ* freight is entirely abolished.

3. If the owner of the cargo, or any part of it, wish to withdraw it before the termination of the voyage, in spite of the offer of the captain to forward it to its destination, such owner, upon taking delivery at an intermediate port or place, shall be liable for freight for the whole voyage, and shall give good and sufficient bail for any General Average or salvage expenses which may attach to the same.

4. The entire freight is due upon goods jettisoned or sacrificed for the common benefit, and for those sold to raise the necessary funds for defraying expenses incurred for the common benefit.

5. No freight is due upon goods lost by perils of the sea, nor for those taken by public enemy or by pirates. Nor upon any goods sold or destroyed in consequence of perils of the sea, in any port or place other than the port of destination.

6. If the captain save the goods from shipwreck, or if he recapture them from the enemy or from pirates, and if, being in a state to be transported to their destination, he delivers them, then he shall be entitled to the whole freight; if not, he shall be entitled to none.

7. The total freight is due upon delivery of the cargo at the port of destination, although diminished or deteriorated by perils of the sea, if the consignee takes delivery, and in this case the consignee is bound to take delivery of all consigned to him by the same shipper, and not to choose the sound and reject the damaged.

If the consignee will not take delivery, the captain, after due authorisation, may sell such goods to pay his freight, but for any deficiency has no resource against the consignee or shipper except there be an express stipulation to that effect.

8. The freight paid in advance is always liable to be refunded in all cases involving non-payment of freight, except where it is stipulated to the contrary.

9. The contribution of the freight to General Average shall be regulated according to the first paragraph of Article X. of the York rules.

This 'projet de loi,' after being submitted to the Executive Council of the National Association for the Promotion of Social Science, was transmitted to all those Governments, bodies of Underwriters and Chambers of Commerce which had appointed delegates to the three previous congresses at Glasgow, London, and York, the following circular being sent with it:—

NATIONAL ASSOCIATION FOR THE PROMOTION OF SOCIAL SCIENCE.

1 Adam Street, Adelphi, London, W.C.
July 1, 1865.

Sir,—The success of the congress for the promotion of our international law of General Average has encouraged the hope that similar advantages may flow from a conference upon the still more important though less intricate question of Freight.

Messrs. Theodore C. Engels and Edouard van Peborgh, the able representatives of the Belgian Government at the York Conference, have drawn up a 'projet de loi' in nine clauses, two copies of which are here annexed.

The Council will feel obliged if your body will return to them, at your early convenience, one of these copies and state thereon, first, whether each clause agrees with the law of your port; if not, what is the law. Secondly, whether you agree with Messrs. Engels and Peborgh as to their views of what the law ought to be, and if not, what you consider ought to be the law.

The conference will meet at Sheffield during the meeting of the Association on October 4, when it is hoped your body will be represented.

It will be interesting to you to learn that the reason that a Bill for General Average has not yet been brought into Parliament, is that Her Majesty's Government are in communication with the French Government with a view to simultaneous action.—I am, Sir,

     Yours obediently,
     GEORGE W. HASTINGS, *General Secretary.*

Although, from the scanty replies received in answer to this circular, it was evident that such an attendance as had been present at the congresses on International General Average would not be attracted by the subject of Freight, the necessary arrangements were made for a full discussion of this important matter, and the first meeting took place at Sheffield on October 5, 1865, under the presidency of Sir Robert I. Phillimore, D.C.L., then Her Majesty's Advocate-General.

MR. PHILIP H. RATHBONE (President of the Liverpool Chamber of Commerce) undertook the duties of honorary secretary, and opened the proceedings with some remarks on the importance of the measure to be discussed and the steps which had been taken for the purpose of preparing an influential meeting for its consideration. He then reported communications from Lord Stanley, M.P., Mr. Scholefield, M.P., Mr. A. de Courcy, the Board of Trade, the Chambers of Commerce at Antwerp, Bristol, Bremen, Dundee, Edinburgh, Glasgow, Gloucester, Hull, Leith, and Tynemouth, the Shipowners' Associations of Glasgow, Greenock, and Sunderland, the General Shipowners' Association of London, the Liverpool Law Society, the Liverpool Steamship-owners' Association, the Committee of Lloyd's, and the Association for the Protection of Commercial Interests as respects Wrecked and Damaged Property in London. The discussions were commenced by Mr. Engels moving, and Mr. Van Peborgh seconding, the adoption of

CLAUSE I.—' As a general rule the freight is not due until the voyage be accomplished, *i.e.* until delivery of the cargo at the port of destination.'

After a few comments, the clause was agreed to with the following addition: 'unless where a special agreement is made to the contrary.'

It may be here remarked that all the clauses were moved and seconded by the above-named Belgian delegates.

CLAUSE II.—'If in the course of the voyage the ship, in consequence of the perils of the sea, and not through any default on the part of the captain or owner, has become unseaworthy and not in a state to accomplish her voyage, the captain shall forward the cargo to its destination by other vessel or vessels, and in this case he shall, upon delivery, have a claim for the whole of the freight due under the original charter-party (or bill of lading), although, in consequence of the cargo having been forwarded, the goods have been transported at a lower freight. But the captain of the original vessel is liable for the forwarding freight.

'If, on the contrary, the forwarding freight is equal to or greater than the original freight, the captain can claim no freight, but the owner of the cargo will be liable for the whole of the forwarding freight.

'If the captain does not forward the cargo, he has not any claim for freight.

'The system of *pro ratâ* freight is entirely abolished.'

I suggested the omission of the words from 'in consequence' to the words 'or owner' inclusive, remarking that if the ship became unseaworthy, from whatever cause, the master should be bound to forward the cargo. Having done so, he would have done his duty to the owners of such cargo, and had therefore a claim to the full freight originally agreed upon. In the clause should be inserted words to show that the master was bound to forward, but only if vessels were obtainable within a reasonable distance or at reasonable terms. The words as they stood looked as if the master might be forced to build a vessel on purpose, and it would surely not be right for him to forward if he was convinced that the freight demanded by the only vessels procurable would exceed the value of the goods at the port of destination, and he could not be bound to forward goods unless in a fit state to be forwarded. In the second part of the clause the words relating to the clause of unseaworthiness might with propriety be inserted, because, if the ship had become unseaworthy from the causes other than the perils of the sea, the owner of the ship should be liable to make good any excess of freight. The master's claim for freight should only be when the freight of the substituted vessel was larger than the original freight. The clause would be better to stand thus:—

'If in the course of the voyage the ship has become unseaworthy, and not in a state to accomplish the voyage, the master shall be bound to forward the cargo to its destination by other vessel or vessels, should such be obtainable on reasonable terms and the cargo be in a condition proper to be forwarded, and he shall, upon delivery, have a claim upon the whole of the freight due under the original charter-party (or bill of lading), when the goods have been transported at a lower or equal freight. But in this case the master of the original vessel is liable for the forwarding freight.'

I then moved this as an amendment, and it was seconded by MR. WHITWILL (Bristol).

MR. R. M. HUDSON (Sunderland) thought, if the ship was not seaworthy on commencing her voyage, the shipowner was clearly liable to all the consequences of her voyage being terminated before the cargo was brought to its destination.

MR. RATHBONE moved the erasure of the words 'shall be bound to forward' and the substitution of the following: 'act as agent for the owner of the cargo, and, if prudent and practicable, to be forwarded.'

MR. WHITWILL seconded this proposal.

MR. ROBERTSON proposed to add after the words 'shall be bound' these: 'under the forfeiture or penalty of 50 per cent. of the freight.'

DR. WADDILOVE seconded this amendment.

MR. ROBERTSON thought the principle involved was, that the shipmaster should be bound in all cases to use every expedient for forwarding his cargo, because, if he did not do so, great occasion for dispute might arise. The risk should be on the captain if he neglected this duty.

MR. CANDLISH thought the last proposition untenable. The master would be bound to give any amount of freight, however exorbitant—perhaps more than the cargo itself. The cargo might be damaged, yet, notwithstanding its damaged condition, he would be bound, irrespective of all consideration, to forward it.

Mr. Robertson's amendment was put and lost, that of Mr. Rathbone being carried, and this disposed of Mr. Hudson's.

THE CHAIRMAN then read the second paragraph: 'If, on the contrary,' when, in lieu thereof, I proposed: 'If, on the contrary, the forwarding freight is greater than the original freight, and if the unseaworthiness of the original vessel has been occasioned by perils of the sea, and not by any default on the part of the master or owner, then the owner of the cargo shall be liable for the whole of the forwarding freight, but the master of the original vessel shall have no claim for freight.'

MR. HUDSON seconded this amendment.

MR. RATHBONE thought that, as the principle was involved in the laws of all countries, if the captain was negligent, and it could be proved he was responsible, the present law would be weakened by inserting these words.

I intimated that they were considering the views of all countries. In some the law was the very reverse of what it was in England. For that reason I thought they ought to accept my amendment, but it was declared lost.

Paragraphs 3 and 4 were agreed to.

CLAUSE III.—' If the owner of the cargo, or any part of it, wish to withdraw it before the termination of the voyage, in spite of the offer of the captain to forward it to its destination, such owner, upon taking delivery at an intermediate port or place, shall be liable for freight for the whole voyage, and shall give good and sufficient bail for any General Average or salvage expenses which may attach to the same.'

On the third clause being read, I said I thought that, under its provisions, the master would be subject to great hardship. Supposing a ship had 200 tons of coal and fifty tons of iron, say, from Newcastle to New York, and in the course of the voyage was driven into Madeira, the owner of the coals might find there a market for them, whilst the iron was unsaleable. Suppose this to be the case, if the owner of the coals were allowed to withdraw, the

iron would be sacrificed, as it would be impossible to find any conveyance for such a small quantity. I would propose the following:
'If the owner of the cargo, or any part of it, wish to withdraw it, or such part of it, at an intermediate port or place before the termination of the voyage, although the master may be willing to forward it to its destination, such owners shall nevertheless be entitled to take it at such intermediate place or port, but shall be liable for freight for the whole voyage, and shall give good and sufficient bail for any General Average or salvage, or other expenses which may attach to the goods so withdrawn, providing always that no owner of a portion of a cargo shall be entitled to withdraw his goods at an intermediate port or place, when such withdrawal would cause any delay or inconvenience in the forwarding of the remainder of the cargo to the safety of the ship.'

MR. RATHBONE approved of my amendment, and seconded it.

MR. ENGELS objected to the amendment.

MR. RATHBONE believed that, according to the English law at present, the captain had full control of the cargo until the port of destination was reached, and that no owner could withdraw at an intermediate port, except under special circumstances.

MR. ROBERTSON said that, if the captain allowed one portion of the goods to be removed, it would entail delay on other parties having goods in the vessel. He thought the rights of those other owners should be protected.

MR. WHITWILL moved the insertion of the words 'or other' after the word 'salvage,' which the Chairman said was agreed to.

After I had replied, my amendment was put and lost.

Clause III. was then agreed to.

CLAUSE IV.—'The entire freight is due upon goods jettisoned or sacrificed for the common benefit, and for those sold to raise the necessary fund for defraying expenses incurred for the common benefit.'

MR. RATHBONE moved an amendment which he thought Mr. Engels would accept. His view was, that the freight was not due on goods jettisoned or sacrificed for common benefit, but that the owner had a claim in General Average for all loss of freight caused by such sacrifice. If the vessel was subsequently lost, there was no General Average on these goods, nor ought there to be on the freight, because the freight had been lost. There were other cases in which the owner ought not to receive the full freight because there was a second General Average, and in that second General Average there were expenses which were thrown on freight which would not be thrown on the freight on goods jettisoned.

MR. ENGELS objected that the value of the goods jettisoned was brought into the General Average with the freight on them. The value of the goods was calculated with the freight on contribution in General Average, consequently he thought they should pay the freight if goods were jettisoned.

MR. WHITWILL said Mr. Engels was in error.

MR. RATHBONE said in English law the freight was deducted from the value of the goods. He thought it would be a pity to alter the law.

MR. HUDSON seconded the amendment, which was the substitution of the words 'no freight' for 'the entire freight,' and the addition, after 'common benefit,' of ' but the owner has a claim in General Average for all loss of freight caused by such sacrifice.'

The amendment was carried.

CLAUSE V.—' No freight is due upon goods lost by peril of the sea, nor for those taken by public enemy or by pirates.

' Nor upon any goods sold or destroyed in consequence of perils of the sea, in any port or place other than the port of destination.'

I then remarked that it seemed very questionable whether the master should be deprived of all freight upon goods sold at an intermediate port in consequence of the perils of the sea. In the first place, the damage at the time of such sale might be slight, although with a certainty of rapid deterioration if the goods were re-shipped; and secondly, masters of ships would have a positive incentive to re-ship damaged goods, even at risk of damage to goods at the time sound, because by so doing they would secure their freight, which by Art. VII. was due in full on all goods delivered, whether sound or not. On the other hand, that was not a case where any deficiency in freight, as shown by a sale, should be made up by a general contribution.

MR. RATHBONE thought there was great justice in what I had

said, but there was great danger. They must recollect who captains were. Were they going to give the captain power to use his own discretion as to whether he was to carry on the goods or not? He thought, if they gave him that power, on many occasions that discretion would be abused, especially in the smaller class—such as fish and fruit vessels. The captain might find it convenient if he could sell the goods and break up the voyage and get the distance freight. It would be almost impossible for anyone to show that he was not justified in what he did. He thought more power would be put into the hands of captains than their education and position would render safe.

MR. HUDSON concurred with Mr. Rathbone. When the owner entered into a contract and took the goods on board, he was bound to see they were in a good condition for carriage. If he carried goods liable to defect, he took extra freight for so doing.

MR. RATHBONE said they had decided that the freight should be at the risk of the shipowner and not of the cargo-owner. The loss of the ship was sufficiently great.

MR. ENGELS asked why, if one possessed a cargo, and it happened to be so damaged that they lost it, why should they aggravate that loss by paying the freight on the goods which they lost?

DR. WADDILOVE could not but think there was some injustice in the rule as it stood. It made the owner responsible for the loss caused by causes beyond his control. He thought the clause ought to be modified so that the whole loss might not fall upon those who could not prevent it.

MR. RATHBONE said that, though the damage was beyond the power of anybody, the loss must fall on somebody. He considered the loss would be much harder if the cargo-owner should pay freight on an utterly useless thing.

MR. ENGELS believed that, if a captain received perishable goods, he should, if a loss arose, forfeit his freight. The owner of the goods lost all his property, and it could not be fair to make him pay.

Clause V. was then agreed to.

CLAUSE VI.—' If the captain save the goods from shipwreck, or if he recaptures them from the enemy, or from pirates, and if, being in a state to be transported to their destination, he delivers them, then he shall be entitled to the whole freight; if not, he shall be entitled to none.' An additional proviso was added to this on the proposal of Mr. Rathbone, at the instigation of the Leith Chamber of Commerce: 'but without prejudice to his claim for wages and expenses while engaged in recovering the goods.'

CLAUSE VII.—'The total freight is due upon delivery of the cargo at the port of destination, although diminished or deteriorated by perils of the sea, if the consignee takes delivery; and in this case the consignee is bound to take delivery of all consigned to him by the same shipper, and not to choose the sound and reject the damaged. If the consignee will not take delivery the captain, after due authorisation, may sell such goods to pay his freight, and for any deficiency has no recourse against the consignee or shipper except there be an express stipulation to the contrary.'

I proposed the clause in a different form: 'The total freight is due upon delivery of the cargo at the port of destination, although diminished or deteriorated by perils of the sea, if the consignee take delivery of all consigned to him by the same bill of lading or (when the goods are in bulk) by the same shipper. If the consignee will not take delivery, the master may, subject to the laws in force at the port of destination, sell such goods to pay his freight, but for any deficiency has no recourse against the consignee or shipper as such, retaining only such claim as he may have upon the charterer under the terms of the charter-party.'

This amendment was not seconded.

MR. RATHBONE proposed another amendment. He supposed the case of a man sending out to Patagonia, Valparaiso, or elsewhere, a cargo of coals. On that cargo the freight was very often by far the larger proportion of the value. It might so happen that the value of the coals in Valparaiso fell below the value of the freight, and, therefore, they make the shipowner a speculator with the cargo-owner. He did not think it a safe principle to go upon. Were this the law, he should, were he a shipowner, make an express stipulation in each case. He proposed to add to the clause: 'But in no case shall the captain be entitled to receive on a cargo deteriorated during the voyage a larger amount for freight than he could have received if the whole cargo had been delivered in the same state in which it was shipped.'

Mr. WHITWILL seconded this amendment.

Mr. ENGELS thought the captain should take his precaution beforehand. He was responsible for what took place.

Mr. POWELL supposed an accident taking place, and part of the cargo, say grain, becoming damaged, and another part heated, and also damaged by sea-water. When that was delivered, freight was paid on the quantity discharged, and was, consequently, from increased bulk, heavier than if the grain had been delivered sound. He thought it should be enacted that no captain should be entitled to receive more freight on a damaged cargo than the amount would be if delivered in a sound condition. The case often happened, and was one of great practical hardship.

Mr. RATHBONE admitted that the hardship was great, but thought it rather one of circumstances than law. It was difficult to find out what the freight was. He presumed the captain had no claim whatever for the increase of weight in the grain, and the only case in which he would get such increase would be where it could not be shown how much the grain had increased.

The amendment was carried, and the following alteration also made: the omission of the words 'shipper and not' to 'damaged' inclusive; and the substitution of 'bill of lading, or when the goods are in bulk, by the same ship.'

CLAUSE VIII.—'The freight paid in advance is always liable to be refunded in all cases involving non-payment of freight, except where it is stipulated to the contrary.' In place of the first four words, the following, 'advance on account of freight,' was adopted.

An additional Clause IX. was inserted, viz.: 'The owner of the ship shall have the absolute lien on the cargo for the freight and dead freight.'

CLAUSE IX. of the 'projet de loi,' but now Clause X., 'The contribution of the freight to General Average shall be regulated according to the first paragraph of Art. X. of the York rules,' was adopted.

The following amended draft was then read:—

I. To establish, as a general rule, that freight should not be due until the voyage be accomplished, *i.e.* until delivery of the cargo at the port of destination, unless where a special agreement is made to the contrary.

II. If in the course of the voyage the ship, in consequence of the perils of the sea, and not through any default on the part of the captain or owner, has become unseaworthy, and not in a state to accomplish her voyage, the captain shall act as the agent for all concerned, and, if prudent and practicable, shall forward the cargo to its destination by other vessel or vessels; and in this case he shall, upon delivery, have a claim for the whole of the freight due under the original charter-party (or bill of lading), although, in consequence of the cargo having been forwarded, the goods have been transported at a lower freight. But the captain of the original vessel is liable for the forwarding freight.

If, on the contrary, the forwarding freight is equal to or greater than the original freight, the captain can claim no freight, but the owner of the cargo will be liable for the whole of the forwarding freight.

If the captain does not forward the cargo, he has not any claim for freight.

The system of *pro ratâ* freight is entirely abolished.

III. If the owner of the cargo, or any part of it, wish to withdraw it before the termination of the voyage, in spite of the offer of the captain to forward it to its destination, such owner, upon taking delivery at an intermediate port or place, shall be liable for freight for the whole voyage, and shall give good and sufficient bail for any General Average, salvage, or other expenses which may attach to the same.

IV. No freight is due upon goods jettisoned or sacrificed for the common benefit, and for those sold to raise the necessary funds for defraying expenses incurred for the common benefit; but the owner has a claim on General Average for all loss of freight caused by such sacrifice.

V. No freight is due upon goods lost by perils of the sea, nor for those taken by public enemy or by pirates.

Nor upon any goods sold or destroyed in consequence of perils of the sea, in any port or place other than the port of destination.

VI. If the captain saves the goods from shipwreck, or if he recapture them from the enemy or from pirates, and if, being in a state to be transported to their destination, he delivers them, then he shall be entitled to the whole freight; if not, he shall be entitled to none, but without prejudice to his claim for wages and expenses while engaged in recovering the goods.

VII. The total freight is due upon delivery of the cargo at the port of destination, although diminished or deteriorated by perils of the sea, if the consignee takes delivery, and in this case the consignee is bound to take delivery of all consigned to him by the same bill of lading, or, when goods are in bulk, by the same ship. If the consignee will not take delivery, the captain, after due authorisation, may sell such goods to pay his freight, and for any deficiency has no recourse against the consignee or shipper, except there be an express stipulation to the contrary. But in no case shall the captain be entitled to receive on a cargo, deteriorated during the voyage, a larger amount of freight than he would have received if the cargo had been delivered in the same state in which it was shipped.

VIII. Advance on account of freight is always liable to be refunded in all cases involving non-payment of freight, except where it is stipulated to the contrary.

IX. The owner shall have an absolute lien on the cargo for the freight and dead freight.

X. The contribution of freight to General Average shall be regulated according to the first paragraph of Section X. of the York rules.[1]

THE CHAIRMAN, having after taken the sense of the meeting, declared the rules to be formally sanctioned, and he requested the honorary secretary to take the necessary steps to get them acted upon.

[1] Vide p. 207.

I have not been able to find traces of any steps which the executive council of the National Association for the Promotion of Social Science took, after the results of the Sheffield Congress had been brought under their notice, in order to prevail upon the Board of Trade to take an interest in promoting the practical use of these deliberations, or whether they met with any success. It appears, indeed, just as with the subject of International General Average, to have been left to the Association for the Reform and Codification of the Law of Nations to resume, in 1879, the consideration of the international law of Affreightment at the very stage it had been left by the Sheffield Congress in 1865.

It should, however, be mentioned that as far back as July 1871, soon after the opening of the Suez Canal, a meeting of merchants and others in the trade to the East took place at the London Tavern for the purpose of trying to agree upon an 'Eastern Trade Bill of Lading.'

The committee then formed included not only representatives of the largest houses engaged in that trade, but the principal shipowners as well as delegates of the Salvage Association.

By the terms of the document then agreed upon after much consideration, steamers were allowed to call at intermediate ports for coaling and other purposes, without such calling to be considered a deviation. They were also permitted to sail with or without pilots, and to tow and assist vessels in distress; and the owner was exempted from loss arising from any act, neglect, or default whatsoever of pilots, master, or crew in the navigation of the ship, but not for any act connected with the stowage or other dealing with the cargo not arising from sea peril.

So long as the traffic to the East was confined to the few and well-regulated lines of steamers, this bill of lading worked satisfactorily, but the immense extension of the mercantile navy which soon afterwards took place inaugurated an altered state of circumstances. Shippers of merchandise hesitated to concede to the general body of shipowners, their masters and crews, the unprecedented concession of the 'negligence clause,' which they had been willing to concede to the lines of steamers referred to above.

A general confusion then arose; the bill of lading which originally was only intended for the few lines which traded to the East and China, was adopted by other steamship owners, not only for those routes but also for Australia and New Zealand; and, as if this was not enough innovation, almost every shipowner issued a separate bill of lading for his steamers, adopting therein any conditions which might appear useful to him, quite irrespective of the interests otherwise affected by the document.

Such was the demand for ships and the influence of the shipowners, that shippers of merchandise had very frequently to submit to conditions in charter-parties and bills of lading which previously had never been thought of, and which were neither equitable nor reasonable between the contracting parties.

It therefore became an absolute necessity to consider by what means the shipowner and the merchant could be brought to an agreement on these matters. The subject of a general Law of Affreightment and a uniform Bill of Lading became henceforward merged together. Henceforward, whether the Law of Affreightment or the Bill of Lading is mentioned, it must be assumed that the larger subject combined in both expressions is under consideration.

To resume the history of the discussion.

At the seventh conference of the Association on

August 14, 1879, in the Guildhall of the city of London, Sir Travers Twiss in the chair, the honorary general secretary, Mr. Jencken, read the following paper, prepared by Mr. H. Reinhold, of Calcutta:—

Eight years ago a committee of merchants trading with the East assembled in London to consider and amend the conditions of bills of lading for steamships passing through the Suez Canal, and after nearly twelve months' deliberation their report on the subject, dated June 18, 1872, unfortunately left the matter in a half-finished state. The gentlemen who undertook the task are well known in the Eastern trade, and their experience and high standing are a guarantee, not only that the matter was thoroughly investigated in all its bearings, but also that the various interests concerned received full consideration at their hands. Although the new route *viâ* Suez was then only beginning to show signs of the great revolution pending in all matters connected with Eastern commerce, it is now, and has been since its construction, absorbing the greater part of the carrying trade from the East to Europe. The attention bestowed at that time upon the subject under discussion proves sufficiently that the members of the committee were fully alive to the alterations required to be made in the form of bill of lading generally in use.

If we admit that shipowners and ship-agents are entitled to claim special exemptions from the ordinary rules and are to have the benefit of exceptional clauses, the merchants, on their part, have equally strong grounds to jealously prevent exceptions being made to override the ordinary legal enactments for the protection of goods entrusted to the care of owners and agents as carriers.

For more easy reference I annex a copy of the report issued by the committee referred to, but regret that no copy of the bill of lading as originally adopted for goods outwards is in my possession; however, those more nearly interested will no doubt have guarded their own interests sufficiently at the time that document was finally determined upon and adopted by common consent, as stated in the report.

Regarding the form and conditions of bills of lading for goods inwards, *i.e.* shipments made from the East to Europe, no such unanimity prevailed, and the various forms of bills of lading now used by different steamship proprietors differ so much with regard to exemptions claimed from acknowledged responsibilities as to demand attention in this respect.

As Calcutta merchants, my firm has on more than one occasion experienced the hardship of certain clauses to which I draw attention with the object of stimulating a discussion. I shall in the first instance point out some glaring inconsistencies between the main part of the bill of lading and the exemption clauses, which are in contradiction to the provisions enacted for the protection of goods; and have no doubt the experience gained by merchants during the six years that have elapsed since the committee closed its labours will now enable them and shipowners to arrive at a more equitable and satisfactory understanding.

1. The old form of bill of lading generally commences: 'Shipped in good order and condition by ———.' There are now some forms in use which add: 'or received to be shipped,' an alteration caused, as I believe, by the altered local arrangements in Calcutta since the introduction of jetties and wharves under Port Commissioners appointed by the Local Government. Of this evidently few people in London are aware, as I know of recent arbitrations where captains had signed such bills of lading, when they had, or I assume that they must have had, the goods fully under their control, but, for the convenience of the ship in the matter of stowing the cargo, the goods were actually taken into the hold a couple of days later. Though the goods were actually thus duly delivered, still it has been interpreted and looked upon as akin to a fraud, and merchants who had in reality nothing to do with the signing of the documents have been mulcted in allowances, whilst the captain, the responsible master who signed the documents, has been left undisturbed.

2. Further, when in the beginning of a bill of lading it is stated that the goods were shipped and received 'in good order and condition,' some bills of lading have adopted an exemption clause which almost totally nullifies the above recital, viz.: 'the

ship is not liable for insufficient packing or reasonable wear and tear of packages.'

3. In the main part of the bill of lading it is said: 'being marked and numbered as per margin,' whilst an exemption clause states that the ship is not liable ' for inaccuracies, obliterations or absence of marks, numbers, address, &c. &c.' On the boat-notes of Calcutta shippers, which accompany the goods with the shipping order and custom-house pass on board, it is generally, we may say universally, stated: 'all packages in bad order, slack bags, or insufficiently marked, &c. &c., to be returned,' by the receiving officer, in order to get from the master a clean bill of lading.

Surely, it is the plain duty of the ship or its receiving officer to see that the goods tendered under such conditions with the shipping order be in good condition, properly marked, and numbered; but on arrival of the vessel cases frequently occur (causing annoyance and loss to consignees) which must have arisen from carelessness, either on the part of the receiving officer, or on the part of the dock employés, by whom delivery is made haphazard.

4. Not a word is said regarding bad stowage, but every merchant is more or less aware that to hurried loading (in order to give quick despatch and save port charges) a great deal of leakage and breakage is due, from which exemption is likewise claimed.

5. A further case in which a ship is not liable according to these exemption clauses is 'loss or damage by dust from coaling on the voyage.'

This is a rather ill-defined, but very expansive, clause under certain circumstances, as may be more clearly judged of by a case in point. A steamer brought home a mixed cargo, comprising, amongst other goods, white rice or table rice, as dead weight, in the lower part of the ship, of which, on arrival, it was found that a portion was mixed with coal dust (small granular parts of coal) and, as a matter of course, subject to a heavy allowance in price for inferior value. As usual, shipowners and agents disclaimed all liability and pointed to the above-cited clause of the bill of lading as protecting them, which clause, according to their account, had been adopted by the general committee of merchants and shipowners.

Anybody reading the committee's report will find that no such bill of lading was adopted, and, even if it had been, it would not free the ship from its obligation to protect the cargo, received in good condition, properly and efficiently, which cargo those interested in the ship bound themselves to deliver in like good order and condition. Thus far goes the law; the rest is the shipowners' own making and interpretation.

6. In some bills of lading it is claimed that, the vessel being ready to unload immediately on arrival, if the owners or consignees are not ready to receive the goods, the same will be landed or put into lighters at the expense of the consignees.

The ordinary custom in London is seventy-two hours' notice to be given that the ship is ready to discharge at a given date and place. Steamship owners have curtailed this to twenty-four hours, and law and equity demand fair and reasonable time to be given to the consignee, which, according to place and circumstances, may proportionately vary; but according to clauses now inserted in some bills of lading the ship may proceed at once to discharge goods, leaving consignees to find them afterwards. The smartness exercised in loading or discharging huge cargoes of merchandise is often praised, but at whose cost this is being carried out is seldom examined into.

7. I cannot fully enter into all details in this paper, but I must not omit to notice the following exemption clause: 'The ship shall not be liable for incorrect delivery, unless each package shall have been distinctly marked by shippers, before shipment, with the name of port of destination.'

By referring to what we have cited under paragraph 3, and more so by reading the bill of lading itself from beginning to end, one cannot but feel the bitter irony of those who, after all, stand under the law referring to carriers.

For the present I think I have said enough to make merchants and others more careful in looking at these documents and to bestow some attention upon this important subject. I think it desirable that the question should be placed before the Chambers of Commerce, or any other commercial associations, of the various ports in the East, for an expression of opinion. Local arrange-

,inents and the diversity in the nature of the various articles of merchandise shipped from different places, demand in many cases special care and conditions, and in my opinion it would be unfair to exclude such considerations from a discussion as to the adoption of a definite form of document which might afterwards obtain or seem to carry weight as settled by special authority.

I take the liberty of suggesting that the London Committee might reassemble to receive and discuss suggestions coming from abroad, and, with their local experience, come to a more satisfactory conclusion as to the general terms of such a document. Moreover, London has the advantage of having representatives of nearly all Eastern firms, as well as the greatest shipping interest, concentrated in its limits, and it affords the best information to be obtained from landing and shipping agents, insurance offices, and others interested in the discussion.

The report of the Committee of Merchants was as follows:—

The Committee entered upon its duties in pursuance of the following resolution, passed at a meeting of merchants and others interested in the trade with the East, which was held at the London Tavern on July 11, 1871:—

'That a committee of merchants be appointed to consider all the special stipulations that have been introduced into bills of lading for steam vessels and to confer thereon with the representatives of the steamship owners and underwriters with a view of drawing up a general form of bill of lading which shall be equitable in its conditions to all parties, and to arrange such a method of settling the freight as may remedy existing irregularities.'

Power was also given to the committee to add to its numbers, and it was finally constituted as follows:—Mr. James Macandrew (Messrs. Matheson and Co.), chairman, Mr. G. Arbuthnot (Messrs. Arbuthnot, Latham and Co.), Mr. W. Broughall (Messrs. Broughall and Co.), Mr. W. H. Crake (Messrs. Crawford, Colvin and Co.), Mr. Lancelot W. Dent (Messrs. Dent, Palmer and Co.), Mr. Horace Farquhar (Messrs. Forbes, Forbes and Co.), Mr. John Fleming (Messrs. Smith, Fleming and Co.), Mr. E. Halton (Messrs. T. A. Gibb and Co.), Mr. F. W. Heilgers (Messrs. Wattenbach, Heilgers and Co.), Mr. John E. Ralli (Messrs. Ralli Brothers), Mr. George

Ross (Messrs. James Wyllie and Co.), Mr. S. L. Schuster (Messrs. Schuster, Son and Co.).

The committee has likewise had the benefit of the valuable advice and assistance of Mr. J. A. W. Harper, Secretary of Lloyd's Salvage Association, who had on behalf of the Association devoted much attention to the conditions of bills of lading.

As convincing proof of the necessity of their inquiries and of the pressing nature of the evils to be remedied in readjusting the freight contract, the committee need only refer to a sheet, published by Lloyd's Salvage Association, and very generally circulated among merchants, in which the exemptions of the ship from liability in various contingencies are classified in a tabular form. There was little difficulty in determining which of these conditions most urgently called for abolition or alteration, and the committee then lost no time in seeking the co-operation of steamship owners, in arriving at a common understanding upon the subject. A meeting of the latter body was called in London, and a committee, of which Mr. C. M. Norwood, M.P., was chairman, was appointed to concert terms with the merchants.

The two committees addressed themselves in the first instance to the examination of the bill of lading outwards, and after prolonged discussion and a series of compromises on both sides the 'Eastern Trade Bill of Lading Outwards' was agreed upon and published in three forms, slightly varied to suit different voyages:—

No. 1.—For an ordinary voyage to the East, direct or trading at intermediate ports.

No. 2.—For a voyage to India, trading at Colombo, Madras, or other open roadsteads on the Malabar or Coromandel coasts.

No. 3.—For a voyage involving transhipment, the steamer not proceeding to the port for which she accepts cargo, such as Rangoon, Batavia, or Japan.

This agreement was promptly announced to merchants in a circular, issued by the chairman of the committee, dated January 20, 1872, appended to which were copies of the revised forms of bills of lading. The new form came into immediate use, and it affords the committee much gratification to testify that it has been very generally accepted, not only in London, but in Liverpool and

Glasgow also, and has proved a useful and successful document. One exception to its universal use is the Liverpool line of steamers to the Straits and China known as Holt's line. The committee in their circular of January 20 recommended that, as far as practicable, shippers should require the Eastern trade bill of lading to be used by any steam vessel in which they engaged to ship goods *viâ* the Suez Canal. Had this recommendation been more generally acted upon, there is no doubt that the managers of Holt's line would have ere now adopted the new form; but, if shippers of goods put it in their power, by continued support of their steamers, to decline compliance with the agreement accepted by all other private steamship-owners in the trade, the efforts of the committee to benefit merchants by the introduction of an improved system are so far frustrated. The committee believe that the results of the agreement have been beneficial alike to shipowner and merchant, and that the advantages of uniformity of system have not been too dearly purchased by the compromises acceded to. If shippers entertain the same view, it rests with themselves alone to necessitate compliance by declining to ship in any line of steamers where the Eastern trade bill of lading is not recognised.

With the two great companies controlling the Overland Route, the Peninsular and Oriental Steam Navigation Company and the Messageries Maritimes of France, no negotiations have yet been entered into. There are many stipulations in their respective bills of lading which seem to the committee to be very prejudicial to the interests of merchants; but it must be conceded on the other hand that their mail contracts and the circumstance of their being essentially passenger lines impose special obligations upon them and render stringent conditions more necessary than in the case of other steamers. At the same time, when the vessels pass through the Suez Canal, as is now very generally done by the French and occasionally by the English company, the committee see no good reason why a slight modification of the Eastern trade bill of lading should not meet all the exigencies of the case; and it rests with shippers to take measures for bringing about an alteration in this respect.

Copies of the three forms of the Eastern trade bill of lading outwards, attested by the chairmen of the two committees, have been deposited in the custody of the Committee of Lloyd's, to serve for purposes of reference as the standard text of the bill of lading agreed upon.

The committee regret that, in the case of the bill of lading inwards, they are unable to report an equally satisfactory result of their labours. It was agreed between the two committees that the bill of lading outwards should be substantially followed, with such verbal alterations as were required by the change of voyage; but that special clauses applicable to the port of London should be introduced respecting the delivery of cargo and payment of freight. The system of discharging ships at Liverpool and elsewhere is very different and might require differently worded clauses, which the trade of the various ports interested would have to adjust.

It was soon found that on these clauses the two committees were essentially at variance. As respects the delivery of cargo, the difference of opinion was not so wide as to preclude the hope of an arrangement, the merchants merely desiring to be protected against a surprise by which their goods would be warehoused by the agents for the ship, before they knew or had the means of knowing of her arrival. The following was the clause proposed by the committee :—

'One clear working day after the day on which the ship reports at the custom-house and is docked is to be allowed for applications for delivery; and if thereafter the goods are not removed without delay by the consignee, the master or agent is to be at liberty to land and warehouse the same, or, if necessary, to discharge into hired lighters at the risk and expense of the owners of the goods.'

The clause finally proposed by the shipowners' committee was as follows :—

'Twenty-four hours (Sundays and holidays excepted) after the ship reports at the custom-house and is docked are to be allowed for applications for delivery; and if thereafter the goods are not removed by the consignee immediately they come to hand in discharging the ship, the master or agent is to be at liberty to land

and warehouse the same or, if necessary, to discharge into hired lighters at the risk and expense of the owners of the goods.'

As it is not customary or practicable in London to give consignees notice of the ship's arrival, except by publication of her report in the bill of entry the morning after it is made, the clause adopted by your committee seems decidedly the more reasonable of the two, especially as the hour of the ship's report is a point on which the consignee of goods cannot possess any evidence. Moreover, the bulk of the warehousing entries would certainly be passed within twenty-four hours, and the steamer's discharge be thus very rarely interrupted, while, if she landed the whole of her cargo on the dock quay, as is most usually done, no interruption at all could take place.

On the more difficult question as to the mode of paying freight some explanations are necessary. When the terms of the bills of lading now used run, ' freight payable in London,' ' freight payable on delivery,' or even ' freight payable as customary,' the shipowners contend that, according to the usage established by themselves since the introduction of steam-vessels into the trade with the East, they are empowered to detain the goods on board or in the dock or a warehouse of their own selection, until the freight is paid in advance of delivery, or, which is practically the same thing, simultaneously with delivery. It will not be forgotten that this is precisely the grievance of which merchants have for years past complained, and to remedy which was one of their principal objects in organising a committee of their number. The shipowners' committee continue to maintain the above position, and their chief arguments for so o ing may be thus expressed:—

I. That payment in advance of delivery is now the established usage of the trade.

II. That it is necessary for their protection against the insolvent or fraudulent consignee of cargo.

III. That it is unreasonable to expect them to follow goods to the wharf or warehouse appointed by the consignee, either for the purpose of collecting the freight upon them or to ascertain the correctness of delivery.

IV. That goods in transit to the wharf or at the wharf may be plundered or damaged by the servants or agents of the consignee, for which, in the absence of distinct proof, the ship would be held liable.

V. That a large proportion of the freight earned is expended in advance on coals, canal dues, and other charges peculiar to steamers, to which, therefore, immediate returns from their earnings are essentially necessary.

VI. That to defer payment of the inward freight for thirty days would render it impossible for steamship owners to carry on their business, owing to the large increase of capital which it would call for.

To these arguments the merchants reply:—

I. That the present usage as to payment is of quite recent introduction, deriving any validity it has from the terms of bills of lading drawn up by shipowners themselves, and that, so far from being established by common consent, it has been constantly objected to by consignees of goods.

II. That the shipowner has a perfect protection for his freight in what is known as the dock or wharf stop, with which there is no intention of interfering, and by which the warehouse-keeper engages not to part with the goods to anyone until he receives a release from the shipowner. To meet the rare case of insolvent or fraudulent wharfingers, the committee were quite willing to concede that the shipowner might object to the goods being delivered into the custody of any such until his freight was paid.

III. That, to constitute proper delivery, the consignee must have the opportunity of ascertaining that his goods are according to bill of lading, while the existing system does not afford this opportunity, either on board ship or on the dock quay. The shipowner, therefore, cannot be absolved from following the goods to their final destination, as, until they are there examined, weighed and measured, it is quite out of his power to render a freight account.

IV. That this objection merely calls for an improved and less hurried method of taking the delivery account as between the dock company, who are the agents of the ship, and the wharfingers, who are the agents of the merchants, and that the merchants' committee would gladly co-operate in the establishment of such an improved system. Cases of plunder could then be traced, without difficulty, to the parties guilty of them.

V. & VI. That it is no part of the merchant's functions to provide capital for carrying on the shipowner's business, and that in London there can be no difficulty whatever in procuring money on so excellent a security as the assignment of a steamer's freight payable in thirty days.

The merchants' committee have likewise to point out that, as a matter of fact, the larger portion of a steamer's freight is voluntarily paid before her discharge, in order that the merchant may obtain possession of the freight release, especially in the common case of goods sold to arrive. They object, however, to being compelled to pay upon the shipowner's estimate of what the freight may eventually amount to, and before he has completed his share of the contract by the delivery of the goods. The term of thirty days has been fixed as the lowest average period in which the landing account of an ordinary cargo can be looked for, there being no desire on the part of the committee to delay payment longer than may be requisite to ascertain the precise amount of freight and the claims, if any, against the steamer for short delivery, ship damage or other default.

Upon this divergence of views the negotiation between the two committees has been broken off. The only concession proposed by the shipowners' committee has been that delivery should be made on prepayment of four-fifths of the estimated freight instead of the whole. This suggestion, however, seemed to your committee to be just as objectionable in principle and inconvenient in practice as the existing system, and it was not seriously discussed. They subjoin the clause as they have drafted it:—

'Freight for the said goods at and after the rate of   per ton of   delivered is to be paid subsequent to the landing thereof by cash in London not later than thirty days after the ship's reporting at the Custom House, or upon any earlier day on which a freight release may be required and received by the consignee;'

While the wording proposed by the shipowners is as follows:—

'Freight for the said goods at and after the rate of   per ton, is to be paid by cash in London, when the ship is ready to discharge.'

The shipowners' committee likewise sought to re-introduce into the bill of lading inwards the exemption for damage by vermin, which by mutual consent had been expunged from the bill of lading outwards. They further proposed for your committee's adoption the following clause :—

'The bill of lading, duly indorsed, is to be delivered to the agent on demand after arrival, in exchange for the master's copy and an order for the delivery of the goods.'

On this latter it will be sufficient to observe that your committee obtained a legal opinion, which was to the effect that the shipowner had no right to require the surrender of an indorsed or cancelled bill of lading, until he had completed delivery of the goods comprised in it.

The committee, having devoted much care to the drafting of the bill of lading herewith, styled the 'Eastern Trade Bill of Lading Inwards, No. 4,' recommend it for adoption by merchants trading to the East, and would urge them to use their best efforts, through their correspondents abroad, to have it recognised and brought into use at the ports of shipment, declining, so far as may prove practicable, to allow their goods to be shipped by steamers the owners of which continue to enforce the use of the old forms.

In the committee's circular of January 20 it was recommended that, to ensure the benefit of a complete protection to sea risks, the policies taken out on voyages by steamer, viâ the Suez Canal, should cover the merchandise 'in terms of the Eastern Trade Bill of Lading.' When this recommendation was brought before underwriters, the clause suggested was at once objected to as imposing upon them new and undefined liabilities. A meeting was held at Lloyd's on February 21, which resulted in the appointment of a committee, representing both the insurance companies and private underwriters, to consider the question further, and, if possible, to come to an agreement respecting it. With this committee the subject has been very fully considered and discussed by your committee. The intention of your committee in their original recommendation was sufficiently evident from their expressing their object to be the more complete protection of the sea risks to which the bill of lading related; but they are quite willing to admit that the language proposed for the clause was too wide and vague in its terms, and might have been interpreted as involving underwriters in some of the liabilities from which shipowners had by the revised bill of lading been specially exempted. In order to draft a clause more exact in its wording, the first matter to be determined was the precise meaning attached, both by the assurers and the assured, to the risks covered by a policy on goods which had been shipped under the Eastern Trade Bill of Lading. On this point the Committee are happy to state that they have arrived at a satisfactory understanding with the underwriters' committee, of which the following is an abstract:—

'The underwriters' risk on the voyage named, calling at the intermediate ports named, is to include—

' Coaling at other intermediate ports not named.

' Taking in and discharging cargo while so coaling.

' Sailing with or without pilots.

' Towing and assisting vessels in all situations of distress.

' Loss or damage arising from the machinery or boilers.

' Dangers and accidents arising from the navigation of the Suez Canal.

' Any act, neglect, or default whatsoever of pilots, master, or crew in the management or navigation of the ship, provided the expression, ' management of the ship,' shall not be held to include any act connected with the stowage or other dealing with the cargo of the ship not arising out of a sea peril—

' In addition to all risks comprehended and provided for in the body of this policy.

' The underwriter is not to be liable for acts or default of the shipper unconnected with sea perils, such as insufficient packing, incorrect marking, improper description, absence of declaration for inflammable or dangerous goods, or insufficient declaration of value for specie and valuables.

' The underwriter, however, is to be liable as heretofore for the consequences of sea damage or sea perils of any kind, such as leakage, breakage, sweat, rust, decay, when traceable to that origin, but not otherwise. Damage by coal-dust, when not mixed up with damage by sea-water, is to be borne by the merchant.

'In case of the goods being placed in quarantine depôt afloat or ashore previous to the final delivery to the consignee, the underwriters' risk will continue until such final delivery, and will cover risk of boats to and from such depôt.

'In case of blockade the underwriters are understood to cover the voyage to the port of discharge selected by the captain as fully and effectually as to the port of discharge named in the policy, their liability ending with the landing of the goods at the former destination.

'Should the voyage be extended beyond the destination named in the policy, as when the goods cannot be found or from stress of weather cannot be landed, the underwriters are to be entitled to receive additional premium for the extra risk incurred.'

It was agreed that it was unnecessary to embody the whole of this understanding in the policy, as most of it is universally accepted by underwriters. It is true that the legal construction of a policy of insurance would not go beyond its expressed conditions; but after a recorded declaration of the meaning attached to it by the representatives of both merchants and underwriters, it need hardly be feared that the latter would contest a claim which clearly fell within the scope of the declaration. The efforts of the two committees were therefore directed to framing a clause which should embody such conditions of the bill of lading as were not sufficiently protected by the ordinary practice of underwriters, and especially a deviation clause which would cover the deviation permitted in the bill of lading for coaling purposes, for towing vessels in distress, and for proceeding to another port in case of blockade. The following is the clause that has been agreed upon by the two committees, to be printed on a slip and attached to the margin of the policy, when so required by the assured:—

'The goods hereby insured being shipped under the Eastern Trade Bill of Lading, No.   , it is agreed that the terms of this policy shall apply to the following sea perils therein referred to, in addition to such risks as are already hereby covered:—

' 1. All deviation of voyage provided for in the said bill of lading with any risk of land carriage incidental to the voyage.

' 2. Sailing with or without pilots; and any act, neglect or default whatsoever of pilots, master or crew in the management or navigation of the ship, improper stowage excepted.

' 3. All risks attending the goods by reason of their discharge into, retention at, and delivery from any quarantine depôt afloat or ashore.

' 4. In case of the goods being carried on to a more distant port through stress of weather, or because they cannot be found, the marine risk of the additional voyage, as well as of the return voyage to their destined port, the assured agreeing to pay for such extra risk such premium as may be agreed upon.

' The attention of your committee has been directed to a discussion, originated in the " Times " newspaper, as to the risk of fire on the dock quays, when cargo is landed there by the ship before its final delivery to the consignee. It seems very doubtful whether a claim for loss so caused would attach under the marine policy, the obligations of which are discharged when the goods "are safely landed." It has even been doubted whether a policy "including risk of boats," would cover the lighterage to a wharf, after the vessel had been docked, and the goods placed in the first instance on the quay. The only sufficient remedy is to introduce a special clause into policies on goods destined for London, whether issued at home or abroad, to the effect that the goods are covered, if landed in transit for delivery to the consignee, or while being conveyed by boats or craft to his warehouse. This, of course, would have to be a matter of special agreement in each case.

' It is only requisite to add that the committee is now dissolved, as its functions terminate with the issue of this report.'

MR. JENCKEN then moved: ' That a committee be appointed to consider the question submitted by Mr. Reinhold on behalf of the Chamber of Commerce of Calcutta, regarding bills of lading for steamships passing through the Suez Canal, and that such committee be empowered and instructed to act in concert with the existing committee of the General Shipowners' Society, the executive council to nominate the members of the committee and to add to their number from time to time as they shall think fit.'

This motion was seconded by MR. H. J. ATKINSON, Chairman of the Hull Chamber of Shipping, and was carried.

Thereupon I read, at the request of the executive council, a paper in which I stated fully what led to the Sheffield Congress, reported its result, and concluded :—

'The executive council of this Association will be glad if the gentlemen who take an interest in this subject will form or appoint a committee for the purpose of considering the Sheffield proposals and reporting at the next meeting the result of their deliberations, with a view to the establishment of an international law of Affreightment.'

DR. E. N. RAHUSEN, of Amsterdam, Counsel to the Nederlandsche Handelsmaatschappij, expressed his concurrence in the views enunciated by me and spoke in support of my suggestion, to which, after listening to some observations from MR. MANLEY HOPKINS and MR. J. E. C. MUNRO, of London, and from the learned Chairman, the conference acceded, it being determined to leave the selection of the members of the committee to the executive council.

According to the report of the proceedings of the eighth conference of the Association, held at Berne in the next year, the following took place on August 26, 1880, Dr. F. Sieveking, of Hamburg, the President of the Conference, in the chair :—

MR. CHARLES STUBBS, of London, read the report of the committee upon Affreightment, which was as follows :—

'In pursuance of the resolution passed by the general conference of the Association on August 14 of last year at the Guildhall, London, the executive council appointed the following gentlemen— Dr. E. E. Wendt (Chairman), Mr. John Glover, Mr. Richard Lowndes, Mr. Ole Möller, Mr. Philip H. Rathbone, and Mr. Charles Stubbs (Hon. Sec.) your committee to consider the subject of an International Law of Affreightment, as originally suggested by Mr. T. C. Engels and Mr. E. van Peborgh of Antwerp, in 1864, and embodied in the Sheffield rules of 1865, and to report the result of their deliberations to the conference at Berne.

'Your committee, having fully discussed the subject, and being unanimous in their opinion, report as follows:—

'That the Sheffield rules, on which the chairman of your committee founded his report to the conference last year, were based on the principle of English common law of no apportionment of freight *pro ratâ itineris peracti* (or distance freight).

'That the reasons in favour of this principle are constantly gaining in force, while the practice of effecting insurances on freight has become so general that the adoption of the principle embodied in the Sheffield rules would involve merely a revision of the terms of freight insurance, which would not be in any way difficult of adjustment.

'That the adoption of this principle by all those maritime nations whose laws still allow *pro ratâ* freight is a preliminary step which must of necessity be taken, before an International Law of Affreightment, based upon the Sheffield rules, has any chance of being accepted.

'That, under these circumstances, your committee suggest that it is desirable that the local committees of the Association, the Chambers of Commerce and any of our members who feel an interest in the subject, should discuss the question and obtain further adhesions to the principle referred to, and should communicate before the end of the year to your committee the result of their discussions and efforts, in order to enable your committee to make a further and more satisfactory report to the next conference.'

Letters upon the subject of the abolition of *pro ratâ* freight from M. E. van Peborgh, of Antwerp, and Mr. Richard Lowndes, of Liverpool, were also read.

DR. HERMAN HALKIER, of Copenhagen, referring to No. 7 of the Sheffield rules, objected to recourse being given to a captain of a ship against a consignee of goods who refused to accept delivery. The consignee was in no way a party to the contract of shipment.

It was right that the captain should be able to resort to the charterer or the shipper, but not to a person who merely stood in the position of having an option to accept or decline delivery.

To this Mr. R. BENEDICT, of New York, answered that the consignee equally with the consignor might be the owner of the goods or the agent of the owner. This being the case, it might frequently be inequitable that the consignee should not be responsible to the captain for non-acceptance.

DR. F. SIEVEKING, of Hamburg, said that there were now two questions before the meeting: 1, the abolition of *pro ratâ* freight; 2, the captain's right of recourse in case of the consignee refusing to accept delivery. It was not the captain's fault if the goods were damaged by the sea, or if the consignee would not accept them; and it was but fair that he should be able to hold some one liable upon such non-acceptance. As his contract was with the consignor, the latter appeared to be the person to whom he should be entitled to look for redress. What precise remedy was to be given to him was another thing: the words always employed in the contract were: 'on right and true delivery of the goods.' A very important objection to *pro ratâ* freight was the difficulty of apportionment. Delivery at the Cape of Good Hope of goods shipped from London for Australia, or *vice versâ*, could not be considered a half performance of the contract to carry. By such delivery the consignor might be placed in a worse position than if he had never shipped his goods. It must not be forgotten that it was always in the captain's power to earn the whole of the freight by forwarding the goods by another vessel. If *pro ratâ* freight were abolished, many doubts and difficulties would be removed, and an uniformity which was much to be desired would be established between the laws of Great Britain and the other commercial countries. The law of his own country, Germany, in no way recognised the principle of *pro ratâ* freight.

M. THÉODORE C. ENGELS, of Antwerp, Chairman of the Belgian Lloyd, pointed out that it was always open to the captain to stipulate for *pro ratâ* freight, where he thought it necessary for the protection of his interests to do so; for instance, in the case of perishable goods. So long as captains of ships knew that they would always earn their distance freight, so long would they be indifferent as to what became of their cargoes. He moved: 'That *pro ratâ* freight should be abolished.' This was seconded by me.

DR. C. C. DUTILH, of Rotterdam, in speaking to the motion, declined to accept all the principles laid down in the Sheffield rules. The provision contained in Rule 5, that ' no freight is due upon goods sold or destroyed, in consequence of perils of the sea, in any port or place other than the port of destination,' would tempt the captain of a merchantman to carry his cargo, however much damaged, at all hazards on to the end of the voyage for the single purpose of earning his freight.

MR. F. R. COUDERT, of New York, moved as an amendment: ' That freight *pro ratâ itineris peracti* should be abolished.'

MR. COUDERT thought that, unless the words '*itineris peracti*' were expressed, then, under the resolution, freight would not be payable upon, say, 400 out of 500 barrels of oil, which was obviously not what was intended.

After some further remarks from MR. C. STUBBS, of London, the amendment was adopted by the mover and the seconder of the resolution and, upon being put to the meeting, was carried by 15 votes to 3.

It was also agreed that the existing committee upon Affreightment should be continued for another year.

We come now to the more practical proceedings in this matter at the ninth conference of the Association at Cologne in August 1881, when, on the 17th of that month, Mr. H. H. Meier, of Bremen, the President of the Conference, in the chair, MR. RICHARD LOWNDES, at the request of the President, then read the

Report of the Committee on an International Law of Affreightment and Bills of Lading.

In compliance with the resolution passed by the Berne Conference of the Association last year, that the Committee on the

International Law of Affreightment should be continued for another year, and in deference to the desire of the executive council that the same committee should also consider the subject of bills of lading as submitted by the Bengal Chamber of Commerce, your committee have taken the necessary preliminary steps to call the attention of those interested in this subject to its discussion, and have also agreed to report to you as follows:—

They have, after careful consideration, come to the conclusion that, inasmuch as objections have been raised against certain clauses of the 'projet de loi' adopted by the Sheffield Conference in 1865, and submitted to this Association in 1879, it would be advisable to obtain, before further action, the adhesion by the leading mercantile communities to certain principles involved in the matters in question, such as the abolition of *pro ratâ* freight (distance freight), and the non-liability of shipowners for the negligence of pilots, masters, and crew, &c., in the navigation of their vessels.

Your committee consider that this adhesion can best be obtained by adopting and introducing common forms of the documents used as contracts of Affreightment, inasmuch as such contracts must necessarily be based upon the principles above referred to.

Your committee think the most important of these documents, and the one of which the adoption of a common form would be most beneficial and expedient, to be the bill of lading. They consider, therefore, that the efforts of the Association should first be directed to agreeing upon a draft bill of lading, the form of which would be generally acceptable. With a view of obtaining a general consensus of opinion upon the question of what this form should be, your committee have communicated with a large number of Chambers of Commerce, and other mercantile associations of various nationalities, requesting them to consider the subject among themselves, and to send representatives to this conference to take part in the discussion. and perhaps assist in the framing of such a document.

Your committee fully appreciate the difficulty in agreeing upon such common form of bill of lading, fair in its terms to all the parties in the maritime adventure, to shipowners and shippers, and to their respective underwriters. They are encouraged, however, by the knowledge that for not years but centuries, and until a comparatively recent date, there was one common form so generally used that it may fairly be said to have been universal among maritime communities.

This form became necessarily obsolete through the introduction of steam and the consequent alterations in the mode of conducting business by sea; and changes by means of additional clauses were gradually introduced, the effect of which has been to put an end to the ancient uniformity, without introducing in its place any other uniform system.

Your committee think that the reform of such a state of things is a fair and proper aim of the Association, and they trust that the discussion hereby introduced may lead to the result desired.

(Signed)   ERNEST E. WENDT, *Chairman.*
JOHN GLOVER.
RICHARD LOWNDES.
OLE MÖLLER.
JAMES POOLE.
PHILIP H. RATHBONE.
CHARLES STUBBS, *Hon. Sec.*

The honorary general secretary then communicated to the conference a paper contributed by Mr. Charles Stubbs, M.A., LL.M., of London,

On the Formulation of a Model Bill of Lading.

A general feeling has for some time been prevalent among shipowners, merchants engaged in export trade, insurance companies, and others interested in questions of Affreightment, that in place of the diverse forms of bills of lading now in use, one common form should by agreement be drawn up, to be used universally in all trades, and whether the carrying ship be a sailing or a steam vessel.

The reasons for the adoption of a single recognised form are sufficiently obvious. At the present time a shipper of goods may be wholly in ignorance, until his merchandise is actually on board a vessel, what the terms of the contract are into which he is entering; he may then have them disclosed to him by the delivery of a bill of lading so comprehensive in its conditions, so voluminous in its exceptions, and, in many cases, so complicated from the mixture of printing and manuscript, and the variety of type, and even of cross printing, that neither he nor anyone else who may have or subsequently acquire rights under the contract, nor the lawyers into whose hands the document frequently comes to be explained, can do much more than guess at its meaning. Even if the particular bill of lading happens to be reasonably clear and fair, the uncertainty as to what its provisions will be, as to what principles it will be based on, is a distinct misfortune to the merchant. He may wish to insure—in the vast majority of cases he does—he cannot even tell his insurer the liabilities the latter is to take on himself. In any case, however, in the complications of modern trading, any practice that causes an element of unnecessary doubt or uncertainty to enter into the transaction conduces to the disadvantage of all the parties concerned, and any attempt to abolish such a practice, if unsuccessful, is praiseworthy; if successful, confers no inconsiderable benefit on the mercantile world in general.

Recognising the work to be of vital importance to commerce, and thus to be within the scope of their duties, the Chambers of Commerce of England, both individually and collectively, have endeavoured to formulate for general adoption a *pro formâ* bill of lading. Their efforts have not indeed, as yet, led to the wished-for result, but they are not the less valuable as showing the growing desire to put an end to the present dubious and unsatisfactory state of the Affreightment question.

Where such practical and influential bodies as the British Chambers of Commerce have failed to achieve the end to which they had devoted their energies, it may at first sight appear to be well-nigh chimerical for a mere law-reforming association to affect an expectation of being successful; but it must be remembered that the Association, owing to its heterogeneous composition, is peculiarly representative of the interests involved, that the intent of its conferences is to afford ample opportunities for the discussion of questions of international moment, and that its object particularly embraces the codification of the regulations governing such questions. As an humble endeavour to afford some slight assistance in the discussion introduced by the committee of the Association on bills of lading, the following brief remarks are offered on the formulation of a typical bill of lading.

It will, it is presumed, be admitted that, in discussing a model bill of lading, the interests of two several parties need alone be considered—the owner of the carrying vessel and the owner of the cargo carried; all other parties concerned must derive their interest from one of these two parties, and should acquire neither more nor less than the just rights of their respective principals. What these rights should be and in what words they can best be enunciated are the two questions to be determined; the former is complex, and its decision a matter of considerable difficulty, the latter is by comparison easy; it should be in simple language, clear, concise and brief.

In discussing the principles on which depend the respective rights of the above-mentioned parties, it may be well to consider what the object of each is in becoming a party to the contract of affreightment.

Now the cargo-owner wishes his merchandise to be carried to its destination safely and speedily, the carrier wishes to earn the freight for the carriage of the merchandise surely and in the shortest possible time. So far, apart from the question of accident, negligence or fraud, their interests are so nearly alike that the contract can easily be arranged and formulated; it is in the determination of their respective liability for damage arising out of the latter events that the practical difficulty arises.

Clearly, on principle, each should bear the damage which is the result of obvious accident, each should endure or be responsible for the damage which is the direct result of the fraud or negligence of himself; but how if it be proximately caused by the act of third parties without any blame being directly attributable to either of the principals, when should this be considered the result of accident, when of negligence?

It would thus appear that the general principles may be considered practically agreed upon; the difficulty arises in determining the applicability of the principles in each particular case.

Assuming that these two principles should govern the contract, it is proposed to consider their applicability in the various instances occurring by examining the clauses, generally termed 'exceptions and conditions,' in use in some of the more usual forms of the bill of lading, briefly commenting on the advisability of inserting or discarding such clauses as they are discussed.

'Weight, measure, quality, contents, and value unknown,' is a condition which appears to be fair to both parties. If any difficulty arises after shipment on any one of the points to cover which this clause is intended, the dispute must resolve itself into the question, Was or was not the merchandise shipped as described in the body of the bill of lading? If it can be shown not to have been so shipped, the cargo-owner can have no claim; in the event of the converse being proved, the shipowner should be considered liable to redeliver the cargo in the same condition as shipped. How is it to be decided in what condition the cargo was shipped? It is submitted that a fair way to determine this may be thus laid down: It should be agreed that a statement in the bill of lading, describing a condition of the cargo naturally obvious to the shipowner or his representative at the time of loading, should be considered as *primâ facie* evidence against him as to such condition when so shipped; otherwise, in the case of the condition not being in accordance with the description, the shipper would be deprived by the shipowner's neglect of the opportunity of detecting and rectifying a possible fraud or mistake at the time when alone such detection or rectification would be easy, without any compensating equivalent for the injury thereby done him. It should be equally agreed that the onus of determining a condition not obvious is a burden which should not fall on the shipowner. The weight, measure, quality, contents, and value are not so naturally obvious without an inspection, which it would be unfair to expect of the shipowner, and the condition protecting him accordingly from bearing this onus may fairly be inserted.

'Reasonable wear and tear' is naturally in the nature of an accident which should fall on the owners of the goods suffering the same. 'Cutting excepted' is a qualifying phrase sometimes added, but this is unnecessary verbiage, for cutting cannot be considered to come under the description of 'wear and tear' in any way.

'Inaccuracies, obliteration, absence, &c., of marks,' and the like, must surely be an improper exception. The shipowner should protect himself by refusing to accept unmarked or insufficiently marked goods; subsequent tampering with the marks cannot be an accident, and consequent loss thereby caused should not fall on innocent shippers.

'Leakage, breakage, heat or decay,' is a phrase of doubtful import; they may all be caused by 'inherent vice,' to use a phrase the meaning of which is well known; in that case, again, obviously cargo-owners' risks; but heat and decay may, on the other hand, be caused by improper stowage or want of ventilation. Improper stowage is a cause beyond the control of the cargo-owner, but particularly within the duty of the shipowner; want of ventilation, again, may be a necessary result of bad weather, an accident of the sea, provided against in a later clause, or it may be caused by the carelessness of the master or crew. It will be submitted, *infra*, that any negligence not solely in the navigation of the ship should not form the basis of an exception; here, therefore, all that it is admitted as necessary for this phrase justly to cover is, the result of 'inherent vice.' This could more simply be done by inserting this latter term alone, but the alteration is after all unnecessary. It has been laid down in the English Courts of Law, that where damage results proximately from a certain cause, such as leakage, for instance, but mediately through some wrongful act or neglect (the *causa causans*), the neglect, and not the proximate leakage, is considered the real cause of damage; the clause, therefore, will mean no more than 'inherent vice' would, and may without modification stand.

'Sweat and rust' can only be caused respectively by want of ventilation, a peril of the sea, or an act of negligence, and by insufficient preparation of the ship for its voyage, an improper omission on the part of the shipowner himself.

'The Act of God, the Queen's enemies, pirates, robbers by land or sea, restraint of princes, rulers, or people.' This is an old and time-honoured phrase, the meaning of which has become, from frequent discussion in the Courts, well known, and against which objection can hardly be maintained.

'Explosion or fire.' The same remark made in reference to 'leakage' applies to 'explosion' and 'fire.'

'Jettison,' if not improper, is a 'danger of the sea,' and the word may be omitted as redundant; if improper, is a default of master or crew, and will be considered under that head.

'Act, neglect or default of master or crew.' This opens up the most difficult question of all—who is to be liable for acts which are apparently beyond the control of both the parties to the contract? The exception, by its obvious meaning, excludes the idea of accident; it points to damage caused by the voluntary act of those navigating the ship. Clearly the cause is entirely independent of the action of the cargo-owner; and since the idea of accident is excluded by the principle laid down, he is entitled to be recouped for the loss sustained. Theoretically he should be reimbursed by the party causing the loss, the master or crew, as the parties by whose immediate default the damage is done; but, as a rule, it would be futile to expect reimbursement from them: not so from the shipowner, and if he is also a party to the act or default, he must also be held liable. Now the shipowner is obviously not, in point of fact, a participator in the act, but (apart from special contract) he is, by reason of the defaulting party being his servant, considered as a participator by the law of most civilised countries. There are two parties: one must suffer, the cargo-owner is absolutely free from blame or carelessness, the shipowner is so likewise, unless it be that he has not exercised due care in the selection of his servants; it is impossible to determine that except by the light of the subsequent event; the servant has been negligent or worse, he is a negligent servant, his act proves it, the law assumes, not, as is frequently said, that the innocent master is liable for the negligence of his servant, but that the master is liable as having been himself guilty of negligence in want of care in selecting his servant. This may seem hard upon the shipowner, but to hold the reverse would be harder on the cargo-owner, who is helpless in the matter; and the experience of centuries has shown the wisdom of the principle involved. There must be a presumption one way or the other, either that, however negligent, however incompetent the servant is, the master is blameless, or that the negligence of the servant is a proof of a certain amount of negligence on the part of the master, sufficient to make him responsible for the resulting damage.

Which of these two presumptions is the most equitable can hardly admit of doubt, which is most in accord with policy is surely equally clear: presume the innocence of the master, and a great inducement to him to exercise care on behalf of parties entirely dependent on him for its exercise is withdrawn.

The reasons in favour of holding a shipowner responsible for the negligence of his servants do not, however, with the same force apply to holding him liable for their simple errors of judgment; there is no necessity for a man ever to be negligent; it is absolutely certain that he must be always liable to commit errors of judgment. Now the great majority of accidents of navigation, not the consequence of inevitable accident, result chiefly from errors of judgment; there may perhaps be some carelessness in addition, but the main cause is error of judgment. It would seem fair, therefore, for the shipowner to exempt himself from liability for the result of such accidents; and to obviate the probability of much discussion as to whether or not the accident was caused solely by an error, and not by any such carelessness, it may be considered fair and proper to insert an exception against 'acts, neglect, or default of master and crew,' but, for the above reasons, strictly restricted by the words 'in the navigation of the ship,' or others to that effect.

'*Act, &c. of Pilots.*'—This is quite unnecessary; the acts of a pilot, if in compulsory employment, do not involve the liability of the shipowner; if employed otherwise than by compulsion of law, he is simply a member of the crew, and the exception as above will cover his acts.

'*Barratry.*'—The reasons for excluding negligence generally from the exceptions apply of course to 'barratry.'

'Dangers or accidents of the seas and rivers' is a proper exception to insert to exempt the shipowner from liability for damage resulting from perils of the sea unconnected with acts of negligence.

Without useless iteration, it would be difficult to deal with the many other conditions annexed to some bills of lading. It is submitted, however, that the above-mentioned clauses include all the exemptions necessary to be inserted.

So far for the exemptions. In the body of the bill of lading it is suggested that there should be omitted all such terms as 'from the ship's tackle,' 'over the ship's side,' 'as customary,' &c., to signify the time of delivery when the shipowner's responsibility should cease. The responsibility should cease 'on delivery;' what delivery is cannot be described in one document to suit all cases; it must depend on the peculiarities of the place of discharge, and the manner of unloading there customary, but it is a question of fact not difficult to determine in each particular case.

Where parties other than the master sign the bill of lading there is always a difficulty, in case of dispute, in proving the authority of the signor to sign; on the other hand, if the master signs it—as he always should—the authenticity of the document and the wording of the terms of the contract are placed beyond dispute.

The number of copies of the bill of lading to be signed is another moot point; but it is clear that the number should be limited, to avoid as much as possible the chance of frauds being successfully perpetrated, such as the one which gave rise to so much litigation in the case of Glyn, Mills and Company *v.* The East and West Indies Dock Company (Law Rep. 5 Q. B. D. 129; 6 Q. B. D. 475).

In order to make these observations more clear and intelligible a draft bill of lading embodying the results arrived at is annexed.

It is not expected that the remarks herein expressed will meet with general approval, neither is it suggested that the model form is in any way perfect; but if as may perchance happen, they should assist in any, even the smallest, degree the deliberations of the Association in their efforts to formulate a bill of lading which will be fair in its terms and generally acceptable, the purpose of the writer will have been more than amply fulfilled.

Model Bill of Lading.

Shipped in good order and condition by A. B. on board the ship X., whereof is master for this present voyage C. D., now lying in the port of Y. and bound for Z.

being marked and numbered as per margin, to be delivered on production of this bill of lading, subject to the exceptions and conditions hereinafter mentioned, in the like good order and condition, when the shipowner's responsibility shall cease, at the aforesaid port of Z., or so near thereto as she may safely get, unto E. F. or to his assigns, on his or their paying freight for the said goods at the rate of

Average as accustomed.

The following are the exceptions and conditions above referred to :—

Weight, measure, quality, contents and value unknown. The shipowner not to be responsible for reasonable wear and tear of packages or goods; nor for leakage, breakage, heat, or decay; nor for loss or damage arising from the act of God, the Queen's enemies, pirates, robbers by land or sea, restraint of princes, rulers or people, act, neglect or default of the master or crew in navigating the vessel, fire, explosion, nor for any dangers or accidents of the seas and rivers.

In witness whereof the master of the said ship has signed two bills of lading exclusive of his own copy, all of this tenor and date, one of which being accomplished the others to stand void.

Dated at Y.   188 .

(Signed)   C. D.

The President then called upon Mr. Richard Lowndes to read a paper he had prepared

On a Common Form of Bill of Lading.

Uniformity in the law of Affreightment, as amongst the maritime countries of Europe and America, is desirable, not merely as simplifying the relative conditions under which the shipowners of different countries are to compete together in the carrying trade, but still more, perhaps, because the ship of any one country is continually placed under the influence of the laws of some other country, so that the English shipowner, for example, has a direct personal interest in the French, German, and American, and every other law of Affreightment; his ship seeking for employment in, or being obliged to visit, sometimes in the ordinary course of navigation, sometimes as the result of accident or sea peril, the ports of every country in the world.

It has been pointed out by M. de Courcy, in his admirable pamphlet recently published, 'La responsabilité des propriétaires de navires en Angleterre et en France,' that courts of law and legislative bodies have been the most tardy, we may almost say have alone been tardy, in recognising the importance of international rules, or, to speak more exactly, of rules common to several, or, if possible, to all nations, in matters of maritime commerce. It is not Governments that are chargeable with this reproach. There exist treaties of commerce, postal conventions, international rules for the prevention of collisions, international conferences, 'on a great number of questions of science, of hygiene, and of political economy.' Nor can private individuals, men engaged in commerce or connected with it in this or that practical relation, be charged with this reproach. There is, I venture to say, no Chamber of Commerce in England, or any other country, which is not more or less in correspondence with those of other countries, on subjects bearing on some branch or other of this large topic—the unification of mercantile law. Indeed, the very existence of this society of ours bears witness to the common impulse. By a strange contrast, says M. de Courcy, nothing, or next to nothing, of the kind is found in the sphere of internal legislation. Each country is conservative of its old laws, or reforms them slowly, without taking concert with its neighbours, and the consequence is that reforms, made in opposite directions, frequently have the effect of widening the differences which existed before. 'I am convinced,' says M. de Courcy, 'that in the 13th century the feudal law of France more resembled that of England than the civil institutions of the two countries resemble one another at the present day.'

Though tardy in their movements, however, courts of law and legislative bodies are to a certain extent amenable to influences from without; and an opinion widely spread and strongly felt amongst mercantile men is sure, sooner or later, to force its way into legislation. What is taking place with regard to the law of General Average, in the direction of unification through the medium of our York-Antwerp Rules, must serve for encouragement to us in this more ambitious and more difficult task of unification of the law of Affreightment.

Hitherto our efforts in this direction have been what we may call empirical. We have taken one striking example of the evils resulting from the divergency of laws—the subject of *pro ratâ* freight—and have endeavoured to establish uniformity with regard to that one point. Something has already been done here in the way of reform—witness the new Belgian Code, in which the rule on this head has been altered, and assimilated to that which prevails in England, and which was recommended for general adoption by this Association. Another empirical reform, if I may call it so—I mean a reform of detail, aiming at a conventional uniformity, in a matter which hardly admits of being reduced to a principle—has recently been recommended to our notice by the well-known name of M. de Courcy, namely, a uniform rule as to the limitation in amount of a shipowner's responsibility for the faults of his servants. To-day we are to consider another aspect of the subject, a proposal which is not empirical, which does not aim at dealing with this or that symptom of the malady, but would strike at the root; that is to say, a proposal to establish uniformity in the law of Affreightment by the adoption of a common form of bill of lading, in which the principal conditions of an international law shall be embodied in express terms.

This, I acknowledge, is a bold undertaking, and one that we

cannot expect to carry to its perfection in a single session. I do not propose, in this paper, to go so far as even to lay before you the complete formula of the proposed bill of lading. I desire only to offer some general observations, mainly for the purpose of eliciting opinions from my present hearers, as to the utility of such a course, and as to the principles on which the proposed international bill of lading should be drawn.

In the first place, then, it will probably be agreed on all hands that the true reason why there are these divergencies of laws on the subject of the contract of Affreightment is, not any difference in the principles or rules of construction adopted by the legislatures or courts of the different countries for interpreting the contract—not this, or this at most in a very minor degree—but the loose and imperfect manner in which the intentions of the contracting parties are set forth on the face of the instrument of contract itself. It is because neither bill of lading nor charter-party is sufficiently explicit—because the instrument is wholly silent where it ought to speak, or speaks vaguely where it ought to be precise; it is for this reason mainly that this instrument has in different countries received a different interpretation. Now for this mercantile men have the remedy in their own hands. They have only to agree amongst themselves as to what they really intend and wish, and then to say so on the face of their contract in words which contain no ambiguity.

I will take, for an illustration of this, the one point which happens to have forced itself principally on my notice—the phrase in the old form of bill of lading, 'the accidents of navigation excepted.' The bill of lading is a receipt for the goods, an acknowledgment of their being in good condition when received, and an undertaking to deliver them, by a specific route, at a place defined, to a person named or to be named, on payment of a stipulated rate of freight. All the conditions of a *prosperous* voyage—conditions comparatively simple—are defined with exactitude; but as for what is to be done, what are to be the respective rights of the contracting parties, in any of the various circumstances which may lead to the voyage not being absolutely prosperous—a case unfortunately too frequent—there is not a word in the ordinary form of contract, beyond this vague expression, 'the accidents of navigation excepted.' Now the question arises, whether this ought to be, or whether we can devise any improvement. Is it not the fact that almost all—that certainly the most important amongst—the divergencies of our different laws concerning Affreightment, have to do with this passage in the bill of lading? If we could only express ourselves a little more distinctly—if we would only say what we mean by this important exception—should we not have made a considerable step towards uniformity? This, of course, is on the supposition that we all mean, or can be brought to mean, the same thing; if not, our conferences here are a mere waste of time.

The clause 'accidents of navigation excepted,' standing in the bill of lading where it does, immediately following and qualifying the undertaking on the part of the shipowner to deliver the goods at their destination in the like good order as when shipped, amounts to no more than the negative proposition that, in the event of such accidents, the shipowner is not bound to do an impossibility. What is to be regarded as an accident of navigation; how to treat a mishap which is due conjointly to a sea peril and to a fault or neglect of the master or seamen, or directly to one and remotely to the other; whether upon the occurring of an accident, the contract is to be regarded as annulled, or suspended, or whether any or what new relation between the contracting parties is thereupon set up; whether, if the ship be disabled by such accident, so that there has been a partial performance of the engagement to carry, the shipowner is to be entitled to a proportionate part of his freight, or whether he is at liberty to earn the whole by sending on the goods in another bottom, or whether he is bound to do so if he can; whether the shipowner shall be answerable for the faults of his crew, and if so, whether he shall be answerable to an unlimited extent; whether, in case of sacrifice made for the sake of all, there shall be a contribution as General Average, and if so by what law, or on what principles, such contribution shall be regulated: concerning all these points, and others like them, the contract is absolutely silent.

Now it is interesting, and indeed important for our present purpose, to consider in what way this omitted or unwritten part of the contract has gradually been filled up. A body of regulations on the subjects here indicated has in the course of time been formed, not in the first instance by the municipal laws of any one country, nor of several countries, but by the usages of seafaring men without distinction of nationality. The oldest written records of these usages were drawn up at places where there were great gatherings of the ships of various countries. I will not speak of the Roman law, or of the Pandects—bodies of law drawn up at a time when the whole civilised world was, at least nominally, the subject of a single empire. Even these codes are said to have been, so far as relates to maritime affairs, not much more than a *résumé* of usages already existing amongst traders by sea. We may confine our attention to what took place in comparatively modern times, when, in the confusion and ignorance which followed the disruption of the Roman Empire, these codes were buried in obscurity, and commercial or at least maritime legislation had to make a fresh beginning. Here we find, according to tradition, the laws or customs of Oleron—the oldest modern written sea-law—drawn up at some gathering of merchant ships off the island of Oleron in the period of the Crusades. Next in antiquity, perhaps, to this may be placed the Ordinances of Wisby; Wisby, in the Baltic, being at that time a mart, or rendezvous, frequented by the ships of all nations. There was nothing municipal, nothing which could be said to belong to one country rather than another, about either of these collections of maritime usages; nor was there anything municipal or local in the authority accorded to them. They were regarded, all over Europe, as declarations of the common law of the sea; they contained the authorised expression of the meaning which merchants and mariners attach to this unwritten portion of their contract of Affreightment. Municipal law on this subject came later. The differences in the laws of different countries on this subject thus appear to have had their origin, not in any difference either in the nature of the contract, or of the understanding of merchants or seafaring men as to what they themselves intended by it, but merely in the circumstance that this understanding had never been sufficiently reduced to writing, and had, in the process of time, come to be interpreted by lawyers in different places, and, naturally enough, in different senses. If, therefore, it should now happen that merchants and shipowners, awakening to a sense of the inconveniences resulting from these differences, should seek to remedy them, by coming to an understanding as to what the common law of the sea, concerning Affreightment, ought to be, and should agree on a form of words completing that which heretofore had been unwritten in the contract, there will in this be nothing revolutionary, but merely the natural development of the original contract itself. I do not for a moment deny that the difficulties in the way of coming to such an understanding are considerable.

One great difficulty—perhaps the principal one—results from the change in the character of sea-traffic resulting from the introduction of steam. It seems probable, if not certain, that before long there will be no important traffic by sea except in steel or iron steamers. Concurrently with this change, there has been growing up in the minds of the owners of these steamships a conviction that there must be one radical change in the old common law of the sea; that is to say, that the shipowner can no longer undertake to be answerable for the faults or neglects of the master or crew. It is enough, they think, if the shipowner engages to do that which a man can do—that he will build a ship fit for her work, and keep her fit, and will man her with a crew sufficient in number, and competent as to quality, so far as competency can be ascertained beforehand, and with a master and officers who have obtained the certificates of competency required by law. To undertake that these men should always do their duty, and in the course of a long voyage shall never once be guilty of a neglect, or mistake, that shall have a mischievous result, involves a liability which these owners of steamships do not care to undertake. I will not stay to discuss the question whether they are right or wrong, wise or unwise, in holding this conviction. It is a fact which we must not ignore, that the great majority do hold it; and that at present they have the power, and exercise it most effectually, of giving effect to this conviction by means of clauses in their bills of lading. Though there are great varieties in these clauses, though some are more comprehensive in their exclusions than others, this ruling idea is in all of them; the owner refuses to be held liable towards the shipper or owner of the cargo for the faults of his crew.

Now, so long as the owners of steamships, speaking of them as a body, hold this conviction so strongly as to unite in refusing to carry merchandise on any other terms, it cannot be denied that they are acting within their rights. No one is bound to build a steamer, or, having built it, to allow some one else to send goods in her on conditions which he himself does not like. And there are some good reasons for thinking that the owners of steamships are likely to persist in this view of the subject. In fact, it is a view which springs almost inevitably from the nature of steam navigation. It is no exaggeration to say that, if not all, certainly the great majority of accidents to steamers are traceable to the fault of some seaman or engineer. A well-built steamer is powerful to resist the adverse forces of nature; she hardly can spring a leak in any gale, and her engines will keep her off a lee-shore; but she is at the mercy of her own servants; a careless engineer or stoker neglecting to keep up water in the boilers may destroy her by an explosion; the rapid pace and the frequent entering of harbours greatly increase the risk of stranding and collision, each mostly traceable to a sailor's fault.

Here, then, is the state of things we have to deal with, a state of things curiously complicated, unsatisfactory, and not likely to last without some change. There is at present no form of bill of lading common to steamships; the old form, still used for sailing ships, is inadequate even for these, since it has been interpreted in different ways in different countries; and the form for sailing-ships on the one hand, and the various forms for steamships on the other, go on different principles in a matter of the most everyday occurrence and most vital importance. It is obvious, therefore, that some change, and perhaps a sweeping one, has become necessary.

What that change should be is a matter as to which we must speak less confidently. Some men doubt—and I cannot say that the doubt is unreasonable—whether we are yet ripe for a change; whether the transition from the sailing-ship to the steamer, and perhaps from the private shipowner to the company, must not first complete itself, or at least reach some kind of a level standing-ground, before the permanent conditions of the bargain between carrier and shipper, under this new state of commerce by sea, can be adjusted. But though this be so, it by no means follows that it would be premature to discuss, and by discussion lay the foundations of, the bill of lading of the age of steam. This bill of lading, which shall express the standing conditions of the contract, will not certainly be invented all at once, nor yet adopted by acclamation: a period of gestation must precede it; and it is this preliminary work to which our attention is now invited.

In the first place, then, so far as regards the liability of the shipowner for the acts of his servants, I cannot think that there should be a permanently different rule for the sailing-ship and the steamer. If sailing-ships continue to exist at all, these, as the less important, will naturally conform themselves eventually to the form of contract adopted for steam. I do not here speak of the temporary question of policy, whether or not it may be to the advantage of the owners of sailing-ships, in their struggle for existence against the rising preponderance of steam, to hold out to shippers the temptation of more favourable terms. Whether this will do them any good is a matter of speculation, interesting, no doubt, to those who own sailing-ships, but of no permanent importance when regarded from the point of view of this Association as a question of maritime legislation.

Turning, then, to the form of bill of lading for steamships, the question which first presents itself is this: Is it wise or desirable that the owners of steamships should exempt themselves from responsibility for all the faults or neglects of their servants, or only for such losses as, though remotely brought about by such faults or neglects, are yet directly caused by the accidents of navigation? There is a broad distinction between the two. At present, most if not all the forms of steamship bills of lading draw no distinction. Most of them contain clauses which exempt the shipowner from responsibility towards the shipper, not merely for losses resulting from a collision or stranding, or accident of a like nature, brought about by the improper conduct of the crew, but also for damage through improper stowage, or careless delivery of goods to the wrong consignee, and, in a word, for every kind of detriment suffered by the owner of the goods through the improper conduct of the shipowner's servants. The question is, whether this is not going too far.

Here again I may exclude from our consideration that which I may call a temporary question of policy, arising under particular circumstances. Some owners of lines of steamships, having a practical monopoly of a particular trade, and therefore a power to dictate their own terms, may conceive it to be to their advantage, so long as they are thus masters of the situation, to concede to the shippers as little as possible. Men in this position may even resent, as an impertinence, what they may describe as an attempt, on the part of persons outside their trade, to dictate to them the terms on which they shall conduct their own business. With all this we have nothing to do. We are to consider the question on broader grounds. Our question is, whether it is not to the advantage of commerce in general, and therefore in the long run to the advantage even of the shipowners placed in the enviable condition I have described, that there should be one general form of contract for the carriage of goods in steamships, subject of course to modification in exceptional cases, but still constituting a standard, which can be recognised and carried out in the legislation of all countries. Such general form, in order to be permanently accepted, must be satisfactory to both parties concerned, and, that it may be so, must be reasonable.

Now it has for centuries been a sort of maxim, or fundamental principle in maritime commerce, that between the shipowner and the underwriter the goods-owner ought to be kept harmless against all losses except those of the market. When once the goods have been put on board, properly packed so as to be fit for carriage, and when they have been fully insured against all risks, the owner of them ought, by one contract or the other, to feel secure. The rule has been that the shipowner undertakes to deliver them, accidents of navigation excepted; and the accidents of navigation are guaranteed by the insurer. It is not to be expected that a new form of contract, which shall destroy the entirety of this security, will be permanently satisfactory to the shippers of cargo. It may for a time be submitted to from a necessity arising from monopoly or a trades-union amongst steamship owners, but the submission will be reluctant; any steamship that should offer better terms in this respect would at once gain a great advantage over her competitors; you would not have a state of things that could be regarded as satisfactory or stable.

On the other side, looking on the question from the shipowner's point of view, the reasons which originally led the owners of steamships to disclaim liability for those misdoings of their servants which relate to the stowage and delivery of the merchandise, and matters of that kind, are such as belong, we may say, to the infancy of steam navigation, are already beginning to lose much of their force and are likely to lose in time almost if not all force. Those reasons may be reduced to one principal head—the peremptory necessity, for steamers, of despatch. Practical men know very well that, in the early days of ocean steaming, this necessity for despatch led to a great deal of hurry and confusion in the loading and discharging of steamships. The old deliberate ways which served for sailing-ships had to be abandoned. The art of methodising haste, of doing the work at once quickly and well, was not acquired all at once. It has been necessary to learn that art; and it may now certainly be said that great progress has been made in the learning of it. But in the early stages of this learning, when it was strongly felt that despatch was essential, while it was not yet seen that despatch was not incompatible with strict precaution against error, the first and easiest way of proceeding naturally seemed to be, to shake off the responsibility for careless loading or careless discharging. This crude device is not now nearly so much needed as it was at first; and the time is certainly coming, if indeed it has not come, when the owners of steamships may safely resume the old wholesome check upon such carelessness which is afforded by their taking the responsibility for it on their own shoulders.

Now let us turn for a moment to the position of a party indirectly, indeed, but intimately connected with the contract—the underwriter. There are, I think, reasons for believing that underwriters as a body, while it would be scarcely possible to induce them to take upon themselves risks so entirely strange to them, of a nature so different from anything they have as yet had to deal with, as the risk of bad stowage or of improper delivery, yet would make no great difficulty in adapting themselves to a contract under which they should merely be asked to make good losses resulting from the perils ordinarily insured against, just as they do now, but without having, as in certain cases they have now, a recourse against the shipowner, when the peril or loss can be traced to the fault of his servants. In truth, such a change would only be a return to the state of things which in England, practically, existed up to about the year 1864 or 1866. It has long been the rule of law in England, as I dare say in all other countries, that, as between insurer and assured, the former is liable, under the old maxim of law, 'Causa proxima, non remota, spectatur,' for losses directly caused by a peril insured against, notwithstanding that the loss may have been remotely brought about by the fault or neglect of someone other than the assured himself. If the shipowner's servant negligently sets the ship on fire, or runs her aground, or into collision with some other ship, the underwriter must bear the loss. It was for a long time generally supposed, I do not say by lawyers, but certainly by mercantile men, that the same rule applied to the contract of Affreightment, and this supposition was for a great length of time generally acted on in practice. The clause 'accidents of navigation excepted' was supposed to free the shipowner, as between himself and the owners of the cargo, from all liability for losses directly resulting from such accidents, so as to render unnecessary any inquiry into the conduct of his servants, the master and crew. In those days Board of Trade inquiries into the causes of maritime disasters did not exist. I well remember the shock to our preconceived notions which was given, in the years I have named, by two decisions of the English courts, which followed one another in rapid succession, both against the same defendant. One of these cases was called Lloyd, the other Grill, against the Screw Collier Company. They laid down the law to be that there was in this matter a fundamental difference of principle between the contract of insurance and that of Affreightment; that, in fact, the 'accidents of navigation' in the bill of lading had not so wide a meaning as the perils of the seas,' &c., in the policy of insurance. The perils which the underwriter takes upon himself, it appears, include losses remotely brought about by the fault of the servants of the shipowner; the 'accidents of navigation,' from which the shipowner exempts himself under an ordinary bill of lading, do not include such losses. The result is that there is a large class of losses, in respect of which the shipper or owner of cargo has a double indemnity; he may, if he pleases, claim from the shipowner damages for loss resulting from the fault of a seaman, or he may claim that loss from his own underwriter, as a loss directly caused by sea peril. If he takes the latter course, his underwriter on payment succeeds to his rights, and may himself sue the shipowner. Now I shall ask practical men to confirm what I am about to say from their own experience; but so far as I have had opportunities for observing, I think I can say with confidence that underwriters generally do not attach much value to the right they have, after paying a loss of cargo, to recover it back from the shipowner on the ground that the loss has arisen through some neglect on the part of his servants. Whether it be that the attempt to enforce such a right almost always leads to litigation, or whether it be due to a feeling that the frequent enforcing of such claims would drive shipowners to a change in the form of their contracts; whatever be the reason, the fact certainly is that such claims are very rarely made. I have myself known many cases in which such a claim might have been made, with very fair hopes of success, but where it has not been attempted, or even seriously thought of.

For these reasons I am inclined to believe that if the owners of steamships would limit their demand in the manner I have suggested—if they would agree to take upon themselves all liability except for the accidents of navigation, on condition that for the results of those accidents they should be exempted from liability, even though the accident itself were brought about by the fault of some one in their employ, all the difficulties and anomalies of the present state of things would be removed; and that this change, whilst highly acceptable to the owners of merchandise, would encounter little or no resistance from underwriters, and would in the long run be decidedly beneficial to the shipowners themselves.

I have dealt, perhaps, at too great length on this point, because of its extreme importance; but before I leave it, there is just one objection which I wish to anticipate.

It may perhaps be urged that a change such as that proposed, if it is likely to do so little hurt to insurer or shipowner, is not likely to do much good to the owner of cargo. In fact, it may be said there exists at this moment no violent dissatisfaction with the present state of things. Anomalous and indefensible in theory it may be, yet it has not worked so very badly. The owners of steamships for the most part use their clauses rather as a safeguard against unreasonable claims, than as a ground for resisting such claims, whether for bad stowage or for non-delivery of goods, as they believe to be well founded; in other words, they do not really avail themselves to the full extent of the power which these clauses give them. On the other hand, as regards sailing-ships, the insurers of cargo do not enforce, to anything like the full extent, the terrible liabilities to which the law exposes the shipowner. They use their power as a menace, put in force only in extreme cases. This being so, why disturb a state of things against which there is as yet no great outcry?

To this the answer surely should be: the uncertainty, both to the merchant and the shipowner, of a state of things which leaves either to the clemency or forbearance of some one else, is in itself a great evil; it operates, so far as it goes, as a discouragement to maritime adventure; and if, as appears to be the case, this uncertainty and this discouragement can be removed by adding a few more words to the printed form of a bill of lading, there is surely no valid reason why the alteration should not be made.

I would suggest, then, for steamers and for sailing-ships, some such form as this: 'Owners not responsible for the accidents of navigation, whether occasioned by the fault or neglect of those in their employ, or otherwise.'

Having now occupied your time more than enough, I propose only, in as few words as possible, to enumerate one or two other principal changes or additional clauses which occur to me as desirable, if we are to have a common form of bill of lading such as may serve for the basis of an international law of Affreightment.

Some fuller specification of the accidents of navigation, particularly in the case of steamships, appears to me desirable. 'Fire' should be mentioned by name. The bursting of boilers, and the breakage of screw-shafts, are accidents, from the effects of which the shipowner should be protected, notwithstanding that either of these occurrences are often attributable either to negligence or wear and tear on some previous voyage, which might legally be construed into unseaworthiness on the voyage in question. These, therefore, should be excepted by name. Very probably other accidents of a like nature may be suggested in the course of our discussions; these, however, are all that at the moment occur to me. It must be remembered, that, without any express words, when goods are shipped in a steamer, 'accidents of navigation' cover all incidents of steam navigation, except such as result from unseaworthiness or fault of the shipowner's servants.

Power to tranship the goods, even without necessity arising from sea-peril, is frequently reserved by the owners of steamships in certain trades. That is a matter of detail, as to which uniformity is not requisite or even particularly desirable. But when such power is intended to be reserved, this must be done by express words.

Careful provision should be made, by an express clause, for the several cases in which the voyage is necessarily broken off in the middle. This raises the whole question of *pro ratâ* freight, and the proper wording of a clause to deal with it will require much consideration. Concerning this, I do not at present propose to go further than to suggest that the framing of such a clause might with advantage be referred to a special committee. The basis of it I take to be that, if the ship is disabled from carrying the goods to their destination, the shipowner is to be at liberty to earn his freight by sending on the goods at his own expense in another bottom. If the goods are by sea-peril rendered unfit to be carried all the way, no freight is to be due. This is apparently the result of our deliberations thus far. I may point out, however, that the latter of these two rules would occasionally lead to most inequitable results. A cargo of coals, for example, though incapable (*e.g.* from being wet and heated) of being carried all the way to its destination, may be sold at the intermediate port at double or treble its original cost; and it certainly appears inequitable that this enhanced value, given to it by the transit, should be taken by the merchant without any payment of freight to the shipowner.

Closely connected with this are two questions, which I believe our Association have already discussed, viz. When goods are damaged by sea-peril, so as to be rendered less valuable, ought there to be a proportionate reduction in the freight on them?—a question which I believe we answer in the negative; and, When goods are thus damaged to such an extent as not to be worth so much as the freight on them, ought the deficit to be reclaimable from the shipper?—which also, I believe, we answer in the negative. It would probably be advisable that both these conclusions should be expressed on the face of our bill of lading.

On the complicated subject of General Average, we already know how to secure a practical uniformity, namely, by the insertion of the York-Antwerp-Rule clause. It would be still better if we could have a York-Antwerp 'Code.' The time has come, I think, when we are ripe for an agreed definition of the principle of General Average. Some few points not touched on by the York-Antwerp Rules ought to be added. The rule as to voluntary stranding, which was somewhat hastily accepted at Antwerp almost without discussion, needs to be reconsidered. As it stands, it appears to me almost the only blemish in these rules. I should like to see a more rational rule of practice substituted for the old deduction of one-third, particularly as regards iron ships and repairs at a port of refuge where the cost greatly exceeds the cost in the home port. Such a code would be the completion of the work done at Antwerp—work which this Association may look back to with some reasonable pride.

Here, then, is the outline—a very crude and imperfect one—of the international bill of lading which the special committee invite you to construct. It is probable that at our present meeting we shall not get further, in any case, than the appointment of a committee, authorised to consult with the accredited representatives of shipowners and merchants in the several countries, and to frame the draft of a bill of lading, to be brought before you for adoption, correction, or rejection, as the case may be, on some future occasion.

The appointment of such a committee, should this meet with your approval, will have been an important step towards the object we have in view.

On the conclusion of the reading of Mr. Lowndes's treatise, SIR TRAVERS TWISS moved the following resolution: 'That the executive council be empowered to nominate a committee to report at the next conference upon the subject of Mr. Richard Lowndes's paper, with power to appoint sub-committees, and directions to print and circulate the said paper.'

I seconded this motion.

On Thursday, August 18, 1881, the conference again met, when MR. H. H. MEIER, the President, who was in the chair, read out the names of the gentlemen who had been added to the Committee on the International Law of Affreightment, namely:—

> THÉODORE ENGELS, of Antwerp.
> H. H. MEIER, of Bremen.
> M. DE COURCY, of Paris.
> PROFESSOR ASSER, of Amsterdam.
> MR. AXEL WINGE, of Christiania.
> JUDGE C. A. PEABODY, of New York.

On the reassembling of the conference on Friday, August 19, 1881, Sir Travers Twiss, in the chair, announced that Mr. Richard Lowndes had kindly promised to form a committee in Liverpool on the important question of the law of Bills of Lading, and moved that Mr. Richard Lowndes, of Liverpool, be appointed honorary secretary of the local committee in Liverpool on the International Law of Bills of Lading, with directions to form a committee, and to report to the executive council of the Association.

In supporting this motion, DR. SYNDICUS MARCUS said that it was very desirable that local committees should be formed to work up any subject which it was agreed to adopt as a question for consideration. The motion was adopted.

The following twelvemonths were utilised to ventilate the subject in all directions, as will be seen from the following very full report of the proceedings of the Association's tenth conference held in the Town Hall of the city of Liverpool on August 8, 1882, under the presidency of the late Lord O'Hagan, who, as will be recollected, presided at the Antwerp Conference of 1877, where the York and Antwerp General Average Rules were promulgated.

I must here express my regret that the attendance of shorthand-writers during these proceedings had not been secured, and therefore only a few of the very acute arguments used during the discussions by the various speakers have been recorded.

The proceedings were opened by DR. CHARLES STUBBS, of London, honorary secretary of the Committee on an International Law of Affreightment and Bills of Lading, reading the following report:—

In accordance with the resolution passed at the Cologne Conference of this Association, that a committee should be nominated by the executive council to consider and report on the subject of the codification of international law, specially with regard to the law of Affreightment and Bills of Lading, the following committee has during the past year been appointed:—

DR. WENDT, London, *Chairman*.
MR. RICHARD LOWNDES, Liverpool, *Deputy Chairman*.
MR. JACOB AHLERS, Hamburg.
PROFESSOR ASSER, Councillor of State, Amsterdam.
MR. H. J. ATKINSON, London and Hull.
MR. L. R. BAILY, Liverpool.
MR. T. C. ENGELS, Chairman of the Belgian Lloyd, Antwerp.
MR. H. W. GAIR, Liverpool.
MR. JOHN GLOVER, London.
DR. GÜTSCHOW, Hamburg.
COL. HILL, C.B., President of the Chamber of Shipping of the United Kingdom, Cardiff.
MR. PHILIP HIRSCHFELD, London.

Mr. E. Hogg, Chairman of the Association of Average Adjusters, London.
Mr. T. H. Ismay, Liverpool.
Mr. W. A. Jevons, Liverpool.
Mr. W. H. Jones, Liverpool.
Mr. S. Lowther, Belfast.
Mr. H. H. Meier, Chairman of the North German Lloyd, Bremen.
Mr. Ole Möller, London.
Dr. W. L. P. A. Molengraaff, Amsterdam.
The Hon. Judge Ch. A. Peabody, New York.
Mr. James Poole, Liverpool.
Mr. J. H. Powell, London.
Mr. P. H. Rathbone, Liverpool.
Dr. Rahusen, Amsterdam.
Mr. H. Reinhold, Calcutta.
Mr. John Riley, London.
Dr. Sieveking, President of the Court of Appeal, Hamburg.
Mr. Ulrich, Secretary-General of the International Underwriters' Association, Berlin.
Dr. Voigt, Hamburg.
Mr. Axel Winge, Christiania; and
Dr. Charles Stubbs, London, *Hon. Sec.*

It has been considered inexpedient, if not impossible, to present a reasoned report, signed by or on behalf of your committee so constituted, on the subject assigned to them. I have, however, been directed to prepare, for the information of the members of the Association at this conference, a report on the proceedings of your committee since the last conference, and the result thereof.

Communications have been addressed to a large number of Chambers of Commerce, associations, leading merchants, shipowners, lawyers, and others in England, America, and the continent of Europe, directing their attention to copies of the papers on bills of lading laid before this Association last year, with the request that they would form local committees in their respective towns, discuss the subject, and transmit to your committee their individual or collective opinions on the same, and, if possible, come, or send representatives, to take part in the intended deliberations at this conference. In response to the request of your committee, local committees have been formed at Liverpool, Newcastle-on-Tyne, Hull, Sunderland, North Shields, Hamburg, Amsterdam and Rotterdam, Antwerp, and New York.

The Liverpool committee, a large and influential body of representatives of Shipowners', Merchants', and Underwriters' Associations and Chambers of Commerce, held many meetings, and, after much discussion, agreed with practical unanimity to two drafts of a common form of bill of lading, one for steam vessels and one for sailing vessels, subject, however, to revision.

These drafts have also been considered by the members of your committee, and widely circulated and submitted to the other local committees, with a view of obtaining opinions as to whether they would meet the views of the various mercantile communities, without or with any alterations.

The letters, accompanied by the documents referred to, have elicited a large number of answers, together with some reasone l reports from the local committees. The general opinion appeared to be in favour of the Liverpool drafts, the approval expressed being, however, as was to be expected, qualified, some of the clauses contained therein being disapproved of in some instances and new clauses suggested in others.

The reports and suggestions referred to are here printed, and may be seen therefore in the full report.

MR. RICHARD LOWNDES, President of the Liverpool Chamber of Commerce, as deputy chairman of this committee and chairman of the Liverpool committee, then introduced the discussion on this subject. He concluded by moving the adoption of the report of the Liverpool committee introducing the draft form of bill of lading.

This report was as follows:—

The 'Association for the Reform and Codification of the Law of Nations' having, in its meeting in Cologne last year, approved of the proposal made to endeavour to establish a common form of bill of lading, so framed as to promote uniformity in the law of Affreightment throughout the mercantile world; and having appointed a special committee to organise this work in the several countries; an invitation was issued, under the sanction of the central committee, to the several shipowning and mercantile associations of Liverpool, to send two representatives from each association in order to constitute a local committee, for the purpose of taking the subject into consideration, and, if possible, framing a bill of lading adapted to the end here proposed.

In response to this invitation, each of the associations sent two representatives. The Shipowners' Association appointed Mr. Donald Kennedy and Mr. John Rankin; the Steamship Owners' Association appointed Mr. James Spence and Mr. W. H. Wilson; the Chamber of Commerce appointed Mr. Richard Lowndes and Mr. Henry Coke; the American Chamber of Commerce appointed Mr. W. D. Heyne and Mr. B. F. Babcock; the East India and China Section of the Chamber of Commerce appointed Mr. Robert Gladstone and Mr. Magnus Mowat; the Iron and General Metal Trade Section appointed Mr. Alexander Sparrow and Mr. George Rae Anderson; the Cotton Section appointed Mr. B. F. Babcock and Mr. Bancroft Cooke; the Underwriters' Association appointed Mr. C. B. Vallance and Mr. S. Cross; and the Liverpool Law Society, who were asked to take part in order to advise the committee on points of law and to assist in the framing of clauses, appointed Mr. H. W. Collins and Mr. A. Bright. These gentlemen, together with the following members of the central committee, who took part *ex officio*—viz. Mr. L. R. Baily, Mr. H. W. Gair, Mr. T. H. Ismay, Mr. W. A. Jevons, Mr. W. H. Jones, Mr. James Poole, and Mr. P. H. Rathbone—constituted the Liverpool Bill of Lading Committee.

This committee, after holding seventeen meetings, now closes its proceedings, at all events until after the approaching annual meeting of the Association on August 8 next, with the following report:—

The committee are practically unanimous on the following points:—

The present state of things, under which almost every steamship company has a form of bill of lading of its own, and there is uncertainty as to the effect of the special clauses constantly introduced, is inconvenient and objectionable.

There is no sufficient reason why the liability of a steamship owner should differ from that of the owner of a sailing-ship, in such matters as damage resulting from improper stowage, or as to loss occasioned by collision or other accident of navigation, brought about through some fault or error of judgment on the part of the master or crew.

If a common form of bill of lading can be drawn up, such as would fairly meet the reasonable requirements of the shipowner on the one hand, and of the owners and insurers of the cargo on the other, its general adoption would be a great convenience to mercantile men.

Admitting that there may be reasons for special clauses in particular trades, and also admitting the principle of freedom of contract, it still would be a great advantage to have any special clauses printed or written in such a manner as to be easily distinguishable from the common form; as, for instance, in the margin of the bill of lading, and not in the body of it. The contracting parties could then readily direct their particular attention to these special clauses, and would know what they were asked to agree to.

The principle of the common form of bill of lading should be this: that the shipowner, whether by steam or sailing ship, should be liable for the faults of his servants in all matters relating to the ordinary course of the voyage, such as the stowage and right delivery of the cargo, and other matters of this kind; but, on the other hand, the shipowner should be exempt from liability for everything which comes under the head of 'accidents of navigation,' even though the loss from these may be indirectly attributable to some fault or neglect of the crew.

It is desirable that the common form of bill of lading should lay down clear and precise rules on every important point as to which the laws of different countries with regard to Affreightment differ from one another, in order that the settlement between shipowner and cargo-owner may be as nearly as possible the same, in whatever country that settlement may have to be enforced.

A common form of bill of lading, based on these principles, was, after much discussion, agreed to, for the most part unanimously by this committee, subject, however, to revision, after being submitted by the representative members to the several associations who had appointed them. It was arranged that, after an interval allowed for that purpose, any suggestions that might be made by the associations should be taken in order.

The first of these happened to be the Shipowners' Association. Their suggestions, which referred only to matters of detail, were discussed and for the most part adopted.

At this stage of our proceedings a letter was received from the secretary of the Steamship Owners' Association, which is printed below. On its being read, the representatives of this association announced to the committee that they considered this letter as putting an end to their representative functions, and that they could thenceforth only speak as individuals.

At the following meeting of the committee the conclusion was come to that, in view of the action thus taken by the Steamship Owners' Association, it was not desirable to proceed further at present in the discussion of the bill of lading, especially as there would be ample opportunity of doing so at the approaching meeting of the Association, on August 8 next. It was therefore resolved to make no further alterations in the form which had been framed by the committee up to that point, and to recommend it as a basis for discussion at that meeting.

In doing so, the committee desire to add the following remarks, in explanation of some of the proposed clauses :—

1. The clause giving liberty 'to deviate so far as reasonably necessary for saving life or property' is inserted to meet what is thought to be the mischievous effect of the recent decision in the case of Scaramanga *v.* Stamp, which subjects the shipowner to the highly penal consequences of a 'deviation,' whenever the master goes out of the direct course, or delays the ship, in order to tow and assist a ship in distress, for the sake of saving property, as distinguished from the saving of life. As a consequence of this

decision, it is well known that peremptory orders are given by the owners of many steamers to their captains, on no account to attempt the towing or assisting of disabled ships, but to take off the crews and passengers and abandon the ships. Another natural consequence of this decision is a material increase in the sums awarded for salvage services. These evils can only be met by a clause in the bill of lading, such as that here proposed.

2. The term 'York-Antwerp Code' is used, in preference to York-Antwerp Rules, in the hope that, by the time the new bill of lading comes into general use, those rules, now coming more and more to be adopted, will be amended and completed, so as to constitute a short code of General Average.

3. The provisions with regard to *pro ratâ* or distance freight have been framed, after much consideration, in the hope that they may be accepted in other countries, as well as our own, as the basis of an equitable settlement of this much-disputed question. That our present English and American law on this subject, which differs from that of almost every other country, does not altogether work well, is shown in a striking manner when cargoes of small cost, such as coal or salt, have been carried for a part of the voyage originally intended, and then, owing to sea-peril preventing the completion of the voyage, are sold for perhaps double or treble their cost. It is plainly unreasonable that the shipowner, by whose expenditure of capital this enhanced value has been created, should receive nothing in return, while the owner of the cargo makes a gain far beyond anything he could have expected had the voyage been completed in the ordinary way. On the other hand, when the voyage is not performed, and the cargo has received no advantage from a partial carriage, the English and American rule, of giving no freight, except as the result of a new bargain, seems to be reasonable enough.

4. The clause giving liberty to the shipowner to earn his freight by forwarding the goods in another bottom, when the original ship has been disabled, notwithstanding that the ship may have been abandoned at sea by the crew, and afterwards recovered by salvors, is inserted to meet the recent decision in the case of the 'Cito,' which determines that such an abandon-

ment totally puts an end to the contract of Affreightment, so that the owner of the cargo may demand delivery of it, at any intermediate port into which the ship has been carried by the salvors, free of all charge for freight. This inequitable result, it would seem, can only be remedied by means of a special clause in the contract.

In conclusion, the committee desire to record the special obligations they are under to their legal members for the valuable time given and services rendered by them to this work, and also to the representatives of the underwriting body for the readiness they have shown to fall in with any reasonable arrangement that may be come to, with the object of protecting the merchant, so far as practicable, as between the bill of lading and the policy.

(Signed, by order of the committee)
RICHARD LOWNDES, *Chairman.*
Liverpool: July 19, 1882.

'COPY OF LETTER REFERRED TO.

'Liverpool: June 19, 1882.

'Dear Sir,—The form of bill of lading prepared by your committee has on two occasions been submitted to the various members of this Association, and has had their careful consideration. It has been found, however, that from the many trades which are represented in the Association, each requiring different provisions, applicable to its trade, it is impossible for the Association to agree to the adoption of any general form of bill of lading. I am desired, however, to state that the various members will give the provisions of any bill of lading, which may be recommended by your committee, their most careful consideration.—Yours truly,

(Signed)   'GRAY HILL, *Secretary.*
'Richard Lowndes, Esq.'

Draft bill of lading presented by the Liverpool committee:—

[1] SHIPPED, in apparent good order and condition, by   in and upon the good *steam* ship called the   now

[1] For the form as finally settled, see p. 379.

lying in the port of   and bound for   with liberty to call at any ports, in any order, to sail without pilots, and to tow and assist vessels in distress, and to deviate so far as reasonably necessary for saving life or property; also with liberty, in case the ship shall put into a port of refuge for repair, to tranship the goods to their destination by any other *steamer* (vessel); and with liberty to convey goods in lighters to and from the ship, at shipper's risk. Such lighterage to be at ship's expense, except that if the cargo is necessarily landed in lighters, the ship being unable to reach the port of destination, the cost of such lighterage shall fall on the cargo.

         being marked and numbered as per margin; and to be delivered in the like good order and condition at the aforesaid port of

The act of God, fire, barratry of the master and mariners, enemies, pirates and thieves, arrest and restraint of princes, rulers and people, collisions, stranding, and other accidents of navigation, excepted, even when occasioned by the negligence, default, or error in judgment of the pilot, master, mariners, or other servants of the shipowners.

Ship not answerable for losses through *explosion, bursting of boilers, breakage of shafts, or* any latent defect *in the machinery or hull*, not resulting from want of due diligence by the owners of the ship, or any of them, or by the ship's husband or manager; nor for decay, putrefaction, rust, sweat, change of character, drainage, or leakage, arising from the nature of the goods shipped or the insufficiency of the packages; nor for any damage or loss occasioned by the prolongation of the voyage; nor for obliteration or absence of marks, numbers, addresses, or descriptions of goods shipped.

unto   , or to his or their assigns, freight, primage, and charges for the said goods, as per margin, to be paid by   . Freight to be paid in cash, without discount; at the rate of exchange for bankers' bills at sight, current on the day of the ship's entry inwards at the custom-house. General Average payable according to York-Antwerp Code.

In witness whereof, the master, or agent, of the said ship hath affirmed to   bills of lading, all of this tenor and date, the one of which bills being accomplished, the others to stand void.

1. Quality marks, if any, to be of the same size as and contiguous to the leading marks; and if inserted in the shipping notes accepted by the mate, the master is bound to sign bills of lading conformable thereto.

2. Ship not liable for breakage of glass, earthenware, or china.

3. Not accountable for goods of any description which are above the value of 100*l*. per package, unless the value be herein expressed and a special agreement made; nor for gold, silver, bullion, specie, documents, jewellery, pictures, embroideries, or works of art, silks, furs, china, watches, or clocks, unless bills of lading are signed therefor, with the value therein expressed, and a special agreement be made.

4. Shippers accountable for any loss or damage to ship or cargo caused by inflammable, explosive, or dangerous goods, shipped without full disclosure of their nature, whether such shipper shall have been aware of it or not, and whether such shipper be principal or agent: such goods may be thrown overboard or destroyed by the master or owner of the ship at any time without compensation.

5. All fines or damages, which the ship or cargo may incur or suffer by reason of incorrect or insufficient marking of packages or description of their contents, shall be paid by the shipper or consignee, and the ship shall have a lien on the goods of such shipper or consignee for the amount thereof.

6. Goods delivered to the ship, whilst on quay awaiting shipment, to be at shipper's risk as regards all the perils excepted in this bill of lading.

7. Goods once shipped cannot be taken away by the shipper except upon payment of full freight, together with the expenses of landing them, and compensation for any damages sustained by the owners through such taking away.

8. In case the ship shall be prevented from reaching her destination by quarantine, blockade, ice, or the hostile act of any power, the master or owners may discharge the goods into any depôt or lazaretto, or at any near available port; all expenses thereby incurred upon the goods to be borne by the owners or receivers thereof.

9. Ship to have a lien on all goods for payment of freight and charges, including back freight, forwarding charges, and charges for carriage to port of shipment, whether payable in advance or not.

10. If the ship is able to carry the goods to their destination, but the goods, by reason of damage sustained or of their own nature, are not fit to be carried all the way, and if such goods have received an enhancement of value by reason of their partial carriage, the ship shall be entitled to a *pro ratâ* freight in proportion to the distance performed, which freight is in no case to exceed the amount of such enhancement of value. *Pro ratâ* freight is admissible in no other case than that dealt with in the preceding sentence, unless there be an acceptance of the goods by the shipper or owner of the goods.

11. When the goods are fit to be carried to their destination, but the ship is unable to carry them, the shipowner may earn full freight by sending the goods to their destination at his own expense in another bottom: this right is not affected by an abandonment of the ship by her crew, or to the underwriters: and the ship is to be, for this purpose, deemed unable to carry the goods to their destination, if she either cannot be repaired at all, or cannot be repaired except at an expense exceeding her value when repaired.

12. Full freight is due on damaged goods; but the consignee is at liberty to abandon his entire consignment for the freight on it, provided he elects to do so before taking delivery.

13. No freight is due on any increase in bulk or weight caused by the absorption of water during the voyage.

14. Freight which by the terms of the bill of lading is made payable by the consignee cannot be demanded from the shipper after the master has parted with his lien on the goods.

15. The goods, if not taken by the consignee immediately on landing, or within such further time as is provided by the regulations of the port of discharge, may be stored by the master, at the consignee's expense and risk.

16. In the event of claims for short delivery, when the ship reaches her destination, the price to be the market price at the port of destination on the day of the ship's reporting at the custom-house, less all charges saved.

NOTICE.—In accepting this bill of lading, the owner of the goods and the shipper expressly accept and agree to all its stipulations and conditions, whether written or printed.

Dated in Liverpool, this   day of   188

Weight and contents unknown.

(*The words printed in italics are to be omitted in the case of sailing ships.*)

MR. ATKINSON, of Hull, as representative of the Chamber of Shipping of London, and of the Hull Chamber of Commerce, seconded the resolution.

A discussion ensued, in which DR. WENDT, MR. JAMES SAMUELSON, MR. SHOTTON, and others took part, in the course of which doubts were expressed as to the meaning to be attached to the resolution; but the President having intimated that, if it were passed, he should rule that members would not be consequently precluded from raising any question on the subject, the resolution was unanimously adopted.

MR. LOWNDES next moved: 'That there should be a common form of bill of lading, and, admitting that there may be reasons for special clauses in particular trades, and also admitting the principle of freedom of contract, it would be convenient that any special or additional clauses should be printed or written in such manner as to be easily distinguishable from the common form.' Adding that this would imply the principle of a common form of bill of lading, without hampering the freedom of contract. The common form would stand like the Lloyd's form of a policy of insurance, as a basis which all knew and understood. Then if the parties wished to vary the common form in any way, as in certain trades, or on particular occasions it might be necessary to do, such variation would be stated in the margin. This was the extent to which he, and the Chamber he represented, advocated a common form.

MR. JOHN GLOVER, of London, seconded the resolution.

MR. LAURENCE R. BAILY, of Liverpool, objected, observing that until it be seen what bill of lading is approved of by the conference, it would be premature to determine whether its adoption would be advisable.

MR. SHOTTON, of Liverpool, supported the resolution.

MR. CORNELIUS WALFORD, of London, said that the bill of lading which was in ordinary use was the same as that used two thousand years ago. There were not thirty words different in the bill of lading which Cicero pleaded upon and that which was in use at the present day. A common bill of lading for international purposes he believed to be an impossibility, although he wished it were otherwise.

MR. GRAY HILL, of Liverpool, remarked that he did not see any probability of so altering the law as it now existed as to lead to any material change. There was a skeleton bill of lading in existence at the present time; the resolution was therefore futile.

MR. WESTGARTH, of Melbourne, thought that, as a national assembly, it was their duty to aim at an international bill of lading, and he supported the resolution.

The resolution was then carried *nem. con.*

MR. RICHARD LOWNDES next moved the adoption of the following clause in the report of the Liverpool committee: 'That the principle of the common form of bill of lading should be this—that the shipowner, whether by steam or sailing ship, should be liable for the faults of his servants in all matters relating to the ordinary course of the voyage, such as the stowage and right delivery of the cargo, and other matters of this kind; but, on the other hand, the shipowner should be exempt from liability for everything which comes under the head of ' accidents of navigation,' even though the loss from these may be indirectly attributable to some fault or neglect of the crew.'

MR. ATKINSON, of London and Hull, seconded the resolution.

I then moved as an amendment: 'That the words, "even though the loss from these may be indirectly attributable to some fault or neglect of the crew," be omitted.'

MR. JAMES SAMUELSON, of Liverpool, seconded the amendment. He held that the shipowner should have such men in his employment as were able to navigate his vessel and look after the interests confided to them. He also objected to the motion, because it seemed to him to be indirectly reviving a principle which it had been sought to abrogate by the Employers' Liability Act. It would practically make the masters and navigators of vessels careless in the performance of their duties; and although by some arrangement the loss, so far as the goods were concerned, might not fall upon the shipper or receiver, it would be indirectly, and in a very marked manner, endangering the lives of passengers and others. He thought the recommendations of the Liverpool committee would have been of more value if there had been attached to it the opinion of the General Brokers' Association, who in reality, to a very large extent, represented the shippers and receivers of goods.

MR. JOHN GLOVER, of London, pointed out that shipowners were not at liberty to select whom they liked to command and navigate their vessels, but they were restricted to persons whose competency was tested by Government examinations. It would be a puzzle to him to find a bill of lading of any shipping line of importance in which the clause contained in the resolution did not appear. One-half or two-thirds of the companies which carried goods to and from our shore, including the Peninsular and Oriental and Royal Mail Steamship Companies, conveyed them on bills of lading containing this clause, and on public grounds they asked that that which was already so general should be made universal. Representing the Shipowners' Society of London, he stated that their reasons for desiring exemption from liability for the acts of their crews were that the responsibility was not really theirs; it had only been put upon them by recent decisions in the Courts, and not by any direct statute; that they had to bear very heavy risks as shipowners in the ordinary prosecution of their business; and, aware of these risks, they took precautions against them, their own vigilance being supplemented in every way by that of the law.

THE HON. DAVID DUDLEY FIELD, of New York, asked whether they would or would not by this resolution change the law. If they put goods upon the London and North-Western Railway in Liverpool for London, and they were lost through the fault of the company's servants, would they not recover from the company? He thought all would agree that the proposal was not in accordance with the law as affecting goods carried by land, and therefore the effect of it would be to have a law for the sea different from that for the land. In his opinion the common form should be: ' Received   certain goods   to be carried to   .' Everything else should be contained, not in the bill of lading, but in a Code of Law. He opposed the motion.

MR. COUDERT, of New York, thought it unwise to adopt the resolution; its effect would be to permit the existence of a liability on land which was abolished on the sea, without any apparent object except the convenience of the shipowner, and the philosophy of this had not been explained. The general interest of the commercial traveller should rather be considered, and the efforts of the Association should be directed to finding out what would be most conducive to diligence on the part of the shipowner.

MR. SHOTTON, of North Shields, supported the motion. He observed that there were such things as Board of Trade inquiries, which by keeping a check on the crews of vessels, to that extent safeguarded the interests of the merchant. Both merchant and shipowner had insurable risks, and it was their duty to insure them.

MR. ENGELS, of Antwerp, held that it was practically impossible to render a shipowner responsible for the faults of all his crew. Some of the men had to be shipped at the last moment in the place of others who had neglected to join, and there was no possibility of examining their character and qualifications.

MR. J. G. ALEXANDER, of London, explained that the limitation of liability of railway companies applied only to valuables, and not to ordinary goods.

Mr. DONALD KENNEDY, of Liverpool, thought that the shipowner, having provided a good ship, and, as far as he could judge, a good crew, had done his duty, and all the rest was a risk which might fairly be covered by insurance, and he supported the resolution.

Mr. GRAY HILL, of Liverpool, said it struck him that there was a most important point of difference between the land-carrier and the carrier by sea. The case of railway companies was not analogous to that of shipowners. Why was it that an employer on land was held responsible for the acts of his servants? He took it that it was partly because he selected his own servants, but still more strongly because he had an opportunity of superintending the servant's acts and of dismissing him if he found he was acting carelessly. A railway company had the conduct of an engineer or guard constantly under its supervision; but a shipowner, having done his best to prepare his ship for sea, and having selected the best officers and men he could get, had no means of communication with her after she left Liverpool or any other port until she reached her port of destination or of call. It was impossible for him to superintend his servants, or to tell what they were doing. If they were doing wrong he had no means of knowing it, and no means of dismissing them and putting proper persons in their places. There was also another distinction between railway companies and shipowners. A railway company had a monopoly. It had gone to Parliament for compulsory powers to take land and houses for the making of the railway, and Parliament had properly said it should not have those powers unless it had certain liabilities. But the shipowner had no monopoly. What was to prevent any number of cargo-owners, who thought the terms of the bill of lading were to their disadvantage, from combining together and starting a line of ships for themselves? Or what was to prevent other shipowners, who were bidding for popularity and custom, from omitting the obnoxious conditions? There was no monopoly in the matter. Nobody was obliged to travel or to send his goods by any particular line or ship, and the matter adjusted itself naturally according to the principles of free trade. Another reason why he opposed the amendment was that he felt satisfied that if it were carried it would lead to no practical esult, because, in order to establish a contract which they were to recommend parties to adopt, they must suppose that the parties were willing to adopt it; and what inducement was there for a shipowner—a steamship owner particularly—to adopt a contract which was going to increase his liabilities very greatly? If the amendment were carried, there was an end to the discussion. He supported the resolution.

MR. G. A. LAWS, speaking on behalf of the Newcastle shipowners, opposed the amendment. The responsibility, he said, for human fallibility, was divided by Mr. Lowndes between both sets of underwriters; it would be made by Dr. Wendt to rest entirely on those of the shipowner.

HERR MEIER, of Bremen, doubted whether anybody would own ships if shipowners were to be made liable for losses arising from the faults, and even errors of judgment, of their crews. The insurance companies had to cover this risk for those who insured. He supported the resolution.

After I had been heard in reply,

The amendment was put to the meeting by the Chairman and negatived by a considerable majority. The resolution, being at once put substantively, was carried by a similar majority.

The meeting then adjourned.

On the conference reassembling, the debate on the proposed International Bill of Lading was resumed.

MR. RICHARD LOWNDES suggested that Mr. Shotton's proposals should be taken first, but, on MR. ATKINSON objecting to this manner of proceeding, withdrew his suggestion.

MR. LOWNDES being then called upon by the Chairman, proceeded to read the draft bill of lading clause by clause.

The following amendments were moved:—

By MR. ATKINSON: 'That the word "either" be inserted before life, in the phrase "for saving life or property."'

The amendment was seconded by Mr. SHOTTON, but after a short discussion was withdrawn.

By Dr. STUBBS: 'That no special clauses be inserted in the bill of lading, but that all such clauses be inserted in a Code of Affreightment instead of a bill of lading.'

Dr. STUBBS said that he moved the amendment as secretary of the committee, and in accordance with the opinions expressed by some of the foreign committees.

THE PRESIDENT ruled this motion out of order in the present stage of the proceedings.

By MR. GRAY HILL: 'That the words "the purpose of" be inserted after the word "for," and before the word "saving," in the phrase "necessary for saving life or property."'

The amendment, being seconded by MR. ATKINSON, was carried unanimously.

By MR. JOHN GLOVER: 'That the words "so far as reasonably necessary" be omitted.'

MR. GLOVER contended that the liberty to save life and property should be an absolute liberty.

I seconded the amendment, remarking that a captain of a vessel ought not to be put in a position of having to weigh in his mind the question whether or not he would be justified in deviating from his course to save life.

MR. WALFORD supported the amendment.

MR. LOWNDES said the question had been very seriously discussed by the committee, and there had been a good deal of argument on both sides, but, in the judgment of the committee, the balance was in favour of retaining the cautionary words.

MR. SHOTTON was afraid that, if the words were retained, a captain of a steam or sailing ship would be very chary about deviating from his course, even for the purpose of saving life, lest he might be held liable for any loss that might unfortunately result.

MR. WESTGARTH supported the amendment.

MR. COUDERT said it was a question whether a deviation for the purpose of saving life could ever be unreasonable. If a captain had that purpose in his mind in deviating from his course, his conduct could not be considered unreasonable. The words were therefore surplusage, and he thought that wherever they could strike out an unnecessary word they should do so.

Mr. Coke thought it would be unreasonable for a ship of 5,000 tons to deviate from its course for the purpose of saving a ship of fifty tons, if the cargo of the larger ship would thereby be put in danger; but if the bill of lading gave the captain power to deviate under any circumstances, his action could not be disputed. He opposed the amendment.

Sir Travers Twiss supported the amendment, remarking that if the clause simply dealt with the saving of property the words would be useful; but, as it dealt also with the saving of life, they would limit very much the discharge of the duties of humanity.

Mr. Atkinson also supported the amendment.

Mr. Sparrow, as one of the committee which had drawn up the bill of lading, protested against the elimination proposed, on the ground that it would be holding out an inducement to captains to go in for saving property at sea for salvage purposes, in the interests of themselves and their owners, quite irrespective of the owners of cargo committed to their charge. No one could for a moment dispute the reasonableness of a deviation for the purpose of saving life, and there could therefore be no fear of life not being saved if the clause stood as printed; but if the words quoted were struck out, there was very great reason to fear that the property in the salvor's ship might be put to very great risk in attempts to save other property merely for the purpose of obtaining salvage for the benefit of the captain or owners of the deviating ship.

Mr. Gray Hill supported the amendment.

Mr. Wilson opposed, and Mr. Hodgkinson spoke in favour of it.

The amendment, being put to the vote, was carried by a majority of 11; 20 members voted for and 9 against it.

By Mr. Atkinson: 'That the words "considerable repairs" be substituted for the word "repair."'

This amendment was not seconded.

By Myself: 'That the words "also with liberty, in case the ship shall put into a port of refuge for repair, to tranship the goods to their destination by any other steamer (vessel)" be omitted.'

Mr. ATKINSON seconded the amendment, observing that in his opinion the liberty proposed should only be given when considerable repairs were necessary, inasmuch as many cargoes deteriorated in value by the number of times they were turned over.

Mr. RICHARD LOWNDES, Mr. ENGELS, Mr. JOHN GLOVER, and Mr. DONALD KENNEDY opposed the amendment, and Mr. BAILY supported it, observing that he had known a master tranship because he could get a better freight by so doing.

On being put to the vote, the amendment was negatived by 15 votes to 8.

By Mr. BAILY: 'That the words " necessarily put into a port of refuge, and such putting in will entail great delay and expense, the master may" be inserted instead of the words " put into a port of refuge for repair, to."'

The amendment was seconded by Mr. ATKINSON, and opposed by Mr. RICHARD LOWNDES, and rejected by 18 votes to 5.

By Mr. ATKINSON: 'That the words "if unavoidable" be inserted after the words "to and from the ship."'

This amendment was not seconded.

By Mr. GRAY HILL: 'That the words "perils of the sea" be inserted after the words "act of God."'

The amendment was seconded by Mr. JOHN GLOVER, and carried by 17 votes to 4.

By Mr. BAILY: 'That the words "barratry of the master and mariners" be omitted.'

Dr. STUBBS seconded the amendment, observing that the word 'barratry' conveyed entirely different meanings in different countries, and was therefore unsuitable for an international bill of lading.

Mr. RICHARD LOWNDES and Mr. WALFORD opposed the amendment, which was, on being put to the vote, negatived by 19 votes to 3.

By JUDGE WARREN: 'That the words "act of God" be struck out, on the grounds that the phrase was superfluous and irreverent.'

PROFESSOR PEABODY, in seconding the amendment, said that he did not like to have the misfortunes and accidents of the sea attributed to the Supreme Being.

Mr. Lowndes deprecated the introduction of theological argument.

The Hon. David Dudley Field thought it was not a question of theology, but of taste and reverence. He suggested the substitution of the words "inevitable accident" or "superhuman cause."

Mr. Westgarth observed that to leave out the old phrase, 'the act of God,' would be tantamount to a revolution.

Mr. Atkinson said there was no more irreverence in inserting the words 'the act of God,' than in using the phrase 'so help me God,' when people gave evidence. He objected most thoroughly to omitting from the bill of lading words which had descended to them as a relic of the piety of their forefathers.

Mr. Grey Hill said the words had received a judicial interpretation for many years, but 'superhuman cause' would cover them.

Mr. Coudert thought the phrase should be retained as an expression of reverence.

M. Clunet supported the rejection of the phrase, as being completely useless. The words '*casus fortuitus*,' which were used in the bills of lading in ancient Rome, appeared to him to be sufficient for all species of bills of lading. If they inserted the words 'the act of God,' they would be equally necessary in a contract for the transport of goods by rail.

I remarked that no such words as 'the act of God' appeared in the German bill of lading.

The resolution was rejected by 27 votes to 12.

The conference then adjourned until two o'clock.

On reassembling, the consideration of the proposed bill of lading was continued, and amendments were further moved as follows:—

By Mr. Hodgkinson: 'That the word "crew" be substituted for the word "mariners," in the phrase "barratry of the master and mariners."'

This was seconded by me, and carried by 8 votes to 5.

By Myself: 'That the words "even when occasioned by the

negligence, default, or error in judgment of the pilot, master, mariners, or other servants of the shipowners," be omitted.'

MR. HOYNE, of Chicago, seconded the amendment, which was supported by DR. MOLENGRAAFF, MR. COUDERT, DR. JACOBSEN, and M. CLUNET; and opposed by MR. ATKINSON, MR. JOHN GLOVER, MR. WALFORD, MR. SHOTTON, MR. RICHARD LOWNDES, and MR. HODGKINSON.

After I had been heard in reply, the amendment was put to the vote, and rejected by 22 votes to 7.

By MR. SPARROW: 'That the following words be added after the phrase "description of goods shipped": "provided that no clause in this bill of lading shall have the effect of relieving the ship from liability for the right delivery of the cargo, or for damage arising from improper stowage."'

The amendment was seconded by MR. COKE, but rejected by 21 votes to 5.

By DR. MOLENGRAAFF: 'That the words "nor for losses or deterioration arising from the nature" be substituted for the words "nor for decay, putrefaction, rust, sweat, change of character, drainage or leakage arising from the nature."'

The amendment was not, however, seconded.

By MR. JOHN GLOVER: 'That the words "on delivery" be inserted after the word "paid," in the phrase "as per margin, to be paid by."'

The amendment was seconded by MR. KENNEDY, and supported by me, and carried unanimously.

By DR. TOMKINS: 'That the word "Rules" be substituted for the word "Code," in the phrase "York-Antwerp Code."'

MR. WILLIAM HOPE seconded the amendment. DR. WENDT having spoken in support of, and MR. LOWNDES against it, it was put to the vote and adopted, the numbers being 24 to 3.

By MR. SHOTTON: 'That the words "if in the United Kingdom of Great Britain and Ireland, but if elsewhere," be inserted after the words "without discount."'

This was seconded by me, but, after some discussion, rejected by 23 votes to 2.

By Mr. Van Eeten: 'That the words " or its equivalent " be inserted after the words " in cash." '

The amendment was seconded by Mr. Engels, but rejected, 8 members voting for it and 4 against.

By Mr. Atkinson: 'That the words " hath affirmed to three bills of lading all of this tenor and date, drawn as first, second, and third, the first of which bills being accomplished, the others to stand void," be substituted for the words " hath affirmed to bills of lading, all of this tenor and date, the one of which bills being accomplished, the others to stand void." '

Mr. John Glover having seconded the amendment, Mr. Westgarth moved the insertion of a clause to the effect that there should be 'certified copies of any number' of the bill of lading.

This proposal was, however, negatived by 11 votes to 4, and Mr. Atkinson's amendment carried by 14 to 1.

A proposition having been made by Judge Warren, and seconded by Mr. Walford, to the effect that the position of the word 'excepted,' in the earlier part of the bill of lading, should be altered, Mr. Atkinson rose to order, and it was overruled by the Chairman.

A discussion then arose as to whether the remaining clauses should be proceeded with by the meeting, or should be referred to a committee; but it was decided to proceed.

It was then moved by Mr. Sparrow: 'That the words " and whether such shipper be principal or agent," in clause 4, be omitted.'

No member rising to second the amendment, it was not put to the vote.

By Mr. Atkinson: 'That the words " as regards all the perils excepted in this bill of lading," in clause 6, be omitted.'

Mr. Shotton seconded the amendment.

Mr. Lowndes and Mr. Sparrow having spoken against it, and Mr. Atkinson replied on the objections, it was put to the meeting and rejected by 13 votes to 4.

By Mr. Atkinson: 'That the words " or mob" be inserted after the word " power," in clause 8.

The amendment, however, was not seconded.

By Mr. Coudert: 'That the words " a lien thereon " be substituted for the words "borne by the owners or receivers thereof," in clause 8.'

M. CLUNET seconded the amendment, but it was lost by 7 votes to 4.

By MR. SHOTTON: 'That the word "demurrage" be inserted after the words "back freight," in clause 9.'

MR. ENGELS seconded the amendment, and it was carried by 9 votes to 4.

By MR. ENGELS: 'That clause 10 be omitted.'

This was seconded by MR. WILLIAM HOPE, and supported by DR. MOLENGRAAFF. MR. LOWNDES having been heard *contrà*, and MR. ENGELS in reply, it was put to the vote and negatived by 18 votes to 6.

By MR. ATKINSON: 'That the words "but the consignee is at liberty to abandon his entire consignment for the freight on it, provided he elects to do so before taking delivery," in clause 12, be omitted.'

MR. SHOTTON seconded the amendment, and it was carried by 15 votes to 9.

By MR. ATKINSON: 'That clause 14 be omitted.'

This was seconded by MR. SHOTTON, but rejected, 9 members voting for and 12 against it.

By MR. HODGKINSON: 'That the words "voluntarily abandoned" be substituted for the words "parted with," in clause 14.'

MR. SHOTTON having seconded, and MR. COUDERT spoken against the amendment, it was negatived by 13 votes to 5.

By MR. GRAY HILL: 'That the words "to the extent of the value of the lien" be inserted at the beginning of clause 14.'

The amendment having been seconded, was carried by 9 votes to 3.

By SIR TRAVERS TWISS: 'That the word "consignee" be substituted for the word "consignees" in the early part of clause 15.'

This was agreed to unanimously.

By M. CLUNET: 'That the following paragraph be inserted at the end of clause 15: "The master shall be entitled to recover from the shipper the difference between the amount of freight stipulated in the bill of lading and the proceeds of the goods, should the consignee neglect or refuse to receive the same."'

This was seconded by MR. ROUSE, and supported by MR. COUDERT, and, being put to the meeting, was carried by 17 votes to 1.

By MR. ENGELS: 'That the words " at the expense and risk of the owner of the goods " be substituted for the words " at the consignee's expense and risk," in clause 15.'

MR. COUDERT seconded the amendment, and it was carried unanimously.

By MR. WALFORD: 'That the word " Liverpool " be omitted.'

This was agreed to unanimously.

By MR. ATKINSON: 'That the word " quality " be inserted after the word " weight " in the phrase " weight and contents unknown."'

The amendment was agreed to unanimously.

By MR. SNAPE: 'That the words " within reasonable time," be inserted after the word " expense," in clause 11.'

The amendment having been seconded by DR. TOMKINS, was agreed to without voting.

Finally, it was moved by MR. SHOTTON, and seconded by MR. ATKINSON: 'That the draft bill of lading so amended be adopted by this conference.'

The resolution was agreed to unanimously amid prolonged applause.

The following is a copy of the bill of lading as adopted:—

SHIPPED, in apparent good order and condition, by   in and upon the good *steam* ship called the   now lying in the port of   and bound for   with liberty to call at any ports, in any order, to sail without pilots, and to tow and assist vessels in distress, and to deviate for the purpose of saving life or property; also with liberty, in case the ship shall put into a port of refuge for repair, to tranship the goods to their destination by any other *steamer* (vessel); and with liberty to convey goods in lighters to and from the ship, at shipper's risk. Such lighterage to be at ship's expense, except that if the cargo is necessarily landed in

lighters, the ship being unable to reach the port of destination, the cost of such lighterage shall fall on the cargo
being marked and numbered as per margin ; and to be delivered in the like good order and condition at the aforesaid port of

The act of God, perils of the sea, fire, barratry of the master and crew, enemies, pirates and thieves, arrest and restraint of princes, rulers, and people, collisions, stranding, and other accidents of navigation, excepted, even when occasioned by the negligence, default, or error in judgment of the pilot, master, mariners, or other servants of the shipowners.

Ship not answerable for losses through *explosion, bursting of boilers, breakage of shafts*, or any latent defect *in the machinery or hull*, not resulting from want of due diligence by the owners of the ship or any of them, or by the ship's husband or manager ; nor for decay, putrefaction, rust, sweat, change of character, drainage, or leakage, arising from the nature of the goods shipped or the insufficiency of the packages ; nor for any damage or loss occasioned by the prolongation of the voyage ; nor for obliteration or absence of marks, numbers, addresses, or descriptions of goods shipped.

unto   or to his or their assigns, freight, primage and charges for the said goods, as per margin, to be paid on delivery by   . Freight to be paid in cash, without discount, at the rate of exchange for banker's bills at sight, current on the day of the ship's entry inwards at the custom-house. General Average payable according to York-Antwerp Rules.

In witness thereof, the master or agent of the said ship hath affirmed to three bills of lading, all of this tenor and date (drawn as first, second, and third), the first of which bills being accomplished, the others to stand void.

1. Quality-marks, if any, to be of the same size as and contiguous to the leading marks ; and if inserted in the shipping notes accepted by the mate, the master is bound to sign bills of lading conformable thereto.
2. Ship not liable for breakage of glass, earthenware, or china.
3. Not accountable for goods of any description which are above the value of 100*l*. per package, unless the value be herein expressed and a special agreement made ; nor for gold, silver, bullion, specie, documents, jewellery, pictures, embroideries, or works of art, silks, furs, china, watches, or clocks, unless bills of lading are signed therefor, with the value therein expressed, and a special agreement be made.
4. Shippers accountable for any loss or damage to ship or cargo caused by inflammable, explosive, or dangerous goods, shipped without full disclosure of their nature, whether such shipper shall have been aware of it or not, and whether such shipper be principal or agent ; such goods may be thrown over-

board or destroyed by the master or owner of the ship at any time without compensation.

5. All fines or damages which the ship or cargo may incur or suffer by reason of incorrect or insufficient marking of packages or description of their contents, shall be paid by the shipper or consignee, and the ship shall have a lien on the goods of such shipper or consignee for the amount thereof.

6. Goods delivered to the ship, whilst on quay awaiting shipment, to be at shipper's risk as regards all the perils excepted in this bill of lading.

7. Goods once shipped cannot be taken away by the shipper except upon payment of full freight, together with the expenses of landing them, and compensation for any damages sustained by the owners through such taking away.

8. In case the ship shall be prevented from reaching her destination by quarantine, blockade, ice, or the hostile act of any Power, the master or owners may discharge the goods into any depôt or lazaretto, or at any near available port; all expenses thereby incurred upon the goods to be borne by the owners or receivers thereof.

9. Ship to have a lien on all goods for payment of freight and charges, including back freight, demurrage, forwarding charges, and charges for carriage to port of shipment, whether payable in advance or not.

10. If the ship is able to carry the goods to their destination, but the goods, by reason of damage sustained or of their own nature, are not fit to be carried all the way, and if such goods have received an enhancement of value by reason of their partial carriage, the ship shall be entitled to a *pro ratâ* freight in proportion to the distance performed, which freight is in no case to exceed the amount of such enhancement of value. *Pro ratâ* freight is admissible in no other case than that dealt with in the preceding sentence, unless there be an acceptance of the goods by the shipper or owner of the goods.

11. When the goods are fit to be carried to their destination, but the ship is unable to carry them, the shipowner may earn full freight by sending the goods to their destination at his own expense within reasonable time in another bottom; this right is not affected by an abandonment of the ship by her crew, or to the underwriters: and the ship is to be, for this purpose, deemed unable to carry the goods to their destination, if she either cannot be repaired at all, or cannot be repaired except at an expense exceeding her value when repaired.

12. Full freight is due on damaged goods.

13. No freight is due on any increase in bulk or weight caused by the absorption of water during the voyage.

14. To the extent of the value of the lien, freight which by the terms of the bill of lading is made payable by the consignee cannot be demanded from the shipper, after the master has parted with his lien on the goods.

15. The goods, if not taken by the consignee immediately on landing, or within such further time as is provided by the regulations of the port of discharge, may be stored by the master, at the expense and risk of the owner of the goods. The master shall be entitled to recover from the shipper the difference between the amount of freight stipulated in the bill of lading and the proceeds of the goods, should the consignee neglect or refuse to receive the same.

16. In the event or claims for short delivery, when the ship reaches her destination the price to be the market price at the port of destination on the day of the ship's reporting at the custom-house, less all charges saved.

NOTICE.—In accepting this bill of lading, the owner of the goods and the shipper expressly accept and agree to all its stipulations and conditions, whether written or printed.

Dated in   , this   day of   188 .

Weight, quality, and contents unknown.

(*The words printed in italics are to be omitted in the case of sailing ships.*)

The following is the report on the form of bill of lading for steamships, proposed by the Committee of the New York Produce Exchange:—

The proposed bill of lading is based upon the form adopted last August at the 'Conference of the Association for the Reform and Codification of the Law of Nations,' but differs from its model in many important respects.

The 'Conference' bill of lading, although far from being a perfect instrument in the sense that under its provisions 'the shipper of goods between the shipowner and the underwriter will be kept harmless from all risks except those of the market,' is still immeasurably superior in the protection it affords to shippers, in these respects, to any of those now issued by the great steamship lines. The modifications that we suggest, we believe, will be more likely to secure for it the approval of underwriters, and thus afford the full protection that shippers are entitled to.

We propose to show, by a comparison of the 'Conference' bill of lading with those now in use in the Atlantic export trade, wherein its provisions are more favourable to the shipper, and to point out the changes that we suggest, and our reasons for so doing.

In the very first sentence, 'Shipped in apparent good order,' we find a qualification introduced which a number of bills of lading now in use do not contain. Out of thirty-six bills of lading examined by us, only fifteen use the adjective 'apparent.' It is evident, however, that any acknowledgment of the condition of the goods which describes them as being 'in good order,' must be based on their external appearance, and therefore we do not consider the addition of this word as material, and have retained it in our proposed form.

The liberty to 'call at any ports in any order' would give as wide a liberty of deviation as any bill of lading now in use provides for, and would not be covered by any ordinary policy of insurance without express agreement.

The various liberties now claimed by the steamship lines are as follows:—

North German Lloyd.—' With liberty to call at any intermediate port.'

Hamburg Am. Pk. Compy.—' No liberty at all.'

Cunard Line.—' With liberty to call at any port, or ports, to receive fuel, to load or discharge cargo, or for any other purpose whatsoever.'

White Star.—' With liberty to call,' &c., exactly as above.

Inman Line.—' To call at any intermediate port for any purpose.'

National Line.—' To have liberty to call at any port or ports.'

Anchor Line, Glasgow service.—' With liberty during the voyage to call at any port, or ports, to receive fuel, to load or discharge cargo, or for any other purpose whatsoever.'

Anchor Line, Liverpool service.—' With liberty to call at any intermediate port for any purpose.'

Anchor Line, Bristol service.—' With liberty,' &c., as per Glasgow service.

Guion Line.—' No liberty at all.'

Monarch Line.—' To call at any intermediate port or ports for any purpose.'

Compagnie Genl. Trans-Atlantique.—' With liberty to call at any intermediate ports.'

Wilson Line.—' No liberty at all.'

Great Western Line.—' With liberty during the voyage to call at any port, or ports, to receive fuel, to load or discharge cargo, or for any purpose whatsoever.'

State Line.—' With liberty,' &c., as Great Western Line.

Red Star Line, Antwerp.—' To call at any intermediate port.'

White Cross Line.—' To call at any port or ports,' &c., as per Great Western Line and others.

Thingvalla Line.—' To call at any port or ports,' &c., as above.

Netherlands' American.—' To call at any port or ports,' &c., as above.

Bordeaux Line, Funch, Edye & Co.—' To call at any port or ports,' &c., as above.

Royal Netherland.—' To call at any port or ports,' &c., as above.

Taurus Line.—' To call at any port or ports,' &c., as above.

Merchants' Line, New York to Havre.—' To call at any port or ports,' &c., as above.

Furness Line.—' To call at any port or ports,' &c., as above.

Centaur Line.—' To call at any port or ports,' &c., as above.

Cambrian Line.—' To call at any port or ports,' &c., as above.

Arrow Line.—' To call at any port or ports,' &c., as above.

Bristol Line.—' To call at any port or ports,' &c., as above.

Edwards Line.—' No liberty at all.'

Red Cross Line.—' With liberty, before shipment or at any period of the voyage, and so often as may be deemed expedient or at any port or place, to ship the whole or part by any other steamer (whether belonging to the owners of the said steamship or not), to tranship or land or store or put into hulk or craft for such time as may be deemed expedient, and thence re-ship on any other steamer, whether belonging to the owners of the said steamship or not, and with liberty for the said steamer or substituted steamer or steamers to proceed to or stay at any ports or places whatsoever on the coasts of Great Britain or Ireland, or on the continent of Europe or Africa, or the islands of the Atlantic, whether in or out of the customary or advertised route, in any rotation and for any purpose whatsoever.'

The steamers of the Red Cross Line are no longer running in the Atlantic trade, and this document has therefore rather an historic than a practical value. We reproduce it to show how far the shipowners may endeavour to exempt themselves from liability if unchecked by united action on the part of shippers.

We suggest as a proper modification of the clause, 'with liberty to call at any ports in any order,' the words, 'with liberty to call at any intermediate ports.'

The next clause, 'To sail without pilots, and to tow and assist vessels in distress, and to deviate for the purpose of saving life or property,' is, with slight verbal modifications, contained in all bills of lading now used by steamers. We have retained this clause for the following reasons :—

It is the invariable rule for steamships to take pilots, the liberty of not doing so being only used in exceptional cases.

The shipowner needs no permission 'to tow and assist vessels in distress, or to deviate for the purpose of saving life;' for the former is already granted by established custom, and the latter is provided for by the law of every civilised country. Deviation to save property only, however, as in the case of towing an abandoned ship into port, will forfeit any policy of insurance, unless as before stated, in regard to the 'liberty to call at any port or ports,' it is provided for by express stipulation.

The law on this subject is clearly laid down by Chief Justice Cockburn in Scaramanga v. Stamp (Law Reports, 5 C. P. D. 316). The Chief Justice gives the result of the American authorities, viz. :—

'Deviation for the purpose of saving life is protected, and involves neither forfeiture of insurance nor liability to the goods' owner in respect of loss which would otherwise be within the exception of "perils of the seas." And as a necessary consequence of the foregoing, deviation for the purpose of communicating with a ship in distress is allowable, inasmuch as the state of the vessel in distress may involve danger to life. On the other hand, deviation for the sole purpose of saving property is not thus privileged, but entails all the usual consequences of deviation. If, therefore, the lives of the persons on board a disabled ship can be saved without saving the ship, as by taking them off, deviation for the purpose of saving the ship will carry with it all the consequences of an unauthorised deviation. But, where the preservation of life can only be effected through the concurrent saving of property, and the *bonâ fide* purpose of saving life forms part of the motive which leads to the deviation, the privilege will not be lost by reason of the purpose of saving property having formed a second motive for deviating.' In these propositions Chief Justice Cockburn entirely concurs, and continues:—

'There would be much force, no doubt, in the argument that it is to the common interest of merchants and insurers, as well as of shipowners, that ships and cargoes, when in danger of perishing, should be saved; and, consequently, that, as a matter of policy, the same latitude should be allowed in respect of saving property as in the respect of the saving of life, were it not that the law has provided another and a very adequate motive for the saving of property by securing to the salvor a liberal proportion of the property saved —a proportion in which not only the value of the property saved but also the danger run by the salvor to life or property, is taken into account, and in calculating which, if it be at once settled that the insurance will not be protected, nor the shipowner freed from liability, in respect of loss of cargo, the risk thus run will, no doubt, be included as an element.'

We cannot help thinking that it would be for the interest of underwriters to extend the liberty of deviation to the saving of property as well as of life, since by so doing claims for salvage in such cases would be materially reduced.

We have retained the clause, 'with liberty, in case the ship shall put into a port of refuge for repairs, to tranship the goods to their destination by any other steamer,' because it has been, for many years past, approved by underwriters as being for the general benefit of all concerned. We have modified the clause, 'with liberty to convey goods in lighters to and from the ship at shippers' risk. Such lighterage to be at ship's expense,' by omitting the concluding sentence, 'except that if the cargo is necessarily landed in lighters, the ship being unable to reach the port of destination, the cost of such lighterage shall fall on cargo;' because this is fully provided for afterwards in section 8 of the 'Conference' bill of lading; in our form, section 7.

The most important clause in all bills of lading is that in which the shipowner describes the perils and accidents from which he claims exemption. The 'Conference' bill of lading is in this, as in all other respects, more moderate than any of those in present use; but, in our opinion, requires still further limitation. Its terms are as follows:—

'The act of God, perils of the sea, fire, barratry of the master and crew, enemies, pirates and thieves, arrest and restraint of princes, rulers and people, collisions, stranding and other accidents of navigation excepted, even when occasioned by the negligence, default or error in judgment of the pilot, master, mariners, or other servants of the shipowners. Ship not answerable for losses through explosion, bursting of boilers, breakage of shafts, or any latent defect in the machinery or hull not resulting from want of due diligence by the owners of the ship, or any of them, or by the ship's husband or manager.'

This clause we propose to modify as follows: 'The perils of the seas, fire, barratry of the master and crew, enemies, pirates, *assailing* thieves, arrest and restraint of princes, rulers and peoples excepted. Ship not answerable for losses by collisions, stranding and other accidents of navigation, even when occasioned by the negligence, default or error in judgment of the pilot, master, mariners, or other servants of the shipowner; nor for losses through explosion, bursting of boilers, breakage of shafts, or any latent defect in hull or machinery, not resulting, in either case, from want of due diligence by the owners of the ship, or any of them, or by the ship's husband, or manager.'

The bills of lading in present use contain exemptions in addition to those made in the 'Conference' bill of lading, viz.:—

North German Lloyd's.—' Robbers, vermin, jettison.'

Hamburg Am. Packet Co.—' Robbers, vermin, jettison.'

Cunard.—' Robbers, vermin, rain, stowage or contact with, or smells or evaporation or taint or breakage from, other goods, negligence, default or error in judgment of stevedores.'

White Star.—' Robbers, vermin, rain, or from stowage or contact with, or smells or evaporation or taint from other goods.'

Inman.—' Thieves of whatever kind, whether on board or not, vermin, riots, strikes, lock-outs or stoppage of labour from whatever cause, rain, spray, stowage or contact with, or smell or evaporation or breakage from, other goods, jettison, or for unseaworthiness of the ship at the commencement of the voyage.'

National.—' Thieves by land or at sea, vermin, rain, spray, coal or coal dust, stowage or contact, &c., jettison, fire before loading or after unloading, heat.'

Anchor Line, Glasgow service.—' Spray, rain, decay or damage by vermin, stowage or contact with, &c., heat, fire on shore.'

Anchor Line, Liverpool service.—' Robbers, thieves of whatever kind, whether on board or not, vermin, riots, strikes, lock-outs or stoppage of labour from whatever cause, rain, spray, stowage or contact with, &c., jettison, heat, fire at any time and in any place, or for the unseaworthiness of the ship at the commencement of the voyage.'

Anchor Line, Bristol service.—' Rain, spray, decay or damage by vermin, stowage or contact with, &c., heat or fire in craft or hulk or on shore.'

Guion Line.—' Vermin, stowage, or contact with other goods, fire in craft or on shore.'

Monarch.—' Robbers, vermin, pilferage, rain, spray, contact with, or smell or evaporation from other goods, jettison, heat, fire at any time or in any place, losses at the port of discharge.'

Compagnie Gen. Trans-Atlantique.—' Robbers, rats or vermin, rain, spray or contact with other goods, &c., heat, fire at sea or on shore.'

Wilson.—' Robbers, vermin, rain, spray, loss or damage or contact with, or smell or evaporation, &c., fire in craft or hulk or on shore.

Great Western.—' Robbers, vermin, stowage, or contact with,' &c.

State.—' Rain, spray, decay, or damage by vermin, stowage, or contact with, &c., heat or fire in craft or hulk or on shore.'

Red Star.—' Robbers, vermin, rain, spray, loss or damage from stowage, or contact with, &c., heat or fire in craft or hulk or on shore, either before lading or after unlading.'

White Cross.—' Robbers, vermin, stowage, or contact with other goods.'

Thingvalla.—' Robbers, vermin, stowage, or contact,' &c.

Netherlands.—' Robbers, vermin, stowage, or contact, &c., fire in craft or on shore before lading or after unlading.'

Bordelaise.—' Robbers, vermin, stowage, or contact, &c., fire in craft or on shore.'

Royal Netherlands.—' Robbers, vermin, stowage, or contact, &c., fire in craft or on shore, before lading or after unlading.'

Taurus.—' Robbers, vermin, stowage, or contact, &c., disease (of cattle), want of space, air or water, fire in craft or on shore, before lading and after unlading.'

Merchant's Ex.—' Robbers, vermin, stowage, or contact, &c., fire on shore or in craft.'

Furness Line.—' Robbers, vermin, rain, stowage, or contact, &c., fire in craft or hulk or on shore.'

Centaur.—' Robbers, vermin, stowage, or contact, &c., fire in craft or hulk or on shore.'

Cambrian.—' Robbers, vermin, contact with, &c., heat or fire in craft or hulk or on shore.'

Arrow.—' Robbers, vermin, rain, spray, contact with, &c., fire in craft or hulk or on shore.'

Bristol City.—' Robbers, vermin, stowage, or contact, &c., fire in craft or hulk or on shore, before lading and after unlading.'

Edwards Line.—' Fire on shore.'

Red Cross.—' Robbers, thieves of whatever kind, whether on board or not, effects of climate, heat of hold, vermin, rain or spray, all injury arising from other goods by stowage, or contact with, or sweating, leakage, smell, or evaporation from steam or otherwise howsoever, heat, fire at any time and in any place whatever, jettison, or unseaworthiness of the ship at the commencement of the voyage,' &c.

We have omitted from the excepted perils, the phrase, ' act

of God.' It is true that these words have a clearly defined legal meaning. Story says: 'By the act of God, a phrase which perhaps habit has rendered too familiar, is meant inevitable accident or casualty.' But as the succeeding phrase, 'perils of the sea,' is wide enough to cover 'inevitable accident and casualty,' we consider the omitted words superfluous.

It is well understood that 'barratry of the master' is not covered by American policies when he is sole or part owner of the ship, even when it concerns innocent shippers of cargo; but this fact is of little practical importance to shippers by steam, and can easily be provided for by insurance in other cases. So, also, can losses arising 'from enemies and pirates and restraints of princes, rulers and peoples.' We have added the adjective 'assailing' before thieves, in conformity with the common law doctrine, which declares 'that shipowners are responsible for theft by their servants, or by others in their employ and confidence, or under their protection, but not for theft committed with armed force or other superior power' ('Story on Bailments'). The exemption of liability of the shipowner for losses directly occasioned by stranding, collision and other accidents of navigation, even when occasioned by the negligence, default or error in judgment of the servants of the shipowner, is now being tested in the United States District Court, in Brooklyn, by a suit brought by the Insurance Company of North America, and the Phœnix Insurance Company, of Brooklyn, against the Williams and Guion Line, to recover a loss paid by these companies, occasioned by the alleged negligence of the master of the 'Montana.' The common law doctrine on this subject is stated by Story as follows: 'A loss from a peril of the sea which might have been avoided by the exercise of any reasonable skill or diligence at the time when it occurred, is not deemed to be such a loss by the perils of the sea as will exempt the carrier, but rather a loss by the gross negligence of the party.' Justice Bradley, in Railroad *v.* Lockwood, held that 'it is not just and reasonable in the eye of the law for a common carrier to stipulate for exemption from responsibility for the negligence of his servants.'

In France, Spain, Holland, Scotland, Louisiana, and the German

States, the carrier is responsible for damage caused by his servants. Story states, however, that the rigour of the common law in this respect has been relaxed in England by statutes, &c., but that none of the statutes have been generally adopted in this country, and, with the exception of some legislative provisions in a few States, the common law prevails.

Mr. Lowndes boldly argues in his pamphlet, 'On a common form of bill of lading,' 'That there has been growing up in the minds of steamship owners a conviction that there must be one radical change in the old common law of the sea; that the shipowner can no longer undertake to be answerable for the faults or neglects of the master or crew. It is enough,' he says, 'if he man her with a crew sufficient in number and competent in quality, so far as competency can be ascertained beforehand, and with a master and officers who have obtained certificates of competency required by law. To undertake that these men shall always do their duty, and in the course of a long voyage shall never once be guilty of neglect or mistake that shall have a mischievous result, involves a liability which they do not care to undertake. It is no exaggeration,' he continues, 'to say that if not all, certainly the great majority of accidents to steamers are traceable to the fault of some seaman or engineer. A well-built steamer is powerful to resist the adverse forces of nature; she can hardly spring a leak in any gale, and her engines will keep her off a lee shore; but she is at the mercy of her own servants: a careless engineer or stoker neglecting to keep up the water in the boilers may destroy her by an explosion; the rapid pace and frequent entrance of harbours greatly increase the risk of stranding and collision, each mostly traceable to a sailor's fault.' Mr. Lowndes goes on to say: 'Now, so long as the owners of steamships, speaking of them as a body, hold this conviction so strongly as to unite in refusing to carry merchandise on any other terms, it cannot be denied that they are acting within their rights. No one is bound to build a steamer, or, having built her, to allow some one else to send goods in her on conditions which he himself does not like,' &c.

This attitude of the shipowners is only to be met by a combination of the shippers, for certainly no one will build steamships except with the intention of carrying merchandise; and, if the shippers unite in demanding a reasonable protection from the carrier, they will be likely to obtain it; but if, without union for self-protection, they accept any bill of lading which the steamship-owner offers them, they have only themselves to blame if they are held to its conditions. In our opinion, the 'Conference' bill of lading should, at least, be modified in the spirit of Mr. Lowndes's remarks, and the same provision should be applied to losses occasioned indirectly by the faults of the servants of the shipowner, as has been applied to those occasioned by explosion, bursting of boilers, breakage of shafts, or any latent defect in hull or machinery. And we have, accordingly, added the clause, 'not resulting *in either case* from want of due diligence by the owners of the ship, or any of them, or by the ship's husband or manager.' Even with this modification the shipper will not be protected by insurance, unless underwriters also agree to this provision, since losses arising from the negligence of master and other servants of the shipowner or from accidents to machinery or latent defects in it, or in the hull, or any unseaworthiness, are not covered by policies of insurance.

The remainder of the clause we have adopted almost as it stands in the 'Conference' bill of lading, changing only the position of one phrase, and adding to the exceptions, 'breakage and land damage, and any damage,' so that it now reads as follows:—

'Nor for decay, putrefaction, rust, sweat, change of character, drainage, leakage, breakage, land damage, or any damage arising from the nature of the goods shipped; nor for the obliteration of marks, numbers, addresses, or descriptions of goods shipped; nor for any damage or loss caused by the prolongation of the voyage.'

The whole of this latter clause, however, is superfluous, as it is well settled law that shipowners are not liable for damage resulting from any of the enumerated causes.

We have also omitted the word 'primage' which occurs between the words 'freight and charges.' It formerly represented the master's commission on the freight, but as it has long since ceased to do this, it is no longer necessary.

The clause 'General Average, payable according to York-Antwerp Rules,' we have retained.

The affirmation clause we have only modified by substituting the words, ' one of which bills of lading being accomplished,' for ' the *first* of which,' &c.

Marginal clause No. 1, as to quality marks, we have adopted as it stands.

No. 2 we have omitted, as it is already fully provided for in the body of the instrument.

No. 3, which we make No. 2, we have modified, viz. :—

'Ship not accountable for gold, silver, bullion, specie, documents, jewellery, pictures, embroideries, or works of art, silks, furs, china, statuary, watches or clocks, unless bills of lading are signed therefor, with the value therein expressed.'

No. 4, in our form No. 3, is made to read, viz. :—

' Shippers accountable for any loss or damage to ship or cargo caused by inflammable, explosive, or dangerous goods, shipped without full disclosure of their nature, whether such shipper be principal or agent ; such goods may be thrown overboard or destroyed by the master or owner at any time without compensation,' omitting the words 'whether such shipper shall have been aware of it or not.'

No. 5, which we make No. 4, is retained unaltered.

No. 6, with us No. 5, we have modified by adding the words : ' except in cases where such goods are detained awaiting shipment for the convenience of the shipowner.'

No. 7, in our form No. 6, is adopted without change.

No. 8, with us No. 7, is retained unaltered, with the exception that we substitute ' shipowners ' for ' owners.'

No. 9, which we make No. 8, is modified by the omission of the concluding phrase, 'whether payable in advance or not.' If freight is paid in advance there can certainly be no lien; what is probably meant is, that charges, demurrage, &c. are to be a lien when the ship's freight is paid in advance, but the phrase is ambiguous and unnecessary.

No. 10, in our bill of lading No. 9, we have adopted without alteration. It introduces a rule as to distance freight, which, although unknown to the law in this country and in England, is but reasonable and just. The clause as to 'enhancement of value' will also properly modify the arbitrary Continental rule, which only looks to the proportion of the voyage completed.

No. 11, in our form No. 10, we have also adopted without alteration. It is already provided for by law in this country, but not distinctly so in Great Britain. The rule as to the circumstances which justify abandonment is in accord with English law, but differs from that prevailing in this country.

No. 12 (11) is adopted without change. It is a well-settled rule of law, although in many cases it may work hardship to shippers.

No. 13 (12) we have not altered.

No. 14 (13) we have adopted as it stands.

No. 15, which in our form is No. 14, reads in the 'Conference' bill of lading as follows, viz. :—

'The goods, if not taken by the consignee immediately on landing, or within such further time as is provided by the regulations of the port of discharge, may be stored by the master at the expense and risk of the owner of the goods. The master to be entitled to recover from the shipper the difference between the amount of freight stipulated in the bill of lading and the proceeds of the goods, should the consignee neglect or refuse to receive the same.'

We propose the following modification :—

'If the goods be not taken by the consignee immediately on landing, or within such further time as is provided by the regulations of the port of discharge, they may be stored by the master at the expense and risk of their owners; provided always, that public notice is given of the arrival of the ship and the commencement of the discharge, and that the same does not begin at night, or at any unreasonable hour. The master to be entitled to recover from the shipper the difference between the amount of freight stipulated for in the bill of lading and the proceeds of the goods, should the consignee neglect or refuse to receive them.'

The final clause, No. 16, in our form No. 15, is adopted without change.

The stipulation to pay for goods short delivered, at the market price at port of destination, is fair and according to law, and is also in marked contrast with the provision in many bills of lading, 'that the shipowner shall only be liable for the invoice or declared value of the goods, whichever shall be the least.'

The concluding clause, 'That in accepting the bill of lading, the owner of goods and the shipper expressly accept and agree to all its stipulations,' &c., we have adopted without modification; and, also, the memorandum 'weight, quality, and contents unknown.

SAMUEL A. SAWYER, *Chairman*,
A. E. ORR,
DAVID BINGHAM,
GUSTAV SCHWAB,
E. R. LIVERMORE,
SILAS C. FORCE,
CHARLES F. WREAKS,
Committee on Bills of Lading.

New York: May 1883.

Form of Bill of Lading proposed by the Committee of the New York Produce Exchange, based on the 'form' adopted at the Conference of the Association for the Reform and Codification of the Law of Nations, August 1882.

SHIPPED, in apparent good order and condition by in and upon the good steamship called the now lying in the port of and bound for with liberty to call at any intermediate ports, to sail without pilots, to tow and assist vessels in distress, and to deviate for the purpose of saving life or property; also with liberty, in case the ship shall put into a port of refuge for repairs, to tranship the goods to their destination by any other steamship, and with liberty to convey goods in lighters to and from the ship at shipper's risk, but at ship's expense being marked and numbered as per margin, and to be delivered in like good order and condition at the aforesaid port of

The perils of the seas, fire, barratry of the master and crew, enemies, pirates, assailing thieves, arrest and restraint of princes, rulers and peoples excepted. Ship not answerable for losses by collisions, stranding and other accidents of navigation, even when occasioned by the negligence, default or error in judgment of the pilot, master, mariners, or other servants of the shipowner; nor for losses through explosion, bursting of boilers, breakage of shafts or any latent defect in hull or machinery (not resulting in either case from want of due diligence by the owners of the ship, or any of them, or by the ship's husband or manager); nor for decay, putrefaction, rust, sweat, change of character, drainage, leakage, breakage, land damage or any damage arising from the nature of the goods shipped or the insufficiency of packages; nor for the obliteration of marks, numbers, addresses, or description of goods shipped; nor for any damage or loss caused by the prolongation of the voyage.

unto   or to his or their assigns, freight and charges for the said goods, as per margin, to be paid on delivery by freight to be paid in cash, without discount, and if in a foreign currency at the rate of exchange for banker's bills at sight, current on the day of the ship's entry inwards at the custom-house. General Average payable according to York-Antwerp Rules.

IN WITNESS whereof, the master or agent of the said ship hath affirmed to three bills of lading, all of this tenor and date, one of which bills being accomplished, the others to stand void.

1. Quality-marks, if any, to be of the same size or and contiguous to the leading marks; and if inserted in the shipping notes accepted by the mate, the master or agent is bound to sign bills of lading conformable thereto.

2. Ship not accountable for gold, silver, bullion, specie, documents, jewellery, pictures, embroideries, or works of art, silks, furs, china, statuary, watches or clocks, unless bills of lading are signed therefor with the value therein expressed.

3. Shippers accountable for any loss or damage to ship or cargo caused by inflammable, explosive, or dangerous goods shipped without full disclosure of their nature, whether such shipper be principal or agent; such goods may be thrown overboard or destroyed by the master or owner of the ship at any time without compensation.

4. All fines or damages which the ship or cargo may incur or suffer by reason of incorrect or insufficient marking of packages or description of their contents, shall be paid by the shipper or consignee, and the ship shall have a lien on the goods of such shipper or consignee for the amount thereof.

5. Goods delivered to the ship whilst on the wharf awaiting shipment, to be at shipper's risk as regards all perils excepted in the bill of lading, except in cases where such goods are detained awaiting shipment for the convenience of the shipowner.

6. Goods once shipped cannot be taken away by the shipper except on payment of full freight, together with the expenses of landing them and compensation for any damage sustained by the shipowner through such taking away.

7. In case the ship shall be prevented from reaching her destination by quarantine, blockade, ice, or the hostile act of any Power, the master or shipowners may discharge the goods into any depôt or lazaretto, or at any near available port; all expenses thereby incurred on the goods to be borne by the owners or receivers thereof.

8. Ship to have a lien on all goods for payment of freight and charges, including back freight, demurrage, forwarding charges, and charges for carriage to port of shipment.

9. If the ship is able to carry the goods to their destination, but the goods by reason of damage sustained or of their own nature are not fit to be carried all the way, and if such goods have received an enhancement of value by reason of their partial carriage, the ship shall be entitled to a *pro ratâ* freight in proportion to the distance performed, which freight is in no case to exceed the amount of such enhancement of value. *Pro ratâ* freight is admissible in no other case than that dealt with in the preceding sentence, unless there be an acceptance of the goods by the shipper or owner of the goods.

10. When the goods are fit to be carried to their destination, but the ship is unable to carry them, the shipowner may earn full freight by sending the goods to their destination at his own expense within reasonable time in another bottom; this right is not affected by an abandonment of the ship by her crew or to the underwriters; and the ship is to be, for this purpose, deemed unable to carry the goods to their destination, if she either cannot be repaired at all, or cannot be repaired except at an expense exceeding her value when repaired.

11. Full freight is due on damaged goods.

12. No freight is due on any increase in bulk or weight caused by the absorption of water during the voyage.

13. To the extent of the value of the lien, freight, which by the terms of the bill of lading is made payable by the consignee, cannot be demanded from the shipper after the master has parted with his lien on the goods.

14. If the goods be not taken by the consignee immediately on landing, or within such further time as is provided by the regulations of the port of discharge, they may be stored by the master at the expense and risk of their owners; provided always, that public notice is given of the arrival of the ship and the commencement of the discharge, and that the same does not begin at night or at any unreasonable hour. The master to be entitled to recover from the shipper the difference between the amount of freight stipulated in the bill of lading and the proceeds of the goods, should the consignee neglect or refuse to receive them.

15. In the event of claims for short delivery when the ship reaches her destination, the price to be the market price at the port of destination on the day of the ship's entry at the custom-house, less all charges saved.

NOTICE.—In accepting this bill of lading the owner of the goods and the shipper expressly accept and agree to all its stipulations and conditions, whether written or printed.

Dated in   this   day of   188

Weight, quality, and contents unknown.

It ought here to be stated that during the last sitting of this conference on August 11, the Hon. W. W. Field, of New York, in the chair,

Mr. Richard Lowndes moved, and I seconded, the following resolution: 'That the powers of the Affreightment Committee be continued, and the names of Messrs. Shotton, Hodgkinson, and Cross be added.'

This was carried unanimously.

Now, when it is considered that, in spite of the general publicity which was given previous to the Liverpool Con ference of its principal object, and of the intention of the English shipowners to secure freedom from liability for the negligence of their masters, officers, and crews, it is certainly extraordinary that the Chambers of Commerce, which are mainly established for the protection of merchant-shippers' interest, did not deem it worth their while to send a sufficient number of delegates to obtain an equitable arrangement on a matter of such vital importance to them.

The natural consequence of this lethargy was, that soon afterwards, from all parts of the world, attempts were made to undo the work of the Liverpool Congress. In proof of this I annex the following important communication received by the hon. gen. sec. of the Association:—

To Dr. Charles Stubbs, Hon. Gen. Secretary, Association for the Reform and Codification of the Law of Nations.

Australian and New Zealand Underwriters' Association
Committee Room, Jamaica Coffee House, London:
August 30, 1883.

Dear Sir,—In anticipation of the coming conference of your Association to be held at Milan, when one of the subjects for discussion is to be the adoption of a common form of bill of lading, and at which such a form is to be submitted to the conference for consideration, and in response to your invitation to send any suggestions that it might be deemed advisable to have presented on that occasion, I beg to enclose two documents protesting emphatically against the adoption of any form of bill of lading which will relieve the shipowner from liability for the negligence of his master and crew, and I shall be obliged by your communicating them to the conference as the deliberate and carefully considered judgment of the two bodies of gentlemen, entitled, in an assembly such as that to which they will be submitted, not only to respectful attention, but also to acceptance.

As you will perceive, one of them bears the signature of all the Australian and New Zealand Insurance Companies, and the other those of the leading London Insurance Companies, and as they may be reasonably taken to represent the views of the whole Underwriting Committees of London and the Colonies of Australia and New Zealand (where precisely the same opinion on the subject has been recently expressed), and yet further, the wishes of all shippers, I am persuaded that they will be regarded by the conference as 'possessed of a gravity and power which it would be right to recognise, and in deference to which the clause now standing in the proposed form of bill of lading will be eliminated.'

At your former conference the insertion of the clause was advocated on the ground that owners were fettered in their choice of masters by the regulations of the Board of Trade, and that, not being free to choose whom they would, they had a claim to be relieved from all responsibility. The argument, if it deserves the epithet, is captivating rather than convincing.

As well might it be urged that a man should be adjudged guiltless of folly who, having appointed one to a position of confidence and trust because he had passed an examination in bookkeeping and accountancy, found himself victimised by the cunning and dishonesty of his nominee, and learned by painful experience that something beyond merely professional or technical knowledge must be required of a man to be placed in such a position. In like manner the shipowner, in his accountability for the lives and property entrusted to his care, ought not to be relieved from all responsibility for the results of his appointments because the masters whom he selects have been required to give proof that they *know* how to manage and *navigate* a vessel—at which point the Board of Trade ceases to exercise control—and beyond which the shipowner's freedom of choice is absolute and perfect. If, therefore, he fail to make choice of wise and fit persons for so high and responsible an office, surely he ought, upon every principle of morality and duty, to be held liable for all the consequences of such a failure. I commend, therefore, these remarks and documents to your care, and remain, dear sir,

Yours faithfully,

(Signed)   E. A. PEARS, *Secretary*.

Resolved: 'That the secretary be instructed to communicate to the secretary of the Association for the Reform and Codification of the Law of Nations, that the members of this Association desire to protest against the adoption of any form of bill of lading for general use which will relieve the shipowner from liability for the negligence of the master or his men; and that any attempt to bring about or perpetuate such relief will meet their strenuous opposition.'

> Adelaide Marine Insurance Company.
> South British Insurance Company.
> National Insurance Company of New Zealand.
> Pacific Insurance Company of Sydney.
> Union of New Zealand, H.G.U.
> Mercantile Marine of South Australia, for United Insurance Company.
> *Pro* Standard Company of New Zealand, H. J. Symons.
> *Pro* Colonial Mutual Marine Insurance, H. J. Symons.
> Sydney Lloyd's, *per* G. W. Holt.
> Sydney Marine Assurance Company, *per* A. Meiklejohn.
> For the Australian Alliance Assurance Company, *per* Young Ehlers & Co. Chas. E. Meeson, agent.
> Australian General Assurance Company. Watt, Gilchrist & Co., agents, *per* E. B.

Derwent and Tanner Assurance Company. Richardson Bros. & Co., agents, *per* U. E. B.

For the South Australian Insurance Company, Limited, J. L. Champion. Agent, T. Galve.

The Colonial Insurance Company of New Zealand. Redfern, Alexander & Co., *per* W. Crandy, agent.

New Zealand Insurance Company. H. J. Bristow, chairman.

The Southern Insurance Company, Limited. Y. F. Watt, secretary.

Victoria Insurance Company, Limited. Agents,

To the Secretary of the Association for the Reform and Codification of the Law of Nations.

London: August 23, 1883.

We, the undersigned, London Marine Insurance Companies, desire to protest against the adoption of any form of bill of lading for general use which will relieve the shipowner from liability for the negligence of the master or crew, and that any attempt to bring about or perpetuate such relief will meet with our strenuous opposition.

London Assurance Corporation, *per* J. S. Mackintosh, underwriter.

Universal Marine Insurance Company, Limited, *per* A. Tozer, secretary.

Royal Exchange Assurance Corporation, *per* J. Davis Browne.

Indemnity Mutual Marine Association. C. J. L. O. Smith.

The Alliance Marine Assurance Company, Limited. Edward Richards.

Ocean Marine Insurance Company. A. Price, secretary.

London & Provincial Marine Insurance Company. S. L. Daniell.

Thames & Mersey Marine Insurance Company. A. B. R.

The Commercial Union Association Company, *per* Hen. D. Rose.

The Marine Insurance Company, Limited. Robert Loop.

The Home & Colonial Marine Insurance Company, Limited. L. Hillman.
The Merchants Marine Company. Thos. Robin.
The Globe Marine, Limited, *per* B. Francis Cobb.

These communications Mr. Stubbs presented on September 13, 1883, to the eleventh conference of the Association at Milan, Sir Travers Twiss in the chair, and they were considered by the executive council of so much importance as to require further and, if possible, more impartial discussion.

In the course of the following year it became apparent that, in the United States of America also, the result of the Liverpool Congress had not been received with anything like general satisfaction, and that the New York Produce Exchange, as well as the Chamber of Commerce of the State of New York itself, had appointed special committees to report on the state of affairs and suggest remedies.

This the latter body—the Chamber of Commerce—did in a very full report on March 6, 1884, which concluded with the proposal of a draft Bill. In this report it was distinctly averred that the shipowners treated the whole matter so brusquely, and with such independent avowal of being masters of the situation, that the Chamber became convinced that only by adoption of such a Bill justice and equity could be obtained for the interest of the merchant-shippers and their underwriters.

The wording of this Bill was to the following effect:—

An Act to regulate the Forms of Bills of Lading and the Duties and Liabilities of Shipowners and others:

Be it enacted by the Senate and House of Representatives of the United States of America in Congress assembled that every vessel publicly offered at any port of the United States for the conveyance of goods and merchandise on the high seas, and all vessels bringing general cargo to any port of the United States, shall be liable to all the conditions and restrictions of this Act.

Section 2. That it shall not be lawful for any such vessel, her owners, master, agent, or manager, to issue any bill of lading which does not clearly specify the exact voyage intended to be made, and any and every port at which it is contemplated she shall touch in the course of said voyage; and every departure from such voyage, save only when compelled thereto by dangers of the sea, unforeseen necessity, *vis major*, or to save life and property in distress at sea, and to tow and convey the same into the nearest or most convenient port of safety, shall be deemed a deviation. But nothing in this Act contained shall prevent or interfere with the right of the vessel to reserve to herself the privilege of calling at or returning to any port or ports named in the bill of lading; and a failure to exercise such privilege shall not constitute a violation of this Act, or be deemed a deviation.

Section 3. That it shall not be lawful for any such vessel, her owners, master, agent, or manager, to insert in any bill of lading any clause, covenant, or agreement whereby the obligations of the owners of said vessel to properly equip, man, provision, and outfit such vessel, and in every way and manner within their, his, or her power to render said vessel seaworthy and capable of performing her intended voyage, shall in any wise be lessened, weakened, or avoided; and all provisions and clauses contained in any bill of lading issued by any such public carrier relieving from liability the vessel, her owners, or master for their or his neglect, or for any improper condition of the vessel, shall be null and void and of no effect in law.

Section 4. That it shall not be lawful for any such public carrier, by any clause or exception in any contract or bill of lading, to be relieved from liability for its, his, her, or their negligence, fault, or failure in proper stowage, custody, and care of all lawful merchandise confided to their charge, nor for failure by reason of negligence to deliver the same, nor to provide for or adopt any other or different transportation than that agreed on by the vessel or voyage specified by which the goods have been shipped, liability for danger of the sea, *vis major*, or unforeseen necessity being in all cases under this Act excepted, nor to limit the extent of their liability to less than an indemnity to the claimant; nor shall anything in this Act contained be construed as enlarging the right of any carrier to limit his liability other than as now established by law.

Section 5. That all goods and merchandise delivered to and received by any such public carrier shall be deemed as shipped subject to the conditions of this Act, and entitled to a bill of lading in accordance therewith; and upon the refusal of the master or agent to issue such bill of lading on demand within a reasonable period after shipment, unless such goods and merchandise have been received from a preceding carrier, and a bill of lading in conformity hereto has been issued, clearance of such vessel upon which said goods were to be or were laden shall be refused by the custom-house authorities of the port until such bill of lading be granted; and such vessel shall be liable to an action *in rem* for all damages and losses suffered by the shippers of goods or merchandise by reason of such refusal or neglect. In case of any dispute as to whether the terms of any bill of lading disagree with this Act, and clearance is refused or delayed in consequence thereof, the following clause may then be inserted in or endorsed on such bill of lading, namely: 'It is hereby declared that this bill of lading, as well as all other copies thereof, are intended to conform in all particulars to the Act of Congress of 1885 on the subject of the form of Bills of Lading; and anything herein contained to the contrary is hereby made null and void.' And thereupon the collector may deem such insertion or endorsement as making the bill of lading conform hereto, and shall grant the clearance if the vessel is otherwise entitled thereto.

Section 6. That if any vessel, her master, agent, or manager, shall plead, in bar or in defence of any suit at law, any clause or exception of any bill of lading contrary to the provisions of this Act, the limitation of liability provided by section 4283 of the Revised Statutes, relating to shipowners, shall not be held to apply to such vessel, owners, or either or any of them.

Section 7. That this Act shall take effect on the first day of July eighteen hundred and eighty-five.

Passed the House of Representatives, February 3, 1885.

    Attest,   JNO. B. CLARK, JUN., *Clerk*.

As will be seen from the above attestation of the Clerk of the House of Representatives, the Act passed this House on February 3, 1885, and was sent to the Senate for approval or amendment, but not having been in time for that session, when, according to the advices received, it would have undoubtedly passed that body, no legislation was undertaken on the subject.

Strange enough, the influence brought about by the parties chiefly interested in the steamer traffic between New York, Liverpool and Glasgow upon the New York Produce Exchange proved so efficacious that this important body adopted, so far back as October 28, 1884, a report recommending with very few and unimportant alterations the adoption of the following, almost identical with the Liverpool Bill of Lading :—

NEW YORK PRODUCE EXCHANGE BILL OF LADING.

RECEIVED, in apparent good order and condition, by from   to be transported by the good steamship now lying in the port of   and bound for   with liberty to call at   being marked and numbered as per margin (weight, quality, contents, and value unknown), and to be delivered in like good order and condition at the port of (or so near thereto as she may safely get) unto   or to his or their assigns, he or they paying freight and primage (if customary) in cash, without discount, on the said goods on discharge, at the rate of   with primage and charges as per margin. General Average payable according to York-Antwerp Rules.

It is mutually agreed that the ship shall have liberty to sail without pilots; to tow and assist vessels in distress; to deviate for the purpose of saving life or property; that the carrier shall have liberty to convey goods in lighters to and from the ship at the risk of the owners of the goods; and, in case the ship shall put into a port of refuge or be prevented from any cause from proceeding in the ordinary course of her voyage, to tranship the goods to their destination by any other steamship.

It is also mutually agreed that the carrier shall not be liable for loss or damage occasioned by causes beyond his control, the perils of the sea or other waters; by fire from any cause and wheresoever occurring; by barratry of the master or crew; by enemies, pirates or robbers; by arrest and restraint of princes, rulers, or people, riots, strikes, or stoppage of labour; by explosion, bursting of boilers, breakage of shafts, or any latent defect in hull, machinery, or appurtenances; by collisions, stranding, or other accidents of navigation, of whatsoever kind (even when occasioned by the negligence, default, or error in judgment of the pilot, master, mariners, or other servants of the shipowner, not resulting, however, in any case, from want of due diligence by the owners of the ship or any of them, or by the ship's husband or manager); nor by heating, decay, putrefaction, rust, sweat, change of character, drainage, leakage, breakage, or any loss or damage arising from the nature of the goods or the insufficiency of packages, nor for land damage; nor for the obliteration, errors, insufficiency, or absence of marks or numbers, address or description; nor for risk of craft, hulk, or transhipment; or any loss or damage caused by the prolongation of the voyage.

1. It is also mutually agreed that the carrier shall not be liable for gold, silver, bullion, specie, documents, jewellery, pictures, embroideries, perfumeries, works of art, silks, furs, china, porcelain, watches, or clocks, in any respect, or for goods of any description whatever above the value of 20 dols. per cubic foot, and in no case is the carrier to be liable beyond 500 dols. per package, unless bills of lading are signed therefor, with the value therein expressed, and a special agreement is made.

2. Also, that shippers shall be liable for any loss or damage to ship or cargo caused by inflammable, explosive, or dangerous goods, shipped without full disclosure of their nature, whether such shipper be principal or agent; and such goods may be thrown overboard or destroyed at any time without compensation.

3. Also, that the carrier shall have a lien on the goods for all freights, primages, and charges, and also for fines or damages which

the ship or cargo may incur or suffer by reason of the incorrect or insufficient marking, numbering, or addressing of packages, or description of their contents.

4. Also, that in case the ship shall be prevented from reaching her destination by quarantine, the carrier may discharge the goods into any depôt or lazaretto, and such discharge shall be deemed a final delivery under this contract, and all the expenses thereby incurred on the goods shall be a lien thereon.

5. Also, that the ship may commence discharge immediately on arrival and discharge continuously, the collector of the port being hereby authorised to grant a general order for discharge immediately on arrival, and upon discharge the goods shall be at the risk of the consignee, and if not taken by him within such time as is provided by the regulations of the port of discharge, they may be stored by the carrier at the expense and risk of their owners.

NOTE.—After Clause 5 all conditions relating to delivery at different ports (also ice and lighterage, blockade and special quarantine clauses, &c.), to be inserted as agreed upon by shippers and carriers in various trades.

6. Also, that full freight is payable on damaged or unsound goods; but no freight is due on any increase in bulk or weight caused by the absorption of water during the voyage.

7. Also, in the event of claims for short delivery when the ship reaches her destination, the price shall be the market price at the port of destination on the day of the ship's entry at the custom-house, less all charges saved.

8. Freight payable on weight is to be paid on gross weight landed from ocean steamship unless otherwise agreed.

9. Parcels for different consignees collected or made in single packages addressed to one consignee to pay full freight on each parcel.

And finally, in accepting this bill of lading, the shipper, owner, and consignee of the goods, and the holder of the bill of lading, agree to be bound by all of its stipulations, exceptions, and conditions, whether written or printed, as fully as if they were all signed by such shipper, owner, consignee, or holder.

In witness whereof, the master or agent of the said ship hath affirmed to   bills of lading, all of this tenor and date, numbered consecutively, one of which being accomplished and given up to the carrier, the others to stand void.

Dated in   this   day of   188 .

The New York Produce Exchange, in reporting upon this bill of lading, added the following statement with reference to the special question of shipowners' liability :—

The most important portion of these clauses—namely, the exemption of the carrier from liability for losses caused by the default of any servant of the ship, provided the owner or manager has done his duty—has been fully preserved. Your committee beg to reiterate the statement made by the framers of the bill of lading submitted to them for revision, in which they pointed out that this exemption is in conflict with the doctrine hitherto held by our Federal Courts, though it has for a long time been sanctioned by custom, and by the all but general practice of underwriters. Your committee are equally decided in their opinion that this exemption is demanded by the circumstances under which modern steamship traffic is carried on, and that our Federal Courts will not much longer be able to resist a change so eminently just and necessary. Your committee may add that the carriers' liability for the seaworthy condition of his ship and for good stowage is in no way affected by these clauses.

It was evident that a declaration from so important a body as the New York Produce Exchange in favour of the shipowners' contentions as expressed in the Liverpool Bill of Lading would carry very great weight in the further consideration of this subject, and it cannot be denied that, until the Legislatures of the different maritime nations take the matter in hand, the united and overpowering influence of the shipowners will carry the day.

We arrive now at the time when, in the city of London, not only the members of Lloyd's, but the merchants and shipowners assembling at the 'Baltic,' as well as the members of the Chamber of Commerce, proceeded publicly to discuss the Bill of Lading question, and in order to do justice to the arguments put forward at these meetings, I think it best to reproduce out of the 'Times' the reports therein contained of them.

In the 'Times' of February 5, 1885, it was stated that :—

A meeting of underwriters of Lloyd's, Liverpool, and Glasgow, and of various London marine insurance companies, was held yesterday at Lloyd's under the presidency of Mr. William Young. The circular convening the meeting, which was issued on the 21st ult. from Lloyd's, stated that 'A deputation of shipowners and other gentlemen connected with various marine insurance clubs had, at their special request, an interview with the Committee of Lloyd's on January 16. They stated that their object was to obtain the consent of Lloyd's to the adoption of a bill of lading which the deputation proposed should be called ' Lloyd's Bill of Lading.' The chief point which the shipowners desire is the introduction of the clause concerning negligence, so that claims against shipowners under that head with regard to cargo may cease. The committee propose to lay this subject before a general meeting,' &c.

THE CHAIRMAN, having apologised for the unavoidable absence of Mr. Goschen (Chairman of Lloyd's), stated that the circular of the 21st ult. pretty well explained the reason of that meeting. The request contained therein from gentlemen in the north was one which could not be ignored by the Committee of Lloyd's, but they had felt that the matter was so important that it was their duty to call that meeting to consult with them and underwriters generally on the document in question. Hence the invitation to Liverpool, Glasgow, to various companies in London, and to other underwriting bodies. As an indication of the opinion of gentlemen in different places he would refer shortly to views which had been expressed in letters which had been received. The Underwriters' Association, Glasgow, were strongly of opinion that it would be undesirable in the interests of the mercantile community generally that the shipowner should have the power to contract himself out of responsibility to the owners of goods by his vessel for loss through the negligence of his officers and crew. The Underwriters' Association, Liverpool, had sent to the meeting Mr. Cross (chairman), Mr. Storey (deputy chairman), and Mr. A. N. Dale, who would be able to speak for themselves; but it was understood that Liverpool generally was in favour of the New York Produce Exchange Bill of Lading. The North of England Steamship Owners' Association approved of the New York Produce Exchange Bill of Lading. The Hull Chamber of Commerce and Shipping were in favour of the form of bill of lading adopted in August 1882. The Newcastle and Gateshead Chamber of Commerce resolved to memorialise Lloyd's Committee in favour of the adoption of a common form of bill of lading to be called 'Lloyd's Bill of Lading.' To that an amendment was moved: 'That such common form of bill of lading shall not contain any conditions which might further limit the existing responsibilities of shipowners as common carriers.' This amendment, they were informed, was lost by one vote. The New York Underwriters' Association had sent the following cablegram: 'New York underwriters object to restoring negligence clause in bill of lading, and will not assume risks of carelessness of shipowners and crew under ordinary policy.' They had also had letters from various gentlemen well known to them, and especially one from a gentleman who, he was afraid, was not at that meeting, Mr. Tozer, who had assisted them on various occasions with his advice. Mr. Tozer had been at first inclined to say: 'Do nothing,' but on having the resolutions which would be submitted to the meeting shown to him, he was converted to the views which were expressed therein, and had authorised him to state so. They would have observed in the circular which had been issued the use of the phrase 'Lloyd's Bill of Lading,' but that was without the leave and authority of Lloyd's Committee. Some had urged that this was a matter of no concern to underwriters at all, and that it lay between the shipowner and the merchant; but in answer to that it might be pointed out that they were employed by both and had duties to both. In his own individual opinion he thought underwriters really represented the public in the controversy; their interest was the interest of the public. They would understand that in moving the resolutions, as he intended to do, he was not in any way speaking for the committee as a whole. That was an open meeting, and the question was not a cabinet question, but one for the meeting to decide. If they wished the matter to go further, they would approve the resolutions; while, if they wished it to end now, they would have nothing to do but to negative them. The resolutions, he thought, bore rather towards the idea of some sort of compromise, and it seemed to him that they would afford some sort of *modus vivendi* between all parties. He concluded by moving the following resolutions:—

'(1). That, in the opinion of this meeting, the proposed relief of shipowners from responsibility for the conduct of their servants would tend to increase preventable loss of life and property at sea, and is not desirable in the interest of the mercantile community.

'(2). That if the responsibility of shipowners as at present limited by law be shown to be unduly onerous, having regard to the conditions of the business, a readjustment of the limits will be the only satisfactory remedy.

'(3). That this meeting, while ready to consider any reasonable proposal with regard to the general limit of responsibility, considers that any alterations of the ordinary conditions of carriage by sea should be effected by legislation and not by private contracts between individual merchants and the shipowner.

'(4). That the risks of merchants who accept charters or bills of lading exempting the shipowners from responsibility for the acts of their servants will be thereby greatly increased, and that the acceptance by merchants of such increased risks will be a material circumstance which ought to be communicated to underwriters when they are invited to insure such risks.

'(5). That the resolutions passed by this meeting be made public.'

Mr. S. I. Da Costa, in seconding the resolutions, stated that the subject had engaged his attention for some time, and he had endeavoured to consider it without prejudice to the many conflicting interests involved. From a shipowner's point of view the present state of things must be very unsatisfactory, and he thought the shipowner was justified in seeking some measure of relief from the liabilities which the common law imposed upon him. It did not, however, follow that the underwriter was to relieve him entirely from all liability arising from negligent navigation, or to endorse every condition which in his contract with the merchant the shipowner desired to impose. During the period last year in which he (the speaker) occupied the position of Mr. Young, the subject came before him and the Committee of Lloyd's on a communication from the United States, and various questions were asked and opinions elicited from the committee and underwriters of the United Kingdom. He had thought it would not be undesirable to have a conference at which underwriters, merchants, and shipowners could express their opinion on the subject, and he used his best endeavours to bring about a conference, but entirely failed. While he deprecated the idea that an underwriter should look upon the recovery from an owner for a loss paid to a merchant for merchandise sacrificed through negligent navigation in the light of a salvage on his underwriting account, he felt convinced that if the clauses which it was proposed to introduce into charter-parties and bills of lading became current the losses arising from negligence would largely increase, and underwriters would suffer accordingly. He took it, therefore, that to accept the conditions proposed, and to give them the *imprimatur* of Lloyd's, was quite out of the question; and it would be necessary for underwriters to make this clearly understood by those effecting insurance on goods with them, and that if new conditions were to be imported into charters they must be communicated to underwriters and an equivalent in premium given. He trusted that the resolutions would meet with the unanimous approval of the meeting, and that they might prove to be the means of eliciting some proposals from shipowners which might in the end be satisfactory to all the parties interested in this most important question.

MR. C. M. NORWOOD, M.P., said he had understood Mr. Da

Costa to say that the question at issue was entirely a matter for underwriters as far as the meeting was concerned. He (the speaker), however, ventured to think, in the first place, that there were many members of Lloyd's, and subscribing members, who were not underwriters; but he also took a broader ground, and he thought it a great pity that they should define the relations between shipowners and underwriters. His view was that they were all—underwriters, shippers, and merchants—mutually interested in the settlement of the question. He entirely dissented from the view of Mr. Da Costa, that if the liability of shipowners for negligence, accidents, and default of their masters and mates at sea were removed or reduced there would be a great increase of losses. The position which he took—and which he believed every shipowner took—was that it was not only his legal but his moral duty to make his ship seaworthy, to man her properly, and to conduct his business, as far as the ship was in his control, to the best of his ability; and if there was any default on the part of the shipowner in a matter in which he had control, he (Mr. Norwood) would be the last to ask to be relieved from the responsibility. The old doctrine was that a voyage by sea was a mutual undertaking consisting of risk all round, and to attempt to saddle the pecuniary responsibility of goods and cargo on a shipowner for the default of his servant thousands of miles away was, he thought, a most monstrous innovation. Every one in that room, too, knew that it was impossible for a shipowner to put in charge of his vessel a captain, mate, engineer, or any responsible person unless that person had the *imprimatur* of the Board of Trade. If, as he believed, the majority of shipowners selected the best men to command their ships, he thought it monstrous that they should be held responsible for the acts of these men, who were selected especially by a Government department to stand between the shipowner, the underwriter, and the merchant. As to an alteration in the bill of lading, he really did think that the request which had been made was not unreasonable—to make clear the limitation of an onerous responsibility; and he maintained that that was not a request which should be lightly rejected. As a body, shipowners had been attacked in a manner which was altogether unjustifiable, and it was an insulting suggestion that the chief object of the shipowner was to lose his ship and draw his money.

MR. W. MATTHEWS (Messrs. Lamplough and Co.) maintained that, if underwriters did not themselves take such risks as those in question, shipowners would form themselves into mutual clubs, and thus underwriters would ultimately become the losers.

MR. F. A. WHITE (Marine Insurance Company) bore testimony to what Mr. Norwood had said from the shipowners' point of view. There was, however, not only the question of the underwriter in this matter, but the merchant who was not insured. He was sure that underwriters, as one of whom he spoke, would discuss the matter fairly and make any reasonable concession. He maintained, however, that the present was not the proper time for discussing the matter, and that they should await the report of the Royal Commission, which had emanated entirely from the shipowners.

MR. J. G. PITCAIRN was understood to contend that shipowners had no control over the officers of their vessels, and to express a wish that the meeting should be adjourned to see whether some arrangement could not be made with shipowners and merchants.

MR. J. PARK said he could remember the time before 1854 when the shipowners' liability was put in the Merchant Shipping Act of that year. In asking underwriters to take the risk in question, shipowners were not asking them to pay anything but what their fathers had paid before them.

MR. G. F. MILLER (underwriter) said they were deeply convinced of the importance of the third resolution. He thought nothing should be done pending the report of the Royal Commission.

MR. DALE (of Liverpool) said the Liverpool Underwriters' Association had given much consideration to the important question under discussion, and had come to the conclusion that it was neither equitable to shipowners nor politic for underwriters to refuse the suggestion of shipowners—that they should be exempted under bills of lading from liabilities in respect of disasters which were absolutely beyond the shipowner's control, and which he had used all due diligence to prevent. He regretted to see, from the expressions of feeling already given, that the meeting took a different view. In New York, however (by no means an unimportant commercial community), the principle had been conceded, and, though the decisions of the American Courts had hitherto been adverse to the shipowners, the steamship-owners and shippers combined had agreed on a bill of lading which was satisfactory to both parties. The Liverpool steamship owners had recently endeavoured to push those concessions somewhat further, and had sought to exempt themselves from responsibility as to seaworthiness and proper stowage. That had been resolutely withstood by Liverpool underwriters. A compromise was probable by which the steamship-owners would withdraw their pretensions in consideration of underwriters conceding what was called the 'negligence clause.' He regretted that the meeting showed so little disposition to favour this compromise. Risk was the parent of premium. It was the business of an underwriter to insure against perils of the sea and to receive an adequate premium for so doing. In the past the errors of judgment of masters and crews had been considered a peril of the sea covered by an ordinary policy; but recent decisions in our Courts had shown there was, as an underwriter in a letter to the 'Times' had expressed it, a flaw in the shipowners' armour. Of that flaw underwriters had taken advantage. He thought it would not be wise to continue to do so; hence he strongly advised conceding to the shipowner the negligence clause, leaving him liable only for that which he could control. The resolutions had not, he thought, been prepared with that care which so important a subject required, and one, at least, was especially offensive to shipowners. He hoped, therefore, that the meeting would be willing to postpone any discussion on them, and would appoint a committee composed of underwriters, shipowners, and merchants to consider the whole subject, and to report to a future meeting. He concluded by moving an amendment to this effect.

MR. DA COSTA, amid some laughter, said he would second the amendment, but

THE CHAIRMAN pointed out that if he did he would negative the resolutions he had seconded.

MR. CROSS (Liverpool) seconded the amendment. He said he knew, indirectly, that a conclusion could not be arrived at by the Royal Commission in less than three years.

Mr. Lodge (the Marine Insurance Company) held that, if the law was to be altered, the application should be made to the Legislature, and not to the Committee of Lloyd's. All that underwriters said, and all that he had power to say, was that they thought it was more proper to await the result of the Royal Commission, and meantime not to commit themselves to any details.

Mr. John Glover asked whether, if the shipowners were contented to wait, as recommended by Mr. Lodge, until the result of the Royal Commission had been ascertained, probably about three years hence, the underwriters would undertake in the meantime not to bring any further actions against steamship-owners to recover the value of cargoes lost through alleged negligence at sea. (Mr. Lodge: Certainly not.) He had anticipated that reply, and, consequently, it was impossible that shipowners could go on having an action over every loss in which it was to be determined between two underwriters who should pay for a loss for covering which only one of the two had received premium. He also thought it was much wiser for men of business, parties to ordinary mercantile transactions, to settle such questions among themselves by the adoption of proper documents, instead of waiting an indefinite period for legislative relief which might never come. He also pointed out that for underwriters to insist on retaining the right to proceed in the name of merchants against shipowners for the occurrence of such losses foreshadowed double insurance arrangements, which were always objectionable, the alternative to which was that any shipowner might find himself ruined through the occurrence of peril attributable to the fault of one of his servants over which he had absolutely no control. The effect of the improved bill of lading recommended would make traffic at sea safer, not more hazardous, for if the master-and-servant doctrine were eliminated from such cases negligent servants would be dismissed promptly, whereas at present it was often necessary to retain them in service because their evidence was wanted in legal proceedings. In fact, the present uncertainty led to nothing but disputes and litigation, the net result of which was that the loss had to be borne by the underwriters *plus* large amounts of law costs. The resolutions pointed to inquiry and the need for full consideration of the whole subject, and he advised the members of Lloyd's to sanction the appointment of a committee for the purpose of making such inquiry and co-operating with other public bodies labouring to settle the matter satisfactorily.

MR. HENRY GREEN (Chairman of the Chamber of Shipping) observed that Mr. Glover had expressed what they felt. He supported the proposal of Mr. Dale for the appointment of a committee.

After a few observations from MR. WREN,

THE CHAIRMAN replied, and stated that, if they passed the resolutions, the second one meant coming to some understanding between the shipowner and the underwriter as to the amount of liability that had to be borne.

MR. MICHAEL WILLS thought they were pretty much agreed on the general question that it was desirable to have a committee on the subject. He supported the proposal of Mr. Dale.

THE CHAIRMAN put the amendment, in favour of which it was stated that there were 47 votes, and it was, therefore, declared lost.

MR. NORWOOD protested against the first resolution.

THE CHAIRMAN expressed his conviction that there was not the slightest intention on the part of anyone in the room to cast any reflection on shipowners.

The opinion of the meeting was taken as to the omission of the first resolution, and 83 hands were held up in favour of this course being adopted. It was therefore struck out.

THE CHAIRMAN then put the remainder of the resolutions as a substantive motion, and 65 voting for it, it was declared carried.

The proceedings then terminated.

Further, the 'Times' of the 11th of the same month stated :—

A crowded meeting was held yesterday at the Baltic, Threadneedle Street, to take into consideration the proposed international bill of lading. Mr. S. W. Keene, of the Corn Exchange, presided.

THE CHAIRMAN, in opening the proceedings, observed that he

had been striving for many years to effect improvements in bills of lading in common use, and at last he thought there was a reasonable prospect of making a very considerable improvement. The meeting was called for the purpose of hearing a statement of the present position of the question, and would be asked to appoint a committee to examine into the whole subject, and to co-operate with other public bodies in the effort to establish a common form of bill of lading.

Mr. JOHN GLOVER proposed a resolution in accordance with the object of the meeting. He pointed out that merchants justly complained of the variety in the terms of bills of lading, and showed that the international bill of lading would place responsibility on shipowners, and very properly so, in respect of any unseaworthiness in vessels and bad stowage, and would make them responsible for any negligence whatever on their own part. In this respect important improvements would be effected in the interests of merchants. It was also proposed by the common bill of lading to insert in all bills of lading what are known as the ' negligence clauses,' which, he said, were now almost universally used in connection with the great steam lines, and in the American, Indian, Australian, China, and New Zealand trades. Notwithstanding the objection of some underwriters to the latter change, there was no difficulty in finding underwriters to take risks, without any additional premium, in bills of lading containing these clauses, as there was a general impression that it was not fair on the part of underwriters to receive premiums against losses and not to bear the losses when they occurred. Shipowners had been rather rudely awakened from a delusion they had entertained, to the effect that the old words in bills of lading—namely, 'all and every other dangers and accidents of the seas, rivers, and navigation of whatever nature and kind soever during the said voyage always excepted'—saved them from liability for errors in navigation inseparable from the employment of human agency. Actions for large sums had lately been brought against shipowners, in which they had been asked to pay for cargoes lost through mistakes, collisions, fogs, and other common causes of loss at sea. Shipowners, therefore, had now come to the conclusion that if they had to bear these risks their only course was to contract for insurance as well as freight, so that out of the premiums they might be able to pay the losses arising from negligence and other causes of the kind referred to. It was felt to be unfair that underwriters who had received premiums against losses should, on the occurrence of such losses, be enabled to keep the premiums and visit the loss on the shipowners.

Mr. John Ross seconded the resolution.

Mr. Stephen Ralli opposed the motion, and expressed his opinion that the bill of lading, as amended by the New York Produce Exchange, was still objectionable. He thought it advisable that the whole subject should stand over until the Royal Commission had made their report.

Mr. Valeri acquiesced in the views of Mr. Ralli.

Mr. C. M. Norwood, M.P., supported the resolution, and stated that there was not the least difficulty in merchants covering the negligence clause asked for without any additional premium. An improvement in bills of lading would result from the adoption of a common form based on the draft before the meeting, and it was, therefore, in his opinion, highly desirable to appoint a committee to further consider the matter.

Mr. Edward Power suggested that the resolution should be amended, so that the subject should be referred for consideration, without reference to the New York Produce Exchange Bill of Lading, and this suggestion was accepted.

On a vote being taken, the resolution, as amended, was carried by a large majority, and a committee was subsequently appointed.

And the 'Times' of March 5 reported the last of these three meetings as follows:—

Yesterday a meeting of members of the London Chamber of Commerce, and of merchants, bankers, shippers, and others interested in a revision of the existing clauses of bills of lading, from a mercantile point of view, was held at the City Terminus Hotel, Cannon Street. Mr. Magniac, M.P., president of the Chamber, occupied the chair, and among those present were—

Mr. J. H. Tritton, chairman, and the following members of the council:—Messrs. John Glover, E. J. Johnson, W. H. Peat, J. G. Hamilton, George Martineau, J. T. Ritchie, J. M'Call, and G. H. Powell; Sir Saul Samuel, Agent-General for New South Wales; Mr. J. F. Garrick, Q.C., Agent-General for Queensland; Sir Francis Bell, Agent-General for New Zealand; Captain Charles Mills, Agent-General for the Cape of Good Hope; Alderman Atkinson, Hull; Mr. Pearce, Glasgow Chamber of Commerce; and Mr. Kenric B. Murray, secretary of the London Chamber of Commerce.

THE CHAIRMAN, in opening the proceedings, observed that from a communication he had received from a very prominent shipowner, he thought there was some misapprehension as to the scope and object of that meeting. It seemed to have been considered that they were going to hold a kind of indignation meeting in opposition to shipowners. That, however, was an entire mistake. The shipowners themselves had held several meetings to ascertain what their views were on the subject, and the present meeting would endeavour to do the same as regarded the shippers. He had received a letter from Mr. Hubbard, the member for the City, who wrote as follows:—

'For some time past I have observed a gradual movement on the part of shipowners to diminish, and even cancel, the liability heretofore held to attach to them as carriers of the goods they received on freight. With this object, clauses have been inserted in bills successively enlarging the excepted causes of loss and damage until they attain for the shipowner an almost perfect indemnity, notwithstanding that the occurrence of such loss or damage may be distinctly traceable to the neglect or the misconduct of the captains or crews. It is easy to discover an origin for this movement in the increased size and costliness of the mercantile marine, in the rapidity of the voyages performed, in the value of time, in the employment of vessels representing a large capital, and in the frequent changes of captain and crew which may probably occur. These considerations, while explaining the anxiety of shipowners to avoid responsibility, cannot satisfy merchants of the wisdom of this new policy, or of the fairness with which it has been advocated. The fundamental principle that an employer of labour is responsible for the acts of his agent in regard to the work for which he is engaged, cannot be set aside for the convenience of the employer without detriment to the community, and the legal axiom, *Qui facit per alium facit per se*, is strictly applicable to the owner as acting through the captain, and by the captain through the crew. Some shipowners, indeed, have repudiated this liability, and renounced any pretence of control over the captain, but this fantastic pretence is cancelled by the fact of ownership, which they unequivocally admit in their title to the ship, and their receipt of its earnings. An irresponsible ownership is a contradiction not to be tolerated. I sincerely trust that an amicable conference of shippers and shipowners may eventuate in a satisfactory adjustment of the conflicting views, and that this desirable result may be forthwith attained without waiting for the report of the Royal Commission, indefinitely protracting the settlement of a question to the solution of which it is wholly unnecessary.' He thought those views commended themselves to the mind of every one present. A bill of lading ought to be the same thing as the goods themselves. It ought to be precisely the same thing as a deed for the conveyance of land, or a bill of exchange representing a commodity. There ought to be absolute certainty about a bill of lading. There should be no uncertainty as to the delivery of the goods, or as to who was responsible if the goods were not delivered. The liability of shipowners and of underwriters ought to be fixed and ascertained; and it was for the benefit and advantage of public policy, for the benefit and advantage of trade in general, and of the different classes engaged in trade, that such certainty should be absolute. Bankers who advanced on bills of lading ought to be perfectly certain that their advances were not on pieces of paper, but on goods. They would not expect him to go through the different ways in which a shipowner might be affected, but he believed that at the present moment there was one particular liability which the shipowner felt very strongly upon, and about which there was undoubtedly some and perhaps a good deal of question—that was his liability for the acts of his servants. Too little responsibility, however, would engender carelessness, which could not be for the advantage of the nation at large. On the other hand, it might be said that if you require over-responsibility, it may become an illusion, and he believed that it was so in many cases now. This condition of things was not to the interest of any one either. The present bills of lading were not what they ought to be. He had seen one bill of lading—he admitted that it was in a very small trade—as to which he asserted that the only liability upon the shipowner was to receive the freight. There was no liability on him to carry or deliver the goods. That was not a right state of things. Many were anxious that whatever bill of lading was arrived at it should be uniform. He was not prepared to say that it was absolutely impossible to make a uniform bill of lading, but he did think that it was quite possible that there might be particular trades in which particular bills of lading were required. As to the Royal Commission, Mr. Hubbard was strongly against any legislative interference in trade which could be avoided. He (the Chairman) felt convinced that if the meeting appointed a committee to meet the shipowners, and the two parties could agree upon a bill of lading, the Royal Commission—if it were necessary to submit the arrangement to them—would jump at the opportunity of being saved the trouble which they might otherwise have.

Mr. Keene moved the first resolution as follows: 'That this meeting, representing mercantile interests, is of opinion that the bills of lading in force at the present time are, in many cases, unacceptable to merchants, in consequence of the clauses exonerating shipowners from their liabilities. It is urgent that some satisfactory modification of these bills of lading should be agreed upon, and with that view this meeting resolves that a committee be appointed to confer with shipowners and others interested on the subject.' Formerly, he said, a bill of lading was a simple receipt given by the captain or owner by which he undertook to deliver goods in the same order and condition in which he had received them, certain contingencies excepted—'the act of God and the perils of the sea.' A steamship bill of lading now, however, contained clauses enumerating every conceivable thing which might cause loss or damage to goods, exempting the shipowner from all liability arising out of them. He maintained that shippers had no freedom of contract with the shipowners. He did not wish to go into politics, but in the Merchant Shipping Bill of last session there were four clauses which would have helped merchants considerably. He thought it unadvisable to wait for legislation. If the Royal Commission were to report that it was advisable to make a bill of lading, he did not believe that the House of Commons would make a bill of lading for them. In the second part of his resolution a compromise was proposed, and he believed that much good would come out of the proposed committee. The international bill of lading of 1882 and the New York Produce Bill of Lading, which was based upon the international bill, were far from perfect, but if they were taken as a starting-point by the committee he thought something might be made out of them.

SIR FRANCIS BELL seconded, and MR. M'ANDREW supported, the motion.

MR. STEPHEN RALLI also supported the motion. He referred to the discussions which had already taken place upon the subject, and observed that at 'the Baltic,' where a great many merchants and shipowners met daily for the transaction of their business, the question had been fully debated, and he was glad to state that he believed some partial agreement had been already come to between the two parties. He believed they might consider as certain that shipowners would in future accept their liability on the arrival of goods for damage. The most difficult question had been in connection with losses arising from errors of navigation. As regarded the pilots, shipowners had pointed out that, although they were paid by them, and were legally their servants, yet they ought not to be responsible for losses arising from the pilots' acts. In that view he must say that merchants generally concurred, because, although the pilots were legally the agents of the shipowners, the latter did not choose them, and were obliged to take on board the pilots who presented themselves. If that great concession were made by the mercantile community, it ought to be appreciated by the shipowners. He believed that he was in agreement with the feeling of the great majority, if not the whole, of the mercantile community in saying that they would go a step further, and would be willing to exempt shipowners from loss arising from errors of judgment on the part of their officers; but he hoped they would never agree to exempt them from loss arising from the culpable negligence or misconduct of their captains or officers. If shipowners were exempted from loss arising from the last-mentioned causes, some of them—the worst of them—would engage at smaller wages an inferior set of men, a proceeding which would lead to increased loss of ships and life at sea. The best proof of the unfairness of this bill of lading was that the British Government had declined to accept clauses in it to which, however, shippers were obliged to submit.

Mr. Harris, M.P., in supporting the resolution, spoke of the advantages of the similarity of contract which had been established in the grain trade, and said he thought there ought to be similar agreement about bills of lading.

Mr. Hollams (solicitor) thought it remarkable, in view of the excited discussion which had taken place, that there had been no change in the law. Until twenty years ago it was supposed that accidents from collisions and errors of judgment protected the shipowner as being dangers of the sea, but the Court decided about twenty years ago that that was not so, and that the shipowner was liable. This decision had brought about this state of things—that, notwithstanding that the merchant was protected by his underwriter, the shipowner was liable; and the underwriter, on paying the loss, became entitled to the rights of the shipper against the shipowner. He believed that the cause of all the irritation had arisen from this modern practice. Although in law there was no difference, there was practically a good deal of difference between negligence and error of judgment, and he thought a vast distinction ought to be made between the two.

Mr. Steinthal (Vice-President of the Manchester Chamber of Commerce) stated that at Manchester they looked upon the question of bills of lading as rather one between shipowners and underwriters, because the merchants were in the habit of insuring the goods and of recovering from the underwriters, even to the smallest Particular Average, any loss they might sustain. He afterwards testified as a shipper to the unfair clauses contained in bills of lading.

Mr. L. Walker (of Dundee) and Mr. J. F. Garrick, Q.C.,

also supported the motion, the latter gentleman expressing an opinion that, generally, those matters which were within the control of the shipper might fairly stand in the bill of lading, exempting the shipowner. The acts over which the shipowner had control were very large, and there were losses which arose from culpable negligence and those which arose from error of judgment. These, he thought, were matters for mutual consideration between the shipowner and the shipper. There were certain matters, in his opinion, where they must appeal to the State.

After a few remarks from MR. M'AUSLAND (J. Connell & Co.) and MR. REINHOLD (of Calcutta) the resolution was passed.

MR. J. A. EWEN (Sargood, Son, & Co.) proposed the next resolution : 'That the following gentlemen be appointed as a committee, with power to add to their number, and with power to amalgamate with existing committees:—Messrs. J. Macandrew (Matheson & Co.), Victor Benecke (Benecke, Souchay, & Co.), W. Adamson (Adamson, Gilfillan, & Co.), Halton (T. A. Gibb & Co), H. Reinhold (Reinhold & Co., Calcutta), J. A. Ewe (Sargood, Son, & Co.), H. M. Steinthal (Delegate from the Manchester Chamber of Commerce), E. Majolier (Harris Brothers), William Dunn (W. Dunn & Co., South Africa), and J. G. Pitcairn.' He expressed his belief that the resolution would open up the means of an equitable adjustment between all parties. The subject had been approached in no hostile spirit to the shipowners.

MR. W. G. SOPER seconded the motion, which was carried, the name of Mr. Paterson (Messrs. Carter, Paterson & Co.) being added to those mentioned.

MR. POWER next proposed, and MR. MAJOLIER seconded, the third resolution, as follows: 'That this meeting considers it desirable that in all charter-parties and bills of lading an arbitration clause should be inserted.'

The resolution was carried with two dissentients.

On the motion of MR. PITCAIRN, seconded by MR. P. HIRSCHFELD, a vote of thanks was passed to the Chairman, and the proceedings then terminated.

There was a further proof given how the principal firms of the mercantile community of this great city looked anxiously forward for a satisfactory settlement of this most vexed question by their addressing the following requisition to the President of the Royal Commission on Loss of Life at Sea, which was at that time occupied in taking evidence :—

To the Right Honourable the Earl of Aberdeen, President of the Royal Commission on Merchant Shipping.

We, the undersigned, bankers, merchants, and brokers of the city of London, desire to see a uniform bill of lading adopted by the owners of British steamships and sailing vessels.

The present system of multiform bills of lading is found to be inconvenient and unsatisfactory by all members of the mercantile community.

Shipowners have recently proposed a form as basis of a bill of lading for general adoption, but as the clauses of the bill of lading are involved in the questions referred to the Royal Commission, shippers, while granting that uniformity is to be desired, hesitate to take definite action in the matter, in view of the exhaustive consideration of the subject by the Royal Commission under your lordship's presidency.

Shipowners, though not denying that such hesitation is proper, plead that the question is a burning one requiring prompt solution, and we, on our part, are desirous to have it settled as soon as possible upon principles sanctioned by authority.

We are, therefore, of opinion that great satisfaction will be felt by the mercantile community if the Royal Commission will give priority in its deliberations to the consideration of any questions the settlement of which the Commission may think a necessary preliminary to the adoption of a uniform bill of lading, and that, if possible, a special report should be made on the subject.

There is a general desire in all countries to have an international bill of lading, and it is probable that the recommendations of a Royal Commission would be accepted by other countries as a basis for agreement.

Besides these expressions of the various interested

opinions, the public press almost daily during the first few months of 1885 contained letters, giving arguments for and against the concession of non-liability to shipowners for the negligence of the master and crew of their vessels. One of the best arguments found in these letters was in these words : ' Do not withdraw from the only persons who can effectually influence the conditions of navigation, an important incentive to care and vigilance, by acquiescing in a claim so exceptional as that shipowners alone, of all employers of labour, shall not be held answerable for the negligence and incapacity of those they employ.' Nobody can assert that any shipowner is bound to engage the first master, mate, engineer, or other officer who presents his certificate of competency from the Board of Trade. He has the choice among those who come forward, who, although equally qualified in the eye of the law, do not have, in virtue of their certificate of competency, the right to claim the first vacancy.

They must, and should, submit to the scrutiny of those whose patronage and employment they seek. Does it not stand to reason, and should it not, as a matter of plain common sense, be assumed that the greater the liability which would fall upon the employer, the shipowner, through the neglect or incapacity of those he employs, the greater will be the incentive for him to employ competent officers, who, in order to retain the confidence of their employer, and consequently the means of earning a respectable livelihood, would be obliged to exercise the greatest vigilance and care in the navigation of the vessel. On the other hand, if nobody but an unknown merchant or his still less known underwriter has to bear the consequences of neglect, how easy would be the inclination to forget the duty to employ trustworthy servants.

The committee which at the meeting at 'the Baltic'

was appointed for the consideration of this question came to the conclusion that the principal clause under discussion should be worded as follows :—

'Strandings and collisions, and all losses and damages caused thereby, are also excepted, even when occasioned by negligence, default, or error in judgment of the pilot, master, mariners, or other servants of the shipowners, but nothing herein contained shall exempt the shipowner from liability to pay for damage to cargo occasioned by bad stowage, by improper or insufficient dunnage or ventilation, or by improper opening of valves, sluices, and ports, or by causes other than those above excepted, and all the above exceptions are conditional on the vessel being seaworthy when she sails on the voyage, but any latent defects in the machinery shall not be considered unseaworthiness provided the same do not result from want of due diligence of the owners, or any of them, or by the ship's husband or manager.'

The 'Times' of July 25, 1885, gave the following report of the meeting summoned to consider the subject :—

Yesterday a meeting was held at the Baltic Coffee-house, Threadneedle Street, to receive the report of the committee appointed last February to consider the subject of bills of lading and proposed charges therein. The chair was taken by the Right Hon. J. G. Hubbard, M.P., and besides the whole of the members of the committee there was a large attendance of the members. The committee consisted of Messrs. S. W. Keene (S. W. Keene & Co.), T. V. S. Angier (Angier Brothers), James Dixon (Harris & Dixon), A. G. Eumorphopulos (Scaramanga, Manoussi, & Co.), John Glover (Glover Brothers), E. P. Maxsted (Keighley, Maxsted, & Co., Hull), William Milburn, jun. (William Milburn & Co.), W. Muller (J. G. Hubbard & Co.), J. Ross (Begbies, Ross, & Gibson), O. Valieri (Mavro, Valieri, & Co.), J. Watson (Watson, Medill, & Co.), J. B. Watt (J. B. Watt & Co.), and E. H. Watts (Watts, Ward, & Co.). The report of the committee stated that they had held fourteen meetings, and had given the matter their most careful consideration. At an early stage of their labours they were forced to come to the conclusion that the varying circumstances of different trades rendered it impossible to agree on any form of bill of lading that would exactly suit all countries, and they had therefore endeavoured to frame forms suitable for the Black Sea, Danube, Mediterranean, and Baltic trades. They had unanimously agreed to recommend for use in these trades two forms, one adapted for full cargoes of grain, the other for mixed cargoes and general merchandise. The Chairman, in opening the proceedings, stated that the object of the committee had been to make trading easier and safer, and to put an end to the conflicts which always arose in connection with the existing bills of lading. MR. VALIERI proposed the following resolution : ' That the two forms of bills of lading as framed by the committee be accepted and adopted for general use in the trades named, by both merchants and shipowners, on and after September 1 next.' He had, he said, come to the conclusion that conciliation was the true policy between the various parties, and he regarded the concessions made to the shipowners as reasonable and fair. MR. JOHN GLOVER, in seconding the motion, observed that what was proposed was a fair compromise between all parties. MR. ROTH (Crédit Lyonnais) moved an amendment proposing in effect a bill of lading of his own composition. No one, however, would second the amendment, which therefore fell through, and the resolution was adopted with a few dissentients. On the motion of MR. E. H. WATTS, seconded by MR. JOHN ROSS, the following resolution was also passed : ' That a copy of the first resolution, together with the two forms of bills of lading, be sent to the Committee of Lloyd's and to underwriters generally.'

Substantially the changes which are effected by these new documents are to define more clearly the liability of the shipowner for damage occasioned to cargo by bad stowage, improper dunnage, insufficient ventilation, improper opening of valves, and by the unseaworthiness of the vessel. Complaint had been made that by some bills of lading, which had come into extensive use, shipowners had exempted themselves from liabilities arising out of these causes for which they ought fairly to be held responsible. On the other hand, the complaint made by shipowners, that they had been recently held answerable for losses which occurred at sea through mistakes and errors of judgment of pilots and master mariners, and from collisions—all of which were quite beyond the shipowner's control—has been met by the use of language which has made it clear that such losses, arising out of strandings and collisions, are to be treated as common sea perils. Briefly, the parties concerned, instead of waiting for relief by legislation, which might not come, have taken the course of agreeing among themselves as to the most suitable documents on which to carry on their business.

No surprise need be felt that such Chambers of Commerce and underwriting bodies as were not convinced by the arguments brought forward, that the freedom of contract should be allowed to any shipowner to contract himself out of his legal obligation to be answerable for the neglect or default of his master or crew, should try to re-open the discussion of this subject on more neutral territory. The Senate of the Hanse town of Hamburg having invited the Association for the Reform and Codification of the Law of Nations to hold their (tenth) conference in that city on August 18, 1885, it was accordingly publicly announced that this question would be again fully considered.

On that day, under the presidency of Dr. Fred. Sieveking, the President of the Hanseatic Court of Appeal, the subject was introduced by my presenting the following report on the International Law of Affreightment and Bills of Lading :—

Some surprise has been expressed that, although the deliberations at our Liverpool Congress (1882) resulted in the adoption of a form of bill of lading intended to be used by the mercantile and ship-owning community of the world, the executive council of this Association has deemed it advisable to re-open this important subject at the present conference. It therefore devolves upon me, as Chairman of the Bill of Lading and Affreightment Committee, to explain the circumstances which have influenced the council in so deciding.

It may be in the recollection of the members of this Association that at our Milan conference (1883) Dr. Stubbs, as hon. secretary of that committee, reported that, although the draft bill of lading adopted at the Liverpool conference had been most favourably received in some quarters, it had also met with considerable opposition in others, and that while he laid upon the table a pamphlet describing the work of the committee during the preceding year, he at the same time presented resolutions signed by the leading insurance companies of London, and all the insurance companies of New Zealand and Australia, formally protesting against the adoption of any bill of lading for general use which would release the shipowners from liability for the negligence of the master or crew. These resolutions, which were practically of an identical tenor, concluded with the statement 'that any attempt to bring about or perpetuate such relief will meet with our strenuous opposition.'

The pamphlet just referred to contains the report of the committee on bills of lading appointed by the New York Produce Exchange, dated May 1883, in which the Liverpool form of bill of lading is criticised, and another form, differing considerably in its details, is proposed in its stead.

This was not all. Not only have the Chambers of Commerce and the boards of underwriters on the Continent awakened to the very dangerous innovations attempted by the Liverpool Bill of Lading, but the Chamber of Commerce of the State of New York, the National Board of Marine Underwriters at New York, and other public bodies in the United States, have had their attention called to the subject. Their opinion on the subject can best be explained by my quoting the opening sentences of the report of the special committee on International Bills of Lading of the New York Chamber of Commerce, dated June 5, 1883. These run as follows :—

'The multiform bills of lading in existence (if the objectionable clauses are taken collectively) are tantamount to giving the owner of merchandise no obligation on the part of the ship to perform *anything*, and risks are excepted which are not recognised as insured in the printed forms of the policies of marine insurance companies. Some forms of bills of lading are not so obnoxious as others, but, in nearly all, the risks excepted and the conditions imposed are such, that the merchant, who thinks he has insured his goods, finds, upon examination, that he has not insured against the exceptions and conditions of the bill of lading he receives.

'Your committee find, virtually, that nearly every line has promptly followed the example of that one which first began the innovation. Like all social evils, the magnitude and heinousness have become so great, that some amelioration must be granted by the authors, or else the indignation of the mercantile world will soon evolve a worse result to the vessel-owners than any of the liabilities they thus seek to avoid. It is the apprehension of some such result that has prompted the friends of the steamship lines to bring before the conference upon international law in Great Britain this subject, and a proposal that a form of bill of lading should be constructed which should be adapted to the present requirements of trade, and which, while granting every fair concession to shipowners, will serve to protect the shipper of cargo from risks to which he should not be subjected, and which properly should be assumed by the shipowner.'

From the different reports since published by this body, it appears that very considerable care has been taken in elucidating the subject in general, and the law as administered by the United States Courts in particular, and with respect to the latter I may be permitted to quote from the judgment delivered on July 31, 1884, by the Hon. Samuel Blatchford, Justice of the Supreme Court of the United States, in the well-known case of the 'Montana,' the following sentence:—

'In view of all these cases, it holds that a carrier having a regularly established business for carrying all or certain articles, and especially if that carrier be a corporation created for the purpose of the carrying trade, and the carriage of the article is embraced within the scope of its chartered powers, is a common carrier; that a special contract about its responsibility does not divest it of that character; that it cannot be permitted to stipulate for immunity for the negligence of its servants; that the business of a carrier is a public one, and those who employ the carrier have no real freedom of choice, and the carrier cannot be allowed to impose conditions adverse to public policy and morality; that freedom from liability for losses through sheer accident or dangers of navigation, which no human skill or vigilance can guard against, or for losses of money or valuable articles liable to be stolen or damaged, unless apprised of their character or value, or for like cases, is just and reasonable, and may be stipulated for, but that a public carrier cannot stipulate for exemptions which are unreasonable and improper, and which amount to an abdication of the essential duties of his employment; that a stipulation for exemption from liability for negligence is not just or reasonable; that a failure to exercise such care and diligence as are due from the carrier is negligence, and that the carrier remains liable for the negligence if the exemption stipulated for is unlawful.'

In such circumstances no surprise can be felt that the United States Government has been requested to move its Legislature to pass such an enactment as would, without the necessity of going to law in individual cases, protect the owners of goods from the desire of the shipowner to avoid his legal obligation.

And after detailing the already above referred to circumstances under which the Act of February 3, 1885, passed the House of Representatives at Washington, I continued:—

From this enactment it will be seen that the introduction of an international bill of lading is possible only if the principal objection to the Liverpool form, *i.e.* with regard to the non-liability of the shipowner for the negligence of the master and crew, is conceded. How little chance there has hitherto been of obtaining this object may be gathered from the lively discussions which have recently taken place on this subject at the meetings at Lloyd's, at the Baltic, and elsewhere in the city of London, and the different letters which have appeared in the public press since the month of February last.

I ought not to omit to state that Dr. Joh. Fr. Voigt at Hamburg, formerly a Judge at the High Court of Appeal in Leipzig, prepared an opinion for the last conference of German jurists on this subject, in which he upholds the contention, in which I fully concur, that it is not equitable to concede to the shipowner the much desired non-liability for the negligence of the master and crew.

As it can hardly be denied that at the present moment the laws of the whole world are identical on this subject, the surprise may easily be understood, which was generally felt, that the shipowners of this country had succeeded in carrying the Liverpool Bill of Lading.

There appears, at least in my opinion, to be no alternative but to reconsider the whole subject. In order, therefore, to facilitate this course of proceeding, I would suggest that a small committee of five gentlemen, viz. one shipowner, one merchant (not holding shipping property), one underwriter, one banker, and one lawyer should be elected by this conference for the purpose of considering the matter and reporting their recommendations at their earliest convenience.

The conference will then be able to base their further resolutions upon what may be justly called equitable recommendations.

I should further mention that very serious objections have been raised to the present forms of the bills of lading in general. It has been observed that it is not only inconvenient, but utterly impossible for any individual, whether he be the shipper of the goods or his underwriter, or the banker with whom he wants to negotiate a loan on depositing the bill of lading as security, to read and examine its contents. It has been suggested that the bill of lading in its original short form should be restored, and should contain simply a reference to a code of Rules of Affreightment in precisely the same way as is done in policies of insurance to the York and Antwerp General Average Rules. It would be the duty of your committee to draw up such a code, which might be styled 'International Affreightment and Bills of Lading Rules.'

By adopting this course the same object would be attained as the parties interested now have in contemplation, namely, the uniformity of the conditions under which bills of lading are to be issued by the shipowner, received by the owner of the goods, and dealt with by him in his transactions with his underwriter and with his banker; while there would be the additional advantage that it would be easy to detect and correct in such a short document any misprint, which in any document of the length of the Liverpool Bill of Lading, would be practically impossible.

With regard to the proposition contained in the report, that a small committee should be appointed to consider and report on the subject, I stated that, having had the opportunity, since my arrival at Hamburg, of conferring with several members and delegates, and finding that nearly all those present at the conference were specially interested in this question, I desired to withdraw the proposal, and to suggest instead that the conference itself proceed at once with the discussion of the subject.

THE PRESIDENT observed that a modification of the Liverpool Bill of Lading had been prepared by DR. STUBBS, as secretary of the committee, with a view of its forming a basis for the discussions of the conference. But as this form was not yet in print, and could not be distributed to the members of the Association until to-morrow morning, he proposed that for the present, in order to avoid any loss of time, the Rules of Affreightment prepared by the Hamburg Chamber of Commerce, which had already been printed for distribution amongst the members of the conference, should be taken as the basis of discussion. This proposal was adopted by the conference. The following are the rules prepared by the Hamburg Chamber of Commerce :—

RULES PROPOSED BY THE HAMBURG CHAMBER OF COMMERCE CONCERNING BILLS OF LADING.

RULE 1.—It shall not be lawful to insert in the bill of lading any clause, covenant, or agreement, whereby the obligations of owners to properly equip, man, provision, and outfit the vessel, and to render her seaworthy and capable of performing her intended voyage, or whereby the liability of owners for the faults or negligence of their servants in all matters relating to the ordinary course of the voyage, such as the stowage and right delivery of the cargo and other matters of this kind, shall in any wise be lessened, weakened or avoided; and all provisions and clauses to the contrary shall be null and void and of no effect in law.

Rule 2.—Owners to be exempt from the perils of the seas, fire, enemies, pirates, assailing thieves, barratry (but not common theft), arrest and restraint of princes, rulers, and peoples; and not answerable for losses by collisions, stranding, and all other accidents of navigation, even though the loss from these may be attributable to some wrongful act, fault, neglect, or error in judgment of the pilot, master, mariners, or other servants of the shipowner, nor for losses through explosion, bursting of boilers, breakage of shafts, or any latent defect in hull or machinery (not resulting in either case from unseaworthiness nor from want of due diligence by the owner of the ship or by the ship's husband or manager); nor for decay, putrefaction, rust, sweat, change of character, drainage, leakage, breakage, land damage, or any other damage arising from the nature of the goods shipped or the insufficiency of package; nor for the obliteration of marks, numbers, addresses, or descriptions of goods shipped; nor for any damage or loss caused by the prolongation of the voyage.

Rule 3.—Ship to be at liberty to call at any intermediate ports, to sail without pilots, to tow and assist vessels in distress, and to deviate for the purpose of saving life or property; also with liberty, in case the ship shall put into a port of refuge for repairs, to tranship the goods to their destination by any other steamship; and with liberty to convey goods in lighters to and from the ship at shipper's risk, but at ship's expense.

Rule 4.—Quality-marks, if any, to be of the same size as and contiguous to the leading marks; and if inserted in the shipping notes accepted by the mate, the master is bound to sign bills of lading conformable thereto.

Rule 5.—Ship not accountable for gold, silver, bullion, specie, documents, jewellery, works of art, or other valuables, unless bills of lading are signed therefor with the value therein expressed and a special agreement is made.

Rule 6.—Shippers accountable for any loss or damage to ship or cargo caused by inflammable, explosive, or dangerous goods, shipped without full disclosure of their nature, whether such shipper shall have been aware of it or not, and whether such shipper be principal or agent; such goods may be thrown overboard or destroyed by the master or owner of the ship at any time without compensation.

RULE 7.—All fines or damages which the ship or cargo may incur or suffer by reason of incorrect or insufficient marking of packages or description of their contents, shall be paid by the shipper or consignee, and the ship shall have a lien on the goods of such shipper or consignee for the amount thereof.

RULE 8.—Goods delivered to the ship, whilst on quay awaiting shipment, to be at shipper's risk, as regards all the perils excepted in these rules, except in cases where such goods are detained awaiting shipment for the convenience of the shipowner.

RULE 9.—Goods once shipped cannot be taken away by the shipper except upon payment of full freight and compensation for any damages sustained by the owners through such taking away.

RULE 10.—In case the ship shall be prevented from reaching her destination by quarantine, blockade, ice, or the hostile act of any power, the master or owners may discharge the goods into any depôt or lazaretto, or at the nearest convenient port; all expenses thereby incurred upon the goods to be borne by the owners or receivers thereof.

RULE 11.—Full freight is due on damaged goods.

RULE 12.—If the goods be not taken by the consignee immediately on landing, or within such further time as is provided by the regulations of the port of discharge, they may be stored or discharged into hulks or lighters by the master at the expense and risk of their owners; provided always, that public notice is given of the arrival of the ship and the commencement of the discharge, and that the same does not begin at night, or at any unreasonable hour.

RULE 13.—Ship to have a lien on all goods for payment of freight and charges, including back freight, demurrage, forwarding charges, and charges for carriage to port of shipment, and to be entitled to recover from the shipper the difference between the amount of freight stipulated in the bill of lading and the proceeds of the goods, should the consignee neglect or refuse to receive them.

RULE 14.—To the extent of the value of the lien, freight, which by the terms of the bill of lading is made payable by the consignee, cannot be demanded from the shipper after the master has parted with his lien on the goods.

RULE 15.—In the event of claims for short delivery when the ship reaches her destination, the price to be the market price at the port of destination on the day of the ship's entry at the custom-house, less all charges saved.

RULE 16.—Weight, measure, quality, contents, and value, although mentioned in the bill of lading, to be considered as unknown to the master, unless expressly recognised and agreed to the contrary.

RULE 17.—General Average to be paid according to York-Antwerp Rules.

RULE 18.—Freight to be paid on delivery in cash, without discount, at the rate of exchange of bankers' bills at sight current on the day of the ship's entry at the custom-house.

HERR JACOB AHLERS, one of the delegates of the Hamburg Chamber of Commerce, explained the grounds upon which that body had proceeded in framing the rules now before the conference. The Chamber would on no account relieve the shipowner from responsibility for seaworthiness, the equipment of the ship, stowage of the cargo, and so forth, but they considered it unjust to hold him responsible for the ability and skill of the crew. No tradesman dealing on a large scale would undertake such responsibility for his staff. The shipowner would certainly do his utmost to make a good selection as regards the captain and the crew; he would have to see that, even in foreign ports, the equipment and stowage are well done, but, on the other hand, it would be absolutely impossible, in view of the present rapidity of communication, for him to make a selection with regard to the crew. He would cite, as an illustration, carriage by post and railway, in which, although certainly responsibility was undertaken, it was only on payment of a high premium; and under such conditions possibly shipowners also might be induced to undertake the liability. The rules of the Hamburg Chamber would make them responsible for everything that could in justice be required of him, but not for the acts of men over whose action it was absolutely impossible for an owner to exercise control. When even the Post Office and the railway, notwithstanding their numerous staff, are unable to supervise every action, how could the shipowner be in a position to assume the responsibility? He concluded by recommending the rules to the consideration of the conference.

The general secretary then read the following extract from a letter received from Mr. Richard Lowndes, of Liverpool, who was prevented by ill-health from taking part in the conference. The letter was dated August 7, 1885 :—

'With regard to the reform of the law and practice of this country as to the bill of lading, I can state with confidence that there is already a great change in the feeling of the steamship-owning companies of Liverpool since the time when your Association met in Liverpool. At that time their opposition to our proposals—or at least the opposition of a large party amongst them—was the great difficulty in our way. Now, I believe— very likely to a great extent from the fear of a still stronger measure threatened by Mr. Chamberlain—many of those steamship owners who were then most hostile have come round to see that we were really their best friends, and will now support us. The Committee of Lloyd's also are taking action in what is likely to prove the same direction.

'There is, however, a certain pause or suspense, and we hardly know how to take action until the Royal Commission on Shipping has issued its report, and Mr. Chamberlain has brought out his promised or threatened Bill. It would be truly wise, in my opinion, to utilise the respite thus offered to the shipowners, by their voluntarily proposing a well-considered reform of the bill of lading. We may fairly hope that the discussion of the subject at Hamburg may operate as a stimulus to this, perhaps by the appointment of a fresh committee. Our bill of lading was certainly too long and cumbrous, but the leading principles of it have, I think, met with general acceptance.'

The following resolutions, adopted by the Chamber of Commerce of Lübeck, were also presented to the conference by the delegates of that Chamber, and distributed to those present, but were not formally moved, in view of the direction taken by the discussion :—

GENERAL LAW OF AFFREIGHTMENT AND BILLS OF LADING.

'1. It is not feasible to include all or all the more important principles concerning the law of Affreightment within the space of the form of a bill of lading, as the number of the provisions which would be required is too great, and the length of the bill of lading must necessarily be limited, in order to secure an easy survey of its contents.

'2. The form of bill of lading hitherto generally used, which contains only the necessary particulars as to the parties, the objects of the contract, and the contract itself, together with the sundry provisions necessary for the case in question, suffices in practice, because the principles which govern the law of Affreightment are fixed by law or custom, and are known to all parties concerned so far as it is necessary.

'3. The wish to abolish the differences which now exist in the law of Affreightment of the different maritime countries can only be realised, in case the legislative powers or the Governments of the maritime countries authorise competent delegates familiar with maritime interests, and particularly owners, merchants, underwriters, and jurists, to deliberate and agree on the draft of a code of maritime law.

'4. Besides such international code of maritime law, it will always be necessary to provide clauses for particular species of shipping as to the mutual rights and duties of the parties concerned, which clauses in every case must be stipulated by those concerned according to circumstances and equity. These provisions, which may exist at the side of the general law or alter the same, are to be incorporated in the bill of lading or to be quoted only, in case their length should make that necessary. A common form of bill of lading suiting all purposes cannot be framed.

'5. The present attempt on the part of shipowners to render, by a common form of bill of lading, the shipowners in future no longer liable for the faults of their servants cannot be approved of, as it would constitute an anomaly in maritime and commercial law.

'The liberty to call at any ports in any order, to sail without pilots, to tow and assist vessels in distress, and to deviate for the purpose of saving property, is not to be granted by general clauses in a common form of bill of lading.'

The conference then proceeded with the discussion of the Hamburg Rules, which were read, one by one, by the General Secretary.

On Rule 1, DR. RAHUSEN (Amsterdam) objected to the limitation of the owners' liability to 'matters relating to the ordinary course of the voyage,' and considered that the wording of this part of the rule was by no means clear.

HERR AHLERS defended the rule, though willing to have the wording modified so as to make the meaning clearer.

CONSUL H. H. MEIER preferred, on this point, the wording of the model bill of lading prepared by the New York Produce Exchange, and approved by the Liverpool Steamship Owners' Association, which he read. He wished to defend the shipowners against the attacks now directed against them. Their position was a very different one from that of the railways, which were monopolies, but a shipowner could not by any means be said to possess a monopoly. The effect of imposing liability upon shipowners for the negligence of their officers and crew, whose conduct whilst at sea and in foreign ports it was impossible for them effectively to control, would be to render it impossible for them to carry on their business. It was only of late times that it had been attempted to make them liable in such cases, and it was not until they had been made to suffer heavily, for acts which they were powerless to prevent, that the great steamship companies had sought to protect themselves by clauses in their bills of lading. When, at the Liverpool conference, what he thought to be unreasonable claims on the part of the shipowners had been advanced and sanctioned by the conference, he had protested, feeling sure that such one-sided decisions would not take effect in practice. Now he desired to urge upon the representatives of the shippers, in their turn, the danger and impolicy of going too far in the opposite direction; if they insisted on doing so, no mutual understanding would ever be arrived at.

DR. VOIGT argued against the right of shipowners to exempt themselves from liability for losses due to negligence.

HERR ULRICH considered the clause as to liability for insufficient packing, &c., to be by no means clear.

HERR AHLERS explained that it was not intended on this point to deviate from the common law.

After some further discussion, in which DR. STAMMANN, DR. MÒNCKEBERG, MR. LAEISZ, DR. RAHUSEN and I took part, the conference unanimously adopted the following portions of the first rule:—

'It shall not be lawful to insert in the bill of lading any clause, covenant, or agreement whereby the obligations of owners to properly equip, man, provision, and outfit the vessel, and to render her seaworthy and capable of performing her intended voyage . . . shall in any wise be lessened, weakened, or avoided; and all provisions and clauses to the contrary shall be null and void, and of no effect in law.'

The clause after 'voyage,' 'or whereby the liabilities of owners for the faults or negligence of their servants in . . . the right delivery of the cargo, and other matters of this kind,' was also adopted by a large majority. The words 'stowage and,' before 'right delivery,' were then adopted by a unanimous vote. The remainder of the rule (consisting of the words 'all matters relating to the ordinary course of the voyage, such as'), giving rise to great difference of opinion, was postponed for further consideration at the next sitting. The conference then adjourned.

On Wednesday, August 19, the conference reassembled at 10 A.M., the President (Dr. Sieveking) in the chair.

The draft bill of lading prepared by Dr. Stubbs, as secretary of the Bill of Lading Committee, was now presented, and copies distributed to the members. It was as follows:—

Model Bill of Lading.

Shipped on board the ship   whereof is master for the present voyage   , now lying in the port of
and bound for   ,   , being marked and numbered as per margin, to be carried and delivered at the port of   , or so near thereto as the ship and goods can be safely brought, unto the holder of this bill of lading, on his paying freight for the said goods at the rate of   .
laydays for loading and discharging, demurrage at the rate of   per day.

Subject to all the conditions of the International Code of Affreightment.

Average according to the York and Antwerp Rules. In witness whereof the master of the said ship has signed two bills of lading exclusive of his own copy, all of this tenor and date, one of which being accomplished the others to stand void.

Dated at   ,   188 .

(Signed)   *Master*.

To this was attached the following draft:—

International Code of Affreightment.

I.

The shipowner is responsible for the safety and right delivery of the cargo at the port of discharge, unless the loss, damage, or non-delivery is directly caused by any of the following perils: reasonable wear and tear of packages or goods; leakage, breakage, heat, or decay; the act of God, the Queen's enemies, pirates or robbers by land or sea, the act, neglect, or default of the master or crew in navigating the vessel; and accidents of the sea.

II.

The shipowner is liable for all loss caused to the owner of the cargo by any unreasonable delay in carrying and delivering the cargo.

An unusual delay is to be considered unreasonable unless caused by—

'The act of God, the Queen's enemies, or pirates or robbers by sea or land;

'The act, neglect, or default of the master or crew in navigating the vessel, accidents of the sea, restraint of princes, rulers or peoples;

Detention in consequence of blockade, quarantine, or ice.'

III.

Full freight is to be paid upon all goods shipped, carried and delivered at the named place of delivery, or so near thereto as the same can be safely brought by the shipowner exercising all reasonable efforts and diligence.

The shipowner shall be considered to have fully exercised such efforts and diligence when the ship has been brought so near the place of delivery as she can come, and be always afloat at the first flood-time without lightening.

IV.

Freight shall be paid upon delivery of the cargo in current coin of the place of delivery, without discount, and shall be calculated at the same rate by which the named freight in the bill of lading could be purchased at that time and place.

Freight shall be payable upon the bill of lading quantities, unless either party, shipowner or consignee, before delivery intimate that he requires the cargo to be weighed or measured at the place of delivery.

In such case the owner or master and the consignee shall join in appointing one or more meters or weighers, whose decision as to the quantity delivered shall, in the absence of fraud, be final. The charge for such weighing or measuring shall be borne in moieties by the shipowner and the consignee.

No freight is due on any increase of bulk or weight caused by the absorption of water during the voyage.

Full freight is due upon all damaged goods delivered, unless the damage is caused by the negligence or default of the shipowner or his servants.

In case the ship shall be prevented from reaching her destination by quarantine, blockade, ice, or hostile act of any Power, the master may discharge the goods into any depôt or lazaretto at the nearest available port. All expenses incurred thereby upon the goods shall be borne by the shipper and consignee, and full freight shall thereupon be due.

Pro ratâ freight is payable in no case, except by special agreement.

V.

In case the cargo is carried to its destination and the consignee refuses to accept delivery, the cargo may be landed by the master and warehoused, and twenty-four hours after written notice to such effect has been given to the shipper or consignee, may be sold by the master or owner of the ship. All landing, warehousing, and sale charges shall be payable by the shipper and consignee.

VI.

All charges incurred in shipping cargo, before the cargo is placed on board or taken to by the ship's tackle, and in landing cargo after it has left the ship's side and tackle, shall be borne by the shipper and consignee of the cargo.

VII.

In the event of claims for short delivery, the damages payable by the shipowner shall be the market price of similar goods at the port of destination on the day of the ship's reporting at the customhouse, less all charges saved, if the ship reaches her destination; and if the ship does not reach her destination, then the market price of the goods at the port of shipment, plus ten per cent. to cover prospective profits, and interest calculated at five per cent. per annum on this gross amount from the day of shipment until payment, less the average length of the voyage.

VIII.

The shipowner shall be liable for all dues upon the ship, and the shipper and consignee for all dues upon the cargo.

The shipper and consignee shall be liable to pay or make good to the shipowner all fines and damages incurred or paid by the shipowner, by reason of incorrect or insufficient marking, or description of the cargo, or otherwise by neglect or default of shipper, consignee, or owner of the cargo.

IX.

Laydays at the port of loading shall commence on the day the ship is reported inwards at the custom-house, if before midday, or the loading commence on that day, and on the following day, if after midday, and the loading do not commence on that day.

Laydays or demurrage days at the place of discharge shall commence on the day the ship is reported inwards at the custom-house, if before midday, or the unloading commence on that day, and on the following day, if after midday, and the unloading do not commence on that day.

Laydays or days on demurrage shall continue to count, up to and including the days on which the loading and discharging of the cargo is finally concluded.

The days both for laydays and for demurrage days shall be consecutive days, without any allowance for non-working days, unless the working has been discontinued solely by the default of the master or crew of the ship.

A day for the purpose of calculating laydays or days on demurrage shall count from midnight to midnight, and the first and last days if part or broken days shall count as whole days.

X.

The shipowner shall have a lien upon the cargo and the proceeds thereof, if justifiably sold by him or his agents, for all freight, demurrage, and other charges and damages herein made payable by the shipper and consignee of the cargo.

XI.

In the course of the voyage, the ship is to be at liberty to call at any intermediate, but not other ports, to sail without pilots, to tow and assist vessels in distress, and to deviate for the purpose of saving life or property.

XII.

In case the ship shall put into a port of refuge for repairs, the master shall be at liberty, at ship's expense, to tranship the goods to their destination, and thereby earn full freight.

Copies of the New York Produce Exchange Bill of Lading [1] were also distributed.

THE PRESIDENT stated that the discussion would now proceed upon the basis of this form, the decisions arrived at yesterday being incorporated in it.

The form of bill of lading having been adopted without comment, subject to revision, Rule 1 of the draft 'International Code of Affreightment' was read.

RESPONSIBILITY FOR NEGLIGENCE.

I proposed that the words 'the act, neglect, or default,' in the phrase 'act, neglect, or default of the master or crew in navigating the vessel,' be omitted, and replaced by the words 'error of judgment.' Although I did not think it necessary to give all my reasons for doing so, I might state that the experience I had gained by my investigations into maritime casualties for many years past, enabled me to assure the conference that at least nine-tenths of all such disasters as strandings, collisions at sea, and so forth, were due to some neglect or other of the crew which might be prevented if due diligence were exercised. I therefore thought that for such 'neglect or default' the shipowner ought to be made answerable, but not for mere 'error of judgment.'

HERR ULRICH seconded this amendment.

DR. FRANCK was of opinion that the words in the draft rule, and those suggested to be substituted, should be alike omitted.

HERR AHLERS contended that it would be extremely difficult for the Courts, in inquiring into the causes of an accident, to istinguish where 'error of judgment' ended, and 'neglect or default' began. In cases of emergency the captain and steersman needed to summon all their energies; yet, even under such circum-

---

[1] See p. 395.

stances, they must depend entirely upon the reliability of the crew. He was of opinion that a decision in the sense of the amendment would be absolutely impossible to carry out, as shipowners would never accept it. If the conference wished to achieve a durable work, it should accept the clause as presented.

M. THÉODORE ENGELS also opposed the amendment, and considered it to be in the highest degree unreasonable. Being to a great extent his own insurer, he had the very strongest interest in getting the best captains and crew for his vessels, and in managing them so as to avoid all losses, but the responsibility proposed to be cast on shipowners by the amendment was one which he held to be unendurable.

I explained that I had expressly proposed to exempt the owner from liability for 'errors of judgment,' and I considered the difference between it and ' neglect or default' to be very clear.

HERR SUCKAU wished both expressions to be omitted.

DR. RAHUSEN considered that it would be by no means favourable to the shipping interest, in those cases in which it came into competition with railways, to drive to such an extent the exemption of shipowners from liability for the negligence of their servants. He also regretted their exemption from liability for default in the unloading of the vessel. He inquired whether the principles now to be laid down were to be considered solely as clauses suggested for a model bill of lading which might be accepted or rejected, or whether it would be understood that they were to be obligatory.

THE PRESIDENT replied that it must be considered that the rules on this question of liability for negligence would be obligatory. The question as to liability for damages in unloading could be taken up later.

DR. VOIGT was of opinion that the most serious cause of liability on the part of shipowners, collision, ought to be provided for by law, and that they should not be allowed arbitrarily to exclude it by private conventions. Besides, in most cases, the shipowner was only responsible to the value of his ship and freight. The consciousness of irresponsibility would certainly lead to much greater negligence. The shipowner would be able to cover his risk by an increased freight.

Consul H. H. Meier drew attention to the significance of the object sought to be attained—that of limiting the right of free contract between the shipowner and the shipper. It would in practice be impossible for the owner to undertake responsibility for his crew. The North German Lloyd, for example, of which he was chairman, employed 3,000 men, and how was it possible to undertake such a responsibility as would be cast upon them by this amendment? From a legal point of view it might sound very well, but practically it was unjust. Although he was speaking *quasi pro domo*, he must at the same time observe that his company were their own insurers and bore the entire risk themselves, so that they had the greatest interest in making the most careful selection of their crews. How could the shipowner in Europe be responsible for the Lascars, for instance, who were taken on board in the Indian archipelago as pilots because of their acquaintance with its intricate navigation? It was practically impossible to discharge such a responsibility; at the best it would be an embodiment of the maxim, *Fiat justitia pereat mundus*. It must be permitted to shipowners to exclude, by private convention, such an obligation.

Herr Steinacker stated that, as the delegate of the Chamber of Commerce of Buda-Pesth, he looked at the question essentially from the point of view of the shippers' interests. In Hungary the shipowning class was insignificant, so that their commerce depended almost entirely on the shipowners of other countries. The shippers in his country were unanimous in calling for an increase of the shipowners' liability. He desired, in fulfilment of his commission, to impress upon the conference the importance of not allowing the shipowners to go too far in limiting their liability towards the shippers. Hungary did not yet possess a commercial code, and the rules adopted by the Association would therefore be of great importance to them.

Herr Ahlers opposed the views both of Herr Suckau and of Consul Annecke. He considered the amendment before the meeting to be entirely unworkable and impracticable. If it were adopted it would be impossible to arrive at any of the amendments in the law which were most urgently required by all seafaring nations.

Herr Woermann entirely agreed with Consul Meier. If the amendment were adopted, shipowners would have to cover themselves by insurance for the whole value of the cargo, which was frequently many times more than that of the ship. This would impose upon them an inordinate burden. The shippers could insure the goods much better than the shipowners. Besides, not even the liability of the shipowners by English law would adequately protect the shippers' interests. The shipowner could only undertake responsibility for his crew to the extent agreed to by the conference yesterday; anything more would be impracticable and unjust.

Consul Preuss, on behalf of the Königsberg Chamber of Commerce, of which he was president, agreed with Consul Meier, that it would be impracticable for the shipowner to protect himself by insurance. He hoped the first rule would be adopted without alteration.

Judge Peabody expressed his regret at not having been able to follow the discussion that had taken place in German, and desired to be excused if on that account he should unconsciously repeat arguments that had already been urged. He wished to point out that, in the case of carriage by sea, the shipper was often in a condition to know very little of the qualifications of the carrier, the shipowner. Although he might be acquainted, by reputation or otherwise, with a few great corporations or firms engaged in business as carriers, yet in many cases great lines of shipowners, with whom he could have no practical acquaintance, would have a practical monopoly of the business, and he would have no alternative but to trust his property to them, and the property once in possession of the carrier was not only out of his control, but beyond his knowledge, and where, with his limited means of acquiring knowledge, it would be out of his power to learn what was done or left undone in respect to it; and this was the reason why the carrier had been usually held to very strict responsibility in respect of property entrusted to him. This rule, under the circumstances, would not seem to be unjust, or hostile to the best interests of society. The power is with the carrier, and on him should rest the responsibility. Great care should be taken in adopting measures which would tend to exempt the shipowner from responsibility, or greatly to diminish the responsibility to which he had hitherto usually been held. The goods might often be hundreds and even thousands of miles from the consignor, and in course of *transitus*, in places of which he had no knowledge, and in the care and control of the servants of the carrier, over whose selection he could exercise no influence, and of whose trustworthiness he could know nothing, but whose employment was by the shipowner, and whose trustworthiness should be known to him. It was therefore to the highest degree in the interests of society at large that those general principles of law should be applied, by which carriers are responsible for the due delivery of goods committed to their charge, and the responsibility would be only commensurate with the obligation. The question where to fix the precise line at which this responsibility should end was a difficult one; but in fixing the line it should be borne in mind that the carrier and his agents are on the spot, and that it is their duty and business to select the men who are to navigate the vessel and take charge of the property. The presumption of law should therefore be in favour of protecting the helpless against the powerful, those who are not in a position to look after their own interests against those who are, and we should be very slow to limit the carriers' liabilities. It is a universal principle of law, and is the law of nature, that every man is responsible for his own acts, and that every man who acts by another in effect acts by himself, is bound for the acts of the persons he employs—bound for their diligence, their honesty, and their capability. The carrier ought to be responsible, with very few exceptions, for that which he undertakes to do for the shipper, and this general rule was a very necessary one for the general interests of commerce. He hoped the conference would not thoughtlessly or lightly do anything to relax that responsibility.

In reply to the criticisms of my amendment, I said that it was not with regard to great companies, like the North German Lloyd and the Cunard, that such a provision was necessary: it was with regard to the innumerable smaller shipowners, owning only two or three steamers apiece. The carelessness with which these steamers were sometimes managed, especially in the selection of officers and crew, was simply indescribable, as I could testify from the experience of many years during which it had been my duty to investigate the causes of accidents. In England this was encouraged by the state of the law, by which vessels could be insured for far more than their real value, and of this I gave an illustration which had lately occurred in my own practice. I proposed that the vote should be taken on the general principle in question, leaving the precise wording of the rules to be dealt with by a committee to be subsequently appointed.

Consul Meier entreated the assembly not to pronounce a onesided judgment on the question: such a decision could not possibly lead to any result. He advocated the adoption of Rule I. of the Hamburg Chamber of Commerce.

Herr Laeisz also preferred the proposition contained in Rule I. of the Hamburg Chamber of Commerce. He pointed out that the shipowner's exemption from liability for unseaworthiness, in cases of latent defect, where he had done all that was reasonably possible to secure seaworthiness, was omitted from Rule I. of the form now under discussion.

The President said that the general principle was now under discussion: any question as to the form of the rules could be discussed afterwards.

M. Le Jeune supported my amendment. He pointed out that there had long been a limitation of the liability of carriers by sea as compared with carriers by land, it having been recognised by the legislation of all countries that the former could not be held responsible to the same extent as the latter, on account of the greater difficulty they had in controlling the actions of their servants. But it was necessary to distinguish between the different degrees of negligence on the part of the crew, between the *culpa lata* and the *culpa levis*. For the former the shipowner ought to be answerable, but it was reasonable that he should be allowed to contract himself out of liability for the latter. He accepted the amendment as a reasonable expression of this difference, and he thought it would be unreasonable to go further in making the shipowner liable. He stated that the most recent decisions of the Tribunal de Commerce at Antwerp had refused to recognise the validity of clauses in bills of lading by which shipowners had sought to protect themselves from responsibility for the negligence of their servants, on the ground that such an exemption was contrary to public policy.

DR. FRANCK considered that, from a legal point of view, 'error of judgment' was included in 'default,' and he held it to be illogical to attempt to separate the two. He repeated his opinion that the words 'act, neglect, or default,' should be altogether struck out.

THE PRESIDENT announced that he proposed in the first instance to put the question, 'Ought the shipowner to be allowed to protect himself, by a clause in the bill of lading, from liability for negligence on the part of the captain, officers, and crew?' and, secondly, if this should be carried in the negative, 'Ought he to be allowed to protect himself against errors of judgment on their part?' He at the same time repeated that the vote was only taken on the principle, *salva redactione*. The vote on the first question showed a majority of 24 votes to 17 in favour of the proposition that the shipowner be not allowed to protect himself against negligence. The second question, whether the shipowner should be allowed to protect himself against errors of judgment, having then been put, was decided in the affirmative by a majority of 23 to 7.

Rule 1 of the committee's draft Code of Affreightment was then passed, the words 'error of judgment' having been substituted for 'act, neglect, or default,' and the words 'the Queen's,' having been struck out before 'enemies.'

On Rule 2, HERR AHLERS thought it important that the word 'fire' should be inserted, as, according to English law, fire was not considered a 'peril of the sea.'

I then proposed that, before going further with the discussion, the conference should appoint a small committee consisting of the President, Herren Ahlers and Duncker, Judge Peabody, and Dr. Rahusen, to settle the wording of the rules in conformity with the votes already taken, and to report to a future sitting.

DR. RAHUSEN suggested that the report should be presented to the next conference of the Association, in a year's time, so as to afford opportunity for a deliberate and careful revision.

I informed the meeting that I thought the committee, if now appointed, would be able to bring in its report on Friday.

THE PRESIDENT supported my proposal.

HERR LAEISZ pointed out that there were still a number of important questions of principle to be discussed, as, for instance, that of *pro ratâ* freight, and thought it would be premature now to appoint a committee of revision.

I replied that, on the question of *pro ratâ* freight, the decision of the Berne conference [1] must be taken as conclusive, and that this subject could not now be reopened.

CONSUL MEIER supported the proposition of Dr. Rahusen.

M. ENGELS reminded the assembly that at Liverpool it had been found possible to go through all the points one by one.

My proposition was then put to the vote and rejected by a large majority.

The discussion on Rule 2 having accordingly been resumed,

HERR ULRICH objected to the retention of the word 'ice' in the rule.

HERR LAEISZ then proposed that the discussion on this subject be adjourned till to-morrow morning; the conference meanwhile proceeding with its other business, as the code now under discussion had been only recently placed in the hands of members.

HERR AHLERS asked whether the committee had prepared any statement of reasons in support of the code, there being no one present to state the reasons on behalf of the committee.

I explained that the code had been prepared, on behalf of the committee, by its secretary, Dr. Stubbs, who was unfortunately prevented from being present.

HERR AHLERS then proposed that the discussion should proceed on the basis of the Hamburg Chamber of Commerce rules.

CONSUL MEIER was also in favour of this course, and of the adjournment of the debate.

It was accordingly agreed that the debate should be adjourned,

[1] See note at p. 329.

On Thursday, August 20, the conference reassembled at 10 A.M., Dr. Sieveking presiding, when the discussion on bills of lading was resumed, and the President suggested that it should be resumed on the basis of the rules prepared by the Hamburg Chamber of Commerce, as this seemed to be the wish of most of the members.

HERR LAEISZ desired, as Dr. Stubbs's draft appeared now to be laid aside, to propose that the conference should not be considered in any way prejudiced by the decisions of yesterday. Otherwise a false impression would be produced outside as to the result of the conference's labours.

THE PRESIDENT, however, stated that the votes taken yesterday must be considered decisive. Only questions of principle would at the present stage be voted upon; all questions merely affecting the precise wording of the rules, or their consistency *inter se*, and with the resolutions previously arrived at, being referred to a committee of revision, to be appointed later on.

On Rule 2 of the Hamburg Chamber of Commerce draft, DR. RAHUSEN asked for an elucidation of the phrase 'common theft.' An explanation having been given by the President, the matter was left for the consideration of the committee.

HERR ULRICH pointed out the importance of observing the difference between the various causes of fire, which might be occasioned by *vis major*, by negligence, or by error of judgment. He also thought the expression 'land damage' by no means sufficiently clear.

HERR AHLERS explained that 'land damage' was intended to mean such as would not be externally discoverable.

DR. WOLFFSON thought 'land damage' should be omitted. 'Barratry' would also have to be omitted, in accordance with the decision arrived at yesterday. And at the end of the rule words should be added to the expression 'prolongation of the voyage' to show that its prolongation by sea was meant. The word 'unseaworthiness' also was too general.

DR. FRANCK wished the insertion of the word 'unless' instead of 'even though' after 'accidents of navigation.'

The conference agreed, without a division, to the omission of the words 'land damage.' The other points raised by different speakers were left to the committee of revision, and the rule was passed, subject to such revision.

On Rule 3, CONSUL MEIER desired the substitution of the words 'any other vessel' for 'any other steamship,' as he thought the shipowner ought to have liberty to tranship into a sailing ship, for the completion of the voyage, if no steamer was available.

HERR AHLERS explained that the rule under discussion was only intended to apply to steamers.

HERR ULRICH pointed out that the rule differed from the second paragraph of the New York Produce Exchange Bill of Lading, by the insertion of 'liberty to call at any intermediate ports,' which he thought ought not to be permitted. Such a permission ought only to be given by a special clause in special cases, not by the common form.

HERR AHLERS replied that in this respect the rule was intermediate between that of the New York Produce Exchange and that of the Liverpool conference, under which the permission was not confined to 'intermediate' ports. As a matter of fact, the great lines made no use of this permission, but the owners of general steamers would always require its insertion.

DR. RAHUSEN objected to the vagueness of the word 'intermediate,' and wished the clause struck out.

HERR AHLERS pointed out, in reply, that it was often impossible for the owner of a general ship to know beforehand at what intermediate ports his vessel would call, as this would depend upon the cargo he might be able to secure. A decision to strike out the permission would have no practical result, as it would be necessary always to insert the clause.

CONSUL MEIER hoped the clause would be retained, and pointed out its practical utility. He did not think there would be any real difficulty in determining what was an intermediate port. Thus, on a voyage from Sydney to Hamburg, Antwerp would, but Trieste would not, be an intermediate port.

DR. RAHUSEN explained that he did not wish to prohibit such a liberty where there was some reason for inserting it; but, unless it were expressly reserved, the shipper ought to be entitled to assume that the ship would sail direct to the port of destination.

THE PRESIDENT pointed out that the rules were not intended all to be obligatory, but that, according to the matters to which they related, some would necessarily be optional, so as to take effect only in the absence of agreement to the contrary.

M. ENGELS thought no shipowner would order his ship to call at any intermediate port without some sufficient reason. He desired the retention of the clause.

DR. FRANCK seconded Herr Ulrich's motion entirely to omit the liberty of calling on the voyage, which was, however, lost by a large majority; only 7 votes being recorded in its favour.

DR. RAHUSEN'S motion to omit the words 'intermediate ports,' having been seconded by HERR ULRICH, was then put, and was also rejected by a large majority, only 6 voting for it.

DR. VOIGT proposed the omission of the words 'to sail without pilots,' on the ground that such a liberty would be contrary to the law, which in many cases imposed penalties on vessels sailing without pilots, and also contrary to public policy.

In reply to the President, DR. VOIGT said he did not wish that the conference should adopt a resolution prohibiting the insertion of such a power, but he desired that it should not be contained in the model rules to be adopted.

CONSUL MEIER pointed out that the captains of liners were often as well acquainted with the navigation of the coasts they were accustomed to as any pilot; as, for instance, in the case of steamers crossing every week between London and Hamburg. In cases like this, practical considerations should override the letter of the law. Often, when a pilot could not be found at the mouth of the Elbe, a Heligolander was taken on board as pilot, and this, in the speaker's opinion, was really more dangerous than to sail without a pilot at all.

HERR AHLERS was of the same opinion. It was not merely a question as to the prescriptions of German law, which were certainly very clear and express, but as to those of other States. He referred particularly to a decision of the highest tribunal in England, which had held that under certain circumstances it was not an act of negligence to sail without pilots.

DR. RAHUSEN agreed with Dr. Voigt. So far as regular liners were concerned he could agree with Herr Meier, but the rules now under consideration were intended for all kinds of ships, and under such a clause other vessels, whose captains were not similarly qualified, would have a dangerous liberty conferred upon them. He seconded the amendment.

HERR AD. WOERMANN objected to the amendment, and pointed out that pilotage was not everywhere compulsory by law. In many parts of the world there were no pilots to be had, whilst on the African coast and in the East Indies they were generally natives, who did not at all answer to European ideas of a pilot, and to whom it would be out of the question to commit the supreme direction of the vessel. In the waters of civilised countries the captain was already compelled by law to employ pilots, and in other places it was often very difficult to ascertain whether any real pilots, in the European sense, were to be had. He wished the clause to be retained.

I also opposed the amendment, which I considered contrary to the spirit of the previous day's decision, but I thought it should be made clear that it would be negligence not to employ a pilot, whenever, under all the circumstances of the case, it was proper to do so.

DR. WOLFFSON reminded the conference that the clause under consideration would only apply to the relation between the shipowner and the shipper or cargo-owner. It would, of course, be impossible for the shipowner to liberate himself from liability in his relations with the public at large, by means of a clause in his bill of lading. The meaning of the clause he understood to be that the fact of not having employed a pilot should not, of itself, be considered as proof of default on the part of the captain.

HERR AHLERS pointed out that the clause was supported by the German law, which does not in all cases impose the necessity of pilotage.

DR. VOIGT, in reply, defended his amendment, which was rejected by a large majority, only 5 voting for it.

Dr. WOLFFSON then proposed that the revision committee should be instructed to add to the rule words distinctly showing its meaning to be that it should not be considered negligence not to take a pilot unless the particular circumstances of the case required it.

HERR MEIER seconded the proposal, which was adopted by 18 votes to 17. Rule 3 was then adopted, subject to this modification.

Rule 4 was passed without objection.

On Rule 5, HERR ULRICH asked whether by this clause, in accordance with the German Commercial Code, a declaration of both the value and the nature of the articles would be required.

HERR AHLERS having replied in the affirmative, the rule was adopted *nem. con.*

On Rule 6, HERR ULRICH did not consider the rule went far enough, as it ought to be extended so as to provide against the danger to other goods shipped in the same vessel.

HERR AHLERS thought that such protection was already given by the legislation of every country, and need not be put into the bill of lading, which constituted a contract only between the shipowner and the shipper of goods.

I thought it should be required that dangerous goods be clearly marked as such on the outside, and suggested that the committee should consider the wording of the rule with this view.

HERR WOERMANN was of the same opinion, but thought the words 'shipped with full disclosure of their nature' sufficiently covered the point.

HERR ULRICH's proposition was withdrawn, and the rule passed, subject to revision.

On Rule 7, DR. RAHUSEN pointed out that it was not sufficiently clearly expressed that the shipowner was entitled to pay the amount of fines or damages, and claim reimbursement from the consignee, or, failing payment by him, from the shipper. The observation was referred to the committee of revision, and the rule adopted.

On Rule 8, DR. STAMMANN (Hamburg) objected to the form of the rule, and desired the addition of words to show that the date of signature of the bill of lading was the moment from which the shipowner's responsibility for the goods would begin and the shipper's would cease.

HERR AHLERS objected to such an addition, and pointed out that bills of lading often had to be ante-dated or post-dated.

DR. STAMMANN replied that he did not object to the rule of German law on the subject, but contended that it was at all events necessary to lay down in the rule that the bill of lading could not be signed, so as to make the shipowner liable, before loading began.

CONSUL PREUSS opposed the addition, which would be entirely inapplicable to the custom at Königsberg, by which cargoes are loaded from lighters. Such an addition would run counter to everyday practice.

DR. RAHUSEN agreed with Herr Ahlers. Bills of lading ought, above all things, to be strictly truthful, and such an addition as proposed would often be opposed to the facts of the case. In Holland the expression in use was, 'Received, for the purpose of being loaded.'

The amendment was not put, for want of a seconder, and the rule was adopted.

Rules 9 and 10 were passed, the latter subject to some observations with regard to the precise wording.

On Rule 11, HERR SUCKAU thought the rule unnecessary. He inquired whether, in conformity with German law, full freight would be payable for liquids absorbed by the remainder of the cargo.

HERR AHLERS said that there was a diversity in the laws of different countries on this point, and the Chamber of Commerce had decided against adopting the rule of German law.

DR. FRANCK proposed the addition of the words 'liquids excepted.'

M. ENGELS inquired whether full freight was also to be paid on grains and other goods which had increased in weight by the absorption of moisture. To him, as a shipowner, such a provision could only be agreeable.

HERR AHLERS stated that the rules were purposely silent on this point, as it was a question to be decided on the facts of each particular case. The object of the rule was simply to exclude the right of abandonment of damaged goods given by the German law.

THE PRESIDENT thought it would be desirable to lay it down distinctly that the right of abandonment of damaged goods for freight is excluded, and would, if the rule were adopted, direct the committee to revise it in this sense.

HERR SUCKAU having proposed that the right of abandonment of damaged goods against freight be retained, which was seconded by Dr. Franck, this proposal was rejected by 21 votes against 11, and the principle of the rule, as stated by the President, was accepted.

Rule 12 was adopted without discussion.

On Rule 13, HERR ULRICH considered that the lien ought also to extend to contributions in respect of General Average, and desired that a clause to this effect should be added to the rule.

HERR AHLERS expressed approval of this suggestion.

M. ENGELS also supported the proposal.

The proposition was accepted, and referred to the committee to carry out.

On Rule 14, M. ENGELS thought there was some inconsistency between it and Rule 13, but on explanations being given, the rule was adopted.

On Rule 15, DR. RAHUSEN thought some indication should be inserted as to the mode of ascertaining the market price at the port of destination.

HERR AHLERS thought this must be left to the laws of the different countries in which the valuation would have to be made.

DR. RAHUSEN suggested the insertion, for the sake of clearness, of the words 'freight and' before 'all charges saved.' The suggestion was unanimously accepted, and the rule passed with this modification.

On Rule 16, DR. RAHUSEN asked what was the precise meaning to be attached to the words 'unless expressly recognised.'

HERR AHLERS replied that the effect of the clause 'weight, measure, quality, contents, and value unknown' was to shift the burden of proof, and it was thought necessary to show that the presumption in favour of the shipowner was not to be rebutted by the mere fact that they were mentioned in the bill of lading. On the other hand, the parties were to remain free to enter into a special contract.

Dr. Franck thought the whole clause ought to be omitted.

Dr. Gensel stated that merchants residing inland complained greatly of this clause, which often stood in the way of their obtaining redress for losses sustained by them. He desired that captains should be compelled to measure and weigh goods delivered to them.

Herr Ahlers replied to Dr. Franck that the rule only expressed a stipulation which had already become universal. No shipowner would be willing, considering the different countries in which goods were received, to undertake the responsibility for weight, &c.

Dr. Franck's proposal to omit the rule was seconded by Herr Suckau, but was lost, only 3 voting for it.

Dr. Gensel thereupon declined to make a formal motion in support of his view.

Herr Steinacker expressed his accord with Dr. Gensel's views, and desired that a resolution embodying them should be adopted.

Herr Woermann pointed out that captains had not usually time to undertake such duties as were proposed to be cast upon them. He strongly opposed the idea.

The rule was then adopted without further objection.

On Rule 17, Dr. Franck preferred its omission, on the ground that the York-Antwerp Rules were often equivocal.

I replied to this objection, but for want of a seconder the motion was not put, and the rule was adopted.

On Rule 18, Dr. Rahusen remarked that the words 'freight to be paid on delivery' ought not to exclude the right of stipulating for post-payment of freight.

Herr Woermann wished the insertion of words making it permissible to stipulate in the bill of lading for payment in any currency therein indicated.

Herr Ahlers replied to Dr. Rahusen that the words ' on

delivery' were only intended to negative the English custom, by which a fortnight or a month was often allowed for payment of freight.

HERR WOERMANN'S proposal was accepted, and the rule was passed, subject to an addition to that effect to be made by the committee.

Pro Ratâ Freight.

The rules having thus been completed, HERR AHLERS said the Hamburg Chamber of Commerce had decided not to insert any provision with regard to *pro ratâ* freight, but simply to raise the question whether such a provision should be introduced by the conference or not. In case the conference should desire to insert any such provision, he would recommend its adoption of Rules 10 and 11 of the form adopted by the Liverpool conference.[1]

DR. RAHUSEN thought it inadvisable to discuss the question at present.

DR. WOLFFSON was also decidedly opposed to its discussion, which he thought impracticable at the present conference.

I hoped the conference would decide that *pro ratâ* freight ought not to be allowed at all, and drew attention to the decision to that effect of the Berne conference.[2]

---

[1] The following are the rules referred to :—

10. If the ship is able to carry the goods to their destination, but the goods, by reason of damage sustained or of their own nature, are not fit to be carried all the way, and if such goods have received an enhancement of value by reason of their partial carriage, the ship shall be entitled to a *pro ratâ* freight in proportion to the distance performed, which freight is in no case to exceed the amount of such enhancement of value. *Pro ratâ* freight is admissible in no other case than that dealt with in the preceding sentence, unless there be an acceptance of the goods by the shipper or owner of the goods.

11. When the goods are fit to be carried to their destination, but the ship is unable to carry them, the shipowner may earn full freight by sending the goods to their destination at his own expense within reasonable time in another bottom: this right is not affected by an abandonment of the ship by her crew or to the underwriters: and the ship is to be, for this purpose, deemed unable to carry the goods to their destination, if she either cannot be repaired at all, or cannot be repaired except at an expense exceeding her value when repaired.

[2] The following resolution was adopted at the Berne conference of the Association, 1880 ('Report,' pp. 124 to 127) by 15 votes against 3 :—

'That freight *pro ratâ itineris peracti* should be abolished.'

HERR SUCKAU was opposed to the introduction of a rule on *pro ratâ* freight, as he feared that its insertion might prove a hindrance to the general adoption of the rules.

HERR LAEISZ was also opposed to such a rule, and pointed out that the Berne resolution, referred to by Dr. Wendt, could no longer be considered binding, as the Liverpool conference had come to a contrary decision.

The question whether any rule on the subject should be inserted having been put to the conference by the President, only two votes were given in favour of that course, and the subject accordingly dropped.

RESPONSIBILITY FOR NEGLIGENCE.

CONSUL MEIER wished to make a suggestion, now that the rules had all been gone through, with the view of making them generally acceptable. He thought it might with some justice be contended that the shipowner, having the personal selection of the captain, ought to be responsible for his negligence, and to this extent he would be willing to accept yesterday's decision on the question. But it seemed to him preposterous to lay down that the shipowner was to be responsible for the acts of the officers and crew, about whom he could personally know very little, often nothing at all, and who were frequently engaged in distant ports where the captain might have to fill up his crew as best he could, with almost no choice. He wished therefore to suggest as a compromise that the decision of yesterday should be modified to this extent, as he felt sure that if the rules were passed as they at present stood on this point they would have no chance of acceptance by shipowners, and the work of the conference would go for nothing.

THE PRESIDENT pointed out that the decision arrived at yesterday could not be modified to-day, and he could not allow it to be again brought into question.

CONSUL MEIER then expressed his willingness to withdraw the proposal, in deference to the President's ruling.

I said that, as mover of the resolution adopted yesterday, I should be willing to accept Consul Meier's proposal so far as it concerned the crew, but I did not think it admissible with regard to the officers any more than the captain.

THE PRESIDENT said that, if a compromise acceptable to both parties could be arrived at by the conference, nothing would be more desirable, and there would be no objection to a modification under such circumstances. But, unless this was the case, he could not allow the decision of yesterday to be modified by, perhaps, a small majority on the other side to-day.

M. ENGELS protested against the owner being held responsible even for the negligence of the captain, whilst he agreed that to make them responsible for their crews was simply preposterous, and he was sure that the resolution of the conference could not, on that account, ever take effect. He pointed out that such responsibility was not excluded by the New York bill of lading, which had been prepared by the shippers themselves, who certainly knew what the shippers' interests were.

CONSUL MEIER submitted that the bill of lading should be read a second time, and that it would be competent to insert modifications on the second reading.

HERR ULRICH was decidedly opposed to reopening the question in any form. The decision of the conference had already been published in the press and gone out into the world, and it would seriously affect the reputation of the Association if it were now varied. Moreover, some delegates who took a special interest in the question had gone home, supposing it to be finally settled, and it would be unfair to them to alter the decision.

THE PRESIDENT said that it was evident, after what had been said, that there was no prospect of arriving at a compromise acceptable to all parties, and he must therefore decline to allow the question to be further discussed. The Association did not recognise any second reading.

The committee of revision was then appointed, consisting of the President, Herr Ahlers, Dr. Rahusen, Judge Peabody, and Herr Ulrich.

On Friday, August 21, the conference reassembled under the presidency of myself, when

DR. SIEVEKING presented, on behalf of the committee of revision, the bill of lading and rules as revised by them. They were as follows:—

MODEL BILL OF LADING (AS BROUGHT IN BY THE COMMITTEE OF REVISION).

SHIPPED, in apparent good order and condition, on board the ship   whereof   is master for the present voyage   , now lying in the port of   and bound for   ,   being marked and numbered as per margin, to be carried and delivered at the port of   unto   or order on his paying freight for the said goods at the rate of

Subject to all the conditions of the Hamburg Rules of Affreightment.

In witness whereof the master of the said ship has signed   bills of lading, all of this tenor and date, one of which being accomplished the others to stand void.

Dated at   ,   188

(Signed)   *Master.*

HAMBURG RULES OF AFFREIGHTMENT.

I.

The shipowner shall be responsible that his vessel is properly equipped, manned, provisioned, and fitted out, and in all respects seaworthy and capable of performing her intended voyage, and for the stowage and right delivery of the goods. He shall also be responsible for the barratry, faults, and negligence, but not for errors in judgment, of the master, officers, and crew.

II.

The shipowner shall not be responsible for loss or damages arising from *vis major*, public enemies, civil commotions, pirates, robbers, fire, explosion, bursting of boilers, breakage of shafts or screws, nor for any latent defect in hull or machinery (not resulting from want of due diligence by the owner, husband, or manager of the ship), nor for the cargo's decay, putrefaction, rust, sweat, change of character, drainage, leakage, breakage, or any damage arising from the nature of the goods shipped, or such defective packing as could not be noticed externally, nor for the obliteration of marks, numbers, addresses, or descriptions of goods shipped, nor for any damage or loss caused by accidental prolongation of the voyage, nor for other accidents of the seas, unless it is proved that such exception comes under Rule I.

III.

Steamship to be at liberty to call at any intermediate ports, to sail without pilots, provided such sailing does not constitute a fault or negligence, to tow and assist vessels in distress, and to deviate for the purpose of saving life or property; also at liberty, in case the ship shall put into a port of refuge for repairs, to tranship the goods to their destination by any other vessels, and at liberty to convey goods in lighters to and from the ship at shipper's risk, but at ship's expense.

IV.

Quality-marks, if any, to be of the same size as and contiguous to the leading marks; and if inserted in the shipping notes accepted by the mate, the master is bound to sign bills of lading conformable thereto.

V.

Ship not accountable for gold, silver, bullion, specie, documents, jewellery, works of art, or other precious articles, unless bills of lading are signed therefor with the value therein expressed, and a special agreement be made.

VI.

Shipper accountable for any loss or damage to ship or cargo caused by inflammable, explosive, or dangerous goods, shipped without full disclosure of their nature, whether such shipper shall have been aware of it or not, and whether such shipper be principal or agent; such goods may be thrown overboard or destroyed by the master or owner of the ship at any time without compensation.

VII.

Shipper and consignee to be responsible for all fines or damages which the ship or cargo may incur, or suffer, by reason of incorrect or insufficient marking of packages or description of their contents.

VIII.

Goods delivered to the ship, whilst on quay awaiting shipment, to be considered as taken on board, as far as the shipowner's responsibility is concerned.

IX.

Goods once shipped cannot be taken away by the shipper except upon payment of full freight, and compensation for any damages sustained by the shipowners through such taking away.

X.

In case the ship shall be prevented from reaching her destination by quarantine, blockade, ice, or the hostile act of any Power, the master or owners may discharge the goods into any depôt or lazaretto, or at the nearest convenient port; the shippers and consignees to be responsible for all expenses thereby incurred upon the goods.

XI.

No goods can be abandoned for freight. This rule does not apply to liquids.

XII.

If the goods be not taken by the consignee without delay, or within such time as is provided by the regulations of the port of discharge, they may be stored or discharged into hulks or lighters by the master at the expense and risk of their owners; provided always, that due notice is given of the arrival of the ship and the commencement of the discharge, and that the same does not begin at night or at any unreasonable hour.

XIII.

Ship to have a lien on all goods for payment of freight and charges, including dead freight, demurrage at the port of destination, forwarding charges, charges for carriage to port of shipment, and the fines, damages, and expenses mentioned in Rules VII.

and X., and for General Average claims, and to be entitled to recover from the shipper the difference between the amount of freight stipulated in the bill of lading and the proceeds of the goods, should the freight not be paid otherwise.

XIV.

To the extent of the value of the lien, freight, which by the terms of the bill of lading is made payable by the consignee, cannot be demanded from the shipper after the master has parted with his lien on the goods.

XV.

In the event of claims for short delivery when the ship reaches her destination, the price to be the market price at the port of destination on the day of the ship's entry at the custom-house, less freight and charges saved.

XVI.

Weight, measure, quality, contents, and value, although mentioned in the bill of lading, to be considered as unknown to the master, unless expressly recognised and agreed to the contrary. Simple subscription not to be considered as such agreement.

XVII.

General Average to be paid according to York and Antwerp Rules.

XVIII.

Freight, if payable on delivery, to be paid immediately after delivery, and in the currency stipulated in the bill of lading, or at consignee's option in cash, without discount, at the rate of exchange of bankers' bills at sight current on the day of the ship's entry at the custom-house.

XIX.

Nothing contained in these rules is to be construed so as to authorise an argument to the contrary.

The form was then again gone through and read clause by clause.

On the form of bill of lading being read, HERR LAEISZ objected to the title 'Hamburg Rules of Affreightment,' and wished the name 'International' to be given them instead. As the rules were entirely contrary, on a main point, to those proposed by the Hamburg Chamber of Commerce, he thought the title calculated to convey a wrong impression.

DR. SIEVEKING pointed out that the word 'International' would not be distinctive, and said that the committee had thought it desirable to adopt some title which, like that of the 'York and Antwerp Rules' on General Average, might soon become universally adopted and understood.

HERR WOERMANN also strongly objected to the word 'Hamburg' in the title.

DR. FRANCK hoped the title would be retained.

On a show of hands, the title was adopted by a large majority.

On Rule 2, CONSUL PREUSS desired the omission of the words, 'or such defective packing as could not be noticed externally.' The proposal was novel, and would be far-reaching in its results.

DR. SIEVEKING pointed out that the proposal was in conformity with the prescription of the German Commercial Code.

HERR LAEISZ desired the addition of the words 'with due care' before 'be noticed externally.'

DR. SIEVEKING replied that the committee had not thought it necessary to be more precise than the German Code, the meaning of which was well understood.

HERREN PREUSS and LAEISZ thereupon withdrew their objections.

On Rule 3, HERR WOERMANN asked whether it might not be inferred from the mention of steamships in this rule that the rules were not intended to apply to sailing vessels.

DR. SIEVEKING replied by referring to Rule 19, as excluding any such inference.

HERR LAEISZ wished the words 'by any conveyance' to be substituted for 'by other vessels.'

DR. SIEVEKING pointed out the extremely wide bearing of such an amendment, which would admit of the transmission of goods by railway across the continent of Europe.

Herr Laeisz withdrew the proposal.

On Rule 8, M. Engels objected that this was not in accordance with the decision of the conference yesterday, but after some observations from Dr. Rahusen and Dr. Sieveking, the objection was not pressed.

Some remarks were made on Rule 11 by Dr. Gütschow, but no amendment was proposed.

On Rule 18, Dr. Martin pointed out that the words 'freight if payable on delivery to be payable immediately after delivery' were liable to be misunderstood, and proposed to substitute the words 'freight if not payable in advance.'

Herr Laeisz proposed the insertion of the words 'at port of destination,' instead of 'on delivery.'

This alteration, with the further substitution of the word 'on' for 'after' next to 'immediately,' was adopted unanimously.

On Rule 19, Judge Peabody proposed the substitution of the words 'in respect of anything not contained in these rules' for the words 'to the contrary,' and the amendment was accepted unanimously.

Mr. Alexander called attention to the fact that the form of bill of lading now adopted restored the expressions providing for a series, of which, one being accomplished, the rest were to stand void, although the Liverpool conference had decided, by a large majority, that it was desirable to have the bills of lading 'drawn as first, second, or third, the first of which bills being accomplished, the others to stand void.' He thought the question should not be passed over in silence.

Herr Ahlers thought it better to keep to the accustomed form, and the conference decided accordingly.

Herr Laeisz thought that the bill of lading and rules ought now to be put to the meeting *en bloc*, as was done at the Liverpool conference.

Dr. Sieveking was decidedly opposed to such a course, as the bill of lading might now be rejected by a small majority on account of a single clause to which they had objected, and which had been carried against them at a previous sitting, and thus the whole work of the conference would be nullified.

As chairman of the sitting, I ruled that this could not be done. The bill of lading, as passed, was as follows :—

MODEL BILL OF LADING (*as finally adopted*).

SHIPPED, in apparent good order and condition, on board the ship   whereof is master for the present voyage   , now lying in the port of   and bound for   , being marked and numbered as per margin, to be carried and delivered at the port of   unto   or order on his paying freight for the said goods at the rate of

Subject to all the conditions of the Hamburg Rules of Affreightment.

In witness whereof the master of the said ship has signed bills of lading, all of this tenor and date, one of which being accomplished the others to stand void.

Dated at   ,   188 .

(Signed)   *Master*.

HAMBURG RULES OF AFFREIGHTMENT.

I.

The shipowner shall be responsible that his vessel is properly equipped, manned, provisioned, and fitted out, and in all respects seaworthy and capable of performing her intended voyage, and for the stowage and right delivery of the goods. He shall also be responsible for the barratry, faults, and negligence, but not for errors in judgment, of the master, officers and crew.

II.

The shipowner shall not be responsible for loss or damages arising from *vis major*, public enemies, civil commotions, pirates, robbers, fire, explosion, bursting of boilers, breakage of shafts or screws, nor for any latent defect in hull or machinery (not resulting from want of due diligence by the owner, husband, or manager of the ship), nor for the cargo's decay, putrefaction, rust, sweat, change of character, drainage, leakage, breakage, or any damage arising from the nature of the goods shipped, or such defective packing as could not be noticed externally, nor for the obliteration of marks, numbers, addresses, or descriptions of goods shipped, nor for any damage or loss caused by accidental prolongation of the voyage, nor for other accidents of the seas, unless it is proved that such exception comes under Rule I.

III.

Steamship to be at liberty to call at any intermediate ports, to sail without pilots, provided such sailing does not constitute a fault or negligence, to tow and assist vessels in distress, and to deviate for the purpose of saving life or property; also at liberty, in case the ship shall put into a port of refuge for repairs, to tranship the goods to their destination by other vessels, and at liberty to convey goods in lighters to and from the ship at shipper's risk, but at ship's expense.

IV.

Quality-marks, if any, to be of the same size as and contiguous to the leading marks; and if inserted in the shipping notes accepted by the mate, the master is bound to sign bills of lading conformable thereto.

V.

Ship not accountable for gold, silver, bullion, specie, documents, jewellery, works of art, or other precious articles, unless bills of lading are signed therefor with the value therein expressed and a special agreement is made.

VI.

Shipper accountable for any loss or damage to ship or cargo caused by inflammable, explosive, or dangerous goods, shipped without full disclosure of their nature, whether such shipper shall have been aware of it or not, and whether such shipper be principal or agent: such goods may be thrown overboard or destroyed by the master or owner of the ship at any time without compensation.

VII.

Shipper and consignee to be responsible for all fines or damages which the ship or cargo may incur, or suffer, by reason of incorrect or insufficient marking of packages or description of their contents.

VIII.

Goods delivered to the ship, whilst on quay awaiting shipment, to be considered as taken on board, as far as the shipowner's responsibility is concerned.

IX.

Goods once shipped cannot be taken away by the shipper, except upon payment of full freight, and compensation for any damages sustained by the shipowners through such taking away.

X.

In case the ship shall be prevented from reaching her destination by quarantine, blockade, ice, or the hostile act of any Power, the master or owners may discharge the goods into any depôt or lazaretto, or at the nearest convenient port; the shippers and consignees to be responsible for all expenses thereby incurred upon the goods.

XI.

No goods can be abandoned for freight. This rule does not apply to liquids.

XII.

If the goods be not taken by the consignee without delay, or within such time as is provided by the regulations of the port of discharge, they may be stored or discharged into hulks or lighters by the master at the expense and risk of their owners; provided always, that due notice is given of the arrival of the ship and the commencement of the discharge, and that the same does not begin at night or at any unreasonable hour.

XIII.

Ship to have a lien on all goods for payment of freight and charges, including dead freight, demurrage at the port of destination, forwarding charges, charges for carriage to port of shipment, and the fines, damages, and expenses mentioned in Rules VII. and X., and for General Average claims, and to be entitled to recover from the shipper the difference between the amount of freight stipulated in the bill of lading and the proceeds of the goods, should the freight not be paid otherwise.

XIV.

To the extent of the value of the lien, freight, which by the terms of the bill of lading is made payable by the consignee, cannot be demanded from the shipper after the master has parted with his lien on the goods.

XV.

In the event of claims for short delivery when the ship reaches her destination, the price to be the market price at the port of destination on the day of the ship's entry at the custom-house, less freight and charges saved.

XVI.

Weight, measure, quality, contents, and value, although mentioned in the bill of lading, to be considered as unknown to the master unless expressly recognised and agreed to the contrary. Simple subscription not to be considered as such agreement.

XVII.

General Average to be paid according to York and Antwerp Rules.

XVIII.

Freight if payable at port of destination to be paid immediately on delivery in cash without discount, and in the currency stipulated in the bill of lading, or, at consignee's option, at the rate of exchange of bankers' bills at sight current on the day of the ship's entry at the custom-house.

XIX.

Nothing contained in these rules is to be construed so as to authorise an argument in respect to anything not expressed in these rules.

HERR LAEISZ then said that he was desired, on behalf of the Hamburg Chamber of Commerce, to present the following protest, and to request that it be entered on the minutes of the conference.

'The delegates of the Hamburg Chamber of Commerce, in the name and on behalf of their constituents, beg to declare that, to their regret, they feel unable to recommend the general adoption of the Rules of Affreightment, the first of which, as amended by this conference, imposes responsibilities upon the shipowner which, in their opinion, he cannot reasonably be expected to take upon himself, thus rendering the rules unacceptable for practical use.'

DR. SIEVEKING wished, although he had been a member of the committee of reference, to express the obligations of the conference to those gentlemen who had so kindly undertaken the task of putting its decisions into shape. They had spent a great deal of time in doing so since the meeting of the previous morning. He also expressed the desire that the executive council would do their best to distribute and give effect to the decisions on this question at which the conference had arrived.

M. ENGELS thought that for the council to take such action would be improper, since the resolutions adopted by this conference were totally opposed to those of the Liverpool conference, and the council was bound by the one as much as the other.

Although the importance of these decisions could not be denied, it soon, however, became apparent that they were yet far from leading to any practical result.

I now come to the labours of another congress, whose duty it was to consider the subject-matter of these pages; I mean the congress which the Belgian Government assembled at Antwerp from September 27 until October 3, 1885, for the purpose of trying to obtain an agreement on certain principles of commercial law. In order to bring together a thoroughly competent assembly for the consideration of these matters, the Royal Commission, which the King of the Belgians had instituted for the organisation of this international congress, had not only invited the different Governments to send efficient delegates, but had likewise addressed formal invitations to the barristers of the principal mercantile cities, the faculties of law of the most important continental universities, the principal learned societies, the courts of commerce, the chambers of commerce, the boards of underwriters, and other equally capable and interested bodies.

A large number of gentlemen, thoroughly conversant with these subjects, had therefore an opportunity of investigating the merits of the arguments brought forward in favour of the different contentions, and I cannot do better than give the resolutions, and the conclusions at which they arrived in their own words.

These were as follows:—

The owners of ships are civilly responsible, to the freighters and shippers, for the acts of their captains and their officers relative to the cargo, provided they cannot prove that the damage was caused by *force majeure*, by vice-proper of the merchandise, or by the fault of the shipper.

It is, however, lawful for the parties to vary this responsibility by special stipulations, with the following exceptions:—

Owners of ships should be prohibited from relieving themselves in advance of their responsibility by inserting a clause in the contract of affreightment, the bill of lading, or by any other agreement:—

(A). For any acts of their captains or their officers tending to compromise the seaworthiness of the ships.

(B). For any act which would cause damage through improper stowage, want of care, or incomplete delivery of the goods confided to their care.

(C). For all barratry, all acts and cases of negligence having the appearance of gross fraud.

The responsibility of shipowners resulting from the acts and engagements of their officials is limited to the value of the ship and freight.

They can rid themselves of this responsibility by abandoning the ship and the freight or their value at the moment of the commencement of suit.

Soon after my return from this Antwerp congress I was requested by the London Chamber of Commerce to join the sub-committee, which, as previously mentioned, had been appointed at the Cannon Street Hotel meeting in the previous March for the purpose of considering this subject in all its bearings, and to make such suggestions as might be deemed most expedient to meet the exigencies of the case.

This sub-committee held repeated meetings and adopted, in the month of December 1885, the following report :—

The sub-committee appointed in March 1885 to consider the best means of bringing into general use a reasonable and workable form of bill of lading have given their careful attention to this difficult subject, and now beg to report to the general committee the leading conclusions at which they have arrived.

They speedily resolved that any attempt to draft in concert with the representatives of the shipowners a model bill of lading would prove useless, and should not be made. This endeavour had been made some years previously by the joint committees of merchants and shipowners who drafted the Eastern Trade Bill of Lading, a form which met with very general acceptance at the time, and was taken as the model for the Australian and other bills of lading subsequently introduced. Several important shipowners and companies, however, from the first declined to use the Eastern Trade form, and others successfully introduced variations from it, so that in a few years there was nearly as much diversity in the forms of bills of lading in this trade as in the American or other trades where the shipowners' forms have long been felt as oppressive. The sub-committee are satisfied that any form now agreed upon would in like manner be departed from by the managers of steamship lines, and that no durable reform could possibly be constructed on this basis.

The sub-committee have consequently resolved, that in their view the object aimed at can only be attained by parliamentary legislation; and their efforts have been mainly directed to drafting the requisite Bill in such form as might prove a proper protection to the shipper, and to the holder of the bill of lading for value, while not unfair to the shipowner.

The Act introduced into the American Congress for regulating bills of lading (but which has not yet been effectively considered there) has been before the sub-committee, as have also the Hamburg rules on bills of lading lately adopted at an international conference for the amendment and assimilation of commercial law. Both have been found of service; but the American draft is considered more stringent than would be likely to pass our House of Commons, and it has consequently had to be extensively modified.

The sub-committee found much difficulty in drafting a form of Bill which would prove workable from a legal point of view; but latterly, by the kindness of the council of the Chamber, they have had the valuable assistance of Mr. J. Macdonell, the standing counsel to the Chamber, placed at their disposal, the result being that with his aid a form of bill has been drafted, which is now submitted to the general committee for their approval.

The committee will observe that the Bill is a short one, as it merely seeks to lay down certain legal principles applicable to the case, from which the shipowners will be unable to exempt themselves by any clauses which they may desire to embody in their bills of lading. Upon the question of the general legal principles involved, the sub-committee append hereto a letter dated March 23, 1885, from Mr. Henry Attlee, solicitor, who has given much attention to this question from the merchants' point of view. In the draft Bill they have endeavoured to give effect to his contention that the shipowner should be relieved from the insurance liability which, in law, at present attaches to him as a common carrier.

The Bill does not propose to recommend or enforce any particular form of bill of lading. The sub-committee recognise that different trades require different forms according to their special circumstances. They think, however, that the forms employed should be as simple and short as practicable, and that, without specifically adopting it, Mr. Charles Stubbs's published form may very usefully be taken as a model from which to draft the various bills of lading required for the various conditions of distinct trades. The essential point to be gained, and the consequent protection for the owner of the goods shipped, is that no condition on a bill of lading can be enforced which is at variance with the principles laid down in the Bill.

One object which has to be sedulously kept in view is that the bill of lading must itself be a complete receipt for the goods shipped, and a complete security that they will be delivered in accordance with its terms, saving only through such losses as are covered by an ordinary policy of insurance. This accomplished, the bill of lading becomes a security on which money may be advanced with unhesitating confidence.

It may be thought that the absence of any recognised form of bill of lading will tend to promote litigation, each case of dispute having to be treated on its own special merits. The sub-committee have had this question under view, and are of opinion that it is impossible materially to stop litigation, considering the infinite variety of circumstances with which commercial transactions have to deal. They feel satisfied, however, that with such a law in operation the merchant may encounter litigation with a sense of security which he could never have felt under the previous indefinite and uncertain system.

In explanation of the delay that has taken place in presenting this report, it may be observed that the sub-committee very early came to the conclusion that it was quite hopeless to do anything in the way of legislation during the Parliamentary Session of 1885. They trust, however, that the general committee will so deal with the matter that a Bill, aiming at settling a practicable system for the future, may be presented to the new Parliament at the earliest possible period in 1886.

  J. MACANDREW, *Chairman* (Matheson & Co.).
  C. VICTOR BENECKE (Benecke, Souchay, & Co.).
  H. REINHOLD (Reinhold & Co.).
  J. G. PITCAIRN (J. G. Pitcairn & Sons).
  A. J. MALCOLM (J. McEwan & Co.).
  E. E. WENDT, D.C.L.
         Members of the Sub-Committee.

I concur in the report, but I strongly urge that a clause should be introduced into the Act, providing for the exemption of the shipowner from liability in respect to any error in the actual navigation, even when occasioned by negligence, default, error in judgment of the pilot, master, mariners, or other servants of the shipowner, not resulting, however, in any case, from want of due diligence by the owners of the ship, or any of them.

  J. G. PITCAIRN (J. G. Pitcairn & Sons),
        Member of the Sub-Committee.

COPY OF LETTER FROM MR. HENRY ATTLEE.

      10 Billiter Square, London, E.C.: March 23, 1885.

Dear Sir,—It seems to me that what is wanted is some arrangement which would place the shipowner and the merchant in an equitable position *vis à vis* each other.

In my opinion it is not a question of settling the precise terms of a bill of lading, for it is impossible by the introduction or elimination of particular words varying the liability of parties in a contract to meet the difficulty; but that it is to be met by an alteration in the principle of the law itself regulating the rights of shipowner and merchant. As the law at present stands, the shipowner carrying goods is a common carrier and, therefore, an insurer, that is apart from any special stipulations introduced into any contract which may limit his liability; he undertakes to carry safely and securely against all accidents and risks whatsoever. Hence it is that the shipowners have from time to time sought to limit this general liability by the introduction of apt words to exclude the varied risks which experience has taught them arise in the course of the carriage, and at last these exceptions have become so numerous that they have to be embodied in diamond print, and make a long document difficult of construction and containing contradictions, and have become in many cases unfair in their operation.

Now, as I understand it, the merchants do not object to reasonable limitations of the common-law liability of a carrier; that is to say, they no longer wish that a carrier by water should undertake to carry against all risks, and I think that the case would be better met by a short Act of Parliament declaring that in future a shipowner or carrier by water should not be liable as an insurer, but that his liability should be limited to any loss occasioned by the want of ordinary care on his part, and that in case of a loss it should lie on him to acquit himself by showing that he was not in fault; in other words, his liability would be assimilated to other custodians of goods, such as warehousemen, &c.

To effect this a short Act of Parliament would be required, and the same Act might declare that it should not be lawful for the shipowner by express stipulation to exclude this general liability thus limited to loss occasioned by the want of ordinary care on his part. It would be easy to add words of definition which would relieve the shipowner from liability for the errors of judgment of captains or officers, or for their negligence, except in cases where the shipowner had knowledge of the officer's unfitness for his duties from proved want of ability, dishonesty, or other defect of character, in which latter alternative he should be liable if the knowledge were such as would satisfy a prudent man of the officer's unfitness.

The Act would also provide that the shipowner or ship should be held responsible to the *bonâ-fide* holder for value of a bill of lading for all goods signed for by the captain, or other duly authorised agent at the port of loading, whether such goods were or were not put on board, or that it should be made imperative upon the ship to declare at the port of loading the agent who should be authorised to sign bills of lading, if any, beyond the captain, by whose signature shipowners should be bound, failing which the captain should be legally held to bind the owner. It seems to me it would be preferable that the shipowner, or the ship itself, be held responsible in damages rather than that penal consequences of a criminal nature should be imposed upon the captain or others, signing bills of lading for goods not actually on board.—I am, dear Sir,

Yours faithfully,

(Signed) HENRY ATTLEE.

AN ACT TO REGULATE AND DEFINE THE DUTIES AND LIABILITIES OF SHIPOWNERS.

Whereas it is expedient to amend the law affecting the duties and liabilities of shipowners,

Be it enacted by the Queen's most excellent Majesty, by and with the advice and consent of the Lords Spiritual and Temporal, and Commons, in this present Parliament assembled, and by the authority of the same, as follows:—

I. This Act may be cited as the Bills of Lading Act, 1886.

II. This Act shall come into effect on   , 1886.

III. In this Act, unless the context otherwise requires,

'Shipowners' includes any corporate body owning a ship, and any managing owner;

'Ship' includes every vessel, whether navigated or propelled by steam, sails, or oars, and every lighter, barge, or craft of any kind;

'United Kingdom' means Great Britain and Ireland;

The expression 'owner of goods' includes every person who is for the time being entitled either as owner, or agent for the owner, to the possession of goods, subject in the case of a lien, if any, to such lien;

'Goods' include every description of wares and merchandise;

'Master' includes every person (except a pilot) having command or charge of a ship within the meaning of this Act;

'Bill of lading' includes every mate's receipt, or other document of the nature of a receipt or acknowledgment, for goods temporarily granted until a bill of lading is issued.

IV. This Act shall apply to all ships carrying goods from any port or place in the United Kingdom, and all ships carrying goods to any port or place in the United Kingdom to be delivered there.

V. (1.) No shipowner shall be liable to the owner, consignee of goods, or the indorsee of a bill of lading, for injury or damage to, or loss of, or in respect of, goods to be carried and delivered, except for injury, damage or loss, in receiving, carrying, or delivering them, caused by the want of ordinary and reasonable care on the part of the shipowner, master, crew, servant, or agent of such shipowner.

(2.) Every shipowner shall be liable to the owner, consignee of goods, or the indorsee of a bill of lading, for injury, damage, or loss, as aforesaid, in receiving, carrying, or delivering, if caused by the want of ordinary and reasonable care on the part of the shipowner, master, crew, servant, or agent of such shipowner; and the onus of proving that such injury, damage or loss, as aforesaid, was not occasioned by want of such ordinary and reasonable care, shall be on the shipowner.

(3.) Every shipowner shall be so liable while the goods to be carried and delivered are temporarily deposited before delivery to the owner, consignee, or indorsee, on any quay or wharf, or in any warehouse or other premises, in charge or under control of the shipowner or his agent.

(4.) Any provision or exception in any bill of lading or any agreement to the contrary of this section, shall be null and void.

VI. (1.) Any provision or exception in any bill of lading, or any agreement purporting to relieve or exonerate in any way any shipowner from any duty to properly equip, man, provision, and fit out any ship, and to render it seaworthy, or from any implied warranty of seaworthiness in a contract of affreightment, shall be null and void.

(2.) The onus of proving that any injury, or damage to, or loss of, or in respect of, goods, to be carried and delivered aforesaid, was not occasioned by a breach of such duty on the part of such shipowner, master, crew, servant, or agent, in properly equipping, manning, provisioning, fitting out, and rendering seaworthy any ship, or by a breach of such warranty of seaworthiness, shall, any provision, exception, or agreement to the contrary notwithstanding, be on the shipowner.

(3.) No shipowner shall be liable for injury, damage, or loss as aforesaid, caused by, or arising from, any latent defects in the hull, machinery, tackle, equipment, or outfit of a ship which could not have been discovered by reasonable care or skill on the part of the shipowner, master, crew, servant, or agent.

VII. In every bill of lading issued in fulfilment of a mate's receipt, or of other document of the nature of a receipt, the exact voyage which is intended to be made, and the ports at which it is intended that the ship shall touch, shall be clearly specified or described; and the master or agent of the shipowner shall sign and deliver to the shipper of the goods, within a reasonable time, such a bill of lading for goods received in conformity with the mate's receipt, or other document of the nature of a receipt.

VIII. If goods are discharged at any port other than the port specified in the bill of lading as their destination, or carried to any port beyond such destination, they shall, until delivered thereat, be at the risk of the shipowner; and he shall be liable, any provision or exception in a bill of lading, or any agreement to the contrary notwithstanding, for injury or damage to, or loss of, or in respect of, such goods, caused by their being so discharged or not delivered at the specified port. Provided always, that he shall not be so liable for such injury, damage, or loss by causes beyond the control of the shipowner, master, crew, servant, or agent.

IX. Every bill of lading in the hands of a *bonâ-fide* holder, representing goods to be shipped on board a ship, and signed by the master or agent of the shipowner, shall be conclusive evidence of such shipment as against the shipowner, as well as against the master or agent signing the same, notwithstanding that such goods, or some part thereof, may not have been so shipped or received. But nothing in this Act shall affect a shipowner's, master's, or agent's rights against the shipper or owner of the goods, or other person, in consequence or by reason of whose fraud or default such goods were not shipped or received, or such representation was made.

X. Nothing in this Act shall make a shipowner liable for injury or damage to, or loss of, or in respect of, goods, caused by the act of God or the Queen's enemies, or affect s. 503 of 17 & 18 Vict. c. 107.

XI. Sec. 3 of 18 & 19 Vict. c. 111, is hereby repealed, except so far as regards bills of lading signed before this Act came into force.

This report was adopted and confirmed by the general committee of the London Chamber of Commerce, but was not followed up by any action of that body, as appears from the following report adopted on April 5, 1886 :—

The special committee of the Chamber of Commerce appointed to consider the question of the terms of existing bills of lading and the best means of amending them upon an equitable basis had regarded their functions as closed with the preparation and presentation of their Report dated in December last. They have, however, reassembled in consequence of the wish expressed by the council of the Chamber in their resolution of January 14, that they should communicate with the representatives of the shipowners so as to obtain their views on the legislation proposed by the committee.

The committee accordingly intimated to the General Shipowners' Society, to the Chamber of Shipping, and to the Steam Shipowners' Association that they were ready to meet any representatives whom these bodies might appoint for the purpose of discussing the Bill drafted by the committee, and seeing whether an agreement could be arrived at as to its terms. The answers received from two of these associations are appended hereto. No answer has been received from the Steam Shipowners' Association. It will be seen that the invitation to discuss the Bill is ignored by the one body and declined by the other, while both advance the old expedient that the merchants and shipowners engaged in any particular branch of trade should meet together and arrange a form of bill of lading which would prove mutually acceptable.

The committee have already reported to the council that an agreed bill of lading is quite useless, because no shipowner is bound by it, and the great steam companies, as a rule, will not entertain such negotiations, but insist on using their own forms.

They also reported that the most promising attempt to establish such a bill of lading by the mutually agreed upon form styled 'the Eastern Trade Bill of Lading' had resulted in complete failure, as many important lines never adopted it, while other shipowners, after using it for a time, introduced variations or additional clauses to suit their own purposes, which clauses are complained of by merchants as oppressive and unfair.

The committee therefore now finally report that there is no expectation whatever on their part of arriving at a preliminary understanding with the shipowners on the legislative measures which they propose. Under these circumstances they recommend that the whole question be submitted to the decision of Parliament by the council pressing forward at the earliest possible opportunity in the House of Commons the Bill already recommended by them as being a measure of relief urgently required by the numerous bankers, merchants and shippers who are injuriously affected by the inequitable conditions of the majority of the bills of lading now in use.

As previously stated, the Royal Commission on Loss of Life at Sea was sitting at this time, and the council of the London Chamber of Commerce accordingly resolved that any further action on their part should be deferred till this commission had issued its report.

Soon after, in the month of May of the same year, it was publicly announced that the Chambers of Commerce of Hamburg and Bremen, as well as the Associations of Shipowners at these ports, had agreed upon the adoption of a uniform bill of lading for steamships, and issued the following:—

STATEMENT RESPECTING ITS INTRODUCTION.

As the deliberations on the above subject during the conference of the Association for the Reform and Codification of the Laws of Nations held in August last year at Hamburg, and of the Congrès International de droit Commercial, which met soon after at Antwerp, did not lead to any practical results, owing to the proposed resolutions being partially unacceptable to shipowners, the undersigned Chambers of Commerce and Associations of Shipowners entered into negotiations together in order to draft a bill of lading for steamers doing justice to all parties interested, and to arrange, if possible, its universal adoption. The result of these negotiations is the following model bill of lading.

It adopts the principle that the shipowner shall be responsible for seaworthiness, proper equipment and outfit of the vessel, as well as for faults and negligence of the crew respecting proper stowage, care, treatment, and delivery of the cargo (Rule I.), thus doing justice to the shippers, who, owing to the shipowner not being responsible for the frequent, although generally small, losses caused thereby, which are often not recoverable from underwriters, had just cause of complaint. On the other hand, owners ought to agree to these clauses, as at present many of the best companies have acknowledged a moral liability in this sense and made compensation for claims of the nature described, even if they were not liable according to the wording of their bills of lading.

The owner, however, is not to be responsible for faults and negligence of the crew arising from the navigation of the vessel (Rule II.). This clause, of vital importance to the owner, does not prejudice the shippers, as, with trifling exceptions they are always insured against such risks, nor have the underwriters any cause to complain, as by accepting the premium they obtain an equivalent for such risk, which many underwriters accept without charging a higher premium.

This settlement of the owners' liability for the faults of their crew agrees in principle with all the bills of lading which have been accepted lately after agreement between shippers and owners (viz. the New York Produce Exchange, as approved for adoption by the Liverpool Steamship Owners' Association, the General Produce, Mediterranean, Black Sea, and Baltic Steamship bills of lading and others), a proof that it is in accordance with the sense of justice of the parties concerned.

This cardinal point in the draft is followed by a series of other important clauses respecting the contract of affreightment for which the resolutions of the Liverpool and Hamburg conference of the

Association for the Reform and Codification of the Law of Nations have given a valuable starting-point.

With respect to the codification, it has been agreed to follow the unanimous decision of the Hamburg conference of the Association to arrange the bill of lading clauses in general rules similar to the York and Antwerp General Average Rules. It appears, however, advisable to have the rules printed on the back of the bill of lading, at any rate until they are generally known.

Finally, in order to meet the existing and just requirements of some trades and shipowners, to add to the general rules special clauses, *i.e.* to alter some of their conditions, space has been reserved on the front side of the bill of lading for such additions and alterations, but with regard to the first principal rule respecting the responsibility of the shipowner, it is expressed that no alterations be allowed.

The undersigned believe that in the bill of lading drafted by them for the rules of a contract of affreightment they have found a suitable model acknowledged by the unanimous opinion of the parties every day more than just and equitable, and would strongly recommend its adoption to all shipowners.

The Chamber of Commerce of Bremen. LUIS ED. MEYER, *Chairman.*

The Association of Owners of the Lower Weser. H. H. MEIER, *Chairman.*

The Chamber of Commerce of Hamburg. ROBERT MESTERN, *Chairman.*

The Association of Hamburg Owners. CARL LAEISZ, *Chairman.*

Hamburg and Bremen: May 1886.

FORM OF BILL OF LADING.

SHIPPED, in apparent good order and condition, by M.   ,
on board the steamship   Captain   from
         , bound to   ,   being marked and numbered
as per margin, to be delivered at   unto M.
or order against payment of freight at the rate of
and charges as per margin. Subject to the general rules on the

other side as far as hereafter, there are no alterations or additions to Rules II. to XVII.

In witness whereof, the master of the said ship has signed bills of lading of the same tenor and date, besides the captain's copy which is marked as such, one of which being accomplished the others to stand void.

Dated at

(Signed)

GENERAL RULES FOR STEAMSHIP BILLS OF LADING RECOMMENDED TO BE ADOPTED BY THE CHAMBERS OF COMMERCE OF HAMBURG AND BREMEN.

Rule I.—The shipowner is responsible for the proper fitting out of the vessel and for its being equipped, manned, and provisioned, and in a seaworthy condition, capable to undertake the intended voyage. Also for errors or negligence of his employés respecting proper stowage, care, treatment, and delivery of the cargo.

All agreements and clauses to the contrary to be null and void and of no legally binding force.

Rule II.—The shipowner is not responsible for the dangers of the seas, fire, pirates, robbers, barratry (theft excepted), arrest and restraint of Governments, nor for damages and losses by collision, stranding, and all other casualties of navigation, even if the damages or losses so caused can be proved to have been caused by an illegal act, fault, negligence, or error of the pilot, captain, crew, or any other servant of the shipowner, nor for damages or losses by explosion, bursting of steam boilers or pipes, breakage of shafts, or for any latent defect in hull or machinery (not caused by unseaworthiness or want of due diligence by the owner or ship's husband), nor for decay, putrefaction, rats, or worms, rust, sweat, decomposition, shrinkage, leakage, breakage, country damage, or any damage arising from the natural condition of the goods shipped, or such defective packing as could not be noticed externally, or finally their contact with or damage caused by the smell of other goods, nor for incorrect or faulty address, nor for errors caused by the obliteration of marks, numbers, addresses, or descriptions of the goods shipped.

Rule III.—Vessel to be at liberty to call at any intermediate ports (whether also of ports not mentioned in the bill of lading is subject to special contract), to sail without pilots, to tow and assist vessels in distress, and to deviate for the purpose of saving life or property, also at liberty, in case the ship shall put into a port of refuge for repairs, to tranship the goods to their destination by any other vessel, and at liberty to convey goods at shippers' risk in lighters to and from the ship.

Rule IV.—Quality-marks, if any, to be of the same size as and contiguous to the leading marks. If inserted in the shipping notes accepted by the mate, the master is bound to sign bills of lading conformable thereto.

Rule V.—Ship not accountable for gold, silver, bullion, specie, documents, jewellery, works of art, or other articles exceeding M. 2,000 per package, unless bills of lading are signed therefor with the value therein expressed, and a special agreement to be made.

Rule VI.—Shippers are accountable for any and every loss or damage to ship or cargo caused by inflammable, explosive, or dangerous goods, if such goods are shipped without special agreement and without full disclosure of their nature, whether such shipper shall have been aware of it or not, and whether such shipper be principal or agent. Such goods may be thrown overboard or destroyed by the master or owners of the ship at any time without compensation.

Rule VII.—Shipper and consignee to be responsible for all fines or damages which the ship or cargo may incur or suffer by reason of incorrect or insufficient marking of packages or description of their weights or contents.

Rule VIII.—If the owner has given a receipt for goods still lying on the quay or in lighters, he is only responsible in so far as if they had been already taken on board.

Rule IX.—Goods once shipped can only be taken away by the shipper against payment of full freight and compensation for any damages sustained by the shipowners through such taking away.

Rule X.—In case the ship shall be prevented from reaching her destination by quarantine, blockade, ice, or the hostile act of any Power, the master or owners may discharge the goods into any depôt or lazaretto, or at a convenient port when his duties are fulfilled. The shippers and consignees to be responsible for all expenses thereby incurred upon the goods.

Rule XI.—For cargo damaged or reduced by leakage full freight to be paid. No freight to be paid for increase in weight by sea damage.

Rule XII.—If the goods be not taken by the consignees without delay or within such time as is provided by the regulations of the port of discharge, they may be landed or discharged into hulks or lighters by the master at the expense and risk of their owners.

Rule XIII.—Ship to have a lien on all goods for payment of freight and charges, including dead freight, demurrage, forwarding charges, and for carrying to port of shipment, and the fines, damages, and expenses mentioned in Rules VII. and X. and for General Average claims. Ship also to be entitled to recover from the shipper the difference between the amount of freight stipulated in the bill of lading and the proceeds of the goods, should the freight not be paid otherwise.

Rule XIV.—In the event of claims for short delivery when the ship reaches her destination, the price to be the market price at the port of destination, on the day of the ship's entry at the customhouse, less freight and charges saved.

Rule XV.—Weight, measure, quality, contents, and value, although mentioned in the bill of lading, to be considered as unknown to the master, unless expressly recognised and agreed to the contrary. Signing the bill of lading is not to be considered as such agreement.

Rule XVI.—General Average to be paid according to York and Antwerp Rules, consignees of goods liable to contribute to General Average to sign an average agreement declaring values, or to give sufficient security, at the captain's option.

Rule XVII.—Freight and charges, if payable at port of destination, to be paid immediately on delivery in cash, without discount and in the currency stipulated in the bill of lading, or at consignee's option, at the rate of exchange, of bankers' bills at sight current on the day of the ship's entry at the custom-house. Freight paid in advance cannot be refunded, even if vessel and cargo are lost.

This was the state of affairs when the council of the Association for the Reform and Codification of the Law of Nations received an invitation from the Lord Mayor and the Common Council of the city of London to hold their thirteenth conference in the Guildhall. Again, in order to see whether a satisfactory arrangement could be brought about upon this much-vexed Bill of Lading question, its rediscussion was announced on the programme. Before, however, I report what took place on that occasion, I cannot refrain from quoting that part from the Hon. Sir Charles Butt's opening address on July 25, 1887, in which this learned Judge alludes to the subject under consideration. He said —:

But let me, in the first instance, say a word on a matter to which your attention is invited, and in respect of which the aims of the Association should run a chance of early realisation.

For a time it seemed as if the efforts of the Association to bring about uniformity of contracts of affreightment were likely to result in a speedy and successful issue.

At the conference held at Hamburg in August 1885, a draft bill of lading was presented to the meeting, which embodied by reference a 'Code of Affreightment,' also submitted to the members attending that conference.

The object of that mode of dealing with the matter was, I understand, to avoid undue length of the bill of lading itself. Now, whilst I agree with the opinions expressed by the majority of members at that meeting, I doubt whether the *modus operandi* then suggested is the best that might be adopted. The rules forming the 'Code of Affreightment' may be good in themselves, but they appear to me to deal with so many matters of detail, with so much that is of comparatively minor importance, that I should despair of inducing shipowners, at the present time, to adopt a form of bill of lading incorporating all those rules. On the other hand, I see no reason why a short bill of lading may not be framed, containing within its four corners all essential stipulations binding shipowner and merchant alike. The real difficulty lies not in the form of the bill of lading, but in the question of the insertion of one provision with reference to which merchants on the one hand, and a large number, if not a majority of shipowners on the other are at issue.

The real difficulty is that shipowners refuse to accept any bill of lading which leaves them responsible for the negligence of their servants, the masters and crews of their vessels.

At a meeting of the members of this Association held at Liverpool in 1882, a form of bill of lading exempting the shipowner from liability for the negligence of his servants was approved of; but at the more recent conference at Hamburg in the month of August 1885, a resolution to the effect that the shipowner ought not to be allowed to protect himself from such liability was proposed, and carried by a considerable majority.

Since that time, the matter has not been allowed to rest. The Chambers of Commerce of two most important commercial cities —Hamburg and London—have given expression to opposite views on this question; the Chamber of Commerce of Hamburg holding that the shipowner should, the Chamber of Commerce of London that he should not, be exempt from liability for the negligence of his master or crew.

The controversy has, it seems to me, been embittered by the use by some of the large lines of steamers of bills of lading exempting them from almost every sort of responsibility. These so-called contracts amount, in reality, to little more than this: ' You pay me the freight, and I will do what I please with your goods.' How comes it that such conditions are ever accepted by the merchant? This question admits of one answer, and one answer alone. He accepts simply because he has no choice. Submission is forced on him, and forced on him in defiance of the fundamental duties of the carrier.

Were the majority of shipowners inclined to insist on the imposition of conditions so manifestly unreasonable, the labours of this Association to reconcile the apparently conflicting interests of merchant and shipowner respectively must of necessity be unavailing. In that case we had better stand aside, and let the Legislatures of the different countries deal with the matter.

I believe, however, that merchants and shipowners, alike, desire only a reasonable solution of the question; and that the real point to be determined is what *is* reasonable.

There are those who think that when once an employer of labour, whether shipowner or other person, has taken due care and precaution to secure, so far as may be, the competence and trustworthiness of his agents, or servants, he ought not to be held civilly, any more than he is held criminally, responsible for their wrongful acts. That is a question of very large dimensions, on which opinions may differ, and which it is not for me to determine; but it may not be out of place to remind those who hold this opinion that it is a view of the employer's liability which the legislation of the great majority of civilised states refuses to sanction.

But apart from this more general question of the responsibility of employers for the negligence of their servants, the shipowners contend that in their case an exception should be made, on the ground of the very large responsibilities necessarily placed upon servants who, from the nature of their occupation and employment, are to an unusual extent beyond the control of the employer. The contention is worthy of careful and respectful consideration; but I would venture to suggest, for the consideration of those by whom it is put forward, whether the directors of a railway company have, for practical purposes, more control over the engine-driver, who fails to see, or neglects to obey, a signal, than has the shipowner over his captain, who runs his vessel on a rock, from failing to observe, or to appreciate, the timely warning of the lighthouse. Again, for all practical purposes, has the man who sends his carriage or his cart along the highway more control over his coachman, or his driver, who runs down the carriage of a third person, than has the shipowner over his captain who runs down the third person on the high seas?

These are matters on which I do not presume to pronounce

an opinion *ex cathedrâ*. I merely desire to suggest them for the consideration of those engaged in the controversy, in the hope that the honesty of purpose, which I am persuaded animates all parties concerned, aided by mutual forbearance, may, ere long, bring your labours, in this branch of your undertaking, to a satisfactory issue.

The discussion on the subject was fixed for Wednesday, July 27, and took place under the presidency of Dr. Sieveking (President of the Hanseatic Court of Appeal at Hamburg) with a result which might have been foreseen, from the large number of gentlemen interested in the shipowning interest who had recently become members of the Association.

THE CHAIRMAN opened the discussion on the above question, and explained the present position of the question, suggesting that the attention of the conference should be directed solely to the negligence clause. The question had twice been before the conference—at Liverpool, and again at Hamburg in 1885. At Liverpool, the form of bill of lading adopted excepted the 'act of God, perils of the sea, fire, barratry of the master and crew, enemies, pirates, and thieves, arrest and restraint of princes, rulers, and people, collisions, stranding and other accidents of navigation, even when occasioned by the negligence, default, or error in judgment of the pilot, master, mariners, or other servants of the shipowners.' The bill of lading adopted at Hamburg contained the following clause: 'The shipowner shall be responsible that his vessel is properly equipped, manned, provisioned, and fitted out in all respects seaworthy and capable of performing her intended voyage and for the stowage and right delivery of the goods. He shall also be responsible for the barratry, faults, and negligence, but not for errors in judgment, of the master, officers, and crew.' Before the Hamburg conference concluded, a protest was handed in by the Hamburg Chamber of Commerce declaring that in the opinion of that Chamber the clause was too strong against shipowners, and that it would not be practicable. He brought the proceedings of the Hamburg conference to a conclusion by expressing the hope that before the next conference there would be an interchange of opinion, and that some compromise would be arrived at. Since 1885 a bill of lading had been approved by the Chambers of Commerce of Hamburg and Bremen, and between this bill of lading and the Liverpool Bill of Lading there was great similarity.

MR. GRAY HILL (Liverpool) moved:—

'That the following principle adopted by the conference of this Association held at Liverpool in 1882 be now confirmed and adopted as the basis of discussion. That the principle of the common form of bill should be this—that the shipowner, whether by steam or sailing ship, should be liable for the faults of his servants in all matters relating to the ordinary course of the voyage, such as the stowage and right delivery of the cargo and other matters of this kind; but, on the other hand, the shipowner should be exempt from liability for everything which comes under the head of accidents of navigation, even though the loss from these may be indirectly attributable to some fault or neglect of the crew.'

He said this bill of lading was not sprung upon the conference which adopted it. On the contrary, it was carefully prepared by a committee composed of representatives of all associations who were interested in the matter. Shipowners were there, underwriters were there, cargo-owners were there, and there was a small delegation of lawyers. Nine associations were represented, and only two of them were shipowners' associations. On the other hand, not one single British shipowner, British underwriter, or British merchant attended the Hamburg conference. He was not able to say how far the same interests were represented from the Continent, but he believed he was correct in stating that the majority of the gentlemen present were jurists who were not sufficiently acquainted with the wants of the mercantile world. This absence of the English mercantile world from the conference was easily accounted for: the mercantile world in this country regarded the matter as having been settled at Liverpool. But even in the assembly to which he had referred, the Hamburg Bill of Lading was adopted by only 24 against 17 votes. The action of Liverpool had been followed almost universally, while the action of Hamburg

K K

had been almost entirely neglected, the reason being that the Liverpool Bill of Lading met the wants of the mercantile world, while the Hamburg Bill did not. 'Error in judgment,' so far as English law was concerned, meant nothing. Either shipowners' servants were negligent or they were not negligent. The question was simply whether there was negligence, and therefore the Hamburg Bill appeared to give what in reality it did not give. They were there not to discuss what the law ought to be, they were there to discuss what form of bill of lading they should recommend to the mercantile world; but if the mercantile world would not adopt that form they were wasting their time at that meeting. If, as the President said on Monday, shipowners were unreasonable and would not adopt the form of bill of lading suggested, the Association might stand aside and leave the matter to be decided by legislation. The decision of an important body like that might have considerable influence on legislation, and he therefore drew attention to the question whether there ought to be a change in the law. As it stood the law was very much against the shipowner, because unless he made special contracts he was liable for any kind of negligence on the part of his servants. It was now proposed that the law should step in and make the shipowner liable, although he said by his contract that he was not liable. What about the freedom of contract? Surely shipowners were able to take care of themselves? They were quite able to make their own arrangements. The monopoly argument was nonsense. This was a contract with regard to the cargo, and nothing else. The shipowner was bound by the terms of this resolution to see that his ship was seaworthy. What more could he do? There were no passengers on board, and if the shipowner provided a vessel which was seaworthy, in whose hands was the question whether there should be loss of life? It was, of course, in the hands of the crew. Surely the probabilities were that the crew would look after their own lives! If they did not, no contract between other parties could affect them at all. He was satisfied that in the minds of lawyers there lurked a prejudice on the question, traceable to the old idea that the carrier was to be liable for everything but the act of God and the Queen's enemy. Some of the Judges who laid down that principle based it on the consideration that the carrier was a dangerous kind of man, who might combine with thieves and robbers to take away the goods consigned to him. But did that state of things apply now? Certainly not; and shipowners asked for power to contract themselves out of such liabilities. He doubted whether the law could prevent a contract being made as the parties to it wished. They had seen many fruitless attempts to interfere with the freedom of contract. If they did that, what would be the result? They might possibly put the risk on the shoulders of the shipowner, but they would not be able to keep it there. They could not transfer the incurrence of this risk without remunerating the person to whom it was transferred. No thimble-rigging would enable them to get over that. And if there was any force behind the Hamburg resolution it was the force of those underwriters who wanted to have their cake and to eat it. He urged the conference to be practical, and to bear in mind they were recommending a document for the acceptance of the mercantile world, and do not let them recommend something with which the mercantile world would have nothing to do.

MR. JOHN GLOVER (London) seconded the motion. He said he would like to remove any prejudice which might exist in the mind of any merchants or other gentlemen present who might not have been able to follow this negligence controversy quite so closely as shipowners had been compelled to do. They were not met to defend bad bills of lading. They had given up that. They all believed there were a good many things in bills of lading in the early days of steamships which were not necessary for the shipowners, and which were contrary to the public interest. Liverpool, after long and careful consideration, had adopted a rational bill of lading, and they defended that rational bill of lading. In the second place, he wished to emphasise the fact that they were not seeking to be exempted from the consequences of their own negligence. So far as a shipowner could make a vessel complete for its intended voyage, it was right that he should be responsible, and the Liverpool Bill of Lading made him responsible. What they were trying to remove was a species of vicarious suffering by which shipowners were made responsible for all the mistakes of the professional men who were put on board their ships. He held in his hand a report, dated 1872, signed by Mr. Macandrew, whom he was glad to see on the platform to-day. That report contained a negligence clause with which he was quite satisfied, and which Liverpool ratified in 1882. This negligence clause had had no effect on merchants in increasing their power of getting paid for damage in the owner's control, for premiums had not increased since 1882. Indeed, he ventured to say, that in the last ten years the premiums of insurance on the leading lines to America and the East had fallen by nearly one-half; and what was still more extraordinary was, that the insurance companies had made good profits out of the reduced premiums. Why? Only one reason was possible—the maritime traffic was greater; it was carried on with such superior ships, and with such consummate skill; it was safer, and no one had suffered since the adoption of this negligence clause. The absence of such clauses had involved shipowners in serious losses, and the Courts had become so apt to split hairs that shipowners did not know where they stood. Every shipowner was obliged to insure, that insurance became double insurance, and they all knew the risk of litigation which was involved in double insurance. It was a question who was to pay the loss if the negligence clause was not there. Our English flag was under a disadvantage in this matter. The liability of shipowners abroad was not in person, but in revenue, so that if a ship went to the bottom the matter ended. In this country, though the ship and the freight were lost, the owner could be sued personally. They were, therefore, forced to look at the question in the light of the responsibility which the English law placed upon the shipowner. They were not free to choose their own captains, mates, and engineers. If a man wanted to be a captain, a mate, or an engineer, he had to serve so many years, and go through a series of examinations, such as a doctor would have to go through, and then he became a professional man. That man exercised a judgment, and shipowners said that it was not fair, when they were restricted in the choice of their servants, that they should be held responsible for the mistakes of their servants. They therefore asked the conference to reaffirm the Liverpool resolution, because of what had happened since it was adopted in 1882. He did not like to see the Association on two sides of the question. The discussion of the subject at Liverpool occupied fifty or sixty pages of the report of their proceedings. They discussed the bill of lading line by line, and at last came to a decision, recommending a bill of lading, which they called an International Bill of Lading. They agreed that a uniform bill of lading was not practicable, but they thought it was possible to have separate bills of lading for various trades on the principle of the line laid down in the resolution. Their American friends had a few objections to offer to what was done at Liverpool, but their criticisms were very reasonable, and some of them were met. With reference to this particular question, that of negligence, the New York Produce Exchange said: 'This exemption is demanded by the circumstances under which modern steamship traffic is carried on, and is a change eminently just and necessary.' In the great coal trade of England the question was taken up at a conference in London, and a simple bill of lading for the coal trade, embodying a negligence clause, was settled in 1885. In the same year there was the meeting at the Baltic, where it was decided that there should be a conference of merchants and shipowners to settle the question. Seven merchants and six shipowners were selected; and, after a great many meetings, they came to a very satisfactory bill of lading, which distinctly confirmed the Liverpool decision. In consequence of what fell from the President the other day, he wished to refer to what had been done in London. He understood Mr. Justice Butt to say that the Chamber of Commerce of London had prepared a bill of lading, in which it was denied that the shipowner should have this negligence clause. It was very singular how that happened, but it did not happen. After the Baltic meeting the Chamber of Commerce of London convened a meeting of merchants, from which shipowners were excluded, and appointed a sub-committee. This sub-committee recommended a resolution which would have left the matter in its present uncertain condition; but when the resolution was brought before the Chamber, the Chamber came to the conclusion that the matter was not ripe for such a step, and it did nothing. Consequently it was not right to say that the London Chamber of

Commerce was in favour of the Hamburg decision. He thought Liverpool had a right to complain of the action of Dr. Wendt. Why was the decision of Liverpool not considered conclusive? He did not think it was right to seize the opportunity, when there was no British shipowner present, to reopen a question which had been the subject of such long and careful consideration. He thought he had said enough to show that, if the Association wanted to render any further service in the matter, there was only one course open to them—they could not be on both sides of the question—they arrived at a decision in Liverpool; they ought to confirm that decision. He appealed to his friend Dr. Wendt to be satisfied. He had scored very well in this controversy. He hoped the Association would take a sensible course. He was sure Her Majesty's Government would not consent to interfere with their liberty of contract; but let the Association take a consistent position and get rid of that which common sense had already so clearly condemned.

I said: I have been requested by the executive council of this Association to explain the reasons why, after the decision of the Liverpool Congress in 1882, this subject had been reopened and debated at the Hamburg Congress in 1885. They were simply that, soon after it had become known that the Liverpool Congress had decided to relieve shipowners from liability for the negligence of their servants (the masters and crews of their vessels), numerous protests were addressed to the officers of the Association by different chambers of commerce and bodies of underwriters, not only in this country, but also in India and Australia, all of which were reported to the Milan Congress in 1883. But further, there had been a great pressure brought to bear upon the executive council by the most important chambers of commerce and underwriting bodies in the interior of Germany—all members of the Association—to reopen this question; and when the Senate of Hamburg honoured us with the invitation to hold our conference in that city in 1885, it was decided to make use of that opportunity to do so. As all the members of this Association had due notice of this intention, not only through the general secretary, but likewise by the public press, which was equally available to such shipowners as had not joined our Association, it is quite evident that if the

English shipowners did not think it advisable to see their interests represented at Hamburg, it was not the fault of the Association. It is well known that I represent as many underwriters of ships as of cargoes. I therefore look at the matter from an impartial point of view; and if I have been in favour of the liability of shipowners, it is because my experience has taught me that nine-tenths of all collisions at sea are clearly caused by the negligence of the crew. But before I sit down, let me add a few words on the most conspicuous line of argument used with regard to the matter at issue between ship and cargo owners and their respective underwriters. Where a ship has been lost through the fault of the master, and the underwriter of cargo on board has sued the shipowner for his loss, it has often been argued that the underwriter should not be allowed to make such a claim, as he had received a premium for this risk; and public opinion has frequently been misled by this line of argument. I may therefore be permitted again to refer to the well-known principle that the contract of insurance is solely a contract of indemnity between underwriter and assured. As soon as the underwriter has paid, he acquires all the rights of the assured against third parties; and as he covers only his insured, and does not also insure the shipowner against the negligence of his servants, I fail to see why he should not make any claim against the shipowner. I have never heard it stated that it is an iniquity if the underwriter of a ship lost by the fault of another vessel recovers the loss from the owner of the latter vessel. This underwriter has likewise received his premium for the risk in question; and why should he be entitled to recover, and the same remedy be refused to the cargo underwriter?

HERR LAEISZ (Hamburg) supported the resolution, and said that he believed the general feeling amongst jurists in Germany was in favour of the negligence clause being embodied in the bill of lading.

MR. BARNES (London) said this was a case in which a good underwriter might exclaim, 'Save me from my friends.' It was only the litigious underwriter who wished to dispute claims. He happened to know that, in consequence of the continual friction between some small underwriters and shipowners, the great lines had it within their intention to issue contracts to deliver; and he put it to Dr. Wendt and his friends whether six months after that course was taken the underwriters would think that the action of the conference had been wise if it adopted the Hamburg Bill of Lading? The London Chamber of Commerce did not represent in any degree mercantile or shipowners' interests on this question. He knew a case where a small committee of the Chamber carried a resolution, and the secretary forwarded it as representing the opinion of the Chamber. As soon as the facts were known, the merchants of the City, headed by Messrs. Rothschild, signed a protest condemnatory of everything that had been done, and a committee was called of people who understood the question. They censured the secretary and the committee for having gone out of their way and adopted such a course without calling the general members together. No shipowner had ever heard of any such idea as that the London Chamber was going to discuss this question, still less that it was going to send a resolution favouring any particular course. If such a thing had been done, it would be necessary that it should be followed up in some other way by getting an association which would really represent mercantile interests. If nine-tenths of the losses at sea were due to negligence, what was the object of insurance, except to provide against loss, and those losses ought to be covered by the underwriters. If that association were to affirm the Hamburg resolution, the great body of shipowners would combine together and have a gigantic insurance association, and they would issue a bill of lading simply receiving the goods and undertaking to deliver them and to cover them against all risks. Shipowners were heartily tired of having to pay for a pipe bursting or other similar things which ought to be paid for by the underwriters, and they had far better meet the difficulty by taking the risk from the outset.

MR. THOMAS SCRUTTON (London) said it had come within his duty in the last year or two to examine rather carefully the records made in connection with the only official documents which we possessed in this country respecting accidents at sea, and unless those records were utterly wrong, there was no foundation for the calculation of Dr. Wendt. The official returns showed that out of a total loss of over 6,000 lives, no fewer than 4,043 were due to the weather alone, and under weather it included heavy gales, hurricanes, calms, currents, fogs, and lightning. He hoped that the Association would distinctly put aside, therefore, the impression that nine-tenths of the accidents were due to the negligence of crews.

Mr. Wreacks (New York) stated that the negligence clause adopted at New York was the same as that resolved upon at Liverpool, the only difference being the transposition of the clause referring to the want of due diligence on the part of the shipowner, with the object of emphasising the feeling that under no circumstances should shipowners be excused for their own negligence; but when they exercised all due diligence in the selection of their servants they were protected in the bill of lading.

M. Clunet (Paris) referred to the decisions on this subject of the Conference on Commercial Law, which met at Antwerp in 1885, and in order to bring the Liverpool Bill of Lading into conformity with its decisions, desired to propose the following amendments to the resolution before the meeting :—

1. 'That the Liverpool form of bill of lading should be amended by the addition, after the words " barratry of the master and crew," of the words " (but not common theft)."

2. 'That it be also amended by the addition after the words, " error in judgment of the pilot, master, or shipowner," of the words, " (but not the acts of the grossest fault and recklessness)." '

Mr. Brown (Glasgow) supported the motion, with which, he said, Glasgow was thoroughly in accord.

Mr. M'Andrew (London) held that it was no use attempting to introduce a set form of bill of lading when past experience showed that it was in the power of anybody to depart from it if they chose. Legislation is necessary in order that the liabilities of the shipowners might be defined, and Mr. Glover, instead of hindering the action of the London Chamber, should have assisted them in bringing the subject before the Legislature. He would be glad if Mr. Glover would now give them that assistance.

Mr. Allen (Liverpool) supported the resolution.

Mr. R. Lowndes (Liverpool) thought it would be far better

that the conference should pass the resolution than leave the question to be settled by the Legislature.

HERR AHLERS (Hamburg) urged the appointment of a commission to consider the question.

M: THÉODORE C. ENGELS (Antwerp) supported the proposal of Mr. Gray Hill.

MR. ELISHA SMITH (Liverpool) complained that only one side of the question had been put forward. He had no objection to the clause, but it would be wrong to let it go forth that the conference wanted only the Liverpool Bill of Lading. The Liverpool Bill of Lading was a compromise. Merchants were prepared to give shipowners all they wanted in this matter. Would shipowners in return not give them fair play? Merchants would release shipowners from all things which were not under their control, if shipowners would only hold themselves liable for the things that were under their control. If they accepted the Liverpool Bill of Lading, he promised them that they should hear nothing more on the question.

THE CHAIRMAN then put the question. M. CLUNET, at the suggestion of the Chairman, withdrew his first amendment, and the second fell to the ground for want of a seconder.

MR. GRAY HILL'S resolution was then put to the meeting, and carried by an overwhelming majority, upwards of 120 voting in its favour and 1 against; a result which was natural, as those who could not agree with the resolution, seeing the large body of shipowners and their friends would put them in a minority, abstained from voting altogether.

After faithfully recording this result, I have now, in order to close the history of this movement with the publication of this volume, only to refer to the report of the Royal Commission on Loss of Life at Sea, to which, as previously stated, the principal firms of the mercantile community of the city of London had addressed a petition, in which they expressed the opinion that if the Royal Commission should think fit to recommend the wording of a bill of lading, such recommendation might be universally adopted.

This report, dated August 27, 1887, evidently proves that the Royal Commissioners have not thought proper to consider the subject very minutely, or, what is perhaps more likely, did not agree on the wording of such a document as they could be sure would meet general approbation. It contains only the following passages relating to—

(2). Responsibility of Shipowners to Charterers and Owners of Cargoes.

By the common law the shipowner is responsible to the owners of the cargo which his vessel carries for the seaworthiness of the ship and for the negligent acts of the captain, in the absence of any contract to the contrary. But having regard to the supposed peculiar character of the trade, the Legislature has for many years given to shipowners the benefit of an exceptional limitation to such responsibility. They are not liable to an extent exceeding 8*l*. per ton on the registered tonnage for injury to property entrusted to their care or to other ships or their cargoes. They have also an entire immunity from liability for loss by fire. There has also grown up of late years a practice among shipowners to make large additional exceptions, by their bills of lading, in respect of their liability.

Mr. Hollams, who has had a large experience as a solicitor in the conduct of shipping cases, says: 'In my opinion some of the modern bills of lading are objectionable upon the ground that they free the shipowner from his ordinary responsibility and thus produce loss of life and loss of property, and on the ground that they are only nominal contracts. They are not contracts really entered into, they are only contracts by a fiction of the law, which holds that a man taking a bill of lading must be presumed to have adopted it. This is a view which has been questioned by eminent Judges, but I take it to be the acknowledged rule of law. It is not a contract in fact.'

The Royal Commission of 1874 recommended that any provision in a bill of lading or other agreement having for its object or effect to avoid or limit the liability of a shipowner in respect of goods shipped under it, should have no legal validity, if the loss has been occasioned by the ship having been sent to sea in an unseaworthy condition, unless he proves that he, or those to whom he commits the management of his business, used all reasonable means to make and keep his vessel seaworthy.

We are of the same opinion.

We think no shipowner ought to be relieved by contract or otherwise from the legal obligation to properly equip, man, provision, outfit, and render said ship seaworthy for performing her intended voyage; nor from the legal obligation to properly stow and deliver her cargo as agreed by the terms of shipment (except as to the stowage of chartered vessels loaded under directions of the charterer).

And the 'Summary of Recommendations' with which the report concludes contains only the following sub.:—

(12). That any provision in a bill of lading or other agreement having for its object or effect to avoid or limit the liability of a shipowner in respect of goods shipped under it should have no legal validity if the loss has been occasioned by the ship having been sent to sea in an unseaworthy condition, unless he proves that he or those to whom he commits the management of his business used all reasonable means to make or keep the vessel seaworthy.

In closing this chapter, let me call attention to the consideration of a few points which seem rather to have been lost sight of during the controversy.

One of the peculiarities of the contract of Affreightment is, that it is sometimes defined in the charter-party and sometimes in the bill of lading, and again both documents have frequently to be examined to find the terms upon which the goods are carried. It is not always easy to see which is the case in particular circumstances, and it may not be out of place, therefore, to add here a few words of explanation.

The charter-party may be either (1) a demise or letting of the ship (*locatio navis*), or (2) of the ship with the services of her master and crew (*locatio navis et operarum magistri et nauticorum*), or (3) a sale of the right to have goods conveyed (*locatio operis vehendarum mercium*).

The first two charter-parties have nothing to do with the affreightment; the last is closely connected with it, and may be the one document which alone defines it.

The bill of lading, on the other hand, is sometimes considered as containing the contract, but, strictly speaking, it is never more than evidence of the agreement, and sometimes it is little more than a receipt for the goods.

Speaking generally, the charter-party to which I have last referred is the sole contract as between the charterer and the shipowner, and in case of any dispute between them the bill of lading is entirely subsidiary to it. These are not, however, the parties alone interested in the affreightment; the vessel may have been put up as a general ship, or the bills of lading may be endorsed over to third parties, in which case the contract as between the shipowners and the holders (without notice of the charter-party) of the bills of lading is defined simply by the bill of lading.

As therefore either the charter-party or the bill of lading may be the governing document, it is of the greatest necessity that equal care should be taken that each should accurately describe the contract which it is intended should be entered into. Either party is naturally at liberty to insist on the terms being inserted which he wishes to be applied; if the other does not consent, the contract need not be made; but it should be remembered that on some points, if the document is silent, the law presumes certain conditions. It is in the nature of the thing that these conditions ought to be fair to all parties, and should not be altered by express terms unless for very cogent reasons. The principal of these implied conditions are, that the vessel should be seaworthy and reasonably fit to carry the described cargo. There is no presumption of law, however, at least in this country, specifying in what cases the non-performance of the contract should be excused. A carrier by land is by the common law held excused if he is prevented from fulfilling his contract by certain dangers. A carrier by sea is not so protected. It is absolutely necessary, therefore, that the perils intended to be excepted should be fully set down in the charter-party and bill of lading. The difficulty of deciding what these excepted perils should be was not great in times gone by. Superior force, whether of the elements or by human agency, has always been considered valid excuse for the non-performance of the contract. Gradually a great number of other exceptions came to be inserted from time to time, and of recent years shipowners have made, as has been seen, strenuous efforts to have excepted all acts of negligence of the persons placed in charge of their vessels. Why this contention has arisen is not difficult to trace. The adoption of steam has created a revolution in the carrying trade in more ways than one. The business is now done with so much greater expedition, and is so much greater in extent than in the old sailing times, that owners cannot give the *personal* supervision which they used; accidents and losses are much more frequent, especially by negligence causing collisions and strandings; competition is greater, and profits are smaller. Owners therefore feel the liability for their servants' negligence to a much greater extent than in times gone by. They may be protected by insurance, but this does not, on the whole, diminish their reluctance to face the liability, for it means enhanced premiums.

On the other hand, the owners of the cargo and their respective underwriters object, and have good cause for objecting, to the insertion of the negligence clause. If anyone can diminish the risk of loss by negligence, it is the shipowner, and no one else. He is the employer, and holds the power of dismissal, and this power alone can have any weight in checking neglect of duty on the part of the officers and crew. The cargo-owner is helpless. Once his goods shipped, he has lost control over them, and he never has any influence to bring to bear upon those on board the ship. His opinion—and it seems manifestly a fair view to take—is that where the power to check negligence is, there should be the responsibility, if notwithstanding loss by negligence does occur. This argument has never been fairly refuted by the shipowners. Their case, put in plain words, is that they are not bound to accept the liability unless they like; they do not like, and the shipper may keep his goods, unless he chooses to ship with the negligence clause inserted.

It may be well to point out that shipowners and shippers and their representatives are not the only, or indeed the chief parties interested in this discussion; the public have a serious stake in the matter. The greater the loss by negligence, the higher price will the consumer have to pay, and he is entitled to say, and enforce his opinion through the Legislature, that such course shall be adopted which naturally must most conduce to diminishing loss by negligence and its consequences to his pocket. He has not done so yet in this country, but unless shipowners accept these natural demands, I shall not be surprised if he certainly will at no distant time. Why shipowners should insist upon their action in this matter is difficult to see, because, after all, as between them and the shippers, out of whom they make their profits, the whole difficulty is susceptible of a perfectly easy solution, which can be described in one sentence: Accept the responsibility and adjust the freight in accordance.

The threat which the managers of some of the largest steamship companies have used, that if the shippers and their underwriters decline to consent to the general demand of the shipowners and accept their bills of lading with the negligence clause, they would force them to insure the goods themselves against all risks, issuing a document which would be both bill of lading and policy of insurance, might certainly obviate a part of the difficulty, but only a part, because there are not very many steamship companies, as at present constituted, whose guarantees for the values of all the cargoes they happened to carry on board of their vessels would be readily taken, and therefore the matter remains in *statu quo*.

III.

CASE OF THE 'MARIE DE BRABANT.'

To the Right Honourable Sir Stafford H. Northcote, C.B., M.P., *President of the Board of Trade.*

Sir,—I have the honour to hand to you a memorial drawn up on behalf of certain merchants, subjects of the kingdom of Belgium, regarding a decision of the Judicial Committee of H.M. Privy Council in a matter of appeal from the High Court of Admiralty.

The appellants were the owners of cargo on board of a Belgian ship, which came into collision with a British ship on the high seas. The British ship was found to blame for the collision, but the redress, which could be awarded to the owners of the Belgian ship and her cargo, was held by the Admiralty Court to be limited by the provisions of the 54th section of the Merchant Shipping Amendment Act to the sum of eight pounds for each ton of the British ship, and the Judicial Committee of H.M. Privy Council confirmed the interpretation which the Admiralty Court had given to that statute. The merchants, on behalf of whom the memorial has been prepared, conceive that the British tribunal, in applying the limitations of the British municipal law to a case of injury done by a British ship to a Belgian ship and cargo on the high seas, have infringed a very important principle of international maritime law, inasmuch as no treaty engagement that such limitation shall apply to Belgian ships in cases of collision beyond the limits of British jurisdiction has been entered into between Great Britain and Belgium, whilst the Belgian tribunals afford to the owners of British ships and cargoes in cases of collision with Belgian ships on the high seas as ample a remedy as heretofore. There is thus no longer any reciprocity between the two nations in respect of the redress which their maritime tribunals afford in cases of collision on the high seas.

The memorial was originally prepared with the design of invoking the diplomatic intervention of the Belgian Government with Her Majesty's Government in the hope of obtaining thereby some more adequate compensation for the injury inflicted upon the Belgian merchants than that which the decision of the British tribunals has supplied. That design having for various reasons been abandoned, I have the honour to submit the subject-matter of the memorial to the attention of the President of the Committee of Privy Council for Trade, in the hope that the principles involved in it may be thoughtfully weighed when the time for the revision of the British Statute Law shall arrive.

I have the honour to be, Sir,
Your obedient humble Servant,
ERNST EMIL WENDT.

15 Fenchurch Buildings, London, E.C.:
    26 November 1866.

MEMORIAL OF J. F. CAIL, A. HALOT, AND COMPANY, OF BRUSSELS, MERCHANTS, AND OTHERS, THE OWNERS OF PART OF THE CARGO LADEN ON BOARD THE BELGIAN STEAMSHIP 'MARIE DE BRABANT.'

Your memorialists are Belgian subjects, owners of merchandise laden on board the Belgian screw steamship 'Marie de Brabant,' which sailed from Antwerp, bound to different ports in the Mediterranean and Black Seas, in the month of April 1863. The Belgian ship was pursuing her voyage in the Mediterranean Sea on May 15, 1863, when at about 2.30 A.M. she was run into by the British screw steamship 'Amalia,' and was, with all her cargo, totally lost. The British ship, at the time of the collision, was bound for the port of Liverpool, where she arrived on May 26, 1863; and on June 8 following an action *in rem* against the British ship was instituted by your memorialists in the High Court of Admiralty of England.

The Judge, assisted by Trinity Masters, heard the cause on August 5, 1863, and pronounced the British ship to be solely to blame.

There were other actions brought at the same time against the British ship on behalf of the owners of the Belgian ship, and also on behalf of the owners of other portions of the cargo lost on board her, and the Judge of the Admiralty Court heard and decided all the actions at the same time.

Your memorialists are perfectly satisfied with the decision of the High Court of Admiralty of England in respect of the blame of the collision, but they find themselves aggrieved by reason of the benefit which they would have derived by proceeding against the British ship in a Belgian Court exercising Admiralty jurisdiction. It has always been regarded as one of the advantages of proceeding *in rem* in the Admiralty, that a foreign plaintiff, in whatever country the Admiralty jurisdiction is exercised, will be entitled to the benefit of the same marine laws which would be administered to him in his own country. Sir Leoline Jenkins, one of the highest of British authorities on matters of maritime law, in reporting to the Crown, that the owners of a French ship might have justice done to them in the Admiralty Court of England, observes: 'Having the authority of two such eminent persons in the law (the Attorney-General and the Solicitor-General) that this cause of spoil is cognisable in the Admiralty, I will only add besides, that it has been always so till some late interruptions, and it is not without special satisfaction to a foreign plaintiff that he shall have the benefit of the same marine laws here that we are judged by in his country' ('Life of Sir Leoline Jenkins,' vol. ii. p. 764).

Your memorialists submit that in the proceedings instituted by them against the British ship in the High Court of Admiralty of England they have not had the benefit of the same marine law in respect of compensation for the damage caused to them by the wrongful navigation of the British ship as would have been administered to them in their own country if the British ship had come within the jurisdiction of the Belgian Crown, and as would have been administered to the owners of the British ship if they had proceeded in a cause of collision against a Belgian ship in a Belgian Court exercising Admiralty jurisdiction.

Your memorialists submit that it is a maxim of Admiralty

law that delictum in respect of a collision between two ships on the high seas gives rise to a maritime lien, which travels with the wrong-doing ship into whosoever possession it may pass. This doctrine was fully recognised by the Judicial Committee of Her Majesty's Privy Council in the case of the 'Bold Buccleugh' (Moore's Privy Council Reports, vii. p. 284). This maritime lien is the foundation of a right of action against the wrong-doing ship in all Admiralty Courts; the action *in rem* being a proceeding which the Admiralty jurisdiction has inherited from the jurisprudence of ancient Rome, which, when it authorised an injured party to proceed by way of arrest against the thing itself which had done the damage, instead of proceeding against the owners of the thing by citing them personally, made the *res* itself liable to the full extent of its value to make good the plaintiff's damage. This measure of compensation, which is the peculiar feature of the proceeding *in rem* under the Roman law, has been found by experience to be so consistent with equity and public policy as regards the navigation of ships, that it has been incorporated by the Legislatures of most European nations into their municipal codes as a governing rule for the Courts which administer their territorial law in regard to the personal wrongs of their subjects, whatever may be the *locus delicti* as distinguished from the common law of nations in regard to maritime torts on the high seas. The result of this positive legislation has been that, until the judgment recently delivered by the High Court of Admiralty of England upon the claim of your memorialists, the same measure of compensation in causes of damage on the high seas has been administered in the municipal courts both of Great Britain and of Belgium, and in the Admiralty Court of each country. It is submitted, however, by your memorialists that the foundation upon which the practice of the Admiralty Court in either country rests is different from that upon which the practice of the municipal courts proceeds, and that whilst the latter is the creation of the territorial legislature, and may be varied at its pleasure, the former can only be subject to regulations which are consistent with the law of nations.

Your memorialists have on this head the support of the high authority of Lord Stowell and Sir John Nicholl, who declined to apply the municipal law of Great Britain on occasions when it was sought to invoke it into the Admiralty Court as the governing rule for measuring the compensation to be awarded for damage in suits between British and foreign vessels; Lord Stowell was called upon to apply the rule of the British statute (53 Geo. III. c. 159, s. 1), which limits the responsibility of the owners of ships to the value of the ship and its freight, in the case of the 'Carl Johan,' a Swedish vessel, which had been in collision on the high seas with the 'Edward,' a British vessel; but he refused, saying that the British statute was one of domestic policy, and that with reference to foreign vessels it only applied to cases where the advantages and disadvantages of such a rule were common to them and to British vessels; that if all States adopted the same rule there would be no difficulty, but that no such general rule was alleged, and that if the law of Sweden adopted such a rule it would apply to both countries, but that Sweden could not claim the protection of the statute without affording a similar protection to British subjects in similar cases. Sir John Nicholl, in quoting this judgment of Lord Stowell, and commenting upon it, in the case of the 'Girolamo' (3 Haggard's Admiralty Reports, 187), observed that—' Lord Stowell's judgment appears to be a direct authority that these acts, however binding on the municipal courts, nay, possibly, even on the Admiralty Court as between subject and subject, yet cannot be set up by a foreign ship in the Admiralty jurisdiction;' and in an earlier part of the same case (p. 184), the same learned Judge explains the principle upon which his view proceeds, remarking that—'There is another ingredient of some importance in this case, this defence (namely, the statutory limitation of responsibility) is set up by a foreign owner in behalf of a foreign ship in a Court governed by the principles of international law, and a question arises whether a foreigner can in a suit in this Court set up as a defence a municipal law made to regulate municipal courts only, and contrary to those general rules of law which prevail amongst commercial nations. Reciprocity or mutuality has always been considered as one of the leading principles of justice in questions arising between nation and nation. For example, by our municipal law this country established the principle of restitution upon payment of salvage in cases of recapture of British property from the enemy notwithstanding *pernoctacio infra præsidia* or any of those old general rules by which the property of the former owners was held to be extinguished, but the application of this rule to the property even of our allies in the late war was held to depend entirely upon its reciprocity. Thus, in the case of the 'St. Iago' (cited in the 'Santa Cruz,' 1 Chr. Rob. p. 63) the property was adjudged as prize to the recaptors on the ground of its not being shown that restitution of the property of an ally upon payment of salvage was the rule of the Spanish law; and in the case of the 'Santa Cruz' itself, the same principle was applied with respect to Portugal, but upon the country afterwards engaging prospectively to restore upon payment of salvage British property recaptured by Portuguese subjects, the rule was made mutual.

Your memorialists submit that the reciprocity which Lord Stowell and Sir John Nicholl require as an essential condition to authorise a Court of International Law to apply a positive rule enacted by the Legislature of the State in which the Court sits to the subjects of another State, does not exist unless the Courts of the other State apply the same rule in analogous cases which come before them; in other words, the Courts of each State must be authorised and allowed by their respective Legislatures to apply one and the same rule; but the learned Judge of the High Court of Admiralty, in dealing with the claim of your memorialists, has proceeded upon a different view of the principle of reciprocity when he says that—'If the statute in question (25 & 26 Vict. cap. 10) gives the right of limited liability to the British shipowner and the foreign shipowner alike, if there be perfect reciprocity, then complete justice is done, and the former objection, that it was unjust to give relief to the British owner when a similar relief was denied to the foreigner, is removed.' Your memorialists submit that Lord Stowell and Sir John Nicholl did not hold themselves precluded by the language of the British statute from giving the same relief to both British and foreign shipowners alike, but they declined to extend to Swedish shipowners the relief which was given to all shipowners in general words by the statute, because there was no reciprocity in such matters between Great Britain and Sweden; in other words, because a different rule prevailed in the Swedish Courts.

The mode in which the learned Judge of the High Court of Admiralty came to apply the British statute to the claims of your memorialists may be thus briefly stated:—

The owners of the British ship, the defendants, immediately upon the plaintiffs instituting their action *in rem* against the ship under the Admiralty law, instituted a suit against the plaintiffs *personally* in the Admiralty Court, under the provisions of two British statutes. One of these statutes (24 Vict. c. 10) was passed in 1861, and enacted, that whenever any ship is under arrest of the High Court of Admiralty, the said Court shall have the same powers as are conferred upon the High Court of Chancery in England by the ninth part of the Merchant Shipping Act, 1854. It may be observed that the ninth part of the Merchant Shipping Act had been held by the learned Judge, up to the passing of 24 Vict. c. 10, to apply only to British ships.

The other statute (25 & 26 Vict. c. 10), entitled the 'Merchant Shipping Act Amendment Act, 1862,' has enacted that ' the owners of any ship, whether British or foreign, shall not in cases where without their actual fault or knowledge any loss or damage is by reason of the improper navigation of such ship caused to any other ship or boat, or to any goods, merchandise, or other things whatever, on board any other ship or boat, be answerable in damages to an aggregate amount exceeding eight pounds for each ton of the ship's tonnage.'

The learned Judge of the High Court of Admiralty held that he was bound to apply the provisions of this British statute to the claim of your memorialists, although the cause of action did not arise in British waters, and to hold that your memorialists were not entitled to compensation up to the value of the *res* itself, but only up to the arbitrary limit of eight pounds per ton of the tonnage of the British ship.

Your memorialists have been led to believe, from studying the course of decisions in the High Court of Admiralty of England, that it was an axiom of international law recognised by those Courts that no State has authority to bind by its territorial law any but its own members or such members of other States as are within its territory, and that it was a principle of international jurisprudence admitted by those Courts, that Courts administering the law of nations are bound so to narrow the interpretation of the general language of municipal statutes as to keep them in harmony with the law of nations. Lord Stowell has affirmed this principle in the case of 'Le Louis' (2 Dodson, 239), when he says that 'neither a British Act of Parliament nor any Commission founded on it can affect any right or interest of foreigners, unless they are founded upon principles and impose regulations which are consistent with the law of nations. That is the only law which Great Britain can apply to them, and the generality of any terms employed in an Act of Parliament must be narrowed in construction by a religious adherence thereto.'

Your memorialists submit that when the owner of an American ship, the 'Wild Ranger,' which had been arrested in a cause of collision in the Admiralty Court by the owner of a British vessel, filed a petition under 24 Vict. c. 10, s. 13, for a declaration of limited liability in its favour under the provisions of the Merchant Shipping Act, 1854, the learned Judge of the High Court of Admiralty held that the American defendant was not within the beneficial operations of the Merchant Shipping Act, 1854, s. 504, although the language of the section is most general, viz. '*No owner of any sea-going ship*, where any loss or damage is by reason of the improper navigation of such ship without his actual fault or privity caused to any other ship or boat, or to any goods, merchandise, or other things whatsoever, on board any other ship or boat, shall be answerable in damages beyond the value of his ship and the freight.' The collision in the case of this American ship had occurred on the high seas, and the American shipowner claimed the benefit of the statute as being the *lex fori* on the principle that the *lex fori* is a conclusive rule in all questions of *remedy*. But the learned Judge of the High Court of Admiralty held that the Court of Chancery had rightly decided in the case of Cope v. Doherty (2 De Gex & Jones, 614) that the British statute giving limited liability did not apply to *foreign ships on the high seas*, and that it made no difference in the construction of the statute whether the foreign ship came into collision with another foreign ship, as in Cope *v.* Doherty, or with a British ship, and the learned Judge went on to cite a passage from the decision of Vice-Chancellor Wood in the General Iron Screw Collier Company *v.* Schurmanns (1 Johnson & Hemming, 193) in the following words: 'I adhere to the opinion which I expressed in Cope *v.* Doherty, that a foreign ship meeting a British ship on the open ocean cannot be abridged of any of her rights by any Act of the British Legislature.'

The learned Judge of the High Court of Admiralty on this occasion held himself bound to put the same construction on the British statute in regard to limited liability as the Court of Chancery had done, and declined to apply it to the owners of foreign ships which came into collision with British ships on the high seas.

The same learned Judge, in deciding upon the claims of your memorialists, has held that he was bound to draw a substantial distinction between the words of the Merchant Shipping Act, 1854, which says that '*no owner of any sea-going ship shall be answerable* in damages,' and the words of the Merchant Shipping Act Amendment Act, 1862, which says that '*the owners of any ship, whether British or foreign, shall not be answerable* in damages.'

In construing the latter section he says: 'I must look to see whether it purports to affect the owners of British ships and the owners of foreign ships, and if I find from the words of the section and from the whole context and subject-matter that it was the intention of the statute to make limited liability for both British and foreign ships, then I consider there is no serious objection to the British Parliament legislating for foreigners' (Moore's Privy Council Reports, N.S. i. 475).

Your memorialists, however, submit that the fact of the British Parliament having legislated for foreigners does not of itself remove all serious objections to its so doing, or establish its right to do so in matters in which the subjects of foreign States are not subject to British jurisdiction, and that the general language of a British statute is not sufficient to warrant the Admiralty Court in applying it to foreigners, unless the place in which the cause of action arose was subject to British jurisdiction. Thus the very words of the Merchant Shipping Act Amendment Act, 1854, which the learned Judge of the High Court of Admiralty distinguishes from the words of the Merchant Shipping Act Amendment Act, 1862, were held by Vice-Chancellor Wood, in the case of the General Iron Screw Collier Company *v.* Schurmanns, 'to be applicable to foreigners where such foreigners were *within British jurisdiction*, and he applied the principle of limited liability, as enacted by the general words of the Act of 1854, to the case of a British ship which had damaged a foreign ship by collision happening within three miles from the shore of the United Kingdom, seeing that the place where the cause of action arose was within British jurisdiction. This decision of the Vice-Chancellor is referred to in the judgment of the Privy Council upon your memorialists' appeal.

Your memorialists submit that, having exhausted the ordinary means of redress which were open to them, by instituting proceedings in the High Court of Admiralty of England, and by appeal to the Judicial Committee of Her Majesty's Privy Council, and having been deprived by an interpretation which those Courts have concurred in giving to the *municipal law* of Great Britain, of the full benefit of the maritime lien, to which they were entitled under the law of nations, they may with reason apply to Her Majesty's Government to make good to them their loss, seeing that Her Majesty's Courts afford them no means of obtaining compensation to which they are entitled under the law of nations for the injurious conduct of Her Majesty's subjects in running down the Belgian ship and sinking their merchandise on the high seas.

Your memorialists submit that the value of their merchandise lost on board the Belgian ship, in consequence of the wrongful act of Her Majesty's subjects on the high seas, is 17,762*l.* 7*s.* 4*d.*, whilst they have only been allowed to recover in the Admiralty Court the sum of 6,757*l.* 8*s.* 3*d.*, being their proportion of the statutory value of the British ship, and that whilst that statutory value has been calculated at the rate of 8*l.* per ton, and no more, under the Merchant Shipping Amendment Act, 1862, the real value of the British ship would have been estimated in the market at about 30*l.* per ton, to the full benefit of which value your memorialists submit they are entitled under the law of nations.

J. F. CAIL, HALOT, & CO.

Molenbeck St. Jean, près Bruxelles,
le neuf février 1800 soixante-six.

Vu par nous, Bourgmestre de la Commune de Molenbeck Saint-Jean, pour légalisation de la signature de MM. J. F. CAIL, HALOT, & CIE.

Pr. le Bourgmestre,
L'Échevin,
CHARLES PIERS.

L.S.

Molenbeck St. Jean, le 10 février 1866.

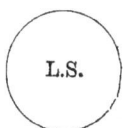

Vu pour légalisation de la signature de Monsieur CHARLES PIERS, qualifié ci-dessus.
Le Gouverneur du Brabant,
DUBOIS THORN.

L.S.

Bruxelles, 10 février 1866.

I certify the above to be the signature of Mr. Dubois Thorn, Governor of the province of Brabant, in the Kingdom of Belgium. Brussels, this tenth day of February 1866.

THOS. JAS. MALTBY,
H.B.M. Vice-Consul at Brussels.

L.S.

Board of Trade, Whitehall:
December 28, 1866.

Sir,—I am directed by the Board of Trade to acknowledge the receipt of your letter of the 26th ultimo, forwarding a memorial from certain merchants, subjects of the kingdom of Belgium, and owners of part of the cargo of the Belgian S.S. 'Marie de Brabant,' protesting against the decision of the Judicial Committee of the Privy Council in the matter of appeal from the High Court of Admiralty, in the case of the collision between the S.S. 'Marie de Brabant,' and the British S.S. 'Amalia,' by which the liability of the owners of the 'Amalia' was held to be limited to the sum of 8*l.* per ton upon the tonnage of the ship, under section 54 of the

Merchant Shipping Act Amendment Act, 1862, and submitting whether the memorialists are not entitled under the General Maritime Law to compensation for their losses to the full extent of the value of the 'Amalia,' which was supposed to be about 30*l.* per ton, also that the above decision is inconsistent with previous decisions of the Court of Admiralty and other British Courts in similar cases.

I am to inform you that the case has received the very careful consideration of this Board.

In reply, I am to observe, in the first place, that the law under which the case in question was decided is based upon the principle of complete reciprocity; because, had the claim been made by the owners of a British ship or cargo against a foreign ship, the liability of the foreign shipowner would be limited just as much as the liability of a British shipowner is limited where the claim is by a foreigner. It appears further to the Board of Trade that the foreigner who comes into the Courts of this country to sue must take the remedy as he there finds it, and can have no ground for complaint if he is treated in the same manner in which British ships and British subjects are treated in the same Courts.

I am to add that the Board of Trade are not aware that there is any uniform maritime law binding upon different nations by which the measure and limit of liability in case of collisions on the high seas is determined. Different nations may and do fix different measures and limits, and all that can be required by principles of reciprocity is, that foreign shipowners shall have the same rights and the same limit of liability as shipowners belonging to this country.

Under these circumstances I am to request that you will be so good as to inform the memorialists that whilst the Court of law has in the case in question decided as it was bound to do, according to the statute law of the country, there is not, in the opinion of the Board of Trade, any reason to suppose that the decision is inconsistent with the principles of international maritime law.

I am, Sir, your obedient Servant,
T. H. FARRER.

E. E. Wendt, Esq.

The Secretary, Board of Trade, Whitehall, S.W.

Sir,—I am favoured with your communication of the 28th instant, and take the earliest opportunity of expressing my grateful thanks to my Lords for the careful consideration which you inform me has been given to the memorial laid before them by me in the case of the 'Marie de Brabant,' and being thoroughly convinced that a reconsideration of the matter would very materially alter the views by which the revision of the Merchant Shipping Act will be influenced, I feel it my duty, in a few words, to express my regret that the Board of Trade should have thought it necessary to proclaim so decidedly their adherence to the principles laid down by the judicial authorities before whom the case was heard; and also to point out how those principles, and the arguments by which they are supported, appear to me to be faulty and untenable.

The whole point at issue seems to rest upon the true meaning of the word 'reciprocity,' for Dr. Lushington in his judgment says: 'If the statute in question gives the right of limited liability to the British shipowner and the foreign shipowner alike, if there be perfect reciprocity, then complete justice is done,' while the Board of Trade now adopt the same mode of expression, and say that the law in question 'is based upon the principle of complete reciprocity,' because a British and a foreign ship would, in our Courts, be treated alike.

Now, I venture to refer to the dictionaries for the exact meaning of the word 'reciprocity,' and I find Johnson defines it as a 'reciprocal obligation,' while 'reciprocal' he holds to mean, 'acting in vicissitude—mutual—done by each to each—mutually interchangable.' Webster defines the word 'reciprocity' to be 'mutual action and reaction.' The meaning which I claim for the expression is quite in accordance with these authorities, and I venture to submit that it cannot properly be narrowed into a synonym for 'similarity or impartiality,' as has been done in the case in question.

By way of illustration, I will assume A and B to be the British and Belgian Legislatures respectively; C to be a British, and D a Belgian shipowner. My contention is, that the Courts of A should give to D the same relief as, *cæteris paribus*, B would give to C, and *vice versâ*; in other words, C and D should know that, whether they apply to A or B, the same justice would be done them; this is complete reciprocity. The narrower view is, that all obligations have been fulfilled if A treats C and D alike, leaving B out of the question altogether; this is impartiality. The former is the proper basis of International Law; the latter of the more narrow municipal legislation.

The further argument that a foreigner coming to our Courts to sue must take the same remedy as we give to our own ships may, I think, be disposed of in a few words. For this purpose it is only necessary to point out that proceedings for damage must, in a majority of cases, be taken before the Courts of the country to which the wrong-doer belongs. The owner of a British ship sunk on the high seas by the default of a Belgian would not be likely to wait until he might happen to find the Belgian ship in one of our own ports, but would at once go to Belgium to claim redress. The effect of the recent decisions is, therefore, to give immunity to our own subject when he is the wrong-doer, leaving him to obtain his remedy in full in a foreign Court, when he is in the right!

In conclusion, as by the comity of nations certain principles of International Law have been generally adopted and adhered to, so the principle first established, as I am advised, by the Code de Commerce, was almost universally adhered to, viz. that the damage caused should be made good by the wrong-doing ship and freight as far as their value went; and this became, therefore, a fundamental principle of General Maritime Law, not adopted by treaty obligations, but by the uniform decisions of the Courts of those countries whose subjects were mostly interested in maritime intercourse, viz. France, the United States, and Great Britain, and so remained until our legislation of 1862,—I have the honour to be, Sir,

Your most obedient Servant,

E. E. WENDT.

15 Fenchurch Buildings: December 31, 1866.

IV.

OBSERVATIONS ON

17 & 18 Vict. cap. 104. The Merchant Shipping Act, 1854.

17 & 18 Vict. cap. 120. The Merchant Shipping Repeal Act, 1854.

18 & 19 Vict. cap. 91. The Merchant Shipping Act Amendment Act, 1855.

25 & 26 Vict. cap. 63. The Merchant Shipping Act Amendment Act, 1862.

15 Fenchurch Buildings,
London: December 1866.

INTRODUCTORY REMARKS.

IT is impossible to deny that the issuing of the Merchant Shipping Act (17 & 18 Vict. cap. 104), 1854, was in so far a complete success, as it not only brought into operation very useful enactments on matters connected with the Maritime Law of the country, which had been previously entirely neglected by the Legislature, but has proved beyond doubt that when in course of time this Principal Act with its Repeal Act (17 & 18 Vict. cap. 120), 1854, and its Amendment Acts (18 & 19 Vict. cap. 91), 1855, and (25 & 26 Vict. cap. 63), 1862, should have been properly revised, so complete and efficient a codification could be arrived at that even foreign Governments would acknowledge its usefulness, and would not be slow in adopting it without much diplomatic interference; by this hitherto unusual but certain process the chances are not very remote that the Legislature of our country may be able to lay the foundation of what is acknowledged to be generally wanting—a Codification of International and General Maritime Law.

No power is so well able to take the initiative in so noble a design as Great Britain, but I admit the difficulties can only be overpowered by doing justice to all acknowledged international principles, and by not attempting to particularise too much.

The more general the views taken in fixing upon principles, the greater the chances of our final success.

The following observations have been prepared with the intention that whenever the Board of Trade should think the time arrived for a proper revision of the above Acts—which I sincerely hope is not far distant—they may be considered as suggestions of a mind for thirty years practically engaged in treating matters of International and General Maritime Law.

That *one* complete Act would generally be preferred to another Amendment Act I ought not to omit to state, and, although enactments as to the Law of General Average, of Freight, of Bottomry, and of Marine Insurance would be very desirable indeed, I would rather recommend the postponement of legislation on the two last subjects, Bottomry and Marine Insurance, than see further delayed what may be called the issue of the first or principal Code on matters of General Maritime Law.

The embodying into the new Maritime Law of the International General Average Rules (framed at York in 1864, under the auspices of the late Lord Chief Baron, Sir Fitzroy Kelly, and of Lord Penzance) and the International Law of Affreightment (framed at Sheffield in 1865, under the auspices of the then Queen's Advocate, Sir Robert Phillimore[1]) would undoubtedly be very acceptable to the mercantile community in general.

How far an alteration in the present system of stating averages could improve its efficiency by establishing a state of things similar to that in practice on the Continent will have to be very carefully considered.

I think it would not be difficult to issue a regulation which, without at all interfering with the independent action of the average stater, would more than hitherto secure a proper execution of the average statements, and prevent the ridiculous delay which now only too frequently takes place before a definite settlement of questions of General Average can be arrived at, to the great prejudice of all parties concerned.[2]

17 & 18 VICT. CAP. 104.

THE MERCHANT SHIPPING ACT, 1854.

PART II.—*British Ships—Their Ownership, Measurement and Registry.*

18. No ship shall be deemed to be a *British* ship unless she belongs wholly to Owners of the following description; that is to say:—
  1. Natural-born *British* subjects:
    Provided that no natural-born subject who has taken the oath of allegiance to any foreign sovereign or state shall be entitled to be such Owner as aforesaid, unless he has, subsequently to taking such last-mentioned oath, taken the oath of allegiance to Her Majesty, and is and continues to be during the whole period of his so being, an Owner, resident in some place within Her Majesty's dominions; or, if not so resident, member of a *British*

---

[1] Late Judge of the High Court of Admiralty.

[2] Since these observations were made, the Average Adjusters' Association has been formed, which has caused a decided improvement in the state of things here complained of.

factory, or partner in a house actually carrying on business in the United Kingdom, or in some other place within Her Majesty's dominions.
2. Persons made denizens by letters of denization, or naturalised by or pursuant to any Act of the Imperial Legislature, or by or pursuant to any Act or ordinance of the proper legislative authority in any *British* possession.

Provided that such persons are, and continue to be, during the whole period of their so being Owners, resident in some place within Her Majesty's dominions, or, if not so resident, members of a *British* factory, or partners in a house actually carrying on business in the United Kingdom, or in some other place within Her Majesty's dominions, and have taken the oath of allegiance to Her Majesty subsequently to the period of their being so made denizens or naturalised.
3. Bodies corporate established under, subject to the laws of, and having their principal place of business in the United Kingdom, or some *British* possession.

It is evident that this section does not sanction the bearing allegiance to two Sovereigns and owning vessels under their two respective flags at the same time; nevertheless it is a fact that a naturalised British subject owning a vessel or vessels registered at the London Custom House, has during the time of his residence in this country reassumed his Prussian nationality, become a citizen and merchant in one of the Prussian ports, and owns vessels under the Prussian as well as under the British flag. The consequences which may only too easily arise from such a state of things in case of war are apparent. A perusal of the return of the number and tonnage of American vessels sold to British subjects in the year 1863 most clearly shows the temptation to which unscrupulous persons are exposed in such times, and the necessity of more strict regulations. I would suggest the addition of the following:—

(4) 'The right to own a British ship ceases at any time that a person, although residing within Her Majesty's dominions, becomes citizen or merchant in another country.'

PART III.—*Masters and Seamen.*

109. The various provisions of the third part of this Act shall have the following applications, unless the context or subject-matter requires a different application; (that is to say),

So much of the third part of this Act as relates to the delivery or transmission of lists of Crews to the Registrar-General of Seamen shall apply to all Fishing Vessels belonging to the United Kingdom, whether employed exclusively on the Coasts of the United Kingdom or not; to all ships belonging to the *Trinity House,* or the Commissioners of Northern Lighthouses, constituted as hereinafter mentioned, or the Port of *Dublin* Corporation, and to all pleasure Yachts, and to the Owners, Masters, and Crews of such ships:

So much of the third part of this Act as relates to the delivery and transmission of lists of Crews, and to the Wages and Effects of deceased Seamen and Apprentices, shall apply to all sea-going *British* ships, wherever registered, of which the Crews are discharged or whose final port or destination is in the United Kingdom, and to the Owners, Masters, and Crews of such ships:

So much of the third part of this Act as relates to the shipping and discharge of Seamen in the United Kingdom shall apply to all sea-going *British* ships, wherever registered, and to the Owners, Masters, and Crews of such ships:

So much of the third part of this Act as relates to Seamen volunteering into the Royal Navy shall apply to all sea-going *British* ships, wherever registered, and to the Owners, Masters, and Crews of such ships, wherever the same may be:

So much of the third part of this Act as relates to rights to Wages and remedies for the recovery thereof; to the shipping and discharge of Seamen in foreign ports; to leaving Seamen abroad and to the relief of Seamen in distress in foreign ports; to the provisions, health, and accommodation of Seamen; to the power of Seamen to make complaints; to the protection of Seamen from imposition; to discipline; to Naval Courts on the high seas and abroad; and to crimes committed abroad; shall apply to all ships registered in any of Her Majesty's dominions abroad, when such ships are out of the jurisdiction of their respective Governments, and to the Owners, Masters, and Crews of such ships:

And the whole of the third part of this Act shall apply to all sea-going ships registered in the United Kingdom (except such as are exclusively employed in fishing on the coasts of the United Kingdom, and such as belong to the *Trinity House*, the Commissioners of Northern Lighthouses, or the Port of *Dublin* Corporation, and also except pleasure Yachts), and also to all ships registered in any *British* possession and employed in trading or going between any place in the United Kingdom and any place or places not situate in the possession in which such ships are registered, and to the Owners, Masters, and Crews of such ships respectively, wherever the same may be.

Under the head of provisions applicable to 'Colonial Ships' should be inserted the words: 'Examinations and Certificates of Masters and Mates.'

The present system of rendering examinations *not* obligatory on all masters and mates sailing vessels under the British flag must improperly and unjustly confer advantages on colonial ships to which they are not entitled, as scarcely any merchant or underwriter is aware of the disadvantages to which he may possibly subject his property on board of a vessel the navigation of which, although under the British flag, is not conducted by two officers whose competency is vouched for, and who consequently cannot be made to bear, what is almost the only effective punishment in case of misconduct, viz. the cancelling or suspending of their respective certificates.

In the case of the 'Trail' which I brought to the

notice of the Board of Trade in 1863, the disadvantages of such a state of things were made most apparent, and in the case of the 'Lucy,' Captain Dahl, which was lost in 1864 while on a voyage from Capetown to East London, and in which most suspicious circumstances came to light, no satisfactory result was arrived at, because neither master nor mate had any certificate whatever. I therefore do not imagine any grave reasons will be adduced against the suggested alteration, with which, of course, an exact definition of the home trade of each colony would be combined.

At all events, public justice demands that the differences which the law permits in the command and navigation of *British* vessels shall be so conspicuously made known that no merchant or underwriter is further misled upon the subject in question.[1]

---

[1] Lloyd's list of August 29 contains the following striking confirmation of the above views expressed by me several months previously:—

'A copy of the following despatch from the Governor of the Straits Settlements, referring to the circumstance that large New South Wales ships are allowed to sail in the China seas without certificated officers, has been received from the Board of Trade.

'Lloyd's: August 29, 1867.

'Government House, Singapore: July 4, 1867.

'My Lord Duke,—At an enquiry recently held here by a Marine Court into the circumstances attending the stranding of the British barque "Othello," of Sydney, Official No. 49,281, of 342 tons burthen, bound from Manilla to Sydney, it appeared from the evidence of the master, Mr. William Sullivan, who was also the owner, that he had no certificate of competency, or service, having been in the colonies since 1827, and during thirty years as master of ships. The mate, Duncan McDougall, also stated that he had no certificate of competency, or service.

'2. I presume your Grace will consider it proper that these circumstances should be brought to the notice of the Board of Trade, as although under the existing law there may be no means of compelling masters and mates of vessels trading solely in the colonies to have certificates of competency, it is probably not known to underwriters in England that large New South Wales ships are allowed to sail in the China Seas without certificated officers.

'I have, &c.

(Signed) 'H. St. George Ord.

'His Grace the Duke of Buckingham and Chandos, &c.'

Volunteering in the Navy.

214. Any Seaman may leave his ship for the purpose of forthwith entering into the Naval Service of Her Majesty, and such leaving his ship shall not be deemed a desertion therefrom, and shall not render him liable to any punishment or forfeiture whatever; and all stipulations introduced into any agreement whereby any Seaman is declared to incur any forfeiture or be exposed to any loss in case he enters into Her Majesty's Naval Service shall be void, and every Master or Owner who causes any such stipulation to be so introduced shall incur a penalty not exceeding twenty pounds.

215. Whenever any Seaman, without having previously committed any act amounting to and treated by the Master as desertion, leaves his ship in order to enter into the Naval Service of Her Majesty, and is received into such service, the Master shall deliver to him his clothes and effects on board such ship, and shall pay the proportionate amount of his wages down to the time of such entry, subject to all just deductions, as follows; (that is to say), the Master of the said ship shall pay the same to the officer authorised to receive such Seaman into Her Majesty's service, either in money or by bill drawn upon the Owner, and payable at sight to the order of The Accountant-General of the Navy; and the receipt of such officer shall be a discharge for the money or bill so given; and such bill shall be exempt from stamp duty; and if such wages are paid in money, such money shall be credited in the Muster-book of the ship to the account of the said Seaman; and if such wages are paid by bill, such bill shall be noted in the said Muster-book, and shall be sent to the said Accountant-General, who shall present the same, or cause the same to be presented for payment, and shall credit the produce thereof to the account of the said Seaman; and such money or produce (as the case may be) shall not be paid to the said Seaman until the time at which he would have been entitled to receive the same if he had remained in the service of the ship which he had so quitted as aforesaid; and if any such bill is not duly paid when presented, the said Accountant-General, or the Seaman on whose behalf the same is given, may sue thereon, or may recover the wages due by all or any of the means by which

wages due to Merchant Seamen are recoverable; and if upon any Seaman leaving his ship in the manner and for the purpose aforesaid, the Master fails to deliver his clothes and effects, or to pay his wages as hereinbefore required, he shall, in addition to his liability to pay and deliver the same, incur a penalty not exceeding twenty pounds; provided that no officer who receives any such bill as aforesaid shall be subject to any liability in respect thereof, except for the safe custody thereof, until sent to the said Accountant-General as aforesaid.

216. If upon any Seaman leaving his ship for the purpose of entering the Naval Service of Her Majesty, the Owner or Master of such ship shows to the satisfaction of the Admiralty that he has paid or properly rendered himself liable to pay an advance of wages to or on account of such Seaman, and that such Seaman has not at the time of quitting his ship duly earned such advance by service therein, and, in the case of such liability as aforesaid, if such Owner or Master actually satisfies the same, it shall be lawful for the Admiralty to pay to such Owner or Master so much of such advance as has not been duly earned, and to deduct the sum so paid from the wages of the Seaman earned, or to be earned, in the Naval Service of Her Majesty.

217. If, in consequence of any Seaman so leaving his ship without the consent of the Master or Owner thereof, it becomes necessary for the safety and proper Navigation of the said ship to engage a substitute or substitutes, and if the wages or other remuneration paid to such substitute or substitutes for subsequent service exceed the wages or remuneration which would have been payable to the said Seaman under his agreement for similar service, the Master or Owner of the said ship may apply to the Registrar of the High Court of Admiralty in *England* for a certificate authorising the repayment of such excess; and such application shall be in such form, and shall be accompanied by such documents, and by such statements, whether on oath or otherwise, as the Judge of the said Court from time to time directs.

218. The said Registrar shall, upon receiving any such application as aforesaid, give notice thereof in writing, and of the sum claimed, to the Secretary to the Admiralty, and shall proceed to

examine the said application, and may call upon the Registrar-General of Seamen to produce any papers in his possession relating thereto, and may call for further evidence; and if the whole of the claim appears to him to be just, he shall give a certificate accordingly; but if he considers that such claim, or any part thereof, is not just, he shall give notice of such his opinion in writing, under his hand, to the person making the said application, or his attorney or agent; and if within sixteen days from the giving of such notice such person does not leave, or cause to be left, at the office of the Registrar of the said Court a written notice demanding that the said application shall be referred to the Judge of the said Court, then the said Registrar shall finally decide thereon, and certify accordingly; but if such notice is left as aforesaid, then the said application shall stand referred to the said Judge in his chambers, and his decision thereon shall be final, and the said Registrar shall certify the same accordingly; and the said Registrar and Judge respectively shall, in every proceeding under this Act, have full power to administer oaths, and to exercise all the ordinary powers of the Court, as in any other proceeding within its jurisdiction: and the said Registrar or Judge (as the case may be) may, if he thinks fit, allow for the costs of any proceeding under this Act any sum not exceeding five pounds for each Seaman so quitting his ship as aforesaid; and such sum shall be added to the sum allowed, and shall be certified by the said Registrar accordingly.

219. Every certificate so given shall be sent by post or otherwise to the person making the application, his attorney or agent, and a copy thereof shall be sent to the Accountant-General of the Navy; and such Accountant-General shall, upon delivery to him of the said original certificate, together with a receipt in writing, purporting to be a receipt from the Master or Owner making the application, pay to the person delivering the same out of the moneys applicable to the Naval Service of her Majesty, and granted by Parliament for the purpose, the amount mentioned in such certificate; and such certificate and receipt shall absolutely discharge the said Accountant-General and Her Majesty from all liability in respect of the moneys so paid, or of the said application.

220. Every person who, in making or supporting any such

application, as aforesaid, to the Registrar of the High Court of Admiralty, forges, assists in forging, or procures to be forged, or fraudulently alters, assists in fraudulently altering, or procures to be fraudulently altered, any document, and every person who, in making or supporting any such application, presents or makes use of any such forged or altered document, or who, in making or supporting any such application, makes or gives, or assists in making or giving, or procures to be made or given, any false evidence or representation, knowing the same to be false, shall be deemed guilty of a misdemeanour.

Volunteering in the Navy.—Cases have frequently occurred where vessels have been entirely unable to complete their crews in consequence of volunteering into the Navy, and very serious losses have thereby arisen to the owners and other parties concerned; the mere restitution of differences in wages seems therefore not to be equitable, and, in fact, in the margin to clause 217 it is stated as follows, viz. : 'If new Seamen are engaged instead of the original Seamen, the owner may apply for repayment of any extra expense he has been put to.' This, I think, should be clearly embodied in the clause itself, and not only excess of wages, but all other expenses and a reasonable sum for detention should, when clearly proved, be cheerfully allowed to the parties aggrieved.

237. Every person who, not being in Her Majesty's Service, and not being duly authorised by law for the purpose, goes on board any ship about to arrive at the place of her destination, before her actual arrival in dock or at the place of her discharge, without the permission of the Master, shall for every such offence incur a penalty not exceeding twenty pounds; and the Master or person in charge of such ship may take any such person so going on board as aforesaid into custody, and deliver him up forthwith to any constable or peace officer, to be by him taken before a justice

or justices or the sheriff of the county in *Scotland*, and to be dealt with according to the provisions of this Act.[1]

238. If, within twenty-four hours after the arrival of any ship at any port in the United Kingdom, any person then being on board such ship solicits any Seaman to become a lodger at the house of any person letting lodgings for hire, or takes out of such ship any effects of any Seaman, except under his personal direction and with the permission of the Master, he shall for every such offence incur a penalty not exceeding five pounds.

The frequent reports of cases of infringement of these two clauses prove evidently that either the punishments attached to the offences enumerated are not sufficiently severe, or the difficulty of bringing offenders to justice is greater than previously anticipated. One of the most noted places in this respect is Cardiff, and it is quite clear that some very different and more efficient measure must be taken in order to stop these evil practices.

243. Whenever any Seaman who has been lawfully engaged, or any Apprentice to the sea service, commits any of the following offences, he shall be liable to be punished summarily as follows; (that is to say),
> (1) For desertion he shall be liable to imprisonment for any period not exceeding twelve weeks, with or without hard labour, and also to forfeit all or any part of the clothes and effects he leaves on board, and all or any part of the wages or emoluments which he has then earned, and also, if such desertion takes place abroad, at the discretion of the Court, to forfeit all or any part of the wages or emoluments he may earn in any other ship in which he may be employed until his next return to the United Kingdom, and to satisfy any excess of wages paid by the Master or Owner of the

---

[1] This section has since been made a little more efficacious by § 5 of the Merchant Seamen (Payment of Wages) Act, 1880.

ship from which he deserts to any substitute engaged in his place at a higher rate of wages than the rate stipulated to be paid to him:

(2) For neglecting or refusing, without reasonable cause, to join his ship, or to proceed to sea in his ship, or for absence without leave at any time within twenty-four hours of the ship's sailing from any port either at the commencement or during the progress of any voyage, or for absence at any time without leave and without sufficient reason from his ship, or from his duty not amounting to desertion or not treated as such by the Master, he shall be liable to imprisonment for any period not exceeding ten weeks, with or without hard labour, and also, at the discretion of the Court, to forfeit out of his wages a sum not exceeding the amount of two days' pay, and in addition for every twenty-four hours of absence either a sum not exceeding six days' pay, or any expenses which have been properly incurred in hiring a substitute:

(3) For quitting the ship without leave after her arrival at her port of delivery and before she is placed in security, he shall be liable to forfeit out of his wages a sum not exceeding one month's pay:

(4) For wilful disobedience to any lawful command he shall be liable to imprisonment for any period not exceeding four weeks, with or without hard labour, and also, at the discretion of the Court, to forfeit out of his wages a sum not exceeding two days' pay:

(5) For continued wilful disobedience to lawful commands, or continued wilful neglect of duty, he shall be liable to imprisonment for any period not exceeding twelve weeks, with or without hard labour, and also, at the discretion of the Court, to forfeit for every twenty-four hours' continuance of such disobedience or neglect, either a sum not exceeding six days' pay or any expenses which have been properly incurred in hiring a substitute:

(6) For assaulting any Master or mate he shall be liable to im-

prisonment for any period not exceeding twelve weeks, with or without hard labour :
(7) For combining with any other or others of the crew to disobey lawful commands, or to neglect duty, or to impede the navigation of the ship or the progress of the voyage, he shall be liable to imprisonment for any period not exceeding twelve weeks, with or without hard labour :
(8) For wilfully damaging the ship or embezzling or wilfully damaging any of her stores or cargo, he shall be liable to forfeit out of his wages a sum equal in amount to the loss thereby sustained, and also, at the discretion of the Court, to imprisonment for any period not exceeding twelve weeks, with or without hard labour :
(9) For any act of smuggling of which he is convicted, and whereby loss or damage is occasioned to the Master or Owner, he shall be liable to pay to such Master or Owner such a sum as is sufficient to reimburse the Master or Owner for such loss or damage ; and the whole or a proportionate part of his wages may be retained in satisfaction or on account of such liability, without prejudice to any further remedy.

Would it not be more practical to substitute for any one under the age of sixteen the punishment of whipping in lieu of imprisonment? The 24 & 25 Vict. cap. 97, gives the power to add, for males under sixteen years, the punishment of whipping; why not substitute it here, where it is clear that a youth is usually led away by others, and would only be brought by imprisonment into the company of bad characters?'[1]

In part 8 of this clause I would omit the words ' wilfully damaging the ship,' as it appears to me this offence

---

[1] Imprisonment cannot now be imposed for offences covered by sub-sections (1) and (2). See the Merchant Seamen (Payment of Wages) Act, 1880, § 10.

is more efficiently treated in the 24 & 25 Vict. cap. 97, and it might perhaps be useful to refer here to this enactment.

260. Any officer in command of any ship of Her Majesty on any foreign station, or, in the absence of such officer, any Consular officer, may summon a Court, to be termed a 'Naval Court,' in the following cases; (that is to say),
- (1) Whenever a complaint which appears to such officer to require immediate investigation is made to him by the Master of any *British* ship, or by any certificated Mate, or by one or more of the Seamen belonging to any such ship:
- (2) Whenever the interest of the Owner of any *British* ship or of the cargo of any such ship appears to such officer to require it:
- (3) Whenever any *British* ship is wrecked or abandoned or otherwise lost at or near the place where such officer may be, or whenever the Crew or part of the Crew of any *British* ship which has been wrecked, abandoned, or lost abroad, arrives at such place.

2. I would suggest to insert the following words, ' or their respective underwriters,' before 'appears,' &c.

261. Every such Naval Court as aforesaid shall consist of not more than five, and not less than three members, of whom, if possible, one shall be an officer in the Naval Service of Her Majesty not below the rank of lieutenant, one a Consular officer, and one a Master of a *British* Merchant ship, and the rest shall be either officers in the Naval Service of her Majesty, Masters of *British* Merchant ships, or *British* Merchants; and such Court may include the Naval or Consular officer summoning the same, but shall not include the Master or Consignee of the ship to which the parties complaining or complained against may belong; and the Naval or Consular officer in such Court, if there is only one such officer in the Court, or, if there is more than one, the Naval or Consular

officer who, according to any regulations for settling their respective ranks for the time being in force, is of the highest rank, shall be the president of such Court.

In the interest of public policy, I think it advisable to order that if the party at whose request the Naval Court is summoned, or who gave such information that its being summoned was decided upon, should not be personally competent to take the position of prosecutor and its adherent functions before such Naval Court, that the officer summoning such Naval Court should appoint any one person of sufficient knowledge to act in such capacity of prosecutor before such Naval Court.

280. The Board of Trade shall sanction forms of official log-books, which may be different for different classes of ships, so that each such form contains blanks for the entries hereinafter required; and an official log of every ship (except ships employed exclusively in trading between ports on the coasts of the United Kingdom) shall be kept in the appropriate sanctioned form; and such official log may, at the discretion of the Master or Owner, either be kept distinct from the ordinary ship's log or united therewith, so that in all cases all the blanks in the official log be duly filled up.

I think it is a dangerous proceeding to allow more than *one* log recognised by law on board of any vessel. The most efficient manner to deal with the matter would be to follow the course adopted by most of the principal Continental Governments, where the ship's log is only legal if it is kept in a book numbered and sealed officially, and in a form prescribed by law, and which might at the termination of the voyage be acted upon as now prescribed for the official log.[1]

[1] Vide page 655.

284. The following offences in respect of official log-books shall be punishable as hereinafter mentioned; (that is to say),
(1) If in any case an official log-book is not kept in the manner hereby required, or if any entry hereby directed to be made in any such log-book is not made at the time and in the manner hereby directed, the master shall for each such offence incur the specific penalty herein mentioned in respect thereof, or where there is no such specific penalty, a penalty not exceeding five pounds.
(2) Every person who makes, or procures to be made, or assists in making, any entry in any official log-book in respect of any occurrence happening previously to the arrival of the ship at her final port of discharge more than twenty-four hours after such arrival, shall for each such offence incur a penalty not exceeding thirty pounds:
(3) Every person who wilfully destroys or mutilates or renders illegible any entry in any official log-book, or who wilfully makes, or procures to be made, or assists in making any false or fraudulent entry or omission in any such log-book, shall for each such offence be deemed guilty of a misdemeanour.

As the concocting of averages and the consequent frauds upon owners and underwriters are only possible by keeping double logs, or by making subsequent entries in the official logs, and as these frauds have lately augmented in a fearful degree, it is absolutely necessary to increase the punishments for such offences in a suitable manner, and it ought to be enacted—
(2) That the offences here designated shall be punished as misdemeanours, and
(3) That the offences here designated shall be punished as felonies.

But I would most earnestly recommend that the opportunity should be taken to make such enactments that the loose and inefficient manner of extending ship's protests would be put a stop to.

Every ship's protest ought to be drawn up in such a manner that it is apparent on the face of the document which part is the real copy or extract of the official log, and which are the additions afterwards thought of; for, as sailors will sign and swear to almost anything that is laid before them, and as in my own experience ship's protests have been issued and executed in the most formal manner, but containing facts entirely false, it is evident that the general public engaged in mercantile adventures, and entirely dependent on the truth of such documents, have a right to expect that all regulations in respect thereto shall be framed so carefully as to render such irregularities next to impossible.

PART IV.—*Safety and Prevention of Accidents.*

292. The following rules shall be observed with respect to boats and life-buoys; (that is to say),

(1) No decked ship (except ships used solely as steam-tugs and ships engaged in the whale fishery) shall proceed to sea from any place in the United Kingdom unless she is provided, according to her tonnage, with boats duly supplied with all requisites for use, and not being fewer in number nor less in their cubic contents than the boats, the number and cubic contents of which are specified in the Table marked S in the schedule hereto for the class to which such ship belongs:

(2) No ship carrying more than ten passengers shall proceed to sea from any place in the United Kingdom, unless, in addition to the boats hereinbefore required, she is also provided with a lifeboat furnished with all requisites for use, or unless one of her boats hereinbefore required is rendered buoyant after the manner of a lifeboat:

(3) No such ship as last aforesaid shall proceed to sea unless she is also provided with two life-buoys:

And such boat and life-buoys shall be kept so as to be at all times fit and ready for use: provided, that the enactments with respect to boats and life-buoys herein contained shall not apply in any case in which a certificate has been duly obtained under the tenth section of the Passengers' Act, 1852.

293. In any of the following cases (that is to say),

(1) If any ship hereinbefore required to be provided with boats and life-buoys proceeds to sea without being so provided therewith, or if any of such boats or life-buoys are lost or rendered unfit for service, in the course of the voyage, through the wilful fault or negligence of the Owner or Master; or,

(2) If, in case of any such boats or life-buoys being accidentally lost or injured in the course of the voyage, the Master wilfully neglects to replace or repair the same on the first opportunity; or,

(3) If such boats and life-buoys are not kept so as to be at all times fit and ready for use;

Then if the Owner appears to be in fault he shall incur a penalty not exceeding one hundred pounds, and if the Master appears to be in fault he shall incur a penalty not exceeding fifty pounds.

294. No officer of customs shall grant a clearance or transire for any ship hereinbefore required to be provided with boats or with life-buoys unless the same is duly so provided; and if any such ship attempts to go to sea without such clearance or transire, any such officer may detain her until she is so provided.

The subject of boats and life-buoys has been so carefully treated at the Society of Arts that I refrain from any observations on the matter in question.

303. For the purpose of the enactments herein contained with respect to the surveys and certificates of passenger steamships, the word 'passengers' shall be held to include any persons carried in a steam ship, other than the Master and Crew, and the Owner, his

family and servants; and the expression 'passenger steamer' shall be held to include every *British* steamship carrying passengers to, from, or between any place or places in the United Kingdom, excepting steam ferry boats working in chains, commonly called steam bridges.

It appears to me that the expression 'passenger steamers' ought to be applied only to those which carry passengers for a monetary consideration.

Quite recently a decision has been given by the Judge of the High Court of Admiralty (the 'Hanna') which strongly demonstrates the necessity of more careful wording of the clause. In this case Dr. Lushington held that a person clearly not belonging to the crew, who was on board for the voyage as a friend of the master, was a 'nondescript, certainly not a passenger!' In my case of the 'Beta,' so fully referred to in my remarks on the question of compulsory pilotage, two persons taken over to Ireland out of charity and paying no fares were held to be passengers.

How far Dr. Lushington was justified in adding to the clear words of this clause the new exemption of nondescripts may be left for others to decide; I must, however, point out and earnestly urge upon the Board of Trade the necessity of so framing and amending the enactments by which the commerce of this great country is governed, that it shall no longer be possible for mere subtleties of reasoning to make a difference of many thousands of pounds to perfectly innocent persons, such being the result of the contradictory decisions above quoted.

319. If the Owner or Master or other person in charge of any passenger steamer receives on board thereof, or on or in any part thereof, or if such ship has on board thereof, or on or in any part thereof, any number of passengers, which, having regard to the

time, occasion, and circumstance of the case, is greater than the number of passengers allowed by the certificate, the Owner or Master shall incur a penalty not exceeding twenty pounds, and also an additional penalty not exceeding five shillings for every passenger over and above the number allowed by the certificate, or, if the fare of any of the passengers on board exceeds five shillings, not exceeding double the amount of the fares of all the passengers who are over and above the number so allowed as aforesaid, such fare to be estimated at the highest rate of fare payable by any passenger on board.

Some means should be adopted for insuring prompter and more certain punishment for offences against this clause; for instance, it is generally understood that on Whit Monday 1867 the 'Alexandra' river steamer left London Bridge with more than 2,000 persons on board, her statutory number being little in excess of 1,000, and she was, in fact, so dangerously overcrowded, that 200 to 300 left her at Blackwall; any accident happening to a steamer in such a state would be attended with such frightful consequences that no mercy should be shown to deliberate offenders.

326. Whenever any steam ship has sustained or caused any accident occasioning loss of life or any serious injury to any person, or has received any material damage affecting her seaworthiness or her efficiency either in her hull or in any part of her machinery, the Owner or Master shall, within twenty-four hours after the happening of such accident or damage, or as soon thereafter as possible, send to the Board of Trade, by letter signed by such Owner or Master, a report of such accident or damage, and of the probable occasion thereof, stating the name of the ship, the port to which she belongs, and the place where she is; and if such Owner or Master neglect so to do he shall for such offence incur a penalty not exceeding fifty pounds.

327. If the Owner of any steam ship have reason, owing to

the non-appearance of such ship, or to any other circumstance, to apprehend that such ship has been wholly lost, he shall, as soon as conveniently may be, send notice thereof in like manner to the Board of Trade, and if he neglect so to do within a reasonable time he shall for such offence incur a penalty not exceeding fifty pounds.[1]

328. In every case of collision, in which it is practicable so to do, the Master shall, immediately after the occurrence, cause a statement thereof, and of the circumstances under which the same occurred, to be entered in the official log-book (if any), such entry to be signed by the Master, and also by the Mate or one of the Crew, and in default shall incur a penalty not exceeding twenty pounds.

I think these clauses can be omitted, as the deposition which the master is bound to make before the Receiver of Wreck, copy of which is by this officer transmitted to the Board of Trade, is sufficient for the object the Board has apparently in view with respect to the report.

PART V.—*Pilotage.*

330. The Fifth Part of this Act shall apply to the United Kingdom only.

331. Every pilotage authority shall retain all powers and jurisdiction which it now lawfully possesses, so far as the same are consistent with the provisions of this Act; but no law relating to such authority, or to the Pilots licensed by it, and no act done by such authority, shall, if inconsistent with any provision of this Act, be of any force whatever.

332. Every pilotage authority shall have power, by bye-law made with the consent of Her Majesty in Council, to exempt the Masters of any ships, or of any classes of ships, from being compelled to employ qualified Pilots, and to annex any terms or conditions to such exemptions, and to revise and extend any exemptions now existing by virtue of this Act or any other Act of

---

[1] Slightly amended by 36 & 37 Vict. c. 85.

Parliament, law, or charter, or by usage, upon such terms and conditions and in such manner as may appear desirable to such authority.

333. Subject to the provisions contained in the Fifth Part of this Act, it shall be lawful for every pilotage authority, by bye-law made with the consent of Her Majesty in Council, from time to time to do all or any of the following things within its districts; (that is to say),

 (1) To determine the qualifications to be required from persons applying to be licensed as Pilots, whether in respect of their age, skill, time of service, character, or otherwise :

 (2) To make regulations as to the approval and licensing of Pilot boats and ships, with power to establish and regulate companies for the support of such boats and ships, and for a participation in the profits made thereby; the companies so established to be exempt from the provisions of the Act passed in the session holden in the seventh and eighth years of the reign of Her present Majesty, chapter one hundred and ten, intituled 'An Act for the Registration, Incorporation, and Regulation of Joint Stock Companies':

 (3) To make regulations for the government of the Pilots licensed by them, and for insuring their good conduct, and their constant attendance to and effectual performance of their duty, either at sea or on shore :

 (4) To fix the terms and conditions of granting licenses to Pilots and Apprentices, and of granting such pilotage certificates as hereinafter mentioned to Masters and Mates, and to make regulations for punishing any breach of such regulations as aforesaid committed by such Pilots or Apprentices, or by such Masters and Mates, by the withdrawal or suspension of their licenses or certificates, as the case may be, or by the infliction of penalties to be recoverable summarily before two justices, so that no such penalty be made to exceed the sum of twenty pounds, and so that every such penalty

be capable of reduction at the discretion of the justices by whom the same is inflicted:

(5) To fix the rates and prices or other remuneration to be demanded and received for the time being by Pilots licensed by such authority, or to alter the mode of remunerating such Pilots, in such manner as such authority may, with such consent as aforesaid, think fit, so that no higher rates or prices be demanded or received from the Masters or Owners of ships in the case of the *Trinity House* than the rates and prices specified in the Table marked U in the Schedule hereto; and in the case of all other pilotage authorities, than the rates and prices which might have been lawfully fixed or demanded by such pilotage authorities respectively under any Act of Parliament, charter, or custom in force immediately before the commencement of this Act:

(6) To make such arrangements with any other pilotage authority for altering the limits of their respective districts, and for extending the powers of such other authority, or the privileges of the Pilots licensed by such other authority or any of them, to all or any part of its own district, or for limiting its own powers or the privileges of its own Pilots or any of them, or for sharing the said last-mentioned powers and privileges with the said other authority and the Pilots licensed by it, or for delegating or surrendering such powers and privileges or any of them to any other pilotage authority either already constituted or to be constituted by agreement between such authorities, and to the Pilots licensed by it, as may appear to such pilotage authorities to be desirable for the purpose of facilitating navigation or of reducing charges on shipping:

(7) To establish, either alone or in conjunction with any other pilotage authority or authorities, funds for the relief of superannuated or infirm qualified Pilots, or of their wives, widows, or children, or to make any new regulations

with respect to any funds already applicable to the above purposes or any of them, with power to determine the amount, manner, time, and persons (such persons to be in the service of such pilotage authority) to and in which and by and upon whom the contributions in support of such existing or future funds may be made or levied; and further, to declare the persons or class of persons (such persons or class of person being confined to men in the service of such pilotage authority, their wives, widows, or children) entitled to participate in the benefits of such existing or future funds, and the terms and conditions upon which they are to be so entitled:

(8) To repeal or alter any bye-law made in exercise of the above powers, and to make a new bye-law or new byelaws in lieu thereof: [1]

And every bye-law duly made by any pilotage authority in exercise of the powers hereby given to it shall be valid and effectual, notwithstanding any Act of Parliament, rule, law, or custom to the contrary.

334. Every bye-law proposed to be enacted by any pilotage authority in pursuance of the foregoing powers shall, before it is submitted to Her Majesty in Council for her assent, be published in such manner as may from time to time be prescribed by the Board of Trade.

335. Every Order in Council made in pursuance of the provisions hereinbefore contained shall be laid before both Houses of Parliament as soon as possible after the making thereof.

336. If the greater part in number of the qualified Pilots belonging to any port, or the Local Marine Board, where there is one, or at any port where there is no Local Marine Board; if any Masters, Owners, or insurers of ships, being not less than six in number, consider themselves aggrieved by any regulation or bye-law in force when this Act comes into operation, or hereafter made under some authority other than the provisions of this Act, or by any defect or omission therein, they may appeal to the Board of Trade, and the said Board may thereupon revoke or alter any such

---

[1] To grant special sea licenses (35 & 36 Vict. c. 73, § 11).

regulation or bye-law, or may make additions thereto in such manner as, having regard to the interests of the persons concerned, may appear to be just and expedient; and every order so made shall be conclusive in the matter.

337. Every pilotage authority shall deliver periodically to the Board of Trade, in such form and at such times as such Board requires, returns of the following particulars with regard to pilotage within the port or district under the jurisdiction of such authority; (that is to say),

(1) All bye-laws, regulations, orders, or ordinances relating to Pilots or pilotage for the time being in force:
(2) The names and ages of all Pilots or Apprentices licensed or authorised to act by such authority, and of all Pilots or Apprentices acting either mediately or immediately under such authority, whether so licensed or authorised or not:
(3) The service for which each Pilot or Apprentice is licensed:
(4) The rates of pilotage for the time being in force, including therein the rates and descriptions of all charges upon shipping made for or in respect of Pilots or pilotage:
(5) The total amount received for pilotage, distinguishing the several amounts received from *British* ships and from foreign ships respectively, and the several amounts received in respect of different classes of ships paying different rates of pilotage, according to the scale of such rates for the time being in force, and the several amounts received for the several classes of service rendered by Pilots; and also the amount paid by such ships (if any) as have before reaching the outer limits of pilotage water if outward bound, or the port of their destination if inward bound, to take or pay for two or more Pilots, whether licensed by the same or by different pilotage authorities; together with the numbers of the ships of each of the several classes paying such several amounts as aforesaid:
(6) The receipt and expenditure of all moneys received by or on behalf of such authority, or by or on behalf of any

Sub-Commissioners appointed by them, in respect of Pilots or pilotage.

And shall allow the Board of Trade, or any persons appointed by such Board for the purpose, to inspect any books or documents in its possession relating to the several matters hereinbefore required to be returned to the Board of Trade.

338. If any of such pilotage authorities as aforesaid (other than the *Trinity House*, or Sub-Commissioners of Pilotage appointed by it, as hereinafter mentioned) fail to deliver to the Board of Trade the periodical returns hereinbefore required within one year of such time as may be fixed by such Board for the purpose, or if any of such authorities do not allow the said Board, or any persons who may be appointed by it for the purpose, to inspect any books or documents in their possession relating to the matters hereinbefore required to be returned by them, it shall be lawful for Her Majesty, by and with the advice of her Privy Council, to direct that all the rights and powers of such authorities in respect of pilotage shall cease or be suspended during such time as Her Majesty directs; and thereupon the *Trinity House* shall thereafter, or during such time as such suspension may continue, have and exercise the same powers of appointing Sub-Commissioners of Pilotage, and of licensing Pilots, and of establishing and altering rates of pilotage, within the district within which the authority so making default has previously appointed or licensed Pilots, as it is by this Act authorised to exercise in any district for which no particular provision is made by any Act of Parliament or charter for the appointment of Pilots, and shall also during such time as aforesaid have and exercise the same rights, title, and powers to and in respect of any pilotage funds or other pilotage property which the said pilotage authorities would or might have had or exercised if not so suspended as aforesaid.

339. The Board of Trade shall, without delay cause the several returns hereinbefore required to be made to such Board to be laid before both Houses of Parliament.

340. The Master or Mate of any ship may, upon giving due notice, and consenting to pay the usual expenses, apply to any pilotage authority to be examined as to his capacity to pilot the

ship of which he is Master or Mate, or any one or more ships belonging to the same Owner, within any part of the district over which such pilotage authority has jurisdiction; and such Master or Mate shall, if such authority thinks fit, thereupon be examined; and if found competent, a pilotage certificate shall be granted to him, containing his name, a specification of the ship or ships in respect of which he has been examined, and a description of the limits within which he is to pilot the same, such limits to be within such jurisdiction as aforesaid; and such certificate shall enable the person therein named to pilot the ship or any of the ships therein specified, of which he is acting as Master or Mate at the time, but no other, within the limits therein described, without incurring any penalties for the non-employment of a qualified Pilot.

341. The pilotage certificate so granted shall not be in force for more than one year, unless the same is renewed, which may from time to time be done by an indorsement under the hand of the Secretary or other proper officer of the authority by whom such certificate was granted.

342. If upon complaint to the Board of Trade it appear to such Board that any such authority as aforesaid has without reasonable cause refused or neglected to examine any Master or Mate who has applied to them for the purpose, or after he has passed the examination has without reasonable cause refused or neglected to grant him a pilotage certificate, or that the examination of any such Master or Mate has been unfairly or improperly conducted, or that any terms imposed or sought to be imposed by such authority are unfair or improper, or that any pilotage certificate granted by such authority has been improperly withdrawn, the Board of Trade may, if in its judgment the circumstances appear to require it, appoint persons to examine such Master or Mate, and if he is found competent may grant him a pilotage certificate, containing the same particulars as would have been inserted in any certificate granted by such pilotage authorities as aforesaid, upon such terms and conditions, and subject to such regulations, as such Board may think fit; and such certificate shall have the same effect as if it had been granted by

such pilotage authority as aforesaid; and such certificate shall be in force for one year, and may be renewed from year to year, either by the said authorities in manner hereinbefore mentioned, or by the Board of Trade, if such Board thinks fit, such renewal to be indorsed on the said certificate, either by such person as the Board of Trade may appoint for the purpose, or in manner hereinbefore provided as to certificates granted by any pilotage authority.

343. All Masters or Mates to or for whom any such pilotage certificates as aforesaid are granted or renewed by any pilotage authority shall pay to such authority, or as it directs, such fees upon their respective certificates and upon the renewals thereof, as are from time to time fixed for that purpose by such authority, with the consent of the Board of Trade; and all Masters and Mates to or for whom any such certificates are granted or renewed by the Board of Trade shall pay to such Board, or as it directs, such fees upon their certificates and upon the renewals thereof as may be fixed by such Board, so nevertheless that in the case of pilotage certificates granted or renewed by the Board of Trade such fees shall in no case be less than the fees payable by the qualified Pilots in the same districts upon their licenses and the renewal thereof; and such fees shall in the case of certificates and renewals granted by pilotage authorities be applicable either to paying the expense of the examinations or any other general expenses connected with pilotage incurred by such authorities, or to the Pilots' Superannuation Fund of the district (if any), or otherwise for the benefit of the Pilots appointed by such authorities, as such authorities think fit; and such fees shall in the case of pilotage certificates granted or renewed by the Board of Trade be applicable to the expense of the examinations, and the surplus (if any) shall be applied for the benefit of the qualified Pilots of the port or district to which such certificates apply, in such manner as such Board thinks fit.

344. If at any time it appears to the Board of Trade or to any pilotage authority that any Master or Mate to whom a pilotage certificate has been granted by such Board or authority has been guilty of misconduct, or has shown himself incompetent to pilot his ship, such Board or such authority (as the case may be) may

thereupon withdraw his certificate, and such certificate shall thenceforth cease to be of any effect whatever.

345. All boats and ships regularly employed in the pilotage service of any district shall be approved and licensed by the pilotage authority of such district, who may, at their discretion, appoint and remove the Masters of such boats and ships.

346. Every pilot-boat or ship shall be distinguished by the following characteristics; (that is to say),

(1) A black colour painted or tarred outside, with the exception of such names and numbers as are hereinafter mentioned; or such other distinguishing colour or colours as the pilotage authority of the district, with the consent of the Board of Trade, directs:

(2) On her stern the name of the Owner thereof and the port to which she belongs painted in white letters at least one inch broad and three inches long, and on each bow the number of the license of such boat or ship:

(3) When afloat, a flag at the masthead or on a sprit or staff, or in some other equally conspicuous situation; such flag to be of large dimensions compared with the size of the boat or ship carrying the same, and to be of two colours, the upper horizontal half white, and the lower horizontal half red:

And it shall be the duty of the Master of such boat or ship to attend to the following particulars: First, that the boat or ship possesses all the above characteristics; secondly, that the aforesaid flag is kept clean and distinct, so as to be easily discerned at a proper distance; and, lastly, that the names and numbers before mentioned are not at any time concealed; and if default is made in any of the above particulars he shall incur a penalty not exceeding twenty pounds for each default.

347. Whenever any qualified Pilot is carried off in a boat or ship not in the pilotage service he shall exhibit a flag of the above description, in order to show that such boat or ship has a qualified Pilot on board; and if he fails to do so without reasonable cause he shall incur a penalty not exceeding fifty pounds.

348. If any boat or ship, not having a licensed Pilot on board,

displays a flag of the above-mentioned description, there shall be incurred for every such offence a penalty not exceeding fifty pounds, to be recovered from the Owner or from the Master of such boat or ship.

349. Every qualified Pilot on his appointment shall receive a license, containing his name and usual place of abode, together with a description of his person, and a specification of the limits within which he is qualified to act; and it shall be the duty of the principal officer of Customs at the place at or nearest to which any qualified Pilot may reside, upon his request, to register his license; and no qualified Pilot shall be entitled to act as such until his license is so registered; and any qualified Pilot acting beyond the limits for which he is qualified by his license, shall be considered as an unqualified Pilot.

350. Every qualified Pilot shall, upon receiving his license, be furnished with a copy of such part of this Act as relates to pilotage, together with a copy of the rates, bye-laws, and regulations established within the district for which he is licensed; and he shall produce such copies to the Master of any ship or other person employing him, when required to do so, under a penalty in case of default not exceeding five pounds.

351. Every qualified Pilot, while acting in that capacity, shall be provided with his license, and produce the same to every person by whom he is employed, or to whom he tenders his services as Pilot; and if he refuses to do so at the request of such person, he shall incur for each offence a penalty not exceeding ten pounds, and shall be subject to suspension or dismissal by the pilotage authority by whom he is licensed.

352. Every qualified Pilot, when required by the pilotage authority who appointed him, shall produce or deliver up his license; and on the death of any qualified Pilot the person into whose hands his license happens to fall shall without delay transmit the same to the pilotage authority who appointed the deceased Pilot, and any Pilot or person failing to comply with the provisions of this section shall incur a penalty not exceeding ten pounds.

353. Subject to any alteration to be made by any pilotage authority in pursuance of the power hereinbefore in that behalf

given, the employment of pilots shall continue to be compulsory in all districts in which the same was by law compulsory immediately before the time when this Act comes into operation; and all exemptions from compulsory pilotage then existing within such districts shall also continue in force; and every Master of any unexempted ship navigating within any such district who, after a qualified Pilot has offered to take charge of such ship or has made a signal for that purpose, either himself pilots such ship without possessing a pilotage certificate enabling him so to do, or employs or continues to employ an unqualified person to pilot her, and every Master of any exempted ship navigating within any such district, who, after a qualified Pilot has offered to take charge of such ship, or has made a signal for that purpose, employs or continues to employ an unqualified Pilot to pilot her, shall for every such offence incur a penalty of double the amount of pilotage demandable for the conduct of such ship.

354. The Master of every ship carrying passengers between any place situate in the United Kingdom, or the islands of *Guernsey, Jersey, Sark, Alderney*, and *Man*, and any other place so situate, when navigating upon any waters situate within the limits of any district for which Pilots are licensed by any pilotage authority under the provisions of this or of any other Act, or upon any part thereof so situate, shall, unless he or his Mate has a pilotage certificate enabling such Master or Mate to pilot the said ship within such district, granted under the provisions hereinbefore contained or such certificate as next hereinafter mentioned, being a certificate applicable to such district and to such ship, employ a qualified Pilot to pilot his ship; and if he fails so to do he shall for every offence incur a penalty not exceeding one hundred pounds.

355. Any Master or Mate of a ship which by the last preceding section is made subject to compulsory pilotage may apply to the Board of Trade for a certificate, and the Board of Trade shall thereupon, on satisfactory proof of his having continuously piloted any ship within the limits of any pilotage district or of any part or parts thereof for two years prior to the commencement of this Act, or upon satisfactory proof by examination of his competency, or otherwise as it may deem expedient, cause to be granted to him,

or to be indorsed on any certificate of competency or service obtained by him under the Third Part of this Act, a certificate to the effect that he is authorised to pilot any ship or ships belonging to the same owner, and of a draft of water not greater than such draft as may be specified in the certificate within the limits aforesaid, and the said certificate shall remain in force for such time as the Board of Trade directs, and shall enable the Master or Mate therein named to conduct the ship or ships therein specified within the limits therein described to the same extent as if the last preceding section had not been passed, but not further or otherwise; and every such Master or Mate shall, upon applying for such certificate or any renewal thereof, pay to the Board of Trade or as it directs such fees not exceeding the fees payable on an examination for a Master's certificate of competency under the Third Part of this Act as the Board of Trade directs; and such fees shall be applied in the same manner in which the fees payable on such last-mentioned examination are made applicable.

356. If any boat or ship, having a qualified Pilot on board, leads any ship which has not a qualified Pilot on board when such last-mentioned ship cannot from particular circumstances be boarded, the Pilot so leading such last-mentioned ship shall be entitled to the full pilotage for the distance run as if he had actually been on board and had charge of such ship.

357. No Pilot, except under circumstances of unavoidable necessity, shall without his consent be taken to sea or beyond the limits for which he is licensed in any ship whatever; and every Pilot so taken under circumstances of unavoidable necessity or without his consent shall be entitled, over and above his pilotage, to the sum of ten shillings and sixpence a day, to be computed from and inclusive of the day on which such ship passes the limit to which he was engaged to pilot her up to and inclusive of the day of his being returned in the said ship to the place where he was taken on board, or up to and inclusive of such day as will allow him, if discharged from the ship, sufficient time to return thereto; and in such last-mentioned case he shall be entitled to his reasonable travelling expenses.

358. Any qualified Pilot demanding or receiving, and also any

Master offering or paying to any Pilot, any other rate in respect of pilotage services, whether greater or less, than the rate for the time being demandable by law, shall for each offence incur a penalty not exceeding ten pounds.

359. If any Master, on being requested by any qualified Pilot having the charge of his ship to declare her draught of water, refuses to do so, or himself makes or is privy to any other person making a false declaration to such Pilot as to such draught, he shall incur a penalty for every such offence not exceeding double the amount of pilotage which would have been payable to the Pilot making such request; and if any Master or other person interested in a ship makes or is privy to any other person making any fraudulent alteration in the marks on the stern or stem-post of such ship denoting her draught of water, the offender shall incur a penalty not exceeding five hundred pounds.

360. A qualified Pilot may supersede an unqualified Pilot, but it shall be lawful for the Master to pay to such unqualified Pilot a proportionate sum for his services, and to deduct the same from the charge of the qualified Pilot; and in case of dispute the pilotage authority by whom the qualified Pilot is licensed shall determine the proportionate sums to which each party is entitled.

361. An unqualified Pilot assuming or continuing in the charge of any ship after a qualified Pilot has offered to take charge of her, or using a license which he is not entitled to use for the purpose of making himself appear to be a qualified Pilot, shall for each offence incur a penalty not exceeding fifty pounds.

362. An unqualified Pilot may, within any pilotage district, without subjecting himself or his employer to any penalty, take charge of a ship as Pilot under the following circumstances; (that is to say),

When no qualified Pilot has offered to take charge of such ship, or made a signal for that purpose ; or

When a ship is in distress or under circumstances making it necessary for the Master to avail himself of the best assistance which can be found at the time ; or

For the purpose of changing the moorings of any ship in port, or of taking her into or out of any dock, in cases where such act can be done by an unqualified Pilot without infringing the regulations of the port, or any orders which the harbour-master is legally empowered to give.

363. The following persons shall be liable to pay pilotage dues for any ship for which the services of a qualified Pilot are obtained; (that is to say), the Owner or Master, or such consignees or agents thereof as have paid or made themselves liable to pay any other charge on account of such ship in the port of her arrival or discharge, as to pilotage inwards, and in the port from which she clears out as to pilotage outwards: and in default of payment such pilotage dues may be recovered in the same manner as penalties of the like amount may be recovered by virtue of this Act; but such recovery shall not take place until a previous demand thereof has been made in writing, and the dues so demanded have remained unpaid for seven days after the time of such demand being made.

364. Every consignee and agent (not being the Owner or Master) hereby made liable for the payment of pilotage dues in respect of any ship may, out of any moneys in his hands received on account of such ship or belonging to the Owner thereof, retain the amount of all dues so paid by him together with any reasonable expenses he may have incurred by reason of such payment or liability.

365. If any qualified Pilot commits any of the following offences; (that is to say),

(1) Keeps himself, or is interested in keeping by any agent, servant, or other person, any public-house or place of public entertainment, or sells, or is interested in selling, any wine, spirituous liquors, tobacco, or tea;

(2) Commits any fraud or other offence against the revenues of Customs or Excise, or the laws relating thereto;

(3) Is in any way, directly or indirectly, concerned in any corrupt practices relating to ships, their tackle, furniture, cargoes, crews, or passengers, or to persons in distress at sea or by shipwreck, or to their moneys, goods, or chattels;

(4) Lends his license;

(5) Acts as Pilot whilst suspended;

(6) Acts as Pilot when in a state of intoxication;

(7) Employs, or causes to be employed, on board any ship of which he has the charge, any boat, anchor, cable, or other store, matter, or thing beyond what is necessary for the service of such ship, with the intent to enhance the expenses of pilotage for his own gain or for the gain of any other person;

(8) Refuses, or wilfully delays, when not prevented by illness or other reasonable cause, to take charge of any ship within the limits of his license upon the signal for a Pilot being made by such ship, or upon being required to do so by the Master, Owner, Agent, or Consignee thereof, or by any officer of the pilotage authorities by whom such Pilot is licensed, or by any principal officer of Customs;

(9) Unnecessarily cuts or slips, or causes to be cut or slipped, any cable belonging to any ship;

(10) Refuses, on the request of the Master, to conduct the ship of which he has the charge into any port or place into which he is qualified to conduct the same, except on reasonable ground of danger to the ship;

(11) Quits the ship of which he has the charge, without the consent of the Master, before the service for which he was hired has been performed;

He shall for each such offence, in addition to any liability for damages at the suit of the person aggrieved, incur a penalty not exceeding one hundred pounds, and be liable to suspension or dismissal by the pilotage authority by whom he is licensed; and every person who procures, abets, or connives at the commission of any such offence shall likewise, in addition to any such liability for damages as aforesaid, incur a penalty not exceeding one hundred pounds, and, if a qualified Pilot, shall be liable to suspension or dismissal by the pilotage authority by whom he is licensed.

366. If any Pilot, when in charge of any ship, by wilful breach of duty, or by neglect of duty, or by reason of drunkenness, does any act tending to the immediate loss, destruction, or serious

damage of such ship, or tending immediately to endanger the life or limb of any person on board such ship; or if any Pilot, by wilful breach of duty, or by neglect of duty, or by reason of drunkenness, refuses or omits to do any lawful act proper and requisite to be done by him for preserving such ship from loss, destruction, or serious damage, or for preserving any person belonging to or on board of such ship from danger to life or limb; the Pilot so offending shall, for each such offence, be deemed guilty of a misdemeanour, and, if a qualified Pilot, also be liable to suspension and dismissal by the authority by which he is licensed.

367. If any person, by wilful misrepresentation of circumstances upon which the safety of a ship may depend, obtains or endeavours to obtain the charge of such ship, such person, and every other person procuring, abetting, or conniving at the commission of such offence, shall, in addition to any liability for damages at the suit of the party aggrieved, incur a penalty not exceeding one hundred pounds, and, if the offender is a qualified Pilot he shall also be liable to suspension or dismissal by the pilotage authority by which he is licensed.

368. The *Trinity House* may, in exercise of the general power hereinbefore given to all pilotage authorities of doing certain things in relation to pilotage matters, alter such of the provisions hereinafter contained as are expressed to be subject to alteration by them in the same manner, and to the same extent, as they might have altered the same if such provisions had been contained in any previous Act of Parliament instead of in this Act.

369. The *Trinity House* shall continue to appoint Sub-Commissioners, not being more than five nor less than three in number, for the purpose of examining Pilots in all districts in which they have been used to make such appointments, and may, with the consent of Her Majesty in Council, but not otherwise, appoint like Sub-Commissioners for any other district in which no particular provision is made by any Act of Parliament or charter for the appointment of Pilots; but no pilotage district already under the authority of any Sub-Commissioners appointed by the *Trinity House* shall be extended, except with such consent as aforesaid, and no Sub-Commissioners so appointed shall be

deemed to be pilotage authorities within the meaning of this Act.

370. The *Trinity House* shall continue, after due examination by themselves or their Sub-Commissioners, to appoint and license under their common seal Pilots for the purpose of conducting ships within the limits following, or any portion of such limits; (that is to say),

- (1) 'The *London* District,' comprising the waters of the *Thames* and *Medway*, as high as *London Bridge* and *Rochester Bridge* respectively, and also the seas and channels leading thereto, or therefrom as far as *Orfordness* to the north, and *Dungeness* to the south; so nevertheless that no Pilot shall be hereafter licensed to conduct ships both above and below *Gravesend*:
- (2) 'The English Channel District,' comprising the seas between Dungeness and the Isle of Wight:
- (3) '*Trinity House* Outport District,' comprising any pilotage district for the appointment of Pilots within which no particular provision is made by any Act of Parliament or charter.

371. Subject to any alteration to be made by the *Trinity House*, the names of all Pilots licensed by the *Trinity House* shall be published in manner following; (that is to say),

- (1) The *Trinity House* shall, at their house in London, fix up a notice specifying the name and usual place of abode of every Pilot so licensed, and the limits within which he is licensed to act:
- (2) The *Trinity House* shall transmit a copy of such notice to the Commissioners of Customs in London, and to the principal officers of Customs resident at all ports within the limits for which such Pilot is licensed; and such notice shall be posted up by the Commissioners at the Custom-house in *London*, and by such officers at the Custom-houses of the ports at which they are respectively resident.

372. Subject to any alteration to be made by the *Trinity House*, every *Trinity House* Pilot, on his appointment, shall execute a bond

for one hundred pounds conditioned for the due observance on his part of the regulations and bye-laws of the *Trinity House*, such bond to be free from stamp duty, and from any other charge, except the actual expense for preparing the same.

373. No qualified Pilot who has executed such bond as is hereinbefore mentioned shall be liable for neglect or want of skill beyond its penalty and the amount of pilotage payable to him in respect of the voyage on which he is engaged.

374. Subject to any alteration to be made by the *Trinity House*, no license granted by them shall continue in force beyond the thirty-first day of January next ensuing the date of such license; but the same may, upon the application of the Pilot holding such license, be renewed on such thirty-first day of January in every year, or any subsequent day, by indorsement under the hand of the Secretary of the *Trinity House*, or such other person as may be appointed by them for that purpose.

375. The *Trinity House* shall have power to revoke or suspend the license of any Pilot appointed by them, in such manner and at such time as they think fit.

376. Subject to any alteration to be made by the *Trinity House*, and to the exemptions hereinafter contained, the Pilotage Districts of the *Trinity House* within which the employment of Pilots is compulsory are the *London* District, and the *Trinity House* Outport Districts, as hereinbefore defined; and the Master of every ship navigating within any part of such district or districts, who, after a qualified Pilot has offered to take charge of such ship, or has made a signal for that purpose, either himself pilots such ship, without possessing a certificate enabling him so to do, or employs, or continues to employ, an unqualified person to pilot her, shall for every such offence, in addition to the penalty hereinbefore specified, if the *Trinity House* certify in writing under their common seal that the prosecutor is to be at liberty to proceed for the recovery of such additional penalty, incur an additional penalty not exceeding five pounds for every fifty tons burthen of such ship.

377. Subject to any alteration to be made by the *Trinity House*, a sufficient number of qualified Pilots shall always be ready to take charge of ships coming from the westward past *Dungeness*; and

the *Trinity House* shall, by bye-law to be made in the same manner as other bye-laws made under the powers herein contained, make such regulations with respect to the Pilots under their control as may be necessary in order to provide for an unintermitted supply of qualified Pilots for such ships, and to insure their constant attendance upon and due performance of their duty, both by night and day, whether by cruising between the *South Foreland* and *Dungeness*, or by going off from shore, upon signals made for the purpose, or by both of such means, or by any other means, and whether in rotation or otherwise, as the *Trinity House* think fit.

378. Subject to any alteration to be made by the *Trinity House*, every Master of any ship coming from the westward, and bound to any place in the rivers *Thames* and *Medway* (unless she has a qualified Pilot on board, or is exempted from compulsory pilotage), shall, on the arrival of such ship off *Dungeness*, and thenceforth until she has passed the south buoy of the *Brake*, or a line to be drawn from *Sandown Castle* to the said buoy, or until a qualified Pilot has come on board, display and keep flying the usual signal for a Pilot; and if any qualified Pilot is within hail, or is approaching and within half a mile, and has the proper distinguishing flag flying in his boat, such Master shall, by heaving-to in proper time or shortening sail, or by any practicable means consistent with the safety of his ship, facilitate such Pilot getting on board, and shall give the charge of piloting his ship to such Pilot; or if there are two or more of such Pilots offering at the same time, to such one of them as may, according to the regulations for the time being in force, be entitled or required to take such charge; and if any such Master fails to display or keep flying the usual signal for a Pilot in manner hereinbefore required, or to facilitate any such qualified Pilot as aforesaid getting on board as hereinbefore required, or to give the charge of piloting his ship to such Pilot as hereinbefore mentioned in that behalf, he shall incur a penalty not exceeding double the sum which might have been demanded for the pilotage of his ship, such penalty to be paid to the *Trinity House*, and to be carried to the account of the *Trinity House* Pilot Fund.

379. The following ships, when not carrying passengers, shall

be exempted from compulsory pilotage in the London District, and in the *Trinity House* Outport Districts; (that is to say),

(1) Ships employed in the coasting trade of the United Kingdom:
(2) Ships of not more than sixty tons burthen:
(3) Ships trading to *Boulogne*[1] or to any place in *Europe* north of *Boulogne*:
(4) Ships from *Guernsey*, *Jersey*, *Alderney*, *Sark*, or *Man*, which are wholly laden with stone being the produce of those islands:
(5) Ships navigating within the limits of the port to which they belong:
(6) Ships passing through the limits of any pilotage district on their voyages between two places both situate out of such limits, and not being bound to any place within such limits nor anchoring therein.[2]

380. Subject to any alteration to be made by the *Trinity House* there shall continue to be paid to all *Trinity House* Pilots, in respect of their pilotage services, such dues as are immediately before the time when this Act comes into operation payable to them in respect of such services.

381. Subject to any alteration to be made by the *Trinity House*, and notwithstanding anything hereinbefore contained, there shall be paid in respect of all foreign ships trading to and from the port of *London*, and not exempted from pilotage, the following pilotage dues; that is to say, as to ships inwards, the full amount of dues for the distance piloted, and as to ships outwards the full amount of dues for the distance required by law; and payment of such pilotage dues shall be made to the Collector of Customs in the port of *London* by some one or more of the following persons; that is to say, the Master or other person having the charge of such ship, or the Consignee or Agents thereof who have paid or made themselves liable to pay any other charge for such ship in the said port of *London*; and such pilotage may be recovered in the same

---

[1] Now Brest. See Order in Council, December 21, 1871.
[2] Extended by 25 & 26 Vict. c. 63, § 41.

manner as other pilotage dues are hereinbefore declared to be recoverable.

382. Subject to any alteration to be made by the *Trinity House*, the said Collector of Customs shall, on receiving any pilotage dues in respect of foreign ships, give to the person paying the same a receipt in writing; and no officer of Customs in the port of *London* shall grant a clearance or transire for any such foreign ship as aforesaid without the production of such receipt; and if any such attempts to go to sea without such clearance or transire, any such officer may detain her until the said receipt is produced.

383. Subject to any alteration to be made by the *Trinity House*, the said collector shall pay over to the *Trinity House* the pilotage dues received by him in respect of any foreign ship; and the *Trinity House* shall apply the same in manner following:

In the first place, in paying to any Pilot who may bring sufficient proof of his having had the charge of such ship such dues as would have been payable to him for such pilotage service if the ship had been a *British* ship, after deducting there from the poundage due to the *Trinity House*:

In the second place, in paying to any unlicensed person who may bring sufficient proof of his having, in the absence of a licensed Pilot, had the charge of such ship, such amount as the *Trinity House* may think proper, not exceeding the amount which would under similar circumstances have been payable to a licensed Pilot, after deducting poundage:

And lastly, shall pay over to the *Trinity House* Pilot Fund the residue, together with all poundage deducted as aforesaid.

384. Whenever any difference arises between the Master and the qualified Pilot of any ship trading to or from the port of *London* as to her draught of water, the *Trinity House* shall upon application by either party, made, in case of a ship inward bound, within twelve hours after her arrival or at some time before she begins to discharge her cargo, and in the case of a ship outward bound before she quits her moorings, appoint some proper officer who shall measure the ship, and settle the difference accordingly, and there shall be paid to the officer measuring such ship by the party against whom he decides, the following sums; (that is to say), one

guinea if the ship be below, and half a guinea if the ship be above the entrance of the *London Docks* at *Wapping*.

385. Subject to any alteration to be made by the *Trinity House*, there shall continue to be paid to them, and carried over to the *Trinity House* Pilot Fund, the sums of money following; (that is to say),

(1) A poundage of sixpence in the pound upon the pilotage earnings of all Pilots licensed by the *Trinity House*:

(2) A sum of three pounds three shillings to be paid on the first day of January in every year by every person licensed by the *Trinity House* to act as Pilot in any district not under the superintendence of Sub-Commissioners, or in any part of such district:

And any qualified Pilot giving a false account of his earnings, or making default in payment of any sum due from him under this section, shall forfeit double the amount payable, and shall further be liable, at the discretion of the *Trinity House*, to suspension or dismissal.

386. Subject to any prior charges that may be subsisting thereon by virtue of any Act or Acts of Parliament or otherwise, the said *Trinity House* Pilot Fund shall be chargeable in the first instance with such expenses as the *Trinity House* may duly incur in performance of their duties in respect of Pilots and pilotage, and after payment thereof shall, subject to any alteration to be made by the *Trinity House*, be administered by the *Trinity House* for the benefit of such Pilots licensed by them after the first day of October one thousand eight hundred and fifty-three as are incapacitated for the performance of their duty by reason of age, infirmity, or accident, or of the widows and children of Pilots so licensed, or of such incapacitated Pilots only.

387. The two corporations of the *Trinity Houses* of the ports of *Hull* and *Newcastle* shall continue to appoint Sub-Commissioners, not being more than seven nor less than three in number, for the purpose of examining Pilots in all districts in which they have been used to make such appointments, and may, with the consent of Her Majesty in Council, but not otherwise, appoint like Sub-Commissioners for any other district situate within their respective

jurisdictions; but no pilotage district already under the authority of any Sub-Commissioners appointed by either of the said Corporations shall be extended, except with such consent as aforesaid; and no Sub-Commissioners appointed or to be appointed by the *Trinity Houses* of *Hull* and *Newcastle* shall be deemed to be pilotage authorities within the meaning of this Act, nor shall anything in this Act contained be held to confer upon the commissioners for regulating the pilotage of the port of *Kingston-upon-Hull* and of the river *Humber* any jurisdiction of a different nature or character from that which they have heretofore exercised.

388. No Owner or Master of any ship shall be answerable to any person whatever for any loss or damage occasioned by the fault or incapacity of any qualified Pilot acting in charge of such ship, within any district where the employment of such Pilot is compulsory by law.

In the discussion of this part of the Act I would at once state that I consider it imperative to do away with compulsory pilotage in its present form altogether as a blot upon our Statute Book, and if it is conceded, as I hope it will be, that the abuses which have grown up with the system are such as to admit of no other remedy, it will be clear that this part of the Act must be entirely remodelled.

I would here refer to the remarks of Mr. Lindsay, in his letter to the President of the Board of Trade in the year 1860, where, at page 217, he treats of this question; he, however, has evidently only been struck by the way in which present legislation increases the burdens of the shipowner without perceiving the injustice to all which it sanctions and perpetuates. He also seems to use the term 'compulsory pilotage' when speaking of an obligation arising out of a policy of insurance; such a use of the term only serves to complicate the questions, which seem to me to be the following :—

(1) Whether it can continue to be part of the legislation of the country that in certain districts vessels shall not be navigated except by a duly licensed pilot specially employed for the purpose.

(2) Whether the enactments by which the employment of such duly licensed pilots is regulated are such as to afford complete and impartial justice to all parties.

Into a separate consideration of the first of these questions I do not propose to enter at any length, as Mr. Lindsay and others have written ably and comprehensively on the subject, but some few remarks may not be out of place.

I can never acknowledge that a pilot ought to be, or was originally intended to be, more than a help to the officers of the ship in avoiding the intricacies or dangers of local navigation. Of course, it cannot be denied that a master of a vessel visiting a port for the first time cannot be so well acquainted with shoals, sands, or beacons, as one who makes his livelihood by conducting vessels at all times in that particular district; on the other hand, how can such pilot, taking charge of a vessel for the first time, be as well acquainted as her own master with the sailing, steaming, or steering qualities, from a defective appreciation of which as many accidents arise as from any other circumstance? There is, it seems to me, no reason whatever why a master of a vessel who has undertaken to perform a voyage, say from Sydney to London, should be relieved of responsibility at any point short of either of these places; by all means allow him to make use at any point of such skilled assistance as may present itself; but if, with the knowledge that such assistance will doubtless be at his command, he does not feel equal to the responsibility of the voyage, it is his fault if he undertake it, and our hardy mariners would look upon it as an insult if it were seriously suggested that they could not find their way anywhere.

This brings me to the second question above propounded; and here, having felt severely the hardships of the law as it at present stands, I must enter more particularly into an examination of the clauses in the Merchant Shipping Act which have brought about a state of things calling, I cannot but think, for a speedy and effectual remedy.

To make myself clear it is necessary that I should point out the clauses and their connection.

By sections 376 to 379 it is made compulsory upon masters of vessels to take on board in certain localities the first qualified pilot who shall offer his services; by section 388 it is enacted that no owner or master of a ship shall be answerable to any person whatever for any loss or damage occasioned by the fault or incapacity of any qualified pilot who has thus compulsorily taken charge; section 372 stipulates that every pilot shall execute a bond for 100*l.*; and section 373 limits the amount recoverable from any such pilot to the amount of such bond, plus the pilotage payable to him for the voyage on which he was engaged.

I say *in certain localities* a pilot must be employed, but it must not, therefore, be supposed that at any given place pilotage must either be or not be compulsory. On the contrary, the two systems are frequently co-existent, and if my illustrations are taken solely from the London district, it must not be supposed that the evils which are here so patent may not be equally felt in other places.

We will now suppose a vessel on her voyage from

the Mediterranean, or elsewhere in the world *south* of *Boulogne*,[1] to have navigated in safety through the dangers of the seas, through the English Channel crowded with shipping, and to have arrived at Dungeness.

Here her officers, if she is bound for the Thames or Medway, become, in the eye of the law, suddenly incapable of taking her any farther, and must employ a licensed pilot, who is supposed to bring with him such consummate skill as to be able to preserve the vessel from dangers, not only below the water, but above it, as collisions, &c., so effectually, that the Legislature has considered itself justified in transferring to him the whole charge and responsibility for the vessel and her cargo. Not so, however, should she be destined for any other port, as Hull, Newcastle, &c.; in such a case the master may, if he chooses, avail himself of the services of the same pilot, but he still remains the responsible person in the event of any accident happening while the pilot is in charge, he having a remedy against the pilot to the extent of 100*l*., which we shall presently see is almost illusory; thus from a comparison of these two cases, where the vessel in one case remains within the pilotage district, in the other passes through it, it is apparent that compulsory pilotage is not rendered necessary by dangers of navigation, and therefore justice demands that the two vessels should be treated alike, at any rate up to the point where their courses diverge.

But it may be stated that when such point is once passed, no hardship remains, and it is therefore necessary to produce further illustrations, for which purpose I must look at the working of the Act as regards wholly unoffending parties. I will therefore suppose that my vessel, the A, is bound down the Thames with a cargo of mer-

[1] Now Brest.

chandise belonging to sundry shippers in all parts of the kingdom, and is brought to an anchor in a proper berth in Sea Reach to wait for tide. While she is lying there motionless, and of course helpless, two steamers are making their way up to London; one, the B, is from St. Petersburg, and has taken a Trinity pilot at Orfordness, the other, the C, is from Odessa, and has taken a Trinity pilot at Dungeness; near the Nore Light, some distance below where my vessel is lying, their courses converge, and from that point upwards they proceed in the same track, while their tonnage, draught of water, speed, and, I may add, their power of doing mischief, are, in all respects, absolutely identical. One of these steamers runs down and sinks my vessel at her anchor, and my whole property is lost; will it be credited that if that steamer is the B, I shall recover from her owners every farthing of my loss; if it is the C, I shall recover nothing? Therefore, although the pilots on board both steamers were licensed by the same authority, although the grossest incapacity may be manifested by the one in charge of the offending vessel, and although my ship was absolutely helpless, the Legislature makes it a matter of life and death to me whether the steamer by which the damage was done cleared originally from St. Petersburg or from Odessa!

It may be said that this is the worst that can happen, and that it is my fault if I have not covered myself by assurance. Although this objection would only amount to an argument, that what would be an injustice towards any other person would be no injustice towards an underwriter, I shall proceed to show that here also the enactments in force are such as to allow even the most complete foresight to be baffled, and that no one can effectually guard against possible utter ruin from unavoidable casualty.

To prove this certainly most serious assertion, I will move my vessel higher up the Thames, and in this case she shall be inward bound, having arrived with a cargo to be discharged into lighters in the stream. A discharging berth is pointed out by the harbour-master, where she is moored between the buoys, and the discharge is commenced, and according to the terms used in almost all marine policies, the underwriters are answerable for all damage occurring to her until she has been 'moored twenty-four hours in good safety'; after the expiration of this period they are absolved from all further liability. In spite of the position of good safety into which she has been ordered, she is run down and sunk by a steamer which is in charge of a pilot, and having no recourse against my underwriters, I look for redress to the owners of the steamer.

Is it sufficient for me to ascertain whether she was bound for a northern or southern port, say for St. Petersburg or for Odessa, as in the last illustration? By no means, for should she be bound to the former port, and not on account of her destination subject to compulsory pilotage, I may be met with the statement that she carried passengers, and on that account was so subjected; in order to procure exemption on this ground it is only necessary to prove that any one person not belonging to the crew was on board, whether any fare had been paid or not; if this can be substantiated, the owners are free from all liability.

Thus utterly foiled in my attempts to obtain compensation from the owners of the wrong-doing steamer, and without recourse against my underwriters, my only chance is to proceed against the pilot himself. It might at any rate be supposed that the Legislature, placing in his hands, as has been shown, such enormous power of inflicting injury, and reducing his liability to such an infinitesimal amount, would have made the remedy against him simple and certain. Such, however, is far from being the case, and it is only by an action at common law, at which all the evidence required for the original action in the Court of Admiralty must be reproduced, that any portion of the 100*l*. can be recovered; that under such circumstances any settlement out of Court mus be preferable to an action cannot be a cause of astonishment.

I may at once state that the illustrations selected by me are not overdrawn, but will be found fully exemplified by the case of the 'Beta,' which was taken by me from the High Court of Admiralty to the Privy Council. The shorthand-writer's notes in this case are at the disposal of all who would like to see the gross injustice which is sanctioned by the law, as at present laid down and interpreted.

The enactments in question are open to further objection from the great temptation they hold out to interested parties to adopt the most discreditable devices to evade responsibility, and even to have recourse to wilful perjury. In the case of the 'Beta,' the owners of that steamer benefited to the extent of at least 5,000*l*., which loss was thrown upon the owners and underwriters of the Mecklenburg barque 'Fides' and her cargo, by the simple fact that they produced two persons who swore that they had been presented with free passages; surely generosity never had a more ample and immediate reward!

Would it, however, be going too far to conjecture that after such experience the owner of a vessel would take care to be provided with a passenger for future occasions?

This, however, is not the worst part of the difficulty,

as will be clear when the mode of procedure is considered, which is as follows. My ship having, while at anchor, as described in the foregoing illustrations, been run down and sunk by a steamer, my first care is to ascertain that all the requirements of the Act of Parliament, as far as they apply to my vessel, were complied with. The result of my investigation being satisfactory, after making an application to the owners of the steamer for compensation, which is at once declined, I put my case in the hands of a proctor, who proceeds in the High Court of Admiralty to prosecute my claim. On behalf of the steamer the only plea is that she was in charge of a duly licensed pilot, employed by compulsion of law, and that therefore, under the 388th section, her owners are exempt from liability, and this plea succeeds unless it can be proved by me that the accident was not solely due to the fault or incapacity of the pilot, but that the crew of the steamer were partly to blame by not having properly carried out the pilot's orders.

But the evidence by which alone I can hope to prove such an allegation must be taken from the crew of such steamer, or from the uncorroborated statement of the pilot himself, and, even if it were to the interest of all the witnesses to be truthful, it may be imagined how difficult it would be to obtain proof sufficient from those quarters. But it is directly to the interest of all to suppress the truth in such a case; the crew, of course, will do all they can to clear themselves from blame, particularly where by so doing they clear their owners from responsibility; while the pilot, having to look to the owners for further employment, and being, in very many instances at least, engaged from year's end to year's end by the same firm, must be, to say the least, very sorely perplexed if he tries to do what is right. In the first place, his evidence will almost certainly be uncorroborated; in the second place, he knows that if he succeeds in throwing the blame upon the crew of the steamer, he will be inflicting upon the owners what may possibly be an enormous loss, and will certainly expect to forfeit their patronage; and, lastly, his own liability, in the case of a decision adverse to himself cannot be more than 100*l.*, and is in most cases *nil*, for if he has any means at all, he will almost certainly be a member of a Club which will undertake to defend him if any proceedings at common law should really be taken against him. If, however, the owners of the steamer agree to indemnify him against any loss, all inducement for him to speak the truth is at an end, except as between his conscience and himself; while for the owners of the steamer a maximum sum of 100*l.* is in one scale, and an unknown liability of many thousands may be in the other, and it is not too much to conclude therefore that such a bargain, however corrupt it may be thought, is not unlikely to have ere this exercised an influence on the decision of the Court where such cases come for hearing.

Having now stated at some length my objections to the present system of compulsory pilotage, I would point out that that system can only be defended by one line of argument, viz. that without it the emoluments of the pilots would be much curtailed, and it would possibly not be worth their while to devote themselves wholly to the business. This argument, however, cannot be suffered to prevail for a moment when it has once been conclusively ascertained that the system in defence of which it is used is in itself an injustice; it is, moreover, clearly based upon a fallacy, as in the northern part of the London district, where pilotage is not compulsory, we do not hear of pilots not earning sufficient to remunerate them, but rather of there being numbers of unlicensed men who enter into competition with them.

These men (watermen, fishermen, old master mariners, or others), without being in possession of any lawful authority, offer their services to any master who may be unacquainted with the part of the coast which he has to navigate, and where the law does not require him to take or pay for a duly licensed pilot.

These men may be thoroughly competent, but the Legislature can never have imagined that their enactments would serve to create a body of men who would get their living by breaking the law, which they now actually do, even when, as is frequently the case, they are shipped as able seamen and entered upon the articles as such.

Fresh hardships have grown out of this state of things, as will be seen by an investigation into the proceedings of the Gravesend Borough Magistrates, who have made it a practice to issue warrants on the simple *ipse dixit* of a pilot against masters of vessels alleged to have employed an unlicensed person within their jurisdiction.

So soon as the vessel in question is reported to have arrived at her place of destination, say, for instance, Sunderland, or some other northern port, the warrant is placed in the hands of police officers, who proceed without delay to arrest the master, bring him in custody to Gravesend for trial, and not unfrequently the charge has after all been dismissed for want of evidence to prove the offence.

The magistrates, however, never give costs against the pilots, and thus the unfortunate master has to find his way back to his vessel, after being mulcted of several pounds for expenses. If, then, the business is so profitable as to excite persons to engage in it who have not the powerful recommendation of the Trinity House license to protect them, there surely can be no fear that the supply of pilots will fail.

Place the pilots under a more stringent authority than at present exists, so that complaints against them, which are now invariably referred to the common law courts, may be promptly investigated by the Trinity House, or any other central authority, and as severely punished as complaints against masters and mates holding certificates of competency; and as a licensed pilot, by virtue of his licence, is empowered to take charge of the property of parties who have no other security than their belief that the British Government will take care to permit only fit and competent persons to be entrusted with a pilot's license, whereas it devolves upon the owner of the ship to employ whatever master or mate he chooses, and in whom he has confidence—I say, this being the state of the case, the duly licensed pilot ought to be subject to a more severe law than either masters or mates can be; at present, however, he can offend with impunity, as, if you hesitate to incur the expenses of legal proceedings without the hope of any pecuniary advantage, you have, virtually, no remedy against him.

I do not wish to enter here into any examination of the question of free-trade in pilotage, nor will I do more than suggest that if the system of licensing pilots is to be continued, there can be no reason why different classes of license should not be adopted, so that every one going on board a vessel for the purpose of taking charge of her, if even only to change docks, should be provided with some sort of a license from the central authority, a system which is very generally adopted on the Continent.

I repeat that all I have desired to do is to point out the abuses of the present system, and I have not the least doubt that the evils and their remedy will receive prompt consideration at the hands of Her Majesty's Government.

To the special clauses I have only to add:

334. Here, most likely, would the order to pay a fine in cases of non-compliance be necessary; this is the mode in which, on the Continent, public bodies are kept to their duties, and it cannot be denied that it has worked satisfactorily.

336. Why not give to every person considering himself aggrieved the right of appeal;—how shall, for instance, as this clause now stands, any foreigner bring his complaint before the Board of Trade?

348. For the reasons stated in my introductory remarks to this part, I would propose to punish this offence, and every one aiding and abetting in it, as a misdemeanour.

362. It will be necessary to take into most serious consideration, if the abolishing of compulsory pilotage should not, in cases of distress, justify the employment of unlicensed pilots.

365. I would propose to add under number

(12) Engages to pilot any vessel out of his regular turn, or makes attempts to enter into engagements to that effect.

372 and 373. It ought to be seriously considered if it would not be far better to raise the amount of bond required, and insist upon substantial securities for its prompt fulfilment, than to retain the present system, which has worked so unsatisfactorily. Pilots very rarely have any property when they are called upon to make good any damage; usually, everything they possess is settled on their families, and it is next to impossible to obtain justice from them under the present state of the law.

374. The decision in the case of the 'Beta,' to which I referred in my introductory remarks to this part of the

Act, proves, beyond all question, that this clause requires alteration.

The 31st of January next following the date of the license was undoubtedly fixed upon as the term beyond which no license should continue in force, in order to give the authorities, viz. the officers of the Trinity House, the Sub-Commissioners of Pilotage, or the Collectors of Customs, a month's time from the end of every calendar year to report to the Trinity House any complaint, or cause of complaint, made, or arising, during the previous year.

In the case under consideration, the Judicial Committee decided that a license, granted on January 21— consequently nine days before the expiration of the time within which such report might have been sent in—was valid in law, because a contrary construction would allow certain districts to be for days, or possibly for weeks, without any qualified pilots.

This interpretation is as unjust as erroneous; unjust, because if the Trinity House had found any difficulty in the working of this clause, it might have given due notice of the necessity of an alteration, and until such notice had been given the public had a right to consider the plain words of the enactment in full force; and erroneous, because it is impossible to believe that if the Legislature meant to give thirty-one days for lodging complaints, any judicial tribunal could have it in their power to reduce such period by one-third. If the words of the clause were not to be interpreted literally, any pilot, knowing that complaints likely to lead to the suspension of his license were in contemplation, would be sure to be the first to interpret the decision in his favour, and present his license for renewal on any day before the time fixed by law for such renewal, viz. January 31.

The want of qualified Pilots could easily be avoided by granting interim certificates, to serve only for the time during which the license was left for renewal.

375. I think the manner in which the revocation or suspension of Pilots' Licenses is to take place ought here to be distinctly stated.

376–379. These clauses will require very material alteration if my suggestions are adopted.

PART VIII.—*Wrecks, Casualties, and Salvage.*

432. In any of the cases following; (that is to say),

Whenever any ship is lost, abandoned, or materially damaged on or near the coasts of the United Kingdom;

Whenever any ship causes loss or material damage to any other ship on or near such coasts;

Whenever by reason of any casualty happening to or on board of any ship on or near such coasts loss of life ensues;

Whenever any such loss, abandonment, damage, or casualty happens elsewhere, and any competent witnesses thereof arrive, or are found at any place in the United Kingdom;

It shall be lawful for the inspecting officer of the Coastguard, or the principal officer of Customs, residing at or near the place where such loss, abandonment, damage, or casualty occurred, if the same occurred on or near the coast of the United Kingdom, but if elsewhere, at or near the place where such witnesses as aforesaid arrive or are found, or can be conveniently examined, or for any other person appointed for the purpose by the Board of Trade to make inquiry, respecting such loss, abandonment, damage, or casualty; and he shall, for that purpose, have all the powers given by the First Part of this Act to inspectors appointed by the said Board.

I would suggest to make these inquiries always compulsory by simply cancelling the words 'It shall be lawful.' It is evident that if any unfair dealing with a ship has taken place, the crew are most ready to confess the truth soon after they have landed, and if one of the two officers referred to in this clause is obliged immediately to institute an inquiry, the execution of the protest, which is always urged forward by the master with all possible despatch, will be postponed, and the whole truth will be more likely to come out; but as the clause now stands Coastguard or Customs' Officials generally find a reason for avoiding to act on their own responsibility, and by a reference to the Board of Trade much time is unnecessarily lost, and, as in the case of the 'Trial' (above referred to), one or other of the principal witnesses may have been sent away in order to prevent his cross-examination.

433. If it appears to such officer or person as aforesaid, either upon or without any such preliminary inquiry as aforesaid, that a formal investigation is requisite or expedient, or if the Board of Trade so directs, he shall apply to any two justices or to a stipendiary magistrate to hear the case; and such justices or magistrate shall thereupon proceed to hear and try the same, and shall for that purpose, so far as relates to the summoning of parties, compelling the attendance of witnesses, and the regulation of the proceedings, have the same powers as if the same were a proceeding relating to an offence or cause of complaint, upon which they or he have power to make a summary conviction or order, or as near thereto as circumstances permit; and it shall be the duty of such officer or person as aforesaid to superintend the management of the case, and to render such assistance to the said justices or magistrate as is in his power; and, upon the conclusion of the case, the said justices or magistrate shall send a report to the Board of Trade, containing a full statement of the case and of their or his opinion thereon, accompanied by such report of or extracts from the evidence, and such observations (if any) as they or he may think fit.

Besides the Stipendiary Magistrates, the County Court Judges, I imagine, would be more fit to conduct the official inquiries here under consideration than any two Justices of the Peace, and I would suggest the substitution of them for the latter.

435. In places where there is a Local Marine Board, and where a stipendiary magistrate is a member of such Board, all such investigations as aforesaid shall, whenever he happens to be present, be made before such magistrate; and there shall be paid to such magistrate in respect of his services under this Act, such remuneration, whether by way of annual increase of salary, or otherwise, as Her Majesty's Secretary of State for the Home Department, with the consent of the Board of Trade, may direct; and such remuneration shall be paid out of the Mercantile Marine Fund.

The same remuneration should be given to the County Court Judges as is to be paid to the Stipendiary Magistrates.

439. The Board of Trade shall throughout the United Kingdom have a general superintendence of all matters relating to wreck; and it may, with the consent of the Commissioners of Her Majesty's Treasury, appoint any officer of Customs or of the Coastguard, or any officer of Inland Revenue, or, when it appears to such Board to be more convenient, any other person, to be a receiver of wreck in any district, and to perform such duties as are hereinafter mentioned, and shall give due notice of every such appointment.

The usefulness of Receivers whenever they are nothing but public officers has been most effectually proved by my own experience in all matters where I have come in personal contact with them, and applied for their assistance in conformity with sections 6 and 14 of their Instructions. It is a very different matter, however, when any other person acts as Receiver, as local and personal interests are almost invariably so powerful as to prevent his acting with vigour and efficiency. For this reason I am of opinion that officers of Customs or Coastguard should always be chosen where practicable.

441. Whenever any ship or boat is stranded or in distress at any place on the shore of the sea, or of any tidal water within the limits of the United Kingdom, the receiver of the district within which such place is situate shall, upon being made acquainted with such accident, forthwith proceed to such place, and upon his arrival there he shall take the command of all persons present, and assign such duties to each person, and issue such directions, as he may think fit with a view to the preservation of such ship or boat, and the lives of the persons belonging thereto, and the cargo and apparel thereof; and if any person wilfully disobey such directions, he shall forfeit a sum not exceeding fifty pounds; but it shall not be lawful for such receiver to interfere between the Master of such ship or boat and his Crew in matters relating to the management thereof, unless he is requested so to do by such Master.

The last part of this clause has been read as if the Board of Trade intended to withhold the Receiver's interference in any case where the master of a ship does not actually desire the same, whereas, it is evident that it was only meant to leave the discipline of the ship's crew in the master's hands.

A more distinct interpretation of this clause is of the utmost necessity, as the clear instructions issued to the Receivers prove that they are intended to assist any master who may be in distress in such a manner that the interests of the owners of the ship and cargo and their underwriters may not be jeopardised by the slippery advice only too often given by parties whose profits would be seriously diminished if these interests were promptly and efficiently protected.

The case of the 'Jeanne,' at Maryport, is one in point; had her master not been advised that he had nothing to do with the Receiver, a very different result would have been obtained; as it turned out, I had to be grateful that the exertions of the Receiver, Mr. Lindsay, exposed the conduct of the parties concerned, and the reports made by that gentleman in this case to the Board of Trade will be found to throw much light upon the practices so rife in many of our outports.

448. Any receiver, or in his absence any justice of the peace, shall, as soon as conveniently may be, examine upon oath (which oath they are hereby respectively empowered to administer) any person belonging to any ship which may be or may have been in distress on the coast of the United Kingdom, or any other person who may be able to give any account thereof, or of the cargo or stores thereof, as to the following matters; (that is to say),
    (1) The name and description of the ship;
    (2) The name of the master and of the owners;
    (3) The names of the owners of the cargo;
    (4) The ports or places from and to which the ship was bound;
    (5) The occasion of the distress of the ship;
    (6) The services rendered;
    (7) Such other matters or circumstances relating to such ship, or to cargo on board the same, as the receiver or justice thinks necessary;
And such receiver or justice shall take the examination down in writing, and shall make two copies of the same, of which he shall send one to the Board of Trade, and the other to the secretary of the committee for managing the affairs of *Lloyd's* in *London*, and such last-mentioned copy shall be placed by the said secretary in some conspicuous situation for the inspection of persons desirous of examining the same; and for the purposes of such examination every such receiver or justice as aforesaid shall have all the powers given by the First Part of this Act to inspectors appointed by the Board of Trade.

Here I may refer to a memorial which was drawn up by me as far back as the spring of 1864, and presented to the Board of Trade with the signatures of the Salvage

Association of Lloyd's and of other parties interested in such questions.[1] We therein urged the necessity of insisting that these depositions should be made not only by British but by foreign masters, and within twenty-four hours of arrival; it is exaggeration to state that the masters are so urgently employed after arrival at any place in distress that they are entirely unable to find time for appearing before the Receiver to make the depositions, which when promptly taken have often proved to be of the very utmost importance to the parties concerned.

But the fact is that immediate action on the part of the Receiver to secure a statement of the principal occurrences during the voyage prevents unscrupulous masters from concocting average claims upon the parties who are unfortunately tied up with them, and, in order to avoid this, the only efficient remedy against such irregularities, all sorts of excuses are brought forward; nay, a former Receiver used to plead as a reason for the impossibility of obtaining these depositions from foreigners that he could not understand their languages and he would not be able to obtain willingly the assistance of an efficient interpreter. I imagine that if the Board of Trade adopts the suggestion of the memorial above referred to, means will be found to secure through the consular officers the attendance of an interpreter, and in case of an isolated refusal energetic steps should be taken to obtain the desired amendment.

Sometimes I have been met in collision cases with the observation that the statements contained in these depositions were only used to the detriment of the parties making them. Now it is evident that they prevent the subsequent setting up of untruthful assertions, and for this reason alone I maintain that they are for the public good, and

[1] Vide p. 655.

when made by both sides can be more easily compared than at any later period.

I admit that injustice might be committed if in a case of collision the deposition of one side were to be published before that of the other had been made; this difficulty will, however, doubtless disappear when my suggestion for taking all depositions within twenty-four hours after arrival is adopted. But there could be no objection to an enactment that in cases of collision the depositions of both sides shall be published simultaneously.

Would it not be a material assistance to the Receiver if leave were given for any party interested to attend the taking of the depositions, and to be at liberty to suggest such questions as he may think fit?

449. Any examination so taken in writing as aforesaid, or a copy thereof, purporting to be certified under the hand of the receiver or justice before whom such examination was taken, shall be admitted in evidence in any Court of justice, or before any person having by law or by consent of parties authority to hear, receive, and examine evidence, as *primâ facie* proof of all matters contained in such written examination.

The Court of Admiralty has objected to admit copies of Receivers' depositions as evidence; how that is possible under this clear enactment I am unable to conceive, but the matter is so important that particular inquiry ought to be made into it. I have myself been obliged to subpœna Receivers from various parts of the coast for the production of original depositions in some Admiralty suits, in order to avoid the objection that copies were no evidence; now this is clearly against the meaning of this clause.[1]

---

[1] This section has since been repealed by 39 & 40 Vict. c. 80, Sch., Part I.

450. The following rules shall be observed by any person finding or taking possession of wreck within the United Kingdom; (that is to say),
- (1) If the person so finding or taking possession of the same is the Owner, he shall as soon as possible give notice to the receiver of the district within which such wreck is found, stating that he has so found or taken possession of the same; and he shall describe in such notice the marks by which such wreck is distinguished
- (2) If any person not being the Owner finds or takes possession of any wreck, he shall as soon as possible deliver the same to such receiver as aforesaid:

And any person making default in obeying the provisions of this section shall incur the following penalties; (that is to say),
- (3) If he is the Owner and makes default in performing the several things the performance of which is hereby imposed on an Owner,

He shall incur a penalty not exceeding one hundred pounds:
- (4) If he is not the Owner and makes default in performing the several things the performance of which is hereby imposed on any person not being an Owner,

He shall forfeit all claim to salvage:

He shall pay to the Owner of such wreck, if the same is claimed, but if the same is unclaimed, then to the person entitled to such unclaimed wreck, double the value of such wreck (such value to be recovered in the same way as a penalty of like amount); and

He shall incur a penalty not exceeding one hundred pounds.

The case of the 'North' shows that it is not only necessary to make the punishments for the offences described under this clause more severe, but that in all counties having partly a seafaring population, the Bench will not be very easily induced to return a conviction or even a committal under such circumstances; and in order to avoid the reproaches which have so frequently emanated from Foreign Governments, it would be advisable, wherever no

Stipendiary Magistrate exists to make the County Court Judges the committing magistrates, and to remove the trial of such cases to the Central Criminal Court, making it obligatory upon the Judge of the Admiralty Court to attend such trials, in order to satisfy everybody that not only nothing but the strictest possible justice is required, but that the Bench is in possession of sufficient knowledge of Maritime Law.

I would further suggest in those parts of the coast where irregularities similar to those of the 'North' have come to light, to make more frequent changes in the Coastguard, who in fact are the real officials upon whom alone the Receiver can depend for information; and if retained too long in one place will only too easily enter into connections with fishermen and others, who require the greatest supervision.

451. If any receiver suspects or receives information that any wreck is secreted or in the possession of some person who is not the owner thereof, or otherwise improperly dealt with, he may apply to any justice of the peace for a warrant, and such justice shall have power to grant a warrant, by virtue whereof it shall be lawful for the receiver to enter into any house or other place, wherever situate, and also into any ship or boat, and to search for, and to seize and detain, any such wreck as aforesaid there found; and if any such seizure is made in consequence of information that may have been given by any person to the receiver, the informer shall be entitled by way of salvage to such sum, not exceeding in any case five pounds, as the receiver may allow.

Where there are no Stipendiary Magistrates, I would here also empower the County Court Judges to grant warrants.

452. Every receiver shall within forty-eight hours after taking possession of any wreck cause to be posted up in the Custom-house of the port nearest the place where such wreck was found or seized,

a description of the same, and of any marks by which it is distinguished, and shall also, if the value of such wreck exceeds twenty pounds, but not otherwise, transmit a similar description to the secretary of the committee at *Lloyd's* aforesaid; and such secretary shall post up the description so sent, or a copy thereof, in some conspicuous place, for the inspection of all persons desirous of examining the same.

The Receiver ought to give to Lloyd's notice of any wreck irrespective of its value, as undoubtedly such information would often lead to further inquiries, by which losses previously unknown would come to light.

460. Disputes with respect to salvage arising within the boundaries of the Cinque Ports shall be determined in the manner in which the same have hitherto been determined; but whenever any dispute arises elsewhere in the United Kingdom between the owners of any such ship, boat, cargo, apparel, or wreck as aforesaid, and the salvors, as to the amount of salvage, and the parties to the dispute cannot agree as to the settlement thereof by arbitration or otherwise,

Then if the sum claimed does not exceed two hundred pounds,

Such dispute shall be referred to the arbitration of any two justices of the peace resident as follows; (that is to say):

In case of wreck, resident at or near the place where such wreck is found:

In case of services rendered to any ship or boat, or to the persons, cargo, or apparel belonging thereto, resident at or near the place where such ship or boat is lying, or at or near the first port or place in the United Kingdom into which such ship or boat is brought after the occurrence of the accident by reason whereof the claim to salvage arises:

But if the sum claimed exceeds two hundred pounds,

Such dispute may, with the consent of the parties, be referred to the arbitration of such justices as aforesaid, but if they do not consent, shall in *England* be decided by the High Court of Admiralty of *England*, in *Ireland* by the High Court of Admiralty of

Ireland, and in *Scotland* by the Court of Session; subject to this proviso, that if the claimants in such dispute do not recover in such Court of Admiralty or Court of Session a greater sum than two hundred pounds, they shall not, unless the court certifies that the case is a fit one to be tried in a superior court, recover any costs, charges, or expenses incurred by them in the prosecution of their claim:

And every dispute with respect to salvage may be heard and adjudicated upon on the application either of the salvor or of the Owner of the property salved, or of their respective agents.

461. Whenever, in pursuance of this Act, any dispute as to salvage is referred to the arbitration of two justices, they may either themselves determine the same, with power to call to their assistance any person conversant with maritime affairs as assessor, or they may, if a difference of opinion arises between them, or without such difference, if they think fit, appoint some person conversant with maritime affairs as umpire to decide the point in dispute; and such justices or their umpire shall make an award as to the amount of salvage payable within the following times; that is to say, the said justices within forty-eight hours after such dispute has been referred to them, and the said umpire within forty-eight hours after his appointment, with power nevertheless for such justices or umpire by writing under their or his hands or hand to extend the time within which they and he are hereby respectively directed to make their or his award.[1]

These clauses are undoubtedly among the most important of the whole Act; and although framed with the best possible intention to avoid litigation, have proved the most vexatious, through the interpretation given to them.

The working of the first clause is threefold, viz.:—

a. That the jurisdiction of the 'Commissioners of Salvage' for the Cinque Ports, as regulated by

---

[1] The summary jurisdiction in small salvage cases is extended by 25 & 26 Vict. c. 63, sec. 49. (See p. 607.)

the 1 & 2 George IV. cap. 126, remains in full force;

b. That elsewhere in Great Britain, claims not exceeding 200*l.* shall be referred to the arbitration of any two Justices of the Peace;

c. That claims exceeding 200*l.* shall be decided by the proper Maritime Court, with the proviso—if claimants do not recover a greater sum than 200*l.* they shall not recover costs unless certified by the Court.

Now what has been the practical result of these enactments?

ad a. With respect to the Cinque Ports Commissioners, that their decisions (especially at Ramsgate and Deal) have been so partial to the fishermen that nobody but an innocent foreigner, who is not cautioned as to the risk he runs by allowing a matter to be referred to them, will ever submit to their arbitration.

ad b. The same objection is made to the decisions of two Justices of the Peace, who are in general so intimately connected with the interests of their county, and frequently so imperfectly acquainted with matters brought before them, that their awards are hardly ever satisfactory.

ad c. The praise which the late venerable Judge of the Admiralty Court[1] has frequently from the Bench bestowed upon the fishermen, and the positive disinclination which he has generally evinced to refuse certifying the claimant's costs even in the most flagrant cases (I may only refer to the case of the 'Adolph Michels,' where costs were certified with an award of only 50*l.*), have made it a usual practice for salvors' agents (their solicitors or proctors) to institute, without any attempts at previous

[1] Dr. Lushington.

settlement, Admiralty proceedings; for, as they can reckon with comparative certainty upon getting their costs whatever may be the award, they will only consent to a compromise out of court when, from fear of the heavy expenses, an amount quite out of proportion to the value of the services is offered.

Such vexatious and very expensive proceedings can only be avoided by positively enacting that nobody shall obtain costs in court who does not receive a judgment for at least 200*l.*; and further by doing away with all arbitrations by Commissioners and Justices of the Peace, appointing in their stead the Stipendiary Magistrates and County Court Judges, two Elder Brethren of the Trinity House to be called in as Nautical Assessors at the request of either party.

These would be cheap and eminently efficient Tribunals, which would very soon convince everybody abroad that our Legislature will see justice done to everybody coming to our shores.

I may mention that the reason why the Commissioners, &c., have given so little satisfaction in deciding salvage differences, is simply that in the majority of cases each Commissioner takes up the position of advocate of the side by which he is appointed, or rather selected, and after a long delay, they agree rather to divide the difference between them than to submit the case to an umpire; therefore, whenever the salvors' agent is sufficiently versed in the mode of proceeding, he makes his original demand outrageously exorbitant, and in the end his clients are proportionate gainers.

This unfortunate mode of compromise has been found so convenient for arbitrators, that I, who about ten years ago was one of their strenuous supporters, since this system has come into almost general practice, have now, in the interests of my clients, peremptorily refused to have anything whatever to do with any kind of arbitration.

I consider that I am the more justified in expressing my candid opinion on this question as I have, through what my clients often denominate too liberal awards, settled a proportionately large number of salvage cases out of court, and have usually succeeded in convincing those claimants who were not satisfied and preferred the decision of the London or Dublin Admiralty Judges, that only in very rare cases they obtained a larger salvage than I had offered.

462. There shall be paid to every assessor and umpire who may be so appointed as aforesaid in respect of his services, such sum not exceeding five pounds as the Board of Trade may from time to time direct; and all the costs of such arbitration, including any such payments as aforesaid, shall be paid by the parties to the dispute, in such manner and in such shares and proportions as the said justices or as the said umpire may direct by their or his award.

The Trinity Masters could not be expected to travel for anything like the amount here fixed; and really no suitor will object to a reasonable charge if only justice can be obtained.

466. Whenever the aggregate amount of salvage payable in respect of salvage services rendered in the United Kingdom has been finally ascertained either by agreement or by the award of such justices or their umpire, but a dispute arises as to the apportionment thereof amongst several claimants, then, if the amount does not exceed two hundred pounds, it shall be lawful for the party liable to pay the amount so due to apply to the receiver of the district for liberty to pay the amount so ascertained to him; and he shall, if he thinks fit, receive the same accordingly, and grant a certificate under his hand, stating the fact of such payment

and the services in respect of which it is made; and such certificate shall be a full discharge and indemnity to the person or persons to whom it is given, and to their ship, boats, cargo, apparel, and effects, against the claims of all persons whomsoever in respect of the services therein mentioned; but if the amount exceeds two hundred pounds, it shall be apportioned in manner hereinafter mentioned.

I would suggest to omit the words '*if he thinks fit*' in the ninth line of the clause. I cannot see any reason why such a matter should be left to the Receiver's discretion.

468. Whenever any salvage is due to any person under this Act, the receiver shall act as follows; (that is to say),
 (1) If the same is due in respect of services rendered in assisting any ship or boat, or in saving the lives of persons belonging to the same, or the cargo or apparel thereof,

He shall detain such ship or boat and the cargo and apparel belonging thereto until payment is made, or process has been issued by some competent court for the detention of such ship, boat, cargo, or apparel.
 (2) If the same is due in respect of the saving of any wreck, and such wreck is not sold as unclaimed in pursuance of the provisions hereinafter contained,

He shall detain such wreck until payment is made, or process has been issued in manner aforesaid;

But it shall be lawful for the receiver, if at any time previously to the issue of such process security is given to his satisfaction for the amount of salvage due, to release from his custody any ship, boat, cargo, apparel, or wreck so detained by him as aforesaid; and in cases where the claim for salvage exceeds two hundred pounds it shall be lawful in *England* for the High Court of Admiralty of *England*, in *Ireland* for the High Court of Admiralty in *Ireland*, and in *Scotland* for the Court of Session, to determine any question that may arise concerning the amount of the security to be given or the sufficiency of the sureties; and in all cases where bond or other security is given to the receiver for an amount exceeding two hundred pounds, it shall be lawful for the salvor or the Owner of the property salved, or their respective agents, to institute proceedings in such last-mentioned courts for the purpose of having the questions arising between them adjudicated upon, and the said courts may enforce payment of the said bond or other security in the same manner as if bail had been given in the said courts.

In some of the outports it has been made a frequent practice immediately after any property brought in liable to salvage has been placed in charge of the Receiver, and without any further inquiry whether the parties to whom such property belongs are willing or able to give sufficient bail for any claim upon them, to telegraph at once to London for an Admiralty Warrant, so as to bring the matter within the jurisdiction of the Court. I think this is a needless expense, which easily might be saved, as it really cannot be pleaded that such a course is adopted for better security, more particularly when, as in the majority of cases, the property is in such a state that, whether arrested or not, it is unable to leave the port.

It would be very easy to improve the Receiver's machinery in order to avoid the taking out of a warrant, as in almost all cases the Receiver actually comes forward as the Agent of the Marshal of the Admiralty Court, and as such takes charge of the property; the result is that a large sum is unnecessarily charged as possession fee, &c., whereas all that claimants have a right to demand is security for salvage, which, of course, ought never to be denied.

469. Whenever any ship, boat, cargo, apparel, or wreck is detained by any receiver for non-payment of any sums so due as aforesaid, and the parties liable to pay the same are aware of such detention, then, in the following cases; (that is to say),

(1) In cases where the amount is not disputed, and payment

thereof is not made within twenty days after the same has become due;

(2) In cases where the amount is disputed, but no appeal lies from the first tribunal to which the dispute is referred, and payment thereof is not made within twenty days after the decision of such first tribunal;

(3) In cases where the amount is disputed, and an appeal lies from the decision of the first tribunal to some other tribunal, and payment thereof is not made within such twenty days as last aforesaid, or such monition as hereinbefore mentioned is not taken out within such twenty days, or such other proceedings as are according to the practice of such other tribunal necessary for the prosecution of an appeal are not instituted within such twenty days;

The receiver may forthwith sell such ship, boat, cargo, apparel, or wreck, or a sufficient part thereof, and out of the proceeds of the sale, after payment of all expenses thereof, defray all sums of money due in respect of expenses, fees, and salvage, paying the surplus, if any, to the Owners of the property sold, or other the parties entitled to receive the same.

Here I would suggest to make it obligatory upon such Receiver to issue public notice in the local and a central paper of the date of sale.

472. If any dispute arises between the receiver and any such admiral, vice-admiral, lord of any manor, or other person as aforesaid as to the validity of his title to wreck, or if divers persons claim to be entitled to wreck found at the same place, the matter in dispute may be decided by two justices in the same manner in which disputes as to salvage coming within the jurisdiction of justices are hereinbefore directed to be determined.

I imagine that no objection could be made to see the authority of two Justices of the Peace superseded by that of a Stipendiary Magistrate or a County Court Judge.

475. If no Owner establishes his claim to wreck found at any place before the expiration of such period of a year as aforesaid, and if no admiral, vice-admiral, lord of any manor, or person other than Her Majesty, her heirs or successors, is proved to be entitled to such wreck, the receiver shall forthwith sell the same, and after payment of all expenses attending such sale, and deducting therefrom his fees, and all expenses (if any) incurred by him, and paying to the salvors such amount of salvage as the Board of Trade may in each case, or by any general rule, determine, pay the same into the receipt of Her Majesty's Exchequer in such manner as the Treasury may direct, and the same shall be carried to and form part of the Consolidated Fund of the United Kingdom.

Public notice of intended sale ought to be required.

478. Every person who does any of the following acts; (that is to say),
- (1) Wrongfully carries away or removes any part of any ship or boat stranded, or in danger of being stranded, or otherwise in distress on or near the shore of any sea or tidal water, or any part of the cargo or apparel thereof, or any wreck; or,
- (2) Endeavours in any way to impede or hinder the saving of such ship, boat, cargo, apparel, or wreck; or
- (3) Secretes any wreck, or obliterates or defaces any marks thereon;

Shall, in addition to any other penalty or punishment he may be subject to under this or any other Act or law, for each such offence incur a penalty not exceeding fifty pounds; and every person, not being a receiver or a person hereinbefore authorised to take the command in cases of ships being stranded or in distress, or not acting under the orders of such receiver or person, who, without the leave of the Master, endeavours to board any such ship or boat as aforesaid, shall for each offence incur a penalty not exceeding fifty pounds; and it shall be lawful for the Master of such ship or boat to repel by force any such person so attempting to board the same.

I think the offences herein described ought to be

punished more severely than is here enacted; the difficulty of proving them is so great, and the inclination to shelter offenders who have, according to the general and customary views among the inhabitants of the coast, only taken what if the wind had blown in a different direction would have been irrecoverably lost, is so universal, that all such offences must be punished with exemplary severity, in order to bring the public mind in those localities to comprehend the wrong which is thereby committed.

Under this part of the Act the suggestion ought to be made that it would be in the interest of public justice to alter the present system of surveying damages to ships. In Continental ports no master of a vessel can obtain a certificate of survey which is of any legal use to him from any other than a surveyor appointed by public authority, sometimes judicial, sometimes mercantile, but always duly sworn to act impartially to the best of his knowledge and belief; we, on the contrary, have fallen into so loose a manner of transacting this sort of business that the most serious irregularities have been the natural result.

According to what is called general custom, any master of a ship, whether British or foreign (in case the law of his country does not force the latter to apply to his consular officer), is at liberty to appoint one or two parties as surveyors, of whom he personally very rarely knows anything, but who are recommended to him by his agent or correspondent as suitable persons for the purpose, who too often do not consider themselves obliged to act in the capacity of impartial surveyors but assume at once the post of partisans, that is to say, they certify to the correctness of anything that is desired, quite immaterial whether truthful or not, if only a colour for their assertion can be found. In fact, in some of our most frequented outports it is publicly asserted that the order to survey a damaged vessel is looked upon in the same light as the retaining fee of a barrister, and is considered to oblige the surveyor to use his official position for the protection of the master of such vessel, without any due consideration for the other interests at stake. How frauds of all descriptions can, with impunity, be practised upon shipowners and their underwriters, when an unprincipled master of a ship combines to that effect with his agent, or the clerks he employs, and finds no effectual resistance on the part of the surveyors, may be readily conceived; and this state of things is the more dangerous as only in very rare instances the underwriters are so efficiently and promptly represented as to prevent by the means which the law affords the serious consequences above described.

One of the methods sometimes available is the appointment of another set of surveyors to prove by a second survey the irregularities in the first; but it is not easy to find in any place men independent enough to go directly against the signed, sealed, and delivered opinions of their townsmen, and if they were to be found much time would be wasted and much useless expense incurred in order to prove the fallacy of the first and the correctness of the second survey. But what can be done when on the faith of an erroneous, or even fraudulent survey, a vessel has been sold and claims made which cannot, under the circumstances stated, be disputed?—a case which has not unfrequently occurred.

It appears to me that the only means of obviating all these serious consequences is to declare that for the interest of all concerned in the case of any damaged ship, or cargo, no survey, valuation, or appraisement shall be good in law or equity, for any purpose whatsoever, unless made by one or two (as the case may be) competent surveyors appointed by the Receiver, and sworn by him in the same way as appraisers are at present under the 50th section of the Merchant Shipping Act Amendment Act, 1862; this would be altogether in accordance with Continental custom, and would conduce to restore the general confidence which recent transactions in our outports have so greatly shaken.

The Receiver will take care that the surveyors he appoints perform their duty efficiently, and as public officials it is to be hoped that their being bribed or tampered with will be altogether out of the question.[1]

PART IX.—*Liability of Shipowners.*

502. The Ninth Part of this Act shall apply to the whole of Her Majesty's dominions.

This part of the Act, although distinctly stated to apply 'to the whole of Her Majesty's dominions,' has been unexpectedly extended in some cases to acts taking place on the high seas, without the jurisdiction of this country or any of her colonies, in which foreign ships have been concerned. The extension gave rise, in the case of the Belgian steamer 'Marie de Brabant,' to a very serious loss to a large numbers of foreigners, as a perusal of the judgments of the Admiralty Court and of the Judicial Committee of the Privy Council will show.[2]

The non-compliance with the fundamental rules of acknowledged principles of international law is so sur-

---

[1] It may be well to state here, that since the foregoing was written, I have—in the interest of my clients—in all cases passing through my hands, and before surveys were held, caused a document to be executed, by which the representatives of the assured and their underwriters respectively appoint each a surveyor, and these two surveyors nominate an umpire, by whose final decision any differences between the two surveyors are finally settled.

[2] For correspondence on this matter, *vide* p. 513.

prising that nothing short of a positive enactment that this part of the Act was intended to be applied only to British ships wherever they meet (of course their laws always travel with them) or to foreign ships when within the limits of British jurisdiction (within three miles from shore), can be expected to alter this highly unsatisfactory state of affairs.

Having submitted to the President of the Board of Trade a memorial especially prepared for the purpose of setting forth the grievances in this case, I may here refrain from entering more minutely upon the subject.

507. Whenever any such liability as aforesaid has been or is alleged to have been incurred in respect of loss of life or personal injury, the Board of Trade may, in its discretion, after giving not less than three days' notice by post or otherwise to the party to be made defendant or defender, by warrant sealed with the seal of such Board, or signed by one of its secretaries or assistant secretaries, require the sheriff having jurisdiction over any place in the United Kingdom to summon a jury at a time and place to be specified in such warrant for the purpose of determining the following question ; (that is to say),

The number, names, and descriptions of all persons killed or injured by reason of any wrongful act, neglect, or default ;

And upon the receipt of such warrant the sheriff shall summon a jury of twenty-four indifferent persons, duly qualified to act as common jurymen in the superior courts, to meet at such time and place as aforesaid.

In the case above referred to of the ' Marie de Brabant,' several lives were lost in consequence of the neglect of the officer in charge of the Liverpool steamer ' Amalia,' and compensation was in due course obtained ; but I have never heard that proceedings were taken in order to suspend or cancel the certificate of such officer ; ought it not to be the duty of the Judge of the Admiralty Court to inform the Board of Trade of such cases?

PART X.—*Legal Procedure.*

519. Any stipendiary magistrate shall have full power to do alone whatever two justices of the peace are by this Act authorised to do.

Here the authorisation of the County Court Judges or Sheriffs, in lieu of the two Justices of the Peace, would have to be recapitulated.

527. Whenever any injury has, in any part of the world, been caused to any property belonging to Her Majesty, or to any of Her Majesty's subjects by any foreign ship, if any time thereafter such ship is found in any port or river of the United Kingdom, or within three miles of the coast thereof, it shall be lawful for the Judge of any Court of Record in the United Kingdom, or for the Judge of the High Court of Admiralty, or in *Scotland* the Court of Session, or the sheriff of the county within whose jurisdiction such ship may be, upon its being shown to him by any person applying summarily that such injury was probably caused by the misconduct or want of skill of the Master or mariners of such ship, to issue an order directed to any officer of Customs or other officer named by such Judge, requiring him to detain such ship until such time as the Owner, Master, or Consignee thereof has made satisfaction in respect of such injury, or has given security, to be approved by the Judge to abide the event of any action, suit, or other legal proceeding that may be instituted in respect of such injury, and to pay all costs and damages that may be awarded thereon; and any officer of Customs or other officer to whom such order is directed, shall detain such ship accordingly.

My observations upon clause 468 will apply equally to this clause.

529. In any action, suit, or other proceeding in relation to such injury, the person so giving security as aforesaid shall be made de-

fendant or defender, and shall be stated to be the Owner of the ship that has occasioned such damage; and the production of the order of the Judge made in relation to such security shall be conclusive evidence of the liability of such defendant or defender to such action, suit, or other proceeding.

In spite of the clear directions contained in this clause, the Judge of the Admiralty Court has persistently refused to recognise underwriters either as plaintiffs or defendants, although they are frequently the only parties who have ultimately anything to gain or lose by the proceedings; this must naturally give rise to very awkward complications.

Apparently unimportant matters of this description have often given rise to irregularities which could not easily be surmounted; let everybody who has an interest in a case have a *locus standi*, and not be obliged to assume another person's capacity and sail under false colours.

PART XI.—*Miscellaneous.*

547. The Legislative authority of any *British* Possession shall have power, by any Act or Ordinance, confirmed by Her Majesty in Council, to repeal, wholly or in part, any provisions of this Act relating to ships registered in such Possession; but no such Act or Ordinance shall take effect until such approval has been proclaimed in such Possession, or until such time thereafter as may be fixed by such Act or Ordinance for the purpose.

If one part of the Act has been made law to the colonies, why not the whole?

Schedule Form B (see Section 38). After perusal of the declaration of ownership I am astonished that the case related by me above[1] could have occurred, but so it is.

[1] Vide *ante*, p. 603.

18 & 19 Vict. cap. 91.

The Merchant Shipping Act Amendment Act, 1855.

19. Whenever any articles belonging to or forming part of any Foreign Ship which has been wrecked on or near the coasts of the United Kingdom, or belonging to or forming part of the cargo thereof, are found on or near such coasts, or are brought into any port in the United Kingdom, the Consul-General of the country to which such ship, or, in the case of cargo, to which the Owners of such cargo, may have belonged, or any Consular Officer of such country authorised in that behalf by any treaty or agreement with such country, shall, in the absence of the Owner of such ship or articles, and of the Master or other Agent of the Owner, be deemed to be the Agent of the Owner, so far as relates to the custody and disposal of such articles.

I would suggest adding to this section a stipulation, that whenever the representative of any underwriter shall be able, to the satisfaction of the Board of Trade or the Receiver, as the case may be, to prove an interest to the wrecked property, such underwriter's representative shall be entitled to the custody and disposal of such articles.

The present mode of effecting insurances, not as formerly at the place where the respective owners of ship or cargo reside, but frequently at very different places, would cause considerable annoyances, delays, and unnecessary expense, if this section remained without the proposed addition.

---

25 & 26 Vict. cap. 63.

The Merchant Shipping Act Amendment Act, 1862.

49. The provisions contained in the Eighth Part of the Principal Act for giving summary jurisdiction to two Justices in Salvage

cases, and for preventing unnecessary Appeals and Litigation in such cases, shall be amended as follows; (that is to say),

(1) Such provision shall extend to all cases in which the value of the property saved does not exceed one thousand pounds, as well as to the cases provided for by th rincipal Act:

(2) Such provisions shall be held to apply whether the Salvage Service has been rendered within the limits of the United Kingdom or not:

(3) It shall be lawful for one of Her Majesty's Principal Secretaries of State, or in *Ireland* for the Lord Lieutenant or other Chief Governor or Governors, to appoint out of the Justices for any borough or county a rota of Justices by whom jurisdiction in salvage cases shall be exercised:

(4) When no such rota is appointed, it shall be lawful for the salvors, by writing addressed to the Justice's Clerk, to name one Justice, and for the Owner of the property saved in like manner to name the other:

(5) If either party fails to name a Justice within a reasonable time, the case may be tried by two or more Justices at Petty Sessions:

(6) It shall be competent for any Stipendiary Magistrate, and also in *England* for any County Court Judge, in *Scotland* for the Sheriff or Sheriff substitute of any county, and in *Ireland* for the Recorder of any borough in which there is a Recorder, or for the Chairman of Quarter Sessions in any county, to exercise the same jurisdiction in Salvage cases as is given to two Justices:

(7) It shall be lawful for one of Her Majesty's Principal Secretaries of State to determine a scale of costs to be awarded in Salvage cases by any such Justices or Court as aforesaid:

(8) All the provisions of the Principal Act relating to summary proceedings in Salvage cases, and to the prevention of unnecessary appeals in such cases, shall, except so far as the same are altered by this Act, extend and apply

to all such proceedings, whether under the Principal Act or this Act, or both of such Acts.

I have in my remarks on the Principal Act entered fully into the necessity of substituting the County Court Judges for the two Justices of the Peace, with respect to the adjudication of salvage cases, and here refer to the arguments there used.

sub. 4. This clause perpetuates the arbitration system which has proved so fallacious, and the consequences of which I have above so fully described.

sub. 6. My suggestions respecting the County Court Judges being here adopted, I see no reason to doubt that the plan, as a whole, will be carried out without very serious opposition.

50. Whenever any Salvage question arises the Receiver of Wreck for the district may, upon application from either of the parties, appoint a Valuer to value the property in respect of which the Salvage claim is made, and shall, when the valuation has been returned to him, give a copy of the valuation to both parties; and any copy of such valuation, purporting to be signed by the Valuer, and to be attested by the receiver, shall be received in evidence in any subsequent proceeding; and there shall be paid in respect of such valuation, by the party applying for the same, such fee as the Board of Trade may direct.

I have myself tried the working of this clause, and its efficiency has principally induced me to propose to give to the Receiver a more extended authority in all matters of average.

54. The Owners of any ship, whether *British* or Foreign, shall not, in cases where all or any of the following events occur without their actual fault or privity; (that is to say),
    (1) Where any loss of life or personal injury is caused to any person being carried in such ship;

(2) Where any damage or loss is caused to any goods, merchandise, or other things whatsoever on board any such ship;

(3) Where any loss of life or personal injury is by reason of the improper navigation of such ship as aforesaid caused to any person carried in any other ship or boat;

(4) Where any loss or damage is by reason of the improper navigation of such ship as aforesaid caused to any other ship or boat, or to any goods, merchandise, or other things whatsoever on board any other ship or boat;

be answerable in damages in respect of loss of life or personal injury, either alone or together with loss or damage to ships, boats, goods, merchandise, or other things, to an aggregate amount exceeding fifteen pounds for each ton of their ship's tonnage; nor in respect of loss or damage to ships, goods, merchandise, or other things, whether there be in addition loss of life or personal injury or not, to an aggregate amount exceeding eight pounds for each ton of the ship's tonnage; such tonnage to be the registered tonnage in the case of sailing ships, and in the case of steam ships the gross tonnage without deduction on account of engine-room:

In the case of any foreign ship which has been or can be measured according to *British* law, the tonnage as ascertained by such measurement shall, for the purposes of this section, be deemed to be the tonnage of such ship:

In the case of any foreign ship which has not been and cannot be measured under *British* law, the Surveyor-General of tonnage in the United Kingdom, and the Chief Measuring Officer in any *British* possession abroad, shall, on receiving from or by direction of the Court hearing the case such evidence concerning the dimensions of the ship as it may be found practicable to furnish, give a certificate under his hand, stating what would in his opinion have been the tonnage of such ship if she had been duly measured according to *British* law, and the tonnage so stated in such certificate shall, for the purposes of this section, be deemed to be the tonnage of such ship.

This clause replaces clause 504 of the Principal Act,

and has been so interpreted by our Courts as to give rise to the most unjust and unheard-of results.

In the first place, it does not deal equal justice to rich and poor; and secondly, it has introduced into this country a state of things utterly at variance with sound principles of law.

It is quite clear that, when the Merchant Shipping Act of 1854 engaged the attention of the Legislature, the necessity of abrogating the system of unlimited liability was strongly urged upon it. By that system the whole property of a shipowner, whether on sea or land, was liable to make good any damage, however great, which might be occasioned by any vessel belonging to him, and this, although he might have taken every precaution which the nature of the case would possibly permit.

Such a state of things, of course, deterred responsible persons from investing their money in shipping property, and, by throwing the carrying trade into the hands of a class who were without adequate means, gave rise to numerous evils, which have been often described and need not be here repeated.

The propriety of admitting the principle of limited liability into maritime matters had already been partly conceded by 7 George II. cap. 15, and by subsequent Acts, and the system now obtained its natural and legitimate extension in the 504th clause of the Act which was the result of mature deliberation, enacting that no owner should be answerable for losses occasioned without his actual fault or privity beyond the value of his ship and the current freight. This new system was qualified, it must be admitted, in cases where liability should be incurred with respect to loss of life or personal injury to any passenger, by the stipulation that the value in such cases should not be taken to be less than 15*l.* per register ton. The reason for this qualification is not apparent, unless it were meant to discourage the taking of passengers at all on board ships of inferior value, in which case it ought to have been made to apply only to liability incurred by the ship on board of which the passengers were. As far as my knowledge goes, however, this stipulation never had any actual influence upon the decisions of our Courts.

Such being the law, as laid down by Parliament in 1854, it soon became apparent that the natural increase in the mercantile navies of the world, together with the general introduction of steam as a propelling power, would produce a great increase in the number of collision cases, and when the Board of Trade had become aware of some defects in the Merchant Shipping Act, and was known to be contemplating the introduction of what afterwards became the Amendment Act of 1862, some of the owners interested in the large steamers, navigating the most frequented parts of the Atlantic, and consequently running the greatest risk of being made liable as above pointed out, really succeeded in prevailing upon the late Government to induce the Legislature to limit the liability of shipowners in the way which now constitutes the law of the land.

A careful perusal of 'Hansard' will show the wonderful argumentation used on both sides of the House when this question was under consideration, and that on May 26, 1862, the then First Lord of the Treasury (Viscount Palmerston) used the following memorable expressions, viz. :—

> 'He could not understand the great tenderness which hon. gentlemen seemed to feel for steamships causing damage to other ships which they met. *If he were not officially connected with his right hon. friend* (the

President of the Board of Trade), but were exercising an independent judgment on his proposal, he should say, that that proposal failed in this, that the true principle which ought to be applied to damage done by steam vessels or any other instrument conducted by man, must be the value of the damage done, not the quality or the value of the instrument causing it. If there was any fault in the proposal of his Right hon. friend it was that it went too far in mitigation of the liability of steamships for damage, and he hoped that the House would not do anything so manifestly unjust as still further to limit their responsibility.'

There cannot be any doubt that a statesman of Lord Palmerston's character would not have uttered those words of complete and entire disapprobation of a measure introduced and strenuously supported in the House by one of his colleagues, had he not been impressed by the strong conviction that great wrong was about to be done, and that if, for party reasons, he were obliged to acquiesce in it, he would at least relieve his conscience by a public declaration, that nothing but his official connection could have induced him to do so.

The Merchant Shipping Act Amendment Act of 1862 having become law, we must now refer to the tenor of subsequent decisions, to see the influence which it has exercised upon the administration of justice in this country.

In the first place, the opening words of the Limited Liability Clause (Sect. 54, 'the owner of any ship, whether British or Foreign, shall not,' &c.) have been held by the Courts to apply to ships of all nations, in all places, whether within British jurisdiction or without. As the most apt illustration of the result of such decisions, I would refer to a separate memorial which I have laid before the Board of Trade,[1] on the subject of the 'Marie de Brabant,' a steamer belonging to Belgian owners, which was run down and sunk by the British steamer 'Amalia,' of Liverpool. The Belgian vessel and cargo were of the value of 38,377*l.* 3*s.* 10*d.*, and this amount would have been completely recovered from the wrong-doing 'Amalia,' the value of which vessel was admitted to exceed the loss she had occasioned, if by any subsequent accident she had been obliged to enter any other than a British port, but, reaching Liverpool instead, the parties interested in the 'Marie de Brabant' were only able to recover 14,600*l.*, and in fact lost 23,777*l.* 3*s.* 10*d.* by being obliged to resort to our Courts for their remedy.

The results of this decision must not be lost sight of. The principles of International Law, which have been adhered to in the most sacred manner by all our most eminent Judges, are now for the first time abandoned, and in their stead we have a sort of *lex fori*, or an assertion by our Courts that a certain fixed measure of relief is all that we can give, and that Foreigners, if they come to our Courts, either as plaintiffs or defendants, must be satisfied with the same limited liability that would be held to apply in the case of one of our own ships; and this while a British shipowner, if plaintiff in the foreign court, would obtain full and complete redress! And there may result from such decisions far worse confusion than has been at present foreseen. For, supposing that a Belgian plaintiff, who had been deprived of his natural international rights by the decision of one of our Courts, in accordance with this British municipal legislation, were subsequently to discover the wrong-doing British ship in a Belgian port; what should prevent him from detaining her there, and

---

[1] Vide p. 513.

obtaining in his own native courts such further redress as he had failed in obtaining here? If such a course is once taken in a foreign country, and it is not at all improbable that it may be, we shall have some of our ships unable to go to France, some to Belgium, and so on; the result being endless confusion and proportionate injury to our trade.

And how has this anomalous and unjustifiable legislation become part of our statute-book? A glance at the first drafts of the Amendment Act, as laid before Parliament for discussion, will show that these words, 'whether British or Foreign,' had no place in them; in the debates they were never referred to; *the House evidently never once remarked that four words had subsequently slipped in* which would be held to bind our Courts to disregard the most obvious duties of international comity, or surely some expression of regret would have been called forth in the House by our departure from the principles which have made our nation famous; on the contrary, the alteration made without any authority by the drawer of the Bill, during its passage through the House, was altogether overlooked, and I will do no more than give the words of a late very eminent Judge, the Lord Justice Knight-Bruce, who thus expressed himself on the point during the hearing of the 'Marie de Brabant' appeal above referred to:—

> 'I do not know why these very extensive Acts of Parliament should have left such an obvious question open to argument. I cannot quite understand it. The questions are so obvious, you know; and a great many people do know that there are other people in the world who have ships besides ourselves.'

In the second place, legislation, in the direction of limited liability, has been by the Amendment Act distorted from its original intention and converted into a powerful engine of oppression and injustice. There can be only one opinion as to what the limitation of a shipowner's liability was originally intended to imply, viz.: that any man investing, say, 100*l*. in the purchase of a 64th share of a ship, should have the certitude that he could not be made to forfeit his share, and a further amount besides. In other words, the owners of any ship inflicting damage were to be allowed to say, 'There is our ship, we give her up to you, and, as far as her value goes, you may pay yourself for any wrong she has done.'

This is the common-sense view of the proposition, and this is what other countries have always acted upon. Our Courts, however, have not held to this interpretation, but have actually made the owners of a ship, which has been found to blame for a collision, liable to make good 8*l*. per ton on her register, when their vessel itself may have been rendered almost valueless or even totally destroyed by the same casualty. And what can be more monstrous than for the law to say that a vessel which has originally cost her owners 4*l*. per ton (and at this rate very excellent vessels may now be bought in open market) which after collision with another vessel may reach a British port in such a state as to be worth only 1*l*. per ton, shall nevertheless be held liable in damages to the extent of 8*l*. per ton or even 15*l*., in case of loss of life, while it is perfectly clear that, if the vessel is a foreigner, more than her *actual market value*, as she reaches port, cannot by any possibility be got out of her, nor ought to be, according to the general law of the sea.[1]

In fact, the creation of this anomalous legislation

---

[1] The records of the Registry of the High Court of Admiralty will show numerous cases illustrative of the above remarks. It is sufficient for my purpose to mention two, viz. the 'Earl of Leicester,' whose owners paid for damages

virtually establishes a monopoly for large and valuable ships to the undue prejudice of small and old ones. In the same debate, to which I have already referred, the then President of the Board of Trade is reported to have said:—

> 'There might, indeed, be a little increase of liability under the present scheme, as far as the owners of worthless ships were concerned, but that was quite right, because an old ship, or one of small value, might do great damage, and might belong to a wealthy owner or company;'

but every practical man would have told the right hon. gentleman that there are many steps between the new A1 ship and that worthless craft which he confesses might probably suffer somewhat under the effects of the clauses supported by him. And I am at a loss to conceive how it can be thought just and equitable to make a poor man who may have invested all his savings in the purchase of a ship, worth 4*l*. a ton, liable to a loss equal to double the amount of his investment, while you, in the same breath, exonerate the rich owner of a very valuable craft from perhaps three-fourths of the amount which, under the General Maritime Law, he might be made liable for, although the latter really could afford to sacrifice more in proportion than the former; and although it is not pretended that the liability in either case bears any proportion to the amount of injury inflicted.

Having now, as I hope, said enough to demonstrate clearly the injustice which is occasioned by the assumption of a fixed arbitrary value for property which is subject to constant fluctuation, and giving it strongly as my

arising out of a collision considerably more than her value; the 'Mindora,' whose owners paid the statutory amount of 8*l*. per ton, although the vessel herself was at the bottom of the sea.

opinion that the late Government, unadvisedly yielding to the influence brought to bear upon it, principally by the Liverpool Chamber of Commerce, gave up, in the 504th clause of the Merchant Shipping Act, a principle against which no reasonable complaint could be urged, I would in conclusion point out what is likely to be the result of this unfair tenderness for large valuable steam-vessels.

Every one must have observed that in the majority of the collision cases now occurring one at least of the vessels is a steamer.

It will also not be denied that the general impression with regard to collisions is, that a vessel going at full speed is not so likely to receive serious damage herself as she is to inflict injury upon another.

Now, bearing this in mind, and remembering that the value of a first-class steamer will often exceed 30*l.* per ton, what would be the position of the master of such a vessel of, say, 1,000 tons register, in view of an inevitable collision? By slackening speed he might receive the blow of the approaching ship, and possibly lose his own, or in figures 30,000*l.*; if he increases his speed he will probably save his own ship though he will certainly sink the other, and if he does his owner's loss cannot exceed 8,000*l.* Surely no words could too strongly condemn legislation which could produce such effects as are here only hinted at.

Long after these observations were made, and only just before the issue of this third edition, another proof has come to my knowledge of the injustice to which this legislation leads.

The British steamer 'Apollo,' belonging to Messrs. Thos. Wilson, Sons, & Co. of Hull, came into collision with and was sunk by the French vessel 'Précurseur.' The Court of Appeal at Rennes on December 21, 1887, held the owners of the 'Apollo' liable for the damages caused to the 'Précurseur' and the cargo on board thereof, to the extent of 8*l*. per register ton. This Court of Appeal, in confirming the judgment of the Court of first instance at Brest, gave its reasons, which are very instructive. They are to the effect that no foreigner can obtain from a French tribunal the advantages of French law (here the freedom from liability by the abandonment of the vessel) if the tribunal of the foreigner does not grant to the French subject the same advantage, or *real reciprocity*. As the French subject would by the English Courts under identical circumstances be held liable for 8*l*. per register ton, the Court of Appeal at Rennes would not absolve Messrs. Wilson & Co. from liability on any other terms than would be granted by the English Courts.

French jurisprudence condemns, therefore, in matters of General Maritime Law, the *lex fori* in similar terms to those used by Lord Stowell and many of our most celebrated and enlightened Judges before the decision in the case of the 'Marie de Brabant' and the 'Amalia.'

34 & 35 VICT. CAP. 110.
The Merchant Shipping Act, 1871.

35 & 36 VICT. CAP. 73.
The Merchant Shipping Act, 1872.

36 & 37 VICT. CAP. 85.
The Merchant Shipping Act, 1873.

39 & 40 VICT. CAP. 80.
The Merchant Shipping Act, 1876.

43 & 44 VICT. CAP. 16.
The Merchant Seamen (Payment of Wages and Rating) Act, 1880.

43 & 44 VICT. CAP. 18.
The Merchant Shipping Act Amendment Act, 1880.

43 & 44 VICT. CAP. 22.
The Merchant Shipping (Fee and Expenses) Act, 1880.

43 & 44 Vict. cap. 43.
The Merchant Shipping (Carriage of Grain) Act, 1880.

45 & 46 Vict. cap. 55.
The Merchant Shipping (Expenses) Act, 1882.

45 & 46 Vict. cap. 76.
The Merchant Shipping (Colonial Inquiries) Act, 1882.

Since the issue of the second edition of this publication, the foregoing Acts have been passed by our Legislature on the subjects here under consideration, but having carefully considered the matters treated therein, they seem to me to require no further observations.

V.

ADMIRALTY JURISDICTION OF COUNTY COURTS.

I HAVE from time to time been requested to express my opinions on the various Legislative Enactments which have been brought forward for conferring a limited jurisdiction in Admiralty matters on County Courts, and if at one time I was induced to urge grave objections to such a course, later experience has shown that to confer on some inferior courts a subordinate jurisdiction, as in salvage cases and in some matters of minor importance, such as Masters' and Seamen's wages, would be a step in the right direction, and a boon to the trading interests of all Countries. The plea of 'bringing justice to everybody's door' appeals strongly to every Legislature, but still it should not be overlooked that the great mass of Admiralty cases are too important and technical to be properly dealt with by the ordinary County Courts, and my experience leads me to believe that Admiralty jurisdiction should only be granted to some few of the County Courts at the leading seaport towns which are presided over by Judges acquainted with maritime law, and which are furnished with special machinery, such as is provided on a larger scale in the Admiralty Division of the High Court.

Admiralty jurisdiction has now been conferred on a number of County Courts for twenty years, but my opinion is strengthened by the fact that cases have frequently come under my notice which show the undesirability of those tribunals for Admiralty matters. Of course, many of the objections I have seen to the County Court Admiralty jurisdiction might possibly have been avoided if legislation had provided methodically for the practice of the High Court to be engrafted into the County Courts in so far as it could be done with a due regard to economy. For instance, the provision for entering a *caveat* against arrest of a ship is a most valuable and economic safeguard to shipowners against arrest and detention of their property, yet no provision is made in either of the County Court Acts, or by the rules made in pursuance of them, for the entry of a *caveat* against arrest. The shipowner is, therefore, left by the Legislature at the mercy of an unscrupulous claimant, who can arrest his ship at the moment she is ready to sail, provided the claim is sufficiently small in amount to confer jurisdiction on the County Court. This is not an imaginary grievance, as the point has arisen in practice; but it is only due to the County Court officials to acknowledge the courtesy with which they always endeavour, so far as lies in their power, to give the shipowner an opportunity of making a money deposit in lieu of entering a *caveat* in order to secure non-arrest. Other curious anomalies have arisen, presumably from the fact that in the wording of the County Court Acts the draftsman has not been careful to follow the wording of the Admiralty Court Act of 1861. The result is that the County Courts have a more extended jurisdiction *in rem* in some cases than that possessed by the High Court.[1] This leads to a still greater anomaly, as the High Court, having no original jurisdiction to try such a case, is the appellate court on these matters from the decision of the inferior court.[2]

Another great objection to the County Courts is that

[1] See Brown *v.* The Alma, 7 M. L. C. (N.S.) 257.
[2] The Rona, Law Rep. 7 P. D. 247.

damages are generally assessed by the Court at the trial instead of being referred to the Registrar, assisted by a Merchant or Merchants. This entails a great amount of unnecessary expenditure of time and money, and does not conduce to a fair settlement of the amount of damages. It is well known that a Judge in Court cannot deal with pure matters of accounts or figures with the same accuracy combined with promptitude which distinguishes a reference. My view is exemplified every day by the Judges referring pure matters of account to a Master or arbitrator for assessment.

It appears to me that a far more satisfactory tribunal for matters of so great importance as Admiralty cases, dealing as they do in a great many instances with the property and right of foreigners, would be to appoint certain of the County Courts as Vice-Admiralty Courts with a similar jurisdiction, up to a limited amount, as that possessed by the Vice-Admiralty Courts abroad, and with the same rules of procedure, except that an appeal should be to the Admiralty Branch of the Supreme Court of Judicature instead of to the Privy Council. The Judges of these Courts, which should each embrace specified areas of seaboard, should be appointed with a view to their knowledge of Admiralty Law as well as their general legal knowledge, and provision should be made for their holding an Admiralty Court whenever necessary. At present great delay and expense frequently occur, owing to the fact that the general business of a County Court occupies so much of the Judge's time that he cannot deal with Admiralty work with the promptitude by which the High Court has earned for itself the grateful acknowledgments of the mercantile marine world.

On this subject I may more particularly refer to my remarks in the preface to the second edition, *sub* V.

VI.

SUGGESTIONS FOR THE IMPROVEMENT OF THE ADMIRALTY PRACTICE.

I CONFESS that I viewed with alarm the merging of the High Court of Admiralty by the Judicature Acts into a branch of one of the Divisions of the Supreme Court of Judicature, for the reasons I have fully set out in the preface to the second edition, *sub* V., and, the new Court of Bankruptcy not having been disturbed, I did not expect that the old and venerable Admiralty Court would be changed.

I felt at once that many and great difficulties would arise. I have frequently pointed out that if the Judge of the Admiralty Division were to go Circuit, as was originally intended, the Admiralty suitor would be a great sufferer. Fortunately a *modus vivendi* has been found, and the two Judges of Probate, Divorce, and Admiralty find their time too fully occupied with the business of that Division to justify either attending assizes. This ensures a prompt despatch of Admiralty business, and has enabled the Admiralty Division to maintain the high reputation for acceleration of business to which I have already alluded in a former chapter.

Whilst on the subject of Judges, I may, perhaps, suggest that when in the future fresh judicial arrangements are made for the Probate, Divorce, and Admiralty Division it would be a great boon to *suitors* if one Judge alone took Admiralty cases. As representative of many underwriters who have cases in the Court, I know they feel the impossibility for two minds to view, in the same light, cases depending so often not on the facts of a case, but on the weight to be given to them. Consequently in very many cases the suitor cannot form any accurate opinion of the result of his case, and therefore misses the great advantage which it is one of the highest aims of a Court to offer, viz. the knowledge that, given certain facts, a certain result may be expected. For salvage cases this is particularly important. As a rule, no two persons would award the same figure on the same state of facts, but a series of awards from the same Judge would enable suitors to form an accurate opinion of the Judge's views of the merits of a service with almost certain accuracy.

This suggestion would entail no loss of judicial power, as, if the Admiralty work was not sufficient, the Judge could, as he does now, take cases from the list of the other branch of the Division.

A great objection to the provisions of the rules made under the Judicature Act is the power to initiate Admiralty proceedings in all District Registries.

It struck me as an anomaly that a District Registrar of some Midland District Registry might issue a warrant to arrest a ship in London or Liverpool in a bottomry action. I doubt if such a contingency was considered when the rules were framed, but surely such a state of things should not be possible. It is a fact that warrants are frequently issued in outport registries, and serious difficulty and delay often occur in obtaining a release, as it is frequently undesirable for a defendant to enter an appearance in the District Registry, and consequently the ship must remain under arrest until the papers are sent to the Principal from the District Registry.

On this question I venture to suggest that, as I have

proposed with Vice-Admiralty in lieu of County Courts, so with the District Registries of the High Court, districts embracing the principal ports should be carved out over which the most important District Registry might exercise jurisdiction, but in all cases I hold it most important that so soon as a District Registry issues a writ or warrant, a copy should be transmitted to the Principal Registry in order that an appearance may be entered and release extracted there without delay, and, if my suggestion in the previous chapter respecting the establishment of Vice-Admiralty Courts is adopted, the District Registries in Admiralty causes might be united with the Vice-Admiralty Courts.

VII.

FREIGHT WHEN SHIP ABANDONED AT SEA.

PROBABLY no decision of our Law Courts, since the remarkable case of the 'Marie de Brabant,' has caused so much surprise among those interested in maritime commerce as that of the 'Cito' (Law Reports, 7 P. D. 5).

The 'Cito,' a Norwegian barque, bound with a cargo of rosin in barrels from Wilmington, U.S., to Rotterdam, was, owing to the perils of the sea, abandoned by her crew off the American coast. Some time afterwards she was picked up by another Norwegian vessel called the 'Colonist,' brought into Plymouth and arrested there with her cargo on board for the salvage services rendered by the 'Colonist' and her crew.

Before the Norwegian owners of the 'Cito' could make arrangements for the release of the vessel, preparatory to sailing her to Rotterdam, in order to complete their contract of Affreightment, the holders of the bills of lading applied to the Admiralty Division for an order that, upon their giving bail to the salvors for any salvage due from the cargo, the same should be released to them without payment of any freight.

Some time previously a somewhat similar case had come before the Court. The 'Kathleen,' an American barque, bound with a cargo of cotton in bales from Charleston to Bremen, after collision in the Channel had been abandoned and brought as a derelict into Dover. An order having subsequently been made by the Court for the cargo to be sold, the owners of the ship moved the Court to set aside the order, or, if it stood, to direct that the freight should be paid out of the proceeds of the sale. The Judge, however, held that the owners of the barque were not entitled to any payment in respect of freight, on the ground that, by the abandonment of the barque, the contract to pay freight had been dissolved.

At first sight it may appear difficult to draw a distinction between these two cases. Both vessels were abandoned in the course of their voyages, and both were afterwards brought in as derelicts. There was, however, a material and, as I consider, a vital distinction between them, inasmuch as the cargo of the 'Kathleen' was in so damaged a state that the properly appointed surveyors considered its transportation to Bremen impossible, and the vessel herself was a complete wreck, quite unfit to carry the cargo on; while the cargo of the 'Cito,' on the other hand, was not injured at all, and the 'Cito' was little damaged, and with very little repair could, without discharging her cargo, have continued and completed her voyage.

Sir Robert Phillimore, however, who was at the time Judge of the Admiralty Division, was unable to see that the circumstances of the two cases were materially distinct, and, considering himself bound by his own previous decision in the 'Kathleen,' he ordered the cargo of the 'Cito' to be delivered to the owners without payment of any freight. The owners of the 'Cito' appealed, but the order was confirmed by the Court of Appeal. The Lords Justices of Appeal did not go the length of saying that the abandonment of the vessel put an end to the contract, but they all expressed the opinion that, by the abandonment of a ship, the shipowner does as far as he can abandon the contract so as to allow the other party to it, the cargo-owner, to treat it as abandoned. The result is much the same; so long as this 'Cito' decision stands, it gives the cargo-owner the full option to take advantage of the common misfortune for the purpose of evading the contract entered into by him. This, I confidentially assert, is opposed to every principle of law and justice. A contract by the law of every civilised country holds good until both parties to it, of their own freewill, agree that it shall not be carried out. Now, how can the abandonment of a ship in such a case as the 'Cito' be taken to be an expression of an agreement on the part of the owners of the vessel to cancel the contract? The action of the crew in leaving a vessel to save their lives is not an act of will at all; they have to desert their vessel under the pressure of a *vis major*; how can this be taken to show an agreement on the part of the shipowner to abandon his part of the contract? He has no power to exercise any option at all. If, when the vessel is recovered and the owner again requires the power to exercise his will in the matter, he then elects not to carry out his contract and the cargo-owner agrees, well and good, the contract is put an end to by mutual consent. To assume, however, such consent on the part of one of the contracting parties from an action forced on his servants by a power which cannot be resisted seems to me to be a doctrine utterly opposed to common sense.

VIII.

REASONS why the making away with or aiding and abetting in scuttling or otherwise destroying a vessel for the purpose of defrauding its underwriters or others who have an interest therein, or in the cargo or freight, should by agreement between the principal maritime nations be deemed and taken to be an ACT of PIRACY.[1]

WHEATON states, in his 'Elements of International Law,' vol. i. p. 256, edition 1864: 'Piracy under the law of nations may be tried and punished in the courts of justice of any nation, by whomsoever, and wheresoever committed,[2] but piracy created by municipal statute can only be tried by that state within whose territorial jurisdiction, and on board of whose vessels, the offence thus created was committed. There are certain acts which are considered piracy by the internal laws of a state, to which the law of nations does not attach the same signification. It is not by force of the international law that those who commit these acts are tried and punished, but in consequence of special laws which assimilate them to pirates, and which can only be applied by the state which has enacted them, and then with reference to its own subjects, and in places within its own jurisdiction. The crimes of murder and robbery, committed by foreigners on board

---

[1] Transmitted to His Grace the Duke of Richmond, K.G., President of the Board of Trade.

[2] 'Every man, by the usage of our European nations, is justiciable in the place where the crime is committed; so are pirates, being reputed out of the protection of all laws and privileges, and to be tried in what parts soever they may be taken.'—*Sir Leoline Jenkins*, vol. ii. p. 714.

of a foreign vessel on the high seas, are not justiciable in the tribunals of another country than that to which the vessel belongs, but if committed on board of a vessel not at the time belonging, in fact as well as in right, to any foreign power or its subjects, but in possession of a crew acting in defiance of all law, and acknowledging obedience to no flag whatsoever, these crimes may be punished as piracy under the law of nations, in the courts of any nation having custody of the offenders.'

This distinction of piracy under the law of nations and piracy under the municipal law has of late become a matter of serious consideration for those interested in the maritime commerce of the world.

For although, thanks to the progress of civilisation, cases of piracy in the common sense of the word have become almost extinct, except in the Chinese and in some parts of the Indian waters, the great extension of maritime commerce and enterprise has brought into prominence a class of people who appear to make it their regular business to defraud underwriters and others, by means of fictitious insurances on ships, on freight, on goods, on advances, or on other insurable risks in respect to voyages on which the ships themselves are intended to be cast away.

And the enormity of their crimes is aggravated by the fact, that for the sake of a gain sometimes comparatively insignificant, property of the greatest value is sacrificed; valuable cargoes, for instance, belonging to innocent owners have sometimes been destroyed simply in order to enable the owners of the vessel or his accomplices to make a profit out of an over-insurance of the vessel.

These crimes, although hitherto not commonly comprised under the designation of 'piracy,' appear to me to deserve to be ranked with that class which Wheaton defines as piracy under municipal statute, a construction adopted also by the late Mr. M'Culloch (Dictionary), who begins an able article on this subject with the following words: 'Piracy consists in committing those acts of robbery and violence upon the seas that, if committed upon land, would amount to felony,' &c.

Now, in searching the statutes of the realm, I find that the following enactments have been passed relating to this subject, viz.:—

I. 27 *Henry VIII. cap.* 4.—An Act declaring the order and punishment of pirates and robbers on the sea.

II. 11 *and* 12 *William III. cap.* 7.—An Act for the more effectual suppression of piracy.

III. 2 *George II. cap.* 28.—An Act for making perpetual an Act therein mentioned for suppressing of piracy.

IV. 18 *George II. cap.* 30.—An Act to amend an Act made in the 11th year of the reign of William III. intituled 'An Act for the more effectual suppression of piracy.'

V. 7 *and* 8 *George IV. cap.* 30.—An Act for consolidating and amending the laws in England relative to malicious injuries to property.

VI. 9 *George IV. cap.* 56.—An Act for consolidating and amending the laws in Ireland relative to malicious injuries to property.

VII. 1 *Victoria, cap.* 88.—An Act to amend certain acts relating to the crime of piracy.

VIII. 1 *Victoria, cap.* 89.—An Act to amend the laws relating to burning or destroying buildings and ships.

IX. 12 *and* 13 *Victoria, cap.* 96.—An Act to provide for the prosecution and trial in Her Majesty's Colonies, of offences committed within the jurisdiction of the Admiralty.

X. 13 *and* 14 *Victoria, cap.* 26.—An Act to repeal an Act of the 6th year of King George IV. for encouraging the capture or destruction of piratical ships and vessels, and to make other provisions in lieu thereof.

XI. 13 *and* 14 *Victoria, cap.* 27.—An Act to provide for the commencement of an Act of the present Session, intituled 'An Act to repeal an Act,' &c. (*see* No. X.).

XII. 24 *and* 25 *Victoria, cap.* 97.—An Act to consolidate and amend the statute law of England and Ireland relating to malicious injuries to property.

The following sections of this last Act especially treat of offences committed against shipping property, and they may be said to constitute the present statute law on the subject:—

'42. Whosoever shall unlawfully and maliciously set fire to, cast away, or in anywise destroy any ship or vessel, whether the same be complete or in an unfinished state, shall be guilty of felony, and being convicted thereof, shall be liable, at the discretion of the Court, to be kept in penal servitude for life or for any term not less than three years, or to be imprisoned for any term not exceeding two years, with or without hard labour, and with or without solitary confinement, and, if a male under the age of sixteen years, with or without whipping.

'43. Whosoever shall unlawfully and maliciously set fire to, or cast away, or in anywise destroy any ship or vessel, with intent thereby to prejudice any owner or part-owner of such ship or vessel, or of any goods on board the same, or any person that has underwritten or shall underwrite any policy of insurance upon such ship or vessel or on the freight thereof, or upon any goods on board the same, shall be guilty of felony, and being convicted thereof, shall be liable, at the discretion of the Court, to be kept in penal servitude for life, or for any term not less than three years, or to be imprisoned for any term not exceeding two years, with or without hard labour, and with or without solitary confinement, and, if a male under the age of sixteen years, with or without whipping.

'44. Whosoever shall unlawfully and maliciously, by any overt act, attempt to set fire to, cast away, or destroy any ship or vessel, under such circumstances, that if the ship or vessel were thereby set fire to, cast away, or destroyed, the offender would be guilty of felony, shall be guilty of felony, and being convicted thereof, shall be liable, at the discretion of the Court, to be kept in penal servitude for any term not exceeding fourteen, and not less than three years, or to be imprisoned for any term not exceeding two years, with or without hard labour, and with or without solitary confinement, and, if a male under the age of sixteen years, with or without whipping.

'45. Whosoever shall unlawfully and maliciously place or throw in, into, upon, against, or near any ship or vessel any gunpowder, or other explosive substance, with intent to destroy or damage any ship or vessel, or any machinery, working-tools, goods or chattels, shall, whether or not any explosion take place, and whether or not any injury be effected, be guilty of felony, and being convicted thereof, shall be liable, at the discretion of the Court, to be kept in penal servitude for any term not exceeding fourteen, and not less than three years, or to be imprisoned for any term not exceeding two years, with or without hard labour, and with or without solitary confinement, and, if a male under the age of sixteen years, with or without whipping.

'46. Whosoever shall unlawfully and maliciously damage, otherwise than by fire, gunpowder, or other explosive substance, any ship or vessel, whether complete or in an unfinished state, with intent to destroy the same or render the same useless, shall be guilty of felony, and being convicted thereof shall be liable, at the discretion of the Court, to be kept in penal servitude for any term not exceeding seven years, and not less than three years, or to be imprisoned for any term not exceeding two years, with or without hard labour, and with or without solitary confinement, and, if a male under the age of sixteen years, with or without whipping.

'47. Whosoever shall unlawfully mask, alter, or remove any light or signal, or unlawfully exhibit any false light or signal, with intent to bring any ship, vessel, or boat into danger, or shall unlawfully and maliciously do anything tending to the immediate loss or destruction of any ship, vessel, or boat, and for which no punishment is hereinbefore provided, shall be guilty of felony, and being convicted thereof shall be liable, at the discretion of the Court, to be kept in penal servitude for life, or for any term not less than three years, or to be imprisoned for any term not exceeding two years, with or without hard labour, and with or without solitary confinement, and, if a male under the age of sixteen years, with or without whipping.

'49. Whosoever shall unlawfully and maliciously destroy any part of any ship or vessel which shall be in distress or wrecked, stranded, or cast ashore, or any goods, merchandise, or articles of any kind belonging to such ship or vessel, shall be guilty of felony, and being convicted thereof shall be liable, at the discretion of the Court, to be kept in penal servitude for any term not exceeding fourteen and not less than three years, or to be imprisoned for any term not exceeding two years, with or without hard labour, and with or without solitary confinement.

'72. All indictable offences mentioned in this Act which shall be committed within the jurisdiction of the Admiralty of England or Ireland, shall be deemed to be offences of the same nature and liable to the same punishments as if they had been committed upon the land in England or Ireland, and may be dealt with, inquired of, tried, and determined in any county or place in England or Ireland in which the offender shall be apprehended or be in custody, in the same manner in all respects as if they had been actually committed in that county or place; and in any indictment for any such offence, or for being an accessory to such an offence, the venue in the margin shall be the same as if the offence had been committed in such county or place, and the offence shall be averred to have been committed "on the high seas;" provided that nothing herein contained shall alter or affect any of the laws relating to the government of Her Majesty's land or naval forces.'

Under the rapid extension of maritime commerce and the more liberal navigation laws of modern times, whereby vessels of all nationalities may not only frequent without restriction the ports of their own country but can trade freely from and to almost any foreign place, the laws now generally in force are insufficient for the suppression of the above described malicious destruction of property.

For instance, if a crime against property upon which insurance has been made in England be committed upon the high seas on board a foreign ship, no steps can be taken against the offender in England, even if he afterwards make his appearance in England, because neither the law of nations nor the statute law of England confers upon English tribunals any jurisdiction over the crime.

A similar state of things exists as regards other nations, and the facilities of locomotion and intercourse with foreign countries make it an easy thing for guilty persons to keep out of reach of the tribunals of the country to which the ship belongs, where alone he can be made amenable to justice. Cases of this description, far from being of rare occurrence, have of late years increased, and are becoming a cause of serious loss to persons concerned in maritime enterprise, more especially to underwriters.

In order to show more clearly the state at which we have arrived, I subjoin abstracts of different cases, distinguished alphabetically, the details of which have come during the last few years under my own personal knowledge and observation, viz. :—

A.

This vessel was lost in 1861, in the English Channel, while on a voyage from France to the Black Sea, with a cargo worth about 1,200*l*., but insured for 14,000*l*. Great suspicions were at the time entertained, but no effectual steps could be taken in this country, and the underwriters therefore were advised to compromise the claim, which they did by payment of 10,000*l*. The matter, coming to the knowledge of the French authorities, was taken in hand by the Public Prosecutor, and the result was that the master of the vessel and five others were brought to trial, when they confessed that they had formed a conspiracy to buy and over-insure vessels and their cargoes, and that the same were then to be fraudulently destroyed; and they stated that the prime mover in the affair was a man living in London, by whom the above cargo had been bought, and who had received the insurance. Subsequent proceedings taken criminally against this person in France were unsuccessful, but he was condemned to repay the 10,000*l*., which, however, have never been recovered.

B.

This was a British vessel which sailed from Belgium for Spain in 1862, with a heavy cargo, and put back under pretence of having broken her windlass. Being grounded on the mud she was there reported to have strained and was discharged to be repaired, but the nature of the repairs done was such as to prove that the ship was from decay unfit to carry the cargo put into her. Being taken out into the roads she was allowed to drift ashore, which necessitated a further repair, and in the end about 2,000*l*. were borrowed on bottomry at exorbitant rates of premium (40 and 45 per cent.), the accounts rendered being even then not satisfactory as to the disposal of so large a sum of money. Sailing at last from Flushing, the ship only got as far as the English Channel, where she put into a port, and as no more money could be obtained on bottomry the master endeavoured to sell part of the cargo, which, however, was prevented by energetic action on the part of the underwriters' representatives; but even then the cargo could not be got out of the captain's hands until the whole freight due by charter to the port of destination was paid him; and besides all the expenses previously incurred the underwriters had to bear the cost of transport for the remaining part of the voyage.

C.

This vessel was the property of a native of Germany, and sailed under the Peruvian flag. On November 4, 1862, she left Bahia for London with a cargo declared to consist of coffee and other goods, which were insured for an enormous amount (upwards of 30,000*l.*) in London, Paris, Bremen, Hamburg, &c. She was scuttled and abandoned on December 19, in the neighbourhood of the Azores, and on investigation it was ascertained that by far the larger portion of the goods thus insured had never been shipped at all, and that the bills of lading or policies of insurance in fact represented goods which had never had any existence. In spite of the fullest evidence given by the crew the laws of this kingdom were powerless in the matter, and no steps could be taken against the master, who, however, fortunately left London for Hamburg to attempt to collect insurances which had been effected there on goods alleged to have been shipped on his own account; he was at once seized and condemned to three years' imprisonment, payment of all costs, and subsequent perpetual banishment from the city and district of Hamburg. He made a full confession of the frauds, the losses occasioned by which fell heavily, not only upon underwriters and insurance offices, but upon London merchants who had made advances on the faith of spurious documents.

The frauds were instigated by a firm of merchants of Bahia, and their complicity was manifest; but one member of the firm was allowed to abscond, and the remaining partner, although brought to trial before a Brazilian court, was acquitted, because he threw all the blame upon the absentee.

A very full report of this case appears in the 'Shipping Gazette' of April 8, 1863.

D.

This Portuguese vessel was owned by a man who had been connected with the firm which was broken up by the detection of their fraudulent complicity in the previous case. The vessel sailed in 1862 from Bahia to a Portuguese port, and very large insurances were effected in Paris, Marseilles, and Genoa upon cargo alleged to have been shipped by her. She was lost very shortly after sailing, and on inquiry it was found that the greater portion of the pretended shipments were fictitious, that all the master's clothes and effects had been removed before sailing, and that the master, who was an uncle of the owner, had been put on board on purpose to make away with the ship. The fictitious shipments were all in the name of the one firm to which reference has already been made.

E.

This was a foreign vessel bound from London to a Dutch port with a cargo of linseed in 1863. She foundered before she left the river Thames, and being subsequently raised by divers it was ascertained that the lashings of the bow-port had been cut from the inside and the port knocked out. The master and crew having disappeared before this was discovered, no steps could be taken against them.

F.

This was a foreign vessel bound, in 1863, from Scotland to an English port, with a cargo of pig-iron, and was abandoned in a sinking state by the crew. On investigation, it turned out that the ship had been doubly insured, and the second insurance, which had already been paid, was refunded to the British underwriters; and as the first insurance done abroad was, by the terms of the policy, avoided, in case of any subsequent insurance being done on the same interest, the underwriters on ship escaped all loss in this case. Those on cargo of course were obliged to pay.

G.

This vessel belonged to one of the South American republics, and was commanded by a German captain, who had traded for some years in that neighbourhood. She sailed in 1863 from Spain for their port of registration, with a light cargo of salt, and on nearing one of the Western Islands, two auger-holes were bored in her by the mate, upon instructions given by the master, and she began to fill rapidly. Being sighted from the island, however, a pilot went off to her, and shaped her course towards the harbour; and as the master soon perceived that she would not sink before reaching it, he himself took the helm and ran her on to the beach, where she remained. During the investigation which followed, the above facts were deposed to on oath by one of the crew, and on examination the auger-holes were actually found in the position described. The underwriters, therefore, refused to pay the demands made upon them, and the question is still being contested.

H.

This vessel, belonging to one of the British colonies, while on a voyage from South America to the Continent in 1863, was compelled by heavy weather to put into a Channel port for repairs, where a new mainmast was put in, for which purpose cargo had to be shifted, and a space made down to the keelson of the vessel; at that time the cargo was perfectly sound and cool. The day after she had resumed her voyage it was noticed that the ship felt warmer than usual, but no steps were taken to ascertain the cause, and on the following day she was totally consumed by fire. Upon investigation made by the underwriters' representative, circumstances came to light which showed the greatest negligence, if not culpability, of the master. The Board of Trade declined, however, to order an investigation, on the ground that the master had no certificate which could be either withdrawn or suspended, because the vessel, although hoisting the British flag, hailed from a colonial port.

I.

This was a Prussian vessel bound from Antwerp to New York, which sailed in December 1863, put into Ramsgate for repairs in the same month, and in April 1864 sailed again for her destination. Six days afterwards she was wilfully sunk off the Scilly Islands, and property insured for nearly 30,000*l.* was thus made away with. On investigation, the circumstances of the case were clearly ascertained, and in order, if possible, to procure a conviction in this country, the carpenter, who had actually bored the holes in the vessel, was arrested and committed for trial at Maidstone; but the only charge of which our Courts could take cognisance was one of conspiring, while in British jurisdiction (at Ramsgate), to commit frauds which were afterwards actually committed beyond the jurisdiction; on this technical question the prosecution failed, although the facts were so little denied that it was actually proved that at the trial both prisoner and witnesses were wearing clothes made out of cloth stolen in Ramsgate from the cargo, thus clearly showing that at that time the ship was intended never to reach her destination.

The owner, master and mate being, after great exertion on the part of the underwriters' representative, arrested and brought to trial in Prussia, were convicted and sentenced to eight, five, and three years' penal servitude respectively.

The underwriters on cargo, residing in Belgium, France, the United States, and elsewhere, were in this case subjected to a loss of about 25,000*l*., all of which they had to pay, solely through a crime committed in order that the owner and his accomplices might make some dishonest profit out of the insurances effected by them on the ship, the freight, and advances.

K.

This colonial vessel was lost by a master who had only been put into her when on a voyage to a neighbouring port in 1864, and, with the cargo, totally destroyed shortly after. Insurances on the hull of the vessel had been effected in Europe to a considerable extent.

No inquiry was made, because, by colonial regulations, the master was not obliged to have a certificate, and there was, therefore, no way of punishing him for gross carelessness, if absolute criminality could not be clearly established.

L.

This foreign vessel sailed from South America in 1864, bound for a Channel port, for orders; and after putting into one of the Brazilian ports to repair damages, proceeded on her voyage. Some months later she was abandoned in the vicinity of the Cornish coast, and shortly afterwards drove ashore near the Land's End, whereby ship and cargo were totally lost.

The whole of the crew signed declarations to the effect that the vessel was improperly abandoned by the master and his brother the mate, who appeared to be joint-owners; the sufferers by the loss of the cargo were, in this instance, British underwriters, who were prevented from lending their assistance to bring the guilty parties to justice in this country by their experience of the difficulty of obtaining a conviction, and the enormous expense and trouble with which it would be attended. The only course remaining was to endeavour, with the aid of detectives, to persuade the criminals to proceed to their own country; but, of course, the proprietors and underwriters of cargo suffered the loss of the whole of their interest.

M.

This foreign vessel sailed from a Belgian port for the West Indies, in 1864; and was shortly afterwards abandoned by the crew and reported by them as having foundered. She was, however, picked up by a steamer and taken into a British port, when it was ascertained that attempts had been made to knock out the bow-port, which, being unsuccessful, three auger-holes had been bored in the bows of the vessel, which would, in a very short time, have insured her destruction.

N.

The facts of this case are so notorious, and the case itself of so recent date, that it will be sufficient briefly to state how, at the Central Criminal Court Session of February 1867, it was proved that this ship, bearing the British flag, and ostensibly proceeding on a voyage from Newport to Shanghai, was purchased, insured, and despatched with the manifest intention that she should be lost on the voyage, and the underwriters thereby defrauded. Four of the parties implicated having been sentenced to twenty, ten, and five years' penal servitude, it was shown in Court that other vessels in which they were interested had been made away with in a similar manner, and it is to be hoped that a most dangerous gang has thus been broken up.

The whole of the evidence given, and the nature of the proceedings, may be seen from a printed report issued by Lloyd's Salvage Association.

The prosecution and conviction of the four parties above referred to cost the underwriters more than 7,000*l*.

O.

This vessel, under a foreign flag, sailed from a Belgian port for South America. Within view of the British coast the master made a deliberate attempt to sink the vessel, which was prevented by the timely appearance of a pilot-boat with several persons on board. The master confessed that what he had done had been instigated by the owner, and the facts were clearly proved by the evidence of the crew. The parties who would have suffered by the loss of ship and cargo, and who will now have to bear the very heavy expenses of salvage, &c., are resident on the Continent and in South America. In spite of all this it was impossible to take any steps in this country, and when, with the help of a detective specially employed for the purpose, the master had been induced to proceed to his native country, he could there be criminally proceeded against only because he had plundered the cargo.

P.

This was a vessel of 194 tons register, under the command of a British captain, which sailed from

Bangkok on August 13, 1866, bound for Hongkong, with a cargo principally shipped by one merchant of the former place. Having been lost in fine weather on the 24th of the same month, suspicions were aroused, which led to the holding of a Naval Court to inquire into the circumstances. The result of the inquiry was, that both captain and mate were arrested, and subsequently the above alluded to principal shipper was also arrested, and the three were tried at Singapore at the January sessions in the present year. It was ascertained that insurances to the extent of 19,000*l.* had been effected upon property valued at not more than 8,500*l.*; and it was conclusively shown that the captain and mate had made away with the vessel at the instigation of the principal shipper, in order to obtain the advantage of their fraudulent assurances. The result was, that the merchant and the master were sentenced to penal servitude for life, and the mate to penal servitude for five years.

As all principles of insurance show distinctly that the underwriter calculates his premium only on what is called 'the common or ordinary maritime risk,' any act intentionally augmenting such risk, is *per se* not only entirely against good faith, but actually destroys the basis upon which underwriting proceeds; and it can only be regretted that, although so many malpractices of this description have, during the last six years, been successfully carried out, it has in very rare instances been possible to bring the offenders to the fate which they so well deserve.

The details above given will show conclusively that the main obstacle to taking efficient action against this class of criminals is the difficulty of bringing them before the proper jurisdiction. This evil is aggravated by the fact that the same opportunities which exist for the offenders to keep out of the way equally facilitate the removal of the witnesses necessary for the prosecution.

What is wanted is, that in case of any wilful destruction of ships or their cargoes, or other crimes against property on the high seas, the suspected persons may be brought before the tribunals of the first place where they can be found, and a proper investigation thereby rendered possible before the crew or the passengers, who probably are the only persons able, by their knowledge of the circumstances under which the crime was committed, to give conclusive evidence, have dispersed, and the possibility of procuring the necessary proofs has thereby vanished.

For these reasons, amongst others, it is necessary, in my opinion, to class such robberies and felonies on the high seas not merely with crimes which Wheaton states to be amenable as piracy under municipal law, but to constitute them piracy under the conventional law of nations, and I propose nothing less than a declaration—

> 'That any one causing to be effected, or aiding and abetting in effecting, fictitious insurances, as well as any one causing to be destroyed, or aiding and abetting in destroying, shipping property, or the merchandise laden on board, or any one causing to be effected, or aiding and abetting in effecting, any insurances on any article knowing the same not to be on board, or on vessels, or their cargoes, or the freight, or advances, knowing the vessels to be intended to be cast away or destroyed at sea, is to be deemed and taken to be a pirate, and to be

justiciable as such by the tribunals of all maritime nations.'

Judging from the facility with which the laws regulating the rule of the road at sea, &c., have been universally adopted, I have no doubt, if the initiative in this important matter were taken by Her Majesty's Government, that all maritime states would be glad to join in the adoption of an international declaration, which would be more likely than anything else to prevent this enormous destruction of property, by bringing to speedy punishment a class of malefactors enjoying hitherto comparative impunity.

15 Fenchurch Buildings, London:
September 1867.

The expectations I had, that Her Majesty's Government would consider it in the interest of maritime commerce to move in the directions I suggested not having been realised, I think it my duty to assert, that the experience I have gained, since the above memorandum was presented, has, if anything, strengthened my opinion as to the advisability of making serious offences against shipping property punishable as crimes under International Law.

To show that at least one well-known authority on International Law has considered my suggestion well worth consideration, I quote the following sentences which appeared in the second edition of the late Sir Robert Phillimore's 'Commentaries on International Law,' vol. iv. p. 775:—

At present there is a practical impunity accorded to savage and brutal men, which encourages them in the commission of acts of cruelty upon the high seas at which human nature shudders; and the true end of International Law, the welfare and safety of individuals as members of States, is sacrificed to an over-scrupulous respect for a general principle which has ceased in this particular instance to be a means of maintaining that end.

A similar remark applies to the fraudulent destruction or casting away of vessels and cargoes, a crime which unhappily often escapes punishment because the country to which the ship is bound or to which the offenders come is not that to which the ship belongs, and its courts have therefore no jurisdiction. It has been proposed, in order to meet this evil, to make these crimes, by the general consent of nations, acts of piracy and justiciable everywhere (*vide* Wendt's ' Maritime Legislation,' 2nd ed. p. 148).

Having referred to this opinion, which was expressed as far back as 1874, it becomes now my duty to mention a case occurring in the following year, which, it might be thought, would have aroused public opinion to such an extent as to have compelled the adoption of my suggestion.

On December 11, 1875, the North German Lloyd steamer 'Mosel' was lying at the quay at Bremerhaven ready to be despatched in a few hours *viâ* Southampton for New York, when, in consequence of the fall of a box which slipped out of the carrier's hands, an explosion occurred, which, besides causing the destruction of property to an enormous amount, killed five passengers and four members of the crew of the 'Mosel,' as well as seventy-six persons who happened to be in the neighbourhood, a very large number more being dangerously wounded.

Shortly after the explosion had taken place, the sound of a shot was heard coming from one of the private cabins of the 'Mosel.' It was found that a passenger called William King Thomas, but whose real name proved to be Alexander Keith, had unsuccessfully attempted to destroy himself. He succumbed eventually, but lived long enough to confess to one of the most diabolical crimes ever committed. The box, which was filled with dynamite, with a clockwork arrangement for exploding it, belonged to the miscreant, who had intended to ship it on the 'Mosel,' and had planned that it should explode during the voyage, when it must have utterly destroyed the vessel and all on board. Further particulars were brought to light at the investigations subsequently set on foot. It appeared that Keith had obtained a clockwork machine from a small watchmaker in the interior of Germany, who had been made to believe that the mechanism he was ordered to make was intended for use in a factory. The instrument was so contrived that it would go for a certain time and then set free a hammer, and it was so fixed by Keith in the chest that the hammer on being freed would explode the contents of the chest. The dynamite, according to the report of Her Majesty's inspector of explosives for the year 1875, was sufficient to cause damage to houses 750 yards away.

From circumstances coming to light at the time it was surmised that the miscreant intended to leave the 'Mosel' at Southampton, and cause extensive insurances to be effected on property declared to be either already on board or to be shipped at that port, when he would have obtained a very large profit by the destruction of that vessel.

Now let us suppose that the miscreant's intentions had partly, but not entirely, succeeded, and that the 'Mosel' had been damaged only after leaving Southampton, and sufficient proof of the diabolical crime had been forthcoming.

Under what jurisdiction could Keith have been indicted in the present state of the law if he had got away and been found, say, in Norway?

I must entirely concur with Professor von Holzendorff of München, who in his 'Observations on the Bremerhaven

Explosion' (*vide* 'Deutsche Rundschau,' II. 6, p. 402) expressed the opinion that in the present state of the law upon these subjects Keith would have escaped punishment altogether.

Before I conclude this chapter I will quote some remarks upon my proposals from a paper prepared by Dr. H. von Spesshardt, of Marburg, on s. 265 of the German Criminal Law, which apparently is the only one treating of crimes such as are now under consideration.

This section is as follows:—

Whoever, with criminal intent, sets fire to an object insured against fire, or causes a vessel, which, or its cargo or freight is so insured, to sink or strand, is subject to penal servitude up to ten years, and at the same time liable to a fine of from a hundred and fifty to six thousand marks. In case of extenuating circumstances, imprisonment for not less than six months, besides a fine not exceeding three thousand marks, may be inflicted.

The observations of Dr. von Spesshardt run thus:—

Although it may appear, from the considerations hitherto entertained, as if the penal conditions of s. 265 entirely fulfilled the practical requirements of maritime intercourse, still one circumstance has not yet been mentioned, which puts upon the crime of marine insurance fraud quite a special mark of danger. Marine insurance fraud is a crime of essentially international importance. The crime of one not only affects the nation to which he belongs, but the criminal attack is moreover directed against the property of subjects of various states. They all have a lively interest in prosecuting the criminal. To this must be added that the scene of the crime is the high sea or some foreign territorial water, on account of which the capture of the criminal is very difficult and at times even legally as well as actually quite impossible. Owing to this personal interest which all maritime nations have in prosecuting maritime fraud energetically, it certainly appears justifiable to apply international measures to combat the same.

In this sense E. E. Wendt made, in a memorial submitted to

the English Government, the noteworthy proposal to treat, by agreement of the seafaring nations, maritime fraud, the destruction of insured vessels, as well as other frauds committed against insurance companies, as piracy and to allow its punishment to each of the contracting states.

If our German penal code were altered in accordance with this principle, and the one-sided national and territorial principle were made less prominent, it cannot be denied that a most important improvement would be effected.

It is a question if and how an insurance fraud, committed by a foreigner against German property, whether the property belongs to Germans or is insured in Germany, can be looked upon as a crime in accordance with the conditions of the penal code. Crimes committed on the high seas by foreigners on board of German vessels, irrespective of the fact whether they are merchant vessels or men-of-war, can undoubtedly be prosecuted criminally on the part of Germany. According to generally recognised international principles, vessels on the high seas are, by means of legal fiction, looked upon as part of the state under whose flag they sail: this applies in the same manner to both men-of-war and merchant vessels. It is otherwise, however, if, for example, a Frenchman commits a crime on board of a German vessel within English territorial waters; in this case, the state in whose waters the deed was committed may, with justice, claim the execution of its territorial authority: only men-of-war, it is agreed, are to be excluded, and are subject to the law of the Home State, even in foreign territorial waters. In the example given, the criminal Frenchman might be prosecuted on the part of Germany, if the German vessel is a man-of-war, and on the part of the English authority, if it is a German merchant vessel; and the same would apply to most states, as the territorial principle has been generally introduced in the penal code.

On the other hand, if a crime is committed by a foreigner abroad, although against German property, our code is powerless, as, for example, if an Englishman destroys, on the high seas, a Spanish vessel laden with German property or insured with a German insurance company. According to our penal code, no crime which can be prosecuted on the part of Germany exists, although Germany has a great interest in capturing the criminal. The states have, therefore, to look to international legal assistance, to extradition treaties; but to whom shall the criminal be surrendered, who in the meantime has gone to America? In this instance the states interested are England, the criminal being a subject thereof, Spain, on whose territory the crime was committed, and Germany, which, if the vessel is again floated and only the cargo is lost, would probably suffer the most. But even if America surrendered to England, no punishment might possibly be inflicted, as England only punishes its subjects for certain crimes committed abroad. Extradition treaties effected between the separate states would, therefore, in view of the doubt arising as to which state should prosecute the criminal, not give suitable assistance. It should therefore be acknowledged that under the circumstances an international crime exists, for the suppression of which all states should cordially unite. In such cases the principle of nationality must be put aside, and each state have the right to put its hand upon the criminal. Certain success will only then be assured, if the arm of justice awaits the criminal wherever he goes.

Although we, therefore, perfectly agree with Wendt's proposal in principle, we should wish it limited to maritime fraud in its technical name. To fictitious insurances, however, or to insurances of cargo not in existence, which actions are not even a completed fraud against the underwriter, cannot, *per se*, without the introduction of any forcible measures, be attributed such importance which would justify the application of the, at any rate, drastic principle.

There remains only one observation for me to make on the latter part of these remarks, in which Dr. von Spesshardt questions whether the conclusion of fictitious insurances ought to be placed in the same category as the other crimes to which I have here referred.

Now it appears to me that the conclusion of a fictitious insurance is an attempt to defraud, a conspiracy to obtain money under false pretences, and therefore ought equally with all other crimes perfected on the high seas, to be punishable as piracy under the law of nations.

But before I conclude this chapter I must not omit to state a most glaring case of piracy which was perpetrated between October 1880 and April 1881, which led to judicial investigations. These are here reported with the names of the parties implicated in these partly successful frauds.

The steam-vessel 'Ferret,' belonging to the Highland Railway Company, was chartered in the year 1880 by James Stewart Henderson. The steamer proceeded in the first instance to Cardiff, there loading a cargo of coals for Marseilles, and in due course passed the Rock of Gibraltar, where her name was signalled. During the night she returned to the Atlantic, at which time a boat and life-buoys were thrown overboard. She next put into San Antonio, Cape de Verde, under the name of 'Bentan,' from which place she proceeded to Santos, where she was chartered for conveyance of a cargo of coffee, which was laden on board for delivery at Marseilles and Genoa. The vessel having cleared from Santos, next appeared under the name of 'India' at Cape Town, at which place Henderson sold the cargo and appropriated the proceeds to his own use, having during the voyage, or previously, forged the various documents in order to show that the coffee had been purchased for his account. From Cape Town he sailed with the proceeds in his possession for the Mauritius, where he discounted one of the drafts for 500*l*., sailing thence for Melbourne, at which place the vessel was seized and Henderson and Wright, the sailing master, were taken into custody, and subsequently tried and convicted for an attempt to defraud the various parties interested. The drafts, amounting to 7,500*l*., then in the possession of Henderson, were attached, but in order to recover the proceeds of said drafts, proceedings in this country, against the Standard Bank of British South Africa and others, were requisite, some of the drafts having been sent forward for encashment by the Sheriff of Melbourne.

These proceedings did not terminate until 1884, and were of a very complicated and expensive nature.

I have no doubt that one of the reasons why the Law Officers of the Crown did not think it worth their while to trouble themselves with the consideration of my suggestions under this head was that, in this age of telegraphic communications over the whole civilised world, the frauds I reported could scarcely be carried out to any large extent.

But I imagine that the two cases I reported since 1867 (and which might have been amplified if I had thought it necessary) are sufficient to prove that, in spite of the facility to communicate by cable with all parts of the world, such frauds are not only contemplated but carried out with a degree of effrontery which has rarely been exceeded.

Let it not be forgotten that within the short space of about seven months the criminal acts perpetrated by these scoundrels would number more than a dozen, and that they escaped with punishments of seven years and three years and a half penal servitude respectively, which would not have been the case if the trial had taken place in this country.

And the best proof that the parties convicted are not the only ones who were implicated in these scandalous proceedings was given by the Telegraphic Code found on board the 'Ferret' at Melbourne; so that we need not be surprised if conspiracies of a similar nature are attempted after the public has forgotten the lesson in question.

IX.

MERCHANT SHIPS' LOGS, PROTESTS AND DE-POSITIONS BEFORE RECEIVERS.

EVERYBODY connected with maritime commerce in any shape or way must agree with me that the above-named subjects are of the most vital importance to those who have a *bonâ fide* interest in any maritime adventure, whether as the owners of ship or cargo, as the underwriters, or as the bankers who have made advances on the security of ship, cargo, or freight.

The laws of almost all maritime nations have indeed from time immemorial very rightly contained stringent enactments as to how during the navigation of a vessel the circumstances of daily occurrence on board must be recorded, and in what manner, after the termination of a voyage, and before the crew is dispersed, the necessary steps are to be taken to obtain their evidence as to the correctness of such records.

In this country, where undoubtedly the largest interests of maritime commerce centre, a state of things has arisen which for its anomaly is unprecedented. This has been often acknowledged, but the various attempts to rectify the law as described in the following pages have been entirely unsuccessful.

As far back as February 4, 1864, the London Salvage Association and the representatives of the principal foreign underwriters addressed the following communication:—

To the Lords of the Committee of Privy Council for Trade.

My Lords,—We, the undersigned, being entrusted with the protection of important mercantile and underwriting interests, both British and foreign, and being continually called upon to inquire into the causes and particulars of casualties occurring in all parts of the coasts of the United Kingdom, have, since the passing of the Merchant Shipping Act of 1854, been brought into constant contact with the Receivers appointed by your Committee, and have carefully watched the working of the regulations laid down by the said Act; and we now beg leave to lay before your Lordships the expression of our opinion that, although the eighth part of the Act makes provision for inquiries and examinations in cases of wreck and casualty, the objects contemplated thereby are not fully attained, and the clauses in question are, therefore, susceptible of improvement. By this eighth part of the Merchant Shipping Act of 1854, Receivers of Wreck are empowered to institute examinations with respect to ships in distress, such examinations to be held as soon as conveniently may be, and two copies of such examination to be taken, one to be transmitted to the Board of Trade and the other to be exhibited by the Committee for managing the affairs of Lloyd's to persons desirous of examining the same. This enactment, therefore, would seem to contemplate the bringing, within a very short period, the facts connected with every casualty under the notice both of the Board of Trade and of the parties interested.

This very desirable result is, however, at present not arrived at. The Act which gives power to the Receiver to take a deposition names no penalty in the event of the master or other of the crew of a ship in distress refusing or neglecting to make one, and the phrase 'as soon as conveniently may be' is almost invariably stretched out to such a time as the master has settled all his other affairs, when his deposition, if made at all, becomes simply an echo of the protest which he is obliged to make in order to claim against his underwriters. Indeed, so far is the great importance of these depositions lost sight of, even by the Receivers of Wreck themselves, that they have been known to tell masters of ships who wished to make their depositions, after the total loss of their vessel, that they need not be in a hurry about that, for it would do just as well when they got home. By this course the clauses of the Act are rendered nugatory, and what was intended to be a clear and succinct narrative from the scene of the casualty becomes comparatively useless.

But when it is considered that cases may occur where frauds may be attempted, then the necessity for ensuring the taking of depositions before the parties leave the spot becomes evident. For it cannot be doubted that the occurrence of a fraud is frequently known to men who, if questioned at once, would gladly tell the whole truth, but when once allowed to leave they are content to remain silent; or if likely to prove disagreeable witnesses, every opportunity is given for their being sent out of the way, so that before the parties who are ultimately to suffer can transmit their instructions the best opportunity of defeating any irregularity is lost.

As the Customs Consolidation Act orders that every ship arriving in the United Kingdom shall, within twenty-four hours after arrival, be reported at the Custom House, or that the master shall incur a penalty for neglecting so to report, in like manner we think that the public interest requires that every master of any ship, whether British or Foreign, which either suffers or inflicts damage, shall, within twenty-four hours after the occurrence of the damage (except where the same may happen at sea, in which case within twenty-four hours after arrival in the first port in the United Kingdom), report himself to the Receiver of Wreck, and there make on oath a deposition in the same form as it is made at present, or in default of so doing shall be liable to such penalty as your Committee may think fit to impose. Further, that in every case of stranding or total loss the deposition of every one of the crew shall be separately taken in the same manner as that of the master. We have further to suggest that a distinct enactment be made with respect to the services of an interpreter in cases where the master of a foreign vessel can speak no language in which he can make himself understood by the Receiver, for the difficulty of communication in such cases often causes the

Receiver to omit altogether the taking of a deposition, and we cannot think that the laws of this country should be allowed to fail in their effect because the Consuls and Vice-Consuls of foreign Powers are so frequently utterly indifferent to the necessity of providing for such communication. By these means, and by impressing upon the Receivers the necessity of the most rigid carrying out of the regulations in this respect, we believe that so complete a record of all casualties may be obtained as will go far to check dishonest and fraudulent practices, which we are afraid are still of too frequent occurrence.

We therefore pray your Lordships to recommend that the Merchant Shipping Act, at as early a period as possible, be amended by the insertion of clauses to the above effect.

This subject was on several occasions brought before the Board of Trade, as will be seen by a return of the copies of letters and correspondence issued on May 15, 1876, and laid before the House of Commons. The letters were from the Secretary of Lloyd's, the Secretary of the Liverpool Underwriters' Association, the Wreck Commissioner, the Secretary to the London and Provincial Marine Insurance Company, the Secretary of the Salvage Association, Messrs. Waltons, Bubb, and Walton, Messrs. Hollams, Son, and Coward, and myself, and in them particulars of numerous and very distinct instances of irregularities and even frauds perpetrated under the present system were made known to the Board of Trade, but nothing to remedy such a state of affairs has been done.

A very glaring case which occurred within my own knowledge induced me to issue in October 1878 the following memorandum :—

Merchant Ships' Protests.

The prosecution lately concluded at Cork of 'The Queen *v.* Minich' has again brought prominently forward the many grave objections there are to the taking and extending of Protests as at present exercised by notaries public.

The Extended Protest being the document intended to be used as evidence of the circumstances therein narrated in cases where claims are to be made by and against the owners, underwriters, and others interested in ship, cargo, or freight, and being in fact in almost all countries other than the United Kingdom the document accepted as conclusive evidence in support of the facts on which the claims are made, the drawing it up should be guarded in the most scrupulous way, that the chance be minimised of its being in any way inaccurate, inefficient, or untrue. The present system of preparing the Protest is open to many and serious objections.

(1) The Protest can be made at any time after the arrival of the ship, thus giving time and opportunity for the master and owner, or others interested, to consult together, and if they are dishonestly inclined, to carefully prepare, or cause to be prepared for them by their legal advisers, a document framed specially to meet some particular necessity, whether it be a claim against their underwriters or a defence to an anticipated action for damage or salvage.

(2) The objection to the manner is also equally grave. In the great majority of cases the draught is sketched out, before the matter comes before the notary, by someone who, although possibly entirely unconnected with the voyage, may nevertheless have an interest in the object to be attained by the Protest, and therefore not be unprejudiced. It is then brought to the notary, and embodied by him in formal words, without reference to the log, and without appealing to or questioning anyone but the master; it is then read over to and signed by those of the crew presented by the master for that purpose, who, though they might, and in all probability would, give a perfectly true version of the facts, if questioned by the notary, yet do not hesitate in their well-known careless manner to sign what is presented to them by an official, though it may contain incorrect or indeed utterly false statements.

(3) Again, as to the person who prepares the Protest—the

notary public. He is a private individual, one of a large number of the same profession, any one of whom may equally well prepare any particular Protest. Now, in the case of a master, who wishes to make a shuffling or untrue Protest, coming to one of these notaries, what power has the latter, if he has his suspicions as to the truth of the tale, to prevent a Protest being made in the terms desired? He may demand the log-book, he cannot compel its production; he may examine those of the crew brought to him, he cannot require the appearance of others not brought; whether he may even swear the appearers is a matter of doubt. He may indeed, as a last resource, refuse to draw up the Protest, and the satisfaction he will then have will be the knowledge that the result of his scrupulousness is that he has lost his fee, and some other less acute or less punctilious notary has received it instead.

The result of this unsatisfactory state of affairs is that the Protest is for all practical purposes worthless. It may even be said truly that it is worse than worthless, for though from the facility of its being made fraudulently it may contain utterly untrue statements, yet it is in appearance a formal and official document; it is attested and sealed by an official functionary, and, in consequence, faith is placed in it and credit given to it, by many, especially abroad, which it in no wise deserves, and instead of being a preventive of fraud, it is actually an official means by which frauds can the more readily be perpetrated.

The validity of the objections I have herein put forward is well shown by the case already referred to of 'The Queen v. Minich.' There a Protest was extended at Cork on behalf of an Italian ship.

The crew were entirely ignorant of the English language, and an interpreter therefore accompanied them to the notary, who was not conversant with Italian. The crew honestly described certain circumstances in connection with the voyage—which description was perfectly in accordance with the statement contained in the ship's log-book—but the interpreter, for reasons of his own, and for the fraudulent purpose of enabling an unjust claim to be made against certain underwriters, inserted in his interpretation an entirely fictitious account of a stranding of the vessel, which was thereupon drafted into the Protest, and sworn to in ignorance by the crew. The log-book was neither required nor produced. The fraud was detected, but the greatest difficulty was experienced in deciding by whom—crew, interpreter, or notary—the fraud had been committed; and even when the fraud was fixed on the interpreter, it was found impossible to find him guilty of perjury, as the right of the notary to swear him was doubtful; for although, with one exception, all the notaries in Cork were shown to have taken Protests on oath from time immemorial, their authority for so doing could not be proved.

To remove the objections above described, and to supply an efficient remedy, is by no means an easy task. Reiterated applications on the subject to the Board of Trade have led to no result; and the chief reason for this may possibly be that no practical plan has yet been devised to introduce the requisite alterations in practice, without disregarding the fact of the existence of a very large number of notaries, to whom the drawing of ships' Protests has been a considerable source of income, and who cannot forcibly be got rid of. The following suggestions, the result of very lengthened connection with and very careful consideration of the subject, are offered in the belief that they will effect the desired result, without interfering with or prejudicing the rights of any parties.

In the first place, as to what should be contained in the Protest. It should in all cases give an exact and accurate transcript of so much of the ship's log as is essential for its compilation. To this should be added such observations or explanations as the various signatories may desire to offer and as the compiler may consider necessary to insert.

To enable the notary, for he may still be retained as the compiler, to draw the Protest in the manner suggested, greater official powers must be given to him, and at the same time stringent regulations in the stead of varying customs must be drawn up to govern his conduct of the matter. He must have authority, and moreover it must clearly be laid down as his duty to demand the log, to summon certain members of the crew (to include at least the master, mate, and two others), to examine them and all other intended signatories separately, and, most important of all, to administer an oath to each signatory and to the interpreters when any are required.

In order that the log-book may be of practical use, the system now obtaining in this country must be entirely remodelled, the present official log-book should be entirely abolished, and the entries therein prescribed should be made in the ship's ordinary log, which should be kept with the same care as is at present applied to the so-called official log. The use of paged and sealed log-books should be made compulsory, the log-book be written up on board every twenty-four hours, the entry be daily read over in the presence of the master, mate, and two others of the crew, and verified by their signatures. In the event of bad weather preventing the completion of this formality during any twenty-four hours, the entry when made should contain a statement to that effect.

For every voyage of not less than seventy-two hours' duration, and for every voyage of less duration when damage to ship or cargo or both has been sustained or is anticipated, it should be compulsory upon the master to deposit his log-book with the Collector of Customs at the time of reporting his vessel, and not later than twenty-four hours after her first arrival in port; the date and time of such deposit should be noted in the log by the official receiving the report, as also the date and time at which the log is returned to the master on the final outward clearance of the vessel. These formalities might supersede the present system of *noting* Protests.

When it is required to extend the vessel's Protest, the notary employed for this purpose should make to the Collector application in writing for the log-book upon a form countersigned by the master or agent of the vessel, the log-book to be delivered to the notary only. Translations, where such may be required of log-books in foreign languages, should be prepared by the notary, or by some competent person appointed by and responsible to him, and the notary should show upon the log-book itself the portions which have been extracted or translated for the purposes of the Protest. The log-book when done with should be returned by the notary direct to the Collector of Customs, together with a statement of the date when and place where the Protest was extended, and of the names of the signatories and of the notary, and such statement should remain attached to the ship's report, and be accessible at all times upon written request and payment of a small fee.

Protests to be made by foreigners not conversant with the English language should be written in parallel columns, and should be read over to the signatories in their own language.

The Protest should be a public document, and the notary by whom it is extended should be empowered to supply copies to persons requiring the same upon payment of a reasonable fee.

A regulation that the Collector of Customs on delivering the log to a notary should register the delivery in the log, and that the notary therein named should be the only one capable of drawing that particular Protest, would prevent the possibility of an attempt to influence or coerce a scrupulous notary by a threat held out directly or indirectly of leaving him for a less punctilious one.

By the adoption of these or similar precautions the Extended Protest would attain, or rather regain its position as a document to be relied on as containing a true statement of facts, and not be, as in many cases it is at present, one framed by the master in conjunction with his owners, their agents or their advisers, either to hold back or conceal the particulars of the occurrences therein referred to to the utmost extent compatible with making any statement whatever concerning them; or, worse still, as it sometimes is, a deliberately false and untrue account of events which never happened at all, instead of an official and reliable record of the fullest and most complete description of the particular occurrences in it contained, such as it is of the utmost importance to shipowners, underwriters, and the mercantile community at large that it should be.

This memorandum was communicated to the Board of Trade, the principal members of both Houses of Parliament, the most important Chambers of Commerce and Underwriting bodies of this Country and the Colonies, and the different replies I received convinced me that it was a subject which was generally considered as requiring attention, but that unfortunately the public was not sufficiently alive to its importance.

Under these circumstances I made use of the Conference of the Association for the Reform and Codification of the Law of Nations, which took place in August 1879, in the Guildhall of the city of London, to read the following report:—

Having had frequent opportunities in the pursuit of my professional avocation for becoming acquainted with the *modus operandi* in keeping the log-books on board of merchant ships, and with the manner in which ships' protests are extended, it has been, in the interest of my clients, my duty to call the attention of Her Majesty's Government and of the Chambers of Commerce and Shipping in this country to the necessity of making alteration in the enactments relating to these two important and, as I will shortly show, intimately connected subjects.

For this reason I have been requested by the executive council of this Association to report to you on the state of the law, and as to the steps desirable to be taken for obtaining the necessary alterations in it.

The log-book on board of merchant ships has been intended from time immemorial to be used for the record of the daily occurrences during the voyage. Everything of any imaginable interest to the ship, its crew, passengers, and cargo was to be carefully and truthfully recorded in it, commencing with the wind and weather in its minutest details, the course steered, the changes of the tide, and the meeting with other vessels, and ending with any births or deaths or other matters concerning the well-being of crew or passengers. Of course, among other entries, particular reports respecting the loading or the discharging of the cargo, and any accidents happening during the voyage, were to be made. In short, these log-books, when properly verified by the signatures of the master, the mate, and, according to some legislations, by one or more of the crew, were intended to and did obtain all credence as public and official documents.

I then referred to my observations on sections 280 and 284 of the Merchant Shipping Act, 1854,[1] and continued:—

It will be also seen that I at the same time called the attention of the public authorities to the necessity for altering the proceedings with regard to the extension of ships' protests, a subject which is so closely connected with the law relating to ships' logs that it cannot be separated from it.

Since then the attention of the Board of Trade has been twice called to this subject:—

First (as will be seen by the return to an order of the House of Commons, dated May 15, 1876, for copies of letters and correspondence between the Board of Trade and others on the subject of sea protests), by the Secretary of Lloyd's, who, addressing the Board of Trade on December 6, 1875, called their attention to the very unsatisfactory manner in which sea protests were prepared, and drew up the following five objections to the present plan of extending protests by a notary, viz.:—

'1. That it may be made at any time after the arrival of the ship, and that it may be and is often framed to meet a particular necessity.

'2. That it is made by a notary who is not competent to verify or correct a statement.

'3. That in the absence of a central office where protests might be registered, opposing owners and captains, notably in collision cases, apply to different notaries and declare to different statements, and, later, swear to them in a court of law.

'4. That faith is not given to a protest which such a document ought to command, owing to the many known and many suspected cases of fraud which have been brought to light.

'5. That the formality of a notary's seal and signature may have the effect in many cases, especially abroad, of giving faith where no faith ought to be given.'

The Secretary of Lloyd's suggested that a public official at the custom-houses should be clothed with a proper authority for extending ships' protests, and made some other very valuable

[1] Vide p. 542.

suggestions, in which he was supported by the present Wreck Commissioner, the Liverpool Underwriters' Association, some other equally important bodies, some leading solicitors, and by me.

Unfortunately, for reasons not difficult to guess, no legislation on the subject was then or has ever yet been attempted.

The second attempt to move in the matter was made by my issuing a memorandum in October 1878.[1]

This memorandum I caused to be presented to the Board of Trade and to those of Her Majesty's Ministers, and the members of both Houses of the Legislature who could be expected to take an interest in the subject; to all the most important bodies of Underwriters, and to the Chambers of Commerce and of Shipping. It was most favourably commented upon by the public press, and was, with few exceptions, in general so satisfactorily received, that I considered myself authorised to write the following letter to Lord Sandon, the President of the Board of Trade, on January 10 last:—

'Relying on the promise your Lordship gave me, that the contents of the memorandum I took the liberty to submit to you on the above subject on October 4 last should have your personal attention, I consider it my duty to state that out of a number of communications I received from public bodies and private individuals, criticising the proposals contained in the memorandum above alluded to, very few deny the desirability of an alteration of the law as far as the extension of "merchant ships' protests" is concerned; and those which really do, base their objection on the ground that as British shipowners as a rule are honourable men, and as in this country protests are not considered as conclusive evidence of the facts on which claims are made, there is no necessity for any legislation on the subject.

'Now I need not point out to your Lordship the fallacy of such an argument.

'The trade of this country brings the vessels not only of British shipowners but of others within its territory. The British banker, merchant, or underwriter is, through the ramifications of his transactions, bound, not by law indeed, but by the equally stringent unwritten code of business honour, daily to pay large amounts on

[1] Vide *ante*, p. 658.

the faith of merchant ships' protests if properly prepared in accordance with the laws and customs of the place of issue.

'As the only safeguard for such banker, merchant, or underwriter is supplied by the notarial seal attached to the protest, and as it is impossible for any such individual to do more than to see that the document in outward appearance shows no sign of fraud, the Government of the country in which such documents are issued is bound to take every care that the chances of fraud in the issue of each document are minimised.

'It is true that in a British court of law a merchant ship's protest is not taken as conclusive evidence of the facts therein related, but it is well known that only a very small proportion of the cases in which such protests are all-important become subject to litigation, and the far greater number, not being litigated, are decided on the statements made in these protests, and depend entirely on their *bona fides*; furthermore, your Lordship will bear in mind that in all foreign courts of law a merchant ship's protest is taken as conclusive evidence. How dangerous it is, therefore, to allow the present state of things (*vide* Parliamentary Return of May 15, 1876) to continue!

'In one of the suggestions I made in my memorandum, at the bottom of page 2, that—

'"The entry be daily read over in the presence of the master, mate, and two others of the crew, and verified by their signatures,"[1]

I understand special objection has been taken, and that some of the Elder Brethren of the Trinity House are of opinion that the carrying out of the suggestion would be subversive of discipline on board. If this view be correct, the withdrawal of this special suggestion can be no impediment to the introduction of the general reform of which I think I have demonstrated the paramount necessity.

'With these observations I recommend this very important subject to your Lordship's most serious consideration.'

It may be considered that in this letter every objection, as far as stated, to my proposals has been answered, but nevertheless up

[1] These words are printed in italics in the Memorandum.

to this present day no change has taken place, no suggestion has been officially made to bring these difficulties to a satisfactory solution.

Strangely enough the Council of the Incorporated Law Society in their last report to the general meeting of their members on July 11 last, suggested that a Bill should be laid before Parliament to enable solicitors to undertake notarial duties without having qualified themselves in the manner at present prescribed by law. In answer to this the public notaries of London issued a printed memorandum in which they state their objections to that proposal of the Incorporated Law Society, and I cannot help expressing the opinion that, notwithstanding the respect and confidence I have for some of those who in some towns of the United Kingdom combine the positions of solicitors and notaries in their own persons, I see very grave objections to such a proposal as that of the Incorporated Law Society. It must be borne in mind that a notary is a public officer who must act *pro bono publico* impartially and independently, whereas a solicitor in his professional capacity and in his usual course of business is liable to be the legal adviser of some or other of the parties to a mercantile transaction affected by the circumstances related in the protest. Now if in such a case he draws up the ship's protest he must be more than human if he is able to separate the usual animus which ought to inspire all his actions in the interest of his client from the official notarial work he attempts to perform.

I mention this circumstance in order to show that the matter brought herewith under your notice must sooner or later come under the consideration of Her Majesty's Government, and that it is, therefore, high time to consider how this subject may most efficiently and beneficially be pressed forward. Of course public opinion will do most, and I therefore beg of you to do your utmost to assist in carrying some such proposal as mine into effect.

A copy of this report was also communicated to all the parties likely to take an interest in this important matter. In February 1880 I was given to understand that a negotiation had been initiated by the Imperial

German Government with our own, with the object of securing by treaty arrangements the taking legally binding evidence within the jurisdiction of the two countries. I then transmitted to the Foreign Office a copy of the above report and suggested that this opportunity should be used for entering into an international arrangement for the improvement of the existing system of preparing, swearing, and issuing merchant ships' protests.

The whole result of this attempt was that I heard from the Foreign Office, on March 10, 1880, ' that Lord Salisbury has been informed by the Board of Trade that, whilst in their opinion some of your suggestions and criticisms deserve consideration, they do not see their way to dealing with the subject at present.'

Since that time nothing has been done, and all the circumstances remain as heretofore, waiting for the improvement which the parties interested in the maritime commerce of this country and the colonies have a right to expect.

X.

VARIOUS PAPERS SHOWING HOW MOST OF THESE SUBJECTS HAVE BEEN URGED UPON THE BOARD OF TRADE.

To show how many years ago the reforms suggested in these pages have been urged upon the Board of Trade, I print the following letter and documents sent by me to the Board in 1867 :—

15 Fenchurch Buildings, London: June 4, 1867.

My Lords,—The kindred subjects of wreck and salvage, and the amendment of our law of merchant shipping, have of late engrossed so large a share of public attention, that I feel sure I need utter no apology for assuming that they have been, and continue to be, favoured with the most particular consideration of the Board of Trade, and that any suggestions or expressions of opinion bearing upon the question will be favourably received and carefully considered.

It is to-day my duty, in my capacity as Representative for the United Kingdom of Great Britain and Ireland of influential foreign underwriters,[1] whose interests I protect in the same manner as the Salvage Association those of certain bodies of underwriters in London and elsewhere, to lay before your Lordships memorials from so many different quarters, bearing signatures so numerous and respectable, that I cannot but think that your Lordships will be astonished at the universality and extent of feeling aroused upon these subjects in countries and places which have, in mercantile

---

[1] The Boards of Underwriters and Insurance Companies of Amsterdam, Antwerp, Bremen, Lübeck, New Orleans, New York, Rostock, Stralsund, and others.

matters, generally shown a very deep-rooted antagonism one to the other.

These memorials, forwarded to me from Amsterdam, Antwerp, Bremen, Colberg (with Stolp and Rügenwalde), Copenhagen, Danzig, Hamburg, Lübeck, Rostock, and Rotterdam, I have been desired to lay most humbly before your Lordships and Her Majesty's Government, and I venture to hope that the sentiments therein expressed may be of service in accelerating the introduction of a reform so long wanted and so universally desired.

It would not become me to take this opportunity of recapitulating at any length the arguments and opinions which have been already expressed by myself on different occasions, and especially:

> In 1864 in a memorial on the subject of the importance of the Receivers of Wreck taking depositions from shipmasters of all nations, which memorial was adopted by the Salvage Association of Lloyd's and others,[1]
>
> In 1866 in my observations on the Merchant Shipping Act, &c., forwarded to the Right Hon. Sir Stafford Northcote, on December 16 last,[2] and
>
> In the present year, in my observations on the Admiralty Jurisdiction Bill, forwarded to the Right Hon. Stephen Cave on April 16.[3]

Even more recently by Mr. Harper, the secretary to the Salvage Association above referred to, in his able and convincing report on the subject of wreck and salvage on the coast of Kent, more particularly in reference to the case of the 'North,' and by many other associations and private persons of far greater capacity and influence than myself.

I must ask permission, however, to recapitulate the principal points upon which my daily experience tells me that amended legislation is imperatively necessary, as will, I think, sufficiently appear upon reference to the papers, documents, and opinions above referred to.

1. The ship's log-book—instead of the present official and

---

[1] Vide p. 655.   [2] Vide p. 527.   [3] Vide p. 133, 2nd edition.

ordinary log-books kept on board every vessel, *one* log-book only to be kept, in a form issued by Government, and duly stamped, signed, and registered, so as to be beyond all possibility of fraud; this regulation has been long introduced in many parts of the Continent.

2. The deposition before the Receiver of Wreck to be compulsory upon Shipmasters of all Nations.

3. The mode of extending protests to be amended.

4. The duties of Receiver to be in all cases discharged by the Collectors of Customs, whose general efficiency cannot be too highly praised. But I cannot refrain from suggesting the necessity of raising the salaries of these very valuable officials, who are too frequently inadequately remunerated for the arduous duties they have to perform, in most cases requiring all their energy, ability, and discretion; a shipwreck may at any moment place in their hands the control of property to an amount greater than in the ordinary course of business would come before them in twenty years. I have known a case, which probably is not singular, where a Collector of Customs, instead of receiving extra payment for performing the important duties of Receiver, has actually been subjected to pecuniary loss, forfeiting during his absence from his own place of business the emoluments for overtime which he was entitled to claim from the public requiring his services.

5. The same limits to be assigned to the districts of Receivers and Principal Officers of Coastguard, in order to promote more harmonious working and more efficient substitution in case of absence.

6. The Coastguardsmen to be moved more frequently from one station to another.

7. In all prosecutions for plunder or illegal receiving of wreck, &c., the obligation to be on defendant to prove lawful possession, as in clauses 210, 215, 245, 305, and 306 of the Customs Consolidation Act.

8. A prompt and inexpensive mode of settlement of salvage claims to be introduced, and costs never to be allowed to salvors when they without due cause apply to higher tribunals

than absolutely necessary. The shamefully extortionate demands made by boatmen themselves, or, even more frequently, by professional or quasi-professional advisers on their behalf, have been fostered into a national evil by the want of local tribunals and by the absolute unwillingness of the present learned Judge of the Admiralty Court to condemn salvors in costs. Nor are these claims generally resisted, for the simple reason that all the parties concerned receive their commission in proportion to the amount paid, a ship's agent being frequently entrusted with the care of the interests both of salvor and ship, and receiving from both his payment.

9. Official surveys of damage to ships or cargoes by competent persons appointed by the Receiver to be provided for, and, if possible, rendered compulsory in every case; but, if not, the power of *underwriters* and their representatives to call for such surveys to be distinctly recognised. This will be the most effectual method of putting a stop to the present system of improper discounts, where fifteen or twenty, or even more per cent. are allowed and divided between the dishonest shipmaster and his even more culpable adviser, to the prejudice of the absent owners and underwriters.

10. The limited liability legislation of the Merchant Shipping Act Amendment Act, having given rise to decisions directly contrary to some of the fundamental principles of International Law, and having been the means of inflicting great injury upon the interests of the less wealthy class of shipowners, to be immediately reconsidered and revised.

11. Seriously to consider the necessity of pointing out to the foreign Governments who complain of the irregularities on our coasts in matters of Salvage and Average, how much they could assist in putting down those abuses by the general adoption of our system of making appointments of paid consular officers only, as it is evident from the wording of the Clauses in the Treaties concluded with reference to the functions appertaining to these officers, that it was never intended to entrust their execution to parties who would derive any pecuniary advantage from the advice they were called

upon to give either in a ministerial or judicial capacity, but at any rate in a perfectly impartial manner.

12. The introduction into this country of the International General Average Rules adopted at York in 1864, and repeatedly brought under the notice of Her Majesty's Government by the United Chambers of Commerce of this country and other influential bodies.

13. The preparing and settling of average statements should be under the immediate control of a public department, say, for instance, the Registry of the High Court of Admiralty, and the adoption of the very useful enactments of the German Law cannot be too strongly recommended.

14. The imperative necessity of doing away with compulsory Pilotage, and of altering the present system of granting and renewing Pilots' licenses in a manner more suitable to the public requirements.

15. The making away with, or aiding and abetting in scuttling, or otherwise destroying, a vessel for the purpose of defrauding its Underwriters or those who have an interest therein, or in the cargo or freight, should, by agreement between the principal maritime nations, be declared an Act of Piracy, otherwise no possibility exists of putting a stop to these fraudulent practices, which have for the last fifteen years been so greatly on the increase, and are the more difficult to prevent, as present legislation is continually defeated in its attempts to punish wrong-doers by questions of jurisdiction.

16. The Masters, Mates, and Engineers of 'Colonial Ships' to be under the same regulations respecting examinations and certificates as those of ships hailing from the United Kingdom.

17. The adoption of the International Law of Affreightment as agreed upon at Sheffield, 1865.

18. To consider if it would be desirable to fix by legislative enactment, as in the German Law, for instance, has been very successfully done, what should constitute a claim for assistance, and what for salvage.

How this amended legislation is to be brought about is not for me to suggest, but it has often struck me that to perform the work efficiently, the issuing of a Royal Commission would be necessary, which would inquire into the above evils so repeatedly complained of, would soon obtain the clear evidence of their existence, and would consider and recommend the fullest means to accomplish a thorough reform.

Your Lordships will always find me ready and willing to assist in any work leading in that direction.

I have the honour to be, my Lords, most respectfully, your Lordships' obedient humble Servant,

ERNST EMIL WENDT.

The Lords of the Committee of Her Majesty's
Privy Council for Trade, Whitehall.

The enclosures in the above were as follow:—

We, the undersigned, being Underwriters of the port of Amsterdam, in the Netherlands, having been informed that Her Majesty's Government have it in contemplation to alter and amend the existing regulations with respect to wrecks, salvage and salvors, and to make better provision for the settlement of salvage claims, and for the management of matters relating to vessels in distress on the coasts of the United Kingdom, do hasten to express to Her Majesty's Government our grateful sense of the inestimable benefit which will be conferred upon the maritime interests of the whole world by the proposed legislative reforms, if carried out in a practical and effectual manner.

We may be pardoned for observing that the frauds practised upon our captains in many parts of the coast of the United Kingdom, the extortionate demands of salvors and their advisers, the unscrupulous manœuvres of shipping agents, the continual inducements to dishonesty held out to inexperienced shipmasters, and, lastly, the enormous outlay attendant upon legal proceedings, aggravate to a most serious extent the consequences of misfortunes unavoidably attendant upon maritime industry; and having ourselves suffered severely from the evils above described, we cannot but rejoice that Her Majesty's Government have appreciated the necessity of carrying out a thorough reform, which we have no doubt will be attended with credit to the country and advantage to the community at large.—*Amsterdam*, February 1867, with forty-nine signatures of the leading underwriters.[1]

> A memorial identical with the above from *Bremen*, February 1867, signed by sixty-six gentlemen, representing the Directors of all the insurance companies and the principal merchants.
>
> A memorial identical with the above from *Colberg*, February 20, 1867, signed by the four principal shipowners.
>
> *Rügenwalde*, February 23, 1867, signed by the four principal shipowners.
>
> and *Stolp*, February 27, 1867, signed by the two principal shipowners.
>
> A memorial identical with the above from *Copenhagen*, signed by thirty-seven gentlemen representing the principal underwriters, shipowners, and merchants.
>
> A memorial identical with the above from *Danzig*, February 19, 1867, signed by twenty-seven shipowners and merchants.
>
> A memorial identical with the above from *Hamburg*, signed by fifty-nine gentlemen representing the different insurance and steamship companies as well as the principal bankers, merchants, and shipbrokers.
>
> A memorial identical with the above from *Rostock*, February 1867, signed by sixty-two shipowners and underwriters.
>
> A memorial identical with the above from *Rotterdam*, February 1867, signed by the representatives of fifty insurance companies and mercantile establishments.

Les soussignés armateurs et assureurs du Port d'Anvers en Belgique ayant été informés que le Gouvernement de Sa Majesté

[1] The names of the parties who signed these memorials having been fully printed in the two previous editions, it is superfluous to repeat them here.

britannique a l'intention de changer et d'amender les lois existantes pour les cas de naufrage et le règlement des services rendus par les sauveteurs à des navires en détresse sur les côtes du littoral anglais, s'empressent d'exprimer au Gouvernement de Sa Majesté britannique leur gratitude pour l'immense bienfait qui résulterait de cette mesure pour les intérêts maritimes du monde entier si les réformes législatives projetées étaient pratiquement et efficacement mises à exécution.

Qu'il leur soit permis d'observer que les fraudes auxquelles nos capitaines sont sujets sur différents points des côtes du Royaume-Uni et les demandes exorbitantes des sauveteurs et de leurs conseillers sont aggravées surtout par les manœuvres déloyales des agents maritimes.

Les énormes dépenses qu'entraînent des poursuites judiciaires rendent cet état de choses fort difficile à remédier ; les intéressés préfèrent se soumettre à un accord quelque désastreux qu'il soit plutôt que de s'engager dans un long et coûteux procès.

Les soussignés ayant été eux-mêmes victimes de cet état de choses déplorable, ne peuvent que se réjouir de la décision prise par le Gouvernement britannique de pousser à une réforme sérieuse, immense bienfait tant pour le pays même que pour le commerce étranger en général.—*Anvers*, 13 Février 1867. Signed by the representatives of twenty-five insurance companies and mercantile establishments.

AN DIE HOHE REGIERUNG IHRER MAJESTÄT DER KÖNIGIN VON GROSSBRITANNIEN UND IRLAND.

Ergebene Vorstellung der unterzeichneten Seeversicherer, Schiffsrheder und Kaufleute zu Lübeck.

Die unterzeichneten Seeversicherer, Schiffsrheder und Kaufleute zu Lübeck haben erfahren, dass die hohe Regierung Ihrer Majestät der Königin von Grossbritannien und Irland beabsichtigt, die jetzt bestehenden Regulative für die Behandlung von Schiffbrüchen Bergung aus Seenoth und Bergerlohn zu ändern und zu vervollkommnen, sowie auch bessere Maassregeln zu treffen für die

Erledigung von Bergelohn-Ansprüchen und für die Handhabung der Angelegenheiten, die sich auf Schiffe beziehen, welche sich an den Englischen Küsten in Seenoth befinden, und eilen, der hohen Regierung Ihrer Majestät der Königin von Grossbritannien und Irland unsere dankbare Anerkennung der unschätzbaren Wohlthat auszusprechen, welche den Interessen zur See der ganzen Welt durch die beabsichtigten legislativen Reformen zu Theil werden wird, wenn sie in practischer und wirksamer Weise ausgeführt werden.

Es wird verzeihlich sein, wenn wir bemerken, dass die Betrügereien, welche gegen unsere Schiffer an manchen Punkten der Englischen Küste verübt werden, die gelderpresserischen Forderungen der Berger und ihrer Rathgeber, die gewissenlosen Kunstgriffe der Agenten, die beständigen Verlockungen zur Unehrlichkeit, denen unerfahrene Schiffer ausgesetzt sind, und schliesslich die enormen Auslagen, welche mit dem gerichtlichen Verfahren verknüpft sind, in hohem Grade die Unfälle noch verschlimmern, welche schon unvermeidlich mit der Schifffahrt verknüpft sind; wir können daher uns nur freuen, dass die hohe Regierung Ihrer Majestät der Königin von Grossbritannien und Irland sich von der Nothwendigkeit einer gründlichen Reform überzeugt hat, und zweifeln nicht, dass dieselbe für England rühmlich und für alle, die Interessen zur See haben, nützlich sein werde. — *Lübeck*, den 16 Februar 1867. Signed by thirteen representatives of insurance companies and mercantile establishments.

The Committee of the Merchant Society, Copenhagen:
March 5, 1867.

Sir,—In your letter of 17th last month you have been pleased to inform the Committee that you have learned from London that the British Government have intended to lay before the present Parliament several proposals, with the view of improving the Maritime Laws hitherto in force in Great Britain, and you submit to this Committee whether the same should not have an occasion —like similar authorities abroad have had—to give their opinion for the purpose of promoting such a reform of the law in England, and specially for the purpose of contributing to an improvement of the British law respecting saving, salvage, and Court charges for settling maritime questions of dispute. In consequence hereof the Committee beg leave to express that they fully approve of the wish that the British law in the said respect should undergo an essential reform. It is a well-known fact, to any one who has been so unfortunate to have been placed under those circumstances, that the detriments and losses to which the seafaring person and the shipping is subject on the British coast is not a little increased by the deficient mode of proceedings in such cases. The expenses connected with the saving alone to the salvors and their assistants generally consume too great and inadequate a portion of the value saved. The want of sufficient laws to regulate the mode of proceedings further exposes the owners and others concerned, through ships' agents and otherwise, to considerable loss; and to seek recourse, by means of law proceedings, is connected with so great expenses that merely from this reason this course is in many cases inexpedient. We therefore do not doubt that a reform might be effected which would be received here, as well as other places, with thankfulness by all persons interested in shipping and trade.

This is the opinion we are ready to give, but we are not certain whether it would be proper to forthcome direct with the same to any authority in England, partly because we do not know how far such a course would meet with approval, partly because we are uncertain whether such a course should not be taken through our own Government; but, authorising you to make use of the present as you may think proper, we beg to limit our answer to these lines. Signed by twelve merchants.

 To S. Gram, Esq.,
Manager of the Copenhagen Maritime Insurance Association.

For a true and faithful translation of the Danish original produced to me.

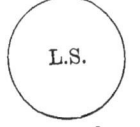

         C. W. LANGE,
 (L.S.) Translator duly sworn and admitted.

Copenhagen: March 14, 1867.

It may be added that an identical memorial to the one previously printed, dated Amsterdam, February 1867, was received by me from New Orleans with the signatures of twenty-five representatives of marine insurance companies and merchants, and transmitted by me to the Board of Trade on June 24, 1867.

XI.

APPELLATE JURISDICTION IN MARITIME CAUSES.

This is another matter in which, according to my humble opinion, serious reform is required. My reasons were fully given in the following memorandum, which I sent on October 31, 1876, to the principal members of both Houses of Parliament and the Chambers of Commerce in this country and the colonies :—

Towards the close of the last Session of Parliament, the Legislature passed, in the 39 & 40 Vict. cap. 59, an Act which, by effecting a radical change in the hearing of appeals in Admiralty causes, affects the general maritime interests of this and many other countries most injuriously.

The change complained of is this: Hitherto in causes brought before the Admiralty tribunal in England, one appeal only has been thought necessary, and one appeal only has there been, but now by this Act it is enacted, for what reasons it is hard to say, that henceforward there shall be, in addition to the existing appeal, a second one, viz. to the House of Lords, quite unnecessary for the performance of justice in those causes, and unasked for by all those most interested in having justice performed therein.

Representing in this country the principal foreign underwriting bodies in the world, and perceiving at once how their interest would be prejudiced by this unfortunate innovation, I addressed a letter, on August 29 last, to the Lord Chancellor, calling the attention of his Lordship to the following facts and reasons to which it is now my wish to draw more general attention, namely—

That at no time, either when the appeals in maritime causes went in accordance with the Act 25 Hen. VIII. cap. 19, to the

High Court of Delegates, or in accordance with the Act 2 & 3 Will. IV. cap. 92, to His Majesty in Council, or in accordance with the Act 3 & 4 Will. IV. cap. 41, to the Judicial Committee of the Privy Council, at no time when the final appeal lay to any one of these varied tribunals had it been considered or even suggested that a second appeal was necessary or even might be beneficial;

That the fact that this was the case until the passing of 36 & 37 Vict. cap. 66, was a strong proof of the adequacy and efficiency of the single appeal in such causes, and the absence of any wish on the part of the suitors to have any second appeal;

That, as a matter of fact, the suitors in Admiralty causes did not want any alteration in the procedure so far as concerns appeals therefrom, and were, on the contrary, much opposed to any second appeal;

That the very Act—the one already referred to—which first clearly throws this burden on the suitors in Admiralty causes, excepts, in its 12th section, all causes in the Courts of Ireland and Scotland from liability to review by the House of Lords which had not been liable to it before;

That it is, therefore, an act of great hardship on the part of the British Legislature to the suitors in Admiralty causes in England to place them not only in a worse position than they have been for centuries past, but also in a worse position than that so reserved to suitors in the Courts of Ireland and Scotland;

That the foreign underwriters, whose representative I am, were all most anxious, and that I was confident the maritime constituencies of this country were so also, to be freed from this most expensive, unnecessary, and cumbersome innovation;

And I, finally, prayed his Lordship to consider the necessity of obtaining the passing of an Amendment Act to reinstate the procedure of Admiralty causes on appeal into the same position as before the passing of 38 & 39 Vict. c. 77.

The answer I received to my communication was as follows:—

'5 Cromwell Houses, S.W.: September 7, 1876.

'Sir,—I am directed by the Lord Chancellor to acknowledge the receipt of your letter of the 29th ult. upon the subject of "Appellate Jurisdiction in Maritime Causes."

'I am, in reply, to inform you that the jurisdiction in Admiralty having, by the Judicature Act of 1873, been made a part of the general jurisdiction of the High Court of Justice, the procedure of appeal is now the same in Admiralty as in other causes.

'I am, Sir, your obedient Servant,
(Signed) 'HENRY J. L. GRAHAM,
'Principal Secretary.'

Now, it may be asserted that the right of appeal to the House of Lords is not a burden but a privilege. It may be so in some cases and to some extent; but it is a burden none the less still more frequently and to a much greater extent. The greatest privilege suitors can have is for their cases to be settled as justly as possible, but, above all things, with the least possible loss of time and money. Every extra and unnecessary appeal causes direct loss both of time and money to the suitors, and is therefore a burden to them; and in this case, where the appeal under discussion is to the House of Lords, and therefore both costly and tedious, the burden is very heavy indeed.

It must be remembered that the tendency of recent legislation has been to limit the liability of shipowners; and the accretion of costs will not in any way increase the extent of the remedy to be obtained by litigation.

It is evident, therefore, that those who are obliged to become suitors in the Admiralty Division of the High Court of Justice of England have two serious grounds of complaint:

Firstly: That they have become burdened with the great expenses and delays of an unnecessary second appeal, to the House of Lords, although during the centuries in which they have had the one single appeal they have never desired, and they do not now desire, any second appeal.

Secondly: That they have been so burdened while such suitors as in the Courts of Ireland and Scotland enjoyed the privilege of being exempt from the appeal to the House of Lords have continued to retain their privilege.

It is not maintained that any advantage accrues to anyone by the creation of this grievance; but the only reason which is and can be assigned for it is the asserted desirability of a uniformity of practice between the Admiralty Division and the other Divisions of the High Court of Justice.

It is for this utterly inadequate reason, then, that while every enlightened Government is doing its best to lessen the burdens which are the inseparable, or rather the natural consequences of commerce and trade, a burden so heavy is laid on two of the principal handmaids of commerce and trade—the Shipping and the Underwriting interests.

In consequence of this memorandum numerous communications have been addressed to me, expressing approval and gratitude for my ventilating this subject and putting it in its proper light, but the *status quo* has not been altered and the grievance remains.

APPENDIX.

APPENDIX.

GERMAN GENERAL MERCANTILE LAW.[1]

FIFTH BOOK.
CONCERNING MARITIME COMMERCE.

FIRST PART.

General Provisions.

Art. 432. A Register is to be kept of all vessels intended for profit by means of sea voyages, and entitled to carry the country's flag.

The Register is public, its inspection being permitted to everybody during the ordinary office hours.

Art. 433. An entry in the Register can only be made after the right of carrying the country's flag has been established.

Before entry in the Register the right of carrying the country's flag cannot be exercised.

Art. 434. The laws of the various countries point out the requirements upon which the right of a vessel to carry the country's flag depends.

They appoint the authorities which have to keep the Register of shipping.

They decide whether, and under what conditions, the entry in the

---

[1] By the law respecting the constitution of the German Empire of April 16, 1871, and the law respecting the introduction of the North German Confederation Laws into Bavaria of April 22, 1871, the German General Mercantile Law Code obtained authority in the whole domain of the German Empire as the law of the Empire —with the modification that where it mentions the North German Confederation, its constitution, borders, members or states, constitutional organisation, officials, flags, &c., the German Empire and its corresponding applications must be understood.

Register of shipping of a vessel acquired from a foreign country may be provisionally replaced by a consular document.

Art. 435. The entry in the Register shall contain—
(1) The facts on which the right of the vessel to carry the country's flag is based.
(2) The facts required for establishing the identity of the ship, and all matters concerning its ownership.
(3) The sea-port from which the vessel is intended to hail. (Home port. Port of Registry.)

A document (certificate) identical with the entry is to be granted.

Art. 436. If subsequently to the entry changes occur in the facts referred to in the foregoing paragraphs, they must be entered in the Register of shipping and stated on the certificate.

In case of the vessel being lost, or forfeiting the right of carrying the country's flag, the vessel is to be struck off the Register of shipping and the certificate has to be returned, unless it be credibly attested that it cannot be returned.

Art. 437. The laws of the various countries determine the space of time within which the facts necessitating an entry or a cancellation are to be notified or proved, and also the penalties which are entailed by neglect of these respites, or by non-compliance with the foregoing provisions.

Art. 438.[1] The laws of the various countries may determine that the provisions of Articles 432 to 437 shall not apply to smaller vessels (such as coasters, &c.).[2]

Art. 439. If a ship or a share therein (ship's-part) be sold, the transfer required according to the principles of the common law, if any, may for the purpose of acquiring a title to the property, be dispensed with by agreement between the contracting parties to the effect that the title to the property shall immediately pass to the purchaser.

Art. 440. In all cases of the sale of a vessel, or of a share therein each of the parties has a right to demand that a certified document respecting the sale should be given to him at his expense.

Art. 441. If a ship, or a share therein, be sold while the ship is engaged on a voyage, it shall, as regards the relative positions of vendor and purchaser, in default of an agreement to the contrary, be

---

[1] *Arts.* 432–438 have lost their practical application, owing to the law respecting the nationality of merchant vessels and their right to carry the flag of the Confederation of October 25, 1867. This law applies to the whole German Empire, and a translation of it will be found on p. 813.

[2] See translation of the Law of May 22, 1881, p. 817.

presumed that the purchaser is entitled to the profits of the current voyage, or responsible for the loss incurred therein.

Art. 442. The personal liabilities of the vendor towards third parties are in no way altered by the sale of a ship or a share therein.

Art. 443. All articles intended for the permanent use of the ship during its navigation are considered to be appurtenances of the ship.

Ships' boats more particularly belong thereto.

In doubtful cases all articles entered upon the Ship's Inventory are considered to be appurtenances of the ship.

Art. 444. For the purpose of this fifth book a ship that has become unseaworthy is considered to be—

(1) *Incapable of repair*, when the repair is altogether impossible, or cannot be done at the place where the ship is, and the ship cannot be moved to a port where the repairs might be carried out.

(2) *Unworthy of repair*, when the cost of the repair without deduction on account of the difference between old and new would amount to more than three-fourths of the previous value.

When a vessel has become unseaworthy in the course of a voyage its previous value is to be taken as that which the ship was worth at the commencement of the voyage; in all other cases, as that which the ship before she became unseaworthy was worth, or would with a proper outfit have been worth.

Art. 445. In the ship's crew are included the master, the seamen, and all other persons appointed to duties on board a ship.

Art. 446. A ship ready to sail cannot be arrested for debts. This provision, however, does not apply to debts contracted for purposes of the intended voyage.

An attachment for debts of goods already laden on board a ship authorises their relanding only in such cases in which the shipper himself would be entitled to demand it, and only upon compliance with all obligations which the latter would at the time have to fulfil.

From the time of the ship being ready to sail a person belonging to the crew cannot be arrested for debts.

Art. 447. When in this fifth book a distinction is made between European and non-European ports, then the non-European ports of the Mediterranean, the Black Sea, and the Sea of Azoff are to be considered as likewise belonging to the former category.

Art. 448. The provisions of this fifth book, which refer to the stay of a vessel in the port of registry, can by the legislation of the various countries be extended to all or any ports situated in the same water as the port of registry.

Art. 449. The provisions of this fifth book apply to the postal establishments only so far as special laws or enactments do not lay down other regulations respecting them.

SECOND PART.

Concerning the Owner and Joint Ownership.

Art. 450. A shipowner is the proprietor of a vessel used by him for the purpose of making a profit by navigation.

Art. 451. The owner is answerable for any damage occasioned to a third party by the fault of any of the crew in the performance of their duties.

Art. 452. The owner is, however, not personally liable for the claim of a third party, but is only answerable to the extent of ship and freight—

(1) When the claim is made on account of a legal transaction, concluded by the master as such, in virtue of the authority he lawfully possesses, and not in consequence of an especial power of attorney.

(2) When the claim is occasioned by the non-performance, or the incomplete or improper performance, of any arrangement made by the owner, as far as the carrying out of such arrangement belonged to the legitimate duties of the master, no matter whether the non-performance or the incomplete or improper performance was caused through the fault of anybody belonging to the crew or not.

(3) When the claim has arisen through the fault of one of the crew.

This section does not, however, apply to the cases stated under Nos. 1 and 2, if any neglect in the performance of the arrangement is attributable to the fault of the owner himself, or if he has especially guaranteed the fulfilment of the arrangement.

Art. 453.[1] The owner is answerable for the claims of persons

---

[1] By § 68 of the law regarding ships' masters and seamen of December 27, 1872 (*vide* translation, p. 790), *Art.* 453 has been altered and reads as follows:—

'The owner is answerable not only to the extent of ship and freight but also personally for claims of the master or any member of the crew arising out of contracts respecting their services and wages.'

The remainder of *Art.* 453 is repealed.

belonging to the crew, and arising out of contracts respecting their services and wages, not only to the extent of ship and freight, but at the same time personally.

If, however, the ship be lost to the owner, without his fault before the termination of the voyage, more especially

> if it be lost by accident,
>
> if it have been condemned as incapable or unworthy of repairs (Art. 444), and if, in the latter case, it be sold without delay by public auction,
>
> if it be captured by pirates,
>
> if it be seized or detained, and condemned as good prize, the

owner is not personally liable for claims arising out of the unfinished voyage, or, when the latter consists of several subdivisions, for claims resulting out of the last portion of the voyage.

The last portion of the voyage commences in the port in which the ship has last taken in or discharged cargo, and from the time at which the loading commenced or the discharging finished. A port of distress is not considered to be a loading or discharging port within the meaning of this clause.

In none of the aforesaid cases is the owner entitled to recover bounties or advances previously paid.

Art. 454. The remaining cases in which the owner is responsible, not personally, but only to the extent of ship and freight, are stated in the following parts.

Art. 455. The owner, as such, may be sued before the court of the port of registry on account of every claim whatsoever, irrespective of the question whether he is personally responsible or only to the extent of ship and freight (Art. 435).

Art. 456. A joint-ownership exists if a vessel belonging jointly to more than one person be employed by them for the purposes of profit by means of navigation.

The regulations respecting joint-ownership do not apply to the case of a vessel belonging to a trading company.

Art. 457. The legal relations of the co-owners to each other are regulated in the first instance by the agreement made between them. Where no agreement has been entered into, the provisions of the following paragraphs are to be applied.

Art. 458. The resolutions of the co-owners are binding with regard to the affairs of the ownership.

Resolutions are passed by a majority of votes. The votes are counted according to the number of shares held. A majority of votes in favour of a resolution exists if the person or persons who have voted for such resolution hold together more than a moiety of the entire vessel. The unanimous consent of all co-owners is requisite for the adoption of resolutions intended to alter the agreement of ownership, or which are contrary to the stipulations of such agreement or foreign to the objects of the ownership.

Art. 459. By resolution of a majority a managing owner (ship's husband, representative owner) may be appointed to carry on the business of the ownership. An unanimous vote is required in favour of a resolution appointing a managing owner, who is not himself one of the part-owners.

The appointment of a managing owner may be revoked at any time by a majority of votes, without prejudice, however, to any claims for compensation arising out of existing agreements.

Art. 460. By virtue of his appointment the managing owner is empowered to carry out all business arrangements and legal acts as against third parties, which the management of a joint-ownership ordinarily requires.

This power extends more particularly to the fitting out, maintaining, and chartering the ship; to the insurance of the freight, the cost of outfit and the outlay necessitated by cases of average; and to the receiving of money in the ordinary course of business.

The managing owner is to the same extent authorised to represent the joint-owners before legal tribunals.

He is empowered to appoint and to discharge the master; the master has to obey only his instructions, and not the instructions, if any, which he may have received from any of the part-owners.

The managing owner is, however, not authorised in the name of the joint-ownership, or of any part-owner or owners, to enter into obligations upon bills of exchange, nor to contract loans, to sell or mortgage the ship or shares therein, nor to insure them, unless a special power of attorney be given to him for such purpose.

In other respects, the special power of attorney, if any, required by the legislation of the various countries, is not necessary for those business and legal acts which by virtue of his appointment he is authorised to carry out.

Art. 461. Any legal act which the managing owner as such may have concluded within the limits of his authority, binds and entitles the joint-owners as against third parties, even when the act has been effected without giving the names of the various part-owners.

In case of responsibility incurred by the joint-owners in consequence of a business matter concluded by the managing owner, the part-owners are responsible to the same extent (Art. 452) as if the transaction had been entered into by themselves.

Art. 462. A limitation of the powers of the managing owner, as stated in Art. 460, can only be pleaded by the joint-owners against a third party, so far as they are in a position to prove that such limitation was known to such third party at the time when the transaction was concluded.

Art. 463. As far as the joint-owners are concerned, the managing owner is bound to act within the limitations which have been stipulated by them as the extent of his powers ; he has also to be guided by the resolutions passed, and to carry the same into effect.

In other respects the extent of his powers, even as against the joint-owners, is to be considered in accordance with the provisions of Art. 460, with this modification, that for new voyages or undertakings, extraordinary repairs, as well as for the appointment or discharge of the master, the consent of the joint-owners must previously be obtained.

Art. 464. The managing owner is bound to apply the attention of a careful owner to the affairs of the joint-ownership.

Art. 465. The managing owner shall keep separate accounts respecting his management of the affairs of the joint-ownership and shall preserve the vouchers relating thereto. He shall, on demand, give to each part-owner information of all matters connected with the joint-ownership, more particularly respecting ship, voyage, and outfit; he is bound to allow him at all times to inspect the books, letters, and papers which have reference to the affairs of the joint-ownership.

Art. 466. The managing owner shall at all times, when called upon by a resolution of the joint-owners, produce to them a balance-sheet. The adoption of the balance-sheet and the approval of the management of the managing owner by the majority does not prevent a majority from enforcing their rights.

Art. 467. Every co-owner shall contribute to the expenses of the ownership, more especially to the expenses of the outfit and the repairs of the vessel, in proportion to the amount of his share.

When a part-owner is in arrear of contributions, and when the money has been advanced by co-owners on his account, he is by law bound to pay them interest from the time the advances have been made. The laws of the various countries decide whether a mortgage-lien is established by such advances upon the share of the part-owner in arrear. Should a mortgage-lien not be so acquired, the advances made give the co-owners an insurable interest in the share in question.

In case this interest should have been insured, the part-owner in arrear is bound to repay the expenses of such insurance.

Art. 468. If it has been decided to commence a new voyage, or after the termination of a voyage to repair the vessel, or to pay off a creditor, to whom the ownership is only liable to the extent of ship and freight, every part-owner who has not assented to the resolution may exonerate himself from making the payments necessary to carry out such resolution by giving up his share without claim to indemnification.

The part-owner intending to exercise this right shall be bound to give judicial or notarial notice of such intention to the part-owners or the managing owner within three days from the date of the passing of the resolution, or, in case he was not present personally or by proxy at the passing of the resolution, then within three days of the time that the resolution shall have been communicated to him.

The share thus given up becomes the property of the remaining co-owners in proportion to the amount of their several shares.

Art. 469. The distribution of profits and losses is made in proportion to the amount of the shares.

The calculation of profits and losses and the distribution of the profits, if any, take place every time that the vessel returns to the port of registry, or whenever it has completed its voyage in another port, and the crew has been discharged.

Monies coming in before the time mentioned, as far as they are not wanted for future expenses, or for satisfying claims of single part-owners against the joint-ownership, shall also be distributed and paid *ad interim* to the several part-owners in proportion to the amount of their shares.

Art. 470. Every part-owner is at liberty to sell his share at any time, either wholly or in part, without the consent of the other part-owners.

The co-owners have no legal right to priority of purchase. The sale, however, of a share whereby the vessel would lose its right to carry the country's flag can only be legally made with the consent of all co-owners. Those laws of the various countries which altogether prohibit such a sale shall not be affected by this provision.

Art. 471. The part-owner who has sold his share is, as regards his connection with the co-owners, considered to be a part-owner until he and the purchaser have notified such sale to the other part-owners or to the managing owner, and continues liable as part-owner to the other part-owners with respect to all obligations contracted previously to such notification.

The purchaser of the share, however, is, as far as the other part-owners are concerned, already liable from the moment of such acquisition. He, like the vendor, is bound, by the stipulations of the agreement of ownership, by the resolutions passed and by the transactions already entered into ; the other part-owners are besides at liberty to enforce against the purchaser the fulfilment of all liabilities attaching upon the vendor with regard to the share in question, the purchaser's right to recover against the vendor being in no way affected thereby.

Art. 472. A change among the part-owners does not affect the continuance of the joint-ownership.

When a part-owner dies or becomes bankrupt, or legally incapable of managing his property, the ownership is not thereby dissolved.

Notice of withdrawal on the part of a part-owner or exclusion of a part-owner are inadmissible.

Art. 473. A dissolution of the joint-ownership may be resolved upon by a majority. A resolution to sell the vessel is to be considered as a resolution to dissolve the ownership.

If it has been decided to dissolve the joint-ownership or to sell the vessel, the sale of the vessel must take place by public auction. The sale shall only take place when the vessel is not chartered for a voyage, and when it is in the port of registry or a home port.

If, however, the vessel has been condemned as incapable or unworthy of repair (Art. 444), it may be sold although under charter, or even in a foreign port. The consent of all part-owners is required if a deviation from the foregoing regulations be contemplated.

Art. 474. As regards their personal obligation to third parties, the part-owners as such are liable only in proportion to the amount of their shares.

In case a share in a ship is sold, both vendor and purchaser are liable with respect to the personal obligations contracted for such share during the period from the sale to the notification mentioned in Art. 471.

Art. 475. The part-owners as such may be sued before the court of the port of registry (Art. 435) for every claim, no matter whether made by a part-owner or by a third party.

This provision applies also to such cases in which an action is entered only against one part-owner or against some of the part-owners.

Art. 476. If two or more persons agree to build a vessel for their joint account and to use the same for the purposes of navigation, then Articles 457, 458, 467 are to be applied, the latter with the modification that it has to include the building expenses, also Articles 472 and

474, and, as soon as the vessel has been finished and handed over by the builder, Articles 470, 471 and 473 likewise apply.

The managing owner (Art. 459) may also be appointed before the vessel has been finished; in this case he assumes from the time of his appointment all rights and duties of a managing owner with respect to the further management of the affairs of the joint-ownership.

Art. 477. Whoever employs for his account a vessel not belonging to himself with the view of profit by means of navigation, and either commands the same himself or entrusts the command to a master, is as against third parties considered to be the owner.

The actual owner cannot prevent anybody who brings forward a claim as ship-creditor, arising out of such employment, from enforcing his claim unless he is in a position to prove that such employment was illegal with regard to himself, and that the creditor has not acted in good faith.

THIRD PART.

Concerning the Master.

Art. 478. The commander of a vessel (ship captain, master) shall exercise the care of a properly qualified master in all matters connected with his duties, but more especially in the fulfilment of contracts to be executed by him. He is liable for every damage occasioned by his fault, particularly for the damage originating in the violation of the duties imposed upon him by this and the following articles.

Art. 479. This liability of the master exists not only towards the owner but also towards the charterer, shipper and receiver of cargo, the passengers, crew, and those creditors of the vessel whose claims arise out of a credit transaction (Art. 497), more especially the bottomry-creditor.

The master is not exonerated from liability as regards the other before-mentioned persons by having acted according to instruction of the owner.

By such instruction, the owner becomes also personally liable if he was acquainted with the position of affairs at the time the instruction was given.

Art. 480. The master, before entering upon a voyage, has to take care that the vessel is in a seaworthy condition, properly furnished and fitted out, properly manned and provisioned, and that the papers required as proofs of identity for ship, crew, and cargo are on board.

Art. 481. The master is responsible for the condition of the gear used for loading and discharging, as well as for proper stowage according to seaman's custom, notwithstanding that the stowage may be performed by special stevedores. He has to take care that the vessel is not overloaded, and that it is provided with the necessary ballast and the requisite dunnage.

Art. 482. If the master when in a foreign country does not comply with the legal provisions there in force, more especially respecting police, customs, and revenue regulations, he shall make good the damage thereby occasioned. In like manner, he shall make good any damage resulting from his taking in goods which he knew or ought to have known to be contraband of war.

Art. 483. As soon as the ship is ready to sail the master shall commence the voyage at the first favourable opportunity.

Even if illness or other causes should prevent him from commanding the ship, he is not allowed unduly to delay its departure or the continuation of its voyage; on the contrary, he shall, if time and circumstances permit, apply to the owner for instructions, inform him without delay of the impediment, and meanwhile make proper arrangements; otherwise he shall appoint another master. He is only responsible for the acts of such substitute in so far as he may have been guilty of carelessness in his selection.

Art. 484. From the commencement of taking in cargo to the completion of the discharge, the master and the mate shall not leave the vessel simultaneously except in urgent cases; in such an event the master shall previously appoint a substitute from amongst the officers or the rest of the crew of the vessel.

The same rule applies, before the commencement of loading and after the completion of the discharge, if the vessel is in an unsafe port or an insecure roadstead.

When the vessel is threatened by any danger, or when it is at sea, the master must be on board, unless urgent necessity should justify his absence.

Art. 485. Although the master, in case of danger, may consult the officers of the vessel, he is nevertheless not bound by the resolutions arrived at; he remains always responsible for the measures taken by him.

Art. 486. On board of every vessel a log-book shall be kept, in which, during every voyage, all important events from the commencement of taking in cargo or ballast shall be entered.

The log-book shall be kept, under the supervision of the master, by the mate, and, in case the latter should be prevented, then by the master himself, or, under his supervision, by another duly qualified member of the crew, selected by him for this purpose.

Art. 487. Daily entries shall be made in the log-book respecting—

The state of wind and weather.

The courses steered by the vessel and the distances run.

The ascertained latitude and longitude.

The state of water at the pumps.

In the log-book shall also be entered—

The depth of water ascertained by heaving the lead.

Every employment of a pilot and the time of his arrival and departure.

Any changes among the persons composing the crew.

The resolutions arrived at in any ship's council.

All accidents happening to ship or cargo, together with a description thereof.

Punishable acts committed, and the disciplinary punishments inflicted, as also births and deaths occurring on board, are likewise to be entered in the log-book.

The entries shall, so far as circumstances will permit, be made daily.

The log-book shall be signed by the master and the mate.

Art 488.[1] The log-book when properly kept and free from suspicion as to form furnishes, as a rule, so far as neither an extended protest (Art. 490) is requisite, nor the production of other vouchers customary, *primâ facie* evidence respecting the occurrences during the voyage, which evidence may be perfected either by oath or other evidence. The judge, however, shall, according to his discretion and guided by consideration of all the circumstances, decide whether the statements of the log-book are more or less deserving of credibility.

Art. 489. The laws of the various countries may determine that on board smaller vessels (as coasters, &c.) the keeping of the log-book shall not be requisite.

Art. 490. The master shall, in conjunction with all the persons forming the crew or a sufficient number thereof, make an extended protest respecting all accidents happening on the voyage, no matter whether entailing the loss or damage of the ship or cargo, a running into a port of distress, or other injury.

The protest shall be extended without delay, and more especially—

In the port of destination or, when there are more than one ports of destination, in that which the vessel first reaches after the accident.

In the port of distress, if the vessel is repaired or discharged therein.

---

[1] Repealed by § 13 of the Civil Process Regulations, d. d. January 30, 1877.

At the first suitable place, if the voyage terminates without the port of destination having been reached.

If the master has died or become incapable to extend the protest the officer next in rank to him is entitled and obliged to do it.

Art. 491. The extended protest must contain a report of all important incidents of the voyage, and in particular a detailed and lucid narration of all accidents sustained, together with a statement of the means adopted to avoid or lessen the damage.

Art. 492. Wherever the provisions of this law are in force notice of the protest shall be given to the competent court, such notice being accompanied by the log-book and a list of all persons composing the crew.

The court shall, after receipt of the notice, proceed with the extension of the protest as soon as possible.

The day fixed for this purpose shall, whenever the circumstances of the case admit of such delay, be made publicly known in an adequate manner.

All persons having an interest in ship and cargo, as well as all other persons who may be affected by the accident, are entitled to be present at the extension of the protest either personally or by deputy.

The extension of the protest is based upon the log-book. When the actual log-book cannot be produced, or when a log-book has not been kept (Art. 489), the reason thereof is to be stated.

Art. 493. The judge is authorised to examine other persons of the crew, if he think proper, besides those that have been produced. He may, for the sake of a more accurate investigation, put suitable questions to be answered by the master as well as by any other person belonging to the crew.

The master and the other members of the crew who may have been summoned shall confirm their depositions upon oath.

The original protocol drawn up respecting the extension of the protest shall be preserved and a certified copy granted on demand to each of the parties interested.

Art. 494.[1] The extended protest drawn up in conformity with Articles 492 and 493 constitutes complete evidence of the incidents of the voyage testified to therein.

Each party interested retains in case of a lawsuit the right to produce counter-evidence.

Art. 495. Legal business which the master transacts while the vessel is in the port of registry is only binding upon the owner when

---

[1] Repealed by § 13 of the Civil Process Regulations, d. d. January 30, 1887.

the master has acted on the authority of a power of attorney, or when there is some other special reason for his obligation to do so.

The master is, however, entitled to engage seamen in the port of registry.

Art. 496. When the vessel is not in the port of registry the master is, as against third parties, by virtue of his appointment authorised to transact on behalf of the owner all business matters whether legal or otherwise rendered necessary by the outfit, manning, provisioning, and maintenance of the vessel and, in general, for the performance of the voyage.

This authority likewise extends to the entering into contracts of affreightment; it extends, moreover, to the instituting of lawsuits having reference to matters connected with his duties.

Art. 497. The master is, however, only entitled to contract loans, to make purchases on credit and to conclude similar transactions on credit, when they are necessary for the maintenance of the vessel and the completion of the voyage, and only so far as is necessary to supply the actual requirement. He is only at liberty to enter into a bottomry transaction when it is unavoidably requisite for the completion of the voyage, and only so far as is necessary to supply the actual requirement.

The validity of the transaction depends neither upon the actual application of the money, nor upon the prudence of the selection made between various modes of raising money, nor upon the question whether the master had at his disposal the money required, except it should be proved that the third party acted in bad faith.

Art. 498. The master is not authorised to conclude transactions on the personal credit of the owner, nor more especially to contract debts upon bills of exchange on his behalf, unless specially authorised by a power of attorney given him to that effect (Art. 452, par. 1). Letters of instruction and orders as to his duties which the master receives from the owner are not sufficient to set up a personal liability of the owner in favour of a third party.

Art. 499. The master is empowered to sell the vessel only in cases of urgent necessity, and when such necessity has been ascertained by the local court after hearing the opinion of experts, and with the assistance of the consul of the country, when one is at hand.

Should there be neither a court of law nor any other authority on the spot to undertake the inquiry, the master shall, in order to justify his actions, take the opinion of experts, and when this is not possible, provide himself with other proofs.

The sale must take place by public auction.

Art. 500. Any owner who has placed restrictions upon the legal authority of the master can only plead against third parties non-observance of such restrictions if he proves that they were known to such parties.

Art. 501. Should the master, without special instructions, have advanced money belonging to himself for account of the owner, or made himself personally liable, he has no greater claim against the owner for indemnification than a third party.

Art. 502. Any transaction within the scope of the master's legal authority entered into by him in his capacity as commander of the vessel, gives the owner a legal claim against a third party, but renders him at the same time responsible to the extent of ship and freight, whether his name appear or not.

The master himself does not become responsible to a third party by such legal transaction, unless he has guaranteed its fulfilment, or has exceeded his authority. The liability of the master in conformity with Articles 478 and 479 is, however, not excluded hereby.

Art. 503. The foregoing articles are likewise binding upon the owner as to the extent of the authority of the master in so far as this authority has not been restricted by the owner.

It is, moreover, the duty of the master to transmit to the owner continual information of the condition of the vessel, the incidents of the voyage, the contracts entered into by him, and the lawsuits that may have become necessary; and, when circumstances permit, to apply to the owner for instructions on all important occasions, particularly in the cases contemplated by Articles 497 and 499, or when he is compelled to alter or abandon a voyage, or when extraordinary repairs and outlay for necessaries are rendered necessary.

The master is only in case of necessity permitted to undertake extraordinary repairs and outlay, even when he may be able to defray the expense with funds belonging to the owner over which he may have control.

If he is unable to procure the requisite funds to provide for an urgent necessity in any other way than either by bottomry or by the sale of superfluous appurtenances or provisions of the ship, he shall adopt that alternative which entails the least detriment upon the owner.

After his return to the port of registry, and otherwise as often as it is demanded, he shall render his account to the owner.

Art. 504. The master shall take every possible care of the cargo during the voyage in the interest of those concerned therein.

When special measures are required in order to avoid or lessen a loss, it is his duty to protect the interest of those concerned in the cargo as their representative; to take their instructions, if possible, and, so far as circumstances admit, to carry the same into effect; otherwise, however, to act according to his own discretion, and generally to take every possible care that those interested in the cargo are speedily informed of such occurrences, and of the measures thereby rendered necessary.

He is particularly in such cases authorised to discharge the whole or a portion of the cargo; in extreme cases, if on account of imminent deterioration or for other causes a considerable loss cannot be otherwise averted, to sell or hypothecate it for the purpose of providing means for its preservation and further transport; to reclaim it in case of capture or detention; or, if it shall have been otherwise withdrawn from his charge, to take all extra-judicial and judicial steps for its recovery.

Art. 505. When the prosecution of the voyage in its original direction is prevented by an accident, the master is at liberty either to continue the voyage in another direction, or to suspend it for a shorter or longer period, or to return to the port of departure, according to the circumstances and to the instructions received, which latter are to be adhered to as closely as possible.

In the case of the cancelling of the contract of affreightment he shall act according to the provisions of Art. 634.

Art. 506. Even in the cases referred to in Art. 504, the master has no right to conclude any business transaction upon the personal credit of the parties interested in the cargo, unless by virtue of a power of attorney authorising him to do so.

Art. 507. With the exception of the cases stated in Art. 504, the master has only the right to hypothecate the cargo, or to dispose of portions thereof by sale or conversion, when and in so far as it is necessary for the purpose of prosecuting the voyage.

Art. 508. If the necessity originates in a General Average, and if the master has an option of remedies, he shall take that alternative which entails the least detriment to the parties interested.

Art. 509. When the case is not one of a General Average, the master shall not take a bottomry bond on the cargo, or dispose of portions of the same by sale or conversion, unless he cannot provide for his requirements in any other way, or unless the adoption of other measures would cause a disproportionate damage to the owner.

In such cases, also, he can only hypothecate or take a bottomry bond on the cargo together with ship and freight. (Art. 681, par. 2.)

He shall resolve upon taking a bottomry bond in preference to sale, unless a disproportionate damage would be caused thereby to the owner.

Art. 510. Taking a bottomry bond on the cargo, or disposing of portions of the same by sale or conversion, shall be considered in the cases contemplated in the foregoing Article as credit transactions (Arts. 497 and 757, No. 7) entered into for account of the owner.

Art. 511. The enactments of Art. 497 are to be applied with respect to the validity of legal transactions entered into by the master in the cases contemplated by Articles 504 and 507-509.

Art. 512. The master does not require the special power of attorney, which may be prescribed by the laws of the various countries, in order to transact the legal and other business to which he is authorised by Articles 495, 496, 497, 499, 504, 507-509.

Art. 513. The master is bound to place to the credit of the owner's account every amount which, in addition to the freight, he may receive from the charterer, shipper, or consignee of the cargo, such as primage or anything in the shape of remuneration or gratuity, or under any denomination whatsoever.

Art. 514. The master shall take no goods on board for his own account without the consent of the owner. If he acts to the contrary, he shall pay to the owner the highest freight charged at the loading port for such voyages and goods at the time of shipment, without prejudice to the right of the owner of enforcing higher damages, which he may be able to prove.

Art. 515. The master can be discharged by the owner at any time, any agreement to the contrary notwithstanding, but without prejudice to his claim of indemnity.

Art. 516. When the master has been discharged because he has been found to be incapable, or because he neglects his duty, he shall receive only so much of his wages, including all other stipulated emoluments, as he has earned up to the time of his discharge.

Art. 517. When the master, who has been engaged for a particular voyage, is discharged, because such voyage cannot be commenced or be continued on account of war, embargo, or blockade, or on account of a prohibition of importation or exportation, or from any other accident happening to ship or cargo, he shall in such cases also receive only so much of his wages, including all other stipulated emoluments, as he has earned up to that time. The same rule applies when a master, appointed for an indefinite period, is discharged after he has undertaken the performance of a particular voyage.

If in any of the above cases the discharge takes place in the course of the voyage, the master is entitled at his option either to a free passage to the port where he has been engaged, or to a corresponding indemnity.

When a claim for a free return-passage is established according to the provisions of this code, it includes also the maintenance during the voyage.

Art. 518. When a master, who has been engaged for an indefinite period, is discharged for other reasons than those stated in Articles 516 and 517 after he has undertaken a particular voyage, he shall receive, besides what is due to him, according to the provisions of the last article, two months' wages if the discharge has taken place in a European port, or four months' wages if it has taken place in a non-European port.

In no case, however, shall he be entitled to more than he would have received if he had completed the whole of the voyage.

Art. 519. Should the pay have been fixed at a lump sum for the whole voyage, the wages earned in the cases contemplated by Articles 516–518 shall be calculated in proportion to the services rendered, to the part of the voyage actually performed, and to the lump sum originally fixed. As basis for the computation of the wages, with respect to the two or four months stipulated by Art. 518, shall be taken the average duration of the voyage, including the time of loading and discharging, due regard being had to the condition of the vessel.

Art. 520. When the return voyage of the vessel does not terminate in the port of registry, the master, who has been engaged for the voyage out and home, or for an unlimited period, shall receive a free return-passage to the port where he had been engaged, with his wages during the voyage, or at his option a corresponding indemnity.

Art. 521. When the master has been engaged for an unlimited period, he is bound as soon as he has entered upon a voyage to remain in such service until the vessel has returned to the port of registry, or to a home port, and its discharge has been completed.

He can, however, demand his discharge after two years' service from the date of his first departure, when the vessel at the time of his giving notice is in a European port, or after three years' service when it is in a non-European port. He shall in such a case allow the owner sufficient time to replace him, and continue his duties meanwhile, and, at all events, complete the current voyage.

If the owner immediately after receiving the notice has given orders for the return voyage, the master is bound to bring the vessel home.

Art. 522. If the master be dismissed against his will, the share which he may have in the vessel as part-owner by virtue of an agreement with the other owners, must at his demand be taken and paid for by the other owners at a valuation to be made by competent persons. This right of the master ceases if he unduly delays the notice that he intends to avail himself of it.

Art. 523. When after the commencement of the voyage the master is invalided or wounded, the owner has to bear the expenses of his care and restoration to health—

(1) If the master returns in the vessel, and if the return voyage terminates in the port of registry, or in the port where he has been hired, up to the termination of the return voyage.

(2) If he returns in the vessel and the voyage does not terminate in either of the aforesaid ports up to the expiration of six months after the termination of the return voyage.

(3) If it has been necessary to leave him behind ashore during the voyage, up to the expiration of six months after the time when the vessel has continued its voyage.

In the two latter cases he is also entitled to a free return-passage (Art. 517) or, at his option, to a corresponding indemnity.

When the master has been invalided or wounded after the commencement of the voyage, he shall receive, if he returns in the vessel, his wages, including all other stipulated emoluments, until the termination of the return voyage, and, if he has been left behind ashore, up to the day on which he leaves the vessel.

If the master has been injured in the defence of the vessel, he is besides entitled to a fair reward, which, if necessary, shall be fixed by the judge.

Art. 524. When the master dies after having entered upon his duties, the owner shall pay his wages, including all other stipulated emoluments, up to the day of his death; if death has occurred after the commencement of the voyage, the owner shall also bear the funeral expenses.

In case the master be killed in defence of the vessel, the owner shall besides make a fair compensation, which, if necessary, shall be fixed by the judge.

Art. 525. The provisions of Art. 453 are also to be applied to the claims mentioned in Articles 523 and 524.

Art. 526. The master shall take care to have the protest extended when the vessel has been lost, and in general he shall protect the interest of the owner as long as it is necessary. He shall, however, continue to receive during such period his wages and payment of the cost of maintenance. The owner is personally liable for such wages and such costs of maintenance. The master retains his claim to a free return-passage (Art. 517), or, at his option, to a corresponding indemnity, subject to the provisions of Art. 453.

Art. 527. This code does not affect the laws of the various countries as regards the qualifications required of the master.

FOURTH PART.[1]

As to the Crew.

Art. 528. The 'crew' comprises all officers of the ship except the master; and in like manner the word 'seaman' includes every ship's officer except the master.

Art. 529. The conditions of the agreement made with the crew shall be stated in the ship's articles.

Art. 530. When a seaman has been engaged after the articles have been drawn up, the stipulations made with the other seamen, according to the contents of the said articles, shall be applied to him in default of any arrangement to the contrary; he shall more especially be entitled only to the same wages which, according to the articles, are due to the other seamen of his class.

Art. 531. The obligation of the crew to go on board and enter upon their duties commences, unless any other agreement has been made, from the time of their engagement. The wages are to be paid from the same period, in default of any arrangement to the contrary.

Art. 532. The master can cause any seaman, who, after having been engaged, neglects to enter upon or continue to do his duties, to be forcibly compelled to perform the same.

Art. 533. The seaman shall unhesitatingly obey the orders of the master with regard to the service of the ship, and he shall at all times perform every work entrusted to him with regard to ship and cargo.

He shall be subject to the disciplinary power of the master. The further regulations concerning the disciplinary power of the master are reserved to the laws of the various countries.

Art. 534. The seaman shall not bring any goods on board without permission of the master. He shall pay the highest freight paid at the loading-port for such voyage and goods at the time of shipment for any

---

[1] The fourth part of the German General Mercantile Law, including *Arts.* 528–556, has been repealed by the law regarding ships' masters and seamen of December 27, 1872. (*Vide* translation, p. 790). But as in several parts of these enactments reference is made to statements contained in the old law, which would be unintelligible if not before the reader, these repealed articles are nevertheless reprinted.

goods shipped by him contrary to this prohibition, whether for himself or for others, without prejudice to any claims for higher damages that may be proved.

The master is also authorised to throw the goods overboard if they endanger the ship or cargo.

The laws of the various countries inflicting additional penalties upon any contravention of this prohibition are not affected by this enactment.

Art. 535. The seaman is bound, if so required, to assist at the extending of the protest and to confirm his deposition by oath.

Art. 536. In default of another agreement the wages shall not be paid to the seaman until after the termination of the voyage; or on his discharge, if the same takes place before that time. The laws of the various countries, and, in default thereof, the custom of the port of registry, shall determine what advances and payments on account shall be made before the commencement of and during the voyage.

Art. 537. The seaman shall not sue the master before a foreign law court. If he acts contrary to this provision he shall not only answer for the loss occasioned thereby, but he shall also forfeit the wages earned up to that time.

In cases of need he may apply to his country's consul, or to that consul who is authorised to act in his place, and in default of such to the consul of any other German State, in order to obtain a provisional decision.

Each party shall provisionally submit to the decision of the consul, without prejudice to the right of enforcing their claims, after the termination of the voyage, before the competent authority.

Art. 538. Unless the agreement contains provisions to the contrary, the seaman shall remain in the service during the whole of the voyage, including intermediate trips, if any, and until the termination of the return voyage.

If the return voyage does not terminate in the port of registry, he is entitled to a free return-passage (Art. 517) to the port where he has been engaged, and to the payment of his wages during the voyage, or, at his option, to a corresponding indemnity.

Art. 539. If, after the termination of the outward voyage, an intermediate voyage has been decided upon, or if an intermediate voyage has been terminated, the seaman may demand his discharge after two years from his engagement, if the vessel, at the time of his giving notice, is in a European port, or after three years if it is in a non-European port. On his discharge the seaman shall receive his wages earned up to that time, but no other indemnity.

But the discharge cannot be demanded when the return voyage has been ordered.

Art. 540. The foregoing Article does not apply when the seaman has engaged himself for a longer time.

An engagement for an unlimited period, or with the general condition that after the termination of the outward voyage the agreement shall be continued for all voyages that might be resolved upon, shall not be considered as an engagement for a longer time.

Art. 541. In default of another agreement, an increase of wages, if payable by time, shall take place for the seamen who shall have served since the outward voyage, in all cases where a vessel remains abroad longer than two years.

The amount of the increase shall be fixed by the laws of the various countries.

Art. 542. The engagement terminates when the owner loses the vessel through an unforeseen incident, more especially—

If it is lost by accident.

If it has been condemned as incapable or unworthy of repair (Art. 444), and if, in the latter case, it is sold, without delay, by public auction.

If it is captured by pirates.

If it is seized or detained and condemned as good prize.

In such a case the seaman shall not only receive the wages he may have earned, but also a free return-passage to the port where he has been engaged, or, at the option of the master, a corresponding indemnity.

He is bound to render assistance in salvage on continuation of his wages, and to assist in the extending of the protest, on payment of travelling expenses and for loss of time. The owner is personally liable for these expenses; but in all other respects he is only answerable subject to the provisions of Art. 453.

Art. 543. The master can, besides in the cases provided for in the agreement, discharge the seaman before the expiration of his time of service—

(1) As long as the voyage has not yet been commenced, if the seaman is incapable for the service for which he has engaged; if such incapacity is not found out until later, the master is entitled to disrate the seaman, and to lower his wages in proportion; the mate is excepted from this provision.

(2) If the seaman commits a gross offence against his duty, more especially if he is guilty of repeated disobedience or continued refractory conduct, of smuggling, or of any action subject to severe punishment.

(3) If the seaman is infected with syphilitic disease, or if, by doing a prohibited act, he has become invalided or wounded, and thereby incapacitated to work.

(4) If the voyage for which the seaman has been engaged cannot be commenced or continued on account of war, embargo, or blockade, or on account of a prohibition of exportation or importation, or on account of any other casualty happening to ship or cargo.

Art. 544. In the cases stated under Nos. 1-3 of Art. 543, the seaman is not entitled to more than the wasge earned; in the cases of No. 4 he is entitled, when the discharge occurs after the commencement of the voyage, not only to the wages earned but also to a free return-passage (Art. 517) to the port where he has been engaged, or, at the option of the master, to a corresponding indemnity.

The laws of the various countries subjecting the seaman to the loss of the wages earned in cases of violation of duty (No. 2) are not affected by the foregoing enactment.

It is also reserved to the laws of the various countries to permit the involuntary discharge of the seamen without any or with only partial indemnity in other cases than those stated in Art. 543.

Art. 545. A seaman engaged for the voyage who may be discharged before the termination of the contract for other reasons than those stated in Articles 543 and 544, shall, if the discharge takes place before commencing the voyage, retain as an indemnity the deposit and advances received, provided the sum is not above the amount usually so advanced.

When no deposits or advances have been given, he is entitled to one month's wages as an indemnity.

If the discharge occurs after the commencement of the voyage, he shall receive, besides the wages earned, two months' wages if he has been discharged in a European port, or four months' wages if he has been discharged in a non European port, but he shall not receive more than he would have been paid if he had only been discharged at the termination of the voyage.

He is, moreover, entitled to a free return-passage (Art. 517) to the port where he has been engaged, or, at the option of the master, to a corresponding indemnity.

Art. 546. When the wages have been fixed in a lump sum, the wages earned (Articles 537, 539, 542, 544, 545) and the wages for one, two, or four months (Art. 545) shall be calculated accor ing ot Art. 519.

Art. 547. The seaman is entitled to demand his discharge when the master is guilty of a gross violation of his duties towards him, more especially of severe ill-treatment, and of withholding food and drink without sufficient reason.

The seaman who takes his discharge for such a reason shall have the same claims as in the case contemplated by Art. 545.

The laws of the various countries may determine whether, and for what other causes, the seaman shall be entitled to demand his discharge.

The seaman demanding his discharge shall not quit the service in a foreign country without the consent of the competent consul (Art. 537).

Art. 548. If a seaman becomes invalided or wounded after having entered the service, the owner shall defray the expenses of his care and restoration—

(1) If the seaman on account of the disease or wound did not commence the voyage, up to the expiration of three months from the time he became invalided or wounded;

(2) If he enters upon the voyage and returns in the vessel to the port of registry, or the port where he has been engaged, up to the expiration of three months from the return of the ship;

(3) If he enters upon the voyage and returns in the vessel, but in case the voyage does not terminate in either of the aforesaid ports, then up to the expiration of six months from the return of the ship;

(4) If he had to be left behind ashore during the voyage, up to the expiration of six months from the time that the vessel has continued its voyage.

In the two latter cases the seaman is also entitled to a free return-passage (Art. 517) to the port where he has been engaged, or, at the option of the owner, to a corresponding indemnity.

Art. 549. The invalided or wounded seaman shall receive his wages—

If he does not commence his voyage, up to the time of discontinuing his duties;

If he enters upon the voyage and returns in the vessel, up to the termination of the return voyage;

If he had to be left behind ashore during the voyage, up to the day on which he leaves the vessel.

If the seaman has been injured in defence of the vessel, he is besides entitled to a fair reward, which, if necessary, shall be fixed by the judge.

Art. 550. The Articles 548 and 549 are not to be applied to seamen whose disease or wounds have been caused by their own prohibited acts or who are suffering from syphilitic complaints.

Art. 551. When a seaman dies after having entered the service, the owner shall pay the wages (Art. 546) earned up to the day of his death and defray the funeral expenses. When a seaman has been killed while defending the vessel, the owner has, in addition, to pay a fair compensation, which, if necessary, is to be fixed by the judge.

As regards the property left on board by the seaman who died during the voyage, the master shall make an inventory thereof, take care of the effects, and sell the same, if necessary.

Art. 552. The enactments of Art. 453 are equally applicable to the claims mentioned in Articles 548, 549, and 551.

Art. 553. It is reserved to the laws of the various countries to define the conditions without which no seaman can be left behind in a foreign country against his will, and, at the same time, to regulate the master's proceedings in such a case.

Art. 554. Persons not belonging to the crew, but appointed on board a vessel as engineers, stewards, or in any other capacity, shall, in so far as the contrary has not been agreed upon, be subject to the same rights and duties as have been enacted in this part with respect to the crew.

No difference shall be made whether they have been engaged by the master or by the owner.

Art. 555. The share in the freight or in the profits which may have been accorded to the seaman shall not be considered as wages in the sense of this part.

Art. 556. It is reserved to the laws of the various countries to complete the provisions of this part, as well with reference to the matter of wages mentioned in the foregoing Article as in other respects.

FIFTH PART.

Concerning Freight earned by the Conveyance of Goods.

Art. 557. The contract of affreightment for the conveyance of goods refers either—

(1) To the whole vessel, or to a proportionate part of, or to a specially defined space in, the same ; or,

(2) To single packages (general cargo).

Art. 558. When the whole vessel, or a proportionate part of, or a specially defined space in, the same, is being let, each party may demand that with respect to the contract a document in writing be executed (charter-party).

Art. 559. When a whole vessel is chartered, the cabin is not included, but without the consent of the charterer, no goods are allowed to be shipped in the same.

Art. 560. In case of a contract of affreightment of whatever nature the shipowner [1] is bound to deliver the vessel in a seaworthy condition (Art. 557).

He is answerable to the charterer for every damage arising from the defective condition of the vessel, unless the defects could not have been discovered in spite of all possible care.

Art. 561. The master shall, for the purpose of taking in the cargo, remove the vessel to the place assigned to him by the charterer, or, when the vessel has been chartered by more than one party, then by all the charterers.

The master shall remove the vessel to the loading-place customary at the port, if the aforesaid notice has not been given in time, or if the same place is not assigned by all the charterers, or if the depth of the water, the safety of the vessel, or the local regulations or arrangements do not permit compliance with their orders.

Art. 562. In default of an agreement to the contrary, or other regulations at the port of loading, or if none exist, then of other local customs, the goods shall be brought free alongside of the vessel by the charterer, while the expense of taking them into the vessel shall be borne by the shipowner.

Art. 563. The shipowner is bound to accept other goods tendered to him by the charterer for shipment to the same port instead of those originally agreed to, provided his position is not thereby altered to his disadvantage.

This provision does not apply when the goods have been specially named in the contract and not merely generally described by their class or sort.

Art. 564. The charterer or shipper who gives a wrong description of the goods shipped, or who ships contraband of war, or goods the exportation of which, or their importation into the port of destination, has been prohibited, or who violates at the shipment the legal regulations, and more especially the laws of police, excise, and customs—if any blame attaches to him—becomes, not only answerable for the delay caused

---

[1] The original expression is ' verfrachter,'—one who lets the vessel; the English language not having a word corresponding to this expression, I have taken ' shipowner ' to designate the party who in almost all cases is the only one justified to let a vessel either himself or through his legal representative.

through his conduct and for all other loss, to the shipowner, but also to all other parties mentioned in the first part of Art. 479.

His liability towards the other parties is not excluded by the fact of his having acted with the consent of the master.

The seizure of the goods gives him no right to refuse the payment of the freight. When the goods endanger the vessel or the remainder of the cargo, the master may land them, or, on urgent necessity, throw them overboard.

Art. 565. Whoever ships any goods on board without the knowledge of the master shall likewise be answerable for any damage resulting therefrom, in conformity with the foregoing Article. The master may reland such goods, or, if necessary, throw them overboard if they endanger the vessel and the rest of the cargo. When the master has kept them on board, they must pay the highest freight charged at the loading port, at the time of shipment, in respect to such voyages and goods.

Art. 566. Without permission being given by the charterer the shipowner is not at liberty to ship the goods in another vessel. If he acts contrary to this provision, he is answerable for all damages of which he does not prove that they would have arisen and remained at the debit of the charterer, even if the goods had not been shipped in another vessel.

This Article does not apply to transhipments in other vessels which in cases of distress take place after the commencement of the voyage.

Art. 567. Without the consent of the shipper his goods shall not be shipped on deck or suspended at the sides of the vessel.

It is reserved to the laws of the various countries to decree that the foregoing enactment, as far as it relates to deckloads, shall not apply to the coasting trade.

Art. 568. When the whole vessel has been chartered, the master shall inform the charterer as soon as he is ready and prepared to take the cargo on board.

The loading-days count from the day after that on which the notice has been given.

If so agreed, the shipowner shall wait for the cargo even beyond the loading-days (days on demurrage).

Unless an agreement to the contrary has been made, no extra remuneration can be demanded for the time fixed for loading. The charterer is, however, bound to pay the shipowner an indemnity for the extra time (demurrage).

Art. 569. If the loading-days have not been fixed by contract, they are determined by the local regulations at the port of shipment, and in default by the local custom. Should such local custom not exist, a fair period of time according to the circumstances of the case shall be taken as the time for loading.

When it has been contracted that a vessel shall wait beyond the lay-days on payment of demurrage, but when the duration of the time has not been fixed, it shall be taken at fourteen days.

When the contract contains only the sum payable for demurrage, it shall be considered that, although the vessel is bound to lie on demurrage, the duration of the time has not been settled.

Art. 570. When the duration of the loading-days, or the day on which they shall expire, has been fixed by agreement, the days on demurrage begin at once at the expiration of the loading-days.

In default of such agreement, the days on demurrage commence only after the shipowner has given notice to the charterer that the loading days have expired. The shipowner can give notice to the charterer even before the termination of the loading-days on what day he considers them expired. In this case no further notice on the part of the shipowner is required at the expiration of the loading-days and the beginning of the days on demurrage.

Art. 571. After the expiration of the loading-days, or in case a further term on demurrage has been agreed to, the shipowner, after the expiration of such term, is not obliged to wait any longer for the cargo. He is, however, bound to give to the charterer at least three days' notice before the expiration of the loading-days, or of the days on demurrage, of his intention not to wait any longer.

When this has not been done, the loading-days, or the days on demurrage, do not expire until the notice has been given and three days have elapsed subsequently to its delivery.

The three days mentioned in this Article shall in all cases be considered to mean running calendar days without interruption.

Art. 572. The notices of the shipowner, mentioned in Articles 570 and 571, need not be given in any particular form. When the charterer refuses satisfactorily to acknowledge the receipt of such a notice, the shipowner may cause a public document to be executed thereupon at the expense of the charterer.

Art. 573. When the demurrage has not been stipulated by contract, it shall be fixed by the judge at his discretion, and, if necessary, after examination of experts.

In fixing the demurrage, the judge shall take into consideration the merits of the case, more particularly the wages, the cost of keeping the crew, and the loss of freight falling upon the shipowner.

Art. 574. In calculating the loading-days and the days on demurrage they are counted as running days, without interruption ; more particularly are included Sundays and holidays, as well as those days on which the charterer is accidentally prevented from delivering cargo. Those days are, however, to be excluded on which, by reason of wind and weather, or from any other accident—

(1) The delivery to the vessel not only of the stipulated, but also of every description of cargo ; or,

(2) The taking in of the cargo

has been prevented.

Art. 575. The shipowner is entitled to demurrage for the days during which he has been longer detained owing to the delivery of any kind of cargo being prevented, even when such prevention has occurred during the loading-days. For those days, however, during which he has been detained in consequence of any prevention having arisen in the taking in of the cargo, no demurrage is due, even if such prevention has occurred during the days on demurrage.

Art. 576. When local regulations or local customs determine the duration of the loading-days according to Art. 569, the two foregoing Articles apply to the calculation of the same only so far as the local regulations or local customs do not decide anything to the contrary.

Art. 577. When the shipowner has stipulated that the loading must be finished by a certain day, he is not obliged to wait any longer because the delivery of every description of cargo (Art. 574, No. I) has been prevented.

Art. 578. In case the shipowner has to receive the cargo from a third party, and when such third party cannot be found, notwithstanding that the readiness of the shipowner to take the cargo on board has been made known in the manner customary at the place, or when such third party refuses to deliver the cargo, the shipowner shall at once inform the charterer thereof, and only wait for the cargo until the expiration of the loading-days, but not during the days on demurrage that may have been stipulated, unless he should receive instructions to the contrary within the loading-days from the charterer or his representative.

When an undivided period of time has been fixed for loading and discharging the vessel together, one-half of such period shall be considered in the above-mentioned case as the time stipulated for loading.

Art. 579. If required by the charterer, the shipowner is bound to enter upon the voyage even without the full cargo contracted for. In such a case, however, he shall not only receive the full freight and demurrage, if any, but he may also demand additional security for so much as the incomplete cargo does not offer sufficient security for the full freight. The charterer shall, besides, repay any additional expenses arising to the shipowner on account of the incompleteness of the cargo.

Art. 580. Should the charterer not have completed the delivery of the cargo at the expiration of the time during which the shipowner is bound to wait for the same (lay-days), the shipowner is at liberty, if the charterer does not withdraw from the contract, to commence the voyage, and to enforce the claims mentioned in the foregoing Article.

Art. 581. Before a voyage has been commenced, whether it be a single or a compound voyage, the charterer may withdraw from the contract, on paying one-half of the stipulated freight as dead freight.

In applying this provision, the voyage shall be considered as having been commenced—

    (1) When the charterer has already given the master his sailing orders;

    (2) When the charterer has already delivered the cargo wholly or in part, and the lay-days have expired.

Art. 582. When the charterer avails himself of the right mentioned in the foregoing Article after delivery of cargo, he shall likewise bear the expenses of loading and discharging, and pay demurrage for the time occupied by the quickest possible unloading, so far as it has not been completed within the period fixed for the loading (Art. 573).

The shipowner shall submit to the delay caused by such unloading even when it exceeds the stipulated time; he shall, however, be entitled to demurrage for the period after the expiration of the same, and to an indemnity for the loss occasioned through any such excess of time, provided that such loss can be proved to exceed the amount of such demurrage.

Art. 583. After the voyage has been commenced in the sense of Art. 581, the charterer can only withdraw from the agreement, and demand the unloading of the goods, on paying the full freight as well as all other claims of the shipowner (Art. 615), and on paying or securing the claims mentioned in Art. 616.

In case of such unloading the charterer shall not only pay the additional expenses thereby incurred, but also indemnify the shipowner for the loss caused by the delay.

The shipowner is not obliged to alter the voyage or to run into a port for the purpose of such unloading of the goods.

Art. 584. The charterer shall only pay two-thirds, instead of the full amount of the freight, as dead freight, in case the vessel has been chartered for the round, or when the vessel, for the purpose of performing the contract, has to make a voyage from another port in order to take in the cargo, and when in both these cases such withdrawal has been notified before commencement, in the sense of Art. 581, of the return voyage or the voyage out of the loading port.

Art. 585. In other compound voyages the shipowner shall receive the full amount of the freight as dead freight if the charterer declares such withdrawal previous to the commencement of the last part of the voyage in the sense of Art. 581 ; a fair portion shall, however, be deducted, if there is reason to suppose that, by the cancelling of the contract, the shipowner has saved expense, and has had an opportunity of earning another freight.

When the parties concerned cannot agree as to the deduction and as to its amount, the judge shall make an order according to the best of his judgment. But in no case shall such deduction exceed one-half of the freight.

Art. 586. When the charterer has delivered no cargo at the expiration of the waiting time, the shipowner is no longer bound by the contract, and is entitled to enforce against the charterer all such claims as he would have had if the charterer had withdrawn from the same (Articles 581, 584, 585).

Art. 587. The freight which the shipowner receives for other goods forming part of cargo shall not be deducted from the dead freight.

The provisions of the first part of Art. 585 are, however, not affected by this enactment.

The right of the shipowner to claim dead freight does not depend upon the actual performance of the voyage contracted for.

The right of the shipowner to demand demurrage and payment of all other claims which he may be entitled to make (Art. 615) is not excluded by the dead freight.

Art. 588. If a proportionate part or a specially defined space of the vessel has been chartered, the Articles 568-587 shall apply with the following modifications, viz.—

(1) In those cases where, in accordance with the foregoing enactments, the shipowner ought to have been satisfied with a portion of the freight, he shall receive the full freight as dead freight, unless all the charterers withdraw from the contract or deliver no cargo.

The freight for such goods, however, which the shipowner has engaged in lieu of those not delivered, shall be deducted from the full freight.

(2) In the cases contemplated by Articles 582 and 583, the charterer cannot demand the unloading of his goods if the voyage would thereby be delayed, or a transhipment be necessitated,

except with the consent of the whole of the charterers concerned. The charterer shall besides repay all costs and make good any loss caused by such unloading.

Should all charterers avail themselves of the right of such withdrawal, the provisions of Articles 582 and 583 remain in force.

Art. 589. When the contract of affreightment has been made for a general cargo, the charterers shall deliver the goods without delay, at the demand of the master.

If the charterer is behind time, the shipowner is not bound to wait for the delivery of the goods ; the charterer, nevertheless, being obliged to pay the full freight, if the voyage has been commenced without them. Allowance is, however, to be made for the freight of such goods as the owner has taken in lieu of those not originally delivered.

The shipowner intending to enforce such claim for the full freight against the charterer in arrear shall, under penalty of the loss of such claim, give notice to the charterer thereof previous to the departure of the vessel. The provisions of Art. 572 apply to the aforesaid notice.

Art. 590. The charterer can, after the shipment has been effected, withdraw from the contract, and demand the discharge of his goods on paying the full freight, as well as all other claims of the shipowner (Art. 615), and on paying or securing all such claims as mentioned in Art. 616, only in accordance with the first part of Art. 588, No. 2.

The provisions of the last paragraph of Art. 583 apply equally to these cases.

Art. 591. When a vessel is laid on the berth for a general cargo, and the time of departure has not been stipulated, the judge shall, on the application of the charterer, and according to the circumstances of the case, fix the date beyond which the commencement of the voyage cannot be delayed.

Art. 592. In all cases of contracts of affreightment, the charterer shall provide the master with all documents required for the shipment of his goods within the period during which such shipment ought to have been effected.

Art. 593. The master shall, for the purpose of discharging the cargo, remove the vessel to such place as is assigned to him by the party to whom the cargo is to be delivered (consignee), or, if the cargo is to be delivered to several parties, to such place as is assigned to him by all the consignees.

If the aforesaid order has not been given in due time, or if the same place is not assigned by all the consignees, or if the depth of the water, the safety of the vessel, or the local regulations or arrangements do not permit compliance with such orders, the master shall remove the vessel to such place of discharge as is customary at the port.

Art. 594. In default of an agreement to the contrary, or of other regulations at the port of discharge, or, if none exist, then, of other local customs, the expenses of unloading out of the vessel are to be borne by the shipowner, but all other expenses relating to the discharge are to be borne by the consignees of the cargo.

Art. 595. When the whole vessel has been chartered, the master shall give notice to the consignee as soon as he is ready and prepared to discharge.

Should the consignee be unknown to the master, the notice shall be given by public advertisement in the manner customary at the place.

The days for discharging commence with the day after that on which the notice has appeared.

Beyond the time fixed for discharging the shipowner has only to wait for the removal of the cargo, when an agreement has been made to that effect (days on demurrage).

Unless an agreement to the contrary has been made, no extra allowance can be demanded for the time fixed for the discharge. For the extra time, however, the shipowner is entitled to an indemnity (demurrage).

When the demurrage has not been settled by contract it shall be fixed by the judge in conformity with Art. 573.

Art. 596. If the days for discharging have not been fixed by contract they are to be determined by the local regulations at the port of discharge, and, in default, by the local custom. Should no such local custom exist, a fair period of time, according to the circumstances of the case, shall be taken as the days for discharging.

In case it has been contracted that a vessel shall wait beyond the lay-days on payment of demurrage, but the duration of such time on demurrage has not been fixed, it shall be taken at fourteen days.

When the contract contains only the amount payable for demurrage, it is to be presumed that, although the vessel is bound to lie on demurrage, the duration of such time has not been finally agreed upon.

Art. 597. Should the duration of the days for discharging, or the day on which they shall expire, have been fixed by agreement, the days on demurrage begin at once with the expiration of such days for discharging.

In default of such an agreement the days on demurrage commence only after the shipowner has given notice to the consignee that the days for discharging have expired. The shipowner can give notice to the consignee, even before the expiration of the days for discharging, on what day he considers them at an end. In this case no further notice on the part of the shipowner is required at the expiration of the days for discharging and at the beginning of the days on demurrage.

The provisions of Art. 572 apply to such notices required of the shipowner as are mentioned in this Article.

Art. 598. In calculating the days for discharging, and the days on demurrage, they are counted as running days without interruption, more particularly Sundays and holidays are included, as well as such other days on which the consignee had been accidentally prevented from receiving the cargo.

Excluded are, however, such days on which, by reason of wind and weather or by any other accident—

(1) The conveyance not only of the goods on board the vessel but of every description of cargo from the ship to the shore ; or,

(2) The unloading out of the vessel

has been prevented.

Art. 599. The shipowner is entitled to demurrage for all days during which he has been compelled to wait in consequence of an impossibility to convey any description of cargo from ship to shore, even should such prevention have occurred during the days stipulated for discharging. For those days, however, during which he has been compelled to wait in consequence of an impossibility to unload the vessel, no demurrage is due, even should such prevention have occurred during the days on demurrage.

Art. 600. When local regulations or local customs determine the duration of the days for discharging according to Art. 596, the two foregoing Articles apply to the calculation of the same only so far as the local regulations or local customs do not decide anything to the contrary.

Art. 601. In case the shipowner has stipulated that the discharge must be finished by a certain day, he is not obliged to wait any longer because the conveyance of any description of cargo from ship to shore (Art. 598, No. 1) has been prevented.

Art. 602. Should the consignee have declared his readiness to receive the goods but delays their reception beyond the time accorded to him, the shipowner may cause their deposit under legal custody or in any other safe manner, giving notice thereof to the consignee.

The master is bound to proceed as herein described, and to give at the same time notice thereof to the charterer, in case the consignee declines to take delivery of the goods or withholds any satisfactory answer upon the notice prescribed in Art. 595, or if the consignee is not to be found.

Art. 603. In so far as, by the delay of the consignee or by any proceeding caused by the depositing of the goods, the days for discharging have been exceeded without any fault of the master, the shipowner is entitled to demurrage (Art. 595), but without prejudice to his right to claim such higher damages as he may be able to prove for such detention, provided it does not come within the period which he has contracted to wait on demurrage.

Art. 604. The Articles 595-603 likewise apply if a proportionate part or a specially defined space of the vessel have been chartered.

Art. 605. The consignee of any general merchandise is bound to receive the same without any delay at the master's demand. In case the consignee is not known to the master such demand shall be made by public advertisement in the manner customary at the place.

The provisions of Art. 602 likewise apply in respect to the right and the obligation of the master to deposit the goods. The notice to the charterer prescribed in Art. 602 may be given by public advertisement in the manner customary at the place.

For those days by which, by the delay of the consignee, or by any proceeding caused by the depositing of the goods, the period within which the vessel ought to have been discharged has been exceeded, the shipowner is entitled to demurrage (Art. 595), without prejudice to his right to claim such higher damages as he may be able to prove.

Art. 606. If the whole vessel, or a proportionate part, or a specially defined space of the same, has been chartered, and the charterer has effected any re-charters for the conveyance of any general merchandise, the Articles 595-603 remain in force respecting the rights and duties of the original owner of the vessel.

Art. 607. The shipowner is answerable for any damage arising through loss of or injury to the goods, from the time of their being shipped until their delivery, unless he can prove that such loss or injury has been caused by the act of God (*vis major*), or by the natural condition of the goods, more particularly by *vice propre*, by diminution in quantity, by ordinary leakage, &c., or by such defective packing as could not be noticed externally.

Loss and injury arising from a defective condition of the vessel, which in spite of all possible caution could not be discovered (Art. 560, par. 2), are to be considered as loss and injury by the act of God.

Art. 608. The shipowner is not answerable for jewels, specie, and valuable documents, unless the description and value of the articles were declared to the master at the time of shipment.

Art. 609. Before the consignee has taken delivery of the goods, he, as well as the master, may, in order to ascertain their condition or quantity, cause a survey of them to be made by the competent authority, or by such surveyors as are officially appointed for the purpose

If circumstances permit, the adverse party, if on the spot, shall be summoned to attend at these proceedings.

Art. 610. When the survey was not effected before delivery was taken, the consignee is bound to cause a supplementary survey of the goods, in conformity with Article 609, to be held within forty-eight hours after the day of the delivery, under penalty of forfeiting all claims for damage or partial loss, no matter whether such loss and damage have been externally perceptible or not.

This clause does not apply to any losses and damages which may have been caused by a malicious act of a person belonging to a crew.

Art. 611. The expenses of the survey shall be borne by the party who has demanded the same.

Should, however, the survey take place at the request of the consignee, and should a loss or damage be ascertained, for which the shipowner is answerable, the expenses have to be borne by the latter.

Art. 612. When, in virtue of Art. 607, compensation has to be made for the loss of goods, such compensation shall only be for the value of the goods lost. This value shall be decided by the market price of goods of the same description and quality at the port of destination of the lost goods at the commencement of the discharge of the ship, or if the cargo is not discharged at that port, then at the time of her arrival. When no market price can be ascertained, or when doubts may arise as to such price or its applicability, more particularly as regards the quality of the goods, the value shall then be settled by competent persons. From the price shall be deducted freight, duties, and expenses saved in consequence of the loss of the goods.

When the port of destination of the goods is not reached, the place where the voyage ends is substituted, or if it ends by the loss of the ship, then the place to which the goods may be brought in safety.

Art. 613. The regulations of Art. 612 are also applicable to those goods for which the shipowner, according to Art. 510, must make compensation.

If, in a case where goods have been disposed of by sale, the net proceeds exceed the value according to Art. 612, then, in place of the latter value, the net proceeds are to be taken into calculation.

Art. 614. When compensation must be made for any damage to goods according to Art. 607, then only the deterioration in their value caused by the damage is to be made good. Such deterioration shall be considered equal to the difference between the market value of the goods in their damaged state—which is to be ascertained by competent persons—and the price stipulated in Art. 612 after deduction of Customs' duties and other expenses as far as they may have been saved in consequence of such damage.

Art. 615. By taking delivery of the goods, the consignee becomes liable to pay the freight and all other charges in conformity with the contract of affreightment or bill of lading, on the basis of which the delivery is made, and further to pay demurrage, if any, to refund Customs' duties and other advances, and besides to fulfil any other obligations devolving upon him.

The shipowner shall deliver the goods to the consignee on payment of the freight and on fulfilment of all other obligations.

Art. 616. The shipowner is not bound to deliver the goods before the amounts due from the same for general average, salvage, assistance, or bottomry have been paid, or security given for the amount.

If a bottomry bond has been given for account of the shipowner, the above regulation holds good in spite of the shipowner's obligation, to free the goods from their liability to the bottomry before they are delivered.

Art. 617. The shipowner is not obliged to accept the goods in payment for the freight, whether they are destroyed or damaged or not.

When, however, vessels [1] filled with liquids have leaked during the course of the voyage to such an extent that they have become altogether or for the most part empty, they may be left to the shipowner in payment of the freight and of his other claims (Art. 615).

By an agreement that the shipowner is not answerable for leakage or by the clause, 'free from leakage,' such right is not prejudiced, but it ceases altogether as soon as the packages have passed into the custody of the consignee.

Should the freight have been fixed in a lump sum, and only some packages totally or for the most part emptied, they can be left to the shipowner in proportionate payment of the freight and of his other claims.

Art. 618. No freight is due for goods lost by any accident, and any freight advanced shall be returned unless an agreement to the contrary has been made.

This provision applies also when the whole ship or a proportionate part or a specially defined space of the same has been chartered. If in such a case the freight has been stipulated in a lump sum, the loss of a part of the goods gives a right to a proportionate deduction from the freight.

[1] Barrels, casks or cases.

Art. 619. Notwithstanding any non-delivery, the freight must be paid for goods that have been lost in consequence of their natural condition (Art. 607), as well as for animals that have died during the voyage.

The provisions concerning General Average will enact to what extent restitution shall take place of the freight for goods sacrificed in cases of General Average.

Art. 620. For goods the conveyance of which has been undertaken without the freight having been agreed upon, the current freight shall be paid which rules in the port of loading at the time of shipment.

For goods beyond the quantity contracted for with the charterer which may have been accepted for conveyance, such freight shall be paid as is in proportion to the originally agreed freight.

Art. 621. When the freight has been stipulated for measure, weight, or quantity, it shall in doubtful cases be considered, that the measure, weight, or quantity delivered, not that taken in, shall decide the amount of freight due.

Art. 622. Primage, gratuities, &c., cannot be demanded in addition to the freight, unless they have been previously agreed upon.

The ordinary and extraordinary expenses of navigation, as: pilotage, harbour dues, light dues, towage, quarantine expenses, charges for cutting passages through the ice, &c., are to be borne by the shipowner alone, unless an agreement to the contrary was effected ; even if the contract of affreightment should not specially bind him to perform the acts causing this expenditure.

Cases of General Average, as well as cases where expenses are incurred for the preservation, saving, or rescuing of the cargo, are not included in this Article.

Art. 623. When a time charter has been entered into, it commences, in default of an agreement to the contrary, from the day following that on which the master has given notice that he is ready and prepared to take in cargo, or to proceed in ballast ; should, however, in the latter case, such notice not have been given on the day before proceeding on the voyage, the freight shall be paid from the day on which such voyage is commenced.

When demurrage or days on demurrage have been agreed upon, the freight per diem begins in all cases only from the day on which the voyage has been commenced.

The freight per diem terminates with the day on which the discharge has been completed.

When the voyage is delayed or interrupted without the fault of the shipowner, the freight must be continued to be paid for the intermediate period, subject to the provisions of the Articles 639 and 640.

Art. 624. A shipowner has a lien upon the goods for the claims mentioned in Art. 615.

The lien exists as long as the goods are retained or deposited ; it remains in force even after the delivery, if it is legally enforced within thirty days after the completion of such delivery ; it ceases, however, as soon as, previous to its judicial enforcement, the goods pass into the custody of a third party, who does not hold them on behalf of the consignee.

Art. 625. In case of a dispute concerning the claims of the shipowner, the latter is bound to give up the goods as soon as the sum in dispute has been deposited with a law court or any other authority or institution empowered to receive deposits.

After the delivery of the goods the shipowner is entitled to receive the sum so deposited, on giving sufficient security for it.

Art. 626. As long as the lien of the shipowner exists, the law court may, at his request, decree that the whole or a proportionate part of the goods be sold by public auction for the satisfaction of his claims.

The shipowner may exercise this right also against the other creditors and the assignees of any bankrupt proprietor of the goods.

Before the decree of sale is issued, the court shall give the interested parties, in case they are present at the place, an opportunity to be heard respecting such request of sale.

Art. 627. When the shipowner has parted with the goods, he cannot make the charterer responsible for any such claims as he may have against the consignee (Art. 615). Only in case the charterer would make a profit out of the loss of the shipowner can any allowance take place.

Art. 628. When the shipowner has not delivered the goods, and avails himself of the right stipulated in the first section of Art. 626, without, however, being fully compensated by the sale of such goods, he can make the charterer responsible for so much of his claim arising out of the contract of affreightment made between him and the charterer, as had not been previously satisfied.

Art. 629. In case the consignee does not take delivery of the goods, the charterer is obliged to satisfy the shipowner for the freight and his other claims, according to the contract of affreightment.

Should delivery of the goods be taken by the charterer, the Articles 593-626 apply in such a manner that the charterer takes the place of the consignee named in these articles. In such a case, the shipowner has more particularly the right of retention and lien in respect to his claims upon the goods, in conformity with Articles 624, 625, 626, as well as the right stipulated in Art. 616.

Art. 630. The contract of affreightment is at an end, and neither party is bound to indemnify the other, if, before the commencement of the voyage, and through an unforeseen incident—

(1) The vessel is lost, particularly—

If it is lost by accident.

If it has been condemned as incapable or unworthy of repair (Art. 444), and if, in the latter case, it is sold without delay by public auction.

If it is captured by pirates.

If it is seized or detained and condemned as good prize.

Or,

(2) The goods described not merely by their class or sort but specially defined in the contract of affreightment are lost.

Or,

(3) The goods, although not specially defined in the contract of affreightment, are lost after they have been delivered on board, or received by the master at the loading berth in order to be taken on board.

Should, however, in the last-mentioned case (No. 3) the loss of the goods have occurred within the lay-days (Art. 580), the contract is not to be considered at an end, in case the charterer has without delay declared his readiness to deliver other goods (Art. 563) instead of those lost, and commenced such delivery within the lay-days. He is bound to complete the shipment of such other goods within the shortest possible time, to bear any additional cost arising in consequence of any such shipment, and to indemnify the shipowner for any damage resulting therefrom in so far as the lay-days have been exceeded.

Art. 631. Either party can withdraw from the contract without being liable for damages—

(1) When before the commencement of the voyage—

The vessel is placed under embargo, or taken possession of for the service of the country or a foreign power.

The trade with the port of destination is prohibited.

The loading port or the port of destination is blockaded.

The exportation of the goods, to be shipped according to the contract of affreightment, from the port of loading, or their importation into the port of destination is prohibited.

The vessel is by a Government order prevented from putting to sea, or the voyage, or the transmission of the goods to be shipped according to the contract of affreightment, is prohibited.

In all foregoing cases, however, the Government order justifies the withdrawal from the contract, only when the impediment that has arisen is apparently not of short duration.

(2) When, before the commencement of the voyage, a war has been declared in consequence of which the vessel, or the goods to be shipped according to the contract of affreightment, or both, can no longer be considered free, and would be liable to risk of capture.

The exercise of the right granted to the charterer in Art. 563 is not excluded in such cases as are provided for by the above enactment.

Art. 632. The contract of affreightment is terminated when, after the commencement of the voyage, the vessel is lost by an unforeseen incident (Art. 630, No. 1).

The charterer shall, however, pay such proportion of the freight for the goods saved or rescued, as the actually performed part of the voyage may bear to the entire voyage (distance freight).

No claim for distance freight shall exceed the value of the goods saved.

Art. 633. In the calculation of the distance freight is to be taken into consideration not only the proportionate distance already performed to that still to be completed, but likewise the comparative proportion of expenditure in cost, time, danger, and labour ordinarily connected with the part of the voyage already performed to that still to be completed.

Should the parties not be able to agree on the amount of the distance freight due, the judge has to decide upon it at his discretion.

Art. 634. The dissolution of the contract of affreightment alters nothing in the obligation of the master to take care of the cargo in the absence of the parties interested, even after the loss of the vessel (Articles 504-506). The master is, therefore, justified and obliged, and in urgent cases even without previous inquiry, as circumstances may require, either to forward the cargo to the port of destination in another vessel for account of the parties concerned, or to have it stored, or sold, and, in case of its being forwarded, or stored, to sell a portion thereof for the purpose of realising the funds necessary thereto and to its preservation, or in case of its being forwarded, to take a bottomry bond on the whole or a part of it.

The master is, however, not obliged to part with the cargo, or to deliver it to another master for the purpose of its being forwarded, unless the distance freight as well as all other claims of the shipowner (Art. 615), and the contributions due from the cargo for General Average, salvage and assistance, and bottomry, have been paid or secured.

The shipowner is responsible for the fulfilment of the duties devolving on the master according to the first section of this Article, to the extent of the value of the ship, so far as anything has been saved of it, and of the freight.

Art. 635. When the goods are lost by any accident after the commencement of the voyage, the contract of affreightment is at an end, without either party being liable to damages ; the freight especially shall not be paid either totally or partially unless the contrary has been enacted by law (Art. 619).

Art. 636. When, subsequent to the commencement of the voyage, any of the incidents occur to which reference is made in Art. 631, either party has a right to withraw from the contract without being liable to damages.

When, however, any of the incidents mentioned in Art. 631, No. 1, have occurred, the parties have, before being able to withdraw, to wait for the removal of the impediment, three or five months respectively, according as the vessel is in a European or in a non-European port.

Such period shall be calculated from the day of receiving notice of the impediment, if the master is then at a port, or from that day on which, after having received such notice, he first reaches a port with the vessel.

The discharge of the vessel shall, in default of an agreement to the contrary, take place at the port at which it is staying at the time of the receipt of the notice of withdrawal.

The charterer is bound to pay distance freight for such portion of the voyage as is actually performed (Articles 632, 633).

When, in consequence of such impediment, the vessel has returned to the port of departure or to any other port, in calculating the distance freight the nearest point to the port of destination, which the vessel had reached, shall be taken as the basis for ascertaining the distance actually performed.

The master is likewise bound to act, in any such cases, before and after the dissolution of the contract of affreightment, in the interest of the cargo, in conformity with the Articles 504–506 and 634.

Art. 637. When the vessel, after taking in its cargo, is detained in the port of loading before the commencement of the voyage, or in an intermediate port or in a port of refuge after its commencement, by any of the emergencies mentioned in Art. 631, then the expenses of such detention (even if the requirements of General Average are not present) are divided among ship, freight, and cargo, according to the principles of General Average, whether the contract is thereby put an end to, or afterwards completely fulfilled. The expenses of the detention include all the expenses enumerated in the second clause of Art. 708, No. 4; but those of putting into and leaving port only when the vessel has put into a port of refuge on account of the obstacle.

Art. 638. When, before the commencement of the voyage, only part of the cargo has met with an incident, which, if it had extended over the whole cargo, would, according to Articles 630 and 631, have dissolved the contract, or have entitled the parties to withdraw from it, the charterer is only authorised either to ship other goods instead of those contracted for, provided the shipowner is not placed at a disadvantage by carrying them (Art. 563), or to withdraw from the contract on payment of one-half of the stipulated freight, and all other claims of the shipowner (Articles 581 and 582). In exercising these rights, the charterer is, however, not bound to observe the time otherwise prescribed. But he is bound to declare without delay which of these two alternatives he intends to adopt, and if he decides upon the shipment of other goods, to effect the same within the shortest possible time, as well as to pay any additional expenses of such shipment, and, should the lay-days have been exceeded, to make good the damage arising to the shipowner in consequence thereof.

When he avails himself of neither of these alternatives, he must pay the full freight for that part of the cargo to which the incident applies. At all events, he is bound to take out of the ship that part of the cargo which is no longer free in consequence of war, prohibition of importation and exportation, or of a Government order.

When the incident occurs after the commencement of the voyage, the charterer shall pay the full freight for such portion of the cargo as is concerned therein, even when the master has been compelled to discharge such portion in a different port from the port of destination, and when he has subsequently continued the voyage with or without delay.

The provisions of Articles 618 and 619 are not affected by this Article.

Art. 639. The delay of the voyage caused by natural events or other incidents before or after its commencement has, except in the cases of Articles 631–638, no influence upon the rights and duties of the contracting parties, unless the apparent object of the contract should thereby have been frustrated.

The charterer is, however, authorised, during every delay caused by an incident, and which appears likely to be of considerable duration, to discharge the goods already laden in the ship at his own risk and expense, and on giving security for their being re-shipped in good time. If he omits to re-ship, he is bound to pay the full freight. In any case he is answerable for all damages occasioned by any discharge originated by him. In case the delay has arisen by a Government order, no freight shall be paid during such delay, if the ship was under time charter (Art. 623).

Art. 640. In case the vessel must be repaired during the voyage, the charterer may, at his option, either take delivery of the whole cargo at the place where the vessel is staying on paying the full freight and the other claims of the shipowner (Art. 615) and on paying or securing the claims stated in Art. 616, or he may wait until the repairs have been completed. In the latter case no freight is due under a time charter during the progress of the repairs.

Art. 641. Should the contract of affreightment be dissolved pursuant to Articles 630–636, the expenses of unloading from the vessel are borne by the shipowner, and all other expenses of the discharge by the charterer. When, however, the cargo only has been affected by the incident, the whole of the expenses of the discharge are borne by the charterer. The same rule applies if, in the case of Art. 638, part of the cargo is discharged. When, in such a case, it was necessary to put into a port for the purpose of discharging, the charterer shall also bear the port charges.

Art. 642. The Articles 630–641 apply likewise, should the vessel have to proceed in ballast to the port of shipment for the purpose of taking in the cargo. In this case, however, the voyage is not considered to have begun before it has actually commenced from the loading port. Has the contract been dissolved subsequently to the vessel having reached the loading port, but before the actual commencement of the voyage thence, the shipowner shall receive for the ballast voyage an indemnity to be fixed according to the principles of distance freight (Art. 633).

In other cases of compound voyages the above Articles shall apply, unless the nature and contents of the contract stipulate anything to the contrary.

Art. 643. Should the contract not extend to the whole of the vessel, but only to a proportionate part, or to a specially defined space of the same or to a general cargo, the Articles 630–642 apply, subject to the following modifications, viz.—

> (1) In the cases of Articles 631 and 636 either party is justified in withdrawing from the contract immediately after the occurrence of the impediment and without regard to its duration.

(2) In the case of Art. 638 the charterer cannot exercise the right of withdrawing from the contract.

(3) In the case of Art. 639, the charterer has only the right of temporary discharge when all other charterers give their consent.

(4) In the case of Art. 640, the charterer can only take delivery of the goods, on payment of the full freight and all other claims, if during the repairs these goods had at any rate to be discharged.

The provisions of Articles 588 and 590 are not affected by this enactment.

Art. 644. After the completion of each separate shipment the master shall sign without delay and on return of the provisional receipt that may have been given on delivery of the goods, as many bills of lading as the shipper may demand.

All copies of the bills of lading must be identical, bear the same date, and state how many copies have been issued. The master is entitled to demand from the shipper a copy of the bill of lading bearing the latter's signature.

Art. 645. The bill of lading contains—

(1) The name of the master.
(2) The name and nationality of the vessel.
(3) The name of the shipper.
(4) The name of the consignee.
(5) The port of lading.
(6) The port of discharge, or the place at which orders for the same are to be obtained (port of call).
(7) The description, quantity, and marks of the goods shipped.
(8) The stipulations respecting the freight.
(9) The place and date on which it has been issued.
(10) The number of the copies issued.

Art. 646. When no agreement to the contrary has been made, the bill of lading can be issued at the demand of the shipper to the order of the consignee or simply to order. In the latter case, the word 'order' means the order of the shipper.

The bill of lading may also name the master as consignee.

Art. 647. The master is bound to deliver the goods at the port of discharge to the legal holder of even only one copy of the bill of lading. The party who is designated as consignee in the bill of lading, or to whom the bill of lading, in case it is issued to order, has been transferred by endorsement, is to be considered as legally entitled to receive the goods.

Art. 648. Should several legal holders of bills of lading apply for such goods, the master shall refuse delivery to all of them, deposit the goods under legal custody or in some other safe manner, and inform thereof those holders of the bills of lading who did apply, stating the reasons for such proceedings.

In case the goods are not deposited in legal custody, the master may cause a public document to be executed stating his proceedings and his reasons for the same, and the outlay thereby occasioned is to be recovered from the goods in the same manner as the freight (Art. 626).

Art. 649. The act of handing over bills of lading issued to order, to the parties who would thereby be authorised to take delivery, after having actually shipped the goods therein specified, is of the same legal consequences respecting the acquisition of the rights depending on the delivery of the goods as the delivery of the goods themselves.

Art. 650. In case several copies of a bill of lading to order have been issued, the holder of one of them cannot enforce the legal rights acquired by the foregoing Article through its transfer, to the prejudice of a party who on production of another copy obtained delivery of the goods from the master in conformity with Art. 647, before the holder of the copy first referred to has claimed their delivery.

Art. 651. Should several holders of bills of lading present themselves before the master has parted with the goods, the latter shall, in so far as their rights arising out of the bills of lading are irreconcilable one with the other, give the preference to that holder whose bill of lading was first received from the common endorser of all of them in such a way as to authorise his taking possession of the goods.

When a copy has been sent to another place, the time of so dispatching it is to be considered the time of delivery.

Art. 652. The master is only obliged to deliver the goods on return of a copy of the bill of lading upon which the delivery of the said goods is duly certified.

Art. 653. The bill of lading is decisive for the legal position of the shipowner and the consignee of the goods towards each other; more especially the delivery of the goods to the consignee shall take place in accordance with the contents of the bill of lading.

Provisions of the contract of affreightment not embodied in the bill of lading have no legal effect as against the consignee, unless special reference has been made to them. When such reference has been made respecting the freight to the contract of affreightment (for instance, by the words 'freight as per charter-party') the stipulations as to the time for discharging, the days on demurrage and the demurrage are not considered to be therein included.

As regards the legal position of the shipowner and the charterer towards each other, the clauses of the contract of affreightment remain conclusive.

Art. 654. The shipowner is responsible to the consignee for the correctness of the description of the goods shipped, as contained in the bill of lading. This liability is, however, limited to the payment of such difference of value as may appear between the actual state of the goods and their description in the bill of lading.

Art. 655. The liability of the shipowner as stipulated in the foregoing article likewise takes effect in case the goods have been delivered to the master in packing, or in closed packages.

Should this be at the same time apparent from the bill of lading, the shipowner is not responsible to the consignee for the correctness of the description of the goods therein contained, provided he proves that notwithstanding the proper attention of a careful master, such incorrectness of the description in the bill of lading could not have been found out.

The liability of the shipowner is not removed by the fact that the identity of the goods delivered with those received may not be disputed, or that the same may be proved by the shipowner.

Art. 656. Should any goods be delivered to the master packed or in closed packages, he may add on the bill of lading the words 'Contents unknown.'

When the bill of lading contains these or any other words to the same effect, the shipowner is, in case of any difference between the contents delivered, and those stated in the bill of lading, only so far answerable as it is proved against him, that he really received other contents than those delivered.

Art. 657. Unless the goods described in the bill of lading by number, measure or weight, have been really counted, measured or weighed to the master on delivery, he may add on the bill of lading the words 'Number, measure, weight unknown.' When the bill of lading contains these or words to the same effect, the shipowner is not answerable for the correctness of the statements in the bill of lading respecting the number, measure, or weight of the goods delivered to him.

Art. 658. In case the freight has been stipulated by number, measure, or weight, and when such number, measure, or weight has been stated in the bill of lading, such statement shall be taken as the basis for the calculation of the freight, unless the bill of lading contains a provision to the contrary. The words 'Number, measure, weight unknown,' or others to the same effect, are not considered to be such provisions to the contrary.

Art. 659. Should the bill of lading contain the clauses, 'Free from breakage,' or 'Free from leakage,' or 'Free from damage,' or any other addition to the same effect, the shipowner is not answerable for breakage or leakage or damage, unless it can be proved to have been caused by the fault of the master or another person for whom the shipowner is responsible.

Art. 660. In case any goods have been delivered to the master which are visibly damaged, in bad condition, or badly packed, he has to state these defects in the bill of lading; otherwise he is responsible to the consignee, although the bill of lading may contain one of the clauses mentioned in the foregoing Article.

Art. 661. After a bill of lading has been issued to order, the master cannot comply with any instructions of the shipper concerning the returning or delivery of such goods, unless all copies of such bill of lading are returned to him.

The same rule applies to any demand made by any holder of a bill of lading for delivery of goods previous to the arrival of the master at the port of destination.

Should he act in contravention of these provisions, he remains liable to any legal holder of the bill of lading.

In case the bill of lading has not been issued to order, the master shall return or deliver such goods even without the production of a copy of the bill of lading, if the shipper and the consignee named in such bill of lading have expressed their proper consent to the returning or the delivery of such goods. When, however, all the copies of the bill of lading are not returned, the master can previously demand security for any losses which might arise in consequence thereof.

Art. 662. The provisions of Art. 661 apply likewise when the contract of affreightment is dissolved, before the port of discharge has been reached, in consequence of any incident contemplated by Articles 630-643.

Art. 663. The enactments of Articles 478, 479, and 502 remain applicable as regards the liabilities of the master upon any contracts of affreightment concluded and any bills of lading issued by him.

Art. 664. In case any sub-contracts of affreightment have been concluded, the shipowner, and not the party letting the ship under such sub-contracts, is answerable to the extent of ship and freight for the fulfilment of the sub-contract of affreightment in so far as its execution belongs to the proper functions of the master and has been so undertaken by him, particularly in consequence of his receiving goods and issuing bills of lading (Art. 452).

Whether, and how far, the shipowner, or the party letting the ship under such sub-contract, can be made answerable by the sub-charterer in all other respects, and whether in the latter case the party letting the ship under such sub-contract is, without limitation, answerable for its fulfilment, or whether he only assumes the limited liability of the owner to the extent of ship and freight, shall not be affected by the foregoing enactments.

SIXTH PART.

Concerning all Matters relating to Freight for the Conveyance of Passengers.

Art. 665. Should the passenger have been named in the passage contract he is not entitled to transfer the right of passage to another party.

Art. 666. The passenger is bound to comply with all instructions of the master concerning the rules on board the vessel.

Art. 667. The passenger who, before or after the commencement of the voyage, does not go on board in due time, shall pay the full passage-money, even if the master commences or continues the voyage without waiting for him.

Art. 668. When, previous to the commencement of the voyage, the passenger gives notice of withdrawal from the passage contract; or when he dies, or when he is compelled by illness or any other incident happening to his person to remain behind, one-half only of the passage-money shall be paid.

When, after the commencement of the voyage, notice of withdrawal is given, or any of the incidents mentioned above occurs, the passage-money shall be paid in full.

Art. 669. The passage contract becomes null and void when the vessel is lost in consequence of a casualty (Art. 630, No. 1).

Art. 670. The passenger may withdraw from the passage contract, when in consequence of a war breaking out, the vessel cannot any longer be considered as free, and would be exposed to the risk of capture, or if the ship's voyage should be delayed by a Government order. The shipowner has likewise the right of withdrawal when, in either of the above cases, he gives up the voyage, or when the vessel is intended principally for the transport of goods, and the adventure cannot be undertaken, because, without any fault on his part, such goods cannot be forwarded.

Art. 671. In all cases in which pursuant to Articles 669 and 670 the passage contract is dissolved, neither party is liable to damages.

When, however, such dissolution takes place after the commencement of the voyage, the passenger shall pay passage-money in proportion of the performed part of the voyage to the whole.

In calculating the amount due the provisions of Art. 633 are decisive.

Art. 672. In case the vessel has to be repaired during the voyage, the passenger shall pay the passage-money in full, although he may not wait for the completion of the repairs. Should he wait for the completion of the same, the shipowner has to provide him with free lodging until the voyage is resumed, and is likewise bound to continue to fulfil his obligations as to subsistence in conformity with the passage contract.

When, however, the shipowner offers to convey the passenger to the place of destination by another vessel equally good, and without prejudice to any further rights, and the passenger refuses to accept such offer, he has no further claim to be provided with lodging and board until the resumption of the voyage.

Art. 673. Beyond the passage-money the passenger shall not pay separately for the conveyance of luggage which, according to the contract, he is entitled to bring on board, unless an agreement to the contrary has been made.

Art. 674. The provisions of the Articles 562, 594, 618 apply to any passenger's luggage brought on board.

When the same has been received by the master or a third party especially appointed thereto, the provisions of the Articles 607, 608, 609, 610, 611 apply in case of loss or damage.

The Articles 564, 565, 566, and 690 apply likewise to all articles brought on board by the passenger.

Art. 675. The shipowner has a lien for the passage-money on any articles brought on board by the passenger. This lien exists, however, only so long as such articles are retained or deposited.

Art. 676. Should the death of any passenger occur, the master shall, according to the circumstances of the case, properly protect the interests of the heirs as to the effects on board.

Art. 677. When a vessel is chartered to a third party for the conveyance of passengers, no matter whether wholly or partially, or in such a manner that a certain number of passengers shall be carried, the enactments of the fifth part apply as regards the legal relations between the shipowner and such third party as far as the nature of the case admits.

Art. 678. When, in the following parts of this book, reference is made to the freight, it shall be considered to comprise also the passage-monies, unless the contrary is enacted.

Art. 679. The laws of the various countries concerning matters of emigration, even where they contain enactments of civil law, are not affected by the enactments of this part.

SEVENTH PART.

Concerning Bottomry.

Art. 680. Bottomry, in the sense of this code, is a loan transaction concluded by the master as such, by virtue of the rights granted to him in this code, under promise of a premium, and under hypothecation of ship, freight, and cargo, or of one or more of these objects, in such a manner that the creditor can enforce his claims only to the extent of the hypothecated (bottomried) objects after the arrival of the vessel at the place where the voyage for which the transaction has been concluded shall terminate (bottomry voyage).

Art. 681. Bottomry transactions may only be concluded by the master in the following cases, viz.—

(1) While the vessel is away from the port of registry, for the purpose of completing the voyage, in conformity with Articles 497, 507–509, and 511.

(2) During the voyage in the sole interest of the parties concerned in the cargo, for the purpose of preserving and forwarding the same in conformity with Articles 504, 511, and 634.

In the case of No. 2 the master may take bottomry on the cargo alone; in all other cases he may take bottomry for the ship or the freight alone, but for the cargo only together with ship and freight.

When a bottomry bond is given on the ship without naming the freight, the latter is not considered as included. When, however, a bottomry bond on ship and cargo is given, the freight is considered to be included in the same.

A bottomry bond on the freight is admissible as long as the latter is exposed to any sea risk.

A bottomry bond can likewise be given for the freight of that part of the voyage which has not yet been commenced.

Art. 682. The amount of the bottomry premium may without any restriction be agreed upon by the contracting parties.

In default of an agreement to the contrary the premium includes the interest likewise.

Art. 683. A bottomry bond shall be executed by the master concerning the bottomry transaction. Should this not have been done the creditor has the same rights as he would have if the master had entered into a simple credit transaction for the purpose of supplying any of his requirements.

Art. 684. The bottomry lender can demand that the bottomry bond shall contain—
  (1) The name of the bottomry creditor.
  (2) The amount of the principal of the bottomry debt.
  (3) The amount of the bottomry premium, or the total amount of the sum payable to the creditor.
  (4) The description of the objects hypothecated by the bond.
  (5) The description of the vessel and the master.
  (6) The bottomry voyage.
  (7) The time at which the bottomry debt shall be paid.
  (8) The place where the payment shall be made.
  (9) The designation of the document as bottomry bond embodied in the document itself, or the declaration that the debt has been contracted as a bottomry debt, or any other declaration sufficiently showing the transaction to be of the nature of bottomry.
  (10) The circumstances which have necessitated the entering into the bottomry transaction.
  (11) The date and place where the document has been executed.
  (12) The signature of the master.

The signature of the master shall be certified if required.

Art. 685. Unless the contrary has been agreed upon, the bottomry bond shall, at the demand of the bottomry lender, be executed to the order of the creditor, or simply to order. In the latter case the word 'order' signifies the order of the bottomry lender.

Art. 686. When the necessity of concluding the transaction has been established previous to the execution of the bottomry bond, by a document from the consul of the country, or from the consul authorised to act for the same, or in default of such consul from any court of law or any other competent authority, of the place of execution, or, in case neither of these exist, from the officers of the vessel, it shall be considered that the master has been duly authorised to conclude the transaction to the extent in question.

Evidence to the contrary, however, shall be admissible.

Art. 687. The bottomry lender can demand the execution of several copies of the bottomry bond.

Should several copies have been issued, the number of such copies has to be stated in each of them.

The bottomry bond is transferable by endorsement, if it has been made out to order.

The plea that the master had not been authorised to enter into the transaction at all, or to the extent in question, is admissible also against the holder by endorsement.

Art. 688. Unless an agreement to the contrary has been made in the bottomry bond itself, the bottomry debt is payable at the port of destination of the bottomry voyage and on the eighth day after the arrival of the vessel in that port.

From the day when it falls due mercantile interest becomes payable upon the whole bottomry debt including the premium.

The foregoing provision does not apply when the premium has been stipulated by time; the time premium runs, however, until the payment of the principal of the bottomry debt has been effected.

Art. 689. The payment of the bottomry debt when due cannot be refused to the legal holder of even only one copy of the bottomry bond.

Such payment can only be demanded upon return of such copy, on which the customary receipt for the payment is to be attached.

Art. 690. In case several legal holders of any bottomry bond apply for payment, such payment shall be refused; the amount shall, in case it is required to obtain possession of the bottomried objects, be deposited with a court of law, or in any other safe manner; and those holders of any bottomry bond who have applied shall be informed of the course taken and of the reasons for the same.

Should such amount not have been deposited with a court of law, the depositor may cause a public document to be issued respecting his proceedings, and his reasons for the same, and he may deduct the expenses thereby occasioned from the bottomry debt.

Art. 691. The bottomry creditor is not liable to contribute to General or Particular Average.

In case, however, the bottomried objects become, by reason of General or Particular Average, insufficient for the payment of the bottomry creditor, he shall bear the loss thereby caused.

Art. 692. All the bottomried objects are jointly and severally liable to the bottomry creditor.

After the arrival of the vessel at the port of destination of the bottomry voyage, the creditor can apply for an arrest of all bottomried objects even before his claim becomes due.

Art. 693. The master shall care for the safe keeping and preservation of the bottomried objects; he shall not without urgent reasons commit any act whereby the risk of the bottomry creditor is increased or altered from what he might anticipate when entering into the contract.

If he acts contrary to these provisions he is answerable to the bottomry creditor for the damage thereby arising (Art. 479).

Art. 694. When the master has arbitrarily changed the bottomry voyage, or when he has arbitrarily deviated from the proper course, or when after its termination he has again exposed the bottomried object to sea risks without having been compelled to do so in the interests of the creditor, the master is personally answerable to the creditor for the bottomry debt, so far as the latter does not receive his payment out of the bottomried objects, unless he proves that the non-payment has not been caused through the change of the voyage or through the deviation or through the new sea risk.

Art. 695. The master shall not deliver the bottomried cargo, either entirely or partially, before the creditor has been paid or properly secured, otherwise the master is personally answerable to the creditor for the bottomry debt so far as he could, at the time of their delivery, have been paid by the goods so given up.

Until the contrary has been proved it shall be considered that the creditor could have been paid in full.

Art. 696. When in the cases of Articles 693, 694, 695 the master has acted by directions from the shipowner, the provisions of the second and third sections of Art. 479 shall apply.

Art. 697. If the amount of bottomry is not paid when due, the creditor may apply to the proper court to order the sale of the ship and cargo on which bottomry has been taken, as also to hand over the bottomried freight.

The action shall be brought, as far as the ship and freight are concerned, against the master or owner; as to the cargo, if before its delivery against the master, after its delivery against the consignee, so long as it is in his own possession, or in the custody of any person holding it for his account.

The creditor can make no use of his rights to the prejudice of a third party who has *bond fide* become possessor of the bottomried cargo.

Art. 698. The consignee, to whom it is known on taking delivery of any bottomried goods, that they are liable for a bottomry debt, becomes personally answerable to the creditor for the debt to the extent of the value which the goods had at the time of their delivery, so far as the creditor could have been paid out of the goods if the delivery had not taken place.

Art. 699. When the adventure is given up before the commencement of the bottomry voyage, the creditor may demand immediate payment of the bottomry debt at the place at which such bottomry has been taken; he must, however, be satisfied with a proportionate reduction of the premium ; in fixing such reduction the proportion of the danger sustained to that undertaken shall be principally considered.

When the bottomry voyage does not terminate in the port of destination, but in another port, the bottomry debt must be paid in the latter port without deduction from the premium, after the expiration of the stipulated time for payment or, in default of any agreement, after the expiration of eight days (Art. 688). Such time of payment to be calculated from the definite abandonment of the voyage.

The Articles 689–698 apply likewise to the foregoing cases where the contrary is not enacted by this Article.

Art. 700. The application of the provisions of this part is not affected by the master being part owner or sole owner of the vessel or of the cargo, or of both of them, or by his having entered into the bottomry transaction upon special instructions from the parties concerned.

Art. 701. It is reserved to the legislation of the various countries to introduce regulations respecting irregular bottomry transactions, *i.e.* such as may not have been entered into by the master as such in the cases contemplated by Art. 681.

EIGHTH PART.

Concerning Average.

First Division.—General Average and Particular Average.

Art 702. All damage intentionally done to ship or cargo, or both, by the master or by his orders, for the purpose of saving both from a common danger, together with any further damage occasioned by such measures and likewise expenses incurred for the same purpose, are General Average.

General Average is borne by ship, freight and cargo in common.

Art. 703. All losses and expenses not belonging to General Average but caused by an accident are Particular Average, as far as they do not come under Art. 622.

Particular Average is borne by the owners of the ship and cargo respectively, each for himself alone.

Art. 704. The application of the rules for General Average is not debarred by the fact that the danger has been occasioned by the fault of a third party, or even of one of the parties interested in the adventure.

The party interested who is in fault can, however, not only make no demand for compensation on account of any damage which is thereby sustained, but is likewise answerable to each contributor for the loss which he suffered through such damage being apportioned as General Average.

Should the danger have arisen through the fault of one of the crew, the owner is likewise answerable for the consequences subject to the conditions of Articles 451 and 452.

Art. 705. Average contribution takes place only when the ship as well as the cargo, each either wholly or in part, have been actually saved.

Art. 706. The obligation to contribute on the part of an article which has been saved is only then completely annulled when the article, owing to its having subsequently suffered Particular Average, is entirely destroyed.

Art. 707. The right to compensation for damage belonging to General Average is only so far set aside by a Particular Average subsequently affecting the damaged article (whether this be again damaged or totally destroyed) as it is proved that the latter accident not only was entirely independent of the former but would have likewise carried with it the former damage if this had not already taken place.

If, however, before the occurrence of the latter accident steps should already have been taken to reinstate the damaged article, then the claim for reimbursement holds good as far as such steps are concerned.

Art. 708. The following cases in particular are General Average, always supposing that the requirements of Articles 702, 704 and 705 are complied with so far as there is nothing to the contrary specially directed by this Article :—

(1) When goods, portions of the ship, or articles belonging thereto, are thrown overboard, masts are cut away, ropes or sails cut adrift, anchors, hawsers, or chain-cables slipped or cut away.

These damages, as well as any further damages caused to ship or cargo by such acts, belong to General Average.

(2) When, in order to lighten the vessel, the cargo or part of it has been discharged into lighters.

To General Average belong as well the hire of the lighters as also any damage done to ship or cargo by discharging into the lighters or by re-shipping into the vessel, and any damage which may have been done to the cargo while in the lighters.

If the lightening of the vessel must have taken place in the ordinary course of the voyage, there is no General Average.

(3) When the ship has been purposely run ashore, but only if prevention of sinking or of capture was thereby intended.

The damages caused by the stranding, as well as by the getting off, as also all the expenses of getting off, belong to General Average.

An average contribution is not made if the ship which has been stranded to avoid sinking is not got off, or after being got off is found incapable of repair (Art. 444).

If the ship has been stranded, without the stranding being purposely done for preservation of ship and cargo, then the damages caused by such stranding are not, but the expenses occasioned by the getting off, and the damages purposely inflicted on ship or cargo with this object are, General Average.

(4) If the vessel has put into a port of refuge in order to avoid a common danger threatening the ship and cargo in case the voyage were prosecuted, more particularly if the putting into port is for the necessary repair of damage done to the ship during the voyage.

To General Average in this case belong the expenses of entering and leaving, the expenses attaching to the ship itself owing to the stay, the wages and provisions of the crew during the stay, also the expense of lodging the crew on shore if and so long as they could not remain on board; further, if the cargo must be discharged as a consequence of the cause which led to the ship's putting into the port of refuge, the expense of discharging and re-shipping, and the expense of warehousing the cargo on shore up to the time when it might have been put on board again.

The several charges for detention are only admitted for the time that the cause of putting into the port of refuge remains in force. If the cause is to be found in a necessary repair of the ship, the charges for detention are only admitted up to that time at which the repair might have been completed.

The expense of repair to the ship belongs to General Average so far only as the damage which is to be repaired is itself General Average.

(5) When the ship is defended against enemies or pirates.

All damage done to ship and cargo in such defence, the ammunition expended, and in case any of the crew is wounded or killed in such defence, then the expenses of his cure or burial, as also the compensations to be paid (Articles 523, 524, 549, 551), are General Average.

(6) When the vessel has been detained by enemies or pirates, and is redeemed by payment.

What is given for ransom together with the cost of maintenance and release of the hostages is General Average.

(7) Losses and expenses incurred in obtaining the monies necessary for payment of General Average during the voyage, or expenses incurred in apportioning the amounts among the parties interested, belong to General Average.

Among these, more particularly are to be reckoned the loss on goods sold during the voyage, the premium on a bottomry loan taken up for the advance of the necessary funds, and, when this is not the case, the premium of insurance or the monies expended, the expenses of determining the damage and drawing up the adjustment.

Art. 709. Not as General Average, but as Particular Average, are to be considered—

(1) Losses and expenses incurred in procuring monies required in consequence of a Particular Average, even if in the course of the voyage.

(2) Expenses of reclaiming, even if the ship and cargo are both reclaimed together, and both successfully.

(3) Damage done to the ship, its appurtenances, or the cargo, by carrying a press of sail, even when the press of sail was carried to avoid stranding or capture.

Art. 710. In cases of General Average, damages and losses occurring to the following articles are not allowed for in making up the statement—

(1) Goods not laden under deck; this regulation does not, however, apply to the coasting trade, when deck cargoes are allowed by the laws of the various countries to be carried in such coasting trade (Art. 567).

(2) Goods for which there is no bill of lading, nor any entry nor the manifest or cargo-book.

(3) Valuables, specie, and securities, respecting which proper notice has not been given to the master (Art. 608).

Art. 711. Damage done to the vessel or its appurtenances, belonging to General Average, must be surveyed and estimated by experts at the port where it is made good, and before the repairs are commenced if it is done in the course of the voyage; otherwise at the port where the voyage terminates. The estimate must include the probable cost of all requisite repairs. If the repairs are done in the course of the voyage, the estimate determines the amount to be allowed for th damage, except when the cost of completing such repairs is less than the estimated amount. If it was not possible to make an estimate, then the amount actually laid out on the necessary repairs is conclusive.

So far as the repairs are not completed during the voyage the estimate alone is conclusive in the settlement of the damage.

In other cases, a deduction is made for the difference between old and new of one-third of the whole amount; in the case of chain-cables, however, only one-sixth, and on the anchors themselves no deduction at all is allowed.

From the total amount are further to be deducted the proceeds or value of the whole articles, if they shall be in existence, which have been or are to be replaced with new.

If such a deduction, and also the deduction for the difference between old and new, have to be made, the latter is first to be deducted, and afterwards the other deduction is to be made from the remainder.

Art. 712. The full amount of the repairs, when settled according to the provisions of the preceding Article, is the amount to be allowed in General Average if, at the time of sustaining the damage, the vessel had not been afloat for a full year.

The same rule applies in allowing for separate parts of the ship, and particularly for the metal sheathing, and for separate parts of the appurtenances, when such parts have not been in use for a full year.

Art. 713. The amount to be allowed for goods which have been sacrificed is determined by the market price of goods of the same kind and quality at the port of destination, at the time when the discharge of the ship was commenced.

If there is no market price, or in case of uncertainty as to such price or its applicability, more particularly with reference to the quality of the goods, the value must then be settled by competent persons.

From the value is to be deducted whatever saving in freight, duties and charges has resulted from the loss of the goods.

As goods sacrificed are to be considered, also, such as have been sold to satisfy General Average (Art. 708, No. 7).

Art. 714. The amount to be allowed for goods which have suffered damage belonging to General Average is determined by the difference between the value of the goods in their damaged state at the commencement of the discharge of the vessel, which is to be settled by experts and the market price, as defined in the preceding Article, after deduction of dues and charges, so far as these may have been saved in consequence of the damage.

Art. 715. In fixing the amount which is to be allowed (Articles 713, 714), a deduction is to be made on account of decrease of value and losses which may have occurred before, at, or after the casualty, not belonging to General Average.

Art. 716. If the voyage does not terminate with regard to ship and cargo at the port of destination, but at another port, such latter port takes the place of the port of destination for the determining of the General Average allowance ; whereas, if the voyage is terminated by the loss of the ship, the place to which the cargo is brought in safety becomes the port of destination in like manner.

Art. 717. The allowance for freight not earned is to be determined by the amount which would have been due on the sacrificed goods, if they had been carried on by the ship to the port of destination ; or, if the ship does not arrive at the port of destination, if they had reached the port where the voyage terminates.

Art. 718. The total amount of the loss which forms the General Average is apportioned among ship, cargo, and freight, in proportion to their respective values.

Art. 719. The ship with its appurtenances contributes—
(1) On its value in the condition in which it was at the end of the voyage, when the discharge was commenced.
(2) On the amount allowable as General Average on the ship and its appurtenances.

From the value under No. 1 is to be deducted the existing value of those repairs and supplies which have been made since the occurrence of the casualty.

Art. 720. The cargo contributes—
(1) On the goods still existing at the end of the voyage when the discharge was commenced, or if the voyage is terminated by the loss of the ship (Art. 716), on the goods that have been brought into safety, so far as at the time of the casualty these goods, in both cases, were on board the vessel or a lighter (Art. 708, No. 2).
(2) On the goods sacrificed (Art. 713).

Art. 721. In determining the contribution, the rate is to be taken—
(1) For goods which are undamaged, or the market value, or the value as fixed by experts (Art. 713), of the goods at the end of the voyage, when and where the discharge was commenced, or, if the voyage is terminated by the loss of the ship (Art. 716), at the time and place of the salvage, after deducting freight, duties, and other expenses.
(2) For goods which have been spoilt during the voyage, or have suffered damage not belonging to General Average, on the value, as fixed by experts (Art. 714) of the goods in their damaged state at the time and place stated in clause 1 of this section, after deduction of freight, duties, and other expenses.

(3) For goods which have been sacrificed, on the amount at which they are estimated under Art. 713 for General Average.

(4) For goods which have suffered damage belonging to General Average, the value, as estimated under clause 2 of this section, of the goods in their damaged state, adding thereto the difference of value which, according to Art. 714, is allowed in General Average as compensation for the damage.

Art. 722. Goods recovered after being jettisoned are not to contribute to a General Average occurring at the same time or subsequently, unless the owner of them makes a claim for contribution.

Art. 723. The freight contributes on two-thirds—

(1) Of the gross amount earned.

(2) Of the amount estimated as General Average according to Art. 717.

The laws of the respective countries retain the powers of reducing the above stipulated proportion of two-thirds to one-half.

Passage-money contributes on the amount which would have been lost if the ship had perished, after deducting the expenses which would in that case have been saved.

Art. 724. If a contributory object is liable for a claim arising out of a subsequent casualty, it must only contribute on its value after deduction of this claim.

Art. 725. The following do not contribute to General Average—

(1) Ammunition and provisions of the ship.

(2) Wages and effects of the crew.

(3) Baggage of passengers.

If objects of this kind have been sacrificed or have sustained damage which comes under General Average, compensation is made for them as provided by Articles 713-717 ; compensation is, however, not made for private effects consisting of valuables, specie, or securities, unless they have been duly notified to the master (Art. 608). Objects of this kind, for which compensation is made, contribute on the value, or difference of value at which they are replaced on the adjustment.

The objects enumerated in Art. 710 contribute as far as they have been saved.

Money advanced on bottomry is not liable to contribute.

Art. 726. If after the casualty, and before the commencement of the discharge at the end of the voyage, a contributory object is totally lost (Art. 706), or partially lost or diminished in value, more particularly in the case stated in Art. 724, a corresponding increase takes place in the amounts to be contributed by the remaining objects.

If the loss or diminution of value occurs after the commencement of the discharge, the amount for which such object is liable to contribute, as far as the object is inadequate to the satisfaction of a claim, falls as a loss on the claimant.

Art. 727. Claimants on account of General Average have the same rights as ships' creditors with respect to the amounts due from the ship and freight.

With respect to goods which have to contribute, they have a lien on the separate goods for the amounts for which each is liable. Such lien, however, cannot, after delivery of the goods, be enforced to the prejudice of third parties, who have *bonâ fide* come into possession of them.

Art. 728. An average loss in itself does not constitute a personal liability for payment of the average amount.

The receiver of goods from which a contribution has to be received, if such fact was known to him when he received the goods, is, however, personally liable for such amount up to the value of the goods at the time of their delivery, in so far as the amount could have been recovered out of the goods themselves if they had not been delivered.

Art. 729. The loss is to be determined and apportioned at the port of destination; or, if that is not reached, at the port where the voyage terminates.

Art. 730. The master is bound to cause the average statement to be made up without any delay. If he acts contrary to this obligation, he renders himself liable to every party interested.

Should the preparation of the average statement be unnecessarily delayed, every party interested may address a request for such preparation and urge its completion.

Art. 731. Under the jurisdiction of this code, the average statement is to be made up by the persons regularly appointed for the purpose, or in their absence by parties especially authorised by the Court (average staters). (Compare Article 57, clauses 1–7 of the Prussian Introductory Law.[1])

---

[1] *Art. 57. Prussian Introductory Law.* The following regulations are hereby laid down for the stating and settling of averages:—
- (1) As soon as the average statement is made up, the average stater shall lay the same before the Court of Commerce. It is the duty of this Court to examine the statement, and if mistakes or omissions are found, to have the same corrected by the average stater.
- (2) After the statement has been examined, and, if necessary, corrected, the parties who have to contribute, if they have announced themselves to the Court, or are known in other ways, more particularly by the ship's papers or cargo accounts, are to be invited to appear before a deputy of the Court on a fixed day if they reside in the district of the Court, or

Every party interested is bound to furnish the average stater with all documents necessary for making up the statement as far as they may be under his control, viz. :—charter parties, bills of lading, and invoices.

To the laws of the respective countries is reserved the right of making further regulations respecting the drawing up of the average statement and the settling of the same.

Art. 732. Security shall be given to the parties interested in the cargo for the amounts due from the ship, before the latter can be allowed to leave the port in which, according to Art. 729, the apportionment and arrangement of the loss is to take place.

Art. 733. The master is not allowed to deliver goods, from which a contribution to average may be due, until the amount of such contribution shall have been paid, or security given for the same (Art. 616); in default of which, in addition to the liability of the goods, he becomes personally liable for the amounts.

If the master shall have acted in accordance with instructions from his owner, then the directions of the second and third parts of Art. 479 are to be acted upon.

> have appointed representatives there; otherwise, in the person of an official agent, who will be appointed to act for them, in order to make their several objections to the statement.
>
> To the summons is to be attached the announcement, that any party not appearing will be considered to have no objection to make to the statement.
>
> (3) If at the stated time no objections are made to the statement, then the Court shall confirm the same.
>
> (4) If an interested party make objections, he must prove them in the sitting appointed, or must reserve the right of putting in a written statement of his grievance. In the latter case the statement must be laid before the Court within fourteen days: if this should not be done, it will be considered that the official record of the sitting is to serve as such statement.
>
> The ordinary legal steps will be taken by the Court on the statement of grievance, or should such not have been reserved, or not have been put in during the interval of fourteen days to be allowed as above, then on the copy of the official record of the sitting which is to serve as statement.
>
> (5) When the objections which may have been brought forward have been settled by a legal decision, or otherwise, then the Court shall proceed to confirm the average statement, the same having first been duly amended in conformity with the settlement of the objections.
>
> (6) When objections are raised which only affect a portion of the average statement, the Court shall at once confirm the statement so far as the same is not affected by the objections.
>
> (7) When the average statement has been so confirmed, immediate execution may be granted upon it.

The lien which parties entitled to compensation have on the contributory goods is exercised for them by the shipowner.

Art. 734. If the master shall have given a bottomry bond on the cargo, or have disposed of a part of the same by sale or otherwise, in order to be able to continue the voyage, although for an expense which does not belong to General Average, then the loss which the party interested in the cargo may sustain, because his claim cannot be satisfied, or can only partly be satisfied by ship and freight (Articles 509, 510, 613), shall be borne by the whole of the parties interested in the cargo, according to the regulations laid down for cases of General Average.

In settling the loss, the compensation fixed in Art. 713 is decisive in all cases, and particularly in such as come under the second part of Art. 613. Goods which have been sold also contribute to General Average, should such occur (Art. 720), with the value at which such compensation may be determined.

Art. 735. With respect to other losses and charges to be divided according to the principles of General Average, the necessary instructions are given in Art. 637.

The amounts and compensations to be paid under the stipulations of Articles 637 and 734 are in all respects placed on the same footing as payments and compensations in cases of General Average.

Second Division.—Damage by Collision.

Art. 736. When two ships come into collision, and either on one or both sides, in consequence of such collision, ship or cargo alone, or ship and cargo, should be damaged or entirely lost, then in case any one of the crew of either ship should have occasioned the accident by any fault of his own, the owner of that ship is answerable according to Articles 451, 452 for the repairs of the damage which may have been done to the other ship or her cargo by the collision.

The owners of the cargo in the two ships are not liable to contribute to the repairs of the damage.

The personal liability of the crew for the consequences of their faults is not altered by this section.

Art. 737. If no fault is attributable to any of the crew of either vessel, or if the collision is occasioned by faults on both sides, then no claim can be established for the damage done to either or both ships.

Art. 738. The two preceding sections are applicable whether both vessels, or either of them, are under sail or drifting with the current, or are at anchor, or fastened to the shore.

Art. 739. When a ship which has been damaged by collision sinks before it can reach a port, it is taken for granted that the sinking of the ship was a consequence of the collision.

Art. 740. When the ship is in charge of a pilot (where pilotage is compulsory) and the crew have performed the duties required of them, the owner of the ship is then not responsible for the damage occasioned by a collision for which the pilot is to blame.

Art. 741. The provisions of this Article are also applicable when more than two vessels come into collision.

When in such a case the collision shall have been occasioned by the fault of any of the crew of one of the vessels, then the owner of such vessel is also answerable for damage which may be occasioned in consequence of the second vessel through the collision being driven into collision with a third.

NINTH PART.

Concerning Salvage and Assistance in Cases of Distress.

Art. 742. When in case of distress a ship or its cargo, being no longer under the control of the crew, or having been abandoned by the same, is taken charge of either wholly or in part by third parties and brought into safety, then such parties have a claim for salvage.

When in any other case than the above, a ship or its cargo is rescued from a state of distress by the help of third parties, then such parties have only a claim for assistance

The crew of the vessel which is lost or in danger can have no claim for salvage or assistance.

Art. 743. When during the danger an agreement has been made as to the amount of the salvage or payment for assistance, such agreement may nevertheless be disputed on the plea that the amount agreed upon was excessive, and the reduction of the same to an amount more in accordance with the circumstances of the case may be demanded.

Art. 744. In the absence of any agreement, the amount of the salvage or assistance shall be fixed by the judge in money, all the circumstances of the case being taken into reasonable consideration.

Art. 745. The amount awarded for the salvage or assistance also includes compensation for any outlay which may have been made for the purposes of the salvage or assistance.

It does not include, however, the costs and fees of the legal authorities, the duties and charges to which the salved articles may be liable, or the expenses of storing, preserving, valuing, and disposing of the same.

Art. 746. The following circumstances are more particularly to be taken into consideration in settling the amount to be awarded for salvage or assistance :—

The zeal shown.
The time expended.
The services rendered.
The outlay incurred.
The number of persons who assisted.
The danger to which they and their vessels were exposed, as also
The danger which threatened the salved or rescued articles, and
The value of the same remaining after deduction of the expenses (Art. 745, clause 2).

Art. 747. The award for salvage or assistance shall not be fixed at a proportion of the value of the salved or rescued articles, unless all parties shall mutually agree thereto.

Art. 748. The amount of the salvage shall not exceed one-third of the value of the articles salved (Art. 746).

Only in exceptional cases may the amount be increased up to the half of the value, as when the salvage was accompanied with unusual exertions and risks, and when at the same time such value is only small.

Art. 749. The amount awarded for assistance shall always be less than the amount of salvage would have been in the same circumstances. In settlement of the amount to be awarded for assistance, the value of the articles rescued is only of secondary importance.

Art. 750. When several persons have taken part in the salvage or rendering of assistance, the amount awarded shall be divided among them in proportion to the services that each may have rendered either personally or with his property, and in case of dispute, according to the number who have to participate.

All those who devote themselves to the saving of human life in a casualty are entitled to participate equally.

Art. 751. When a ship or its cargo is either wholly or in part salved or preserved by another ship, then the amount awarded for salvage or assistance is divided between the owner, the master, and the rest of the crew of the other ship, unless it shall have been otherwise specially agreed between them, in such proportion, that the owner shall take one-half, the master one-quarter, and the rest of the crew the other one-quarter. Among the latter the amount shall be divided in proportion to the pay to which each is entitled, or to which each would be entitled according to rank.

Art. 752. No person has any claim for salvage or assistance—

APPENDIX. 753

(1) Who has forced the acceptance of his services, or more particularly has gone on board the ship without permission of the master, when the latter was present.

(2) Who has not immediately given notice to the master, the proprietor, or the proper authority respecting such salvage.

Art. 753. With respect to the expenses for salvage and assistance, which shall be understood to include the amount awarded for such salvage and assistance, the creditor has a lien on the salved or preserved articles, and with respect to the salved may detain them until security for the amount has been given.

In enforcing the lien, the stipulations of the second and third clauses of Art. 697 shall be applied.

Art. 754. The master may not deliver the goods, either wholly or in part, until the creditor has been paid or has received security, otherwise he makes himself personally liable to the creditor, so far as the latter's claim could have been satisfied out of the delivered goods at the time of their delivery.

If the master has acted in accordance with instructions from his owner, then the directions of the second and third clauses of Art. 479 come into operation.

Art. 755. Salvage and rendering of assistance do not of themselves impose a personal responsibility for payment of salvage and assistance expenses.

But the receiver of goods, when it is known to him at the time he received them that the same were liable for salvage or assistance expenses, becomes personally liable for such expenses, so far as they could have been satisfied out of the goods themselves, had they not been delivered.

If other articles have been salved or preserved together with the goods which have been so delivered, then the personal liability of the receiver only extends to the amount which falls upon the goods delivered, when the expenses are divided among the whole of the articles.

Art. 756. The laws of the respective countries retain the right to amend the provisions of this ninth part.

They can enact that other than legal tribunals shall, with the reservation of an appeal to law (Art. 744), be called upon to decide questions as to liability to the payment of salvage or assistance claims, or as to the amounts to be awarded in such cases.

The regulations of the different countries as to the recapture of a ship taken by the enemy do not come under the provisions of this part.

TENTH PART.

Concerning the Ship's Creditors.

Art. 757. The rights of a ship's creditor are acquired by virtue of the following claims, viz.—

(1) Expenses of a compulsory sale of the vessel, to which belong also the expenses connected with the distribution of the purchase-money, the cost of watching, keeping, and maintaining the vessel and its appurtenances from the application for the compulsory sale or from the arrest preceding such sale ;

(2) Expenses, not included in No. 1, of watching and keeping the vessel and its appurtenances, from the time of its being brought into the last port, in case it has been sold by order of a court of law ;

(3) All official, ship, navigation, and port duties, more particularly tonnage, light, quarantine, and port dues ;

(4) The claims of the crew arising out of contracts respecting their services and wages ;

(5) Pilotage monies, and expenses for salvage, assistance, redemption, and reclamation ;

(6) The contributions of the vessel to General Average ;

(7) Claims of the creditors, to whom the vessel has been bottomried, as well as the claims arising out of other credit transactions which the master as such has concluded in urgent cases while the vessel was away from the port of registry (Articles 497, 510), even if he is part-owner or sole owner of the vessel. Claims for supplies furnished or services rendered enjoy the same privilege as the aforesaid claims on credit transactions, if such supplies have been furnished or services rendered in cases of necessity, while the vessel was away from the port of registry, and for the preservation of the vessel or for the performance of the voyage, to the master as such and not on his personal credit, so far as the supplies furnished or services rendered were required to make good the necessity ;

(8) Claims for non-delivery of or damage to goods forming part of cargo and to baggage coming under the second section of Art. 674 ;

(9) Claims, not coming under one of the above heads, arising out of law transactions which the master as such has concluded by virtue of his legitimate authority and not of a special

power of attorney (Art. 452, No. 1); also claims, not coming under one of the above heads, arising out of non-fulfilment or incomplete or imperfect fulfilment of a contract made by the owner, so far as the carrying out of the latter belonged to the duties of the master (Art. 452, No. 2);

(10) Claims arising out of the fault of a person belonging to the crew (Articles 451 and 452, No. 3), although he may at the same time be part-owner or the sole owner of the vessel.

Art. 758. Ship's creditors to whom the vessel has not already been bottomried have a legal lien upon the vessel and its appurtenances.

The lien may be enforced against third parties who may have possession of the vessel.

Art. 759. The legal lien of each of these ship's creditors extends also to the gross freight of that voyage out of which his claim has arisen.

Art. 760. As a voyage within the meaning of this part shall be considered that voyage for which the vessel is fitted out anew, or which is commenced either in consequence of a new contract of affreightment or after complete discharge of the cargo.

Art. 761. The ship's creditors specified in Art. 757, par. 4, have, in respect of their claims arising out of a later voyage, a legal lien also upon the freight of former voyages, so far as they are performed under the same agreement as to service and wages (Articles 521, 536, 538, 554).

Art. 762. The provisions concerning the legal lien of the other ship's creditors apply equally to the lien to which bottomry creditors are entitled according to Art. 680.

The extent of the lien of the bottomry creditor is, however, determined by the contents of the bottomry contract (Art. 681).

Art. 763. The lien of a ship's creditor exists in like manner for principal, interest, bottomry premium, and costs.

Art. 764. A ship's creditor enforcing his lien may sue the shipowner as well as the master, the latter even when the vessel is in the port of registry (Art. 495).

A judgment given against the master is, as regards the lien, valid against the shipowner.

Art. 765. The rights of a ship's creditor are not impaired by the fact that the shipowner became personally liable for the claim, either at the time of its origin or subsequently.

This provision applies more particularly to the claims of the crew founded upon agreements of service and wages (Art. 453).

Art. 766. When the vessel belongs to a joint-ownership the ship and freight are liable to ship's creditors in the same manner as if it belonged to a single owner.

Art. 767. The lien of the ship's creditor upon the vessel becomes void—
  (1) By a compulsory sale of the vessel in a home port. The purchase-money takes the place of the ship as regards the ships creditors.
     The ship's creditors must be publicly summoned to protect their rights; in other respects the provisions regulating the proceedings for a sale are reserved to the laws of the various countries;
  (2) By the sale of the vessel effected by the master by virtue of his legal authority in a case of urgent necessity (Art. 499); the purchase-money takes the place of the vessel as regards the ship's creditors so long as it is not paid by the purchaser or is still in the hands of the master.

Art. 768. It is reserved to the laws of the various countries to enact, that liens shall also become void in other cases of sale when the ship's creditors have without effect been publicly summoned to give notice of their liens, or when the ship's creditors have not given notice of their liens to the competent court of law within a fixed period from the time of the vessel's arrival in the port of registry or another home port.

Art. 769. Art. 767 does not apply when only one or more shares are sold, but not the whole vessel.

Art. 770. With respect to the ship, the expenses of the compulsory sale (Art. 757, No. 1) and the outlay for watching and keeping the vessel from the time of its arrival in the last port (Art. 757, No. 2) have precedence over all other claims of ship's creditors.

The expenses of the compulsory sale have precedence over the costs of watching and keeping the vessel from the time of its arrival in the last port.

Art. 771. As regards other claims, those relating to the last voyage (Art. 760), in which are included those arising after the termination of the last voyage, have precedence over the claims connected with former voyages.

As regards claims not relating to the last voyage, those relating to a later voyage have precedence over those relating to a former one.

As regards the ship's creditors mentioned in Art. 757, No. 4, their claims relating to a former voyage have the same precedence as those relating to a later voyage, provided the different voyages are performed under the same contract of service or wages.

When the bottomry voyage includes several voyages in the sense of Art. 760, the bottomry creditor shall rank after those ship's creditors whose claims refer to the voyages commenced after the termination of the first of such voyages.

Art. 772. Claims relating to the same voyage, as also those which are to be considered as relating to the same voyage (Art. 771), are to be paid in the following order, viz.—
   (1) All official, ship, navigation and port dues (Art. 757, par. 3).
   (2) Claims of the crew arising out of agreements concerning their services and wages (Art. 757, par. 4).
   (3) Pilotage monies and expenses for salvage, assistance, redemption, and reclamation (Art. 757, par. 5), contributions of the vessel to General Average (Art. 757, par. 6), claims arising out of bottomry and other credit transactions entered into by the master in cases of necessity, as well as such claims as are to be treated on the same footing therewith (Art. 757, par. 7).
   (4) Claims for non-delivery of or damage to goods and baggage (Art. 757, par. 8).
   (5) Claims mentioned in Art. 757, pars. 9 and 10.

Art. 773. Of the claims referred to in pars. 1, 2, 4, and 5 of Art. 772, those comprised under one and the same head shall be considered to have equal rights.

Of those claims, however, mentioned in par. 3 of Art. 772, a more recent claim shall have precedence over one of an earlier date ; those arising simultaneously have equal rights.

When the master has concluded several transactions in consequence of the same case of necessity (Art. 757, par. 7), the claims resulting therefrom shall be considered to have arisen simultaneously.

Claims arising out of credit transactions, more particularly out of bottomry contracts entered into by the master for the purpose of paying earlier liabilities under the third head of Art. 772, as well as claims arising out of contracts concluded by him in order to extend the term of payment of, to acknowledge or to renew such former liabilities, shall only have the same priority as the earlier claim, although the credit transaction or contract may have been necessary for the continuation of the voyage.

Art. 774. The ship's creditors' lien upon the freight (Art. 759) is only valid so long as the freight is still unpaid, or the monies paid in satisfaction of the freight are still in the hands of the master.

To such lien apply likewise the provisions of the foregoing articles concerning priority.

Should the freight have been transferred, the lien of the ship's creditors may be enforced likewise against the transferee so long as the freight is still unpaid or the money is in the hands of the master.

For so much of the freight as the shipowner has received he is personally liable to the ship's creditors who have been thereby entirely or partially deprived of their lien ; to each for such amount as he would have received as his proportion if the said money had been distributed according to the legal order of priority.

The same personal liability attaches to the shipowner, with respect to goods shipped on his own account, to the extent of the current freight at the loading port at the time of shipment.

Art. 775. When the shipowner uses the freight to satisfy one or more creditors having any lien thereupon, he is answerable to creditors who would have had a prior claim only so far as it is proved that he has knowingly wronged them.

Art. 776. In so far as the shipowner has received the purchase-money in the cases mentioned in the first or second heads of Art. 767 he is personally responsible for the amounts received to all ship's creditors, to the same extent as he is to the creditors of a voyage in case of encashment of the freight (Articles 774, 775).

Art. 777. When the shipowner, after having received notice of the claim of a ship's creditor for which his liability extends only to the ship and freight, sends the vessel to sea on a new voyage (Art. 760), should such a course not be indispensable in the interest of the ship's creditor, he becomes likewise personally responsible for the claim to the extent of that amount which the creditor would have realised if the value of the vessel at the commencement of the voyage had been distributed amongst the ship's creditors according to the legal order of priority.

Unless proved to the contrary, it shall be considered that the creditor would have received payment in full by such distribution.

The personal liability of the owner arising out of the encashment of freight which is subject to the lien of the creditor (Art. 774) is not affected by this Article.

Art. 778. In cases of General Average, the compensation for sacrifice or damage takes, as against the ship's creditor, the place of that which the compensation is to make good.

The same rule applies to the indemnity which, in case of loss or damage to the vessel or of non-payment of freight when goods have been lost or damaged, is due to the shipowner by the party who has caused the damage by his illegal conduct.

When the compensation or indemnity has been received by the shipowner, he is personally responsible to the ship's creditors to the extent of the amount received in the same manner as to the creditors of a voyage in case of encashment of the freight (Articles 774, 775).

Art. 779. In case of any competition between ship's creditors enforcing their lien and other creditors on mortgage or otherwise, preference is due to the ship's creditors.

Art. 780. The provisions of Articles 767, 769, concerning the extinction of any liens of such ship's creditors, apply likewise to other liens acquired in accordance with the laws of the various countries either by voluntary declaration or legal process against the ship or a share therein and enforceable against a third holder.

The provision of Art. 767, No. 1, applies likewise to any liens to which a share of the vessel is subject in case of a compulsory sale of such share.

In other respects the rights of the mortgage creditors mentioned in the first paragraph are not subject to the enactments of this part, but to the laws of the various countries.

Art. 781. Of liens upon the goods for freight, bottomry monies, contributions to General Average, claims for salvage and assistance (Articles 624, 626, 680, 727, 753), the lien for freight ranks after all others; amongst these claims the more recent have priority over the earlier claim, those of simultaneous origin enjoy equal rights. Claims originating in transactions which the master has concluded in consequence of the same case of necessity are considered to be of simultaneous origin.

The provisions of Art. 778 apply in the cases of General Average, and of loss or damage by illegal conduct; the provisions of Art. 767, No. 2, apply in the case of a sale effected by the master for the purpose of avoiding or lessening a loss according to the third section of Art. 504; and the provisions of Art. 776 apply when the party for whose account the sale has taken place receives the purchase-money.

ELEVENTH PART.

Concerning Insurances against the Dangers of Maritime Navigation.

First Division.—General Principles.

Art. 782. Every interest computable in money, which any person has at stake in the preservation of ship or cargo from the dangers of maritime navigation, may be the subject of marine insurance.

Art. 783. The following more particularly may be insured:—
  the vessel;
  the freight;
  the passage-monies;

the cargo;

the bottomry monies;

the average monies;

other claims for the payment of which vessel, freight, passage-monies, or cargo, are liable;

the benefit expected from the arrival of the cargo at the port of destination (imaginary profits);

the commission to be earned;

the risk taken by the underwriter (re-insurance).

One of these insurances does not include the other.

Art. 784. Claims of the master and the crew for wages are not insurable.

Art. 785. The party insuring may either insure his own interest (insurance for own account) or the interest of a third party (insurance for account of another, as agent), and in the latter case may or may not give the name of the assured.

The contract may also leave it undecided whether the insurance has been effected for own account or as agent (for account of 'whom it may concern'). If in the case of an insurance on account of 'whom it may concern,' it should turn out that the same has been effected on account of a third party, the provisions concerning insurance as agent come into application.

The insurance is considered to have been effected for the account of the party taking the insurance when it does not appear upon the face of the contract that it has been effected as agent or for account of 'whom it may concern.'

Art. 786. An insurance as agent is only binding upon the underwriter when either the party taking the insurance has been authorised by the assured to effect it, or when the absence of such authorisation has been notified to the underwriter by the party taking the insurance at the time of completing the contract.

When this notification has been omitted, the want of authorisation cannot be made good by the subsequent approval of the insurance by the assured.

When the notification has been given, the validity of the insurance as against the underwriter is not dependent upon the subsequent approval of the assured.

The underwriter on whom, according to the provisions of this article, the insurance contract is not binding, is entitled, even when he proves the invalidity of the contract, to the full premium.

Art. 787. When the insurance has been effected by an empowered substitute, by a manager without authorisation, or by some other representative of the assured in the name of the latter, such representative is neither an insurer within the meaning of this act, nor is the assurance itself an insurance done by an agent.

In doubtful cases it shall be considered, that even when an insurance refers to the interest of a named third party it is an assurance done as agent.

Art. 788. The underwriter is obliged to deliver to the party effecting the insurance at his request a written document (policy) relating to the insurance contract and bearing his signature.

Art. 789. The validity of the insurance contract is not affected by the question whether at the time of its conclusion there is no longer any possibility of a claim occurring for damage, or whether a claimable damage has already occurred.

The contract is, however, invalid as an insurance contract if both contracting parties were aware of the position of affairs.

If the underwriter alone was aware that the possibility of a claimable damage no longer existed, or if the insured party alone was aware that a claimable damage had already occurred, the contract is invalid as regards the other party to whom the position of affairs was unknown In the second case the underwriter is entitled to the full premium, even when he relies upon the invalidity of the contract.

When the contract has been concluded for the party taking the insurance by a representative, the stipulations of the second section of Art. 810 apply ; in case of an insurance as agent, the provisions of Art. 811 ; and in case of an insurance of several objects or of a collection of objects, the provisions of Art. 814.

Art. 790. The full value of the insured object is the insurable value.

The sum insured shall not exceed the insurable value.

The insurance has no legal validity, so far as it exceeds the insurable value (over-insurance).

Art. 791. When in the case of a simultaneous conclusion of various insurance contracts, the total amount of the sums assured exceeds the insurable value, all underwriters together are only answerable to the extent of the insurable value, each of them being liable for such a percentage of the insurable value as the sum he has insured represents in proportion to the total of the amounts insured. When doubts arise in such cases the contracts shall be considered as simultaneously concluded.

Insurance contracts for which a common policy has been given, as also insurance contracts concluded on the same day, are considered as simultaneously concluded.

Art. 792. When an interest which has already been insured to its full value is again insured, the latter insurance is legally invalid so far as the interest has already been insured for the same time and against the same danger (double insurance).

If the full value is not covered by the earlier insurance, the later insurance is only valid for that part of the value not previously insured, so far as the insurance has been taken for the same time and against the same danger.

Art. 793. The later insurance is, however, legally valid notwithstanding the previous insurance—

(1) When at the conclusion of the later insurance, it is agreed with the underwriter that rights arising out of the previous insurance shall be ceded to him.

(2) When the later insurance is concluded with the condition that the underwriter shall only be answerable so far as the assured may be unable to enforce payment against the former underwriter on account of insolvency, or so far as the former insurance may be legally invalid.

(3) When the former underwriter is by formal notice released from liability so far as is necessary to avoid a double insurance, the later underwriter being informed thereof at the conclusion of the later insurance. In this case the former underwriter is entitled to the full premium although he is freed from his obligation.

Art. 794. In case of double insurance the later insurance, not the previous one, is legally valid, when the previous insurance has been taken as agent without authorisation, the later insurance on the other hand being effected by the assured himself, provided the assured at the time of effecting the later insurance was not informed of the previous one, or gives notice to the underwriter at the time of its conclusion that he repudiates the previous insurance.

The provisions of Articles 900 and 901 apply in such cases as far as regards the rights of the former underwriter to the premium.

Art. 795. When several insurances have been made simultaneously or successively, a subsequent renunciation of rights attaching against one underwriter cannot influence the rights and obligations of the remaining underwriters.

Art. 796. When the insured sum falls short of the insurable value, the underwriter in case of a partial damage shall make good the amount of such damage only in the same proportion as the sum insured bears to the insurable value.

Art. 797. When by arrangement of the parties the insurable value is fixed at a stated sum ('valuation,' 'valued policy.'), such stated sum is binding upon the parties as the insurable value.

The underwriter is, however, entitled to demand a reduction of the valuation, if he proves it to be considerably overstated ; if an imaginary profit has been insured at a valuation, he shall, if he disputes such estimate, prove that it exceeded the profit which, at the time of the conclusion of the contract, could, according to commercial calculation, possibly have been expected.

A policy containing the clause 'provisionally valued' shall, so long as a definite valuation has not been inserted, be considered as an unvalued (open) policy.

When freight has been insured the valuation shall only influence the amount claimable against the underwriter when such has been expressly stipulated.

Art. 798. When several objects, or a collection of objects, are included in a policy under the same assured sum, and for some of them special valuations have been agreed to, the objects specially valued are considered as separately insured.

Art. 799. Unless the parties have agreed upon another basis of value, the insurable value of ship shall be considered to be its value at the time when the underwriter's risk begins.

This rule applies even when an estimate of the insurable value of the vessel has been inserted.

Art. 800. The cost of outfit, the wages, and the cost of insurance may be insured together with the ship or separately, so far as they may not have been previously covered by insurance of the gross freight. They are considered to be insured together with the ship only when such has been mutually agreed upon.

Art. 801. The freight may be insured to the extent of its gross amount in so far as it may not have been previously covered by insurance of the cost of outfit, of wages, and cost of insurance.

The amount of freight stipulated by the contracts of affreightment shall be considered as the insurable value of the freight, and when a fixed amount of freight has not been agreed upon, or so far as goods have been shipped on account of the shipowner, the amount of the current freight (Art. 620).

Art. 802. When an insurance upon freight does not mention whether the whole or only a part thereof is insured, the whole freight shall be considered as insured.

When it is not stated whether the gross or net freight is insured, the gross freight shall be considered as insured.

When the freight of the outward voyage and the freight of the homeward voyage have been covered in one insurance, and it has not been stated what proportion of the insured sum shall apply to the freight of the outward voyage and what to that of the homeward voyage, one moiety of such sum shall be accounted as the freight of the outward voyage, and one moiety as the freight of the homeward voyage.

Art. 803. Unless the parties have agreed upon another basis of value, the value which the goods may have at the place and time of shipment, including all expenses incurred till they have been received on board, together with the cost of insurance, shall be considered as the insurable value.

The freight and the charges during the voyage and at the place of destination are only included when a special agreement has been made to that effect.

The provisions of this Article are also applicable when the insurable value of the goods has been inserted.

Art. 804. When the cost of outfit or the wages are insured, whether separately or by insurance of the gross freight, or when in the case of an insurance on goods, the freight or the charges during the voyage and at the place of destination are insured, the underwriter is not iable to pay for that portion of the same which in consequence of a casualty has not become due.

Art. 805. In the case of an insurance upon goods, imaginary profit or commission is only considered as included in the assurance if such has been stipulated by the contract, even though the insurable value of the goods may have been declared.

If when imaginary profit has been included in the insurance the insurable value has been declared, but without stating what proportion of the said value relates to the imaginary profit, it shall be considered that ten per cent. of the said value is intended to cover the imaginary profit. If when imaginary profit has been included in the assurance, the insurable value has not been declared, then ten per cent. of the insurable value of the goods (Art. 803) is considered to have been insured as imaginary profit.

The provisions of the second paragraph are applicable also to cases where commission has been included in the insurance, with the modification, however, that two per cent. is to be substituted for the ten per cent.

Art. 806. If imaginary profit or commission has been separately insured, but the insurable value not declared, it shall in doubtful cases be considered that the insured sum is to be taken also as the insurable value.

Art. 807. Monies advanced upon bottomry may be insured on account of the bottomry creditor together with the bottomry premium.

If an insurance on bottomry monies does not mention what interests have been bottomried, it shall be considered that the bottomry advances are insured upon ship, freight, and cargo. If the whole of these interests have not actually been bottomried, the underwriter alone is entitled to claim the benefit of the foregoing enactment.

Art. 808. When the underwriter has fulfilled his engagement, he acquires, so far as he has paid a loss which the assured was entitled to claim against a third party, the rights of the assured against such third party, without prejudice, however, to the provisions of the second paragraph of Art. 778, and the second paragraph of Art. 781.

The assured shall, at the request and at the expense of the underwriter, provide him with a certified document acknowledging his assumption of all rights against the third party.

The assured party is responsible for any action by which he prejudices those rights.

Art. 809. In case of the insurance of a claim the payment of which is secured upon some interest exposed to the perils of the sea, the assured in case of damage shall cede to the underwriter, when the latter has fulfilled his engagement, his rights against the debtor to the same extent to which the underwriter has made good the loss.

The insured party is not bound to enforce his rights against the debtor before claiming against the underwriter.

SECOND DIVISION.—CONCERNING STATEMENTS MADE AT THE TIME OF CONCLUSION OF THE CONTRACT.

Art. 810. The party taking the insurance, whether acting on his own account or as agent, shall inform the underwriter at the time of conclusion of the contract of all circumstances within his knowledge, which, as being of importance for the due appreciation of the risk which the underwriter is taking upon himself, are of a nature to influence him in his decision either to enter into the contract at all or on what conditions.

When the contract is concluded by a representative on behalf of the party taking the insurance, the circumstances known to the representative must also be stated.

Art. 811. In the case of an insurance as agent, the underwriter must at the conclusion of the contract be likewise informed of all circumstances known to the assured himself or to any intermediate agent.

This does not, however, apply to facts within the knowledge of the assured or of an intermediate agent when such circumstance has come to their knowledge so late that, without resorting to extraordinary measures, they would be unable to notify it to the party taking the insurance before the conclusion of the contract.

Nor does it apply to facts within the knowledge of the assured when the assurance has been effected without his authority or knowledge.

Art. 812. When the obligation mentioned in the two foregoing Articles is not fulfilled, the contract is not binding upon the underwriter.

This rule, however, does not apply when the fact not notified was known to the underwriter, or when it might be taken for granted that it was known to him.

Art. 813. When the party taking the insurance as at the time of concluding the contract made an incorrect statement concerning an important fact (Art. 810), the contract is not binding upon the underwriter unless the incorrectness of the statement was known to him.

This provision applies irrespective of the question whether the incorrectness of the statement was wilful or accidental, and whether with or without fraudulent intention.

Art. 814. In the case of insurance of several objects or of a collection of objects, if the provisions of Articles 810-813 have been infringed with respect to a circumstance relating only to a portion of the insured objects, then the contract continues in force against the underwriter as regards the remaining portion. The contract is, however, invalid against the underwriter with respect to this portion also, if it is clear that he would not have insured such portion alone on the same conditions.

Art. 815. The underwriter is entitled to the full premium in cases contemplated by Articles 810-814, even when he relies upon the total or partial invalidity of the contract.

Third Division.—Obligations of the Assured Arising out of the Contract of Insurance.

Art. 816. In default of a special agreement to the contrary, the premium is payable immediately after the conclusion of the contract, and, when a policy is required, against delivery of such policy.

The party taking the insurance is liable for the payment of the premium.

In case of an insurance effected as agent, if the party taking the insurance has become insolvent and has not received the premium from the assured, the underwriter may claim payment of the premium likewise from the assured.

Art. 817. When before commencement of the underwriters risk another voyage has been substituted for the voyage insured, the underwriter is exonerated from all liability in case of insurance upon ship and freight; with respect to other insurances the risk of the substituted voyage only attaches to the underwriter when the alteration in the voyage has neither been made by the assured nor by his orders nor with his approval.

When the insured voyage is altered subsequently to the commencement of the underwriter's risk, the latter is not answerable for accidents occurring after the alteration in the voyage. He is, however, answerable for such accidents when the alteration has been made neither by the insured nor by his orders nor with his approval; or when the alteration has been occasioned by a casualty, unless such casualty results from perils which are not at the risk of the underwriter.

The voyage is altered so soon as the determination to direct it to another port of destination has been carried into effect, although the routes to the two ports of destination may not have as yet diverged. This rule applies as well to cases referred to in the first as to those referred to in the second paragraph of this Article.

Art. 818. If the commencement or the termination of the voyage be unduly delayed by the assured or by his orders or with his approval; or if the ordinary course of the insured voyage be deviated from, or a port be entered the putting into which cannot be considered to be included in the insured voyage; or if the assured otherwise cause an augmentation of or alteration in the risk, more especially by the non-fulfilment of a promise expressly made in this respect; then the underwriter is not answerable for accidents which may afterwards occur.

This result, however, does not take place—
(1) If it is clear that the augmentation of or alteration in the risk could have had no influence upon the subsequent casualty;
(2) If the augmentation of or alteration in the risk, subsequently to the risk attaching upon the underwriter, has been occasioned by a casualty, provided the latter does not result from a danger for which the underwriter is not answerable;
(3) If the master has been impelled by the dictates of humanity to deviate from the course of the voyage.

Art. 819. If at the conclusion of the contract the name of the master has been given, this fact alone does not imply a promise that such master shall retain the command of the vessel.

Art. 820. In case of insurance upon goods the underwriter is not responsible for any casualty, if and so far as such goods have not been forwarded by the vessel designated for their conveyance. He is, however, responsible to the extent of the contract, if, subsequently to the commencement of his risk, without orders from or approval of the assured, the goods are forwarded in some other manner than by the vessel designated for their conveyance, or when this has been done in consequence of a casualty, unless such casualty results from a risk for which the underwriter was not responsible.

Art. 821. When an insurance is effected on goods without stating the name of the vessel or vessels (insurances on 'ship or ships'), the assured, immediately he has received intelligence of the name of the vessel on board of which the insured goods have been shipped, shall communicate this information to the underwriter.

In case of non-fulfilment of this obligation the underwriter is not responsible for any casualty happening to the goods so shipped.

Art. 822. Every casualty must be notified to the underwriter so soon as the party effecting the insurance or the assured, if the latter is aware of the insurance, receives information thereof; otherwise the underwriter is entitled to deduct from the claim for damage such amount as might have been saved if the notification had been made in due time.

Art. 823. When a casualty happens the assured is bound to do everything in his power to save the insured objects, as well as to avoid greater loss.

He shall, however, if possible, previously communicate with the underwriter respecting the steps to be taken.

FOURTH DIVISION.—CONCERNING THE EXTENT OF THE RISK.

Art. 824. The underwriter is responsible for all risks to which vessel or cargo is exposed during the period of the insurance, so far as no stipulation to the contrary is contained in the following regulations or in the special agreement.

He shall bear more particularly—
(1) Risk arising from the element and other perils of the sea, even when occasioned by the default of a third party, such as: penetration by the sea-water, stranding, shipwreck, sinking, fire, explosion, lightning, earthquake, damage by ice, &c.;
(2) Risk of war and of any Government dispositions;
(3) Risk of arrest on the application of a third party, and not caused by the default of the assured;
(4) Risk of theft, as also the risk of piracy, plunder, and other acts of violence;
(5) Risk of the hypothecation of the insured goods for the prose-

cution of the voyage, or of their disposal, sale, or conversion for the same purpose (Articles 507-510, 734);

(6) Risk of dishonesty or default of any member of the crew, so far as a loss may thereby be entailed upon the insured object;

(7) Risk of collision, no matter whether the assured sustains loss from the collision directly, or indirectly by being required to make good damage inflicted upon a third party.

Art. 825. The following damages are not at the charge of the underwriter—

(1) In the case of an insurance on ship or freight—

Damage occasioned in consequence of the vessel having been sent to sea in an unseaworthy condition, or improperly fitted out or manned, or without the necessary papers (Art. 480);

Damage which, except in the case of collision, arises out of the liability of the owner to make good damage occasioned to a third party by a member of the crew (Articles 451 and 452).

(2) In the case of an insurance upon the ship—

Damage to the vessel and her inventory resulting only from wear and tear in the ordinary employment of the vessel;

Damage to the vessel and her inventory arising only from old age, decay, or worm.

(3) In the case of an insurance upon goods or freight—

Damage arising from the natural condition of the goods, more particularly from internal corruption, diminution, ordinary leakage, &c., or from defective packing of the goods, or occasioned thereto by rats or mice; when, however, the voyage has been unusually protracted by an accident, for which the underwriter is responsible, the latter shall make good the damages described under this head to the same extent as they are attributable to the delay;

(4) Damage arising out of any default of the assured, and in the case of insurance of goods or imaginary profit such damage also as may have been occasioned by a default of the shipper, consignee, or supercargo in their respective capacities.

Art. 826. The liability of the underwriter to make good a damage attaches also when the assured has a claim for compensation against the master or some other person. The assured may in the first instance require payment from the underwriter. He shall, however, give all necessary assistance to the underwriter for the effectual prosecution of such claim, and shall likewise, at the underwriter's expense, exercise all suitable precaution according to the circumstances of the case for securing the claim by withholding the freight, by causing the vessel to be arrested, or by other proper means (Art. 823).

Art. 827. When a vessel is insured for a voyage the risk of the underwriter begins from the time when the taking on board of cargo or ballast commenced, or, if neither cargo nor ballast is to be taken on board, from the time of the departure of the vessel. It terminates with the completion of the discharge of the cargo or ballast at the port of destination.

When the discharge is unduly delayed by the assured, the risk terminates at the time when the discharge would have been completed if such delay had not taken place.

When, before completion of the discharge, cargo or ballast has been taken in for another voyage, the risk terminates at the time when such shipment of cargo or ballast has been commenced.

Art. 828. When the insurance is effected upon goods, imaginary profit, or the commission to be earned on account of goods shipped, the risk commences at the time when the goods leave the shore for the purpose of being loaded in the vessel or the lighters; it terminates at the time when the goods again reach the shore at the port of destination.

When the discharge is unduly delayed by the assured, or, in the case of an insurance on goods or imaginary profit, by the assured or by one of the persons mentioned in Art. 825, No. 4, the risk terminates at the time when the discharge would have been completed if such delay had not taken place.

The underwriter takes the risk of such use of lighters in connection with the shipment or discharge as may be in accordance with the custom of the port.

Art. 829. In the case of insurance upon freight, the risk arising out of accidents to which the ship and through it the freight are exposed commences and terminates at the same moment at which the risk would commence and terminate in the case of an insurance upon ship for the same voyage; the risk arising out of accidents to which the goods and through them the freight are exposed commences and terminates at the same moment at which the risk would commence and terminate in case of an insurance upon goods for the same voyage.

With respect to insurance upon passage-monies, the risk commences and terminates at the same moment as it would commence or terminate with an insurance upon the ship.

The underwriter on freight and passage-monies is only responsible for a casualty happening to the vessel so far as contracts of affreightment or for the conveyance of passengers have already been entered into ; and, when the owner ships goods on his own account, only so far as such goods have already left the shore for the purpose of being loaded in the vessel or in lighters.

Art. 830. In the case of insurance upon bottomry and average-monies the risk commences at the time the advances are made, or, when the assured has himself provided the average-monies, at the moment of their being expended ; it terminates at the moment at which it would terminate if the insurance were taken upon the objects which have been hypothecated, or for which the average-monies have been expended.

Art. 831. The underwriter's risk when commenced continues throughout the stipulated period or the insured voyage without interruption. The underwriter more particularly takes also the risk of casualty during the stay in a port of distress or an intermediate port, and, in the case of an insurance upon an out-and-home voyage, during the stay of the vessel in the port of destination of the outward voyage.

When the goods must be temporarily discharged or when the vessel must be taken ashore for repairs, the underwriter is liable also for the risk during the time that the goods or the vessel are ashore.

Art. 832. If, after inception of the risk, the insured voyage is voluntarily or by compulsion abandoned, the port in which the voyage terminates takes the place of the port of destination with respect to the termination of the risk.

When, after abandonment of the voyage, the goods are forwarded to the port of destination otherwise than by the vessel named for their conveyance, the risk continues to attach with respect to such goods even if they are forwarded wholly or in part by land. The underwriter in such cases bears also the expense of the previous discharge, the expense of the temporary warehousing, and the excess of expense incurred in forwarding the goods even if they have been forwarded by land.

Art. 833. Articles 831 and 832 apply only when not in contradiction to the stipulations of Articles 818 and 820.

Art. 834. When the period of insurance is stipulated in days, weeks, months, or years, the time shall be computed according to the calendar, and the day from midnight to midnight. The underwriter bears the risk during the day of its commencing as well as of its terminating.

With respect to computation of time, the reckoning at the place where the ship happens to be is decisive.

Art. 835. Should the vessel be insured upon a time-policy, and at the expiration of the period agreed therein be in course of a voyage, the insurance shall be considered, in default of an agreement to the contrary, to be prolonged until the arrival of the vessel in the next port of destination, and, if the discharge takes place in such port, until the termination of the discharge (Art. 827). The assured is, however, at liberty to waive such prolongation by notice to the underwriter before the sailing of the vessel.

In case of prolongation the assured shall continue to pay the agreed time-premium for the period of such prolongation, and, if the vessel should be missing, then until the expiration of the time when the assured becomes entitled to claim payment upon her as a total loss for want of news.

In case of waiver of the prolongation no claim can be made upon the underwriter on the ground of the ship being missing, if the period allowed for receipt of news does not terminate until after the expiration of the period of insurance.

Art. 836. In the case of an insurance effected for one or other of several ports, the assured may select one from amongst these ports; in the case of an insurance for two or more ports, the assured is entitled to visit every one of the ports mentioned.

Art. 837. When the insurance has been effected for several ports or when the assured has reserved the right to call at several ports, the assured is permitted to visit such ports only in the stipulated order, or in default of any agreement then in the order which the ordinary course of the voyage would demand; he is, however, not obliged to visit all the various ports named.

So far as the contrary does not appear upon the face of the policy, the order in which the ports are named therein is considered to be the order stipulated.

Art. 838. The underwriter is responsible for—
(1) Contributions to General Average, including such as the assured has himself to bear on account of damage sustained by him; contributions to which, in conformity with Articles 637 and 724, the principles of General Average apply, being placed on the same footing as contributions to General Average;
(2) Sacrifices which would belong to General Average if the vessel had had goods on board other than such as belonged to the owner;
(3) Other outlay necessarily or judiciously incurred with the view of saving the property, as also of avoiding heavier loss

(Art. 823), even if the measures resorted to have proved unsuccessful ;

(4) Expenses rendered necessary for the investigation and determination of the loss falling upon the underwriter, more especially expenses of survey, valuation, sale, and of making up the average statement.

Art. 839. The liability of the underwriter to make good contributions to General Average and such other contributions as are placed on the same footing as General Average is regulated by the average statement made up at the proper place, whether at home or abroad, in conformity with the laws in force at the place where it is made up. More especially, the assured who has sustained a General Average loss shall not demand from the underwriter more than the amount of the loss as shown by the average statement; but the underwriter on the other hand is liable for the whole of such amount, the insurance value more particularly not being taken into consideration.

Neither is the assured entitled to claim against the underwriter payment of damages which according to the law of the place where the average statement has been prepared do not belong to General Average, on the plea that such damages would be General Average, according to other law, more particularly according to the law in force at the place where the insurance has been effected.

Art. 840. The underwriter, however, is not responsible for contributions referred to in the foregoing Article so far as they result from an accident for which the underwriter is not responsible according to the contract of insurance.

Art. 841. When the average statement has been made up by a person authorised thereto either by law or custom, the underwriter may not contest its correctness because the laws of the place where it has been made up have not been adhered to and the assured has suffered loss thereby, unless the latter has been himself the cause of such additional loss by insufficient attention to his rights.

The assured shall, however, cede to the underwriter his claims against parties unduly benefited at his expense.

On the other hand, the underwriter is at liberty in all cases to dispute the correctness of the average statement as against the assured, in so far as a loss sustained by the assured himself for which he would not have been entitled to indemnification according to the law of the place where the average statement was made up, shall nevertheless have been treated as General Average.

Art. 842. With respect to a loss suffered by the assured, and either belonging to General Average or claimable on the same footing as

General Average, the underwriter, if the regular course of procedure necessary to ascertain and apportion the damage has been commenced, is liable to make good amounts payable to the assured only so far as the assured has not been able to recover even by an action at law the compensation due to him, if such a course were properly open to him.

Art. 843. If, without the fault of the assured, the regular course of procedure has been neglected, he may claim against the underwriter direct, subject to the stipulations of the contract of insurance, the whole amount of his loss.

Art. 844. The underwriter is liable for the damage only to the extent of the amount insured.

He shall, however, make good in full the expenses mentioned in Art. 838, heads 3 and 4, even if the total claim so arising should exceed the sum insured.

If in consequence of a casualty such expenses have already been occasioned—for example, if an outlay has been incurred for redemption or reclamation, or if liabilities have already been incurred for the purpose of replacing or repairing any objects damaged by such casualty, for instance, if average-monies have for such purpose been expended, or if the assured have already paid contributions to the General Average or if the assured have already become personally liable to pay such contributions, and should, at a subsequent period, a new accident happen, the underwriter is liable to make good claims arising out of the later accident to the extent of the whole sum insured, irrespective of the former outlays and contributions for which he is responsible.

Art. 845. After the occurrence of a casualty, the underwriter is entitled, by payment of the full amount insured, to exonerate himself from all further liability arising out of the contract of insurance, more particularly from the obligation to reimburse expenses rendered necessary for the salving, preservation, and rehabilitation of the interest insured.

When at the time of the occurrence of the casualty a portion of the insured objects had already ceased to be exposed to the risk which the underwriter has taken upon himself, the latter, if he avail himself of his rights under this section, shall not be required to make good that proportion of the assured sum which would have been due from such portion.

The underwriter by payment of the insured sum acquires no right to the objects assured.

Notwithstanding the payment of the insured sum the underwriter is liable to make good such expenses as may have been incurred for the salving, preservation, or rehabilitation of the objects insured, before the assured had received notice of his intention to avail himself of this right.

Art. 846. The underwriter, under penalty of forfeiture of the right granted to him by Art. 845, shall make known to the assured his intention to avail himself of such right at latest on the third day from the expiration of that day on which the assured has informed him, not only of the casualty, its nature and immediate consequences, but also, so far as they are known to the assured, of all other circumstances connected therewith.

Art. 847. When the insurance has not been effected upon the full value, the underwriter is only responsible for the contributions, sacrifices, and expenses mentioned in Art. 838 under heads 1 to 4, in the same proportion that the sum insured bears to the insurable value.

Art. 848. The obligation of the underwriter to make good a loss is neither cancelled nor diminished by the occurrence of a fresh casualty or even of a total loss arising out of a danger which is not at the risk of the underwriter.

Art. 849. The underwriter is not liable to make good particular averages when, irrespective of the expenses necessary to investigate and ascertain the amount of the damage (Art. 838, No. 4), they do not exceed three per cent. of the insurable value; when, however, they amount to more than three per cent., the underwriter shall make good such losses without deduction of the three per cent.

When the vessel has been insured for time or for several voyages, the three per cent. shall be calculated for each single voyage. The meaning of the term 'voyage' is defined by the provisions of Art. 760.

Art. 850. The underwriter shall make good the contributions, sacrifices, and expenses defined under Art. 838, heads 1–3, even when they do not amount to three per cent. of the insurable value. The same, however, are not to be taken into consideration in computing the three per cent. mentioned in Art. 819.

Art. 851. Should it have been agreed that the underwriter shall be exempted from a certain percentage, the provisions contained in Articles 849 and 850 are to be applied, with this modification, that the amount of percentage mentioned in the contract is substituted for the three per cent. therein enacted.

Art. 852. Should it have been agreed that the underwriter shall not be answerable for the risk of war, and that the insurance against other risks shall only run until a molestation of war occurs, which agreement is more particularly presumed to have been made when the contract has been concluded with the clause, 'free from molestation of war,' the underwriter's risk terminates at the moment when the danger of war begins to exercise an influence upon the voyage, more particularly, therefore, when the commencement or continuation of the voyage is prevented by men-of-war, privateers, or by blockade, or delayed for the purpose of avoiding the dangers of war; or when the vessel from such a cause deviates from its course, or when the master loses the free control over the vessel through molestation of war.

Art. 853. Should it have been stipulated that the underwriter shall be exempt from the risk of war, but be liable for all other risks even after a molestation of war has commenced, which stipulation is more particularly presumed to have been made when the contract has been concluded with the clause 'only against dangers of the sea,' the underwriter's risk terminates only with the condemnation of the insured object, or so soon as it would have terminated if the risk of war had not been excepted; the underwriter is, however, not responsible for the damages caused immediately by danger of war; he is therefore not answerable more particularly—

For confiscation by any Powers engaged in war;

For seizure, damage, destruction, and plunder by men-of-war or privateers;

> For expenses arising out of arrest and reclamation, out of blockade of the port where the vessel is lying, or warning away from a port under blockade, or out of voluntary delay on account of risk of war;
>
> For the following consequences of such a delay: deterioration and diminution of the goods, expense and risk of their discharge and warehousing, expense of their forwarding.

In doubtful cases it is presumed that a damage has not been occasioned by risk of war.

Art. 854. If the contract has been concluded with the clause 'for safe arrival,' the underwriter's risk terminates at the moment when the vessel has anchored, or been moored in the port of destination at the customary or proper place.

The underwriter is further only responsible—

(1) In case of insurance on the ship, when either a total loss occurs, or when the vessel is abandoned (Art. 865) or sold as incapable or unworthy of repair in consequence of a casualty happening previous to its arrival at the port of destination (Art. 877).

(2) In case of insurance on goods, when the goods, or a portion of them, in consequence of a casualty do not reach the port of destination, more particularly when before reaching such

port they are sold in consequence of an accident. If the goods reach the port of destination the underwriter is neither answerable for an injury nor for a loss resulting from an injury.

The underwriter shall, moreover, under no circumstances be liable for the contributions, sacrifices, and expenses coming under Art. 838, heads 1-4.

Art. 855. If the contract has been concluded with the clause 'free of damage except in case of stranding,' the underwriter is not liable to make good a loss arising out of a damage, no matter whether such loss consists in a diminution of value, or in a total or partial loss, and more particularly in the arrival of the goods at the port of destination in an utterly spoiled and altered state, or from their having been sold during the voyage on account of damage and immediate deterioration, unless the vessel or the lighter in which the insured goods are laden has been stranded. The following perils of the sea are considered equivalent to a stranding, viz. : capsizing, sinking, breaking up of the hull, shipwreck, and every other casualty of the sea by which the vessel or lighter has become incapable of repair.

If a stranding or some other casualty of the sea considered as equivalent thereto has occurred, the underwriter is liable for every loss exceeding three per cent. (Art. 849) arising out of such casualty, but not for any other injury. Until the contrary be proved, any injury which might possibly have been caused by the accident which has befallen the vessel shall be considered to have been actually caused thereby.

For every loss not arising out of a damage the underwriter is liable, no matter whether a stranding or another of the above-mentioned accidents has happened or not, in the same manner as if the contract had been concluded without the clause. Under all circumstances he is liable for contributions, sacrifices, and expenses mentioned in Art. 838, heads 1, 2, and 4 ; for those expenses, however, mentioned under head 3 of the same Article only when they have been expended in order to avoid a loss which would have fallen upon him.

A damage proved to have been caused by fire without spontaneous combustion or by extinction of such fire, or by bombardment, is not considered as an injury from which the underwriter is exonerated by the above clause.

Art. 856. If the contract has been concluded with the clause 'free of breakage except in case of stranding,' the enactments of the previous Article are applicable with the modification that the underwriter is liable for breakage to the same extent as according to the previous Article he is liable for damage.

Art. 857. A stranding in the sense of Articles 855 and 856 takes place when the vessel under circumstances not incidental to the ordinary navigation takes the ground, and either—

is not got off ; or,

is got off, but either—

(1) Only by resorting to extraordinary measures, such as : cutting away masts, jettison or discharge of a portion of the cargo, &c., or by the occurrence of a tide unusually high, not, however, solely by the application of ordinary measures, such as heaving on the anchor, backing the sails and the like ; or,

(2) Only after the vessel has sustained material damage to the hull from having taken the ground.

FIFTH DIVISION.—EXTENT OF THE DAMAGE.

Art. 858. A total loss of the vessel or the goods occurs when the vessel or the goods have been destroyed, or when they have been withdrawn from the assured without hope of their recovery, particularly when they have been irrecoverably sunk or have been so damaged as to lose their original properties or have been declared good prize. A total loss of the vessel is not nullified by separate portions of the wreck or of the inventory being saved.

Art. 859. A total loss of the freight occurs when the whole freight has been lost.

Art. 860. A total loss, with regard to imaginary profit or to commission expected on arrival of the goods at the place of destination, occurs when the goods have not reached their place of destination.

Art. 861. A total loss with regard to bottomry or average-monies occurs when the objects which have been bottomried, or for which average-monies have been advanced or expended, have either been subjected to total loss or to other accidents in such a degree that in consequence of injuries, hypothecations, or other liabilities thereby occasioned nothing has been left to cover such monies.

Art. 862. In case of total loss the underwriter has to pay the full amount insured, without prejudice, however, to such deductions, if any, as may be allowed according to the stipulations of Art. 804.

Art. 863. If in case of total loss anything has been saved before the payment of the sum insured, the proceeds of the objects saved shall be deducted therefrom. If the insurance was not effected for the full value, only a proportionate part of the value saved is to be deducted from the sum insured.

On payment of the sum for insurance the rights of the assured upon the insured object pass to the underwriter.

If a total or partial salvage occurs after the payment of the insured sum, the underwriter alone is entitled to such subsequent salvage. If the insurance was not made for the full value, the underwriter is only entitled to a proportionate part of what has been saved.

Art. 864. If in case of a total loss with regard to imaginary profit (Art. 860) the goods have during the voyage been so advantageously sold that the net proceeds amount to more than the insurable value of the goods, or when more than that value has been paid as indemnity for them, if they have been sacrificed in case of General Average or if they are to be made good in conformity with Articles 612 and 613, the surplus is to be deducted from the insured sum of the imaginary profit.

Art. 865. The assured is entitled to demand payment in full of the insured sum upon cession of his rights against the insured object in the following cases (abandonment)—

1. When the vessel is missing ;
2. When the object of the insurance is in danger from the fact of the vessel or goods being laid under embargo or seized by a belligerent or otherwise arrested by order of Government, or captured by pirates, and not being released within a period of six, nine, and twelve months, according as the detention, seizure, or capture has occurred—
    - (*a*) In a European port or on a European sea, or in any port, even if not belonging to Europe, of the Mediterranean and Black Sea, or of the Sea of Azof ; or,
    - (*b*) In any other water, but on this side of the Cape of Good Hope or of Cape Horn ; or,
    - (*c*) In any water on the other side of either of these promontories.

The periods are to be calculated from that day on which the accident has been notified to the underwriter by the assured (Art. 822).

Art. 866. A vessel which has commenced a voyage is to be considered as missing when it has not reached the port of destination within the time allowed, and when the interested parties have received no news about it within such period.

The time allowed as the period of presumptive loss amounts—
  (1) To six months for sailing vessels and four months for steamers, when both the port of departure and the port of destination are European ports ;
  (2) To nine months for sailing and steam ships if either the port of departure or the port of destination is a non-European port, but situate on this side of the Cape of Good Hope and of Cape Horn ; and to twelve months for sailing and steam

vessels if the said non-European port is situate on the other side of either of the said promontories;

(3) To six, nine, or twelve months respectively for sailing and steam vessels, when both the ports of sailing and destination are non-European ports, according as the average duration of the voyage may be taken as not more than two, not more than three, or more than three months.

In doubtful cases the longer term must be allowed.

Art. 867. The period of presumptive loss is calculated from the day on which the vessel commenced her voyage. If, however, since the sailing, intelligence respecting her have been received, the term allowed for presumptive loss shall be calculated from the day to which the last information reaches for such a period as would be granted if the voyage had commenced at the point where according to reliable information the vessel was last seen.

Art. 868. The declaration of abandonment must have been communicated to the underwriter within the period allowed for abandonment.

The period allowed for abandonment amounts to six months, when in case of presumptive loss of the vessel (Art. 865, No. I), the port of destination is a European port, and when in the case of detention, seizure, or capture (Art. 865, No. 2), the same has taken place in a European port or a European sea or in a part of the Mediterranean or Black Sea or of the Sea of Azof, even though not belonging to Europe. In other cases the period allowed for abandonment amounts to nine months. The period allowed for abandonment commences at the expiration of the terms mentioned in Articles 865 and 866.

In case of re-insurance the period allowed for abandonment begins at the expiration of the day on which the re-insured underwriter has received the declaration of abandonment from his assured.

Art. 869. After the expiration of the period allowed for abandonment an abandonment is inadmissible, without prejudice to the rights of the assured to claim compensation for a loss upon other grounds.

When in case of a presumptive loss of the vessel the period allowed for abandonment has not been kept, the assured, although entitled to demand payment of a total loss, shall nevertheless, in case the assured object is again brought to light, and it appears thereby that no total loss had occurred, refund the sum insured to the underwriter at his request and on his relinquishing the rights acquired under Art. 863 by payment of the sum insured, and shall be contented to receive instead compensation for a partial loss if any has been sustained.

Art. 870. In order to be valid the declaration of abandonment must be made without reserve or condition, and must extend to the whole object insured, so far as the latter at the time the accident happened was exposed to the perils of the sea.

If, however, the insurance was not concluded for the full value, the assured is only bound to abandon a proportionate part of the insured object.

The declaration of abandonment is irrevocable.

Art. 871. The declaration of abandonment is devoid of legal effect, if the circumstances upon which it is based are not confirmed or have ceased to exist at the time the declaration is made. On the other hand, it continues binding upon both parties even when, at a subsequent period, circumstances supervene the earlier occurrence of which would have precluded the right to abandon.

Art. 872. By the declaration of abandonment all rights of the assured with respect to the insured object are transferred to the underwriter.

The assured is bound to secure the underwriter against all real property liens attaching to the abandoned object at the time of the declaration of abandonment, unless the same arise out of perils for which the underwriter would be liable according to the contract of insurance.

If the vessel is abandoned, the underwriter is entitled to the net amount of freight of the voyage on which the casualty has occurred, so far as the freight has not been earned until after the declaration of abandonment. This portion of the freight shall be calculated in conformity with the principles laid down for ascertaining the amount of distance freight.

If the freight has been separately insured the underwriter thereon shall make good the loss thereby entailed upon the assured.

Art. 873. Payment of the sum insured can only be demanded when the documents justifying the abandonment have been communicated to the underwriter and a proper interval has been allowed for their examination. If the abandonment takes place on account of presumptive loss of the vessel the documents to be communicated must include reliable certificates respecting the date of sailing from the port of departure and respecting its non-arrival at the port of destination during the period allowed for presumptive loss.

The assured shall at the time of making his declaration of abandonment, so far as lies in his power, inform the underwriter whether any and what other insurances have been effected upon the object abandoned, and whether any and what bottomry liabilities and other incumbrances thereon are in existence. If this information has been omitted the underwriter may refuse payment of the sum insured until the information has been supplied; if a term of payment has been agreed, such term commences only from the time when the supplementary notification has been given.

Art. 874. The assured is obliged, even after declaration of abandonment, to give attention to the saving of the insured objects and the prevention of increased loss as laid down by Art. 823, and shall continue to do so until the underwriter himself is in a position to take the matter in hand.

If the assured should receive information that any object looked upon as lost has been again brought to light, he shall immediately acquaint the underwriter thereof, and shall at his request render him every assistance necessary for the recovery or realisation of the object in question.

The underwriter shall repay the expenses; he shall also provide the assured at his request with a sufficient advance.

Art. 875. If the underwriter acknowledges the validity of the abandonment the assured shall supply him at his request and expense with a certified attestation of the transfer of rights effected in consequence of the declaration of abandonment according to Art. 872, and shall deliver to him the documents relating to the objects abandoned.

Art. 876. In case of a partial damage to ship the damage consists of the amount of the expense of repairs to be ascertained in conformity with Articles 711 and 712, so far as the same relate to damages at the risk of the underwriter.

Art. 877. When the ship has in the manner prescribed in Art. 499 been pronounced incapable or unworthy of repair (Art. 444) the assured may, as far as the underwriter is concerned, put the vessel or the wreck up for sale by public auction, and in case of sale the loss consists of the difference between the net proceeds and the insured value.

The risk of the underwriter terminates only with the sale of the vessel or of the wreck; the underwriter is also answerable for the due payment of the purchase-money.

In estimating the value of the ship in a sound state, which is necessary for the purpose of determining whether it is unworthy of repair, its insurable value, no matter whether such value have or have not been estimated, is left altogether out of the question.

Art. 878. The commencement of such repairs does not preclude the exercise of the rights of the assured under the previous Article, when important damages have only subsequently appeared, which the assured had innocently failed to discover.

When the assured avails himself subsequently of this right, the underwriter shall pay separately the amounts already expended in repairs, so far as in consequence of such repairs a higher price has been realised at the sale of the ship.

Art. 879. When goods arrive at the port of destination in a damaged state, the percentage of value lost upon the goods shall be ascertained by a comparison of their actual gross value there in damaged state, with the gross value which they would have had there in their sound state. The same percentage of the insurable value is to be taken as the amount of the damage.

The value of the goods in damaged state is to be ascertained by public sale, or, if the underwriter consents, by valuation. The value which the goods would have had in a sound state is to be ascertained agreeably to the regulations laid down by the first and second paragraphs of Art. 612.

The underwriter shall also make good the expenses of survey, valuation, and sale.

Art. 880. When a portion of the goods has been lost in the course of the voyage, the damage consists in the same percentage of the insurable value as has been lost of the value of the goods.

Art. 881. When goods have been sold in the course of the voyage in consequence of a casualty, the damage consists in the difference between the net proceeds of the goods after deduction of the freight, duties, and sale expenses, and their insurable value.

The risk taken by the underwriter terminates only upon the sale of the goods; the underwriter is also answerable for due payment of the purchase-money.

The stipulations of Articles 138–842 are not affected by the provisions of this Article.

Art. 882. In case of partial loss of the freight, the loss consists of such portions of the stipulated freight, or, if no freight has been stipulated, then of the current freight, as shall have been lost.

If the freight has been valued, and such valuation is, in conformity with the fourth paragraph of Art. 797, decisive as to the loss to fall upon the underwriter, then the loss consists of the same percentage of the valuation as has been lost of the stipulated or current freight.

Art. 883. If, in the case of imaginary profit or of commission expected upon arrival of the goods, the latter arrive in a damaged condition, the damage consists in the same percentage of the amount insured upon profit or commission as the damage to the goods ascertained according to Art. 879 bears in proportion to the insurable value of the goods.

If some portion of the goods have not reached the port of destination the damage consists of the same percentage of the amount insured upon profit or commission as the value of the goods not arrived in the port of destination is to the value of all the goods.

If in the case of insurance upon imaginary profit the stipulations of Art. 864 apply to the non-arrived portion of the goods, the excess referred to in Art. 864 shall be deducted from the loss.

Art. 884. With respect to bottomry and average-monies in case of partial loss the damage consists of the deficiency resulting from the fact that the object bottomried, or upon which average-monies have been advanced or expended, may from subsequent accidents have become insufficient to cover the bottomry or average-monies.

Art. 885. The underwriter shall pay the full amount of the damage calculated according to Articles 876–884, when the full value has been insured, without prejudice, however, to the provisions of Art. 804 ; if the insurance has not been effected upon the full value, the underwriter shall only make good a proportionate part of such damage as stipulated by Art. 796.

SIXTH DIVISION.—PAYMENT OF LOSSES.

Art. 886. In order to be entitled to claim compensation for a loss the assured shall lay before the underwriter a statement of the claim.

He shall at the same time satisfy the underwriter by means of sufficient vouchers—

(1) Of his interest.
(2) That the insured object has been exposed to perils of the sea.
(3) Of the casualty which gives rise to the claim.
(4) Of the damage and its extent.

Art. 887. When the insurance has been effected by an agent the assured shall further show that the party taking the insurance was authorised by him to do so. When the insurance has been effected without authority (Art. 786) the assured must show the circumstances by which it is proved that the insurance was taken for his account.

Art. 888. Vouchers which owing, for instance, to the difficulty of procuring other evidence are ordinarily accepted in mercantile transactions without objection are generally to be considered as sufficient, such as for proof of interest :

(1) The ordinary documents of ownership, in case of insurance on ship ; the invoices and bills of lading so far as from their contents is apparent that the assured is entitled to the ownership of such goods in case of insurance on goods.

The charter-parties and bills of lading in case of insurance on freight.

(2) The bills of lading as proof of shipment of the goods.

(3) The extended protest, and the ship's log-book (Articles 488 and 494), as proof of the casualty ; the sentence of the prize court in case of condemnation ; reliable certificates as to the date of sailing of the vessel from the port of departure, and as to its non-arrival at the port of destination within the period allowed for presumptive loss in case of the latter.

(4) Documents of survey, valuation, and sale by public auction, drawn up conformably to the laws or usages of the place where the damage was verified, also estimates of the expenses drawn up by experts, also the receipted accounts for repairs executed and other receipts for payments made, as proof of the damage and its extent ; with respect to partial damage to the vessel (Articles 876, 877), however, the documents of survey and valuation, and the estimates of repairs, are only admissible when damages arising from wear and tear, age, decay, or worm are duly specified therein, and when, at the same time, so far as was practicable, such experts have been employed as have either been permanently and officially appointed or especially selected by the local tribunal, or by the consul of the country, or in default or in the absence of such officials, then by some other public authority.

Art. 889. Even in case of a lawsuit the documents mentioned in Art. 888 are usually, and so far as special circumstances do not give rise to suspicion, to be received as evidence.

Art. 890. An agreement, to exonerate the assured from the burden of proving the circumstances mentioned in Art. 886, or any portion thereof, is valid, without prejudice, however, to the right of the underwriter to prove the contrary.

An agreement made at the time of the insurance of goods, that production of the bill of lading should be dispensed with, does away only with the necessity of proving the shipment.

Art. 891. When an insurance is effected by an agent, the party taking the insurance may, without production of a power of attorney from the assured, make use of the powers reserved to the assured by the contract of insurance, and may receive and enforce payment of the sums insured. Should, however, a policy have been issued. this rule applies only when the party taking the insurance produces the same.

If the insurance has been taken without instructions, the party taking the insurance requires the consent of the assured in order to receive or enforce payment of the sums insured.

Art. 892. When a policy has been issued the underwriter shall pay the sums insured to the assured upon production of the policy.

Art. 893. The party taking the insurance is not bound to deliver the policy to the assured or to his creditors or to his assignees in bankruptcy before his claims against the assured, with reference to the insured object, have been satisfied. In case of a loss the party taking the insurance may pay himself for such claims out of the amounts due from the underwriter, and retain the amounts out of the insured sums when received in preference to the assured and his creditors.

Art. 894. The underwriter makes himself responsible to the party taking the insurance, if he, while the latter is still in possession of the policy, prejudices his rights under Art. 893, either by payments to the assured or his creditors, or his assignees in bankruptcy, or by agreements entered into with such parties.

The provisions of the common law determine how far the underwriter makes himself responsible to third parties who have acquired an interest in the policy, by entering into agreements respecting their interests or by paying over sums insured without requiring cession of the policy, or without making the necessary endorsement thereon.

Art. 895. If the underwriter is called upon to pay the sums insured, he may not, in case of an insurance effected as agent, set off claims which he may have against the party taking the insurance.

Art. 896. The assured may cede to a third party not only claims for compensation due to him on account of an accident which has already occurred but also possible claims to arise out of future accidents. If a policy has been issued to order, the same may be transferred by endorsement, the provisions of the Articles 301, 303, 305 being applicable as concerns such endorsement. In case of insurance as agent the endorsement of the party taking the insurance is sufficient for the validity of the first transfer.

Art. 897. When after the expiration of two months from the notification of the casualty the statement of claim (Art. 886) has, without fault of the assured, not as yet been produced, but the lowest amount due by the underwriter has been approximately ascertained, the latter shall pay this amount as on account of his liability, not however until expiration of the period stipulated for the payment of the sum insured. If the period allowed for payment is to commence from the time when the statement of claim has been laid before the underwriter, such period shall in the sense of this Article be calculated from the time when the underwriter has received the *pro formâ* estimate.

Art. 898. The underwriter shall make payment in advance of—

(1) Two-thirds of the amount claimable from him in cases of average

on account of his liability to be subsequently ascertained, towards the expenses of salving, preservation or rehabilitation of the insured object ;

(2) In case of capture of the ship or goods the full amount due from him towards the costs of the suit of reclamation, so far as the same may be rendered necessary.

Seventh Division.—Cancelling the Insurance and Repayment of the Premium.

Art. 899. When the adventure to which the insurance relates is wholly or partially abandoned by the assured, or when without his agency the insured object wholly or in part is not exposed to the risk which the underwriter was to bear, either the whole or a proportionate part of the premium may be reclaimed or withheld, less a suitable bonus due to the underwriter (ristorno).

When no specified amount is agreed upon or usual at the place where the insurance is effected, the bonus (allowance for ristorno) consists of one-half per cent. of the entire sum insured or of the corresponding portion thereof ; if, however, the premium does not amount to one per cent. of the sum insured, then of one-half of the whole premium or of the proportionate part thereof.

Art. 900. If the insurance is invalid on account of want of insurable interest (Art. 782), or on account of over-insurance (Art. 790), or on account of double insurance (Art. 792), the premium may here also be reclaimed or withheld, with the exception of the bonus stipulated in Art. 899, provided that the party taking the insurance has acted *bonâ fide* in effecting the same, and in case of an insurance as agent the assured has also acted *bonâ fide* at the time of giving the order.

Art. 901. The rules laid down by Articles 899 and 900 apply even if the insurance contract is void as against the underwriter on account of violation of the rules for giving information, or for other reasons, even if the underwriter notwithstanding such invalidity would be entitled to the full premium.

Art. 902. A return of premium does not take place if the underwriter's risk has already attached.

Art. 903. If the underwriter has become insolvent, the assured may at his option either withdraw from the contract and reclaim or withhold the whole premium, or may take a new insurance at the expense of the underwriter according to Art. 793. He, however, may not exercise this option, if, previous to his withdrawing from the contract or taking a new insurance, sufficient security is given to him for the fulfilment of the liabilities of the underwriter.

Art. 904. If the insured object changes hands, the rights appertaining to the assured by virtue of the insurance contract, as regards possible future accidents, may be transferred to the new owner in such a manner that the new owner is entitled to claim against the underwriter to the same extent as if no transfer had taken place and as if the assured himself enforced the claims.

The underwriter takes no responsibility for perils which would not have arisen if no transfer had taken place.

He may not only make use of the same pleas and counter-claims to which he would be entitled against the new owner direct, but also of those which he might have been entitled to make use of against the assured ; not, however, of such as do not arise out of the contract of insurance, except so far as they have been in existence previous to the notification of the transfer.

The legal effects of a transfer by endorsement of a policy made out to order are not affected by the foregoing enactment.

Art. 905. The provisions of Art. 904 are also applicable to insurances upon a share in a vessel.

If the vessel itself is insured, the same apply only when the vessel has changed owners in the course of the voyage. The commencement and termination of the voyage are determined according to Art. 827. When the vessel has been insured for time or for several voyages (Art. 760), the insurance only remains in force, in case of a change of ownership during a voyage, up to the discharge of the vessel in the next port of destination (Art. 827).

TWELFTH PART.

Statutory Limitations.

Art. 906. The claims enumerated in Art. 757 are only in force for one year. The limit extends, however, to two years—
   (1) For claims of the crew arising out of contracts of service or wages when the discharge has taken place on the other side of the Cape of Good Hope or of Cape Horn ;
   (2) For claims for compensation arising out of the collisions of vessels.

Art. 907. The limitation imposed by the previous Article extends also to personal claims of the creditor against the shipowner or a person belonging to the crew.

Art. 908. The period of limitation is reckoned—

(1) With respect to claims of the crew (Art. 757, No. 4), from the expiration of the day on which the contracts of service or wages come to an end, and, if the institution of legal proceedings is sooner possible and admissible, from the expiration of the day on which such possibility and admissibility takes place; the right, however, to demand payments in advance or on account does not affect the commencement of the period of limitation;

(2) With respect to claims for injury to or for undue delay in the delivery of goods and personal effects (Art. 757, Nos. 8 and 10) and for contributions to General Average (Art. 757, No. 6), from the expiration of the day on which the delivery has taken place; with respect to claims for non-delivery of goods, from the expiration of the day on which the vessel reaches the port where the delivery should have taken place, and, if such port is not reached, from the expiration of the day on which the party interested has first had notice of that fact as well as of the damage;

(3) With respect to claims caused by the default of a member of the crew (Art. 757, No. 10) not coming under head 2 of this Article from the expiration of the day on which the party interested receive notice of the damage; with respect, however, to claims for compensation arising out of the collision of vessels, from the expiration of the day on which the collision occurred;

(4) With respect to all other claims, from the expiration of the day on which the claim becomes due.

Art. 909. One year is also the period of limitation for the claims for which the goods are responsible with respect to the freight and all extra charges connected therewith, to demurrage, to outlay for duties and other expenses, to bottomry monies, contributions to General Average, salvage and assistance expenses, as also for all personal claims against parties interested in the cargo and for claims on account of passage-monies.

The period of limitation commences, as regards contributions to General Average, from the expiration of the day on which the contributory goods have been delivered, with respect to other claims from the expiration of the day on which they have become due.

Art. 910. Claims of the underwriter and of the assured arising out of the contract of insurance are not enforceable after five years.

The period of limitation commences from the expiration of the last day of the year in which the insured voyage has terminated, and, in case of insurance for time, from the expiration of the day on which the insured period terminates. In case of presumptive loss of the vessel, it commences from the termination of the day on which the period allowed for receipt of news comes to an end.

Art. 911. A claim which, according to Articles 906–910, has lapsed cannot be enforced as a counter-claim or otherwise by way of set-off, if it had already lapsed at the time that such other claim originated.

I.

REGULATION FOR SEAMEN OF DECEMBER 27, 1872.

WE, William, by the grace of God, German Emperor, King of Prussia, &c., &c., order in the name of the German Empire, with the consent of the Confederate Council and of the Parliament, as follows :—

FIRST SECTION.

Introductory Regulations.

§ 1. The provisions of this law apply to all merchant vessels (law of October 25, 1867) which have the right to carry the national flag.

§ 2. Master in the sense of this law is the commander of the vessel (ship-captain), and in default, or if he is prevented, his substitute.

§ 3. The 'crew' includes all officers of the ship except the master; and in like manner the word 'seaman' includes every ship's officer except the master.

Persons not belonging to the crew, but appointed on board a vessel as engineer, steward, or in any other capacity, shall be subject to the same rights and duties as have been enacted in this law with respect to the crew, there being no difference whether they have been engaged by the master or by the owner.

§ 4. Seamen's Offices, within the limits of the Confederation, are the authorities for engaging the crews in the several confederate states and the consulates of the German Empire abroad.

The establishment of the authorities for engaging the crews, or so-called shipping offices, within the limits of the Confederation, belong to the function of the territorial government in accordance with their respective laws. The business conduct thereof is subject to the supervision of the Empire.

SECOND SECTION.

Sea Voyage Books and Articles

§ 5. No one within the limits of the Confederation may take service as a seaman, unless he has previously proved his name and age before a Seamen's Office and received from it a sea voyage book.

If the seaman is a German, he must not be allowed to take service on board ship before he is fourteen years of age; he must also prove his military relations, and if he is still subject to parental control or a minor, the consent of the father or guardian to take service on board ship.

A copy of the 'Regulation for Seamen,' and the law respecting the duty of German merchant vessels to take seamen in distress on board, must be handed to the seaman together with the sea voyage book.

§ 6. The parental consent, or that of the guardian, unless limited, is considered as given once and for ever.

In virtue of it the minor will be treated as of age in so far as wages agreements are concerned, as well as regarding the rights and duties and legal proceedings connected therewith.

§ 7. Whoever has received a sea voyage book must, in order to obtain a new sea voyage book, produce the old one or prove its loss. That this has been done will be certified in the new sea voyage book by the Seamen's Office.

If the loss be proved, a statement from the Seamen's Office will be added to this certificate respecting the former rank and service details, as well as respecting the length of service, in so far as the seaman can sufficiently prove the same.

§ 8. Whoever, according to the contents of the sea voyage book, has been engaged must not be allowed to enter a new engagement before he can prove the termination of the previous service by the proper entry in the sea voyage book (§§ 20, 22). If in the opinion of the Seamen's Office such an entry cannot be adduced, but the termination of the service can otherwise be credibly proved, a statement entered into the sea voyage book by the Seamen's Office is to be of the same effect.

§ 9. The arrangement and price of the sea voyage book are fixed by the Confederate Council. The expedition thereof is free of charge and stamp duty.

The sea voyage book must state the military relations (§ 5) of the holder.

§ 10. The master has to regulate the engagement (shipping, discharging) of the crew according to the provisions of the following articles (§§ 11 to 22).

The seaman must be present at the engagement unless an unavoidable obstacle prevents him.

§ 11. The engagement consists in the announcement of the wages agreement concluded with the seaman before a Seamen's Office. It must take place for vessels lying within the limits of the Confederation under production of the sea voyage books before the commencement or continuation of the voyage, and for other vessels as soon as a Seamen's Office be reached.

§ 12. The engagement proceedings will be drawn up by the Seamen's Office as the ship's articles. If the persons belonging to the crew of a vessel are not engaged at the same time by one act, the further expedition will be on the basis of the first proceedings.

The ship's articles must contain : Name and nationality of the vessel, name and domicile of the master, name, domicile and rank of each seaman, and the conditions of the wages agreement, including any special arrangements.

In the ship's articles must be more especially stated what is due to the seaman for food and drink per day. Otherwise the arrangement of the articles will be fixed by the Confederation.

§ 13. If a seaman has been engaged after the ship's articles have been drawn up, the Seamen's Office has to enter such engagement on them.

§ 14. At every engagement effected within the limits of the Confederation, the Seamen's Office enters a statement thereof and the date of commencement of the service into the sea voyage book of each seaman, which at the same time serves as a departure or sea passport. Beyond the limits of the Confederation such entry is only made when the sea voyage book is produced for this purpose.

The sea voyage book has for the duration of the service to be taken in charge by the master.

§ 15. If a seaman who has been engaged is, owing to an unavoidable occurrence, prevented from entering the service, he is obliged to render as soon as possible an account thereof to the master and to the Seamen's Office before which he was engaged.

§ 16. The discharge consists in the announcement of the termination of the services on behalf of the master and such of the crew as are to be discharged. It must take place as soon as the service is terminated and, unless otherwise agreed, before the Seamen's Office of the port where the vessel lies, and after loss of the vessel before the first Seamen's Office which can be reached.

§ 17. Before the discharge takes place the master must certify in the sea voyage book of the seaman about to be discharged the rank which he occupied, his other duty-relations and the time of his service, likewise, if particularly requested, a character as to ability. The latter must not be entered in the sea voyage book.

§ 18. The signatures of the master to these entries and to the certificate of character (§ 17) are to be attested free of charge and stamp duty by the Seamen's Office before which the discharge takes place.

§ 19. Should the master refuse to give a certificate of character (§ 17), or should it contain accusations the correctness of which the seaman disputes, the Seamen's Office has to investigate the matter at the request of the latter, and to certify to the seaman the result of such investigation.

§ 20. The discharge of a seaman has, by the Seamen's Office, to be noted in the sea voyage book and on the ship's articles.

§ 21. After the expiration of the voyage or of the time to which the ship's articles and the therein contained engagement-proceedings refer, the same have to be delivered to the Seamen's Office before which the discharge took place.

The latter forwards the same to the Seamen's Office of the port of registry.

§ 22. Should any changes take place with the complement of the crew at a time when circumstances do not permit of such engagement (shipping, discharging) (§ 10) to be carried out in accordance with the above regulations, the master is obliged, as soon as he can reach a Seamen's Office, to complete the engagement there, giving the reasons which prevented this from being previously done, or, in case even this subsequent act is no longer possible, to report the fact.

An entry as to such report will be made by the Seamen's Office on the ship's articles as well as in the sea voyage book of the seamen concerned.

§ 23. The costs of such engaging and discharging, inclusive of the expedition of the ship's articles, have to be paid by the shipowner.

The stipulation of the costs to be fixed in equal amounts for all Seamen's Offices within the limits of the Confederation is reserved for the Confederate Courcil.

Until this has taken place the territorial governments shall stipulate the amount of the costs to be charged.

THIRD SECTION.

Contract.

§ 24. The validity of the wages agreement does not depend upon being in writing.

§ 25. If on concluding the wages agreement no arrangement as to the amount of the wages is expressly arrived at, and any doubt arises as to its amount, those wages will be considered as agreed upon which the Seamen's Office of the port where the seaman was engaged declares as usual at the time of the engagement.

§ 26. If a seaman engages himself for any period, for which he is bound by a previous agreement, then the first concluded engagement has in preference the claim to be fulfilled.

If, however, an official engagement based on the later agreement has been effected, this has the preference should *no* official engagement for the first agreement have taken place.

§ 27. When a seaman has been engaged after the ship's articles have been executed, the stipulations made therein with the other seamen shall be applied to him in default of any arrangement to the contrary ; he shall more especially only be entitled to the same wages, which, according to the articles, are due to the other seamen of his rank.

§ 28. The obligation of the seaman to go on board with his effects and to enter upon his duties commences, unless any other agreement has been made, from the time of his engagement.

If the seaman delays to enter upon his duties for more than twenty-four hours, the master is authorised to withdraw from the engagement. The demands for any additional expenses to provide a substitute and for other losses arising out of the delay are not affected thereby.

§ 29. The seaman who after the engagement avoids entering upon or continuing his duties, can be forced by the master, through the Seamen's Office, to its fulfilment.

The costs arising therefrom have to be made good by the seaman.

§ 30. The seaman is obliged to obey unhesitatingly the orders of the master with regard to the service of the ship, and to perform at all times every work entrusted to him with regard to ship and to cargo.

He has to perform these duties not only on board of the vessel and in its boats but in lighters and ashore, as well under ordinary circumstances as when under average.

Without permission of the master he is not allowed to leave

the vessel until he is discharged. Should he have received such permission, he must return at the time fixed, but should no time have been fixed, before eight o'clock in the evening.

§ 31. Should the vessel be in port, the seaman may only under pressing circumstances be obliged to work more than ten hours per day.

§ 32. Should any danger of the seas arise, especially if shipwreck be threatened, or should any violence and attack against ship or cargo be contemplated, the seaman must unhesitatingly render all assistance ordered for the preservation of ship and cargo, and he dare not, without permission of the master, leave the vessel so long as the master himself remains on board.

He is at the time of shipwreck, bound to render every assistance necessary for the safety of persons and their effects, as well as to take care and secure any parts belonging to the ship, its gear and the cargo, and all this in accordance with the master's orders, and to assist during any salvage operations on continuation of his wages and maintenance.

§ 33. The seaman, if so required, is bound to assist at the extending of the protest, and to confirm his depositions by oath. He has to fulfil this obligation on payment of travelling expenses and compensation for loss of time, even if the wages agreement has been terminated in consequence of the loss of the vessel (§ 56).

§ 34. If after the voyage has been commenced it is found that any seaman, with the exception of the mate, is incapable for the service for which he was engaged, the master is entitled to reduce his rank and to lower his wages in proportion.

If the master makes use of this power, he must, as soon as possible thereafter, inform the party concerned of such resolution, and to enter in the ship's log that this has been done, and when; before such intimation and entry have been given and made, the lowering of the wages does not take effect.

§ 35. In default of any other arrangement the wages shall be paid from the time of the engagement.

§ 36. In default of any other agreement the wages shall not be paid to the seaman until after the termination of the voyage or on his discharge, if such should previously take place. Should the vessel wholly or in part discharge the cargo in the first port of an intermediary voyage, the seaman may, if six months have elapsed since his engagement, demand one half of the wages due to him. In like manner the seaman is, after the expiration of a further six months from such date, entitled to the payment of half of the wages earned since.

§ 37. In default of any agreement the usage of the port where the seaman is engaged determines if, and to what extent, before the commencement of the voyage advances on account of wages shall be made or any earnest-monies are to be paid.

§ 38. All payments to seamen must, according to their choice, be made, unless otherwise agreed, either in cash or by sight draft on the owner.

§ 39. Before commencement of the voyage the master must open an account-book, in which all advances and payments on account of wages, as well as such earnest-monies as have been paid, are to be entered. In this account-book the seaman must give a receipt for each payment. The master is likewise obliged to give to each seaman who demands it a special wages book and to enter equally therein any payment made on account of the wages of the holder.

§ 40. If the number of the crew decreases during the voyage and is not made up again, the amount of the wages thus saved is, unless otherwise agreed, to be divided amongst the remaining seamen in proportion to their respective wages. No claim to division exists, however, if the decrease of the crew be caused by desertion and the effects of the deserted seaman did not remain on board.

If the number of the crew during the voyage be reduced by more than one-sixth, the master, at the request of the remainder of the crew, is obliged, should circumstances permit, to make up the deficiency.

§ 41. In all cases in which a vessel remains more than two years abroad, and should no other arrangement have been made, such seamen as have been two years in the service are entitled to an increase of wages if these are agreed for time.

This increase is to be determined as follows:—

(1) The ship's boy receives at the beginning of the third year the wages of an ordinary seaman as fixed by the ship's articles or the average amount shown by them, and at the beginning of the fourth year the wages of an able seaman as fixed by the ship's articles.

(2) The ordinary seaman receives at the beginning of the third year the wages of an able seaman as fixed by the ship's articles, and at the beginning of the fourth year one-fifth more.

(3) The remainder of the crew receive at the beginning of the third year one-fifth more and at the begininng of the fourth year a further one-fifth of the original amount of wages stated in the ship's articles. In the case *sub* No. 2 the ordinary seaman enters at the beginning of the third year into the rank of an able seaman.

§ 42. The demands of the master and of all persons belonging to the crew which arise out of any service and wages agreements, and who have been on board of a vessel which, according to Articles 866 and 867 of the German General Mercantile Law, is to be considered as missing, are due at the expiration of the time allowed for the calculation of the presumptive loss.

The termination of such service relations are to be reckoned from half a month after the day on which the last news from the vessel was received.

The amount of the demands has to be handed to the Seamen's Office of the port of registry, which has to arrange the payment to those entitled to receive them.

§ 43. The seaman is entitled to nourishment for account of the vessel from the time the service begins. He is only allowed to use the food and drink served out to him for his own requirements, and must not dispose, waste, or do away with it in any manner whatever.

§ 44. The crew is entitled to a protected and sufficiently ventilated space on board the vessel intended solely for them and their effects, and corresponding to their number and the size of the vessel.

If the seaman in consequence of a casualty or from other reasons cannot obtain shelter on board the vessel, other suitable provision is to be provided for him.

§ 45. The minimum of food and drink to be served out to the seaman per day (§ 43), the size and fitting up of the space set apart for the crew, as well as the minimum of medicines to be carried, are, in case of doubt, to be determined by the law of the port of registry.

The issue of more particular stipulations belongs to the Governments of the different countries.

§ 46. The master is, in case of an unusually long duration of the voyage, or in case any casualties should have occurred, entitled to reduce the rations or to make a change respecting the choice of food and drink.

He must enter in the log-book when, why, and in what way the reduction or change took place.

If this is omitted, or if the arrangements made by the master prove unjustifiable and caused by his fault, the seaman is entitled to such an allowance as is equivalent to the privations suffered. The Seamen's Office before whom the discharge takes place shall decide about such demand under reservation of recourse to law.

§ 47. If an officer of a ship, or not less than three seamen, complain before a Seamen's Office that the vessel for which they were engaged is unseaworthy, or that the provisions which are on board for the wants of the crew as food and drink are insufficient or spoiled, the Seamen's Office must cause the vessel or the provisions to be examined and to enter the result in the log-book. It must also take care, in case the complaint is proved to be well founded, so provide the necessary remedy.

§ 48. If a seaman after having entered the service falls ill or is wounded, the owner shall defray the expenses of his care and curing.

(1) If the seaman, on account of the disease or the wound, did not commence the voyage up to the expiration of three months from the time he became ill or was wounded.

(2) If he enters upon the voyage and returns in the vessel to a German port up to the expiration of three months from the return of the ship.

(3) If he enters upon the voyage and returns in the vessel, but if such voyage does not terminate in a German port, then up to the expiration of six months from the return of the ship.

(4) If he had to be left behind ashore during the voyage up to the expiration of six months from the time that the vessel has continued such voyage.

Should the vessel not return to the port from which it started, the seaman is likewise entitled to be returned free of expenses to that port (§§ 65, 66) or, at the option of the master, to a corresponding compensation.

§ 49. The sick or wounded seaman shall receive his wages—

If he does not commence the voyage, up to the time of discontinuing his duties

If he enters upon the voyage and returns in the vessel up to the termination of the return voyage.

If he had to be left behind ashore during the voyage, up to the day on which he leaves the vessel.

If the seaman has been injured in defence of the vessel, he is besides entitled to a fair reward, which, eventually, shall be fixed by the judge.

§ 50. Paragraphs 48 and 49 are not to be applied to seamen whose decease or wounds have been caused by their own unlawful acts or who are suffering from syphilitic diseases.

§ 51. Should the seaman die after having entered the service, the owner shall pay the wages (§ 67) earned up to the day of his death and defray the burial expenses.

If a seaman is killed while defending the vessel, the owner has to pay in addition a fair reward, which, if necessary, is to be fixed by the judge.

§ 52. Documentary evidence must be produced by the master, attested by two ship's officers or other credible persons, as to the death of any seaman occurring after commencement of the service.

The document must contain day and hour of the death, the Christian and surname, the place of birth or domicile, and the age of the deceased as well as the supposed cause of death. It must be executed by the master and the witnesses called in.

As far as the property of the deceased seaman is on board, the master has to cause an inventory to be made to take care of it, and, if necessary, to sell it.

The inventory is to be made in the presence of two ship's officers or other credible persons.

The property itself, or the proceeds realised by its sale, as well as any wages due, are to be given to the Seamen's Office at which it first can be done, together with the inventory and certificate of death.

If the Seamen's Office abroad refuses to take charge of the property from special reasons, the master must deliver it to the first Seamen's Office at which the matter can best be arranged.

The rules of the laws respecting the keeping of the civil registers are not affected by the regulations of this first and third section.

§ 53. If the master dies during the voyage, the mate is bound to produce a document as to the death, and to take care of the property left in accordance with the above regulations (§ 52).

§ 54. The seaman is obliged to remain during the entire voyage, including compound voyages, in the service up to the conclusion of the return voyage, unless otherwise agreed in the contract of his engagement.

Under return voyage in the sense of above rule must be understood the voyage to the port from which the vessel started. If, however, the vessel comes from a non-European port, or from a port in the Black Sea, or Sea of Azof, and began the voyage at a German port, any of the voyages named hereafter are to be considered as return voyages, provided the master, immediately after arrival, declares to the crew the voyage as ended there, viz. :—

(1) The voyage to any German port.
(2) The voyage to any non-German port in the North Sea or to a Channel port or port in Great Britain.
(3) If the vessel commenced her voyage from the Baltic, the voyage to a non-German port of the Baltic or to a port in the Sound or Cattegat.

If the return voyage does not end in the port from which the vessel originally sailed, the seaman is entitled to a free return-passage (§§ 65, 66) to that port and to his wages during the voyage, or, at his option, to a corresponding compensation.

§ 55. After the voyage is ended, the seaman cannot demand his dismissal before the cargo is discharged, the vessel cleaned and properly secured in port, or at any other place, and, if required, the protest extended.

§ 56. The engagement terminates when the owner loses the vessel through an unforeseen accident, more especially—

 If it is lost.

 If it has been condemned as incapable or unworthy of repair (Art. 444 of the German General Mercantile Law) and if, in the latter case, it is, without delay, sold by public auction.

 If it is captured by pirates.

 If it is seized or detained and condemned as good prize.

In such a case, the seaman shall not only receive the wages he may have earned (§ 67), but also a free return-passage to the port where the vessel sailed from, or, at the master's option, a corresponding compensation.

§ 57. The master may, irrespective of the cases provided for in the agreement, discharge the seaman before the expiration of his time of service—

(1) As long as the voyage has not yet been commenced, if the seaman is incapable for the service for which he has been engaged.

(2) If the seaman commits a gross offence against his duty, more especially if he is guilty of repeated disobedience and continued refractory conduct or smuggling.

(3) If the seaman is guilty of theft, fraud, faithlessness, embezzlement, concealment of stolen goods, forgery, or any action punishable, under the penal law by penal servitude.

(4) If the seaman is infected with syphilitic disease, or if, by doing an unlawful act, he has become invalided or wounded, and thereby incapacitated to work.

(5) If the voyage for which the seaman has been engaged cannot be commenced or continued on account of war, embargo or blockade, or on account of the prohibition of exportation or importation, or on account of any other casualty happening to ship and cargo.

The dismissal and reason thereof must be announced to the seaman, and, in cases of Nos. 2, 3, 4, be recorded on the ship's log.

§ 58. In the cases stated under Nos. 1–4 of § 57, the seaman is not entitled to more than the wages earned; but in case of No. 5 he is, when the discharge occurs after the commencement of the voyage, not only entitled to the wages earned, but likewise to a free return passage (§§ 65, 66) to the port from which the vessel sailed, or, at the option of the master, to a corresponding compensation.

§ 59. The seaman who is engaged for a voyage and may, for other reasons than those stated in § 57, be discharged before the termination of the contract, shall, if such dismissal takes place before the commencement of the voyage, retain as a compensation the earnest-money and advances received in so far as they do not exceed the usual amount.

When no earnest-money or advances have been paid, he is entitled to one month's wages as a compensation.

If the dismissal occurs after the commencement of the voyage he is entitled to a free return-passage (§§ 65, 66) to the port from which the vessel sailed, or, at the master's option, to a corresponding compensation. Besides the wages so earned he shall receive two months' wages if he be dismissed in a German port, or four months' wages if he be dismissed in a non-European port, but he is never to receive more than he would have been paid in case he had been dismissed at the termination of the voyage.

§ 60. Should, in conformity with the stipulation at the close of the preceding paragraph, the seaman after termination of the voyage be dismissed in a German port, then, in order to ascertain the wages due to him, besides those previously earned, the duration of the voyage of a sailing vessel is to be reckoned as follows :—

From Ports	To Ports Of the North Sea	To Ports Of the Baltic
	Months	Months
(1) Of the North Sea up to 61° N. L. and of the English Channel, as	1	$1\frac{1}{2}$
(2) Of the Baltic and neighbouring waters, as	$1\frac{1}{2}$	1
(3) In Europe, outside of the Channel and up to the Straits of Gibraltar, inclusive of the Azores, as well as of the North Sea beyond 61° N. L. and outside of the North Sea up to the North Cape inclusive, as	$1\frac{1}{2}$	2
(4) Of the Mediterranean, Black Sea, and Sea of Azof, as	2	2
(5) In Europe, eastwards of the North Cape, as	2	2
(6) Of the East Coast of America, from Quebec to Rio de Janeiro inclusive, as	2	$2\frac{1}{2}$
(7) Southwards from Rio de Janeiro to Cape Horn, inclusive, as	$2\frac{1}{2}$	3
(8) Of the West Coast of America, from Cape Horn to Panama, inclusive, as	$3\frac{1}{2}$	4
(9) Of the West Coast of Africa, north of the Equator, inclusive of the Canary and Cape Verd Islands, as	2	$2\frac{1}{2}$
(10) Southwards from the Equator up to Cape of Good Hope, inclusive, as	$2\frac{1}{4}$	$2\frac{3}{4}$
(11) On the other side of the Cape of Good Hope, this side of Cape Cormorin, inclusive, the Red Sea and Persian Gulf	$3\frac{1}{2}$	4
(12) Not included in the above	4	4

§ 61. The seaman is entitled to demand his discharge—
(1) If the master is guilty of a gross violation of his duties towards him, more especially of ill-treatment and of withholding food and drink without sufficient cause;
(2) If the vessel changes its flag;
(3) If, after the termination of the outward voyage, an intermediate voyage has been decided upon, or if after termination of an intermediate voyage in case, two or three years having elapsed since the original engagement, the vessel is in a European (§ 70) or in a non-European port.

Change of owner or master does not entitle the seaman to demand his discharge.

§ 62. In case of § 61, *sub* 3, the dismissal cannot be demanded—
(1) If the seaman has engaged himself for a longer time than therein stated; but an engagement for an unlimited period, or with the general condition that after the termination of the outward voyage the service is to continue for all voyages that might thereafter be decided upon, shall not be considered as an engagement for such time;
(2) If the return voyage has been ordered.

§ 63. In cases *sub* 1 and 2 of § 61 the seaman has the same claims as in the case contemplated by § 59; in the case *sub* 3 he is not entitled to receive more than the wages earned (§ 67).

§ 64. The seaman, except the vessel changes its flag, shall not without consent of a Seamen's Office (§ 105) quit the service in a foreign country.

§ 65. Should, according to this law, a claim for a free return-passage be established, it likewise includes maintenance during the voyage.

§ 66. The claim for a free return-passage is satisfied if the seaman, who is able to work, should, with the consent of the Seamen's Office, be provided with such employment as is equivalent to his former position and with corresponding wages, on board of a German merchant vessel, which goes to the port from which his vessel originally sailed, or to a port near thereto; in the latter case of course under payment of the corresponding allowance for the further free return-passage (§ 65) to the port of original departure.

If the seaman is not a German, a vessel of his own nationality will be considered equivalent to a German vessel.

§ 67. In the cases of §§ 36, 51, 56, 58, 59 & 63, the wages earned—if they have originally been fixed at a lump sum for the whole voyage shall be calculated in proportion to the services rendered and to the part of the voyage actually performed, taking, of course, into consideration the lump sum originally fixed.

In order to ascertain the wages for a single month, as referred to in §§ 59 and 60, the average duration of the voyage, including the time for loading and discharging—of course considering the general condition of the vessel—is to be taken as basis for such compensation.

§ 68. The owner is answerable for the claims of the master, as well as of the other persons belonging to the crew, which arise out of all contracts respecting their services and wages, not only to the extent of ship and freight, but personally.

This provision takes the place of Art. 453 of the German General Mercantile Law.

§ 69. The share in the freight or in the profits which may have been accorded to the seaman as reward shall not be considered as wages in the sense of this law.

§ 70. In the cases of §§ 59 and 61, the non-European ports of the Mediterranean, the Black Sea and the Sea of Azof are to be considered as equal to European ports.

§ 71. The master shall not, without the consent of the Seamen's Office, leave a seaman behind in a foreign country. Should it be feared that, in case of such leaving behind, a seaman may become destitute, the granting of the necessary permission may be made dependent upon the master providing for a term a proper security against such an event up to three months.

The provisions of § 103 are not affected hereby.

FOURTH SECTION.

Disciplinary Regulations.

§ 72. The seaman is subject to the disciplinary power of the master.

The same begins with the commencement of the service and expires at its termination.

§ 73. The seaman is obliged always to be sober and to observe towards everybody a proper and peaceable behaviour.

He is bound to treat the master and his other superiors with respect and to obey unhesitatingly their several orders.

§ 74. The seaman must, at the master's request, communicate truly and completely to him what he knows respecting all matters relating to the ship's service.

§ 75. The seaman shall not bring any goods on board without the master's permission ; for any goods shipped by him contrary to this prohibition, whether for himself or for others, he shall pay the highest freight charged at the loading-port for such voyages and goods at the time of shipment, without prejudice to any further claims for higher damages that may be proved.

The master is likewise authorised to throw the goods overboard should they be a danger to the ship or the cargo.

§ 76. The provisions of § 75 also apply if the seaman, without the master's permission, brings or causes to be brought on board brandy or other spirituous liquors or more tobacco than he requires for his own use on the intended voyage. Such spirituous liquors and tobacco as are brought on board in contravention of this provision are forfeited to the ship.

§ 77. The measures adopted by the master in conformity with the provisions of §§ 75 and 76 have to be entered into the log-book as soon as this can be done.

§ 78. If the ship is lying in port, the master is authorised, in order to prevent desertions, to take charge of the effects of the seamen until the departure of the vessel.

§ 79. The master is authorised to take all the requisite measures to uphold order and to secure the regularity of the service. For this purpose he may inflict as punishment the customary extra labour or moderately reduce the food ; the latter, however, at the most for three days. Fines, corporal punishment, or imprisonment he must not inflict as correction.

The master is authorised to use every means necessary to enforce obedience to his orders in cases of opposition or continued disobedience.

He may adopt the proper measures of safety against the parties concerned, and, if necessary, put them in irons during the voyage.

Every seaman, if required, is obliged to render assistance to the master for the purpose of upholding order as well as for prevention or suppression of any refractoriness.

Abroad the master must apply, in pressing cases, to the commanders of the available men-of-war of the Empire for assistance in order to uphold the necessary discipline.

§ 80. Every measure taken by the master in accordance with the provisions of § 79 has, as soon as this can be done, to be entered in the ship's log, stating likewise the cause thereof.

FIFTH SECTION.

Punishments.

§ 81. A seaman who, after signing the ship's articles, absents himself in order to avoid entering on the service, is liable to a fine up to twenty thalers. But proceedings will only be taken if required.

If a seaman deserts or absents himself in order to avoid continuation of the service, he is liable to a fine up to one hundred thalers, or imprisonment up to three months. But proceedings will only be taken if required.

A seaman who deserts or secretes himself with the advance received in order to avoid the service engaged for, is liable to imprisonment up to one year, as threatened by § 298 of the penal code.

§ 82. In the case of the two last provisions of § 81, the seaman loses all claim to the wages earned unless he, for the purpose of continuing the service, before the departure of the vessel, either voluntarily returns or is brought back by force. The wages, and in so far as they are insufficient, his effects, may be taken to cover the demands of the owner arising out of the wages and hire agreement; and, in so far as the wages are not required for these purposes, they will be treated in accordance with § 107.

§ 83. Has the seaman withdrawn from the service in one of the cases of § 61, *sub* 1 and 3, without permission of the Seamen's Office (§ 64), he is liable to a fine up to the amount of one month's wages.

§ 84. A seaman who is guilty of gross violation of his duties is liable to a fine up to the amount of one month's wages.

As violation of the duties in this sense are to be specially considered—

Carelessness while on watch;

Disobedience against an order of a superior concerning the service;

Improper behaviour towards superiors, towards other members of the crew, or towards passengers;

Leaving the vessel without permission, or overstaying leave;

Taking one's own or strange property from shipboard, or bringing goods or other objects on board without permission;

Allowing strangers on board, or any craft to come alongside the vessel;

Drunkenness on duty;

Waste, unauthorised disposal or putting away of provisions.

As far as regards ship's officers, the fine may be increased up to the amount of two months' wages.

If the wages are not agreed to be paid by time, the fine is fixed at an amount which, according to the opinion of the Seamen's Office, is equivalent to the monthly hire. But proceedings will only be taken if required. Such requisition is valid if made before the discharge of the person.

§ 85. The master, as soon as it can be done, has to enter every violation of duty (§ 84) in the ship's log-book with an exact statement of the facts, and, if practicable, to inform the seaman of the contents of such entry with express reference to the punishment threatened by § 84. Should such information not have been practicable, the reasons thereof are to be recorded in the log-book. If no entry has been made, no proceedings can be taken.

§ 86. A seaman who refuses lawful obedience to the repeated commands of the master or another superior is liable to imprisonment up to three months, or to a fine up to one hundred thalers.

§ 87. If two or more persons belonging to the ship's crew refuse lawful obedience to the master or another superior, the parties concerned are liable to imprisonment up to one year. The ringleader is liable to be punished with imprisonment up to three years.

If there are extenuating circumstances, a fine up to two hundred thalers may be adjudged.

The ringleader to be punished with imprisonment up to two years.

§ 88. A seaman who incites two or more persons belonging to the ship's crew to commit an action which is punishable according to §§ 87 and 91, is liable to the punishment as a ringleader if the incitement causes the punishable action or a punishable attempt thereof.

If the incitement was without result, then in case of § 87 a fine up to one hundred thalers, in case of § 91 a fine up to two hundred thalers, or imprisonment up to one year, is to be inflicted.

§ 89. A seaman who undertakes to necessitate the master or another superior by force or threat of force, or by refusal of any duty, to take or not to take any action which he was in duty bound to perform, is liable to imprisonment up to two years. If there are extenuating circumstances, a fine up to two hundred thalers may be adjudged.

§ 90. The same terms of punishment (§ 89) are to be applied to the seaman who resists the master or another superior by force or by threat of force or who assaults the master or another superior.

§ 91. Should one of the acts designated by §§ 89, 90, after preconcertion, be mutually committed by several seamen, the punishment may be increased up to the double amount of the threatened maximum.

The ringleader, as well as those who assault the master or another superior, are liable to penal servitude up to five years or to imprisonment of equal duration (even police supervision may be added if considered desirable). Should there be extenuating circumstances, an imprisonment of not less than three months' is to be adjudged.

§ 92. A seaman who refuses to obey such commands of the master or another superior which are required for the prevention or suppression of the actions designated by §§ 89, 90, is liable to punishment as an accessory.

§ 93. A seaman is liable to a fine up to twenty thalers, or imprisonment up to fourteen days, who—

(1) In order to deceive a Seamen's Office in any proceeding as to the granting of a sea voyage book, or any entry therein, or respecting an engagement, distorts or suppresses true facts or insinuates false ones;

(2) Omits to be present at the engagement in accordance with § 10;

(3) Or, should he be prevented from entering the service, does not present the necessary proofs thereof to the Seamen's Office in accordance with § 15.

The contents of § 271 of the penal code are not affected by the provision as above, *sub* 1.

§ 94. Whoever makes a complaint before a Seamen's Office as to the unseaworthiness of the vessel, or the deficiency of provisions, although he is perfectly aware of the untruth of his assertions, and causes thereby a survey to be held, is liable to imprisonment up to three months.

Whoever makes a complaint before a Seamen's Office as to the unseaworthiness of the vessel, or the deficiency of provisions, although he might with a little care have ascertained the untruth of his assertions, and causes thereby a survey to be held, is liable to a fine up to one hundred thalers.

§ 95. The infliction of the punishment threatened by this section, or by that of any other legal penal code, is not excluded in consequence of the guilty party having already been subjected to disciplinary punishment on account of the deed of which he is accused. A disciplinary punishment suffered may, however, be taken into consideration in the decision of the Seamen's Office (§ 101), as well as in the judgment of any legal tribunal when the punishment is apportioned.

§ 96. The master or other superior who exceeds his disciplinary authority towards a seaman is liable to a fine up to three hundred thalers, or imprisonment up to one year.

§ 97. The master who intentionally neglects to fulfil his obligations to provision the vessel properly, is liable to imprisonment; and he may, in addition, be adjudged to a fine of five hundred thalers, as well as to the loss of his civil rights.

If the master has carelessly omitted to fulfil his obligations, he is, should the crew in consequence thereof not have been able to receive proper food, liable to a fine up to two hundred thalers, or imprisonment up to one year.

§ 98. A master who, without the consent of the Seamen's Office (§ 71), leaves a seaman abroad, is liable to a fine up to one hundred thalers, or to imprisonment up to three months.

§ 99. A master is liable to a fine up to fifty thalers, or to imprisonment, who—

(1) Does not comply with any of his obligations respecting the engagement (shipping and discharging) of the crew (§ 10);

(2) In order to deceive a Seamen's Office respecting the engagement (shipping, discharging) of the crew, or respecting an entry into the sea voyage book, distorts or suppresses true facts or insinuates false ones;

(3) Does not obtain and produce such evidence as is required in cases of death, or neglects his duty to attend to the property left (§§ 52, 53);

(4) Does not cause such entries in the ship's log-book to be made as are ordered by §§ 77 and 80;

(5) Does not, in case of misdemeanour or crimes, fulfil his duties in accordance with §§ 102 and 103;

(6) Refuses to the seaman, without reasonable cause, the opportunity to obtain the decision of the Seamen's Office (§§ 105, 106);

(7) Keeps a seaman without food or drink without proper cause.

(8) Does not take care that a copy of this law, as well as of the rules respecting the food and lodging of the crew, is accessible in their respective space (§ 108). § 271 of the penal code is not affected by the regulation *sub* 2.

§ 100. The designations of §§ 81–91 apply likewise if the punishable actions have been committed beyond the limits of the Confederation.

The period of limitation of the prosecution does not commence, in this case, before the day on which the vessel, to which the wrongdoer at the time belonged, first reaches a Seamen's Office.

§ 101. In the cases of §§ 81, art. I., 84, 93, 99, the investigation is made, and decision given, by the Seamen's Office. It has summarily to examine the accused and to ascertain the facts. Witnesses are not to be sworn. At the close of the examination, a decision supported by reasons has to be given, of which the accused is to be informed, verbally should he be present, but by a written communication should he be absent.

Should a punishment have been decreed, the duration of the imprisonment has to be fixed in case the accused is unable to pay any fine.

The accused may appeal against the decision within ten days of the publication or the receipt thereof.

The notice of appeal has to be lodged with the Seamen's Office in writing.

If the Seamen's Office is abroad, the further proceedings have to be taken before that court in whose district the port of registry is situated, and in default of such, of that German port which the vessel first reaches after the conviction.

The decision of the Seamen's Office, with respect to the collection of the fine, is provisionally to be executed.

§ 102. Should a seaman commit a misdemeanour or a crime during the time the vessel is at sea or abroad, the master must, in the presence of ship's officers or other trustworthy persons, take a record of everything which could be used as evidence of the deed, and have an influence on the punishment. More especially has the nature of the wounds to be correctly described in cases of murder or dangerous bodily injury, and likewise has to be stated how long the injured person lived, whether and what remedies were applied, and what nourishment he took.

§ 103. The master is authorised to search at any time the effects of the crew who are suspected of any punishable deed. The master is further authorised to arrest the seaman guilty of any act which is subject to heavy punishment (§ 57, *sub* 3). He is obliged to do so if there is any fear of escape.

The accused has to be surrendered, together with all the proceedings recorded, to that Seamen's Office where it can first be done. Should for special reasons a Seamen's Office abroad decline to take action, the master must cause the surrender to that Seamen's Office where it otherwise can first be done. If in urgent cases a Seamen's Office cannot be timely reached, the master is authorised to surrender the accused to foreign authority for delivery to the competent authority of the port of registry. Notice of this has to be given to the first Seamen's Office where it can be conveniently done.

SIXTH SECTION.

General Conditions.

§ 104. Every Seamen's Office is bound to attempt an amicable settlement of all such disputes as have arisen between the master and the seaman and are brought to its notice. The Seamen's Office before which the discharge of a seaman takes place is more especially obliged to make such an attempt at amicable adjustment.

§ 105. The seaman shall not sue the master before a foreign tribunal. If he acts contrary to this provision he shall not only answer for the loss occasioned thereby, but he shall also forfeit the wages earned up to that time.

In cases of need he may apply to the Seamen's Office for a provisional decision. The opportunity for this is not without pressing reasons to be denied by the master.

Each party has provisionally to submit to this decision of the Seamen's Office without prejudice to the right of enforcing their respective claims after the termination of the voyage before the competent authority.

In case of a forced sale of the vessel, the provisions of the first article respecting the enforcement of the demands of the seaman arising out of the hire or wages agreement do not apply.

§ 106. At home any disputes which arise after the engagement between the master and the seaman as to the commencement or continuation of the service have to be adjudicated upon by the Seamen's Office with the reservation of the right of recourse to law. The decision of the Seamen's Office is to be executed provisionally.

§ 107. The fines which are fixed or adjudged, according to the provisions of the fifth section, go to the Seamen's Fund, and, in the absence of one, to the poor-box of the port of registry of the vessel, to which the accused at the time of committing the punishable action belonged, in case by territorial legislation such fines have not been decreed for other similar objects.

§ 108. A copy of this law, as well as of the rules respecting food and lodging of the crew (§ 45), is to be at any time accessible in the crew's space, for inspection by the seamen.

§ 109. The application of §§ 5 to 23 and of §§ 48 to 52 to smaller vessels (coasters &c.) may, by decree of the territorial governments, be excluded.

§ 110. This law enters into force on March 1, 1873. On the same day the fourth part of the fifth book of the General German Mercantile Law is to be considered null and void.

§ 111. Should reference have been made in other laws to provisions which are cancelled by this law, the corresponding provisions of the latter take the place of the first.

Done at Berlin, Dec. 27, 1872.

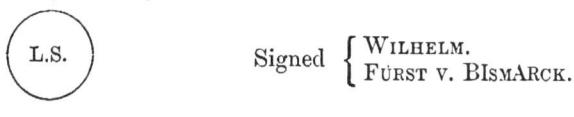

(L.S.)   Signed { WILHELM.
FÜRST V. BISMARCK.

II.

LAW RESPECTING THE OBLIGATION OF GERMAN MERCHANT VESSELS TO TAKE HOME DISTRESSED SEAMEN OF DECEMBER 27, 1872.

We, William, by the Grace of God, German Emperor, King of Prussia, &c. &c., order in the name of the German Empire, with the consent of the Confederate Council and of the Parliament, as follows:—

§ 1. Every German merchant vessel which is bound from a non-German port to a German port or to a port in the Channel of Great Britain, the Sound, or of the Cattegat, or to a non-German port in the North Sea or the Baltic, is, at the written request of the Seamen's Office, obliged to take against compensation (§ 5), to her port of destination, any German seamen, who find themselves abroad in a condition of distress, for the purpose of being finally forwarded to Germany.

With respect to foreign seamen who, immediately after having taken service on board of a German merchant vessel, find themselves out of Germany in a condition of distress, a similar obligation devolves upon German merchant vessels which are bound to the native country of such foreign sailors. The master may, by the Seamen's Office, be forced to fulfil such obligations.

§ 2. If several vessels offer an opportunity for passage, the seamen to be so sent home are to be distributed by the Seamen's Office on board of the several vessels according to their size and the number of their respective crews.

§ 3. The passage can be refused—

(1) If and in so far as there is no suitable room on board for those to be taken;

(2) If the seaman who is to be taken is ill in bed, or suffering

from syphilitic or such other disease as is dangerous to the health or safety of the crew, or who is to be sent home on account of a misdemeanour or crime;

(3) If and in so far as the number of those to be taken is in excess of one-fourth of the crew;

(4) If the passage is not demanded at least two days before the time the vessel is ready to sail.

The decision as to the cause of the refusal rests with the Seamen's Office.

§ 4. During the passage the seaman taken on board receives food and lodging for account of the ship. He is subject to the disciplinary authority of the master.

§ 5. In default of an agreement as to a lower rate, the compensation (§ 1) amounts for each day on board—

(1) For a master, mate, surgeon, engineer, assistant engineer or paymaster, to one thaler on board of sailing vessels and to one-and-a-half thaler on board of steamers.

(2) For every other seaman, to half a thaler on board sailing vessels and two-thirds of a thaler on board steamers.

§ 6. The payment of the compensation is, at the port of destination, made by the Seamen's Office against delivery of the written request for the passage (§ 1).

§ 7. The person brought home is answerable for the expenses caused by the passage.

The directions which bind the owner or other persons to the repayment of such expenses are not affected by this law.

§ 8. Whoever avoids the fulfilment of an obligation due according to § 1 is liable to a fine up to fifty thalers, or to imprisonment. The provisions contained in § 101 of the Regulations for Seamen apply likewise for the adjudication of the punishment and for all further proceedings as herein mentioned.

§ 9. This law enters into force on March 1, 1873.

Done at Berlin, Dec. 27, 1872.

(L.S.)   Signed { WILHELM.
FÜRST V. BISMARCK.

ANNEX A.

LAW RESPECTING THE NATIONALITY OF MERCHANT VESSELS AND THEIR RIGHT TO CARRY THE FLAG OF THE CONFEDERATION OF OCTOBER 25, 1867.

We, William, &c. &c.

§ 1. All vessels of the confederate states intended to obtain profit by means of sea voyages have in future to carry as national flag the flag of the Confederation only (Arts. 54 and 55 of the Constitution of the Confederation).

§ 2. Only such merchant vessels are entitled to carry the flag of the Confederation which are the exclusive property of such persons who are subjects of the Confederation (Art. 3 of the Constitution).

Limited liability companies and companies composed of personally liable shareholders established within the territory of the Confederation in Prussia, likewise such fellowships as are registered in accordance with the law of March 27, 1867, in so far as these companies and fellowships have their seat within the territory of the Confederation, and that they are composed of such personally liable shareholders as are subjects of the Confederation, have to be considered as on a level with these persons.

§ 3. Within the states of the Confederation which border on the sea, registers of all merchant vessels entitled to carry the flag of the Confederation have to be kept. The laws of the Confederation designate the authorities who have to keep the registers of shipping.

§ 4. The register of shipping is public, its inspection being permitted to everybody during the ordinary office hours.

§ 5. A vessel can only be entered on the register of shipping of that port from which the vessel is intended to be employed in navigation (home port—port of registry).

§ 6. The entry in the register of shipping shall contain—

(1) The name and description of the vessel (whether barque, brig, &c.).

(2) Its size and the carrying capacity calculated according to the size.

(3) The date and place of building, or, if it had carried the flag of a country not belonging to the North German Confederation, the circumstances under which the right to carry the flag of

the Confederation was acquired, and besides, if possible, the date and place of building.

(4) The port of registry.

(5) The name and particular designation of the owner, or, if there are several owners, the names and particular designations of each co-owner, and the amount of the share each holds ; if a commercial association is owner or co-owner, the firm and place where the association is established ; and if the association is not a limited liability company, the name and particular designation of each member forming the commercial association ; respecting companies composed of personally liable and of limited shareholders, the registration of all such members as are personally liable instead of the registration of all members will be sufficient.

(6) The legal title according to which the property in the vessel or in the several shares was acquired.

(7) The nationality of the owner or of the co-owners.

(8) Date of registration of the vessel.

Each vessel must be entered in the register of shipping under a separate regular number.

§ 7. An entry in the register of shipping cannot be made before the right to carry the flag of the Confederation, and all the items required by § 6, have been credibly established.

§ 8. The registration authority has, in virtue of the entry of the vessel in the register of shipping, to grant a document (certificate) identical therewith.

The certificate must further declare that all proofs required by § 7 have been supplied, as well as that the vessel has the right to carry the flag of the Confederation.

§ 9. The right of the vessel to carry the flag of the Confederation is attested by the certificate. No sea-pass is required in order to prove particularly this right.

§ 10. The right to carry the flag of the Confederation must not be exercised before the registration of the vessel in the register of shipping nor before the granting of the certificate.

§ 11. If subsequently to such entry changes occur in the matters of fact referred to in § 6, they must be recorded in the ship's register and stated on the certificate.

In case of the loss of the vessel, or of having forfeited the right to carry the flag of the Confederation, the vessel is to be struck out of the register of shipping and the certificate is to be returned, unless it be credibly attested that it cannot be returned.

APPENDIX. 815

§ 12. The circumstances which, according to § 11, necessitate an entry or a cancellation in the register of shipping have to be reported and credibly proved by the owner to the registration authority in compliance with the provisions of § 11, within six weeks after expiration of the day on which he received notice thereof, and eventually returning the certificate at the same time.

The obligation of the report and proof rests—

(1) If there is an ownership, with all the co-owners;
(2) If a limited liability company is owner or co-owner, with all the directors thereof;
(3) If another commercial association is owner or co owner, with all the personally liable members thereof.
(4) If the change consists in a transfer of ownership, by which the right to carry the flag of the Confederation is not affected with the new owner of the vessel or share.

§ 13. If a vessel which, according to the provision of § 2, is not entitled to carry the flag of the Confederation, nevertheless sails under the flag of the Confederation, the master of such vessel is subject to a fine up to five hundred thalers or to imprisonment up to six months; the vessel may likewise be confiscated.

§ 14. If a vessel which, according to § 10, must abstain from carrying the flag of the Confederation, because the entry in the register of shipping or the granting of the certificate has not yet taken place, nevertheless sails under the flag of the Confederation, the master of the vessel is subject to a fine up to one hundred thalers, or proportionate imprisonment in case he cannot prove that the unauthorised hoisting of the flag of the Confederation was done without his fault.

§ 15. Any one who does not fulfil the obligation resting upon him in accordance with § 12 within the prescribed period of six weeks is liable to the punishment threatened by § 14 in case he cannot prove that he was faultless in not complying with the regulation. The punishment cannot be inflicted if before the expiration of the time such obligation was fulfilled by another person who was equally obliged to perform the same duty. The punishment is doubled towards such person as likewise neglects to fulfil the obligation within six weeks after the day on which the judgment becomes valid in law.

§ 16. If a foreign vessel outside the territory of the Confederation becomes by transfer the property of a person who is a subject of the Confederation, and acquires thereby the right to carry its flag, the entry in the register of shipping and the certificate may be replaced by a certificate issued by the consul of the Confederation in whose district the vessel at the time of the transfer was, and by which this official attests the acquisition of the right to carry the flag of the Confederation; but such consular certificate is only valid for the duration of one year from its date, and beyond this year only for such time as the voyage may be prolonged by *force majeure*. As long as consulates of the separate states of the Confederation exist, the certificate in question may be granted by the consul of such state of the Confederation to which the buyer of the vessel belongs, and no such consul nor a consul of the Confederation being appointed, by the consul of another state of the Confederation (Art. 56 of the Constitution of the Confederation).

§ 17.[1] It is reserved for the laws of the Confederation to determine whether and which smaller vessels (coasters, &c.) are entitled to carry the flag of the Confederation without previous entry in the register of shipping and the grant of the certificate.

§ 18. Vessels which, in accordance with § 2, are entitled to carry the flag of the Confederation, and which in consequence of the provisions of Art. 432 of the General German Mercantile Law are already entered on the ship's register of a confederate state, and are therefore already provided with certificates as to the right of carrying the flag of the Confederation, do not require to be entered again on the register of shipping or to be provided with new certificates in order to exercise the right to carry the flag of the Confederation.

§ 19. The provisions of the laws of the Confederation respecting the keeping of the existing registers of shipping apply likewise to the keeping of registers of shipping according to this law in so far as they are in accordance with the provisions of the same, and without prejudice to later alterations by the laws of the Confederation.

§ 20. This law enters into force on April 1, 1868.

Respecting such vessels as are at present entitled to carry the flag of Mecklenburg-Schwerin, the provisions of § 2 as to the requirements of the nationality do not enter into force before April 1, 1869.

Done at Castle Babelsberg, October 25, 1867.

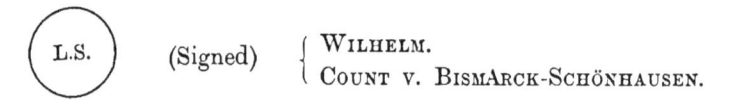

(L.S.) (Signed) { WILHELM.
{ COUNT V. BISMARCK-SCHÖNHAUSEN.

[1] Repealed by the law of June 28, 1873. (See p. 817.)

REGISTRATION AND DESIGNATION OF MERCHANT VESSELS. IMPERIAL LAW OF JUNE 28, 1873.

We, William, &c. &c.

§ 1. In place of § 17 of the law respecting the nationality of merchant vessels and their right to carry the flag of the Confederation, dated October 25, 1867, the following regulation is substituted :—

'Vessels of not more than fifty cubic metres gross tonnage are entitled to carry the national flag without entry into the register of shipping and the grant of the certificate.'

§ 2. The change of name of a vessel once entered in the register of shipping may only, from specially urgent reasons, be allowed. The consent of the Imperial Chancellor's Office is requisite for it.

§ 3. Every vessel entered in the register of shipping must have—

(1) Its name on each side of the bow, and
(2) Its name, and the name of the port of registry, on the permanent parts of the stern, in good, visible, and securely fastened letters.

§ 4. In case of contravention against the provisions of § 3, the master of the vessel is subject to a fine up to one hundred and fifty marks, or imprisonment.

§ 5. This law enters into force on January 1, 1874.

Done at Castle Babelsberg, June 28, 1873.

(L.S.)   (Signed)   { WILHELM.
                     { FÜRST V. BISMARCK.

LAW RESPECTING COAST TRADING VOYAGES, DATED MAY 22, 1881.

§ 1. The right to load goods in a German seaport, and to carry them to another German seaport in order to be discharged there (coast trading voyages) belongs exclusively to German vessels.

§ 2. This right may be granted to foreign vessels by State treaty, or with consent of the Council of the Confederation by imperial decree.[1]

§ 3. The master of a foreign vessel who, unauthorised, pursues coast trading voyages, is subject to a fine up to three thousand marks.

And the vessel, as well as the goods so illegally forwarded, may, besides the fine, be adjudged to be confiscated, irrespective of whether they belong to the party condemned or not. § 42 of the penal code is accordingly to be applied.

§ 4. Existing treaty stipulations as to coast trading voyages are not affected by this law.[2]

§ 5. This law enters into force on January 1, 1882.

[1] By decree of December 29, 1881: 'The right to load goods in a German seaport, and to carry them to another German seaport in order to be discharged there (coast trading voyages), has been granted to vessels of Belgium, the Brazils, Denmark, Great Britain, Italy, and Sweden-Norway.'

[2] The present treaty regulations to which § 4 of the above law refers are given in detail by the proclamation of the Imperial Chancellor, dated December 29, 1881. They concern Austro-Hungary, Roumania, Siam, and Tonga.

INDEX.

ADM

ADMIRALTY Jurisdiction of County Court, 621-623

Admiralty Practice, suggestions for the improvement of, 624-626

Affreightment, principles originally proposed, 295-297; circulated by Social Science Association, 297-298; Discussion upon them at Sheffield Congress, 298-306; Draft agreed upon at Sheffield Congress, 306-308; Résumé of early Bill of Lading Discussions, 309-310; proposed law of, and uniform Bill of Lading. *See* Bill of Lading

Appellate jurisdiction in maritime causes, 681-684

Average. *See* General Average, German law concerning, 741-750

BILLS of lading, résumé of early discussions on Eastern trade, 309; proposed uniform, 310; Mr. Reinhold's paper on, at London Conference 1879, 311-325; committee proposed to deal with subject, 326; Report of Committee to Berne Conference, 326-327; Discussion at Berne Conference, 327-329; Report of Committee to Cologne Conference, 329-331; Dr. Stubbs' paper on the formulation of a Model Bill of Lading at Cologne Conference, 331-339; Mr. Lowndes' paper on a common

BIL

form of Bill of Lading, 340-355; Committee nominated to consider subject, 355; Liverpool Conference on, 356 Report of Hon. Secretary, Dr. Stubbs, to Liverpool Conference, 356-358; Report of Mr. Lowndes, 358-366; Discussion and Resolutions at Liverpool Conference, 366-379; Liverpool draft bill of lading as adopted, 379-382; New York Produce Exchange, Report on Liverpool Bill of Lading, 382-397; Bill of Lading proposed by that Committee, 395-397; New Zealand and Australian underwriters' protest against Negligence Clause, 398-401; London Insurance Companies' protest, 401-402; Both considered at Milan Conference, 402: Proposed United States Bill of Lading Act, 402-405; New York Produce Exchange Bill of Lading, 405-408; Meeting called by Lloyd's to agree to a 'Lloyd's' Bill of Lading, 409-417; 'Baltic' meeting called to agree to a common form of bill of Lading, 417-419; London Chamber of Commerce, Meeting for same purpose, 419-425; Memorial on same subject to President of Royal Commission on Merchant Shipping, 426; 'Baltic' meeting to consider report of their committee, 428-430; Reconsideration of subject at Ham-

BIL

burg Conference, 430-476; Rules prepared by Hamburg Chamber of Commerce, 435-438; Ditto, by Chamber of Commerce of Lubeck, 440-441; Dr. Stubbs' Draft International Code of Affreightment, 443-447; Bill of Lading and Rules of Affreightment as drawn by Committee, 466-470; Ditto as passed by Hamburg Conference, 472-475; Protest of Hamburg Chamber of Commerce against, 476; Resolutions passed at Antwerp Conference, 477-478; Report of London Chamber of Commerce Committee, 478-486; Act of Parliament suggested by this Committee, 483-486; Final Report of Committee, 486-487; Hamburg and Bremen Chambers of Commerce Bill of Lading and Rules of Affreightment, 487-493; London Conference (1887), 493-506; Sir Charles P. Butt on the Negligence Clause, 493-496; Discussion on this Clause, 496-506; Report of Royal Commission on Loss of Life at Sea; their views on the responsibility of shipowners to cargo-owners, 507-508; authors' argument in favour of a Bill of Lading being agreed upon, 508-512. *See* also Affreightment

Bottomry, German law concerning, 737-741

Coast Trading voyages, German law concerning, 817, 818

Collision, limited liability in cases of. *See* Limited Liability of Shipowners, German law concerning, 751-754

County Courts, Admiralty jurisdiction of, 621-623

Creditors' ships, German law concerning, 754-759

Crew, German law concerning, 706-711

GEN

Depositions. *See* Merchant ships' logs

Distressed seamen, German law concerning passage home of, 811, 812

Eastern Trade Bill of Lading, 209

Freight, when ship abandoned at sea, 627-629

General Average :—Initiation of movement leading to York Antwerp Rules, 1; Glasgow Conference, Discussion, and Resolutions, 1-70; Draft Bill embodying Glasgow Resolutions, 71-94; remarks upon by Antwerp Delegates, 95-107; Amendment of Bill at London Preliminary Meetings, 1862, 107-109; report of Preliminary Committee, 111; return of attendance of such Committee, 112; resignation of Committee of Lloyd's, 113; correspondence upon such resignation, 113-116; London Conference, 117; Amended Draft Bill, 117-119; Committee appointed to settle the Bill, 120; epitome of members' opinions, 121-125; Final Draft Bill, 126-128; York Congress discussion and resolutions, 128-205; rules as framed at York Congress, 205-209; Bremen Conference, 210-213; Committee then appointed, 213-214; Antwerp Conference, 214; alterations made in the York Rules, 244-245; the York and Antwerp Rules, 245-247; protest of Lloyd's, 248; report of Committee to Frankfort Conference, 249-254; Frankfort approval of rules, 255-256; report to London Conference 1879, 255-259; discussion thereon,

GEN

259-262; report to Berne Conference, 262-280; report to Hamburg Conference, 280-294

German General Mercantile Law:—
Maritime Commerce, 687-759; general provisions, 687-690; ownership, 690-696; the master, 696-706; the crew, 706-711; freight (goods), 711-735; freight (passengers), 735-737; bottomry, 737-741; Average, 741-750; damage by collision, 750; salvage, 751-754; ships' creditors, 754-759. *Maritime Insurance*, 759-790; general principles, 759-765; statements to be made by assured, 765-766; obligations of assured arising out of contract, 766-768; extent of the risk, 768-778; extent of the damage, 778-784; payment of losses, 784-787; cancelling the insurance, 787-788; time limitation of liability, 788-790

German law concerning goods, 711-735; passengers, 735-737

German Maritime Law, regulation for seamen of 1872, 790-811; introductory regulations, 790; sea voyage books and articles, 791-793; seamen's contract and wages, 794-803; disciplinary regulations for seamen, 803-804; punishment of seamen, 805-809; general conditions, 810-811

German Maritime Law, Distressed Seamen, regulation of 1872, 811-812

German Maritime Law, nationality of merchant vessels, 813-816

German Maritime Law, registration of merchant vessels, 817

German Maritime Law, regulation concerning coast trading voyages, 817-818

HAMBURG Chamber of Commerce Rules of Affreightment, 435-438, 487-493

MER

Hamburg and Bremen Chambers of Commerce Bill of Lading and Rules of Affreightment, 487-493

Hamburg Rules of Affreightment and Bill of Lading, 472-475

INSURANCE, German Law, 759-790

LEGISLATION, necessity for amending, 670-680

Limited liability of shipowners (*see* the 'Marie de Brabant' case), 513-526; under the Merchant Shipping Acts, author's observations on, 610-619

Liverpool Bill of Lading, 379-382

Lloyd's Bill of Lading proposed, 409-417

Log-books, proposed reform in. *See* Merchant ships' logs

Lubeck Chambers of Commerce Rules of Affreightment, 440-441

'MARIE DE BRABANT,' case of, 513-526; memorial to Board of Trade, 513-523; Board of Trade answer, 523-525; author's reply, 524-526

Masters, German law concerning, 696-706

Merchant Shipping Acts 1854, observations on, 527-607; 1855, 607; 1862, 607

Merchant ships' logs, protests, and depositions before receivers, 655-669; letter from London Salvage Association to Privy Council, 656-658; author's memorandum on merchant ships' protests, 658-663; report on merchant ships' protests and log-books to London Conference, 664-668

Merchant ships, German law concerning. *See* under German General Mercantile Law and German Maritime Law

NEW

New York Produce Exchange Bill of Lading, 395-397, 405-408

Ownership of merchant ships, German law concerning, 690-696

Passenger freight, German law concerning, 735-737

Piracy, wilful destruction of property at sea to be regarded as, 630-654

Protests. *See* Merchant ships' logs

Salvage, German law concerning, 751-754

Sea voyage books, German law concerning, 791-793

Seamen, German law concerning,

YOR

790-812. (*See* under German Maritime Law.)

Ships' Articles, German law concerning, 791-793

United States Bills of Lading Act, 402-405

Wages, German law concerning seamen's, 794-803

Wilful destruction of property at sea, 630-654; memorandum by author, 630-647; the 'Mosel' case, 648-649; Dr. Von Spesshardt's observations on, 650-652; the 'Ferret' case, 653-654

York and Antwerp Rules of General Average, 245-247